Papers on
REGULATION OF GENE ACTIVITY DURING DEVELOPMENT

D1482494

Edited by

WILLIAM F. LOOMIS, JR.

University of California
San Diego

HARPER & ROW, PUBLISHERS
New York, Evanston, and London

Papers on
REGULATION OF GENE ACTIVITY
DURING DEVELOPMENT

Library of Congress Catalog Card Number: 71-105245

ACKNOWLEDGMENTS

I would like to thank the copyright owners and the authors who permitted reprinting these papers. I am particularly grateful to those authors who supplied reprints, from which the copy has been made. I am indebted to the staff of Harper & Row for encouragement and advice in this enterprise. Finally, I wish to acknowledge the patient clerical assistance of Mrs. Betty Vrooman.

CONTENTS

ix

Papers on
REGULATION OF GENE ACTIVITY
DURING DEVELOPMENT

INTRODUCTION

Unifying concepts which can account for all the variety of differentiations which occur during the development of an egg into an embryo or a cell into a tissue have yet to be formulated. However, the general problems in developmental biology are fairly well defined. How do genetically identical cells become functionally diverse? How is the size and shape of a tissue or organism controlled? How are separate metabolic activities integrated into a functional pattern? How are temporal changes mediated?

It is clear that the cells of an organism with distinct tissues must be responsive to conditions which elicit metabolic decisions to alter the possible functions. These decisions result in new cell types which are distinct from each other and from the original cell type. These cell types must be metabolically stable and often must be able to pass on their particular functional attributes to progeny cells in a stable hereditary fashion.

One theory to account for these alterations in function which was considered until recent years held that unused genetic material was discarded as specialization of function proceeded. However, the demonstration that the genetic material of a single intestinal cell is sufficient for the formation of a complete embryo if transplanted to an enucleated frog egg (Gurdon, 1962) and that a complete carrot plant can be cultured from a single differentiated cell (Braun, 1959; Steward et al., 1958) proved that essential genetic material is not lost in the process of development of either animal or plant cells.

Currently the theory of differential gene activity is invoked to explain many developmental phenomena. The theory is derived from studies on bacterial physiology which have been most elegantly described by Jacob and Monod (1961). The theory postulates that the action of specific genetic regulatory elements, operators and repressors, can activate or inactivate specific genes depending on the environment of the nucleus. Thus, in a given environment, certain genes will be active while others will be inactive. Under different conditions, a different spectrum of active genes will exist. If one considers that a gene is active only when its product is active then the concept of regulation of gene activity can account for most biochemical differentiations.

Many studies on eukaryotic cells support the Jacob-Monod model for gene control and several are included in this collection. However, the detailed genetic evidence required for confirmation of the model has yet to be acquired in eukaryotic cells. Moreover, as studies with higher organisms progressed, it became apparent that many details of physiological differentiation were not controlled by regulation of the synthesis of enzymes but by regulation of the activity of existing enzymes. Often, stabilization of the enzymes as well as activation and inhibition of activities were found to account for alterations in metabolic activity. However, definitive methods for the study of *in vivo* control of enzyme activity are not presently available.

Cellular metabolism is such a highly sensitive matrix of interacting pathways that experimental alteration of one step often results in a complex series of adjustments in other steps which minimize the net effect. An exception to this "biological uncertainty principle" is the synthesis of specific proteins. All evidence to date indicates that expression of one gene or

1

operon does not affect the expression of another operon. Therefore, the study of differentiation has been most incisive when focus was directed at the regulation of specific gene activity. Although the metabolic role of many of the enzymes and structural proteins which form the basis of these studies is only guessed at, it is felt that evolutionary pressures have restricted developing cells to synthesizing proteins which will be of immediate or ultimate use in the function of the cell within the whole organism. Thus, even if we do not know the physiological function of a particular control mechanism, our understanding of development is increased if we know the primary steps in its unfolding.

The papers of this collection are directed at the elucidation of the mechanisms involved in regulation of gene activity. They have been chosen on the basis of clarity and homogeneity within this structure and not necessarily for historical importance. Thus, many studies which provided fresh insights and new avenues for experimentation have been omitted because the background required for appreciation of the contribution was too extensive or subsequent work has simplified the understanding of the problem. Moreover, many studies of developing systems which are being pursued by molecular techniques have not been included for reasons of space. It is envisioned that as this field matures, these early studies of the chemical basis of development will appear as primitive probes. It is hoped this collection may help in this process.

Braun, A. (1959)   Proc. Nat'l Acad. Sci. *45*, 932-938. A demonstration of the recovery of the crown gall tumor cell with the use of complex tumors of single-cell origin.

Gurdon, J. (1962)   Devel. Biol. *4*, 256. Adult frogs derived from the nuclei of single somatic cells.

Jacob, F., and J. Monod (1961)   J. Mol. Biol. *3*, 318. Genetic regulatory mechanism in the synthesis of protein.

Steward, F., M. Mapes, and K. Mears (1958)   Am. J. Botany *45*, 705-708. Growth and organizational development of cultured cells. II. Organization in cultures grown from freely suspended cells.

Section I

ENDOGENOUS CONTROL OF ENZYME SYNTHESIS IN EUKARYOTIC MICROORGANISMS

MONOD, J., and F. JACOB, 1961. Cold Spring Harbor Symp. Quant. Biol. *26*, 389. General conclusions: teleonomic mechanisms in cellular metabolism, growth, and differentiation.

TAURO, P., and H. O. HALVORSON, 1966. J. Bacteriol. *92*, 652. Effect of gene position on the timing of enzyme synthesis in synchronous cultures of yeast.

LOOMIS, W. F., JR., 1969. J. Bacteriol. *97*, 1149. Acetylglucosaminidase, an early enzyme in the development of *Dictyostelium discoideum*.

ROTH, R., J. M. ASHWORTH, and M. SUSSMAN, 1968. Proc. Nat'l Acad. Sci. *59*, 1235. Periods of genetic transcription required for the synthesis of three enzymes during cellular slime mold development.

LOOMIS, W. F., JR., and M. SUSSMAN, 1966. J. Mol. Biol. *22*, 401. Commitment to the synthesis of a specific enzyme during cellular slime mold development.

YANAGISAWA, K., W. F. LOOMIS, JR., and M. SUSSMAN, 1967. Exp. Cell Res. *46*, 328. Developmental regulation of the enzyme UDP-galactose polysaccharide transferase.

The differential rate of synthesis of specific proteins in bacteria can vary depending on the presence or absence of specific chemicals in the environment. For example, when lactose is present in the medium, cells of *Escherichia coli* synthesize β-galactosidase almost a thousand times more rapidly than in its absence. Recent studies have shown that the control of the β-galactosidase gene is determined by two specific genetic elements, the *lac* repressor gene, *i,* and the *lac* operator. The operator is located very near the *lac* structural genes on the bacterial chromosome. The *i* gene codes for a protein, the *lac* repressor, which interacts with the *lac* operator DNA and inhibits transcription of the *lac* operon (Gilbert and Müller-Hill, 1966; Riggs et al., 1968). When a specific small molecule, a β-galactoside, binds to the repressor, the repressor no longer interacts with the operator DNA and the operon becomes active. In this instance the small molecule inducer is chemically related to the substrate of the enzyme, but this need not be so since the inducer only interacts with the repressor, a protein unrelated to the enzyme.

This detailed biochemical understanding of the control mechanisms operative during adaption in bacteria has stimulated studies on similar problems in multicellular organisms. From a theoretical point of view, the concept of regulator genes, the only function of which is to control other genes, can account for almost every biochemical observation in developmental physiology. Ingenious circuitry which will result in stable or periodically alternating states are presented in the first paper of this collection (p. 7). It is not known if these mechanisms are operative in eukaryotic cells. In fact, one of the present challenges in developmental

biology is to provide evidence in support or opposition to these models.

The studies of Halvorson and his colleagues (p. 20) on potential gene activity in relation to the division cycle of yeast clearly demonstrated a mechanism for regulating the time of accumulation and the amount of accumulation of a specific protein. Thus, if all else is constant, the product of a gene expressed at the start of a cell cycle will be present at twice the concentration of the product of a gene expressed at the end of a cell cycle. The application of this mechanism to differentiation in all dividing cells is clear.

However, many cells undergo biochemical differentiations in the absence of cell division. A useful example of this is the development of the cellular slime mold, *Dictyostelium discoideum*. Several enzymes in this organisms have been shown to be developmentally controlled (pp. 30, 36). Both the temporal and quantitative aspects of these biochemical differentiations appear to be regulated. Studies utilizing actinomycin D to preferentially inhibit RNA synthesis have delineated specific periods during which RNA must be synthesized for the various enzymes to accumulate. The differences in the periods of RNA and protein synthesis for different enzymes suggest that control of both transcription and translation of specific mRNA molecules may be involved in these biochemical differentiations.

Preliminary delineation of the intercellular interactions which occur in this organism has been made. It can be shown that certain biochemical differentiations proceed in the absence of normal multicellular topography while others require normal morphogenesis (p. 44). Intercellular interactions can be clearly demonstrated in synergistic development of pairs of mutant strains, neither of which can develop alone (p. 48). An understanding of the chemical factors involved in synergy would greatly advance our knowledge of development.

Gilbert, W., and B. Müller-Hill (1966)   Proc. Nat'l Acad. Sci. *56*, 1891. Isolation of the *lac* repressor.

Riggs, A., S. Bourgeois, R. Newby, and M. Cohn (1968)   J. Mol. Biol. *34*, 365-368. DNA binding of the *lac* repressor.

RELATED READING

Fulton, C., and A. Dingle (1967)   Devel. Biol. *15*, 165. Appearance of the flagellate phenotype in populations of *Naegleria amebae*.

Halvorson, H. (1965)   Symp. Soc. Gen. Microbiol. *15*, 343. Sequential expression of biochemical events during intracellular differentiation.

Spencer, T., and H. Harris (1964)   Biochem. J. *91*, 282-286. Regulation of enzyme synthesis in an enucleate cell.

Zetsche, K. (1966)   Biochim. biophys. Acta *124*, 332-338. Regulation der UDP-glucose 4-epimerase synthesis in kernhaltigen und kernlosen acetabularian.

Reprinted from Cold Spring Harbor Symposia on Quantitative Biology
Volume XXVI, 1961
Printed in U.S.A.

General Conclusions: Teleonomic Mechanisms in Cellular Metabolism, Growth, and Differentiation

by Jacques Monod and François Jacob

Services de Biochimie Cellulaire et de Génétique Microbienne, Institut Pasteur, Paris

I. INTRODUCTION

Before attempting to draw the conclusions, or some of the conclusions, which emerge from the discussions of the past eight days, we would like to express the unanimous feeling of the participants that the choice of the subject and the timing of this conference were excellent, as shown by the exceptional and sustained interest of the sessions. For this we are deeply indebted to our host Dr. Chovnick, Director of the Long Island Biological Laboratory, and to Dr. Umbarger who had a major share in the planning of the conference.

We shall not attempt here to summarize the proceedings of a meeting where such an abundance of observations, pertaining to a wide variety of systems, were presented. We would rather try to reconsider the problem of cellular regulation as a whole, in perspective so to say, as it appears to us as a result of this confrontation.

One conclusion which was repeatedly emphasized is the wide-spread occurrence and the extreme importance of regulatory mechanisms in cellular physiology. Since this aspect has been treated, with characteristic elegance and insight by Dr. B. Davis, in his introductory paper, we shall not dwell on it here. Let us however recall, for instance, the systems described by Dr. Kornberg (see this Symposium, page 257) which illustrate the fact that essential enzymes of intermediary metabolism, such as the condensing enzyme (a typical "amphibolic" enzyme according to the useful terminology proposed by Davis), are submitted to wide regulatory variations, depending on the substrates present in the medium. The idea, often expressed in the past, that adaptive effects are limited to "unessential" enzymes is thus evidently incorrect. Let us also recall that the genetic breakdown of a regulatory mechanism has repeatedly been found (cf. the cases of β-galactosidase, alkaline phosphatase, aspartate and ornithine transcarbamylase) to lead to enormous overproduction of the enzyme concerned; it is evident that no cell could survive the breakdown of more than two or three, at most, such systems. Finally, let us also point to the wide variations observed, in relation to different diets, in the level of liver enzymes, and to the significant observation that, in certain hepatic tumors, the same enzymes appear to obey altogether different rules of conduct (see Van Potter, this Symposium, page 355).

In the present discussion, we wish to center attention on the mechanisms, rather than on the physiological significance, of the different regulatory effects. It is clear that great progress has been accomplished in this respect, allowing us now clearly to distinguish between different types of mechanisms, and also to recognize that certain systems which appeared entirely different from one another a few years ago, are in fact submitted to similar, if not identical, controls. This is particularly striking in the case of inducible and repressible enzyme systems and of lysogenic systems, all three of which would seem to obey fundamentally similar controlling elements, merely organized into different circuits.

The major part of this paper will then be devoted to the discussion of mechanisms. However, the analysis of these mechanisms has been, so far, largely restricted to microbiological objects. A constantly recurring question is: to what extent are the mechanisms found to operate in bacteria also present in tissues of higher organisms; what functions may such mechanisms perform in this different context; and may the new concepts and experimental approaches derived from the study of microorganisms be transferred to the analysis and interpretation of the far more complex controls involved in the functioning and differentiation of tissue cells? We shall consider this question in the last section of this paper.

II. REGULATORY MECHANISMS

A. Possible, Plausible, and Actual Cellular Control Mechanisms

To begin with, we might try to classify and define *a priori* the main types of cellular regulatory mechanisms, including any likely or plausible mechanism which may or may not have been actually observed, or discussed during the present conference.

1. *Mass action*

Since many, if not most, metabolic reactions are largely reversible, mass action might have a significant share in regulation. However most pathways involve one or several irreversible steps which could not be controlled by mass action. Moreover, it is a general observation that the intracellular concentration of most intermediary metabolites in the cell is vanishingly small, indicating that mass action only plays a limited role, and also suggesting that other mechanisms must intervene in metabolic regulation. Mass action effects were, in fact, not discussed during this conference.

2. *Enzyme activity*

By virtue of the buffering effect implied by Henri-Michaelis kinetics, an enzyme constitutes, by itself, a controlling element. The rate of the reaction which it catalyzes depends upon its characteristic kinetic constants, in particular on its relative affinity for substrate and product. It is worth noting that these constants are related to the equilibrium constant, i.e., to the free energy change of the reaction itself, by the Haldane equation, thus reintroducing mass action as one of the controlling factors in any enzyme-catalyzed reaction. The relative values of the forward and backward reaction constants in the Haldane equation may be supposed to present, in some systems at least, a physiological, controlling significance. For instance, the fact that alkaline phosphatase, which catalyzes a virtually irreversible reaction, has a very high affinity for orthophosphate may result in control of this reaction by the product, in spite of irreversibility. The "teleonomic" significance of this correlation, where it obtains, is emphasized by the fact that in other irreversible systems, the enzyme shows very low affinity for the products. This is the case, for instance, for the β-galactosidase reaction. Thus, intracellular phosphate esters may be protected by intracellular orthophosphate, while galactosides would not be so protected by galactose. The products of an enzyme necessarily are *analogues* of the substrate, and competitive inhibition is expected in any case: whether it is physiologically significant or not depends upon the specific construction of the enzyme site.

Competitive inhibition of enzymes by organic substances other than steric analogues of the substrate (including product) is not observed, in general. But the specific construction of enzyme sites offers yet other regulatory possibilities, as revealed by the discovery of the "feedback" or "endproduct" inhibition effect. As we have seen, this type of effect actually turns out to be extremely wide-spread and physiologically highly significant. We shall discuss it at some length.

3. *Enzyme activation and "molecular conversion"*

The well known conversion of zymogens into active proteases evidently plays an important regulatory and protective role. On this basis, one might expect various types of alteration of molecular structure ("molecular conversion") to occur in the regulation of activity of intracellular enzymes. Actually, relatively few observations of such effects have been reported. However, the

mechanisms described by Tompkins and by Rall and Sutherland may be considered as "molecular conversions" and this may also be true of the effects reported by Hagerman. We shall discuss the possible implications of these mechanisms in a later section.

4. *Specific control of enzyme synthesis*

Since it is well known that cells of different tissues within the same organism do not exhibit the same enzyme (or protein) patterns, while all these cells presumably contain the same genome; and since the same may be said of bacteria from a single clone grown in different media, it is evident that specific mechanisms exist, which control the expression of genetic potentialities with respect to specific protein synthesis. In bacteria, adaptive enzyme systems have been the subject of much work, and we shall discuss these systems at some length. The occurrence of similar mechanisms in differentiated organisms is highly probable, although, as the discussions here have shown, not conclusively demonstrated in any single case. It would appear that some of the "adaptive" effects observed in tissue cells are due to enzyme stabilization rather than to control of enzyme synthesis. This will be discussed in the last section of this paper.

From this brief review and classification of the main plausible and/or actually observed mechanisms of cellular control, it is apparent that *all* these mechanisms—except mass action—are directly related to the specific molecular structure of the enzymes, or other proteins, concerned. The fundamental problem of specific determinism in protein synthesis is, therefore, coextensive to our field of investigation. This would be the justification, if any were needed, for the fact that a major part of this conference was devoted to this problem. We shall discuss it in connection with enzymatic adaptation since, as we have seen, induction and repression are directly related to the mechanisms of information transfer from genes to proteins.

B. The Novick-Szilard-Umbarger Effect: *Endproduct or "Allosteric" Inhibition*

In 1954, Novick and Szilard discovered that the synthesis of a tryptophan precursor (later identified as indol-3-glycerol-phosphate) in *E. coli* was inhibited by tryptophan. They formulated the hypothesis that tryptophan specifically inhibited the activity of an *early* enzyme in tryptophan biosynthesis and that this effect had regulatory significance. Observations of the Carnegie group on isotopic competition (Roberts *et al.*, 1955) between endogeneous and exogeneous metabolites suggested the occurrence of similar effects in the synthesis of several amino acids. The work of Umbarger (see this Symposium, page 301), directly at the enzyme level, indeed demonstrated that, in many pathways, an early enzyme is so constructed as to be strongly and specifically inhibited by the metabolic endproduct of the pathway.

As the reports here have shown, endproduct inhibition is extremely widespread in bacteria, insuring immediate and sensitive control of the rate of metabolite biosynthesis in most, if not all, pathways. From the point of view of mechanisms, the most remarkable feature of the Novick-Szilard-Umbarger effect is that the inhibitor *is not a steric analogue of the substrate.* We propose therefore to designate this mechanism as "allosteric inhibition." Since it is well known that competitive behavior toward an enzyme is, as a rule, restricted to steric analogues, it might be argued that an enzyme's concept of steric analogy need not be the same as ours, and that proteins may see analogies where we cannot discern any. That this interpretation is inadequate is proved by many observations which were reported here. Umbarger and others have shown that in general, only *one* enzyme, the first one in the specific pathway concerned, is highly sensitive to inhibition by the endproduct. If steric analogy were involved, the different enzymes of the pathway would then be considered to hold private and dissenting opinions about stereochemistry. And the same would have to be said of two different enzymes catalyzing an *identical* reaction in the *same* organism, as in the remarkable case of β-aspartokinase, reported by Cohen and Stadtman (see this Symposium, page 319).

Such observations leave no doubt that the construction of the binding site of enzymes subject to allosteric inhibition is exceptional and highly specialized. The findings of Changeux (see this Symposium, page 313) actually show that the groups involved in the binding of inhibitor, in the case of threonine-deaminase, may be inactivated without parallel inactivation of the enzyme. They show, moreover, that the abnormal reaction kinetics of this enzyme (already noted by Umbarger) are directly related to its competence as a regulatory enzyme, and may be experimentally normalized by inactivation of the inhibitor binding groups. This leads to the conclusion that two distinct, albeit interacting, binding sites exist on native threonine deaminase. Competitive inhibition in this system, therefore, is not due to *mutually exclusive* binding of inhibitor and substrate, as in the classical case of steric analogues.

Closely similar observations have been made independently and simultaneously by Pardee (private communication) on another enzyme sensitive to endproduct (aspartate-carbamyl-transferase). This situation may therefore be a general one for enzymes subject to allosteric inhibition and these findings raise several interesting new problems of enzyme chemistry. Studies of the structure of the two sites and of their interaction, using analogues of the substrate and inhibitor, might conceivably lead to interpretations in terms of the "induced-fit" theory of Koshland (1959).

In any case, one may predict that "allosteric enzymes" will become a favorite object of research, in the hands of students of the mechanisms of enzyme action.

Since the allosteric effect is not *inherently* related to any particular structural feature common to substrate and inhibitor, the enzymes subject to this effect must be considered as pure products of selection for efficient regulatory devices. This raises a question concerning the genetic determinism of allosteric enzymes. If indeed these enzymes generally possess two different binding groups, they might be supposed to represent the association, favored by selection, of two originally independent enzyme-proteins. If such were the case, one might expect the structural gene corresponding to such an enzyme to be, as a rule, composed of two cistrons, governing respectively the structure of each of the two components of the molecule. In vitro dissociation and reassociation of the two components might also be observed, and would help greatly in the analysis of the effect itself.

A particularly interesting possibility is suggested by this discussion. Namely that, since again there is no obligatory correlation between specific substrates and inhibitors of allosteric enzymes, the effect *need not be restricted to "endproduct" inhibition.* (This in fact is the main reason for avoiding the term "endproduct inhibition" in a general discussion of this mechanism. We feel that endproduct inhibition may turn out to constitute only *one class* of allosteric effects.) It is conceivable that in some situations a cell might find a regulatory advantage in being able to control the rate of reaction along a given pathway through the level of a metabolite synthesized in another pathway. Wherever favorable, such "cross inhibition" might have become established through selection. In other words, *any* physiologically useful regulatory connection, between any two or more pathways, might become established by adequate selective construction of the interacting sites on an allosteric enzyme. This, we feel, may be a very important point, to which we shall return later.

Another aspect should be mentioned. As is well known, the principle of steric analogy has been widely used in attempts to rationalize the design of synthetic drugs, particularly in the case of antibacterial and antitumoral agents. The results have been rewarding, although not as much, perhaps, as one might have anticipated. Yet the principle is evidently valid. But it may prove even more rewarding to look for analogues of the natural controlling agent, rather than for analogues of the substrate of the reaction which one proposes to hit. An example of such an analogue is furnished by 5-methyl-tryptophan, which does not compete with tryptophan for incorporation into protein, while it does efficiently block tryptophan synthesis by allosteric inhibition (and also by repression) (Trudinger and Cohen, 1956).

Similar considerations evidently apply to the analysis of the mode of action of drugs and antibiotics.

C. Molecular Conversion

As we already noted, the well-known example of the zymogens seemed to suggest that alterations, reversible or not, of the molecular structure of certain enzymes might represent an important type of regulatory mechanism. Surprisingly enough, very few examples of such mechanisms have been discovered. It would be unwise to conclude that "molecular conversions" are not a significant type of mechanisms, especially in view of some of the observations reported here. Tomkin's work on the glutamic-alanine dehydrogenase conversion (see this Symposium, page 331) does more than reveal a possible mechanism of steroid hormone action. His observations show that the same protein may acquire different specific activities, depending upon a reversible alteration of molecular structure. This discovery would seem for the first time to justify the idea, often expressed in the past, that an enzyme might possess, in vivo, several different activities (alternative or not) which might be difficult to recognize in vitro. In Tomkin's case, the conversion involves interaction of the protein with itself. In other cases, it might conceivably depend upon interaction of two different proteins, and might remain undetected for this reason. Such possibilities are also suggested by the work of Yanofsky on the two components of tryptophan synthetase. Whether or not the glutamic-alanine dehydrogenase conversion affords a physiologically valid interpretation of steroid action, it does propose a model of a possibly important type of regulatory mechanism.

To a certain extent, the phosphorylase "conversion" discussed here by Rall and Sutherland (see this Symposium, page 347) pertains to the same general type of mechanism, since the activity of phosphorylase eventually depends upon its interaction with two other specific proteins, which phosphorylate and dephosphorylate respectively the metabolic enzyme. (In passing, it may be of interest to note that certain types of suppressor mutations could be due to interactions of this type.) It will be interesting to see whether the transhydrogenase activation, described by Hagerman, also belongs to the class of molecular conversions. In microorganisms, the formation (induced by aerobic conditions) of L-lactic from D-lactic dehydrogenase has been reported by Labeyrie, Slonimsky and Naslin (1959). Whether or not this is pure molecular conversion, or involves de novo synthesis of part of the enzyme molecule is not established as yet.

We would venture to predict that in the next few years several new examples of molecular conversions will be discovered.

Little has been said during this conference of the mechanisms which control cell division. It should be noted that these mechanisms presumably involve, or govern, certain types of "molecular conversions." This is most clearly indicated by the work of Mazia (1959) following the pioneer investigations of Rapkine (1931). Lwoff and Lwoff (1961) have stressed the fact that in the cycle of the polio virus, cyclic dissociation and association of the coat protein occurs, and they have suggested that similar events, affecting certain proteins, may play an important role in cell division. Systematic inquiries based upon this suggestion would certainly be justified.

D. Specific Control of Protein Synthesis

1. The determinism of protein structure

The discussions at this conference have shown, once more, that the one gene-one enzyme hypothesis is now considered as established beyond reasonable doubt. The early difficulties of the theory were evidently due to insufficient biochemical analysis of the apparent exceptions. In the case of several enzyme-proteins, known to be made up of two or more polypeptide chains, it is now apparent that the structure of each polypeptide chain is governed by an independent gene or cistron. This constitutes a remarkable confirmation of the theory and an important step forward in understanding the mechanisms which govern protein structure. The work of Yanofsky (see this Symposium, page 11) on tryptophan-synthetase has been particularly illuminating in this respect.

Even when the one gene-one enzyme theory is redefined and qualified as the one cistron-one polypeptide chain theory, some complications remain, the interpretations of which are still not elucidated. We refer to intracistronic complementation and to the occurrence of suppressor mutations.

Although the first problem, intracistronic complementation, was not discussed during this conference, it should be briefly mentioned here. It is now generally believed to be often associated with a polymeric state of the normal enzyme protein. Observations made with a number of complementary mutants of glutamic dehydrogenase (Fincham, 1959) and β-galactosidase (Pasteur group) are in keeping with this assumption. The active enzyme, in both cases, is known to be a polymer, while certain mutations, in the case of β-galactosidase, result in the formation of an inactive monomer (Perrin, 1961). Studies of in vitro complementation may be expected to throw much light on the building of tertiary and quaternary structures of proteins. In any case, intracistronic complementation does not seem to offer a serious challenge to the concept that the gene or cistron acts as a *unit* in determining polypeptide structure.

The difficulty of interpreting suppressor mutation appears to be much greater. It has generally been a umed that suppressor mutations acted in some way at the tertiary level of protein synthesis, in contrast to true structural mutations assumed to operate at the primary level. The observations reported by Yanofsky indicate that certain suppressor mutations may actually restore the wild-type peptide structure in a *fraction* of the molecules. The working hypothesis proposed by Yanofsky following earlier suggestions of Benzer (namely that these suppressor mutations modify the specificity of an amino acid-activating-enzyme in such a way that compensatory errors would occur with a certain frequency in the choice of the corresponding amino acid) appears particularly interesting since it involves precise predictions. One of these predictions of course is that in such mutants the properties of one of the 20-odd amino acid activating enzymes should be detectably modified. If so, proof would be virtually obtained that the corresponding sRNA fraction does play the role of an adaptor as assumed by Crick (1958) and others, and a new method of determining amino acid substitutions resulting from structural mutations might become available. Another prediction is that the same suppressor mutation might be found to correct in part the effects of two primary mutations affecting two different enzymes. And lastly one would not expect such suppressor mutations to occur at more than about 20 loci. Thus, confirmation of Yanofsky's hypothesis will be awaited with particular interest.

The two fundamental problems with which we are now faced are the nature of the code and the mechanisms of information transfer from DNA to enzyme-synthesizing centers.

A few years ago, following the beautiful work of Benzer (1957) which demonstrated the linear structure of the genetic material at the ultrafine level and the work of Ingram (1957) on sickle-cell hemoglobin, it seemed that the basic assumption of all coding hypotheses, namely collinearity, would soon be proved. The only proof that has been obtained so far is that optimism is essential to the development of Science; collinearity still remains to be formally demonstrated. However, the reports of Yanofsky, of Streisinger and of Rothman at the conference, and what is known of the work of other laboratories, notably Brenner's, again encourage optimism; one feels confident that the final demonstration will soon be at hand.

The nature of the code itself is another matter. But the new experimental approaches, notably the study of chemical mutagens, are developing so rapidly (cf. Benzer and Freese, 1958; Freese, 1959) that cautious and patient optimism is justified. The study of the effects of reverse mutations occuring at the same site as the primary alteration, may also permit the elimination of certain types of codes. Finally a direct, chemical attack, involving the determination of partial (terminal) sequences in both a protein and the corresponding messenger RNA, may become possible, assuming the mRNA theory to be correct, if and when methods of isolating a specific message will be available.

A new experimental approach to the problem of the universality, or otherwise, of the code has been opened up by the observation of Falkow et al. (1961) of genetic transfer between *E. coli* and *Serratia*. Preliminary observations by the Pasteur Institute and M.I.T. groups on β-galactosidase and alkaline phosphatase suggest that the *E. coli* genes are transcribed correctly in *Serratia*. This would seem to indicate that the 20% difference in the G + C/A + T ratio between the two genera is not due to the use of different codes, and would agree with Sueoka's universalist conclusions. Further and more detailed studies of proteins synthesized by such "displaced" genes are evidently required. If the codes in *Serratia* and *Escherichia* and perhaps a few other bacterial genera turn out to be the same, the microbial-chemical-geneticists will be satisfied that it is indeed universal, by virtue of the well-known axiom that anything found to be true of *E. coli* must also be true of Elephants.

However, the remarks of Benzer, and also Yanofsky's interpretation of his suppressor mutations suggest that discrete differences of coding, concerning only one or a few amino acids, might exist between different groups, due to differences in specificity of the activating enzymes. The possibility that the code is universal for certain amino acids, and non-universal for others, seems interesting from an evolutionary point of view.

Assuming the problem of the code to be advancing, albeit slowly, the problem of how the tertiary structures are determined remains very open. But while this question was posed only in general terms until recently, it is now very precisely defined by the beautiful studies of the Cavendish group on the structures of myoglobin and of the α and β chains of hemoglobin. These studies have revealed that the tertiary structure of all three polypeptide chains are closely similar, while the primary structure of myoglobin differs widely from that of both hemoglobin chains, except however for about twelve residues which appear to occupy identical strategic positions in the three proteins (Perutz, 1961). This is a remarkable confirmation of the idea (Crick, 1958) that the tertiary folding is governed by a certain number of key residues, while being largely independent of the nature of residues in other positions. It remains to be seen whether it will ever be possible to formulate any general "folding rules" which would allow one approximately to deduce the tertiary configuration of a protein from knowledge of its primary structure. Yet, this is the goal that one would wish to reach, since this deduction, which we cannot begin to make, seems to be made unfailingly by the protein-synthesizing machinery in the cell.

This brings up another issue which must be mentioned at this point, although it was not discussed during the conference, evidently because it is implicitly considered as settled. A few years ago, the question was often debated whether any further (non-genetic) *structural* information needed to be furnished, or might conceivably be used in some cases, at the stage of tertiary folding in protein synthesis. Such a "finishing touch" has been considered as one of the possible mechanisms which might account for the effect of antigen in antibody synthesis (Pauling, 1940) and of inducer in enzymatic adaptation (Monod and Cohn, 1952). In the latter case, no evidence for, and a great deal of evidence against this possibility has accumulated (cf. Monod, 1956, Jacob and Monod, 1961) and proof has been obtained that inducer action is completely unrelated to the structure of the binding site of the induced enzyme (Perrin *et al.*, 1960). In the meantime, speculations on the origin of antibodies reverted from "instructive" to purely "selective" theories (Burnet, 1959; Lederberg, 1959). While this evolution is justified, in the case of antibodies, by general considerations, direct experimental evidence is yet to be found that would allow "selection" of the correct theory.

2. *The control of gene expression*

As we already pointed out, the purely structural (one gene-one enzyme) theory does not consider the problem of gene expression. The discovery of a new class of genetic elements, the regulator genes, which control the *rate* of synthesis of proteins, the *structure* of which is governed by *other* genes, does not contradict the classical concept, but it does greatly widen the scope and interpretative value of genetic theory. In all the adequately studied cases, it is established that the regulator genes act negatively (i.e. by blocking rather than provoking the synthesis of the proteins which they control) through the intermediacy of a cytoplasmic "aporepressor". Although the chemical nature of the aporepressor is still unknown, we feel that the term "regulator gene", as operationally defined, for instance, in the case of the lactose system of *E. coli*, should not be applied indiscriminately to any gene found to influence, in an unknown way, the formation of an enzyme: it is clear that a *structural* gene might exert such an effect by, e.g. controlling an enzyme which synthesizes an inducer of another system (cf. the observations of Horowitz in this Symposium, page 233)

To avoid confusion, the term "regulator" should be applied only to genes identified by *recessive constitutive mutations* affecting a protein structurally controlled by *another gene*.

In any case, the most urgent problem with respect to regulator genes is to identify their active product. Although it is almost certain that this product cannot

be a small molecule, and while it seems likely that it i not a protein, there is no positive evidence to identify it as a nucleic acid. Only when this question is solve shall it be possible to study directly the interaction o inducer or repressor with aporepressor, and to ac count for the specificity of this interaction.

Concerning this last point, the only statement tha can be made at present is a strictly negative one namely that the specificity of induction or repressio is completely independent of the specificity of actio of the enzymes involved. Although inducers are in gen eral substrates, or analogues of the substrate, and re pressors are products (often distant) of the controlle enzyme, the mechanism of the effect itself imposes n restriction upon the "choice" of the active agent. The specificity therefore must be considered purely as result of selection, as in the case of allosteric inhibition This selective freedom may have some important the oretical implications which will be discussed later.

As we have seen (Jacob and Monod, this Sympo sium, page 193) there are very strong reasons to be lieve that the site of action of the repressor is genetic; that in fact it is identical with the "operator" locus itself. Besides the arguments derived from the kinetics of enzyme synthesis, to which we shall return, the main reason is the existence, in certain systems, of genetic units of coordinate expression, i.e. of "operons" including several structural genes, controlled by a singl operator. So far, operons have been recognized only in bacteria, where genes controlling sequential enzymes are frequently, if not generally, tightly clustered (Demerec and Hartmann, 1959). One may wonder whether the concept of operon also applies to organisms where genetic clustering is not usually observed. The fact that pseudoalleles have been discovered in *Drosophila* and maize, wherever genetic methods attained sufficient resolution, suggests that the clustering of cistrons involved in controlling the same biochemical step may in fact be very widespread. It is tempting to speculate that the loci where pseudoallelism is observed control the synthesis of proteins containing two or more different polypeptide chains and that they involve two or more linked cistrons. Thus the operon, in higher organisms, might often correspond to the "gene" as defined by the one gene-one enzyme concept. Moreover, as we have seen, the results obtained with bacteria also permit one to define the operon in a somewhat different manner, namely as the *unit of transcription*. This definition remains valid and useful independently of the number of cistrons covered by a given operon.

Long before regulator genes and operator were recognized in bacteria, the extensive and penetrating work of McClintock (1956) had revealed the existence, in maize, of two classes of genetic "controlling elements" whose specific mutual relationships are closely comparable with those of the regulator and operator: the

"Activator" of McClintock appears to work as a *transmitter* of signals, presumably cytoplasmic since they act both in *cis* and in *trans*. By contrast the specific *receiver* of these signals only acts in *cis* upon genes directly linked to it. Although, because of the absence of enzymological data in the maize systems, the comparison cannot be brought down to the biochemical level, the parallel is so striking that it may justify the conclusion that the rate of structural gene expression is controlled, in higher organisms as well as in bacteria and bacterial viruses, by closely similar mechanisms, involving regulator genes, aporepressors, operators and operons.

A last point concerning the operator should be made. As we have seen, the operator locus of the Lac operon in *E. coli*, appears to be part of one extremity of the structural gene controlling galactosidase. In the arginine system (see Vogel; Maas; and Gorini; this Symposium) a single regulator appears to control the expression of several unlinked genes (or clusters) governing the different enzymes of the sequence. The operator segment for each of these genes or clusters presumably has the same structure, and if so one would expect the different enzymes of the system to contain the same sequence in one of their terminal peptides. Apart from the interest of providing a possible test for the preceding assumptions, the evolutionary implications of such a situation are evident.

3. *Messenger RNA*

The assumption that regulation, in inducible and repressible systems, operates at the genetic level by blocking or releasing the synthesis of the primary genetic product is intimately related to the problem of "messenger-RNA". On the basis of the kinetics of induction and repression, this assumption necessarily implied that the primary product in question is a short-lived intermediate (Jacob and Monod, 1961) and it led to a systematic search for an intermediate endowed with the proper kinetic properties. As we have seen, this search has been remarkably successful.

All or most of the evidence available at present on the so-called "messenger-RNA" fraction has been discussed in detail during the conference and we need not consider it at any length here. It might be useful however to summarize the main conclusions as follows:

a. A RNA fraction endowed with an exceptionally high rate of turnover exists not only in phage-infected cells (Volkin and Astrachan, 1957) but also in normal cells (Gros *et al.*, see this Symposium, page 111).

b. The base ratios in this fraction, in contrast to all other RNA fractions approximate the characteristic (group specific) base ratios of DNA (Volkin and Astrachan, 1957; Yčas and Vincent, 1960; Hayes, Hayes and Gros, 1961).

c. "mRNA" appears to form hybrids with homologous but not with heterologous DNA, indicating that the sequences in "mRNA" complement the sequences in DNA (Spiegelman, see this Symposium, page 75).

d. An enzyme system able to synthesize RNA polynucleotides using DNA as primer and reproducing the DNA base ratios in its product exists in *E. coli* from which it has been isolated and purified (Hurwitz *et al.*, see this Symposium, page 91).

e. *Escherichia coli* ribosomes appear to be able to synthesize either bacterial protein or viral protein depending on whether the "mRNA" with which they are associated is viral or bacterial; in other words, ribosomes appear to be non-specific with respect to the type of protein which they synthesize. (Brenner *et al.*, see this Symposium, page 101).

f. In reconstructed subcellular systems, the presence of DNA appears essential both for the incorporation of amino acid into protein, and for the synthesis of RNA, presumably mRNA, as shown in particular by Tissières' recent results; in the absence of DNA, partially isolated mRNA stimulates incorporation.

The very significant recent findings of Wood, Chamberlain and Berg (1961, in preparation) should be recalled here although they were not discussed at the conference. Using reconstructed systems containing washed ribosomes, they found that amino acid incorporation into protein was almost completely dependent upon the addition of purified polymerase, DNA, and triphosphonucleotides, the absence of any one of these additions resulting in 90 to 95% inhibition of incorporation.

The sum of these observations is impressive and seems to justify the optimistic feeling shared by most of us that the primary product of the genes, the intermediate responsible for the transfer of structural information to protein-forming centers, has been identified, as well as the enzyme system which synthesizes this product by transcribing DNA into RNA. However it must be pointed out that formal proof of the structure-determining function of "mRNA" will be obtained only when the synthesis of a specific protein, known to be controlled by an identified structural gene, is shown to take place in a reconstructed system containing messenger-RNA from genetically competent cells, while all other fractions were prepared from cells known to lack this particular structural gene.

It should also be emphasized that, while the existence of a fraction possessing the properties of "mRNA" was predicted largely on the basis of the assumption that repressive regulation operates at the genetic level, it remains to be proved, also by direct experiments, that inducers and repressors do control the synthesis of the specific messengers corresponding to the proteins which they are known to induce or repress in vivo.

Many other problems are raised by the recent findings on messenger-RNA. One of them is the stoichiometry of the intermediate. The possibility that the stoichiometry is one to one (that is to say that one molecule of messenger is destroyed for each molecule of protein synthesized) is interesting, but it seems to meet with serious difficulties. The possibility that the messenger may be endowed with different stability in different species or groups is at least equally likely, and it may eventually be found to account for the conflicting reports in the literature concerning the effects of enucleation on protein synthesis.

A question which was in the minds of many participants of the meeting was what the role of ribosomes and ribosomal RNA in protein synthesis might be, if indeed all of the specific structural information is provided by mRNA. Among various speculations, for which there is at present no basis and little immediate hope of devising experimental tests, one may mention the possibility that ribosomal RNA can form base pairing bonds with mRNA and thereby stretch it into the correct position for protein synthesis. In addition, the configuration in space of the ribosome-mRNA complex might restrict the freedom of folding of the polypeptide chain and thereby provide certain folding rules.

E. THE GLUCOSE EFFECT

One of the oldest known regulatory effects in enzyme synthesis is generally known today as the "glucose effect" although it is recognized that almost any carbon source may inhibit the synthesis of a wide variety of enzymes, the magnitude of the inhibition depending mostly on the rate of metabolism of the compound. The widespread occurrence and the physiological importance of this effect were illustrated in particular by Magasanik's report (see this Symposium, page 249). Concerning mechanisms however, few conclusions can be drawn at present. The most urgent question in this respect is whether the inhibition by glucose, or other carbon sources, of synthesis of an inducible enzyme is related or not to the mechanism of induction itself. The data summarized by Brown would seem to indicate that, in contrast with previous views, the glucose effect is largely independent of the specific aporepressor-inducer interaction. Brown's findings (Brown and Monod, 1961) would be consistent with a model involving the synthesis, in the presence of glucose, of a more or less non-specific inhibitory compound, indifferent to the presence or absence of the specific aporepressor as well as of the inducer.

The findings of Magasanik and of Neidhardt (see this Symposium, page 249 and 63) on the other hand indicate that the inhibitory agent ultimately responsible for the glucose effect must have some degree of specificity. On the basis of the knowledge acquired concerning the mechanism of specific induction and repression, it would seem that the following questions, concerning the nature of the glucose effect, should be asked and could receive an experimental answer:

a. Is the inhibitory agent specific for certain groups of enzymes? If it is, one would expect to find mutants which have lost the capacity to synthesize this compound and therefore would have lost the glucose effect for certain types of enzymes while retaining it for others.

b. Does the inhibitory agent act at the same level as the specific aporepressor? If so, certain mutations in the operator region might modify quantitatively the glucose effect towards enzymes belonging to the corresponding operon.

c. If the glucose effect does *not* work at the operator level, but rather at the cytoplasmic level (as suggested by some findings of Halvorson (discussion at this Symposium, see page 231), the quantitative regulatory coordination within an operon, characteristic of specific induction and repression, would not be observed with respect to inhibition by glucose.

III. REGULATION AND DIFFERENTIATION IN HIGHER ORGANISMS

1. GENERAL REMARKS

The regulatory problems posed by (or to) differentiated organisms are not only of an order of a complexity immeasurably greater than in microorganisms, they are of a different nature. Higher organisms may therefore be expected to possess certain types of cellular regulatory mechanisms which are not found in microorganisms. On the other hand, it seems very unlikely that the main mechanisms recognized in lower forms: allosteric inhibition, induction and repression, should not be used also in differentiated organisms. But it is clear that these mechanisms, by their very nature, can be adapted to widely different situations, and would serve entirely different purposes in *E. coli* and Man, respectively. As we have already pointed out, the specificity of allosteric inhibition, as well as the specificity of induction and repression is inherently "free", in the sense that it results exclusively from the teleonomic construction of the regulatory system. As it turns out, allosteric inhibitors, inducers, and repressors of bacterial systems are, in general, directly related to, or identical with, metabolites of the pathway which they control. This should be considered to reflect the relatively unsophisticated regulatory requirements of free-living unicellular organisms, whose only problems are to preserve their intracellular homeostatic state while adapting rapidly to the chemical challenge of changing environments, and whose success in selection depends on a *single* parameter: the rate of multiplication. Tissue cells of higher organisms are faced with entirely different problems. Intercellular (and not only intracellular) coordination within tissues or between different organs, to insure survival and reproduction of the organism, becomes a major factor in selection, while the environment of individual cells is largely stabilized, eliminating to a large degree the requirements for rapid and extensive adaptability.

2. *Nutritional adaptation*

These rather obvious *a priori* considerations may perhaps account in part for the somewhat discouraging results which seem to have been obtained so far in attempts to demonstrate induction by substrate or repression by metabolites of enzyme systems in various tissues. Several reports at the conference did illustrate the fact that the level of liver enzymes may vary greatly, depending on the type of diet to which the animals are submitted. But these reports have also illustrated the difficulties of analyzing the mechanisms involved. As Hiatt (see this Symposium, page 367) and also Feigelson, (unpublished) have pointed out, it may be that some of these effects are due to simple stabilization of the enzyme by substrate, rather than to control of their rate of synthesis. Simple stabilization, admittedly, is not a very exciting mechanism. It may well be a physiologically significant one, especially in the liver. The microorganisms have a simple way of getting rid of an enzyme-protein for which there is no more inducer-substrate; they only need to outgrow the protein which has ceased to be synthesized. This simple device is not available to liver cells, and this may justify the selection of the apparently wasteful method of synthesizing enzymes which are stable only in presence of their substrate. It should be added however that many of the systems described here would be difficult to interpret on this basis alone; and one feels confident, in spite of the lack of formal proof, that true induction and/or repression plays an important role in nutritional adaptation of higher organisms.

In any case, it seems clear that nutritional adaptation is not the most important, nor perhaps the most fruitful, field for the investigation of regulatory effects in higher organisms. The development and functioning of these differentiated cellular populations poses three major problems which have hardly begun to be solved at the biochemical and genetic level, namely, differentiation itself, the control of cellular multiplication, and the mechanism of hormone action. Although these three problems are intimately related, we will discuss them separately.

3. Possible Mechanisms of Hormone Action

As we have already seen, there are now several recognized cases of "molecular conversion" where a natural hormone appears to be involved, directly or indirectly. Although it is not clear to what extent these particular effects may account for the physiological action of the hormones in question, the suggestion is that many hormones may act primarily by similar mechanisms. The fact that such mechanisms have not been observed, so far, in bacteria may possibly be significant. It may be recalled that the bacteria, alone among all other forms of life, do not synthesize any steroid. It may also be remarked that an unknown, probably very large, number of microbiologists have at one time or another hopefully added steroids (or adrenalin or insulin) to their bacterial cultures, without ever observing any effect (except catabolic reactions). One is led to wonder whether not only the compounds themselves, but also the type of regulatory mechanism which they control may not be a privilege of differentiated organisms. It would be very unwise however to base such a conclusion on such scanty evidence. And it is to be hoped that, in future years, systematic attempts will be made to verify whether or not certain hormones may not actually act as allosteric inhibitors, inducers, or repressors of certain enzyme systems. The main difficulty of this research will be that no guiding *chemical* principle (based on steric analogy, reactivity, etc.) will help the investigator in the selection of which enzyme systems to test, since again the specificity of induction-repression and of allosteric inhibition is apparently completely independent of the structure and specificity of the controlled enzyme itself. Also, and for the same reasons, it is quite possible that the same hormone may prove to act on different systems, if not by different mechanisms, in different tissues.

4. Differentiation

It may be in the interpretation and analysis of differentiation that the new concepts derived from the study of microorganisms will prove of the greatest value. One point at least already seems to be quite clear: namely that biochemical differentiation (reversible or not) of cells carrying an identical genome, does not constitute a "paradox", as it appeared to do for many years, to both embryologists and geneticists.

This point may require some elaboration. The control mechanisms discovered in microorganisms govern the *expression* of genetic potentialities. Most of the actual systems however are entirely reversible, in the sense that the effects of inhibitors, inducers, or repressors do not survive for any length of time after elimination of the active agent, and the cells soon return to their initial state.

Differentiation, on the other hand, is stable, and persists once it has been induced. Whether differentiation is ever *completely* irreversible (except in non-growing cells), is an exceedingly difficult question, because the experimental operations which might decide this issue generally cannot be performed. In any case, we need not go into this discussion; let us consider that differentiation may be more or less stable, even attaining irreversibility in some cases. It might then be argued

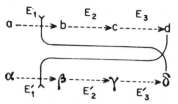

FIGURE 1. Model I. The reactions along the two pathways $a \to b \to c \to d$, and $\alpha \to \beta \to \gamma \to \delta$, are catalyzed by enzymes E_1, E_2, E_3 and E_1', E_2', E_3'. Enzyme E_1 is inhibited by δ, the product of the other pathway. Conversely, enzyme E_1' is inhibited by metabolite d, produced by the first pathway.

that since the microbial systems are completely reversible, similar mechanisms could not account for stable differentiation. But it should be clear that the microbial systems must have been geared precisely for reversibility, since selection, in microorganisms, will necessarily favor the most rapid response to any change of environment. Moreover, it is obvious from the analysis of these mechanisms that their known elements could be connected into a wide variety of "circuits", endowed with any desired degree of stability. In order to illustrate some of these possibilities, let us study a certain number of theoretical model systems in which we shall use only the controlling elements known to exist in bacteria, interconnected however in an arbitrary manner.

Consider for instance the following model, which uses the properties of the allosteric inhibition effect, assuming two independent metabolic pathways, giving rise to metabolites a, b, c, d, and α, β, γ, δ (Fig. 1). Assume that the enzymes catalyzing the first reaction in each pathway are inhibited by the final product of the *other* pathway. By such "crossfeedback" a system of alternative stable states is created where one of the two pathways, provided it once had a head-start or a temporary metabolic advantage, will permanently inhibit the other. Switching of one pathway to the other could be accomplished by a variety of methods, for instance by inhibiting temporarily any one of the enzymes of the active pathway. It should be noted that a model formally identical with this one was proposed by Delbrück (1949) (long before feedback inhibition was discovered) to account for certain alternative steady-states found in ciliates.

The following model corresponds to a classical induction system, with the only specific assumption that the active inducer is not the substrate, but the *product* of the controlled enzyme. (Fig. 2). Such a system is autocatalytic and self-sustaining. Although it is not self-reproducing in the genetic sense, it should mimic certain properties of genetic elements. In the absence of any exogenous inducing agent, the enzyme will not be synthesized unless already present, when it will maintain itself indefinitely. When the system is locked, temporary contact with an inducer will unlock it permanently. Actually, certain inducible permease systems in *E. coli* may be described in this way, and behave accordingly, as shown by Novick and Weiner (1959), and by Cohn and Horibata (1959). A similar mechanism appears to account for the so-called "slow adaptation" of yeast to galactose, without having recourse to some kind of "plasmagene" as previously believed by Spiegelman (1951).

Two different inducible or repressible systems may be interconnected by assuming that each one produces the metabolic repressor or the inducer of the other. In the first case, as illustrated below (Fig. 3) the enzymes would be mutually exclusive. The presence of one would permanently block the synthesis of the other. Switching from one state to the other could be accomplished by eliminating temporarily the substrate of the live system. In the second case, which may be represented as shown in Fig. 4, the two enzymes would be mutually dependent; one could not be synthesized in the absence of the other, although of course they might function in apparently unrelated pathways. Temporary inhibition of one of the enzymes, or elimination of its substrate, would eventually result in the permanent suppression of both.

In the preceding models, the systems were interconnected by assuming that the metabolic product of one is an inducer or a repressor of the other. Another type of interconnection, independent of metabolic activity,

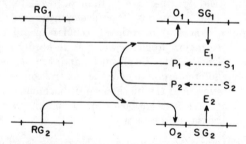

FIGURE 3. Model III. Synthesis of enzyme E_1, genetically determined by the structural gene SG_1, is regulated by the regulator gene RG_1. Synthesis of enzyme E_2, genetically determined by the structural gene SG_2 is regulated by the regulator gene RG_2. The product P_1 of the reaction catalyzed by enzyme E_1 acts as corepressor in the regulation system of enzyme E_2. The product P_2 of the reaction catalyzed by enzyme E_2 acts as corepressor in the regulation system of enzyme E_1.

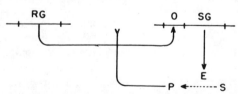

FIGURE 2. Model II. Synthesis of enzyme E, genetically determined by the structural gene SG is blocked by the repressor synthesized by the regulator gene RG. The product P of the reaction catalyzed by enzyme E acts as an inducer of the system by inactivating the repressor.

would be obtained by assuming a regulator gene controlled by an operator, sensitive to another regulator. For instance, in the system shown below (Fig. 5) a regulator gene controls the synthesis of enzymes within an operon which includes another regulator gene acting upon the operator to which the first one is attached. Such a system would be completely independent of the actual metabolic activity of the enzymes, and could be switched from the inactive to the active state by transient contact with a specific inducer, produced for instance only by another tissue. Once activated, the system could not be switched back except by addition of the aporepressor made by the first regulator gene. The change of state would therefore be virtually irreversible. It is easy to see that, conversely, starting from the active state, transient contact with an inducer acting on the product of RG_2 would switch the system, permanently, to the inactive state.

Finally the following type of circuit might be interesting to consider in relation to cyclic phenomena. In this circuit, the product of one enzyme is an inducer of the other system while the product of the second enzyme is a corepressor (Fig. 6). A study of the properties of this circuit will show that, provided adequate time constants are chosen for the decay of each enzyme and of its product, the system will oscillate from one state to the other.

These examples should suffice to show that, by the use of the principles which they illustrate, any number of systems may be interconnected into regulatory circuits endowed with virtually any desired property. The essential point about the imaginary circuits which we examined, is that their elements are not imaginary. The particular properties of each circuit are obtained only by assuming the proper type of specific interconnection. Such assumptions are freely permitted. since, as we have already seen, the specificity of induction-repression and of allosteric inhibition is not re-

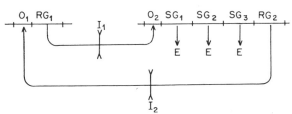

FIGURE 5. Model V. The regulator gene RG_1 controls the activity of an operon containing three structural genes (SG_1, SG_2, SG_3) and another regulator gene RG_2. The regulator gene RG_1 itself belongs to another operon sensitive to the repressor synthesized by RG_2. The action of RG_1 can be antagonized by an inducer I_1, which activates SG_1, SG_2, SG_3 and RG_2 (and therefore inactivates RG_1). The action of RG_2 can be antagonized by an inducer I_2 which activates RG_1 (and therefore inactivates the systems SG_1, SG_2, SG_3 and RG_2).

stricted by any chemical principle of analogy, and apparently is *exclusively* the result of selection for the most efficient regulation.

The models involving only metabolic steady-states maintained by allosteric effects are insufficient to account for differentiation, which must involve directed alterations in the capacity of individual cells to *synthesize* specific proteins. Such models would seem to be most adequate to account for the almost instantaneous, and thereafter more or less permanent, "memorization" by cells of a chemical event. The problem of memory itself might usefully be considered from this point of view.

It has long been recognized, by embryologists and biochemists alike, that "enzymatic adaptation" might offer an experimental approach toward the interpretation of differentiation. The realization that induction and repression are governed by specialized regulatory genes, that both eventually operate by controlling negatively the activity of structural genes, and that the specificity of inducers or repressors is entirely

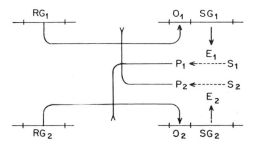

FIGURE 4. Model IV. Synthesis of enzyme E_1, genetically determined by the structural gene SG_1 is blocked by the repressor synthesized by the regulator gene RG_1. Synthesis of another enzyme E_2, controlled by structural gene SG_2 is blocked by another repressor synthesized by regulator gene RG_2. The product P_1 of the reaction catalyzed by enzyme E_1 acts as an inducer for the synthesis of enzyme E_2 and the product P_2 of the reactions catalyzed by enzyme E_2 acts as an inducer for the synthesis of enzyme E_1.

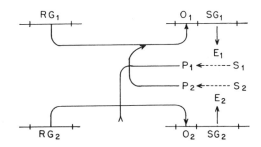

FIGURE 6. Model VI. Synthesis of enzyme E_1, genetically determined by the structural gene SG_1, is blocked by the repressor synthesized by the regulator gene RG_1. Synthesis of another enzyme E_2, controlled by structural gene SG_2, is blocked by another repressor synthesized by regulator gene RG_2. The product P_1 of the reaction catalyzed by enzyme E_1 acts as an inducer for the synthesis of enzyme E_2 while the product P_2 of the reaction catalyzed by enzyme E_2 acts as a corepressor for the synthesis of enzyme E_1.

suigeneris, allows, as we have just seen, the construction of models capable, in principle, of accounting for virtually any type of differentiation. The fact that these mechanisms are not only genetically controlled, but operate directly at the genetic level, and may be in some cases quite independent of any metabolic event in the cell itself, is evidently of special value, since the transitions of state in such systems should very closely mimic true transmissible alterations of the genetic material itself. That differentiation involves induced, specific, and permanent alterations of the genetic information of somatic cells has often been proposed as the only possible interpretation of the "paradox". It should be clear that this type of hypothesis, which meets with almost insuperable difficulties, is in fact completely unnecessary (except perhaps in certain exceptional cases, such as that of the reticulocytes and red cells), since as we have seen the transcription of a gene, not only in a cell, but in a whole cell lineage, may be permanently repressed, or derepressed, depending on an initial, transient event, which would not involve any alteration of the information carried by the gene. And it might be noted that this type of interpretation would not, in any way, be incompatible with the beautiful experiments of Briggs and King (1955) which showed that the nuclei of certain embryonic tissues, in the frog, had lost certain potentialities of expression possessed by the original nucleus of the egg.

The microbial systems actually offer some examples of irreversible effects resulting from repression or derepression. For instance, both lysogenization by an infecting temperate phage, and induction of a lysogenic bacterium, are irreversible consequences of transient conditions favoring, in the first instance, the establishment of a permanent state of self-repression, and in the second a release of the repressed condition. In the repressed (prophage) state which is maintained indefinitely in the absence of inducing agents, the viral genes are inactive in transcription; they are fully active in the vegetative state. Yet the transition from one to the other does not involve any alteration of the information contained in the genetic material of the phage.

The lysogenic systems may also be of some use in thinking about the problem of the control of cellular multiplication. In the prophage (i.e., repressed) state, the phage DNA replicates synchronously with the host cell DNA. In the derepressed state, it replicates about 20 times as fast. The presence of the repressor cannot, by itself, account for this difference. But it is a fact that the decision between synchronous or "wild" replication depends initially upon the regulator-operator interaction. It is most probable that in tissue cells the regulation of multiplication is very complex, since it must simultaneously control several systems which have to be kept in pace. And it may be of some interest to note that even relatively simple regulatory systems may go astray in several different ways. We know for instance that the constitutive state may be obtained by mutation of either the regulator or the operator. In a system such as the one shown in Fig. 6, mutations of either one of the two operators, or of one of the regulator genes, would abolish the repressive control, resulting either in a constitutive or in a "super-repressed" phenotype. In addition even *temporary* inactivation of one of the loci (for instance by reversible lesions such as are known to be produced by UV light) or temporary blocking of one of the repressors by a complexing agent, would lead precisely to the same permanent phenotypes, which might or might not be reversible by an inducer, depending upon the specific properties of the system. Only by a very thorough genetic and biochemical analysis of such a system could one decide whether the transition was brought about by true mutation, or by temporary inactivation.

These observations may have some bearings on the problem of the initial event leading to malignancy. Malignant cells have lost sensitivity to the conditions which control multiplication in normal tissues. That the disorder is genetic cannot be doubted. That, following an initial event, mutations within the cellular population are progressively selected, leading towards greater independence, i.e., heightened malignancy, is now quite clear, due in particular to the work of Klein and Klein (1958). But while the initial event, responsible for setting up the new selective relationships, may of course be a genetic mutation, it might also be brought by the transient action of an agent capable of complexing or inactivating *temporarily* a genetic locus, or a repressor, involved in the control of multiplication. It is clear that a wide variety of agents, from viruses to carcinogenes, might be responsible for such an initial event.

As a conclusion to this discussion of theoretical models, one would like to turn to experimental examples, and see whether they might, or might not, fit with the interpretations. Unfortunately, in the face of formidable technical difficulties, the study of differentiation either from the genetic or from the biochemical point of view has not attained a state which would allow any detailed comparison of theory with experiment. This is our excuse for using microbial systems as models for the interpretation of differentiation. Eventually, however, differentiation will have to be studied in differentiated cells. The remarkable advances achieved in the methodology of cell cultures encourage optimism. The greatest obstacle is the impossibility of performing genetic analysis, without which there is no hope of ever dissecting out the mechanisms of differentiation. But it should be noted that actual genetic mapping may not necessarily be required. Adequate techniques of nuclear transfer, combined with systematic studies of possible inducing or repressing agents, and with the isolation of regulatory mutants, may conceivably open the way to the experimental analysis of differentiation at the genetic-bio-chemical level.

REFERENCES

BENZER, S. 1957. The elementary units of heredity. pp. 70–93. *"The Chemical Basis of Heredity"*. ed. W. D. McElroy and B. Glass, Baltimore: Johns Hopkins Press.

BENZER, S., and E. FREESE. 1958. Induction of specific mutations with 5-bromouracil. Proc. Nat. Acad. Sci., *44:* 112–119.

BRIGGS, R. W., and T. J. KING. 1955. Specificity of nuclear functions in embryonic development. pp. 207–228. *Biological Specificity and Growth*, ed. E. G. Butler. Princeton: Princeton University Press.

BROWN, D. D., and J. MONOD. 1961. Carbon source repression of β-galactosidase in *E. coli.* Federation Proc., *20:* 222.

BURNET, F. M. 1959. The clonal selection theory of acquired immunity. Cambridge: Cambridge University Press.

COHN, M., and K. HORIBATA. 1959. Analysis of the differentiation and of the heterogeneity within a population of *Escherichia coli* undergoing induced β-galactosidase synthesis. J. Bact., *78:* 613–623.

CRICK, F. H. C. 1958. On protein synthesis. "Biological Replication of Macromolecules". 12th Symp. Soc. Exp. Biol., 138–163.

DELBRÜCK, M. 1949. In "Unitès biologiques douées de continuité génétique", Edit. du CNRS, Paris, 33–34.

DEMEREC, M., and P. E. HARTMAN. 1959. Complex loci in microorganisms. Ann. Rev. Microb., *13:* 377–406.

FALKOW, S., and L. BARON. 1961. An episomic element in a strain of *Salmonella typhosa.* Bact. Proc. (G 98), 96.

FINCHAM, J. R. S. 1959. The role of chromosomal loci in enzyme formation. Proc. Xth Int. Cong. Genetics, *1:* 355–363.

FREESE, E. 1959. On the molecular explanation of spontaneous and induced mutation. *Structure and Function of genetic elements*, Brookhaven Symposia, *12:* 63–75.

HAYES, D., F. HAYES, and F. GROS. 1961. In preparation.

INGRAM, V. M. 1957. Gene mutation in human haemoglobin: the chemical difference between normal and sickle-cell haemoglobin. Nature, *180:* 326–328.

JACOB, F., and J. MONOD. 1961. Genetic regulatory mechanisms in the synthesis of proteins. J. Mol. Biol., *3:* 318–356.

KLEIN, G., and E. KLEIN. 1958. Histocompatibility changes in tumors. J. Cell. Comp. Physiol., *52:* 125–168.

KOSHLAND, D. E., JR. 1959. Enzyme flexibility and enzyme action. J. Cell. Comp. Physiol., *54:* 245–258.

LABEYRIE, F., P. P. SLONIMSKY, and N. NASLIN. 1959. Sur la différence de stéréospécificité entre la déshydrogénase lactique extraite de la levure anaérobie et celle extraite de la levure aérobie. Biochim. Biophys. Acta, *34:* 262–265.

LEDERBERG, J. 1959. Antibody formation by single cells. Science, *130:* 1427.

LWOFF, A., and M. LWOFF. 1961. In preparation.

MAZIA, D. 1959. Cell Division. Harvey Lectures, 1957–1958, *53:* 130–170.

MC CLINTOCK, B. 1956. Controlling elements and the gene.

Cold Spring Harbor Symp. on Quant. Biol., *21:* 197–216.

MONOD, J. 1956. Remarks on the mechanism of enzyme induction. *"Enzymes: Units of biological Structure and Function"*, Henry Ford Hospital. Intern. Symp. pp. 7–28. New York: Academic Press.

MONOD, J., and M. COHN. 1952. La biosynthèse induite des enzymes (adaptation enzymatique). Adv. Enzymol., *13:* 67–119.

NOVICK, A., and L. SZILARD. 1954. Experiments with the chemostat on the rates of amino acid synthesis in bacteria. p. 21. *"Dynamics of Growth Processes"*. Princeton University Press.

NOVICK, A., and M. WEINER. 1959. The kinetics of β-galactosidase induction. Symp. on Molecular Biology. ed. R. E. Zirkle, University of Chicago Press, 78–90.

PARDEE, A. B. Personal communication.

PAULING, L. 1940. A theory of the structure and process of formation of antibodies. J. Am. Chem. Soc., *62:* 2643–2657.

PERRIN, D. 1961. In preparation.

PERRIN, D., F. JACOB, and J. MONOD. 1960. Biosynthèse induite d'une protéine génétiquement modifiée, ne présentant pas d'affinité pour l'inducteur. C. R. Acad. Sci., *251:* 155–157.

PERUTZ, M. 1961. 50th Anniversary Symposium of the Biochemical Society, London. In press.

RAPKINE, L. 1931. Sur les processus chimiques au cours de la division cellulaire. Ann. Physiol. Physicochim. Biol., *7:* 382–418.

ROBERTS, R. B., P. H. ABELSON, D. B. COWIE, E. T. BOLTON, and R. J. BRITTEN. 1955. Studies of biosynthesis in *Escherichia coli.* Carnegie Institution of Washington Publ., 607.

SPIEGELMAN, S. 1951. The particulate transmission of enzyme-forming capacity in yeast. Cold Spring Harbor Symp. on Quant. Biol., *16:* 87–98.

TRUDINGER, P. A., and G. N. COHEN. 1956. The effect of 4-methyltryptophan on growth and enzyme system of *Escherichia coli.* Biochem. J., *62:* 488–491.

VOLKIN, E., and L. ASTRACHAN. 1957. RNA metabolism in T2-infected *Escherichia coli.* pp. 686–694. *"The Chemical Basis of Heredity"*, ed. W. D. McElroy and B. Glass, Baltimore: Johns Hopkins Press.

WOOD, W. B., M. CHAMBERLAIN, and P. BERG. In Preparation.

YČAS, M., and W. S. VINCENT. 1960. A ribonucleic acid fraction from yeast related in composition of desoxyribonucleic acid. Proc. Nat. Acad. Sci., *46:* 804–810.

DISCUSSION

UMBARGER: Although I have a right to object to only one-third of the term, "NSU," I should like to offer one more plug for my suggestion that the word "end-product inhibition" be employed as an operational term for examples of the endproduct of a biosynthetic inhibiting an early step in its own biosynthetic pathway. Like "repression," the term can be used to describe an empirical observation and should subsequent study so indicate, it can be further described as a feedback mechanism. Should the inhibitory interaction have no such physiological consequence, the operational term is still appropriate.

JOURNAL OF BACTERIOLOGY, Sept., 1966
Copyright © 1966 American Society for Microbiology

Vol. 92, No. 3
Printed in U.S.A.

Effect of Gene Position on the Timing of Enzyme Synthesis in Synchronous Cultures of Yeast

PATRIC TAURO AND HARLYN O. HALVORSON[1]

Department of Bacteriology, The University of Wisconsin, Madison, Wisconsin

Received for publication 2 May 1966

ABSTRACT

TAURO, PATRIC (The University of Wisconsin, Madison), AND HARLYN O. HALVORSON. Effect of gene position on the timing of enzyme synthesis in synchronous cultures of yeast. J. Bacteriol. 92:652–661.—In synchronously growing cultures of *Saccharomyces cerevisiae*, enzyme synthesis is periodic. The effect of various factors on the timing of α-glucosidase synthesis has been investigated. The period of the cell cycle during which α-glucosidase is synthesized is unaffected by the method employed to induce synchrony, as well as other environmental conditions. However, a definite relationship exists between the number of nonallelic structural genes present for α-glucosidase and the number of periods of synthesis during the cell cycle. It is concluded that the periodic synthesis of enzymes observed in synchronously growing cultures of yeast is probably the result of an ordered process of transcription of the various structural genes.

In synchronously dividing cultures of yeast, deoxyribonucleic acid (DNA) synthesis is discontinuous (1, 7, 28), and the different classes of ribonucleic acids (RNA) and protein are synthesized throughout the cell cycle (5). In contrast to this, the synthesis of many enzymes is periodic (1, 5, 21, 24). The time during which a given enzyme is synthesized occupies only a fraction of the division time. This period is characteristic for each enzyme, and the same pattern occurs in subsequent cell cycles. These and similar observations made in bacteria (1a, 10–13, 19) have led to a renewed interest in the mechanism controlling the timing of enzyme synthesis during the cell division cycle.

Our initial findings in interspecific yeast hybrids, that the parental genes for a given enzyme are expressed at different periods of the cell cycle (5) and that addition of inducer does *not* change the time of induced enzyme synthesis (6a), led us to propose early (7) that the genome was transcribed in an ordered manner during the cell cycle.

The present paper provides further evidence for this conclusion and also illustrates some of the methodology and controls in experiments with synchronous cultures. In particular, these experiments were designed to provide answers to two

questions concerning the time of enzyme synthesis during the cell cycle. (i) Is the time of enzyme synthesis determined by the method employed to induce synchronous growth? (ii) For a given structural gene, what is the relationship between the gene position (centromere distance) and the time of its expression?

MATERIALS AND METHODS

Table 1 summarizes the various strains of yeast employed.

Materials. Chemically pure grade maltose was obtained from Matheson, Coleman and Bell, East Rutherford, N.J., and contaminating glucose was removed by the method of Halvorson and Spiegelman (8). α-*p*-Nitrophenyl-D-glucopyranoside (α-PNPG) and β-*p*-nitrophenyl-D-glucopyranoside (β-PNPG) were obtained from General Biochemicals Corp., Chagrin Falls, Ohio. Disodium-*p*-nitrophenyl phosphate (PNPP) was a product of Calbiochem.

Methods. Two methods were employed to obtain synchronously growing cultures of yeast. Method A consisted of phasing a selected fraction of yeast cells by a modification of the method described by Sando (20). The procedure consisted of growing the yeast cells in 250 ml of Wickerham's medium (26) and harvesting the cells in the late logarithmic phase of growth. The larger cells, without buds, were selected from the heterogenous population by first allowing the cells to settle at 25 C for 2 hr and then repeatedly centrifuging at 100 × *g*. The cells were washed and suspended in 100 ml of starvation medium (27) at 10^8 to 10^9 cells per milliliter and aerated for 10 to 12

[1] National Institutes of Health Research Career Professor.

TABLE 1. *Yeast employed in this study*

Strain	Source	Culture no.	Genotype[a]
Hybrid yeast (*S. fragilis* × *S. dobzhanskii*	L. J. Wickerham	Y-42	—
S. cerevisiae	Ö. Winge	Y-55	M_1m_1 m_2m_2 m_3m_3 m_4m_4
S. cerevisiae	Ö. Winge	Y-62	M_1m_1 m_2m_2 M_3m_3 m_4m_4
S. cerevisiae	Ö. Winge	Y-70	M_1m_1 M_2m_2 M_3m_3 m_4m_4

[a] The M genes govern the synthesis of α-glucosidase.

hr at 25 C. The cells were then collected by slow centrifugation, washed, and resuspended at a high cell density (10^9 to 10^{10} per milliliter) in 10 ml of synthetic growth medium (5) and aerated for about 10 to 12 hr. The cell suspension was then diluted 500-fold with fresh synthetic growth medium containing 1% maltose, unless otherwise indicated, and was incubated at 25 C. The final suspension was uniform in size and morphology and contained over 95% of viable cells. This method takes about 2 to 3 days before the cells are ready for use.

Method B was essentially that described by Mitchison and Vincent (16). One-liter cultures of *Saccharomyces cerevisiae* grown in synthetic medium containing 1% maltose were harvested in the mid-logarithmic phase of growth and suspended in 5 to 6 ml of sterile water. A 2-ml amount of this suspension was layered on a 10 to 40% (w/v) linear sucrose gradient in a glass tube (19 by 170 mm) and centrifuged for 10 min at 500 × *g* in a swinging bucket rotor at 20 C. After centrifugation, the top 10 to 30% (v/v) of the gradient was collected, washed immediately, and suspended in fresh growth medium at 25 C. This fraction represents 3 to 4% of the population placed on the gradient. Microscopic examination and analysis of the size distribution (Fig. 1) showed that the selected fraction was homogenous.

Determination of growth and division. Samples (2 ml) were collected from synchronously growing cultures at intervals, and growth was arrested by adding 0.1 ml of 36% formaldehyde. Cell numbers were determined either with a hemocytometer, as described by Williamson and Scopes (27), or with an electronic cell counter (Coulter counter). For the latter, yeast samples were diluted 200-fold in 0.9% sodium chloride solution by use of an automatic diluter, and 0.5 ml of the diluted sample was counted, each time in triplicate, with the use of a 70-μ orifice tube. In experiments with strains which showed tendencies to aggregate, mild sonic treatment for about 10 sec with a 20-kc MSE ultrasonic probe (21) facilitated counting of the yeast cells without visible damage to the cells. For determination of the cell size distribution, the electronic particle size distribution plotter was set to count for a time period of 4 sec at each electronic window. Standard polyvinyl latex particles of uniform size were used to standardize the Coulter counter. Changes in optical density of the culture were measured with a Beckman DU spectrophotometer at 600 mμ with the use of a 1-cm cuvette.

Dry-weight determination. Samples (10 ml) of the

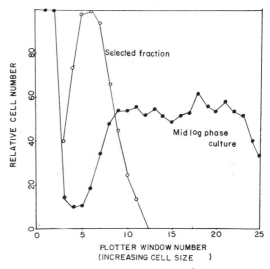

FIG. 1. *Cell size distribution of a culture in exponential growth and a fraction selected by sucrose density centrifugation.*

synchronously growing culture were withdrawn at intervals, and filtered rapidly through a tared 0.45-mμ membrane-filter disc (Millipore Filter Corp., Bedford, Mass.). This was washed with 20 ml of cold distilled water and dried at 85 C to a constant weight.

Enzyme assays. At intervals, samples were removed, washed twice by centrifugation, and prepared for enzyme assay as previously described (3). α-Glucosidase was assayed by the method of Halvorson et al. (9). β-Glucosidase was measured by the method of Duerksen and Halvorson (3), and alkaline phosphatase was determined by the method of Torriani (25). In all cases, a unit of enzyme is defined as millimicromoles of substrate hydrolyzed per 100 sec. When enzyme levels are plotted as a function of the fraction of a generation (Fig. 9 and 12), the amount of enzyme present at the beginning of the cell cycle is normalized to unity.

RESULTS

Use of interspecific hybrids in synchronous growth experiments. Interspecific hybrids, which one would expect to contain numerous nonallelic genes, provide ideal experimental materials for examining the effect of gene position on the timing of specific enzyme synthesis during the cell cycle.

As previously noted (5, 7), cultures of such an interspecific hybrid (Y-42), synchronized by the phasing method of Williamson and Scopes (27), exhibit balanced growth (the amount of any component doubles in subsequent generations). Further characteristics of this system are illustrated in Fig. 2. Increases in the dry weight of cells during synchronous growth occurred at about the same time that the optical density began to increase and that the first signs of budding were observed microscopically. Once growth was initiated, the dry weight increased continuously, with the rate doubling with the beginning of each generation and the total amount essentially doubling during each generation. In similar experiments with this organism, the rate of protein synthesis was nearly linear over the generation cycle (7). In synchronous cultures of *S. cerevisiae* (21), as well as during the cell cycle of *S. cerevisiae* (15), *total* dry mass increases linearly, whereas protein and RNA increase in an exponential manner.

Inherent variables, such as a degree of asynchrony in the population and fluctuating pool levels, make precise determinations of the overall kinetics of macromolecular synthesis difficult. However, measurements such as those shown

in Fig. 2 can be useful guides to monitor the extent to which a synchronous culture is under conditions of balanced growth.

In cultures of the hybrid yeast (Y-42), synchronized by the drastic phasing method of Williamson and Scopes (27), periodic enzyme synthesis has been observed (5). It was, therefore, of interest to re-examine the timing of enzyme synthesis in cultures synchronized by milder methods. Figure 3 illustrates such an experiment with the same hybrid yeast (Y-42) phased by method A. After a delay of 320 min, cell numbers increased periodically over two generations. In each generation, two periods of alkaline phosphatase and β-glucosidase synthesis and one period of α-glucosidase synthesis were observed. In these and parallel experiments, the fraction of the generation during which each of these enzymes was synthesized was closely approximated in subsequent generations and was in agreement with our earlier findings (5).

Determination of the degree of synchrony in populations of S. cerevisiae. The degree of synchrony was a function of the inherent characteristics of the cells and of the phasing method employed. Since the generation time of a synchronous culture did not represent only the period during which division of cells occurred, generation times were calculated from the theoretical growth curves, as shown by the dashed line T in Fig. 4. The growth curves, as determined either by use of the Coulter counter or by direct counting of the cells, showed similarity in pattern, although the cell numbers, as determined by the two methods, differed slightly. The bud ratio fluctuated in close agreement with the growth and

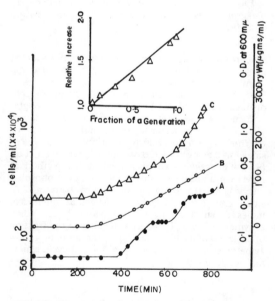

FIG. 2. *Dry-weight changes in a phased synchronous culture of a hybrid yeast (Y-42). (A) Cell number. (B) Optical density. (C) Dry weight.*

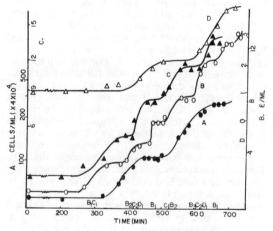

FIG. 3. *Enzyme synthesis in a phased culture of the hybrid yeast Y-42. (A) Cell number. (B) Alkaline phosphatase. (C) β-Glucosidase. (D) α-Glucosidase.*

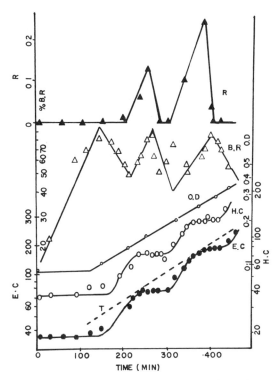

FIG. 4. *Determination of the degree of synchrony in a yeast population. Saccharomyces cerevisiae was grown synchronously in synthetic medium containing 1% maltose. E.C., Coulter Counter, total cells per milliliter times 4×10^{-4}; T, theoretical growth curve; H.C., microscopic, total cells per milliliter times 5×10^{-4}; O.D., optical density (600 mμ); R, normalized rate of division per hour; and B.R., bud ratio.*

division of the yeast cells, reaching a level of 90% just before division, and this is consistent with a high degree of synchronization of the population. The degree of synchrony can also be followed by calculating the normalized rate of cell division (R) according to the equation of Engelberg (2):

$$R = (dn/dt)/N \text{ per unit of time}$$

where n is the total number of cells dividing and N is the total number of cells present at time t. The plot of R against time (Fig. 3) shows the same periodicity as observed in the bud ratios.

The synchronization index (SI) for this experiment was calculated from the equation of Scherbaum (22):

$$SI = (N/N_0 - 1)(1 - t/g)$$

where N_0 and N are the total number of cells before and after division, respectively, t is the

time period during which division occurs, and g is the generation time of the culture. An SI of 0.7 for the first division and 0.6 for the second indicates that the culture possesses a fair degree of synchrony; these values are in close agreement with the values reported by Scherbaum (22) for a number of synchronous microbial systems.

In practice, the individual division steps in synchronous growth have been monitored by following the frequency size distribution with the use of an electronic particle size distribution plotter. This procedure is illustrated in Fig. 5, in which a part of the spectrum representing different periods during a generation of synchronous growth of *S. cerevisiae* is presented. Initially, the population was composed mostly of single cells. During growth, the peak gradually dropped and the distribution shifted to the right as individual cells enlarged and produced buds. At the end of the generation, the curve showed a dramatic return to the original position and showed a near doubling of the relative cell number. These changes closely parallel the shifts in bud ratios (Fig. 4).

Use of S. cerevisiae for synchronous growth experiments. A clearer insight into the relationship between the position of a gene and its time of expression during the cell cycle would be afforded if the timing of the *same* structural gene could be examined at different positions along the chromosome. The M genes determining the synthesis of α-glucosidase in *Saccharomyces* provide such an opportunity. Six nonallelic genes have been described; all are unlinked and two have been centromere-linked on different chromosomes (17). The same enzyme is coded by each of these genes (9), each functions independently (18), and all are induced in a similar manner. With the use of appropriate diploids, it should be possible to examine the *function* of each of these genes in the presence of a *common* regulatory system. Stepwise synthesis of α-glucosidase in synchronous cultures has already been reported (6a, 7; and Fig. 3).

Effect of the method of phasing on the timing of α-glucosidase synthesis. The diploid heterozygous strain of *S. cerevisiae* (Y-55) carrying one structural gene (M_1m_1) for the synthesis of α-glucosidase was phased by the method A, and the synthesis of enzyme was examined during two generations of growth (Fig. 6). After a period of 200 min, the cell numbers increased periodically, and, in each of the two generations examined, only one period of α-glucosidase synthesis was observed, which began at about the middle of the generation.

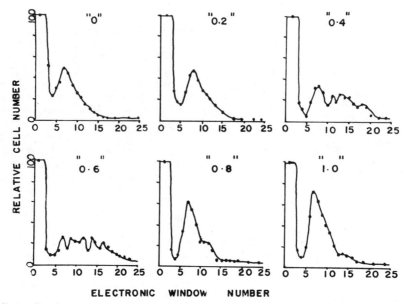

Fig. 5. *Cell size distribution in a synchronously dividing culture of Saccharomyces cerevisiae. The distribution spectrum was measured for cultures at 0, 0.2, 0.4, 0.6, 0.8, and 1.0 fraction of a generation.*

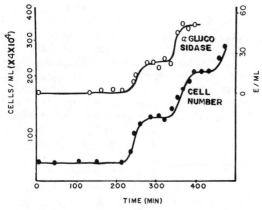

Fig. 6. *Enzyme synthesis in a phased, synchronously dividing culture of Saccharomyces cerevisiae (Y-55).*

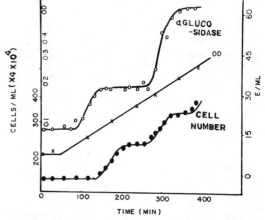

Fig. 7. *Enzyme synthesis in an unphased, synchronous culture of Saccharomyces cerevisiae (Y-55).*

To determine whether the periodicity was influenced by the method of inducing synchronous growth, a synchronous fraction from the same yeast was physically separated as in method B, and the synthesis of α-glucosidase was examined during two periods of synchronous growth (Fig. 7). After a very short lag, the cell number increased periodically, and, in each generation, a single period of enzyme synthesis was observed during the same fraction of the cell cycle observed in the experiment of Fig. 6.

As a further control to test the possibility that exposure and centrifugation introduced periodic enzyme synthesis in the population, the following

experiment was conducted. A cell suspension of *S. cerevisiae* (Y-55) was centrifuged on a sucrose gradient in the same manner as described in Fig. 7. After centrifugation, the entire contents of the centrifuge tube were mixed, diluted into fresh growth medium, and allowed to grow. As shown in Fig. 8, the cell number in this asynchronous culture increased continuously. The synthesis of α-glucosidase was continuous and no bursts in synthesis were observed, further supporting the conclusion that periodic enzyme synthesis is not caused by the method employed to induce synchronous growth.

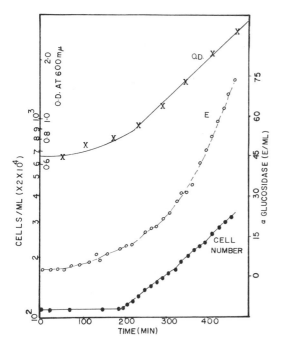

FIG. 8. *Enzyme synthesis in an asynchronous culture of Saccharomyces cerevisiae Y-55). The culture was first centrifuged in a sucrose density gradient. See text for details.*

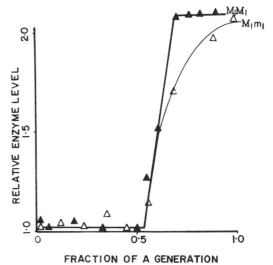

FIG. 9. *Timing of enzyme synthesis in homozygous and heterozygous diploid strains of Saccharomyces cerevisiae. See Fig. 7 for data for* M_1m_1 *and Halvorson et al. (6a) for data for* M_1M_1.

Comparisons of diploids homozygous and heterozygous for M_1. One might expect that allelic copies of the same gene would be expressed during the same period of the cell cycle. This is confirmed by the results in Fig. 9, where increases in the level of α-glucosidase as a function of the fraction of the generation time are compared in diploids of *S. cerevisiae* hetcrozygous (M_1m_1) and homozygous (M_1M_1) for the structural gene for α-glucosidase. In each case, only one period of enzyme synthesis was observed, and this period was initiated at about the middle of the generation. Both genes were apparently expressed simultaneously.

Effect of gene position on the timing of enzyme synthesis. The various M genes function independently in exponential cultures, and the level of induced α-glucosidase is strictly additive to the gene dosage (18). Further, in synchronous cultures, the times of basal and induced α-glucosidase synthesis are identical; induction does not change the time of expression of the genome (6a). Therefore, since these various M genes are scattered over the yeast genome, examination of the time of α-glucosidase synthesis in synchronous cultures enables one to test further whether the time of expression is determined by the position of the structural gene.

To examine this hypothesis, a series of experiments were carried out in which α-glucosidase synthesis was followed in synchronous cultures carrying one or more of the various M genes. The following two typical experiments illustrate the methodology and determination of the time of expression of each gene. Two strains of *S. cerevisiae*, one carrying two structural genes, M_1 and M_3 (Y-62), and the other carrying three structural genes, M_1, M_2, and M_3 (Y-70), were synchronized by method A, and the synthesis of α-glucosidase was followed. As shown in Fig. 10, the synthesis of enzyme in the heterozygous diploid with two different structural genes for α-glucosidase occurred as two distinct steps which repeated in each generation. One step occurred shortly after the initiation of each cell cycle, whereas the second occurred approximately in the middle of the cell cycle. From the results of Fig. 6 and 7, it is clear that the second step occurs at the same time enzyme synthesis commences in cultures carrying only the M_1 gene. Presumably, the earlier step in enzyme synthesis is determined by the M_3 gene.

An example of enzyme synthesis in a synchronous culture with three structural genes for α-glucosidase (M_1m_1, M_2m_2, M_3m_3) is shown in Fig. 11. As shown in this experiment, three periods of enzyme synthesis occurred in each cell cycle; these periods also recurred in subsequent generations. Two periods occurred during the same fraction of the generation cycle shown in

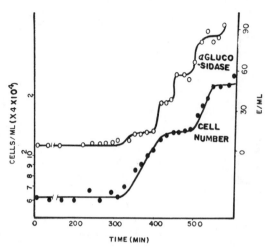

FIG. 10. *Enzyme synthesis in a synchronous culture of Saccharomyces cerevisiae (Y-62) having two structural genes for α-glucosidase (M$_1$M$_3$).*

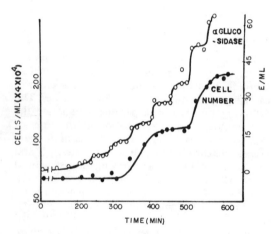

FIG. 11. *Enzyme synthesis in a synchronous culture of Saccharomyces cerevisiae (Y-70) having three structural genes for α-glucosidase synthesis (M$_1$M$_2$M$_3$).*

Fig. 10, and presumably correspond to the products of the M$_1$ and M$_3$ genes. The third period of enzyme synthesis began at about 0.75 fraction of the generation cycle, which is apparently the time of expression of the M$_2$ structural gene.

In parallel experiments, a burst in enzyme synthesis at 0.25 fraction of a generation was seen in cultures carrying the M$_4$ gene (6a). In Fig. 12 are summarized the times of expression of the four different M genes, as determined from the second generation of synchronous growth.

Our interpretation of these and similar experiments can be summarized as follows. (i) The number of periods of enzyme synthesis in the

cell cycle corresponds to the number of unlinked structural genes present. (ii) The time of expression of a given structural gene is unaffected by the presence of other structural genes. (iii) Each of the structural genes has a unique time of expression in the cell cycle.

These findings led us to conclude that the M genes are expressed independently of each other at different times of the cell cycle.

DISCUSSION

An ordered transcription of the genome, which parallels the probable order of gene replication, has been explained by either of two distinct hypotheses. (i) The gene is continuously available to transcription; periodicity in enzyme synthesis is the result of end-product repression. (ii) Transcription is ordered or sequential, or both; each gene is available for transcription only during a specific period in each cell cycle.

As stated earlier (5, 7), evidence obtained with synchronous cultures of yeast makes the first hypothesis untenable. Addition of high concentrations of inducers, which one would expect to overcome the cyclic control by end-product inhibitors, has no effect on the time in which enzyme synthesis commences or ceases during the cell cycle (6a). Their only effect is to increase the differential rate of enzyme synthesis during a limited period of the cell cycle. These results may explain the well-known phenomenon in yeast where, under conditions of full induction or derepression, the maximal level of a given enzyme comprises only a fraction of a per cent of the total cell protein (6). This is in marked contrast to the situation found in bacterial cells.

If the periodicity of enzyme synthesis was regulated by repression (end-product or otherwise; 4), then one would expect the time of gene expression to be subject to alteration by drastic environmental changes. Such changes are, in fact, encountered in the methods of phasing cultures in which prolonged starvation is employed. As reported here, in experiments with a hybrid yeast, the timing of enzyme synthesis was the same in cultures phased either by the 13-day repeated starvation method of Williamson and Scopes (28) or by the short-cycle starvation method A. Further, in *S. cerevisiae*, α-glucosidase synthesis occurs at the same time of the cell cycle in cultures synchronized by starvation or by sucrose density centrifugation, a procedure which does not induce periodic synthesis in control experiments. Finally, attempts to interfere with levels of repressors by reducing the growth rate or following enzyme synthesis under conditions of glucose repression have not dissociated the time of enzyme synthesis from cell division.

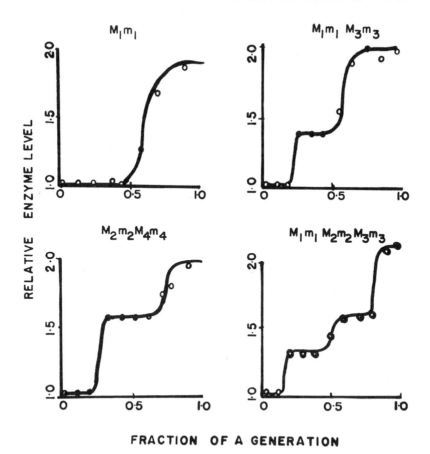

FRACTION OF A GENERATION

FIG. 12. *Timing of α-glucosidase synthesis in various M strains of Saccharomyces cerevisiae. The relative rate of enzyme synthesis is plotted as a function of the generation time. The data are derived from the second generation of synchronous growth (data from Fig. 7, 10, 11, and M.S. Thesis of P. Tauro, Univ. of Wisconsin, 1965).*

Our evidence is consistent with the second hypothesis. This conclusion is best summarized by recalling the predictions of this hypothesis which have been experimentally verified. (i) Closely linked genes are expressed at approximately the same time during the cell cycle (7). (ii) Genes which are located on the same chromosome, equidistant from the centromere (allelic), are expressed at exactly the same time (Fig. 9). (iii) The time of expression of genes, which *code for precisely the same enzyme* and *are located at different distances from the centromere*, varies.

One would anticipate that the third prediction is a common phenomenon in interspecific hybrids, since, in these strains during the course of evolution, one would expect not only the appearance of isozymes, but also considerable chromosomal rearrangement. This possibility was examined in the hybrid produced by crossing *S. dobzhanskii* × *S. fragilis* (5). Only one period of β-glucosidase synthesis occurs per generation in

each of the parental strains. In the hybrid, however, two periods of enzyme synthesis were observed per cell cycle, each corresponding to the time of enzyme synthesis in the parental strains. In this hybrid, several periods of alkaline phosphatase were also observed per cell cycle. The separation of two distinct alkaline phosphatases by chromatography (Nakao and Halvorson, *unpublished data*) may provide an explanation for these observations.

A more direct test has been afforded by the existence of different M genes in yeast, each responsible for the production of the enzyme α-glucosidase (9). These genes have been mapped (17). Of importance here is the fact that these genes are unlinked and are associated with different linkage groups. Each of these functions independently and, as shown here, is expressed at a different period of the cell cycle.

In cultures of *Shizosaccharomyces pombe*, synchronized by gradient sedimentation, single steps of aspartic transcarbamylase and ornithine transcarbamylase were observed per cell cycle (1). However, sucrase, maltase, and alkaline phosphatase increased continuously over the division cycle. These findings led Bostock et al. to conclude "that similar modes of enzyme synthesis are found in both prokaryotic and eukaryotic cells." However, the lack of information on the genetics of S. pombe limits this conclusion. Since more than three steps of enzyme per cell cycle are difficult to determine, and numerous maltase (α-glucosidase) and sucrase genes (17), as well as types of alkaline phosphatases, are known in yeast, it is not clear whether these are exceptions to the finding in S. cereviseae of one transcriptional period per structural gene during each cell cycle.

One possible explanation of sequential enzyme synthesis in yeast is that transcription is linked to replication of the genome. This possibility would seem unlikely, since DNA synthesis occupies only a portion of the cell cycle (1, 7, 28), whereas protein and enzyme synthesis are continuous throughout the cell cycle, both preceding and following the period of DNA synthesis. This possibility has been clearly eliminated in Bacillus. Periodic enzyme synthesis is observed both in a thymineless strain of B. subtilis in which DNA synthesis is inhibited by 5-fluorodeoxyuridine (12) and during outgrowth of spores of B. cereus (23) in which the few per cent increase of DNA observed is blocked by mitomycin (W. Steinberg, M.S. Thesis, Univ. of Wisconsin, Madison, 1965).

Findings such as these might lead one to suspect that similar mechanisms control transcription in both prokaryotic and eukaryotic cells. However, it is by now clear that some essential differences exist between these systems, making a unified hypothesis unlikely. The initial finding in yeast that transcription is ordered and related to gene position (5, 7) was later demonstrated for basal enzyme synthesis in bacteria (14). Despite these similarities, the two systems respond differently to the presence of inducers. Contrary to the findings in yeast (6a), in Escherichia coli and B. subtilis enzymes can be induced or derepressed at any period of the cell cycle (10, 12, 13), suggesting that the genome is accessible to transcription at all times. In these organisms, periodicity of enzyme synthesis during the cell cycle is difficult to interpret, being subject to all those regulatory systems known to influence enzyme levels in exponential cultures.

In summary, the present evidence in yeast favors an ordered, sequential transcription of the genome, the time of expression of a given gene being determined by its spatial arrangement on the yeast chromosome. Experiments are in progress to determine whether this order is from the centromere to its extremities or the reverse.

ACKNOWLEDGMENTS

This investigation was supported by grants from the National Science Foundation (B-1750) and Air Force Office of Scientific Research [AF 49 (638) 314].

LITERATURE CITED

1. BOSTOCK, C. J., W. D. DONACHIE, M. MASTERS, AND J. M. MITCHISON. 1966. Synthesis of enzymes and DNA in synchronous cultures of Schizosaccharomyces pombe. Nature 210:808–810.
1a. DONACHIE, W. D. 1965. Control of enzyme steps during the bacterial cell cycle. Nature 205:1084–1086.
2. ENGELBERG, J. 1964. The effect of non-dividing cells on the synchronization of cell cultures. Exptl. Cell Res. 34:111–119.
3. DUERKSEN, J. D., AND H. O. HALVORSON. 1958. Purification and properties of an inducible β-glucosidase in yeast. J. Biol. Chem. 233:1113–1120.
4. GOODWIN, B. C. 1966. An entrainment model for timed enzyme synthesis in bacteria. Nature 209:479–481.
5. GORMAN, J., P. TAURO, M. LA BERGE, AND H. O. HALVORSON. 1964. Timing of enzyme synthesis during synchronous division in yeast. Biochem. Biophys. Res. Commun. 15:43–49.
6. HALVORSON, H. O. 1964. Genetic control of enzyme synthesis. J. Exptl. Zool. 157:63–76.
6a. HALVORSON, H. O., R. M. BOCK, P. TAURO, R. EPSTEIN, AND M. LA BERGE. 1966. Periodic enzyme synthesis in synchronous cultures of yeast, pp. 102–116. In I. L. Cameron and G. M. Padilla [ed.], Cell synchrony—studies in biosynthetic regulation. Academic Press, Inc., New York.
7. HALVORSON, H. O., J. GORMAN, P. TAURO, R. EPSTEIN, AND M. LA BERGE. 1964. The control of enzyme synthesis in synchronous cultures of yeast. Federation Proc. 23:1002–1008.
8. HALVORSON, H. O., AND S. SPIEGELMAN. 1952. The inhibition of enzyme formation by amino acid analogues. J. Bacteriol. 64:207–221.
9. HALVORSON, H. O., S. WINDERMAN, AND J. GORMAN. 1963. Comparison of the glucosidases of Saccharomyces produced in response to five non-allelic maltose genes. Biochim. Biophys. Acta 67:42–53.
10. KUEMPEL, P. L., M. MASTERS, AND A. B. PARDEE. 1965. Bursts of enzyme synthesis in the bacterial duplication cycle. Biochem. Biophys. Res. Commun. 18:858–867.
11. MAALØE, O. 1962. Synchronous growth, p. 1–32. In I. C. Gunsalus and R. Y. Stanier [ed.], The bacteria, vol. 4. Academic Press, Inc., New York.
12. MASTERS, M., AND W. D. DONACHIE. 1966. Repression and the control of cyclic enzyme synthesis in Bacillus subtilis. Nature 209:476–479.

13. MASTERS, M., P. L. KUEMPEL, AND A. B. PARDEE. 1964. Enzyme synthesis in synchronous cultures of bacteria. Biochem. Biophys. Res. Commun. 15:38–42.

14. MASTERS, M., AND A. B. PARDEE. 1965. Sequence of enzyme synthesis and gene replication during the cell cycle of *Bacillus subtilis*. Proc. Natl. Acad. Sci. U.S. 54:64–70.

15. MITCHISON, J. M. 1958. The growth of single cells. II. *Saccharomyces cerevisiae*. Exptl. Cell Res. 15:214–221.

16. MITCHISON, J. M., AND W. S. VINCENT. 1965. Preparation of synchronous cultures by sedimentation. Nature 205:987–989.

17. MORTIMER, R. K., AND D. C. HAWTHORNE. 1966. Genetic mapping in *Saccharomyces*. Genetics 53:165–174.

18. RUDERT, F., AND H. O. HALVORSON. 1963. The effect of gene dosage on the level of α-glucosidase in yeast. Bull. Res. Council Israel 11A:337–344.

19. RUDNER, R. B., B. PROKOPACHNEIDER, AND E. CHARGAFF. 1964. Rhythmic alterations in the rate of synthesis and the composition of rapidly labelled RNA during synchronous growth of bacteria. Nature 203:479–483.

20. SANDO, N. 1963. Biochemical studies on the synchronized culture of *Schizosaccharomyces pombe*. J. Gen. Appl. Microbiol. 9:233–241.

21. SCOPES, A. W., AND D. H. WILLIAMSON. 1964. The growth and oxygen uptake of synchronously dividing cultures of *Saccharomyces cerevisiae*. Exptl. Cell Res. 35:361–371.

22. SHERBAUM, O. H. 1964. Comparison of synchronous and synchronized cell division. Exptl. Cell Res. 33:89–98.

23. STEINBERG, W., H. O. HALVORSON, A. KEYNAN, AND E. WEINBERG. 1965. Timing of protein synthesis during germination and outgrowth of spores of *Bacillus cereus* strain T. Nature 208:710–711.

24. SYLVÉN, B., C. A. TOBIAS, H. MALMGREN, R. OTTOSON, AND B. THORELL. 1959. Cyclic variations in the peptidase and catheptic activities of yeast cultures synchronized with respect to cell multiplication. Exptl. Cell Res. 16:77–87.

25. TORIANI, A. 1960. Influence of inorganic phosphate in the formation of phosphatase by *Escherichia coli*. Biochim. Biophys. Acta 38:460–479.

26. WICKERHAM, L. J. 1951. Taxonomy of yeast. U.S. Dept. Agr. Tech. Bull. 1029.

27. WILLIAMSON, D. H., AND A. W. SCOPES. 1962. A rapid method for synchronizing division in the yeast *Saccharomyces cerevisiae*. Nature 193:356–357.

28. WILLIAMSON, D. H., AND A. W. SCOPES. 1960. The behavior of nucleic acids in dividing cultures of *Saccharomyces cerevisiae*. Exptl. Cell Res. 20:338–349.

JOURNAL OF BACTERIOLOGY, Mar. 1969, p. 1149–1154
Copyright © 1969 American Society for Microbiology

Vol. 97, No. 3
Printed in U.S.A.

Acetylglucosaminidase, an Early Enzyme in the Development of *Dictyostelium discoideum*

WILLIAM F. LOOMIS, JR.

Department of Biology, University of California, San Diego, La Jolla, California 92037

Received for publication 23 September 1968

The specific activity of acetylglucosaminidase has been found to increase more than 10-fold during the first 10 hr of development in the cellular slime mold *Dictyostelium discoideum*. The specific activity then remained essentially constant until after germination. The activity was purified 36-fold and found to behave as a single protein species. The increase in specific activity required concomitant protein synthesis. If ribonucleic acid synthesis was preferentially inhibited during the period of synthesis of acetylglucosaminidase, further increase in enzymatic activity stopped after 2 hr. The increase in activity did not occur in a mutant strain which did not undergo the first step in morphogenesis. Mutant strains, blocked slightly later in morphogenesis, synthesized the enzyme at the normal rate but for an extended period. It was concluded that the initiation and termination of synthesis of acetylglucosaminidase are controlled by the developmental program.

It has been thought for many years that development of multicellular organisms may result from differential gene activation (10). Changes in the specific activity of enzymes during development can give evidence on differential gene action when the relation to protein and ribonucleic acid (RNA) synthesis is determined.

The development of the cellular slime mold *Dictyostelium discoideum* presents a favorable system for genetic and biochemical studies, because large numbers of cells can be induced to undergo multicellular development synchronously (16) and techniques for clonal isolation of mutants with altered developmental capacities have been perfected (24). The specific activity of a large number of enzymes does not change appreciably during the development of *D. discoideum* (3, 23). However, three enzymes have been found which are synthesized only during discrete periods of slime-mold development and which require prior RNA synthesis: trehalose-phosphate synthetase (EC 2.3.1.15) activity increases during the pseudoplasmodial stage (14), and uridine diphosphate (UDP)-glucose pyrophosphorylase (EC 2.7.7.9) and UDP-galactose polysaccharide transferase activities increase when the pseudoplasmodia culminate to form spores and stalk cells (1, 18, 20).

This study concerns an enzyme activity which increases by more than 10-fold early in slime-mold development during the period of aggregation prior to multicellular organization. The increase

in specific activity requires concomitant protein synthesis and previous RNA synthesis.

MATERIALS AND METHODS

Chemicals. *p*-Nitrophenyl derivatives of β-D-*N*-acetylglucosamine, β-D-glucuronide, β-D-glucoside, α-D-glucoside, β-D-xylopyranoside, and *o*-nitrophenyl β-D-galactoside were purchased from Calbiochem. *p*-Nitrophenyl β-D-*N*-acetylgalactosamine was purchased from the Cyclo Chemical Corp. (Los Angeles, Calif.). Cycloheximide (Acti-Dione) was purchased from The Upjohn Co. (Kalamazoo, Mich.). Actinomycin D was a gift from Merck Co., Inc. (Rahway, N.J.).

Membrane filters were purchased from the Millipore Filter Corp. (Bedford, Mass.).

Chromatographic methods. Carbohydrates were separated on Whatman no. 1 paper with ascending solvent systems either of *t*-butyl alcohol-methyl ethyl ketone-formic acid-water (8:6:3:3) or of isopropyl alcohol-water-HCl (65:18.4:16.6; reference 4). The sugars were located by use of an Ag(NO₃) stain.

Organism. *D. discoideum* strain NC-4 (haploid) and strain KY-3 (the morphological mutant) have been previously described (24). Five strains which fail to aggregate normally (VA-3 to VA-7) were isolated from strain NC-4 by Diane Van Alstyne who used the method of Yanagawa, Loomis, and Sussman (24). Two other strains which fail to aggregate (min 4 and min 5) were isolated by Loomis and Ashworth (8).

The amoebae were grown in association with *Aerobacter aerogenes* (16). Development was initiated by removal of the bacteria and was allowed to proceed at

22 C on membrane filters (Millipore HABP 047) saturated with phosphate buffer salt solution (16).

Acetylglucosaminidase assay. Approximately 5 × 10^7 cells were collected from the membrane filters and suspended in 3 ml of distilled water. The samples were frozen, thawed, and treated for 30 sec on a Branson Sonifier. Assays on crude extracts were performed immediately with 20 to 200 μg of protein per ml in 10^{-2} M acetate buffer, pH 5, which contained 8 × 10^{-3} M p-nitrophenyl N-acetylglucosamine. After incubation at 35 C for 5 to 100 min, the reaction was stopped by the addition of an equal volume of 1 M Na_2CO_3. Substrate-dependent absorption at 420 nm was determined with a Zeiss spectrophotometer. A unit of activity is defined as the amount which will liberate 1 nmole of p-nitrophenol per min under the above conditions. Specific activity is expressed as units per milligram of protein. Protein was determined by the method of Lowry et al. (9).

Acetylglucosamine determinations. The concentration of N-acetylglucosamine was estimated by the method of Reissig, Strominger, and Leloir (12) with p-dimethylaminobenzaldhyde reagent.

RESULTS

Characteristics of the reaction. The activity of acetylglucosaminidase (EC 3.2.1.30) was estimated by observation of the increase in optical density at 420 nm after incubation of the extract with p-nitrophenyl N-acetyl β-D-glucosamine. The reaction product had an absorption spectrum from 310 to 500 nm, which is identical with authentic p-nitrophenol. When 1 μ mole of substrate was totally hydrolyzed by incubation with partially purified enzyme (600 units/mg of protein), the only observable reducing compound cochromatographed with authentic N-acetylglucosamine in two solvent systems. It was concluded that the enzyme activity under study catalyzes the following reaction: p-nitrophenyl N-acetylglucosamine + H_2O → p-nitrophenol + N-acetylglucosamine.

The formation of p-nitrophenol is linear with respect to time up to 100 min, and linear with respect to amount of extract up to 0.5 mg of protein per ml at 35 C until more than 0.1 μmole has been formed. The Michaelis constant (K_m) for p-nitrophenyl N-acetyl β-D glucosamine is 10^{-3} M under standard assay conditions. The enzyme has a broad pH optimum in the range pH 4.5 to 5.5. It is stable to freezing and thawing; the activity is stable for more than 10 min at 50 C, but it is inactivated by 5 min at 80 C. The rate of the reaction is linearly dependent on temperature from 20 to 45 C and shows a Q_{10} of 2 in this range.

Partial purification of acetylglucosaminidase. Approximately 5 × 10^9 amoebae of *D. discoideum* strain NC-4 were allowed to develop on membrane supports for 16 hr before they were col-

lected in 10^{-3} M phosphate buffer, pH 6. The cells were concentrated by slow-speed centrifugation, and the pellet was resuspended in buffer. All activity was found associated with the cells. After it was frozen, thawed, and sonically treated, the extract was made 0.5% in streptomycin sulfate. The supernatant liquid, after centrifugation at 3,000 × g for 15 min, was brought to 60% saturation with ammonium sulfate. After 2 hr at 0 C, the precipitate was collected by centrifugation and was found to contain 85% of the acetylglucosaminidase activity present in the starting material.

Material, partially purified by the above steps, was chromatographed on a diethylaminoethyl (DEAE)-Sephadex column that was equilibrated with 0.2 M NaCl, 10^{-4} M phosphate buffer (pH 6), and eluted by an NaCl gradient from 0.2 M to 0.7 M. The enzyme eluted as a single peak at about 0.4 M NaCl (Fig. 1). This procedure resulted in a 36-fold purification of the enzyme. The activity was found to be excluded by Sephadex G100. At no time during the purification was there evidence for more than a single molecular species with acetylglucosaminidase activity.

The kinetics, pH optimum, and temperature

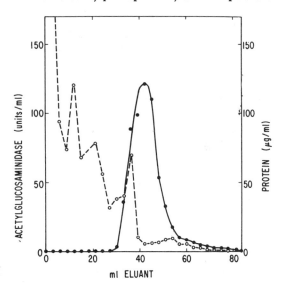

FIG. 1. *Purification of acetylglucosaminidase. Acetylglucosaminidase (1,500 units), purified to a specific activity of 320 units/mg of protein from a crude extract of* D. discoideum *pseudoplasmodia, was applied to a column (1 by 10 cm) of DEAE-Sephadex in 10^{-4} M potassium phosphate buffer, pH 6, containing 0.2 M NaCl. The enzyme was eluted with a linear gradient of NaCl from 0.2 M to 0.7 M in 100 ml of the phosphate buffer. Samples (3 ml) were collected and assayed for protein (O) and acetylglucosaminidase (●).*

characteristics of the reaction catalyzed by the partially purified enzyme were similar to those catalyzed by the crude extract; this suggests that no diffusable cofactors, activators, or inhibitors of the enzyme are present in crude extract. The specificity of the partially purified material was tested on a variety of compounds (Table 1). Only *p*-nitrophenyl *N*-acetylglucosamine and *p*-nitrophenyl *N*-acetylgalactosamine were hydrolyzed to a significant extent under standard assay conditions. A highly purified sample of acetylglucosaminidase from pinto beans also catalyzes the hydrolysis of *p*-nitrophenol galactosamine (2).

Kinetics of enzyme synthesis during development. When the food supply of *D. discoideum* is depleted or removed, the solitary vegetative amoebae aggregate over a period of several hours into masses of about 10^5 cells. During the next few hours, these masses organize into migratory pseudoplasmodia. After an additional period of about 8 hr, the pseudoplasmodia settle down on the support and form tall gently tapering stalks. At the top of each stalk, about 5×10^4 cells encapsulate to form the spores (legend, Fig. 2). This developmental sequence occurs in the absence of exogenous food supply or significant cell division (11, 21).

Samples were taken for determination of acetylglucosaminidase activity at various times after initiation of development (Fig. 2). The specific

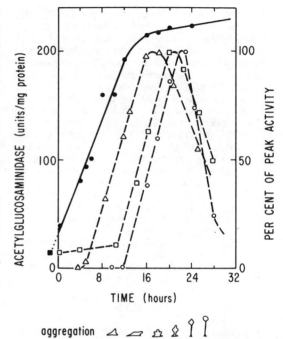

aggregation

FIG. 2. *Kinetics of accumulation of acetylglucosaminidase. Cells of D. discoideum were collected from the membrane filters at various times after the initiation of development and the specific activity of acetylglucosaminidase was determined* (●). *A single determination on vegetative amoebae growing exponentially was performed* (■). *Kinetics of accumulation of other developmentally controlled enzymes are from the data of Roth et al. (14) and are presented as per cent of peak activity: trehalose-phosphate synthetase* (△), *UDP-glucose pyrophosphorylase* (□), *UDP-galactose polysaccharide transferase* (○). *Schematic representation of morphogenesis in D. discoideum is presented with the time scale.*

TABLE 1. *Substrate specificity of acetylglucosaminidase*

Compound[a]	Relative reaction rate
p-Nitrophenyl *N*-acetyl β-D-glucosamine	100
p-Nitrophenyl *N*-acetyl β-D-galactosamine	46
o-Nitrophenyl β-D-galactoside	0.2
p-Nitrophenyl β-D-glucuronide	<0.1
p-Nitrophenyl β-D-glucoside	<0.1
p-Nitrophenyl β-D-xylopyranoiside	<0.1
p-Nitrophenyl α-D-glucoside	0.1
Hyaluronic acid	<0.1
Chitin (poly *N*-acetylglucosamine)	<0.1

[a] Concentration in reaction mixture was: *p*-nitrophenyl *N*-acetyl β-D-glucosamine and *p*-nitrophenyl *N*-acetyl β-D-galactosamine, 8×10^{-3}M; hyaluronic acid, 5 mg/ml; chitin, 15 mg/ml; and all other compounds at 10^{-2}M. Reaction with hyaluronic acid and chitin was assayed by estimation of release of *N*-acetylglucosamine; reaction with other compounds was assayed by increase in absorbance at 420 nm. All compounds were incubated with at least 10 units of partially purified enzyme (specific activity, 6,000) up to 1 hr at *p*H 5 and 35 C.

activity of acetylglucosaminidase increases by a factor of about 10 during the first 8 to 10 hr of development; it then remains essentially constant. The gradual rise in specific activity during the latter part of development may be due to preferential protection from protein catabolism rather than enzyme synthesis since total protein per cell decreases considerably during that period (5, 22).

When samples taken at 0, 12, and 24 hr of development were mixed in all possible combinations, the activities were strictly additive; this suggests that no diffusable inhibitors or activators can account for the difference in specific activity in the different samples.

Cycloheximide has been shown to inhibit protein synthesis preferentially more than 85% within 15 min in *D. discoideum* (1, 15). When protein synthesis was blocked at different times during the aggregation of the amoebae, the accumulation of acetylglucosaminidase ceased, while the activity which was present appeared stable (Fig. 3). It was concluded that the majority of the increase in specific activity requires concomitant protein synthesis.

Actinomycin D has been shown to inhibit RNA synthesis preferentially in *D. discoideum* more than 95% within 30 min (17, 20). When this drug was added at 0 or 4 hr after the initiation of de-

velopment, acetylglucosaminidase continued to accumulate for only about 2 hr; it then remained approximately constant (Fig. 4). It appears that RNA synthesis must occur during development for the normal amount of acetylglucosaminidase to accumulate. Enzyme-forming capacity, expressed in the absence of RNA synthesis, is never more than 20% of maximum activity. This finding is in contrast to results with two other developmentally controlled enzymes which continue to accumulate at the normal rate for 8 hr or more after RNA synthesis is inhibited (1, 20).

Relationship of acetylglucosaminidase synthesis to morphogenesis. Many morphogenetically aberrant mutants of *D. discoideum* have been described (19, 24). Seven strains which fail to aggregate normally were independently isolated after treatment with nitrosoguanidine. All but one of these strains accumulated acetylglucosaminidase to a specific activity higher than that in wild-

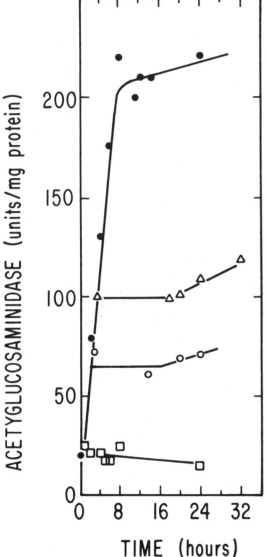

FIG. 3. *Inhibition of accumulation of acetylglucosaminidase by cycloheximide. Membrane filters with developing amoebae were transferred to pads containing cycloheximide (500 µg/ml) at 0 (□), 2 (○), 4 (△) hr. after the initiation of development. Control cells were not transferred (●).*

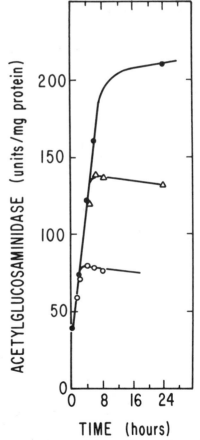

FIG. 4. *Inhibition of accumulation of acetylglucosaminidase by actinomycin D. Membrane filters with developing amoebae were transferred to pads containing actinomycin D (100 µg/ml) at 0 (○) and 4 (△) hr. Control cells were not transferred (●).*

type cells after the initiation of development. The exceptional strain, VA-5, showed no sign of aggregation and failed to synthesize significant amounts of the enzyme (Fig. 5). Thus, an early morphological aberration affects synthesis of acetylglucosaminidase, but completely normal aggregation does not appear to be required for the synthesis of this enzyme.

The increase in specific activity of acetylglucosaminidase in the six semi-aggregateless strains (min 4, min 5, VA-3, -4, -6, and -7) does not stop after 8-hr development, as in wild-type cells (Fig. 5). To determine whether continued enzyme synthesis in one of these strains, VA-4, requires continued RNA synthesis, actinomycin D was added to cells of this strain at 0 and 8 hr of development. Samples were collected at 8, 20, and 34 hr for determination of acetylglucosaminidase activity. The specific activity increased for less than 2 hr in cells treated with the drug, while previously accumulated activity remained constant. It is concluded that continuous RNA synthesis is required for the prolonged enzyme synthesis in this semi-aggregateless strain.

Strain KY-3 is a morphological mutant which forms pseudoplasmodia but fails to culminate (24). Accumulation of acetylglucosaminidase in this strain follows kinetics similar to those in the wild-type strain (Fig. 4).

Absence of spatial localization. During the development of *D. discoideum*, cells of the initially homogeneous population of amoebae differentiate to either of the two terminal forms, spores or stalk cells. To determine whether acetylglucosaminidase activity is restricted to one or the other

of these cell types in mature fruiting bodies, spores and stalk cells were separated by micromanipulation from a 24-hr preparation. There was no significant difference in the specific activity of acetylglucosaminidase in these cell types (Table 2).

DISCUSSION

The increase in specific activity of acetylglucosaminidase reported here is a facet of the development of *D. discoideum*. The increase does not occur in a mutant strain that is unable to accomplish the first step in morphogenesis (aggregation), but it does occur in strains which form imperfect aggregates. The termination of enzyme synthesis appears to be another facet of the development of this organism, since a mutation which affects aggregation also affects termination of accumulation of acetylglucosaminidase.

The increase in activity does not appear to be an artifact of the assay or the result of diffusable activations or inhibitors. Concomitant protein synthesis is required for accumulation of activity, a result which suggests that the increase in specific activity may result from de novo synthesis of the enzyme. In support of this view is the observation that concomitant RNA synthesis must also occur for the majority of the activity to accumulate. Synthesis of messenger RNA molecules has been shown by similar methods to be required for de novo enzyme synthesis in bacteria (7, 19).

A requirement for RNA synthesis during development of *D. discoideum* has been shown for the synthesis of three other developmentally controlled enzymes (13). The full complement of enzyme-forming capacity for two of these enzymes is stable for at least 6 hr in the absence of RNA synthesis (13). Enzyme-forming capacity for the third enzyme, trehalose-phosphate synthetase, like that for acetylglucosaminidase, decays within 2 hr in the absence of RNA synthesis. Thus, protein synthesis in *D. discoideum* appears to depend on both stable and unstable RNA species.

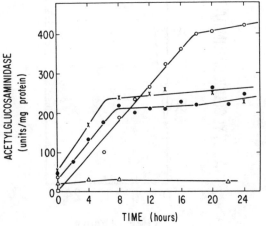

FIG. 5. *Acetylglucosaminidase in morphologically aberrant mutants of D. discoideum: strain VA-5, △; VA-4, ○; KY-3, ×; NC-4 wild type, ●. A single determination of vegetative cells of strain VA-4 growing exponentially was performed (□).*

TABLE 2. *Specific activity of acetylglucosamidase in various cell types*

Cell type	Acetylglucos-aminidase[a]
Aerobacter aerogenes.............	<2
Vegetative amoebae..............	16
Mature fruiting body............	210
Spore cells.....................	218
Stalk cells.....................	194

[a] Assays were performed as described in Materials and Methods. Values are expressed as units per milligram of protein.

Unlike the three previously described developmentally controlled enzymes, acetylglucosaminidase is stable throughout morphogenesis. The specific activity decreases to that of vegetative cells only after germination of the spores.

It must be emphasized that the physiological role of acetylglucosaminidase is unknown. However, the primary purpose of these studies is to define the product of a single gene under developmental control; acetylglucosaminidase appears to be such a molecule. Studies on the factors which control the formation of this enzyme are in progress.

ACKNOWLEDGMENTS

I am indebted to Stuart Brody for stimulating discussion and to Karen Howard for expert technical assistance.

This investigation was supported by grant GB-5830 from the National Science Foundation.

LITERATURE CITED

1. Ashworth, J., and M. Sussman. 1967. The appearance and disappearance of uridine diphosphate glucose pyrophosphorylase activity during differentiation of the cellular slime mold *Dictyostelium discoideum*. J. Biol. Chem. **242**:1696–1700.
2. Bahl, O., and K. Agrawal. 1968. Glycosidases of *Phaseolus vulgaris* I. Isolation and characterization of β-N-acetyl-glucosaminidase. J. Biol. Chem. **243**:98–102.
3. Cleland, S., and E. Coe. 1968. Activities of glycolytic enzymes during the early stages of differentiation in the cellular slime mold *Dictyostelium discoideum*. Biochim. Biophys. Acta **156**:44–50.
4. Fink, K., R. Cline, and R. Fink. 1963. Paper chromatography of several classes of compounds: correlated R_F values in a variety of solvent systems. Anal. Chem. **35**:389–398.
5. Gregg, J., A. Hackney, and J. Krivanek. 1954. Nitrogen metabolism of the slime mold *Dictyostelium discoideum* during growth and morphogenesis. Biol. Bull. **107**:226–235.
6. Hartwell, L., and B. Magasanik. 1964. The mechanism of histidase induction and formation in *Bacillus subtilis*. J. Mol. Biol. **10**:105–119.
7. Leive, L. 1965. Some effects of inducer and utilization of β-galactosidase messenger RNA in actinomycin-sensitive *Escherichia coli*. Biochem. Biophys. Res. Commun. **20**:321–327.
8. Loomis, W. F., Jr., and J. Ashworth. 1968. Plaque size mutants of the cellular slime mold *Dictyostelium discoideum*. J. Gen. Microbiol. **53**:181–186.
9. Lowry, O. H., N. Rosenbrough, A. Farr, and R. Randall. 1951. Protein measurement with the Folin phenol reagent. J. Biol. Chem. **193**:265–275.
10. Morgan, T. 1934. Embryology and genetics. Columbia University Press, New York.
11. Raper, K. 1935. *Dictyostelium discoideum*, a new species of slime mold from decaying forest leaves. J. Agr. Res. **50**:135–147.
12. Reissig, J., J. Strominger, and L. Leloir. 1955. A modified colorimetric method for the estimation of N-acetylamino sugars. J. Biol. Chem. **217**:959–966.
13. Roth, R., J. Ashworth, and M. Sussman. 1968. Periods of genetic transcription required for the synthesis of three enzymes during cellular slime mold development. Proc. Natl. Acad. Sci. U.S. **59**:1235–1241.
14. Roth, R., and M. Sussman. 1968. Trehalose 6-phosphate synthetase (uridine diphospho glucose: D-glucose 6 phosphate 1-glucosyltransferase) and its regulation during slime mold development. J. Biol. Chem. **243**:5081–5087.
15. Sussman, M. 1965. Inhibition by actidione of protein synthesis and UDP-Gal polysaccharide transferase accumulation in *Dictyostelium discoideum*. Biochem. Biophys. Res. Commun. **18**:763–767.
16. Sussman, M. 1966. Biochemical and genetic methods in the study of cellular slime mold development p. 397–410. *In* D. Prescott (ed.), Methods in cell physiology, vol. II. Academic Press Inc., New York.
17. Sussman, M., W. F. Loomis, Jr., J. Ashworth, and R. Sussman. 1967. The effect of actinomycin D on cellular slime mold morphogenesis. Biochem. Biophys. Res. Commun. **26**:353–359.
18. Sussman, M., and M. Osborn. 1964. UDP-galactose polysaccharide transferase in the cellular slime mold *Dictyostelium discoideum*: appearance and disappearance of activity during cell differentiation. Proc. Natl. Acad. Sci. U.S. **52**:81–87.
19. Sussman, M., and R. Sussman. 1953. Cellular differentiation in *Dictyosteliaceae*: heritable modification of the developmental pattern. Ann. N.Y. Acad. Sci. **56**:949–960.
20. Sussman, M., and R. Sussman. 1965. The regulatory program for UDP-galactose transferase activity during slime mold cytodifferentiation: requirement for specific synthesis of ribonucleic acid. Biochim. Biophys. Acta **108**:463–473.
21. Sussman, R. R., and M. Sussman. 1960. The dissociation of morphogenesis from cell division in the cellular slime mold *Dictyostelium discoideum*. J. Gen. Microbiol. **23**:287–293.
22. White, G., and M. Sussman. 1961. Metabolism of major cell components during slime mold morphogenesis. Biochim. Biophys. Acta **53**:285–293.
23. Wright, B. 1966. Multiple causes and controls in differentiation. Science **153**:830–837.
24. Yanagisawa, K., W. F. Loomis, Jr., and M. Sussman. 1967. Developmental regulation of the enzyme UDP-galactose polysaccharide transferase. Exptl. Cell Res. **46**:328–334.

Reprinted from the PROCEEDINGS OF THE NATIONAL ACADEMY OF SCIENCES
Vol. 59, No. 4, pp. 1235–1242.   April, 1968.

PERIODS OF GENETIC TRANSCRIPTION REQUIRED FOR THE SYNTHESIS OF THREE ENZYMES DURING CELLULAR SLIME MOLD DEVELOPMENT*

BY R. ROTH,† J. M. ASHWORTH,‡ AND M. SUSSMAN§

DEPARTMENT OF BIOLOGY, BRANDEIS UNIVERSITY, WALTHAM, MASSACHUSETTS

Communicated by Sol Spiegelman, January 24, 1968

Various aspects of mRNA synthesis and stability have been examined in acteria by permitting transcription to occur over a known, usually brief, period and then determining how much of a specific protein subsequently accumulates in the absence of further RNA synthesis.   Thus, bacterial cells have been exposed to an inducer for very brief periods during which RNA synthesis could proceed normally and were then permitted to synthesize the enzyme *de novo* in the absence of both the inducer and further transcription.   The latter restriction was accomplished with base analogues,[1] uracil deprivation,[2] actinomycin D,[3, 4] and by infection with lytic viruses.[5]   In an arginine- and uracil-requiring strain of *E. coli* infected with phage T6, protein and RNA synthesis were sequentially (and reversibly) restricted by successive precursor deprivations in order to study the accumulation of enzymes required for phage development.[2, 6]   Under all of the above conditions, the amounts of enzymes synthesized were assumed to reflect in a simple fashion the over-all quantities and net concentrations of the corresponding mRNA species, and the subsequent decays of enzyme-forming capacity with time were assumed to reflect the manner in which the mRNA disappeared.

This approach has also been exploited to investigate the transcriptive and translative events required for accumulation and disappearance of the enzyme uridine diphosphate galactose:polysaccharide transferase during slime mold development.   This enzyme, undetectable in the vegetative cells of *Dictyostelium discoideum*, appears at a specific morphogenetic stage, accumulates to a peak of specific activity, is preferentially released by the cells, and is then rapidly destroyed.[7, 8]   The accumulation of the enzyme was shown to be sensitive to coincident inhibition of protein synthesis (by cycloheximide) and to prior inhibition of RNA synthesis (by actinomycin D).[9, 10]

By adding actinomycin at later and later times during the developmental sequence and then determining how much, if any, transferase activity subsequently accumulated, it was possible to define the limits of this transcriptive period and the temporal and quantitative relations between it and the translative period that followed.   This was done both in *D. discoideum* wild type and in a temporally deranged mutant Fr-17.[10]   This approach has now been extended to two other enzymes which accumulate at different times during cellular slime mold development, uridine diphosphate glucose (UDPG), pyrophosphorylase (EC 2.7.7.9)[11] and trehalose-6-phosphate synthetase (EC 2.3.1.15).   The present communication describes the temporal and quantitative relations between the transcriptive and translative periods for the accumulation of all three enzymes. The results indicate that: (*a*) the three transcriptive periods, though many hours (7–9) in length, occupy relatively restricted portions of the total number of hours (24) required for morphogenesis to be completed under these conditions;

(b) they are initiated at different times during the developmental sequence; (c) during each transcriptive period, there is a linear or possibly sigmoid relation between the time over which transcription is permitted to occur (before addition of actinomycin) and the amount of the corresponding enzyme which subsequently accumulates; (d) the transcriptive periods begin, respectively, one, five, and seven hours prior to the appearances of the corresponding enzymes.

Materials and Methods.—Organism and culture conditions: D. discoideum strain NC-4 (haploid) was grown in association with *Aerobacter aerogenes*[12] to the beginning of the stationary phase. The cells were then harvested, washed free of the remaining bacteria, and aliquots of 1×10^8 cells were dispensed on 47-mm Millipore filters (AABP 047 00) resting on pads saturated with buffer–salts–streptomycin solution in 60-mm Petri dishes.[12] Under these conditions the cells aggregate and construct fruiting bodies over a 24-hr period with a high degree of synchrony.

Enzyme assays: For the UDP-gal transferase and trehalose-6-phosphate synthetase assays, the cells were harvested in 0.01 M Tris (tris-(hydroxymethyl)aminomethane), pH 7.4, with 0.005 M thioglycollate, or in 0.1 M tricine (N-tris (hydroxymethyl)methylglycine), pH 7.5, for the UDPG pyrophosphorylase assay and were stored at −20°C. The samples were then thawed, sonicated in a Branson sonifier for 1 min at a level of 2 amp, and assayed immediately.

UDP-gal transferase:[8] The reaction mixture contained 15 μmol dimethylglutarate, pH 7.4, 4 μmols KCl, 0.5 μmol MgCl₂, 36 mμmols UDP-galactose-(C¹⁴) at a specific activity of 1.8 μc/μmol, purified mucopolysaccharide acceptor in a volume of 0.08 ml, and 0.2 ml of enzyme extract. The mixture was incubated 60 min at 30°C. Then 0.25 ml of 0.1 M HCl was added and the mixture was incubated 13 min at 100°C to hydrolyze the remaining UDP-gal. Three ml absolute ethanol were added to precipitate the acceptor. After 30 min in the cold, the precipitate was deposited on a Millipore filter (EHWPO2500), washed three times with 80% ethanol, cemented to a planchette, and counted. Acceptor-dependent enzyme activity was measured in mixtures containing and lacking a standard concentration of the acceptor (a 20-fold difference at peak activity) and expressed as cpm/hr/mg protein.

UDPG pyrophosphorylase:[11] The reaction mixture contained 2.5 μmols MgCl₂, 5 μmols uridine triphosphate (UTP), 2.5 μmols glucose (C¹⁴)-1-phosphate at a specific activity of 0.04 μc/μmol in a volume of 0.15 ml, and 0.35 ml of extract in 0.1 M Tricine pH 7.5 buffer. The mixture was incubated 10 min at 35°C and 1.5 min at 100°C. Alkaline phosphatase (25 μg of crystalline bacterial enzyme) was added and the mixture incubated 30 min at 45°C to destroy the remaining G-1-P. Then 0.01 ml of 5 N HNO₃, 0.3 ml of 14% mercuric acetate in 10% acetic acid, and 0.5 ml of 95% ethanol were added to precipitate the UDPG. After 10 min in the cold, the precipitate was deposited on a Millipore filter (EHWPO 2500), washed three times with 80% ethanol, cemented to a planchette, and counted. Activity was expressed as μmols UDPG produced/min/mg protein.

Trehalose-6-phosphate synthetase: This enzyme, previously demonstrated in D. discoideum,[13] catalyzes the reaction G6P + UDPG → trehalose-6-P + UDP.[14] The above stoichiometry was confirmed, and a quantitative enzyme assay based on the procedure of Cabib and Leloir[14] was devised[15] and has been employed in the present study. The reaction mixtures contained 15 μmols MgCl₂, 0.5 μmol ethylenediaminetetraacetate (EDTA), 100 μmols KCl, 8 μmols disodium glucose-6-phosphate, 2 μmols UDPG in 0.09 ml (pH 7.0), and 0.16 ml extract. The mixture was incubated 30 min at 37°C and the reaction was stopped by incubating 5 min at 100°C. The UDP that had been generated was assayed by adding 1.0 μmol neutralized phosphoenolpyruvate and 10 units of pyruvate kinase in 0.07 ml and incubating 60 min at 30°C. The pyruvate thereby produced was determined colorimetrically. Activity was expressed as μmols UDP (or trehalose-6-phosphate) produced/min/mg protein.

Actinomycin treatment: Actinomycin D was stored dry at 0°C in the dark and solutions were prepared a few hours before use. Washed cells, harvested from growth plates, were deposited on the Millipore filters and allowed to develop for varying periods.   The filters were then shifted to fresh pads saturated with buffer–salts–streptomycin solution containing 125 μg/ml actinomycin.   All operations were carried out in dim light and the cells were incubated in light-proof containers.

Reagents: Labeled glucose-1-phosphate and UDP galactose were purchased from New England Nuclear Corp., and unlabeled UDPG, UDP-gal, and glucose-1-phosphate from Sigma.   Phosphoenolpyruvate and pyruvate kinase were purchased from Boehringer. Alkaline phosphatase purified from *E. coli* was purchased from Worthington.   Actinomycin D was graciously donated by Dr. Clement Stone of Merck, Sharp and Dohme, Inc.

Results.—The morphological features of the development of washed *D. discoideum* amoebae deposited on Millipore filters are schematically summarized in Figure 1.   The initially smooth lawn of cells concentrates into conical, multicel-

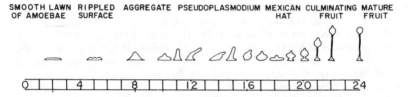

SMOOTH LAWN RIPPLED   AGGREGATE PSEUDOPLASMODIUM MEXICAN CULMINATING MATURE
OF AMOEBAE   SURFACE   HAT   FRUIT   FRUIT

Fɪɢ. 1.—*D. discoideum* wild-type amoebae were harvested from growth plates, washed, and deposited on Millipore filters (see *Materials and Methods*). The various morphogenetic stages were attained at the times (hours after deposition on the Millipores) designated on the abscissa.   Under routine conditions, this time sequence is precise within ±45 min.

lular aggregates, and these are transformed into organized fingerlike pseudoplasmodia.   Subsequent morphogenetic movements result in the construction of fruiting bodies, each composed of a mass of spores surmounting a cellulose ensheathed stalk above a basal disk.   The entire process requires 24 hours under these conditions.   Figure 2 shows the changes in the specific activities of the three enzymes during the developmental sequence.   In agreement with previously published results, trehalose-6-phosphate synthetase starts accumulating at 5 hours from a previously undetectable level, peaks at 16–17 hours, and then disappears.[15]   UDPG pyrophosphorylase is initially present at low activity, remains relatively constant until 12 hours, and then increases rapidly to a peak

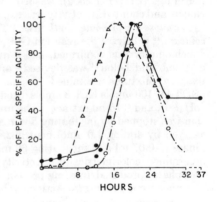

Fɪɢ. 2.—Developmental kinetics of the three enzymes.   Cells were harvested from growth plates, washed, and deposited on Millipore filters as described in *Materials and Methods*.   After incubation for the times indicated in the abscissa, the cells were harvested, frozen, sonicated, and assayed for three enzyme activities: trehalose-6-P synthetase (*triangles*); UDPG pyrophosphorylase (*closed circles*); UDP-gal:polysaccharide transferase (*open circles*). The specific enzyme activities thereby measured are expressed as percentages of their peak activities which were, respectively, 0.017 μmol trehalose-6-phosphate produced/min/mg protein; 0.25 μmol UDPG produced/min/mg protein; and 1500 cpm C[14]-galactose transferred/hr/mg protein.

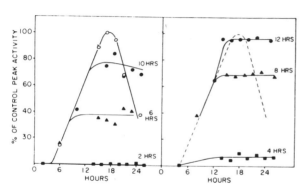

FIG. 3.—Effect of actinomycin on the accumulation and disappearance of trehalose-6-phosphate synthetase activity. Washed cells were deposited on Millipore filters at 0 time. At various times thereafter, one set of Millipores was shifted to new pads saturated with a solution containing actinomycin, 125 μg/ml of pad fluid, and a second (control) set was shifted to pads lacking actinomycin. The cells were collected at intervals thereafter for enzyme assays. The control curves varied only with respect to the absolute levels of peak enzyme activity ($\pm$ 8%), and one of them is shown on the left (*open circles with solid line*) and is reproduced on the right (*dotted line*). All the curves were normalized to this one. Next to each experimental curve is the time after deposition of the cells on the Millipores at which they were exposed to actinomycin.

9 hours later. Part of this activity (the fraction associated with the stalk cells of the mature fruit) then disappears. The rest, associated with the spores, remains.[11] The accumulation and disappearance of UDP-gal transferase activity follow closely (30–60 min) behind those of the pyrophosphorylase.[8, 11]

The effect of actinomycin D on RNA and protein synthesis and on over-all morphogenesis in *D. discoideum* has been described in detail elsewhere.[16] The rate of uridine incorporation was depressed to *ca.* 20 per cent of the normal level and this residue was confined exclusively to the 4S region of sucrose gradient sedimentation profiles. In contrast, amino acid incorporation remained unaffected for periods of four to six hours after addition of the agent. Morphogenetic changes, both gross and cytological, were inhibited in a specific manner. Where further morphogenesis did occur after exposure to the drug, it was at the same rate as in untreated controls.[16] There was no indication of generalized damage to the cells nor of aberrations other than those stemming directly from the inhibition of RNA synthesis. Figures 3–6 show the effect of actinomycin D addition on the accumulation and disappearance of trehalose-6-phosphate

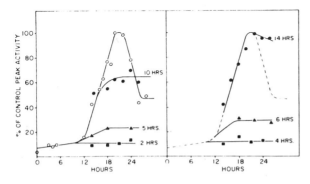

FIG. 4.—Effect of actinomycin on the accumulation and disappearance of UDPG pyrophosphorylase. The control curve (*open circles, solid line*) on the left, reproduced as a dotted line on the right, gives the combined data from two separate experiments and represents the time course of pyrophosphorylase accumulation and disappearance in the absence of actinomycin. Companion sets of Millipores were exposed to actinomycin at the times shown next to each of the experimental curves and were sampled at the times indicated in the abscissa for determinations of specific enzyme activity.

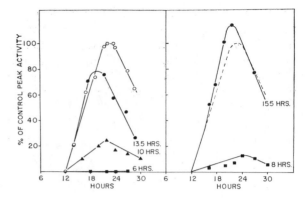

FIG. 5.—Effect of actinomycin on the accumulation and disappearance of UDP-gal polysaccharide transferase. See Fig. 4 for explanation. Two of the curves (*squares, triangles*) were published previously.[10]

synthetase, UDPG pyrophosphorylase, and UDP galactose:polysaccharide transferase, respectively. In the case of the synthetase, addition of actinomycin prior to 4 hours prevented significant synthesis of enzyme; addition after 13 hours permitted synthesis approximately at the normal rate and to a peak 100–105 per cent of that attained by the controls; addition betweentimes permitted intermediate amounts of enzyme to be synthesized, such that the later actinomycin was added, the more enzyme accumulated. Also, the disappearance of enzyme observed in the controls was prevented or interfered with by addition of actinomycin even as late as 12 hours. The same general pattern of inhibition was observed in the case of the pyrophosphorylase but over a different time period. Thus addition of actinomycin prior to 5 hours prevented synthesis of the enzyme; addition after 12 hours permitted synthesis at approximately the normal rate and to a peak 100–110 per cent of the control; addition between times permitted intermediate amounts to be synthesized. Addition of actinomycin even as late as 14 hours, though it did not interfere with accumulation of the pyrophosphorylase, did significantly affect its disappearance. In the case of the UDP-gal transferase, the pattern of inhibition is in agreement with previously published data.[10] Addition of actinomycin prior to 7.5 hours prevented any synthesis of enzyme; addition after 14–15 hours permitted synthesis at approximately the normal rate and to a level 100–110 per cent of the controls; addition at times in between permitted synthesis to intermediate levels. The precise relationships between the time of actinomycin addition and how much of each enzyme could subsequently be synthesized are shown in Figure 6 and are approximately linear

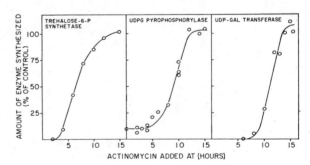

FIG. 6.—Relation between the times at which actinomycin was added and the peak level of enzyme activity that subsequently accumulated, expressed as per cent of the control peak. The points are calculated from curves shown in Figs. 3–5 and from others not shown. The data for UDP-gal transferase were published previously.[10]

or perhaps sigmoid.   The data (i.e., peak levels of enzyme which accumulated) are taken from the curves in Figures 3–5 and from curves not shown.

Discussion.—The results described above indicate that during cellular slime mold morphogenesis, the accumulation of each of three enzymes requires a specific period of genetic transcription.   The temporal relations of these periods with each other and with the ensuing translative events are summarized in Figure 7.   In

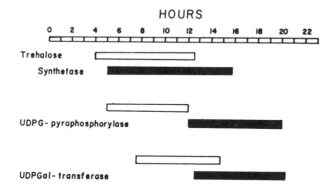

Fig. 7.—A schematic summary of the transcriptive and translative periods for accumulation of the three enzyme activities, derived from Figs. 3–6.

considering what kind of transcription is involved, it should be noted[17] that: (*a*) RNA synthesis goes on throughout the developmental sequence of both *D. discoideum* and a sister genus, *Polysphondylium pallidum;* (*b*) the RNA which is synthesized includes ribosomal and transfer RNA and material whose relative stability, association with polysomes, and size indicate it to be mRNA; (*c*) although considerable ribosomal turnover and resynthesis do occur during the developmental sequence, no differences could be detected between the ribosomes of vegetative amoebae and mature fruiting bodies with respect to protein composition or the sedimentation properties, base compositions, and specific hybridizability of the rRNA.   While these data do not permit an unequivocal judgment, it is at least reasonable to suppose that the transcriptive products required for the accumulation of the three enzymes are the mRNA species which respectively dictate their primary structures.

It is noteworthy that these transcriptive periods apparently occupy restricted portions (*ca.* one third) of the time required for completion of the total morphogenetic sequence and of the time over which RNA synthesis occurs.   This implies that not only the initiation of a transcriptive act but also its duration is under developmental control, a conclusion supported by the fact that in the temporally deranged mutant of *D. discoideum* (strain Fr-17) in which developmental events generally begin too soon and are completed too fast, the period of transcription required for the synthesis of UDP-gal transferase not only starts sooner than in the wild type but is of shorter duration (4 vs. 7–8 hr) in correspondence with the relative periods over which the enzyme accumulates in the two strains.[7, 10] Figure 6 indicates that, within each transcriptive period, there appears to be a linear or perhaps a sigmoidal relation between the time over which transcription is allowed to proceed (before addition of actinomycin) and the amount of enzyme subsequently synthesized.

Figure 5 indicates time lags of one, seven, and five hours, respectively, between the initiation of each transcriptive period and the appearance of the corresponding enzyme. The possibility that they represent times needed for the combination of subunits into enzymatically active polymers, as observed in similar experiments with bacteria,[4] is ruled out by the fact that, in *D. discoideum*, addition of cycloheximide during the periods of enzyme accumulation froze the levels of all three enzyme activities immediately.[9, 11, 15] Thus, appreciable pools of preformed subunits do not appear to exist. The extents of the time lags (up to 7 hr) and the extreme differences (1–7 hr) among the three may imply the existence of specific translational controls or controls over the rate at which mRNA species might be conducted through the nuclear envelope to the site of translation.

The time lags also imply functional life spans of the RNA (up to 7 hr) greatly in excess of those encountered in bacteria and more comparable with values postulated for higher plants and animals.[18, 21] Unlike the situation obtaining in bacteria, the kinetics of enzyme synthesis either in untreated or actinomycin-poisoned cells display no hint of first-order decay. Furthermore, as seen in Figures 2–4, even when actinomycin was added early enough to limit significantly the extent of enzyme synthesis, the residue was synthesized at the same rate as in the controls. Finally, it should be noted that in the case of UDP-gal transferase, the five-hour time lag could be experimentally extended by at least three hours (by addition and then removal of cycloheximide) without significant detriment to the amount of enzyme subsequently synthesized.[22]

Figures 3 and 4 indicate that, for two of the enzymes at least, transcriptive periods are required for disappearance as well as accumulation of activity. Even in the case of the transferase, the requirement was demonstrable in mutant strain Fr-17[10] but not in the wild type where the two transcriptive periods apparently coincide. The meaning of these results is not clear since they could equally be due to genetically determined acts which specifically eliminate these enzymes or merely be the secondary consequences of the fact that actinomycin stopped morphogenesis short of the stages at which these enzymes normally do disappear.

Summary.—In the development of the cellular slime mold *Dictyostelium discoideum*, three different enzyme activities accumulate rapidly at specific morphogenetic stages and then disappear partly or completely. The enzymes are trehalose-6-phosphate synthetase, UDPG pyrophosphorylase, and UDP gal: polysaccharide transferase. The accumulations of all three enzymes are sensitive to prior inhibition of RNA synthesis by actinomycin D. The three transcriptive periods differ with respect to the times of their initiation and duration. They begin one, seven, and five hours before the appearances of the corresponding enzymes, thus indicating the existence of specific controls over the translation of mRNA into protein or over the migration of the former through the nuclear envelope to the site of translation.

* This work was supported by a grant (GB-5976X) from NSF.

† Predoctoral trainee, graduate training program in developmental biology (NIH T1 HD-22).

Part of these results were taken from a thesis offered by the senior author in partial fulfillment of the requirements for the Ph.D. degree.

‡ Harkness Foundation fellow. Present address: Department of Biochemistry, Leicester University, Leicester, England.

§ Recipient of a Career Development Award from NIH.

[1] Nakada, D., and B. Magasanik, *Biochim. Biophys. Acta*, **61,** 835 (1962).

[2] Cohen, S. S., M. Sekiguchi, J. L. Stern, and H. D. Barner, these Proceedings, **49,** 698 (1963).

[3] Hartwell, L. H., and B. Magasanik, *J. Mol. Biol.*, **10,** 105 (1964).

[4] Leive, L., *Biochem. Biophys. Res. Commun.*, **20,** 321 (1965).

[5] Kaempfer, R. O. R., and B. Magasanik, *J. Mol. Biol.*, **27,** 453 (1967).

[6] Sekiguchi, M., and S. S. Cohen, *J. Mol. Biol.*, **8,** 638 (1964).

[7] Sussman, M., and M. J. Osborn, these Proceedings, **52,** 81 (1964).

[8] Sussman, M., and N. Lovgren, *Exptl. Cell Res.*, **38,** 97 (1965).

[9] Sussman, M., *Biochem. Biophys. Res. Commun.*, **18,** 763 (1965).

[10] Sussman, M., and R. R. Sussman, *Biochim. Biophys. Acta*, **108,** 463 (1965); Loomis, Jr., W. F., and M. Sussman, *J. Mol. Biol.*, **22,** 401 (1966).

[11] Ashworth, J. M., and M. Sussman, *J. Biol. Chem.*, **242,** 1696 (1967).

[12] Sussman, M., in *Methods in Cell Physiology*, ed. D. Prescott (New York: Academic Press, 1966), vol. 2, p. 397.

[13] Roth, R., and M. Sussman, *Biochim. Biophys. Acta*, **122,** 225 (1966).

[14] Cabib, E., and L. F. Leloir, *J. Biol. Chem.*, **231,** 259 (1958).

[15] Roth, R., Ph.D. Thesis: Brandeis University (1967).

[16] Sussman, M., W. F. Loomis, Jr., J. M. Ashworth, and R. R. Sussman, *Biochem. Biophys. Res. Commun.*, **76,** 353 (1967).

[17] Sussman, R. R., *Biochim. Biophys. Acta*, **149,** 407 (1967).

[18] Hotta, Y., and H. Stern, these Proceedings, **49,** 648, 961 (1963).

[19] Stewart, J. A., and J. Papaconstantinou, these Proceedings, **58,** 95 (1967).

[20] Wessells, N., *J. Exptl. Zool.*, **157,** 139 (1964).

[21] Marks, P., E. R. Burka, and D. Schlessinger, these Proceedings, **48,** 2163 (1962).

[22] Sussman, M., these Proceedings, **55,** 813 (1966).

Reprinted from *J. Mol. Biol.* (1966) **22**, 401–404

Commitment to the Synthesis of a Specific Enzyme during Cellular Slime Mold Development

W. F. LOOMIS, JR. AND M. SUSSMAN

During morphogenesis in the slime mold *Dictyostelium discoideum*, the enzyme UDP-galactose polysaccharide transferase first appears when the individual amoebae have already entered into multicellular aggregates, about 12 hours after the start of the developmental sequence. The specific activity rises linearly to a peak toward the end of construction of the fruiting body about nine hours later. During the following few hours, the enzyme is preferentially released into the extracellular space and is rapidly inactivated or destroyed (Sussman & Osborn, 1964; Sussman & Lovgren, 1965).

The accumulation of transferase activity has been shown to be sensitive to coincident inhibition of protein synthesis by cycloheximide (Sussman, 1965) and prior inhibition of RNA synthesis by actinomycin D (Sussman & Sussman, 1965). The transcriptive period, as delineated by sensitivity to actinomycin, begins seven to eight hours after the start of morphogenesis and ends about seven hours later. Within this period, a simple linear relation exists between the time of addition of actinomycin and the total enzyme activity subsequently accumulated.

Previous results have indicated that, although the accumulation, extrusion and disappearance of the enzyme as well as the transcriptive preliminaries are all correlated with specific morphogenetic events, there is in fact limited dependence on the gross topography of the system (Sussman & Sussman, 1965). The present study reveals an even more limited dependence on topography, namely, cells permitted to begin the developmental sequence but then dissociated and incubated under conditions which prevent reaggregation are nevertheless committed to accumulate and destroy the enzyme in normal fashion even though they remain as a smooth lawn of amoebae. The initial period of undisturbed cell association required for this commitment ends before the transcriptive period starts.

(a) Chemicals

UDP-[^{14}C]galactose (uniformly labelled) ($1 \cdot 2$ μc/μM) and [^{14}C]algal hydrolysate ($1 \cdot 8$ μc/μg) were purchased from the New England Nuclear Corp., Boston, Mass. Actinomycin D was kindly supplied by Merck, Sharp & Dohme, Inc. The drug was stored dry at -20°C in the dark.

(b) Conditions of development

D. discoideum NC-4 (haploid) was grown in association with *Aerobacter aerogenes* on nutrient agar plates and collected in cold distilled water at the first signs of depletion of the bacteria. The washed cells were allowed to develop on Millipore filter supports (AABPO47) as described by Sussman & Lovgren (1965).

(c) Assays

UDP-galactose polysaccharide transferase was assayed according to Sussman & Osborn (1964). Protein was estimated according to the method of Lowry, Rosebrough, Farr & Randall (1951). Incorporation of ^{14}C-labeled amino acids into 10% trichloroacetic acid-insoluble material was determined according to Sussman (1965).

Washed *D. discoideum* amoebae deposited on Millipore filters in portions of 10^8 cells form completed multicellular aggregates by 10 hours, pseudoplasmodia by 13 to 14 and mature fruits by 23 to 24 hours. If such populations are harvested at stages up to and including the pseudoplasmodial and are mildly triturated in cold water, a homogeneous suspension is obtained in which most of the cells are separate and the remainder in very small clusters. When these are redeposited on Millipore filters, they reaggregate rapidly and proceed through morphogenesis in normal fashion, re-accomplishing within two to three hours at most, what required up to 15 hours the first time. The presence of 10^{-2} M-EDTA in the incubating fluid has been shown previously to prevent aggregation if added at zero time and to prevent reaggregation of cells dissociated from pseudoplasmodia (Gerisch, 1961). When 10^{-2} M-EDTA was added at zero time, the cells remained as a smooth lawn of amoebae. When EDTA was added to cells dissociated from pseudoplasmodia, reaggregation did not occur. No spores were observed but some of the amoebae attained a swollen vacuolated appearance similar to that of stalk cells. This effect of EDTA on morphogenesis was readily reversible at all times either by removal of EDTA or by the addition of equimolar $CaCl_2$. Cells dissociated and incubated in the presence of 10^{-2} M-EDTA at either time were found to be more than 80% viable and able to incorporate ^{14}C-labeled amino acids at the same rate as undissociated cells.

Figure 1 shows the effect of cell dissociation on the developmental kinetics of UDP-galactose polysaccharide transferase activity. Amoebae, permitted to develop for eight hours on the filters before being dissociated and redeposited in the presence of EDTA (1 to $1 \cdot 5 \times 10^{-2}$ M) accumulated transferase activity at the same rate and to the same level as did the controls. In contrast, cells incubated from time zero in the presence of 10^{-2} M-EDTA accumulated transferase activity to a level only 15% that of the control and, with $1 \cdot 5 \times 10^{-2}$ M, less than 1%.

The data described above indicate that a period of incubation in the absence of EDTA is necessary for the cells to become committed to the subsequent accumulation of transferase activity in its presence. To delineate this period, enzyme activity was measured in cells allowed to develop normally for various lengths of time and then dissociated and incubated in the presence of 10^{-2} M-EDTA. Figure 1(b) indicates that between zero and eight hours, an approximately linear relationship exists between the number of hours during which the cells were incubated in the absence of EDTA and the amount of transferase subsequently synthesized.

Figure 1(b) also shows the limits of the transcriptive period required for the subsequent accumulation of transferase activity as delineated by sensitivity to actinomycin D. In agreement with previous results (Sussman & Sussman, 1965), this period is found to begin about seven and a half hours after the start of the morphogenetic sequence. Thus the cell population is fully committed before the start of this transcriptive period.

The results described above are not peculiar to EDTA. A previous study (Sonneborn, Sussman & Levine, 1964) demonstrated that at least one new antigenic determinant appears during *D. discoideum* aggregation and that the γ-globulin fraction of suitably absorbed rabbit serum containing the corresponding antibody would inhibit aggregation without affecting cell viability. In the present study it has been found that amoebae incubated on Millipore filters for 14 hours and then dissociated and re-incubated in the presence of this γ-globulin fraction could synthesize the transferase to the same level as the controls while remaining unaggregated. In contrast, cells

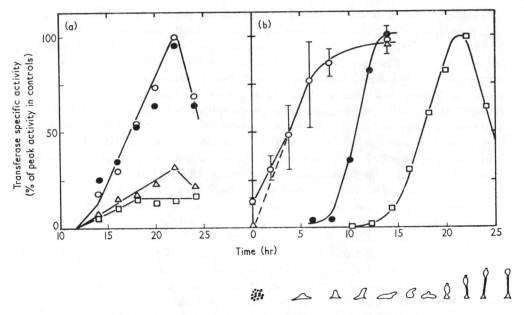

FIG. 1. Transferase synthesis following addition of EDTA.

Dictyostelium discoideum cells were allowed to develop for various periods of time on Millipore filters. They were dissociated and redeposited in the presence of 10^{-2} M-EDTA. UDP-Galactose polysaccharide transferase activity and protein content were determined.

(a) (—O—O—) Control; (—□—□—) EDTA at T=0; (—△—△—) EDTA at T=4 hr; (—●—●—) EDTA at 8 hr. (b) (—□—□—) transferase activity in controls; (—●—●—) peak transferase activity accumulated in cells incubated in the presence of actinomycin D added at the times indicated; (—O—O—) peak transferase activity in cells incubated in the presence of 10^{-2} M-EDTA added at the times indicated (the points are the mean of at least three independent determinations; vertical lines show the standard deviations); (△) peak transferase activity in cells incubated in the presence of 1.5×10^{-2} M-EDTA added at the times indicated. Cell extracts of control cells incorporated a maximum of 2·13 mμmoles galactose/hr/mg protein into ethanol-insoluble material.

The morphogenesis of control cells is shown schematically below the graph.

incubated from time zero in the presence of the γ-globulin accumulated less than 10% of the control level.

Previous work has indicated that UDP-galactose polysaccharide transferase in *D. discoideum* is a developmentally regulated enzyme (Sussman & Osborn, 1964; Yanagisawa, Loomis & Sussman, 1966). The present results show that the synthesis of the enzyme depends on cellular functions carried out during the first few hours of development which are inhibited when association of the amoebae is prevented by either EDTA or a specific antibody preparation. After this initial period of commitment however, the synthesis of transferase appears to be independent of gross morphogenetic topography.

One interesting feature of the commitment process lies in the fact that it is gradual rather than all or none. Thus an approximately linear relation exists between the extent of the initial period of undisturbed development and the total enzyme activity which accumulates after dissociation and incubation in the presence of EDTA. Two possible explanations emerge: (a) that this results from a gradual increase in the state of commitment within all of the cells; (b) that an increasing proportion of cells become fully committed with time. The latter is particularly attractive since the commitment period coincides with the period of cell aggregation and it might be supposed that the cells become committed at times bearing a relationship to the order in which they entered the aggregate. Previous work has shown that this order does exert a profound developmental influence and may determine whether a given amoeba differentiates into spore, stalk cell, or basal disc cell (Raper, 1940; Bonner, 1944). In addition, Takeuchi (1963), in an immunohistochemical study of spore-specific antigens of *D. discoideum*, has found that the appearance of these combining groups within cell aggregates and pseudoplasmodia is correlated with the positions of the individual cells.

Another interesting feature is the fact that a cell can be committed prior to the period during which the transferase-specific RNA is fabricated. Thus, commitment may not be merely a reflection of the presence of mRNA synthesized already. This is in direct contrast to inductive processes in bacteria as, for example, the mobilization of the *Lac* operon by IPTG (Nakada & Magasanik, 1964; Kepes, 1963).

This work was supported by a National Science Foundation Grant (GB-1310). The senior author is a postdoctoral trainee in the developmental biology graduate training program (NIH T1 HD-22).

Brandeis University					WILLIAM F. LOOMIS, JR.†
Waltham, Massachusetts					MAURICE SUSSMAN
U.S.A.

Received 22 August 1966, and in revised form 19 October 1966

REFERENCES

Bonner, J. T. (1944). *Amer. J. Bot.* **31**, 175.
Gerisch, G. (1961). *Exp. Cell. Res.* **25**, 535.
Kepes, A. (1963). *Biochim. biophys. Acta*, **76**, 293.
Lowry, O. H., Rosebrough, N. J., Farr, A. L. & Randall, R. J. (1951). *J. Biol. Chem.* **193**, 265.
Nakada, D. & Magasanik, B. (1964). *J. Mol. Biol.* **8**, 105.
Raper, K. B. (1940). *J. Elisha Mitchell Scient. Soc.* **56**, 241.
Sonneborn, D. R., Sussman, M. & Levine, L. (1964). *J. Bact.* **87**, 1321.
Sussman, M. (1965). *Biochem. Biophys. Res. Comm.* **18**, 763.
Sussman, M. & Lovgren, N. (1965). *Exp. Cell. Res.* **38**, 97.
Sussman, M. & Osborn, M. J. (1964). *Proc. Nat. Acad. Sci., Wash.* **52**, 81.
Sussman, M. & Sussman, R. (1965). *Biochim. biophys. Acta*, **108**, 463.
Takeuchi, I. (1963). *Develop. Biol.* **8**, 1.
Yanagisawa, K., Loomis, W. F., Jr. & Sussman, M. (1966). *Exp. Cell. Res.* in the press.

† Present address: Department of Biology, University of California, LaJolla, Calif., U.S.A.

© 1967 by Academic Press Inc.

Experimental Cell Research **46**, *328–334 (1967)*

DEVELOPMENTAL REGULATION OF THE ENZYME UDP-GALACTOSE POLYSACCHARIDE TRANSFERASE[1]

K. YANAGISAWA[2], W. F. LOOMIS, JR.[3], and M. SUSSMAN

Brandeis University, Waltham, Mass., U.S.A.

Received October 5, 1966

THE enzyme UDP-Gal polysaccharide transferase, absent in vegetative amoebae of the slime mold *Dictyostelium discoideum*, appears some time after multicellular aggregates have formed and accumulates to a peak of specific activity during construction of the fruiting body. It is then preferentially released into the extracellular space and is rapidly destroyed or inactivated [13, 14]. Both accumulation and disappearance require concomitant protein synthesis and a prior period of RNA synthesis [10, 11].

That this enzyme is developmentally regulated has been suggested by the performances of 3 mutant strains which display morphogenetic abnormalities [8, 16]. One of them, strain Agg-204, cannot aggregate and after growth the amoebae remain as separate individuals. Another, strain FR–2, can aggregate but stops development at this point, the component cells retaining their amoeboid form. Neither strain accumulates detectible transferase activity [14]. A third mutant, strain FR–17, is temporally deranged, reaching its terminal stage of development in about half the time required by the wild type to construct fruits. The terminal stage is a flattened, irregular, papillated aggregate within which the amoebae differentiate into normal spores and stalk cells. In accord with the overall acceleration of morphogenesis, a variety of end and by products detectible by biochemical and immunochemical assays have been found to appear sooner and to accumulate more rapidly than in the wild type. UDP-Gal transferase is also formed and disappears precociously in this strain.

In the present study, the performance of five other morphogenetically deficient mutant strains further supports the conclusion that the transferase is developmentally regulated. The steps in the pattern of control appear to be correlated with specific morphogenetic events in such a way that (a) a

---

[1] This work was supported by a grant from the National Science Foundation (GB 1310).

[2] Postdoctoral Trainee (Graduate Training Program) in Developmental Biology for NIH (T1 HD–22).

[3] *Present address:* Department of Biology, University of California, San Diego, Calif., U.S.A.

mutant strain incapable of developing beyond a particular morphological stage is also incapable of applying those controls over UDP-Gal transferase activity which the wild type brings into play during subsequent development; (b) when deficient mutants undergo synergistic morphogenesis [9], the synergism extends to the control of transferase activity.

METHODS

Organisms and conditions of experiment.—*D. discoideum* NC-4 (haploid) and mutant derivatives were grown on SM medium in association with *Aerobacter aerogenes* [12]. When exponential growth had ceased, after about 40–44 hr of incubation, the cells were harvested in cold water, washed 3 times by centrifugation for 5 min at 1200 × *g*, suspended in water at 2×10^8 cells/ml and distributed in 0.5 ml aliquots on black 2 inch millipores. The millipores rested on absorbent pads saturated with buffer-salt-streptomycin solution inside 60 mm petri dishes. The incubation temperature was 22°C. Development is highly synchronous under these conditions. For enzyme assays, the cells from single millipores were harvested in 3 ml of Tris (0.01 *M*), thioglycolate (5×10^3 *M*), pH 7.5 buffer and frozen. Immediately before assay, they were thawed and broken in a Branson Sonifier (intensity level = 2 amps; time = 45 sec).

Transferase assay.—A detailed description is given elsewhere [14]. The reaction mixture contained a buffer-salt solution, extract, UPD-^{14}C-galactose (1400 cpm/mμmole) and a standard concentration of mucopolysaccharide acceptor. After 1 hr incubation at 30°C, the mixture was heated in 0.05 *M* HCl for 10 min at 100°C to hydrolyze the remaining UDP-galactose, precipitated with 80 per cent ethanol, deposited on a millipore, washed with 80 per cent ethanol and counted at 35 per cent efficiency in a gas flow counter. Enzyme activity was measured by the acceptor dependent transfer of ^{14}C-galactose into the mucopolysaccharide fraction (cpm/hr/mg protein). In active preparations the incorporation of galactose into the alcohol-insoluble fraction in the absence of acceptor was about 5 per cent of that in its presence, probably due to endogenous mucopolysaccharide.

Protein determination.—This was performed by the method of Lowry *et al.* [6].

RESULTS

Induction of mutants with nitrosoguanidine

N-methyl-N'-nitro-N-nitrosoguanidine (NG) has been shown to be a remarkably potent mutagen for bacteria [1, 7]. It is equally so for the cellular slime molds. Amoebae were harvested from growth plates, washed three times with 0.05 *M* potassium phosphate buffer pH 6 by centrifugation in the cold, suspended in this buffer containing 1 mg/ml NG[1] and incubated for

---

[1] It is vital that the NG be stored dry and in the cold and that fresh solutions be prepared for each treatment. Even if stored in the manner described, color changes (and the loss of potency) occur after two or three months.

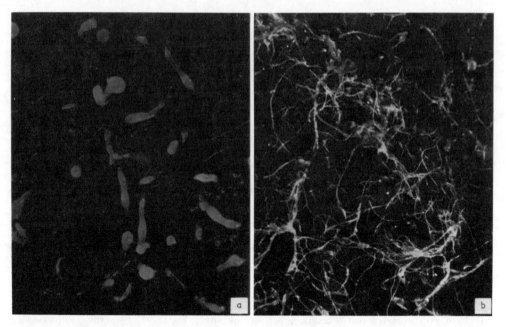

Fig. 1.—Photomicrographs of KY–3. *Left:* pseudoplasmodia (15 ×). *Right:* aerial filaments produced during pseudoplasmodial migration (ca 15 ×).

20–30 min at 22°C. The cells were then spun down, washed twice with buffer, diluted appropriately and plated on SM agar with bacteria. At a survival rate of 10–20 per cent, about 1 out of 15 of the resulting clones displayed a stable morphogenetic anomaly. Most of these mutant strains were either unable to aggregate or unable to form mature fruits similar to mutant types previously observed as a result of spontaneous mutation or after UV ir-radiation [16]. Two novel classes of mutants were also observed. One class consists of strains which develop beyond aggregation to produce normal pseudoplasmodia but remain in this form without completing development. The other class consists of strains which give rise to spherical aggregates within which practically all the cells transform into spores without evidence of stalk formation.

Description of mutant strains employed in the transferase study

Strain KY–28 forms perfectly smooth colonies on growth medium without any sign of aggregation. Likewise, washed cells incubated on millipore filters remain as a smooth lawn of amoebae.

Experimental Cell Research **46**

Strains KY–11 and KY–5 form irregular papillated aggregates both on growth medium and on millipores.

Strain KY–13 forms normal aggregates and these transform into upright, finger-like pseudoplasmodia.

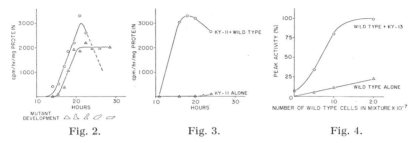

Fig. 2. Fig. 3. Fig. 4.

Fig. 2.—Developmental kinetics of UDP-Gal transferase activity in mutant KY–3 (△) and wild type *D. discoideum* (○).

Fig. 3.—Transferase synthesis and destruction during synergistic development by mixtures of KY–11 and wild type amoebae (cell ratio, 10:1, respectively).

Fig. 4.—Relation between peak scientific transferase activity accumulated and the number of wild type present in synergistic mixtures with 10^8 KY–13 amoebae.

Strain KY–3 forms normal aggregates and these transform into migrating slugs. Further development on both growth plates and millipores is dependent on population density. At 10^8 cells/millipore, no further development occurs. At slightly lower densities, as the slugs migrate they spin out very thin viscous material in a manner reminiscent of stalk formation in *D. mucoroides* [2]. This results in the construction of fine aerial filaments terminated by small, nippled, pear-shaped pseudoplasmodia. At still lower densities, 4×10^6–1×10^7 cells/millipore, just above the minimum cell density required for aggregation to occur, viable spores are produced at the termini. These breed true on replating. Fig. 1 shows photo micrographs of the migrating slugs and the aerial filaments.

Developmental kinetics of UDP-Gal transferase in the mutants

Strains KY–11, KY–13 and KY–28 were separately incubated on millipores. Extracts of the mutant strains harvested during the period in which the wild type accumulates peak transferase activity, contained only a few per cent of the peak transferase activity found in wild type cells (see Fig. 3 and Table I for data). Strain KY–3 was found to accumulate transferase activity at the usual rate and to a level only slightly below that of the wild type (Fig. 2). However this activity did not subsequently disappear as it does in the wild

Experimental Cell Research **46**

type. Furthermore, when duplicate cell samples were centrifuged at $2,500 \times g$ for 5 min and the cell pellets separated from the supernatants, all of the enzyme activity was found to be associated with the cells, none with the supernatants. In contrast, it has been previously shown that shortly after the peak activity is attained in the wild type, at least 80 per cent of the enzyme is

TABLE I. *Transferase accumulation during synergistic development.*

Strains	Specific activity at 22 hr (as % of peak wild type activity)
KY-5	5
KY-11	5
KY-28	4
KY-5 + KY-28	32
KY-5 + KY-11	17
KY-28 + KY-11	42

Washed amoebae were mixed at cell ratios of 1:1 and incubated at 10^8 cells/millipore. The cells were harvested after 22 hr at 22°. Specific activities of transferase are compared with the peak activity attained by 10^8 wild type cells under comparable conditions.

released into the supernatant at a specific activity 30-fold higher than in the cells [13]. Thus, while strain KY–3, at the population density employed, can accumulate transferase activity it can neither extrude the enzyme nor inactivate it.

Developmental kinetics of the enzyme during synergistic development

When cells of each of the 3 mutant strains KY–11, KY–13 and KY–28 were mixed with small numbers of wild type amoebae (cell ratios of 10:1 and 5:1) and incubated on millipores, normal, mature fruiting bodies appeared. Synergistic development of this kind has been previously explored [3, 4], but not at the biochemical level. All three combinations accumulated considerable amounts of transferase activity, far more than could be accounted for by the number of wild type cells present. Fig. 3 shows the time course of transferase activity in strain KY–11 alone and in a 10:1 mixture with wild type cells. Fig. 4 shows the peak activities accumulated by mixtures of 10^8 cells of strain KY–13 with different numbers of wild type amoebae.

Strains KY–5, KY–11 and KY–28 when paired with each other in 1:1 cell ratios and incubated (10^8 cells/millipore) also developed synergistically. Unfortunately the level of synergism is not easily reproducible but in general, combinations of strains KY–11 and KY–5 and combinations of strains

Experimental Cell Research **46**

KY–5 and KY–28 yielded incomplete and aberrant fruits while combinations of strains KY–11 and KY–28 yielded normal, mature fruits. When the level of synergistic development was high, considerable transferase activity accumulated as shown in Table I.

DISCUSSION

As mentioned previously UDP-Gal polysaccharide transferase first appears in wild type *D. discoideum* when cell aggregates are transformed into pseudo-plasmodia, accumulates to a peak at a late stage of fruit construction, is preferentially released by the cells, and then is rapidly destroyed. A study of 8 mutant strains, here and elsewhere [14] permit the following statements:

(1). Strain FR–17 proceeds through the flow of morphogenetic events more rapidly than the wild type. The pattern of control over transferase activity in strain FR–17 while remaining qualitatively the same as in the wild type is correspondingly accelerated.

(2) Strains FR–2, Agg–204, KY–28, KY–5 and KY–11 stop development at stages prior to that which is normally accompanied by the appearance of the transferase in the wild type. Mutant strain KY–13 stops shortly thereafter. All of these strains accumulate little or no transferase activity.

(3) Strain KY–3 develops to a late pseudoplasmodial stage. This, in the wild type, marks the period of transferase accumulation but is prior to attainment of peak activity as well as enzyme extrusion and inactivation. In strain KY–3, transferase activity appears at the usual time and accumulates at the normal rate to a level somewhat less than in the wild type but is neither extruded nor inactivated.

(4) Strains KY–11, KY–13 and KY–28 can develop synergistically when mixed with small numbers of wild type cells. Under these conditions, they accumulate the normal level of transferase and then destroy it. Mutant strains KY–5, KY–11 and KY–28 can develop synergistically when paired with each other. Here too, appreciable levels of transferase activity accumulate.

The correlation between changes in transferase activity or location and the attainment of specific morphogenetic states cannot be taken to imply a mandatory coupling between them but rather as the reflection of parallel events controlled by a common source. This stems from the finding that wild type cells permitted a period of undisturbed development (coinciding with the formation of early aggregates) and then dissociated and incubated under conditions which prevent reaggregation, can nevertheless accumulate the normal level of transferase activity and destroy it at the usual times while remaining as a smooth lawn of amoebae [5].

SUMMARY

During development of *Dictyostelium discoideum* wild type, the enzyme UDP-galactose polysaccharide transferase appears and accumulates to a peak of specific activity, is preferentially released by the cells, and is then destroyed. These events are correlated with the occurrence of specific morphogenetic events. A comparative study of morphogenetically deficient mutants has revealed that (a) strains incapable of proceeding beyond a particular developmental stage are likewise incapable of applying those controls over transferase activity which the wild type exerts during the subsequent development; (b) mutants which ordinarily accumulate little or no transferase activity can synthesize considerable levels of enzyme when they develop synergistically in mixtures with other mutants or with the wild type.

A highly effective procedure for induction of slime mold mutants using nitrosoguanidine is described.

REFERENCES

1. ADELBERG, E. A., MANDELL, M. and CHEN G., *Biochem. Biophys. Res. Comm.* **18**, 788 (1965).
2. BONNER, J. T., *Quart. Rev. Biol.* **32**, 232 (1957).
3. ENNIS, H. L. and SUSSMAN, M., *J. Gen. Microbiol.* **18**, 433 (1958).
4. KAHN, A. J., *Develop. Biol.* **9**, 1 (1964).
5. LOOMIS, W. F. JR. and SUSSMAN, M., *J. Molec. Biol.* In press (1966).
6. LOWRY, O. H., ROSEBOROUGH, N. J., FARR, A. L. and RANDALL, R. J., *J. Biol. Chem.* **193**, 265 (1951).
7. MANDELL, J. D. and GREENBERG, J., *Biochem. Biophys. Res. Comm.* **13**, 575 (1960).
8. SONNEBORN, D. R., WHITE, G. J. and Sussman, M., *Develop. Biol.* **7**, 79 (1963).
9. SUSSMAN, M., *J. Gen. Microbiol.* **10**, 110 (1954).
10. SUSSMAN, M., *Biochem. Biophys. Res. Comm.* **18**, 763, 7 (1965).
11. —— *Proc. Natl Adac. Sci.* **55**, 813 (1966).
12. —— *in* D. PRESCOTT (ed.), Methods in Cell Physiology, vol. **2**, pp. 397–409. Academic Press, New York, 1966.
13. SUSSMAN, M. and LÖVGREN, N., *Exptl Cell Res.* **28**, 97 (1965).
14. SUSSMAN, M. and OSBORN, M. J., *Proc. Natl Acad. Sci.* **52**, 81 (1964).
15. SUSSMAN, M. and SUSSMAN, R. R., *Biochim. Biophys. Acta* **108**, 463 (1965).
16. SUSSMAN, R. R. and SUSSMAN, M., *Ann. N. Y. Acad. Sci.* **56**, 949 (1953).

Section II

DIFFERENTIAL SYNTHESIS OF PROTEINS IN DEVELOPING ORGANS

MARKERT, C. L., 1963. In "Cytodifferentiation and Macromolecular Synthesis," ed. M. Locke. Acad. Press, p. 65. Epigenetic control of specific protein synthesis in differentiating cells.

CAHN, R. D., N. O. KAPLAN, L. LEVINE, and E. ZWILLING, 1962. Science *136,* 962. Nature and development of lactic dehydrogenases.

PLAGEMANN, P. G. W., K. F. GREGORY, and F. WRÓBLEWSKI, 1960. J. Biol. Chem. *235,* 2282. The electrophoretically distinct forms of mammalian lactic dehydrogenase. I. Distribution of lactic dehydrogenases in rabbit and human tissues.

REEDER, R., and E. BELL, 1967. J. Mol. Biol. *23,* 577. Protein synthesis in embryonic chick lens cells.

STEWART, J. A., and J. PAPACONSTANTINOU, 1967. J. Mol. Biol. *29,* 357. Stabilization of mRNA templates in bovine lens epithelial cells.

SCOTT, R. B., and E. BELL, 1964. Science *145,* 711. Protein synthesis during development: control through messenger RNA.

KIRK, D. L., and A. A. MOSCONA, 1963. Devel. Biol. *8,* 341. Synthesis of experimentally induced glutamine synthetase (glutamotransferase activity) in embryonic chick retina *in vitro.*

MOSCONA, A. A., and R. PIDDINGTON, 1967. Science *158,* 496. Enzyme induction by corticosteroids in embryonic cells: steroid structure and inductive effect.

MOSCANA, A. A., M. H. MOSCONA, and N. SAENZ, 1968. Proc. Nat'l Acad. Sci. *61,* 160. Enzyme induction in embryonic retina: the role of transcription and translation.

VARNER, J. E., and G. RAM CHANDRA, 1964. (P. 456) Proc. Nat'l Acad. Sci. *52,* 100. Hormonal control of enzyme synthesis in barley endosperm.

CHRISPEELS, M. J., and J. E. VARNER, 1967. Plant Physiol. *42,* 1008. Hormonal control of enzyme synthesis: on the mode of action of gibberellic acid and abscisin in aleurone layers of barley.

HEYWOOD, S. M., and A. RICH, 1968. Proc. Nat'l Acad. Sci. *59,* 590. *In vitro* synthesis of native myosin, actin, and tropomyosin from embryonic chick polyribosomes.

HEYWOOD, S. M., and M. NWAGWU, 1968. Proc. Nat'l Acad. Sci. *60,* 229. *De novo* synthesis of myosin in a cell-free system.

The development of a fertilized egg into a metazoan embryo dramatically demonstrates the process of differentiation of a single cell into various cell types as diverse as spleen, lens, muscle, or brain. The obvious differences in function in these tissues convince us that these cell types must have radically different protein complements.

Studies on lactic dehydrogenase activity in various tissues have significantly increased our understanding of biochemical differentiation during embryogenesis. By focusing attention on a single biochemical characteristic and ignoring for the time being the confusion of simultaneous changes in a large number of enzymes, it was possible to analyze the regulatory processes involved in organogenesis (p. 59). The study was enriched by the finding that lactic dehydrogenase in vertebrates is not a single protein enzyme but is a family of enzymes resulting from the association of two different protein subunits (p. 79). The electrophoretic separation of these "isozymes" allowed an analysis of the relative abundance of each subunit in various cell types. Thus, these studies simultaneously focused on the developmental control of the accumulation of two related proteins. Not unexpectedly, dramatic differences in subunit concentrations were found in different tissues. Some of the physiological mechanisms which result in the differences and the physiological consequences of the differences are discussed in the papers included in this collection (p. 87).

Differentiation of lens tissue is chiefly characterized by the progressive accumulation of a family of proteins, the crystallins. Metabolically active lens epithelial cells become more and more specialized to lens function as crystallins accumulate until at the terminal stage few proteins other than crystallins are synthesized, and metabolism and cell division are strongly suppressed. When attention was focused on the biochemical steps involved in this process, the results indicated that the preferential synthesis of crystallins results from the exceptional stability of the mRNA molecules which direct the synthesis of these proteins (p. 93 and p. 103). A correlation of the stability with mitotic index provides one avenue for further study.

The mechanism of differentiation which utilizes preferential stability of mRNA does not seem to be restricted to lens development but may occur in feather and red blood cell development as well, as is discussed by Scott and Bell (p. 117).

Somewhat different mechanisms seem to be involved in the accumulation of glutamine synthetase in developing retinal cells (p. 120). Embryonic retinas can be cultured in large quantities in vitro permitting high resolution biochemical techniques to be applied to the study of the differentiations which occur in this tissue. It was found that certain steroid hormones which occur in developing chicks in vivo and in adult horse serum in the in vitro system can stimulate a precocious accumulation of glutamine synthetase in retinal cells (p. 137). The accumulation of this enzyme requires protein and RNA synthesis. Considerable enzyme accumulation was found to occur after inhibition of RNA synthesis by actinomycin D when the cells had been incubated in the presence of steroid for several hours. However, the extent of accumulation depends on the amount of actinomycin D added. A possible explanation is discussed in one of the papers included in this collection (p. 139). Another possible explanation, involving stabilization of the enzyme as a result of actinomycin treatment, can be derived from the work of Reel and Kenney (p. 314).

A detailed study of hormonal stimulation of accumulation of several enzymes in germinating barley seeds has been carried out by Varner and his colleagues (pp. 147, 154). When a seed is hydrated, a series of metabolic changes occur which result in germination. One of the more striking events is the metabolism of the storage compounds of the endosperm. The enzymes responsible for this process appear to be localized in a tissue not destined to become part of the seedling, i.e., the aleurone layer. Cells of the aleurone layer can be maintained in culture free of other tissue and thus provide useful material. Filner and Varner (1964) have shown that the plant growth hormone, gib-berellic acid, regulates the *de novo* synthesis of α-amylase in aleurone cells. Gibberellic acid appears to increase production of mRNA for amylase (pp. 147, 154).

Differentiation of muscle cells is chiefly characterized by the accumulation of three proteins, myosin, actin, and tropomyosin. By using an *in vitro* protein synthesizing system to analyze the specificity of different size classes of polysomes, Heywood and Rich (p. 163) were able to show that mRNA which can synthesize actin accumulates several days before mRNA for myosin or tropomyosin during chick muscle embryogenesis. Confirmation of the technique was provided by Heywood and Nwagwu (p. 171) who isolated RNA from embryonic chick muscle which could direct the synthesis of myosin. This is one of the first direct studies of a specific mRNA in eukaryotic cells.

Filner, P., and J. E. Varner (1967) Proc. Nat'l Acad. Sci. *58,* 1520-1526. A test for *de novo* synthesis of enzymes: density labeling with H_2O^{18} of barley α-amylase induced by gibberellic acid.

RELATED READING

Hotta, Y., and H. Stern (1963) Proc. Nat'l Acad. Sci. *49,* 648. Molecular facets of mitotic regulation. I. Synthesis of thymidine kinase.

Hotta, Y., and H. Stern (1965) J. Cell Biology *25,* 99. Inducibility of thymidine kinase by thymidine as a function of interphase stage.

Konigsberg, I. (1963) Science *140,* 1273. Clonal analysis of myogenesis.

Rutter, W., W. Clark, J. Kemp, W. Bradshaw, T. Sanders, and W. Ball (1968) In "Epthelial-mesenchymal interactions," 18th Hahneman Symposium. R. Fleischmajer and R. Billingham, eds. Baltimore, pp. 114-131. Multiphasic regulation in cytodifferentiation.

Rutter, W., N. Wessels, and C. Grobstein (1963) Symp. on Met. Control Mech. Nat'l Cancer Inst. *13,* 51. Control of specific synthesis in the developing pancreas.

Sato, G., and V. Buonassisi (1964) In Wistar Instit. Mono 1, pp. 27-34. Philadelphia, Pa. Hormone synthesis in dispersed cell culture.

Voytovich, A., and Y. Topper (1967) Science *158,* 1326. Hormone-dependent differentiation of immature mouse mammary gland *in vivo.*

Reprinted from
CYTODIFFERENTIATION AND MACROMOLECULAR SYNTHESIS
1963
Academic Press Inc., New York, N. Y.

Epigenetic Control of Specific Protein Synthesis in Differentiating Cells

CLEMENT L. MARKERT

Department of Biology, The Johns Hopkins University, Baltimore, Maryland

The recognition of the chromosomal basis of inheritance some 60 years ago immediately posed a dilemma which has not yet been resolved and which in fact sums up what may be the fundamental problem of embryonic development. It was observed that during cell division each daughter cell received an identical set of chromosomes, presumably therefore an identical set of hereditary potentialities. Yet these daughter cells commonly followed their own independent pathways of development until finally at late stages of differentiation they exhibited very different phenotypes. Thus the dilemma: identical genotypes give rise to very different phenotypes—as different as nerve, and muscle, and pigment cells. With the tremendous expansion of our knowledge of genetics and biochemistry, of the structure and function of genes, of deoxyribonucleic acid (DNA), ribonucleic acid (RNA), and protein, and of their complementary structural and chemical relationships, this basic dilemma has become sharper and its solution so much the more important for our understanding of cell differentiation and embryonic development.

We know now that the metabolic machinery of a cell is largely regulated by enzymes and that the structure of enzymes, like other proteins, is ultimately encoded in the DNA of the chromosomes and probably also in RNA. So far as we can presently judge, the cells of a metazoan have constant identical supplies of DNA, but their enzymatic composition varies enormously. In fact the enzymatic content of a cell is the principal feature by which we assess the biochemical state of differentiation of the cell. Clearly some mechanism must regulate gene expression and this mechanism, whatever it may be, should provide the key to our dilemma and simultaneously elucidate the most basic problems of development. In searching for a mechanism that could selectively and differentially control gene expression in terms of the enzymes produced, we might profitably examine each step leading to the synthesis of an enzyme from the DNA to messenger RNA to ribosome to released enzyme. A limitation imposed anywhere along this sequence could regulate the enzymatic repertory of a cell and thus specify its state of differentiation. However, the problems of control seem to enlarge rapidly as the distance from the chromosome increases.

At the level of the chromosome we can easily imagine a single molecule activating or inhibiting a gene, turning it on or off, as it were. But at all later steps many molecules in many locations would be required to stifle the enzymatic expression of a functioning gene. Effective control of the enzyme molecules themselves would seem to involve enormous logistic problems and constitute a profligate drain on the resources of the cell, but then, perhaps the cell does not view economy the way we do. It should be remembered that the titer of any given enzyme per cell may range from many millions of molecules to none so far as we can tell, or at least to a number so low as to have no physiological significance for the cell. Turning the gene off seems to be the most satisfactory method of completely preventing the appearance of a particular enzyme in the cell. But what of the problem of regulating the amount of enzyme produced once the gene is turned on? Again the problem seems easiest to solve at the gene itself, but we have few facts to guide us in constructing a hypothesis of molecular regulation of the quantity of gene function. Taking a cue from the exciting work on the regulation of bacterial genes summarized by Jacob and Monod (1963), we might assume that the quantitative control of gene function is determined by the duration of gene activation which in turn is a function of the abundance of unstable activating molecules. The more abundant the activator, the greater would be the time during which the activator and gene were associated, and thus the more numerous would be the gene products.

In our efforts to formulate a mechanism for regulating gene function, it is important to bear in mind that the mechanism cannot be an autonomous expression of the genome of any particular cell. The mechanism is clearly dependent upon external influences. Transplanting an embryonic cell from one tissue environment to another will commonly change the fate of the transplanted cell to conform with its new location. Thus gene expression is dependent upon the extracellular environment, although more immediately upon the environment within the cell. Obviously a cyclical, dynamic interaction between the genome and its environment occurs, so that the environment specifies which part of the genome is to function and to what degree, and the functioning genome in turn modifies the environment. This reciprocal interplay of genome and environment drives the cell along the path of differentiation and is basically responsible for embryonic development.

Perhaps the most important, and certainly the most neglected, portion of this cycle is the chromosomes themselves—particularly the structural and chemical changes which occur in them as their function changes (Gall and Callán, 1962; Beermann, 1961; Clever, 1961). Our knowledge of chromosome change as related to function is still meager, but other parts of this cycle of interaction, particularly the synthesis of specific proteins, can more profitably be reviewed today. The mechanisms—genetic and epigenetic—that bring about the synthesis of protein molecules can best be studied by focusing on a specific protein. The enzyme lactate dehydrogenase (LDH) has been extensively investigated by many laboratories, and now provides a rich source of information for analyzing problems of protein synthesis. This oxidoreductase is ubiquitous in vertebrate tissues and is found in many other organisms as well. It catalyzes the interconversion of pyruvate and lactate and simultaneously of $NADH_2$ and NAD.* Lactate appears to have little metabolic importance other than as a temporary storage reservoir for hydrogen during periods of relative anaerobiosis. Pyruvate, of course, occupies a key position in carbohydrate metabolism.

Isozymes

From our understanding of the gene control of enzyme synthesis, the encoding of a single protein by a single gene would lead us to suppose that all the molecules of LDH within a single individual should be identical, except possibly for rare accidents. We were surprised, therefore, a few years ago (Markert and Møller, 1959), to find that LDH exists in several distinct molecular varieties, five in fact, in the tissues of vertebrates. These multiple molecular forms, or isozymes, of LDH, present in a sharp fashion the problems involved in the genetic and also in the epigenetic control of specific protein synthesis in differentiating cells.

The fact that LDH exists in more than one molecular variety in a single organism was first recognized by Meister (1950) and later confirmed by Neilands (1952). Using zone electrophoresis, Wieland and Pfleiderer (1957) and Pfleiderer and Jeckel (1957) were later able to demonstrate additional molecular varieties of LDH and to show that they existed in tissue- and species-specific patterns. Other enzymes have also been shown to exist in multiple molecular forms, but generally the early observations were considered, at best, to be biochemical curiosities or, at worst, evidence of defective preparative procedures leading to artifacts in the form of partially degraded but still active enzyme molecules. A full appreciation of the fact

---

* NAD = nicotinamide-adenine dinucleotide, replacing DPN (diphosphopyridine nucleotide); $NADH_2$ = dihydronicotinamide-adenine dinucleotide, replacing DPNH (diphosphopyridine nucleotide, reduced form).

that many enzymes normally exist in several different isozymic forms depended upon the development of analytical procedures that permitted a direct assay of the isozymic content of tissues with a minimum of manipulation and without the use of conventional preparative procedures.

The development of techniques (Smithies, 1955) for the resolution of protein mixtures by electrophoresis in starch gels provided the basic analytical procedure. The employment of histochemical staining techniques to visualize enzymes separated on starch gels (Hunter and Markert, 1957) provided a simple procedure for direct analysis of enzymes in tissue homogenates. By these methods the isozymes of numerous enzymes, particularly those of LDH, were readily separated and identified (Markert and Møller, 1959). These stained starch strips (Fig. 1), or zymograms, revealed the existence of five isozymes of LDH in all the mammals so far examined (Fig. 2).

The common occurrence of the same number of LDH isozymes in different mammals suggested that the isozymes probably had biological significance. This conclusion became obvious when a variety of different tissues were analyzed. Nearly every tissue contained all five isozymes of LDH in precise relative proportions—that is, the zymogram of each tissue showed a characteristic constant pattern of isozymes. These patterns are very stable and are not easily modified by procedures commonly employed in the purification of enzymes. Homogenizing different tissues together resulted in zymograms that showed merely the summation of the patterns of the constituent tissues.

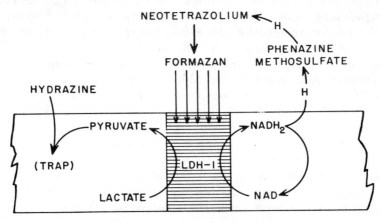

FIG. 1. Diagram of the reactions involved in visualizing the isozymes of LDH after resolution by starch gel electrophoresis. The method essentially provides a colorimetric test for the production of $NADH_2$.

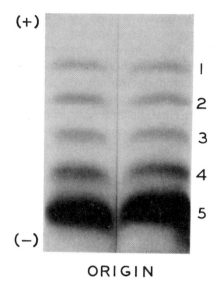

FIG. 2. Photograph of zymograms of two independent preparations of mouse LDH from skeletal muscle. Note that all five isozymes are present. Electrophoresis occurred at pH 7.0 at room temperature for about 6 hours at a voltage gradient of 6 V/cm.

Neither inhibition nor activation of individual isozymes occurred. Moreover, during the several steps involved in purification the isozymic pattern remains essentially constant. From these observations it seems clear that isozyme patterns, as seen on zymograms, reflect conditions within the tissue and are definitely not artifacts of the analytic procedures.

Since these analyses were performed on tissues that were, of course, composed of heterogeneous populations of cells, it seemed possible that the pattern of isozymes observed represented a corresponding pattern of cell types, each contributing a single isozyme to the total. Two lines of investigation provided at least a partial answer to this possibility. First, a single cell type—mouse erythrocytes—was obtained in pure form. These erythrocytes were separated from the cells of the blood by centrifugation, washed thoroughly in physiological saline solution, lysed in distilled water, and the resulting solution electrophoresed. This single cell type produced a complex pattern of several isozymes. Thus, one might conclude that a single cell can synthesize more than one isozyme, although these observations do not preclude the possibility that the erythrocytes themselves are a heterogeneous population in terms of isozymic content. This reservation seems unlikely in view of the work of Nace *et al.* (1961). By using fluorescent labeled antibodies to different LDH isozymes of the frog, these investigators were able to demonstrate the presence of three isozymes in the egg of the frog *Rana pipiens*. It seems probable, therefore, that single cells do produce more than one isozyme. However, the diverse cells composing a tissue do not make identical contributions to the isozyme pattern of the tissue. This is easily demonstrated by dividing a complex organ, such as the stomach, into distinct parts and analyzing each of these separately. Quite different isozyme patterns are commonly obtained from these different parts of an organ. The pattern of any organ or tissue is merely the summation of the patterns of its constituent parts.

It is obvious from an examination of the zymograms (Fig. 3) of the different tissues of the mouse that the specific characteristics of each tissue or organ is based upon the specific proportions of the several isozymes present

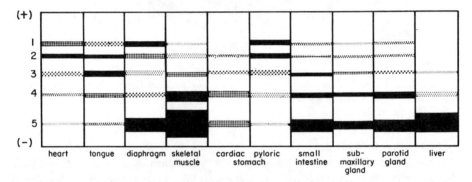

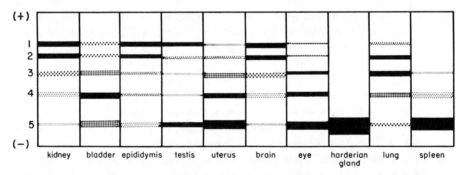

FIG. 3. Diagrammatic representation of the LDH zymogram patterns from 20 tissues or organs of the adult mouse. The darkness of the isozyme bands is a rough indication of the amount of enzyme activity in the band. (From *Develop. Biol.*, **5**, 363–381.)

in the tissue and not upon the presence or absence of an isozyme (Markert and Ursprung, 1962). The concept of a tissue-specific isozyme is entirely inappropriate. Furthermore, all of the isozymes appear to be equally important. Although LDH-5 predominates in many mouse tissues, each isozyme is the most abundant in some tissue. Nearly all tissues contain measurable amounts of all five isozymes, and the few exceptions probably represent cases in which the titer of the isozyme is too low to be detected by these techniques. The range of variation on a zymogram from the faintest to the darkest band represents about a hundredfold difference in isozyme titer.

The fact that each cell can synthesize more than one isozyme raises the question as to where these isozymes may be located within the cell. Reliance must be placed on cytochemical techniques for identifying the location of enzymes within cells. Such techniques are difficult to apply to LDH because of the ready solubility of this enzyme. However, some progress has been made. Allen (1961) demonstrated that LDH is not uniformly distributed throughout the cell and, in fact, different cell types show characteristic distributions of the LDH. His results did not permit the identification of the different isozymic forms of LDH but only located the enzymatic activity. However, the use of fluorescent labeled antibodies (Nace *et al.*, 1961) against individual isozymes did permit localization to individual cells, and even intracellular location could be ascertained with some accuracy, particularly in large cells such as the frog egg. Nace and his associates eluted fluorescent labeled antibodies from precipitin bands in Ouchterlony plates. With these antibodies they then stained tissue sections and demonstrated the differential location of individual isozymes. For example, LDH-1 was identified on yolk platelets of the egg and in the connective tissue of the oviduct. LDH-3 was found in the egg cytoplasm and in certain cells of the oviduct epithelium and in jelly-secreting glands of the oviduct. The location of LDH-2 in the egg was not determined but it was found in certain cells of the oviduct epithelium. Walker and Seligman (1963) have also described precise intracellular localizations of LDH activity which were characteristic for different cell types, although the techniques used by these investigators do not resolve the individual isozymes. All these data suggest that each isozyme may be located in a prescribed site in the cell. Presumably the difference in net charge by which we are able to separate the isozymes electrophoretically is an important molecular property in allowing each isozyme to be held at specific sites in the cell.

The specificity of isozyme distribution in the various tissues of vertebrates strongly implies biological significance. Moreover, since the patterns of adult tissues are different, it follows that these patterns must have arisen during the

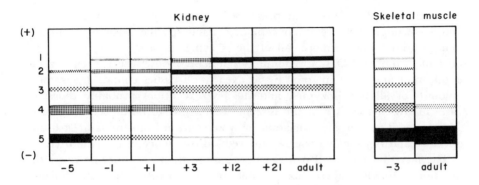

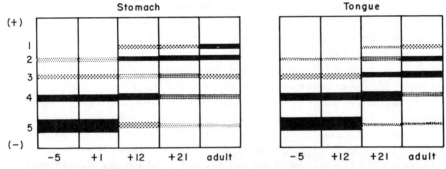

Fig. 4. Diagrammatic representation of changing LDH patterns during the development of several mouse tissues. Note that patterns do not change synchronously. The numbers along the abscissa indicate days before (−) or after (+) birth. (From *Develop. Biol.*, **5**, 363–381.)

course of embryonic development. Direct analysis of tissues at successive steps in development shows this to be so. The adult patterns gradually emerge and in so doing exhibit remarkable regularities of change from the embryonic precursor patterns (Fig. 4). In the mouse, the most extensively investigated mammal, the largest part of the pattern change occurs during early neonatal existence, although progressive changes also occur during embryonic life. Once adulthood is reached, no further change is observed, even in very old mice. All embryonic tissues first exhibit a predominance of LDH-5. As development proceeds a gradual shift in pattern occurs so that enzyme activity is progressively transferred toward the LDH-1 end of the spectrum. The extent of this shift varies enormously in different tissues. In skeletal muscle, for example, very little change in pattern occurs, nearly all

LDH activity being in LDH-5, both in the embryo and in the adult. Heart muscle exhibits quite another picture. In this tissue enzyme activity is progressively shifted from LDH-5 toward LDH-1. In the adult heart nearly all LDH activity is found in isozymes LDH-1 and LDH-2 with almost none remaining in the previously dominant LDH-5. Yet other tissues show intermediate degrees of change from the embryonic emphasis on LDH-5 to the increased abundance of LDH-1 generally characteristic of adult tissues.

This progressive transposition of enzyme activity from one end of the spectrum of isozymes to the other does not occur synchronously throughout the developing mouse. Some tissues mature faster than others so far as their isozyme patterns are concerned. At the same stage of development, for example, the kidney shows a more nearly adult pattern than does the heart, even though the heart functions in the embryo much as it does in the adult. Each tissue evidently matures at its own characteristic rate, largely independently of other tissues.

The pattern changes characteristic of mouse development are paralleled in the development of the chick (Lindsay, 1962) but with certain conspicuous and instructive exceptions. LDH-5 is not the principal isozyme in the chick embryo as it is in the mouse, but rather LDH-1 first appears. In certain tissues such as breast muscle, LDH activity is gradually shifted along the spectrum of isozymes until in the adult only LDH-5 is detected. No change occurs in the chick heart pattern; LDH-1 remains predominant throughout life. Thus adult patterns in the chick are similar to those of the adult mouse, but the starting patterns in the embryo are quite different and therefore the sequence of pattern change is also different. As will be discussed later these differences between chick and mouse are probably related to the availability of oxygen during embryonic development.

Physicochemical Nature of LDH

A full appreciation of the biological significance of isozymes depends upon a detailed knowledge of the physical and chemical differences among them. Accordingly we have undertaken to analyze the physicochemical nature of the LDH isozymes (Markert and Appella, 1961). Highly purified, crystalline preparations of LDH have been made from beef, pig, mouse, and chicken muscle. The most extensive analysis has been made with beef LDH (Table I) but the same general results also seem to apply to LDH from the other organisms.

Beef LDH has a molecular weight of 135,000 as determined from measurements with the ultracentrifuge and by light scattering. In the ultracentrifuge crystalline preparations from beef skeletal muscle, containing all five iso-

TABLE I
PHYSICOCHEMICAL PROPERTIES OF LDH ISOZYMES[a]

Physicochemical property	LDH-1	LDH-5
Molecular weight	135,000	135,000
Sedimentation coefficient ($S_{20,w}^0 \times 10^{-13}$ cm/sec)	7.0	7.0
Diffusion coefficient ($D_{20,w} \times 10^{-7}$ cm²/sec)	5.10	5.10
Partial specific volume (W_{20} ml/gm)	0.750	0.750
Isoelectric point	4.5	9.5
Subunit size	35,000	35,000
Electrophoretic mobility (pH 7.2, 0.1 ionic strength phosphate buffer)	−4.90	+0.63

[a] From beef tissues.

zymes, show a single symmetric peak. This monodisperse behavior in the ultracentrifuge suggests that all five isozymes are the same size. By contrast, free boundary electrophoresis or zone electrophoresis in starch gels reveals five distinct molecular species. Thus the net charge on each isozyme is different. At pH 7.0 the isozymes are equally spaced along the starch gel after electrophoresis. This arrangement suggests that each isozyme differs from the next in the series by the same increment of charge. A plausible molecular basis for such regularity will be discussed later. Each of these isozymes may be separated from the crystalline preparation by electrophoresis in a column of cellulose powder followed by elution with buffer. Such purified isozymes have the same molecular weight as the crystalline preparations containing several isozymes. Thus the possibility that isozymes are polymers is excluded. They are all the same size. They are not equally stable, however. The curves depicting the course of denaturation by heat for beef LDH-1 and LDH-5 reveal that LDH-5 is noticeably less stable. This fact suggests that the tertiary structure of the two molecules might be significantly different. The tertiary structure relies heavily upon hydrogen bonds to hold the molecule in a stable configuration. Agents that rupture hydrogen bonds might then reveal differences among isozymes if indeed the differences lie in the tertiary structure.

Subunit Hypothesis

When hydrogen bonding reagents such as 12 M urea and 5 M guanidine hydrochloride were added to solutions of the isozymes, they were readily denatured; all enzymatic activity disappeared, as was expected. However, more important was the fact that the molecule was split into four polypeptide chains of equal size as shown by measurements in the ultracentrifuge (Fig.

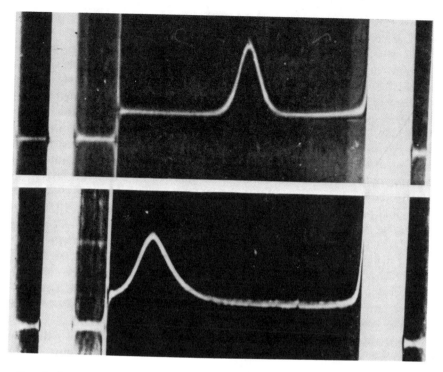

Fig. 5. Schlieren photographs taken at the same time after the beginning of ultracentrifugation. Upper photo is of intact LDH preparation; lower photo is after dissociation of LDH into subunits. The difference in sedimentation constants indicates that the subunits are one-fourth the size of the intact molecule. Note that each preparation is monodisperse.

5). Low pH will also dissociate the LDH molecule into its constituent polypeptides. These polypeptides have no enzyme activity and may be separated into at least two electrophoretically distinct forms. The subunits obtained from LDH-1 and from LDH-5 each appear to be electrophoretically homogeneous but different from each other. The subunits of LDH-2, -3, and -4 all appear to be mixtures of the two kinds of subunits found in LDH-1 and -5. Complex crystalline preparations containing several isozymes also dissociate into two kinds of subunits. Assorting these two kinds of subunits in all possible combinations of four would yield five distinct molecular varieties (Appella and Markert, 1961). It is surely more than coincidence that five LDH isozymes are found in nearly all mammalian tissues so far examined. If the two subunits are designated A and B, then the formulas for the five isozymes can be written A^0B^4, (LDH-1); A^1B^3 (LDH-2); A^2B^2 (LDH-3); A^3B^1 (LDH-4); A^4B^0 (LDH-5). This hypothesis (Markert, 1962; Appella and Markert, 1961), which owes much to our knowledge of hemoglobin composition and synthesis, not only provides a plausible explanation for the structure of isozymes, but is readily subject to experimental test. At least three tests are apparent. (1) Recombination of equal numbers of the dissociated subunits of LDH-1 and LDH-5 should produce all five isozymes in the ratio of 1:4:6:4:1. The major difficulty in this approach is to discover the conditions required to promote reassociation of the subunits. Some success has been achieved but satisfactory completion of this test will require more experimentation. (2) Total amino acid analyses of LDH-1, LDH-3, and LDH-5 should demonstrate whether LDH-3 has an amino acid composition that could be formed by equal numbers of the subunits found in LDH-1 and LDH-5 as the hypothesis predicts. The results of this test will be presented below. (3) If each type of subunit is antigenic, then immunochemical tests should demonstrate that LDH-1 and LDH-5 are not cross-reactive but that each is cross-reactive with LDH-2, -3, and -4. Such tests have been conducted in several laboratories and the results are consistent with the hypothesis (Plagemann *et al.*, 1960a; Cahn *et al.*, 1962; Lindsay, 1962; Markert and Appella, 1963).

Recombination of dissociated subunits to form new isozymes is the most critical test. Although this test is not yet complete it is interesting to note that most of the patterns of isozymes as seen in zymograms of mouse tissues (Fig. 3) could be produced by a random assortment of subunits, provided that the proportions of the subunits were fixed at an appropriate ratio (Fig. 6). Thus in mouse skeletal muscle the ratio of A to B should be about 30:1, in kidney about 1:10, and in adult heart about 1:3. At about the time of birth the mouse heart should contain equal numbers of subunits A and B, thus producing mostly LDH-3. The few exceptions to the possibility of randomly generated patterns, such as the diaphragm, can be attributed to the heterogeneity of the tissue components, each contributing a quite different isozyme composition to the over-all pattern of the organ.

Analysis of the isozyme patterns in fragments of the stomach (Fig. 3) demonstrates the local heterogeneity that can exist in complex organs or tissues. It is perhaps surprising that the organ patterns agree as closely as they do with patterns predicted upon the basis of random assortment of subunits. The fact that the spectrum of isozymes in any tissue is continuous is also in accord with the subunit hypothesis. No isozymes are skipped in the series and the quantities of each generally follow a smooth gradient of diminution from the most abundant to the least. These characteristics of the

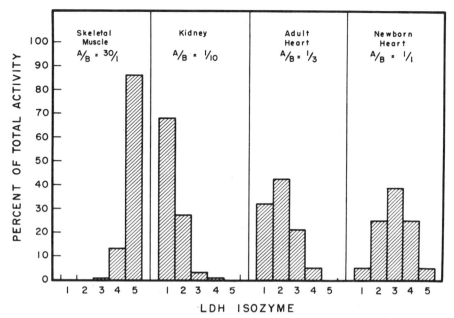

FIG. 6. Relative abundance of each LDH isozyme in tissues as predicted on the assumption of a random assortment of different initial numbers of the polypeptide subunits A and B.

distribution pattern would be predicted from the subunit hypothesis, provided the subunits were assorted at.random.

Chemical Composition

By investigating the chemical composition of isozymes some insight may be obtained into their synthesis and perhaps into their function. Two general approaches are available: determination of total amino acid composition by means of an amino acid analyzer and determination of peptide patterns ("fingerprinting") after trypsin digestion. Both procedures have been applied to crystalline preparations containing several isozymes and also to pure preparations of LDH-1 and LDH-5 from beef tissues. The amino acid composition of these preparations is shown in Table II. It is obvious that LDH-1 and LDH-5 differ considerably although they appear to be related proteins. Moreover the differences correspond with the electrophoretic behavior of these isozymes. At pH 7.0 LDH-1 has a greater net negative charge than LDH-5 and accordingly is richer in aspartic and glutamic acids, but poorer in the basic amino acids, arginine, lysine, and histidine. The basic amino

TABLE II

AMINO ACID COMPOSITION OF LDH ISOZYMES FROM BEEF MUSCLE

Amino acid	Number of amino acid residues per molecule of enzyme[a]	
	LDH-1	LDH-5
Lysine	94	95
Histid ne	25	34
Arginine	34	52
Aspartic acid	123	104
Threonine	56	62
Serine	92	61
Glutamic acid	124	135
Proline	42	63
Glycine	91	100
Alanine	72	122
Valin	135	82
Methionine	32	20
Isoleuc ne	86	73
Leucine	130	118
Tyrosine	26	35
Phenylalanine	19	26

[a] Based upon a molecular weght of 135,000 (including 12 residues of cysteine and 30 residues of tryptophan in each isozyme).

acids are all more abundant in LDH-5. The subunit hypothesis predicts that the amino acid composition of LDH-3 should be equal to one-half the sum of the amino acids of LDH-1 and LDH-5. Unfortunately, pure preparations of LDH-3 in sufficient quantity to provide a critical test of this hypothesis have not yet become available, and preliminary results with small quantities have been ambiguous.

Since the amino acid compositions of LDH-1 and LDH-5 are different, their peptide patterns should also be different, and this is so. Peptides are obtained by digesting the LDH with trypsin, which splits the molecule at each arginine and lysine residue. The resulting peptides are resolved on paper by chromatography and electrophoresis and visualized with the aid of ninhydrin. Such peptide patterns show that some of the peptides from LDH-1 and LDH-5 appear to be the same. The N-terminal residue appears to be threonine in both LDH-1 and -5 and the C-terminal residue is aspartic acid for both isozymes. These similarities argue for a common origin during the biochemical evolution of these isozymes. The two different genes which presumably encode the constituent polypeptides of LDH probably arose by duplication from a single precursor gene and then diverged through the accumulation of spontaneous mutations.

The peptide analysis also tends to confirm the subunit hypothesis. The number of arginine + lysine residues found in LDH-1, for example, is about 130. If only a single long polypeptide were involved, then digestion with trypsin should yield approximately 130 peptides. However, only about one-fourth this number is actually observed (Fig. 7)—a result to be expected

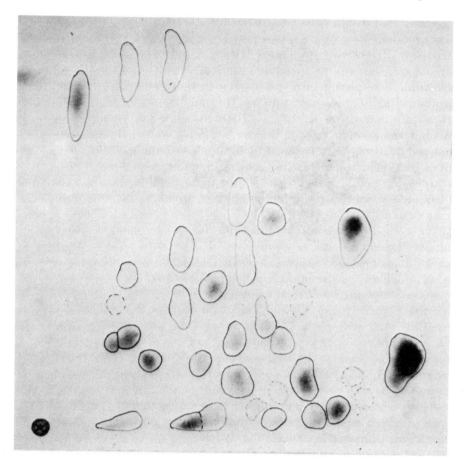

FIG. 7. Peptide pattern of LDH-1 from beef heart. Isozyme digested with trypsin and peptides resolved on paper by electrophoresis and chromatography. The peptide pattern of LDH-5 is conspicuously different. Note that the number of peptides is about 30 or one-fourth of the number of arginine + lysine residues in the intact enzyme molecule.

if the molecule is composed of four identical subunits. It is interesting to note that four molecules of NAD are bound to each molecule of LDH, presumably one per subunit, although once dissociated the subunits do not bind NAD.

Immunochemical Properties

Recently Lindsay (1962) and Cahn *et al.* (1962) have completed extensive immunochemical analyses of LDH isozymes obtained principally from the chicken. These studies show that LDH-1 and LDH-5 are immunochemically distinct although both are related to LDH-2, -3, and -4. Antisera to either LDH-1 or LDH-5 will precipitate LDH-2, -3, and -4 as well as the immunizing antigen, but will not precipitate the isozyme at the opposite end of the spectrum. These results are consistent with the assumption that the polypeptides A and B are distinct antigens. It would then follow that the immunochemical properties of the intact LDH molecule would be a function of its subunit composition. In fact Lindsay's (1962) analysis indicates that one antibody molecule is sufficient to inhibit one enzyme molecule. Thus complete inactivation of LDH-2, -3, and -4 by antisera to either LDH-1 or -5 is to be expected. The data on quantitative precipitin tests by Cahn *et al.* (1962) also supports this expectation. Earlier studies of the immunochemical properties of LDH isozymes of the rabbit (Plagemann *et al.*, 1960a) and frog (Nace *et al.*, 1961) can also be fitted into this general analysis although the subunit hypothesis was not considered in this work. These investigators tended to picture each isozyme as distinct, as indeed it is, but not necessarily in the qualitative sense implicit in their discussions.

Recent immunochemical investigations of beef, pig, and mouse LDH isozymes (Markert and Appella, 1963) also support the conclusions drawn from the work with chick LDH. Isozymes from these different species did not cross-react in agar gel diffusion analyses, but such species specificity is not surprising. During the long course of evolution the genes encoding the structure of LDH in different species would surely become different in some degree. In fact the electrophoretic behavior of the LDH isozymes of different species is commonly different, and the different mobilities indicate a difference in amino acid composition—that is, in the primary structure of the constituent polypeptide chains. This species specificity opens up the possibility of a fruitful examination of the synthesis of LDH. The favored hypothesis of LDH synthesis assumes that two nonallelic genes produce two different polypeptides which, assorting at random in groups of four, produce the five isozymes observed. A hybrid between two species would possess four such genes, each producing a different polypeptide. Assorting four different polypeptides in all possible combinations of four would give rise to 35 different molecular varieties of LDH. Thus an examination of LDH patterns in hybrid tissues should prove very instructive.

Function of Isozymes

From the point of view of cell function it seems strange that a cell should synthesize precise patterns of isozymes, all performing exactly the same catalytic function. One type of molecule would seem sufficient. However, a detailed examination of the catalytic properties of the LDH isozymes shows that they are not identical although each exhibits the basic properties of LDH. The extensive work of Kaplan and his associates (Kaplan *et al.*, 1960; Kaplan and Ciotti, 1961) has clearly demonstrated that the different isozymes of LDH have significantly different catalytic efficiencies, particularly when various NAD analogs are substituted for the normal coenzyme in the assay mixture. This behavior of the isozymes *in vitro* with abnormal substrates probably reflects differences in their normal behavior *in vivo*, although no direct test of this assumption has been made. It seems quite likely that the fundamental role of LDH is to regulate the ratio of NAD to $NADH_2$ with the production of lactate as only an essential by-product of this activity. The $NAD/NADH_2$ ratio is of critical importance in regulating numerous biochemical reactions in the cell. Each isozyme may serve to regulate this ratio at specific locations in the cell where that particular isozyme is bound by virtue of its unique charge.

The catalytic efficiency of the different isozymes has been measured in the presence of different concentrations of the normal substrates, lactate and pyruvate, by several investigators (Plagemann *et al.*, 1960b; Kaplan and Ciotti, 1961; Lindsay, 1962; Cahn *et al.*, 1962; Markert and Ursprung, 1962). These investigations all agree in demonstrating that high pyruvate concentrations inhibit LDH (Fig. 8). However, the substrate optimum for LDH-1 is much lower than for LDH-5, and with increasing concentrations of pyruvate LDH-1 activity is inhibited long before LDH-5 activity is depressed. This behavior has interesting physiological implications and provides a metabolic rationale for the existence of LDH isozymes. Mammalian skeletal muscle, for example, is rich in LDH-5. During periods of vigorous activity this muscle produces large quantities of pyruvate that is then reduced to lactate by LDH-5 with a simultaneous oxidation of $NADH_2$ to NAD. This reaction enables the muscle to use glucose as a source of energy even after oxygen is exhausted, because essential supplies of NAD can be regenerated from $NADH_2$ by transferring the hydrogen to pyruvate (to yield lactate) rather than to oxygen. Thus lactate can serve as a temporary hy-

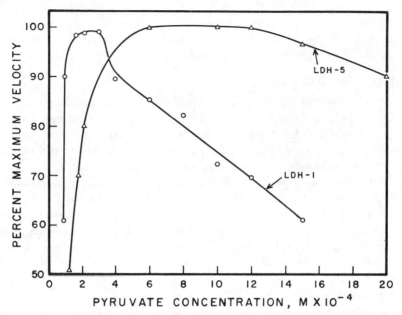

Fig. 8. Effect of pyruvate concentration on the velocity of the reaction with human LDH isozymes LDH-1 and LDH-5 at pH 7.0. (Redrawn and modified from the data of Plagemann *et al.*, 1960.)

drogen storage reservoir until increased oxygen supplies become available. However, at high levels of lactate, muscle function is impaired. This is not usually serious in skeletal muscle but it might be fatal in heart muscle. Since heart muscle contains principally LDH-1, large quantities of lactate are not likely to accumulate during rapid metabolism of glucose because the enzyme would be increasingly inhibited by the increased concentration of pyruvate. Thus in heart muscle, lactate production should be maintained at a relatively constant low level even in the face of fluctuating pyruvate concentrations. Only tissues capable of tolerating relatively anaerobic conditions are rich in isozymes at the LDH-5 end of the spectrum. Other tissues are equipped principally with LDH-1 or LDH-2. It is interesting to note that mammalian embryos have a preponderance of LDH-5 in accord with their relatively anaerobic environment. The tissues of chick embryos, on the other hand, appear to be as well oxygenated as adult tissues and these embryonic tissues synthesize mostly LDH-1. Only later in adult tissues subject to anaerobiosis, such as skeletal muscle, does LDH-5 become a prominent part of the enzymatic repertory.

These observations not only give meaning to the existence of isozymes, but suggest that the epigenetic control of their synthesis may in some way involve the oxygen tension in the cell. The metabolic mechanisms which bring about the differential function of genes still remain one of the greatest mysteries in biology, but it does seem clear that regulation of the relative levels of function of two genes for the A and B polypeptides is sufficient to account for the LDH isozymic patterns observed in adult tissues, as well as the changing patterns apparent during embryonic development.

Whether differential gene function is a plausible explanation for the origin of the isozymic forms of enzymes other than LDH, only further investigation will reveal. Although the isozymes of any enzyme carry out the same catalytic function, their distinguishing physical properties may enable them to be integrated into distinct metabolic pathways in different locations in the cell. This arrangement should permit a more precise and sensitive control of cell metabolism and thus should have proved biologically advantageous during the course of evolution. The large number of enzymes which have so far been demonstrated to exist in multiple molecular forms indicates that organisms have frequently exploited the advantages of synthesizing isozymes. These specialized forms of an enzyme must now be accorded a position of general biological significance. Further study of the nature of isozymes and of the genetic and epigenetic mechanisms that regulate their synthesis will surely advance our understanding of the processes of cellular differentiation, and may even bring a solution of the dilemma posed by different phenotypes arising from the same genotype.

ACKNOWLEDGMENTS

The work from the author's laboratory reviewed here has been supported by grants from the National Science Foundation, the American Cancer Society, and by contracts with the Atomic Energy Commission. Most of the research was carried out in collaboration with Drs. Ettore Appella and H. Ursprung. The skillful assistance of Joanne Yundt and Sheila Hutman is gratefully acknowledged.

REFERENCES

ALLEN, J. M. (1961). Multiple forms of lactic dehydrogenase in tissues of the mouse: Their specificity, cellular localization, and response to altered physiological conditions. *Ann. N. Y. Acad. Sci.* **94,** 937–951.

APPELLA, E., AND MARKERT, C. L. (1961). Dissociation of lactate dehydrogenase into subunits with guanidine hydrochloride. *Biochem. Biophys. Research Communs.* **6,** 171–176.

BEERMANN, W. (1961). Ein Balbiani-Ring als Locus einer Speicheldrüsenmutation. *Chromosoma* **12,** 1–25.

CAHN, R. D., KAPLAN, N. O., LEVINE, L., AND ZWILLING, E. (1962). Nature and development of lactic dehydrogenases. *Science* **136,** 962–969.

CLEVER, U. (1961). Genaktivitäten in den Riesenchromosomen von *Chironomus tentans* und ihre Beziehungen zur Entwicklung. I. Genaktivierungen durch Ecdyson. *Chromosoma* **12,** 607–675.

GALL, J. G., AND CALLAN, H. G. (1962). H³ Uridine incorporation in lampbrush chromosomes. *Proc. Natl. Acad. Sci. U.S.* 48, 562–570.

HUNTER, R. L., AND MARKERT, C. L. (1957). Histochemical demonstration of enzymes separated by zone electrophoresis in starch gels. *Science* 125, 1294–1295.

JACOB, F., AND MONOD, J. (1963). Regulation of protein synthesis in bacteria as a model for genetic repression, allosteric inhibition and differentiation. This volume, pp. 30–64.

KAPLAN, N. O., AND CIOTTI, M. M. (1961). Evolution and differentiation of dehydrogenases. *Ann. N. Y. Acad. Sci.* 94, 701–722.

KAPLAN, N. O., CIOTTI, M. M., HAMOLSKY, M., AND BIEBER, R. E. (1960). Molecular heterogeneity and evolution of enzymes. *Science* 131, 392–397.

LINDSAY, D. T. (1962). Developmental patterns and immunochemical properties of lactate dehydrogenase isozymes from the chicken. Thesis, Johns Hopkins University, Baltimore, Maryland.

MARKERT, C. L. (1962). Isozymes in kidney development. *In* "Hereditary, Developmental, and Immunologic Aspects of Kidney Disease" (J. Metcoff, ed.), pp. 54–63. Northwestern Univ. Press, Evanston, Illinois.

MARKERT, C. L., AND APPELLA, E. (1961). Physicochemical nature of isozymes. *Ann. N. Y. Acad. Sci.* 94, 678–690.

MARKERT, C. L., AND APPELLA, E. (1963). Immunochemical properties of lactate dehydrogenase isozymes. *Ann. N. Y. Acad. Sci.* in press.

MARKERT, C. L., AND MØLLER, F. (1959). Multiple forms of enzymes: Tissue, ontogenetic, and species specific patterns. *Proc. Natl. Acad. Sci. U. S.* 45, 753–763.

MARKERT, C. L., AND URSPRUNG, H. (1962). The ontogeny of isozyme patterns of lactate dehydrogenase in the mouse. *Develop. Biol.* 5, 363–381.

MEISTER, A. (1950). Reduction of α, γ-diketo and α-keto acids catalyzed by muscle preparations and by crystalline lactic dehydrogenase. *J. Biol. Chem.* 184, 117–129.

NACE, G. W., SUYAMA, T., AND SMITH, N. (1961). Early development of special proteins. *Symposium on Germ Cells and Development (Inst. Intern. Embryol. and Fondazione A. Baselli), 1960* pp. 564–603.

NEILANDS, J. B. (1952). Studies on lactic dehydrogenase of heart—purity, kinetics, and equilibria. *J. Biol. Chem.* 199, 373–381.

PFLEIDERER, G., AND JECKEL, D. (1957). Individuelle Milchsäuredehydrogenasen bei verschiedenen Säugetieren. *Biochem. Z.* 329, 370–380.

PLAGEMANN, P. G., GREGORY, K. F., AND WRÓBLEWSKI, F. (1960a). The electrophoretically distinct forms of mammalian lactic dehydrogenase. I. Distribution of lactic dehydrogenases in rabbit and human tissues. *J. Biol. Chem.* 235, 2282–2287.

PLAGEMANN, P. G., GREGORY, K. F., AND WRÓBLEWSKI, F. (1960b). The electrophoretically distinct forms of mammalian lactic dehydrogenase. II. Properties and interrelationships of rabbit and human lactic dehydrogenase isozymes. *J. Biol. Chem.* 235, 2288–2293.

SMITHIES, O. (1955). Zone electrophoresis in starch gels: Group variations in the serum proteins of normal human adults. *Biochem. J.* 61, 629–641.

WALKER, D. G., AND SELIGMAN, A. M. (1963). The use of formalin fixation in the cytochemical demonstration of DPN and TPN dependent dehydrogenases in mitochondria. *J. Cell Biol.* in press.

WIELAND, T., AND PFLEIDERER, G. (1957). Nachweis der Heterogenität von Milchsäuredehydrogenasen verschiedenen Ursprungs durch Trägerelektrophorese. *Biochem. Z.* 329, 112–116.

Reprinted from Science, June 15, 1962, Vol. 136, No. 3520, pages 962-969

Nature and Development of Lactic Dehydrogenases

The two major types of this enzyme form molecular hybrids which change in makeup during development.

R. D. Cahn, N. O. Kaplan, L. Levine, E. Zwilling

Many enzymes have been reported to exist in more than one form within the same species. By several methods a number of molecular forms of lactic dehydrogenase (LDH) have been found in differing amounts in the various organs of one individual (1–4). This article describes studies which were undertaken in an attempt to elucidate the molecular nature of these multiple enzymatic forms and to follow their development. Most of the developmental studies were made on the chicken.

Two "pure" lactic dehydrogenases occur in the chicken. One of them (CM) is found principally in the breast muscle, and the other (CH) in the heart, of adult chickens. These two enzymes are separate entities as judged by physical, enzymatic, and immunochemical criteria (1, 2, 5). During embryonic development the LDH enzymes of the chicken breast muscle shift from the enzymes related to CH, through several intermediate enzyme types, and appear in the adult as pure CM. The characterization of these intermediate enzyme types by several independent methods has led to the development of the hypothesis, which we present in this article, that the intermediate enzyme types which appear during embryonic development are "hybrid" enzymes, consisting of both CM and CH components. Furthermore, these "hybrids" also occur in the adult tissues of the chicken and in other animals.

Immunological Approach

In order to use immunological methods for the study of the development and structure of specific proteins, it is necessary that the immune systems be fully characterized. Two immune systems were used in this study: (i) CH-LDH rabbit anti-CH-LDH (anti-CH) and (ii) CM-LDH rabbit anti-CM-LDH (anti-CM). Anti-CM was shown to be homogeneous when measured by double diffusion in agar (6), immunoelectrophoresis (7), and quantitative precipitation analyses (8, 9). Anti-CH was shown to be heterogeneous when measured by double diffusion in agar. After absorption with CM, two bands remained when tested with crude chicken heart extracts, only one of which showed LDH activity (10, 11). This absorption did not decrease the complement (C') fixation titer of CH-anti-CH (Fig. 1), nor did it remove antibody capable of neutralizing CH enzymatic activity. Thus, the heterogeneity in anti-CH reflected antibodies to impurities in the CH immunizing antigen (probably CM) and not anti-CH cross-reacting with CM.

Figure 1 shows the C' fixation curves of CM and CH with anti-CM and anti-CH. After absorption with CM, anti-CH showed no reduction in titer against CH. Moreover, the C' fixation curves were identical when either crystalline CH or crude heart extracts were used as antigen. At the dilutions of antisera used (1/5000 for anti-CH and 1/2200 for anti-CM) no cross reactions between CM and CH are detectable. Figure 2 demonstrates the ability of C' fixation to resolve a mixture of pure CM and CH. The heights of the curves at peak fixation are the same in the mixture as in the two pure systems. By the shift in the abscissa at peak fixation it is possible to calculate the percentage of total enzyme activity which reacts with either anti-CM or anti-CH (9, 12). In an artificial mixture of pure CM and CH (Fig. 2), the percentages calculated by C' fixation are equal to the percentages obtained by enzymatic assay.

Figure 3 illustrates the results of enzyme inhibition with homologous and heterologous antisera. Anti-CM was found to have no inhibitory effect toward CH. Unabsorbed anti-CH, however, did neutralize CM, although much more antiserum was required than with CH. After absorption with crystalline CM, anti-CH was specific for CH (Fig. 3). No reduction in the enzyme neutralizing titer of anti-CH toward CH was effected by the absorption with CM (Fig. 3B)—a finding that confirmed our conclusion from earlier C' fixation and gel diffusion analyses that anti-CH had a small amount of antibody to CM. Anti-CM, which was prepared against a highly purified recrystallized enzyme, showed absolute specificity for CM and appeared to be homogeneous.

Development of CM in Chick Embryos

Figures 4 and 5 represent the C' fixation analyses of extracts of breast muscle of chick embryos of increasing age as measured by the reaction with anti-CH and anti-CM, respectively. Figure 4 shows that in the 6-day-old embryo essentially all of the LDH activity is identical with adult heart lactic dehydrogenase (CH). It should be noted that this same sample gave a very weak reaction with anti-CM. On the other hand, essentially all of the lactic dehydrogenase from breast muscle of an 8-day-old newly hatched chick was identical with the adult muscle lactic dehydrogenase (CM). At intermediate times during development (at 13.5, 16.5, 17.5, 19.5, and 22 days of incubation), reactivity with anti-CH decreases, whereas reactivity with anti-CM increases. These changes are most rapid just prior to and during hatching.

Quantitative C' fixation is advantageous in that it can measure qualitative changes in protein structure as well as resolve quantitatively two independent antigens in admixture. As in quantitative precipitin analyses, maximum C' fixation with a constant amount of antibody is a function of the extent of antigen-antibody aggregation. A protein whose determinant groups differ in

Dr. Cahn and Dr. Zwilling are affiliated with the biology department, and Dr. Kaplan and Dr. Levine with the graduate department of biochemistry, of Brandeis University, Waltham, Mass.

number or structure from those of the homologous antigen will fix less C′ with the homologous antibody. Thus the decrease in the amount of C′ fixed at equivalence (peak fixation) (Fig. 4) and the increase in the same parameter (Fig. 5) reflect a change in LDH antigenic structure during development. The amount of lactic dehydrogenase (as measured by enzymatic activity) which is required to reach peak fixation, however, is a function of the fraction of the lactic dehydrogenase in the enzyme mixture which reacts with a particular antibody. For example, the lactic dehydrogenase in the breast muscle of the 6-day-old embryo gives maximum fixation with anti-CH at 0.08 enzyme units, essentially the same amount as that required for maximum fixation with pure CH. The same enzyme of the 6-day-old embryo reaches maximum fixation with anti-CM at 10 enzyme units; maximum fixation is reached with 0.1 enzyme unit with pure CM. From these data we have estimated the percentage of the extracts that react with either anti-CM or anti-CH (*11*, *13*). In Fig. 6 is presented a summary of these calculations: the percentages of lactic dehydrogenase reacting with anti-CH and anti-CM, respectively, in the chicken breast muscle during development. Figure 7 summarizes the changes in antigenic structure of the same extracts as measured by the maximum amount of C′ fixed as compared to the maximum amount for the homologous antigen (CM or CH). From an analysis of these data it can be shown that the lactic dehydrogenase of chicken breast muscle changes from CH to CM through intermediate antigenic enzyme types during development.

Further evidence that the lactic dehydrogenase in the breast muscle is changing qualitatively as well as in overall composition (that is, in the proportions of CM to CH) was obtained from studies of the precipitation of enzyme activity by the specific antibodies. Figure 8 summarizes the results from several series of enzyme precipitation experiments. The pattern of change in the amount of enzyme activity precipitable with anti-CM and anti-CH is very similar to the summaries in Figs. 6 and 7. One striking fact is evident from an analysis of these data. More than 100 percent of the enzyme activity can be precipitated from embryos of intermediate stages (Table 1); that is, the sum of the amounts precipitated separately by

Table 1. Percentage of total enzyme activity precipitated. Each extract was tested separately against anti-CM and anti-CH. Tests on normal rabbit serum controls were made for each point, to check for nonspecific inhibition. Each value represents results for three tubes containing increasing amounts of anti-CM and anti-CH. After incubation at room temperature for 1 hour and overnight at 0° to 4°C, the tubes were spun and enzyme activity was determined on the supernatant fluid. The percentage of total activity was calculated at the point of maximum precipitation, on the basis of the normal-serum control for that amount of antiserum.

Tissue	Anti-CM	Anti-CH	Total
Adult heart extract	0	100	100
6-day breast muscle	14	100	114
11-day breast muscle	44	96	140
12.6-day breast muscle	54	95	149
13.8-day breast muscle	58	96	154
16.7-day breast muscle	64	96	160
17.3-day breast muscle	74	83	157
17.7-day breast muscle	83	67	150
19.5-day breast muscle	94	29	123
22-day breast muscle	94	18	112
Adult breast muscle extract	>98	<1	99
Mixture of breast-muscle and heart-muscle extracts (roughly 50–50)	43	57.5	100.5

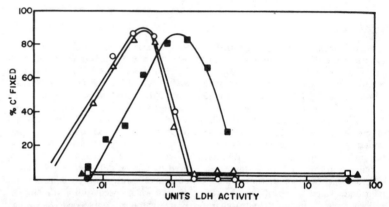

Fig. 1. Complement fixation by CM-anti-CM and CH-anti-CH. Open circles, CH-anti-CH; open triangles, CH-anti-CH absorbed with CM; solid squares, CM-anti-CM; open squares, CH-anti-CM; solid circles, CM-anti-CH; solid triangles, CM-anti-CH absorbed with CM.

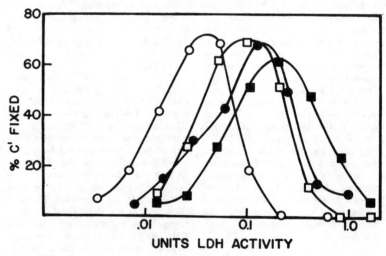

Fig. 2. Complement fixation analysis of a mixture of CM and CH. Open circles, CH-anti-CH; solid circles, CM-anti-CM; open squares, mixture of CM and CH-anti-CH; solid squares, mixture of CM and CH-anti-CM.

anti-CM and anti-CH is greater than the amounts of enzyme added. If a known mixture of pure CM and pure CH is treated with anti-CM and with anti-CH in a similar· manner, the amounts of enzyme precipitated (Table 1) add up to exactly the amounts added. This is interpreted to mean that some enzyme molecules in the embryonic extracts are being precipitated by both anti-CM and anti-CH. Since no CM is ever precipitated under these conditions by anti-CH, nor any CH by anti-CM (Fig. 3), the only conclusion to be drawn is that, during development, LDH molecules arise which contain antigenic structures common to

both CM and CH. These conclusions were confirmed directly when we looked at the change in the electrophoretic patterns of breast muscle from chick embryos of increasing age (Fig. 9).

In the very young blastoderm the CH form of lactic dehydrogenase predominates, but there is a trace of a more slowly moving component. Gradually a third, even more positively charged, band appears, and these two intermediate bands increase slowly in intensity at the expense of CH, up to about 16 days. Then, suddenly, there is a rapid appearance of a band corresponding to CM and one slightly more negatively charged. This qualita-

tive picture agrees remarkably well with the kinetics of development of CM and the disappearance of CH-related lactic dehydrogenase (Figs. 6–8), as judged by C' fixation and enzyme neutralization with the specific antibodies. The sequential development of the more negatively migrating bands is mirrored in the increase in reactivity with anti-CM and the decrease in reactivity with anti-CH.

Table 2 summarizes the results of enzyme precipitations carried out with anti-CM and anti-CH on all five electrophoretic bands in the chicken. It may be seen that the intermediate bands arising during development are completely precipitated by both antisera, whereas there is no cross reaction between the extremes.

Still another method of approaching this problem has yielded the same answer as the immunochemical and electrophoretic approaches. The CM and CH forms of lactic dehydrogenase differ in their substrate saturation curves (Fig. 10) as well as in their · ability to reduce coenzyme analogs (*1, 2, 5, 11*). The ratio of the rate of oxidation of reduced diphosphopyridine nucleotide (DPNH) with $0.01M$ pyruvate to the rate of oxidation of deamino DPNH with $0.00033M$ pyruvate can be used to measure the relative amounts of CM- and CH-related lactic dehydrogenases in a mixture. These data are plotted in Fig. 8. The ratio falls during the development of the chick breast muscle in a manner markedly similar to the way in which the amount of anti-CH-related lactic dehydrogenase changes (Figs. 6–8). Thus, all four of the methods used give the same result: the level of CM-related lactic dehydrogenase rises during the development of the breast muscle, and the level of CH-related lactic dehydrogenase falls. During the period in which both CM- and CH-like enzymes are present in about equal amounts, there is a large amount of enzyme present which is related to both CM and CH. We have called these intermediate enzyme types "hybrid" lactic dehydrogenases.

When cells from embryonic chicken tissues (heart, liver, leg muscle) are placed in tissue culture, their LDH pattern shifts from heart-related to muscle-related lactic dehydrogenases. These changes occur much faster than the normal, *in ovo*, shifts. We are at present investigating possible causes of these shifts (pO_2, pCO_2, yolk constituents, and so on).

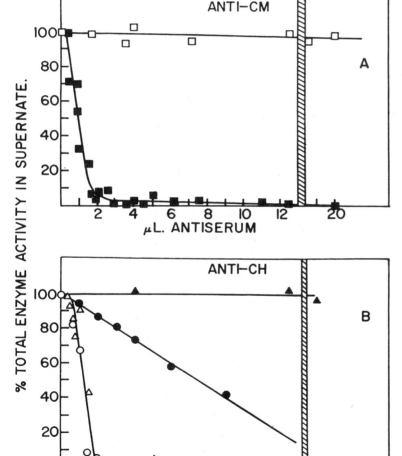

Fig. 3. Enzyme precipitation with anti-CM and anti-CH. Open circles, CH-anti-CH; open triangles, CH-anti-CH absorbed with CM; solid circles, CM-anti-CH; solid triangles, CM-anti-CH absorbed with CM; solid squares, CM-anti-CM; open squares, CH-anti-CM. Precipitations were carried out as described in Table 1.

Number of Multiple Forms

Although there have been a number of reports which suggest that more than five molecular forms of lactic dehydrogenase have been found on electrophoretic analysis, we believe that only five distinct types exist in any given animal species (Fig. 11). Under certain conditions, the most slowly migrating band appears to split into a major band and a minor satellite band. However, the catalytic and immunological characteristics of the two bands appear to be identical. Irwin Freedberg of our laboratory has found that many artifacts can be introduced if the gel is overloaded with lactic dehydrogenase, and more than five bands can be observed under these conditions. The additional bands do not occur, however, if the preparation is diluted before application to the gel. The bands detected in the undiluted solution were strong enough so that they could still have been detected after dilution if they had been genuine molecular species (14).

Physical Nature of Hybrid
Lactic Dehydrogenase

In most vertebrates so far studied there are two chief categories of lactic dehydrogenase. One type predominates in heart, the other in muscle. In the chicken these heart and muscle lactic dehydrogenases are completely different. They have widely differing amino acid composition, electrophoretic mobility on starch grain and gel, substrate inhibition kinetics, and analog oxidation ratio, and they elicit antibodies in the rabbit that are non-cross-reacting (1, 2, 5, 11). The heart enzymes of the various vertebrates studied (Table 3) show striking similarities, as do the muscle enzymes. There are much greater differences between the heart and muscle enzymes of the chicken than between beef-heart and chicken-heart enzymes (1, 2, 5, 11).

The lactic dehydrogenases of most vertebrates can be separated into five equally spaced, distinct components by starch gel electrophoresis (15). In the chicken, pigeon, beef, rat, mouse, rabbit, and human the most positively moving of these bands is the heart type, whereas the most negatively moving is the muscle type (Fig. 11). The intervening bands show intermediate properties, as determined by all of the criteria mentioned above, and vary in a regular way from the heart

band to the muscle band. (Tables 4 and 5). Different tissues from the same animal have characteristic distributions of the five bands, but these distributions are quite species specific. For example, in the human, band 1 (the muscle band) is predominant in the liver, whereas in the chicken, bands 4 and 5 (the hybrid and heart bands) are predominant in the liver. The fact that only five bands are found in most well-documented, careful studies with vertebrate tissues has suggested to us that there must be some fundamental significance in this number and that any hypothesis that attempts to explain "hybrid" enzymes must adequately account

for these five bands. In an attempt to devise such a theory we have used the following facts.

The chicken muscle, chicken heart, beef muscle (beef M), and beef heart (beef H) forms of lactic dehydrogenase all bind four molecules of diphosphopyridine nucleotide (DPN) per molecule of enzyme. Recently, Appella and Markert (3) reported that beef H lactic dehydrogenase can be dissociated into four subunits by treatment with 5M guanidine HCl + 0.1M mercaptoethanol. In collaboration with Amadeo Pesce, we carried out this type of experiment on CM and CH. The results show that both of these enzymes can be bro-

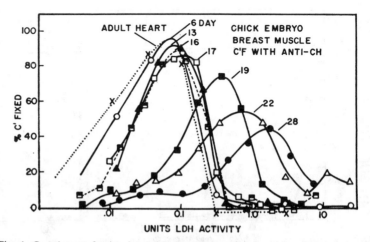

Fig. 4. Complement fixation by developing chicken breast muscle when tested with anti-CH. ×'s, adult heart; open circles, 6-day-old embryo breast muscle; solid triangles, 13-day-old embryo; half-solid squares, 16-day-old embryo; open squares, 17-day-old embryo; solid squares, 19-day-old embryo; open triangles, 22-day-old embryo; solid circles, 28-day-old embryo.

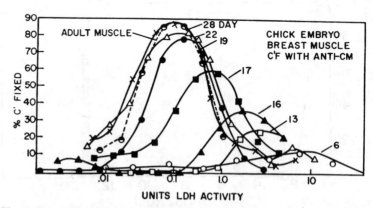

Fig. 5. Complement fixation by developing chicken breast muscle when tested with anti-CM. Half-solid circles, adult breast muscle; open circles, 6-day-old embryo breast muscle; open squares, 13-day-old embryo; solid triangles, 16-day-old embryo; solid squares, 17-day-old embryo; solid circles, 19-day-old embryo; open triangles, 22-day-old embryo; ×'s, 28-day-old embryo.

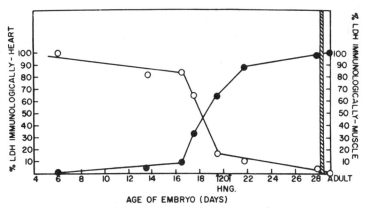

Fig. 6. Summary of LDH composition of developing chicken breast muscle, from complement fixation analyses (see text). Open circles, anti-CH; solid circles, anti-CM; *HNG*, hatching.

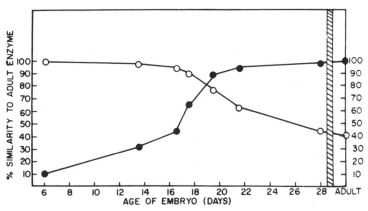

Fig. 7. Summary of change in immunochemical similarity to CM and to CH of LDH in developing chicken breast muscle, as shown in complement fixation analyses (see text). Open circles, anti-CH; solid circles, anti-CM.

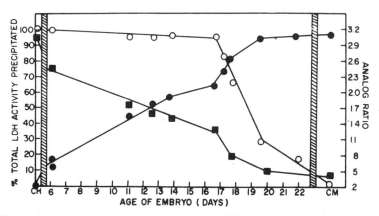

Fig. 8. Immunological and catalytic analysis of LDH in developing chicken muscle. Ordinate at left: Open circles, precipitation of enzyme wth anti-CH; solid circles, precipitation of enzyme with anti-CM. Ordinate at right; Solid squares, ratio of rate of oxidation, by breast muscle extracts, of deamino DPNH to rate of oxidation of DPNH, at concentrations of sodium pyruvate of $3.3 \times 10^{-4}M$ and $1.0 \times 10^{-2}M$, respectively.

ken down into four subunits of equal molecular weight by treatment with $5.5M$ guanidine HCl plus $0.1M$ mercaptoethanol (*16*). Electrophoretic-chromatographic "fingerprints" of tryptic digests of CM and CH show only roughly 35 amino acid spots. Furthermore, there are only one-quarter the number of arginine plus lysine spots as there are residues of these amino acids in the entire molecule. These data, taken together with the results, cited above, indicating the presence of several species of LDH molecules with antigenic groupings common to both CM and CH, have led us to formulate the following hypothesis: CH is a tetramer, composed of four identical subunits (HHHH) of molecular weight about 31,000; CM also is a tetramer, composed of four identical subunits (MMMM) that differ in many respects (including net charge at *p*H 7.0) from the subunits that compose CH; H and M are probably elaborated by two different genes. If both the H and M genes are active in the same cell, then the primary gene products (monomer units) recombine in some manner in groups of four, yielding five different molecular species (HHHH, HHHM, HHMM, HMMM, and MMMM) all possessing LDH activity. The order of the arrangement of the subunits may affect the antigenic specificity of the molecule, but the subunits, according to the hypothesis, operate independently in respect to their substrate inhibition and rates of reaction with DPN analogs. This hypothesis predicts *five* electrophoretically distinct bands[1] of lactic dehydrogenase on starch gel electrophoresis if, and only if, subunits H and M differ in net charge at the *p*H used. It also predicts that the five bands should be spaced at approximately equal intervals and should show regular changes in their antigenic and enzymatic properties. It is conceivable that a species may possess subunits H and M with identical net charges, so that only one band can be detected, and yet that there might still exist the basic heterogeneity predicted. We propose to call the three intermediate lactic dehydrogenases "hybrid" enzymes, since they differ quantitatively and qualitatively from the "parental" types much as genetic hybrids do. We feel that this categorization is much more suitable than the terms previously used—*isoenzymes* or *isozymes*—since the enzymes are not the same but show properties differing in a regular way from one extreme to the other. It is

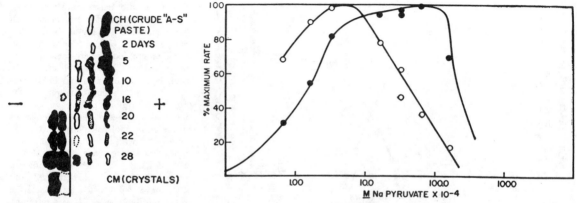

Fig. 9 (left). Electrophoretic patterns of LDH during the development of chicken breast muscle. Tracing of starch gels (Connaught, 14 percent) stained for LDH with nitro blue tetrazolium (10, 11). Blocks, 19.5 by 6.9 by 0.6 centimeters; run, 15 hours; temperature, 0°C; current, 27 milliamperes, 7.5 to 12.5 volts per centimeter across the block. Citrate-phosphate buffer, pH 7.0 (11). Solid bands, very intense staining; striped bands, intense staining; speckled bands, moderate staining; clear bands, weak staining; broken outline, barely visible. A–S, ammonium sulfate. Fig. 10 (right). Effect of pyruvate concentration on the activity of CM and CH. Open circles, CH; solid circles, CM.

likely that many other cases where enzymes exist as "hybrid" enzymes will come to light, but there are also cases where electrophoretically distinct bands may represent other modifications of enzyme molecules (17). We wish to emphasize that when one observes that a given enzyme has multiple bands, this does not necessarily imply that hybrids are involved. To have hybrids, it is essential that at least two distinct types of enzymes be present.

Various studies by Markert and Appella, as well as by us, have indicated that there are no distinguishable catalytic differences between the two electrophoretically separated lactic dehydrogenases found in the crystalline beef heart preparation. We have now been able to show, through more detailed studies with the coenzyme analogs, that the two bands do have some significantly different characteristics. The major band is the pure heart type (HHHH), whereas the minor component has the properties of the hybrid (MHHH) (Table 4).

Significance of Multiple Forms

The data presented in this article support the suggestion, made previously, that there are two types of lactic dehydrogenase (1, 2). Our view that the synthesis of the two types of subunits is controlled by two separate genes has also been supported by comparative studies. We have reported previously that the heart lactic dehydrogenase in the Heterosomata or flatfish

(halibut, sole, flounder) differs greatly from that in other teleosts. We have now compared the properties of a number of skeletal muscle lactic dehydrogenases in members of several other orders of teleost fish and in the flatfish. An example of such a comparison is given in Table 6, where the ratios of the rates of reaction of tuna and flounder lactic dehydrogenase with some coenzyme analogs are summarized. It may be seen from the data that the skeletal muscle lactic dehydrogenases are quite similar in tuna and flounder. However, the heart enzymes are very different in the two species. From the characterizations given in Table 6, it appears that the skeletal muscle enzymes and the heart enzymes of the flounder

are identical. It is of interest to note (Table 6) that an antibody to the purified halibut muscle lactic dehydrogenase completely precipitates muscle lactic dehydrogenases of both tuna and flounder. The antibody, however, reacts with the flounder heart enzyme but not with the tuna heart enzyme. We have obtained similar data indicating that the heart and muscle lactic dehydrogenases of the sole and halibut are identical. The flatfish are the only group of vertebrates for which we have found identical types of lactic dehydrogenase in heart and muscle in the adult stage. Furthermore, we have been unable to detect evidence of more than one type of lactic dehydrogenase in any of the tissues of the adult flatfish; on

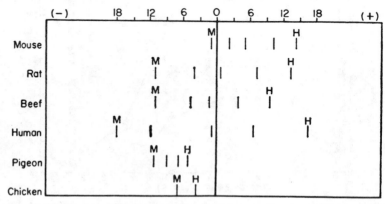

Fig. 11. Starch-grain electrophoresis of lactic dehydrogenases of different animals. M, most negatively migrating band, or muscle LDH; H, most positively migrating band, or heart LDH. Electrophoresis was continued for 18 hours at 10 volts per centimeter, with sodium veronal buffer, 0.05M, pH 8.6, at 2° to 4°C.

electrophoresis, only one band has been observed in any of the tissues studied. These results suggest that the flatfish may represent a mutant in which lactic dehydrogenase of the heart type is lost, at least in the adult stage.

Further evidence suggesting that the two types of lactic dehydrogenase are under the control of different genes has been obtained from studies with amphibians. Through analysis with coenzyme analogs we have found that the skeletal muscle lactic dehydrogenase of several species of frog and toad appear to be almost identical. However, the heart enzyme of the bullfrog (*Rana clamitans*) appears to dif-fer distinctly from that of the other species studied. Not only does it differ with respect to reaction with the analogs but it differs greatly from the heart enzymes of the other amphibians studied in electrophoretic mobility on starch grain. However, the muscle enzyme of the bullfrog has electrophoretic characteristics almost identical to those of the other species studied. Differences in immunological and thermal stability have also been found between the heart enzyme of the bullfrog and that of other amphibian species. From its catalytic, physical, and immunological properties, it appears that the lactic dehydrogenase of the bullfrog heart may be a mutant enzyme. However, the lactic dehydrogenase of the bullfrog skeletal muscle appears to be very similar to that of the skeletal muscle of other amphibian species. This indicates that a modification of one type of enzyme can take place without an alteration in the second type. It seems reasonable to assume from such data that the two types of lactic dehydrogenase are controlled by different genes.

It should be emphasized that the electrophoretic migration, on starch, of the hybrids depends on the migration of the two pure types. In the case of the bird enzymes, the two pure types migrate relatively close together toward the negative pole at pH 8.6, and observation of the hybrid forms under these conditions is very difficult. On the other hand, the two types of lactic dehydrogenase in mammals usually differ greatly in their migratory characteristics, and the hybrids in mammals therefore can be detected more easily as electrophoretic entities. It can be said with considerable certainty that the more widely the two basic enzymes differ in charge, the more separable the hybrids will be after electrophoresis on starch.

Each species appears to possess both a heart and a muscle type of lactic dehydrogenase. For example, the muscle enzyme from the rat migrates considerably more negatively than the corresponding enzyme from the mouse (Fig. 11). Hence, the locations of the hybrid enzymes of the two rodents on electrophoresis are somewhat different. Although the muscle enzymes of the rat and mouse differ electrophoretically, they still appear to be closely related, as indicated by their reaction with the coenzyme analogs (Tables 5 and 7). The electrophoretic mobilities of the lactic dehydrogenases are not accurate criteria of the relationship between species and should not be used as indicators in evolutionary studies. In this connection, it is valuable to note that we have found some slight but significant differences in the migration of the same LDH moiety in different tissues of the same animal.

We have suggested previously (*11, 18*) that the differences in properties of the heart and muscle lactic dehydrogenases are of functional significance. There is a great difference in the degree to which pyruvate inhibits activity of the chicken heart and of the chicken muscle enzymes (see Fig. 10). A similar difference was found previously for purified bovine skeletal muscle and heart enzymes (*2*). Our view is that these marked differences are not *in vitro* curiosities but are physiologically important factors in the regulation of cellular metabolism. In evaluating the role of lactic dehydrogenase in skeletal and cardiac muscle, it is important to emphasize the difference in metabolic

Table 2. Percentage of enzyme activity precipitated. The assays were carried out as described in Table 1.

Type	Anti-CH	Anti-CM
MMMM (band 1)	0	100
MMMH (band 2)	95	100
MMHH (band 3)	100	70*
MHHH (band 4)	100	43*
HHHH (band 5)	100	0

* Since very little of these two bands was available, the enzyme precipitations may have been incomplete, due to the fact that the proportion of antibody to antigen was 7 to 10 times that in assays of the other bands. This reaction is inhibited when there is antibody excess (*11*) as well as when there is antigen excess, and this probably accounts for the low values observed (see *22*).

Table 3. Ratios of rates of reduction of $TNDPN_1$ to $APDPN_3$* in crude extracts of vertebrate heart and skeletal muscle.

Animal	Skeletal muscle	Heart
Turkey	0.48	5.3
Chicken	0.50	5.2
Pigeon	0.63	5.0
Tuna	0.22	8.2
Toad	1.60	6.2
Green frog	1.62	6.8
Rabbit	0.73	5.4
Human	2.2	5.7
Mouse	1.7	5.6
Beef	1.2	5.8

* APDPN, 3-acetylpyridine DPN; TNDPN, thionicotinamide DPN. Subscript 1 or 3 indicates that $3.3 \times 10^{-4}M$ lactate, or $1.0 \times 10^{-2}M$ lactate, respectively, was used in the assay.

Table 4. Comparison of the rates of oxidation of $DeDPNH_1/DPNH_3$* ratio for molecular forms of lactic dehydrogenase from beef chest muscle and heart.

Type	Chest muscle	Heart
MMMM (band 1)	0.53	
MMMH (band 2)	0.70	0.78
MMHH (band 3)	1.23	1.29
MHHH (band 4)	1.83	1.74
HHHH (band 5)	2.78	2.50

* DeDPNH, nicotinamide hypoxanthine dinucleotide; DPNH, reduced DPN. Subscript 1 or 3 indicates that $3.3 \times 10^{-4}M$ pyruvate, or $1.0 \times 10^{-2}M$ pyruvate, respectively, was used in the assay.

Table 5. Comparison of the rates of oxidation of $DeDPNH_1/DPNH_3$* ratio for various bands from mouse and rat tissues (*23*).

Type	Rat	Mouse
MMMM (band 1)	0.73	0.83
MMMH (band 2)	1.25	1.12
MMHH (band 3)	1.57	1.42
MHHH (band 4)	1.80	2.02
HHHH (band 5)	2.40	2.58

* DeDPNH, nicotinamide hypoxanthine dinucleotide; DPNH, reduced DPN. Subscript 1 or 3 indicates that $3.3 \times 10^{-4}M$ pyruvate, or $1.0 \times 10^{-2}M$ pyruvate, respectively, was used in the assay.

Table 6. Analog and immunological properties of lactic dehydrogenase in tuna and flounder.

Part	$APDPN_1/$ $TNDPN_1$*	Percentage precipitated by antibody to halibut skeletal-muscle LDH
	Tuna	
Heart	0.34	0
Muscle	11.5	100
	Flounder	
Heart	11.2	100
Muscle	12.0	100

* APDPN, 3-acetylpyridine DPN; TNDPN, thionicotinamide DPN. The subscript 1 indicates that $3.3 \times 10^{-4}M$ lactate was used in the assay.

Table 7. Analog reactivities of MMMM type lactic dehydrogenase from mouse and rat.

Ratio*	Mouse	Rat
$DPNH_3/DPNH_1$	0.80	0.87
$DPNH_3/APDPNH_1$	0.62	0.45
$DPN_3/TNDPN_1$	3.2	2.8
$TNDPN_3/APDPN_3$	3.5	6.2

* APDPN, 3-acetylpyridine DPN; TNDPN, thionicotinamide DPN. Subscript 1 or 3 indicates that $3.3 \times 10^{-4}M$ pyruvate, or $1.0 \times 10^{-2}M$ pyruvate, was used in the assay.

properties of the two tissues. Skeletal muscle depends particularly on the anaerobic breakdown of carbohydrates for utilizable energy during exercise, and this results in a large production of lactic acid. This generation of lactic acid is essential for anaerobic metabolism; otherwise, reduced DPN would cease to be formed by the oxidation of triose phosphate. Hence, in skeletal muscle, the activity of lactic dehydrogenase must be compatible with the formation of lactate from pyruvate. Therefore, one might expect the skeletal muscle enzyme to operate in the presence of relatively high levels of pyruvate. On the other hand, heart activity depends more on aerobic metabolism than on anaerobic processes. There is no sudden requirement for energy in the heart. Pyruvate metabolism in the heart is directed toward oxidation rather than toward reduction to lactate. The marked inhibitory effect, on heart lactic dehydrogenase, of increasing concentrations of pyruvate permits pyruvate metabolism to proceed toward oxidation through the citric acid cycle. We suggest that the characteristic catalytic properties of the two lactic dehydrogenases are important in regulating the physiological activities of the tissues in which they are found (11, 18). We believe that the heart enzyme is a catalyst geared for activity in an aerobic environment, whereas the muscle enzyme functions in an anaerobic environment.

It is of interest that the heart enzyme appears first in the chick, even in the breast muscle. Grabowski (19) has reported that lactic acid is toxic to the early chick embryo; hence, one might expect that the embryonic tissues would have a system for keeping the formation of lactate low. The heart enzyme allows for formation of less lactate than the muscle enzyme. Therefore, it is possible that the chick tissues rely more on an aerobic than on an anaerobic metabolism, since the embryo may have no mechanism for removing the lactate.

In contrast to the chick embryo, the fetal rat heart appears to develop the skeletal muscle enzyme first (20). After birth, there is a changeover from the primarily muscle type to the heart type of enzyme. It appears likely that metabolism in the fetal tissues is more anaerobic than in the chick embryo, and thus one might expect the enzyme of the muscle type to be the primary embryonic form. Furthermore, lactate probably can be removed quite efficiently by diffusion through the placenta.

The variation in lactic dehydrogenase which has been described suggests that an intriguing type of molecular lability may have been evolved, somewhat similar to that seen in hemoglobins and visual opsins, which provides considerable selective advantage to organisms. The lactic dehydrogenase in a given organ may differ in different species (for example, the liver of most mammals— among them rat, mouse, and human— contains the muscle type of the enzyme, whereas beef liver and liver of other ruminants contains primarily the heart type), and, as emphasized in this article, different LDH molecules may predominate at various times during the development of a given structure. It is possible that particular molecular configurations are most efficient for given sets of metabolic conditions. While little is known of the significance of LDH hybrids in the metabolism of the cell, it may be speculated that a tissue whose metabolism is intermediate between that of heart and that of muscle may function best with a mixture of both types of lactic dehydrogenase. At any rate, the evolution of a system in which there are two basic molecular units and a mechanism for altering the relative proportions not only of the "pure" molecules but of molecules with intermediate properties (hybrid molecules) as well, offers distinct adaptive advantage to an organism. We may presume that such alterations in response to metabolic requirements have occurred with respect to two time scales: that of the evolution of species and that of the development of an individual.

We are not certain of the precise role of the LDH hybrids. It is possible that they are not important as distinct entities, since the individual subunits appear to be operating independently of each other within an enzyme molecule. This is indicated by the intermediate catalytic characteristics. We have as yet obtained no evidence to suggest that a single subunit has catalytic activity by itself. All four subunits seem to be necessary for any enzymatic activity. The subunits appear to be held together by hydrogen or hydrophobic bonds, and it seems likely that the interaction of the four units is essential for stability as well as to give the molecule the tertiary structure that may be necessary for the catalytic function. What may be of importance to the cell is the relative amounts of muscle and heart subunits present at any one time (21).

References and Notes

1. N. O. Kaplan, M. M. Ciotti, M. Hamolsky, R. E. Bieber, Science 131, 392 (1960).
2. N. O. Kaplan and M. M. Ciotti, Ann. N.Y. Acad. Sci. 94, 701 (1961).
3. E. Appella and C. L. Markert, Biochem. Biophys. Research Comm. 6, 171 (1961).
4. C. L. Markert and F. Møller, Proc. Natl. Acad. Sci. U.S. 45, 753 (1959); P. G. W. Plagemann, K. F. Gregory, F. Wroblewski, J. Biol. Chem. 235, 2282 (1960); F. Wroblewski and K. F. Gregory, ibid. 94, 912 (1961).
5. R. McKay, R. D. Cahn, J. Everse, N. O. Kaplan, in preparation.
6. O. Ouchterlony, Acta Pathol. Microbiol. Scand. 25, 186 (1948).
7. P. Grabar and C. A. Williams, Biochim. Biophys. Acta 17, 67 (1955).
8. M. Heidelberger and F. E. Kendall, J. Exptl. Med. 50, 809 (1929).
9. E. A. Kabat and M. M. Mayer, Experimental Immunochemistry (Thomas, Springfield, Ill, 1961).
10. G. W. Nace and T. Suyuma, J. Histochem. and Cytochem. 9, 596 (1961); ———, personal communication.
11. R. D. Cahn, Ph.D. dissertation, Brandeis University (1962).
12. A. Peterkofsky, L. Levine, R. K. Brown, J. Immunol. 76, 237 (1956).
13. The proportions of lactic dehydrogenase reacting with anti-CM and anti-CH were determined at the point of maximum C' fixation. For this calculation it was assumed that the turnover numbers of CM and CH were equal at the pH used. One must also assume that maximum fixation in a cross-reacting system occurs with the same amount of protein as in the homologous system. The turnover number of pure CM under the conditions of the assay is about 70,000 and that of CH is about 60,000. J. Orlando, L. Levine, and M. Kamen [Biochim. Biophys. Acta 46, 126 (1961)] and L. Levine (unpublished data) have shown that the second assumption also is valid in several immune systems.
14. I. Freedberg and R. D. Cahn, unpublished data.
15. Dr. Allan Wilson of this laboratory has found recently that the lobster and many other invertebrates also have five electrophoretically distinct lactic dehydrogenases.
16. A. Pesce and R. Cahn, unpublished data.
17. E. Margoliash and J. Lustgarten, Ann. N.Y. Acad. Sci. 94, 731 (1961); A. Kaji, J. A. Trayser, S. P. Colowick, ibid. 94, 798 (1961); M. L. Bach, E. R. Signer, C. Levinthal, I. W. Sizer, Federation Proc. 20, 255 (1961).
18. N. O. Kaplan, Mechanism of Action of Steroid Hormones (Pergamon, Oxford, 1961), p. 247.
19. C. T. Grabowski, Science 134, 1359 (1961).
20. H. Fine, N. O. Kaplan, S. White, Federation Proc., 21, 409 (1962).
21. Part of this paper has been taken from a Ph.D. dissertation submitted by R. D. Cahn to the faculty of Brandeis University. We acknowledge the excellent assistance of Shirley White, Howard Fine, and Natalie Grimes. This article is publication No. 158 of the graduate department of biochemistry, Brandeis University, Waltham, Mass. The study was aided in part by a training grant in developmental biology of the National Institutes of Health (CRT-5043 and 2G-883) and by grants from the American Cancer Society and the National Institutes of Health.
22. M. Schlamowitz, J. Immunol. 80, 176 (1958). Phosphatase from dog intestine has been shown by Schlamowitz to be soluble in antibody excess. Probably all antigens are soluble in antibody excess, but this has not been demonstrated because available techniques for detecting small amounts of protein antigen in the presence of large amounts of serum are not sufficiently sensitive. This solubility in antibody excess indicates that all of the antigenic groupings on the LDH molecule may be covered with antibody, thus preventing formation of a three-dimensional lattice (see 11).
23. The work summarized in Table 5 was carried out in collaboration with Barbara Cunningham of this laboratory.

THE JOURNAL OF BIOLOGICAL CHEMISTRY
Vol. 235, No. 8, August 1960
Printed in U.S.A.

The Electrophoretically Distinct Forms of Mammalian Lactic Dehydrogenase

I. DISTRIBUTION OF LACTIC DEHYDROGENASES IN RABBIT AND HUMAN TISSUES[*]

PETER G. W. PLAGEMANN, KENNETH F. GREGORY, AND FELIX WRÓBLEWSKI

From the Department of Microbiology, Ontario Agricultural College, Guelph, Canada; and the Sloan-Kettering Institute of the Memorial Center for Cancer and Allied Diseases, New York, New York

(Received for publication, February 2, 1960)

In a preliminary note (1) it was reported that at least two serologically and electrophoretically distinct lactic dehydrogenases were present in rabbit tissues. Nisselbaum and Bodansky (2) recently reported similar serological differentiation of lactic dehydrogenases from various rabbit organs. Heterogeneity of this enzyme derived from different tissues of mammalian species has also been shown by the use of diphosphopyridine nucleotide analogues (3). The lactic dehydrogenases of human sera and various animal tissues have been separated by elution from a column of Hyflo Super Cel with decreasing concentrations of ammonium sulfate (4) and electrophoretically (4–14) into several distinct components. Several other enzymes have also been shown to exist in multiple forms, not only within a single organism but even within a single tissue (13). Markert and Møller (13) suggested that these distinguishable molecular types of enzymes be called isozymes, a terminology we shall follow.

In the present investigation the cross reactions of lactic dehydrogenases derived from various rabbit and bovine tissues with antibodies produced against the lactic dehydrogenases of rabbit skeletal muscle and bovine heart muscle were studied. Starch gel electrophoresis was used to separate the lactic dehydrogenase isozymes of rabbit and human tissues. It will be shown that each tissue has a characteristic distribution of these isozymes and that the isozyme patterns of rabbit and human tissues have many similarities.

EXPERIMENTAL PROCEDURE

Lactic Dehydrogenase Assay—Activity was determined by measuring the rate of optical density decrease at a wave length of 340 mμ resulting from the oxidation of DPNH in the presence of 0.00084 M sodium pyruvate and a suitable dilution of enzyme (15). All measurements were made with a Beckman DU spectrophotometer at pH 7.4 and 30°. One unit of LD[1] was defined as the amount of enzyme required to produce a decrease in optical density of 0.001 per minute under the above conditions.

[*] This work was supported by grants of the National Cancer Institute of Canada (Project 203) and the National Cancer Institute (U. S. A.) (Grant CY 3809). It forms part of the program of the senior author for the M.S.A. degree.
[1] The abbreviations used are: LD, lactic dehydrogenase; anti-LD, antibody inhibitive to lactic dehydrogenase; LD$_1$···LD$_5$, slowest to fastest electrophoretically migrating forms of lactic dehydrogenase, respectively; R_{BH}, distance of electrophoretic migration relative to the migration front of bovine hemoglobin.

Antilactic Dehydrogenase Production—Antibody inhibitive to commercially purified rabbit muscle LD (Nutritional Biochemicals Corporation) was produced in chickens and purified by fractional precipitation with ammonium sulfate as previously described (16). Antibody was similarly prepared against commercially purified bovine heart muscle LD (Worthington Biochemical Corporation). The degree of inhibition of LD by anti-LD was expressed as the percentage inhibition of 40 ± 4 units of LD per cuvette when two cuvettes were simultaneously prepared with and without anti-LD and correction applied for the trace of LD activity in the anti-LD preparation (16). One unit of anti-LD was defined as the amount required to inhibit 50% of the activity of the homologous LD under these test conditions.

Tissue Extracts—All rabbit tissues employed for electrophoresis studies were taken from rabbits killed by exsanguination. These included a transplantable carcinoma, Vx-2, originally developed by Dr. Peyton Rous and in its 135th and 136th transplant generations. Tissue extracts were prepared by grinding tissues, within 1 hour of the death of the animal, in barbital buffer, ionic strength = 0.05, pH 8.6, with a motor driven Potter-Elvehjem, Teflon pestle, tissue grinder. The extracts were clarified by centrifugation. Erythrocytes and plasma were separated from heparinized blood by centrifugation; the erythrocytes washed twice in 0.85% NaCl, suspended in 10% saturated ammonium sulfate and lysed by treatment for 30 seconds in a Raytheon sonic oscillator. Human tissues[2] were obtained from two autopsies performed 12 and 14 hours after death from cancer and nephritis, respectively. These tissues were immediately frozen and kept frozen until extracted as described for the rabbit tissues. Human plasma and erythrocytes were separated from heparinized blood of normal subjects.

Nitrogen content of the tissue extracts was determined by a micro-Kjeldahl procedure (17). Corrections were made for the nitrogen content of the barbital buffer, which was small in relation to the total amounts of nitrogen in the extracts.

Electrophoresis—Zone electrophoresis, with the use of a gel prepared from specially hydrolyzed starch[3] and barbital buffer (ionic strength = 0.05, pH 8.6), was used. Most separations were made with the gel in a horizontal position and the crude

[2] Kindly supplied by Dr. E. L. Barton, Pathologist, General Hospital, Guelph, Ontario and Dr. F. Foote, Memorial Hospital, New York, New York.
[3] Connaught Medical Research Laboratories, University of Toronto, Toronto, Canada.

extracts inserted into a slit in the gel with a supporting medium of starch granules (18). Vertical starch gel electrophoresis as described recently by Smithies (19), in which no supporting medium was used at the origin, was used in some separations with similar results, but proved to be less satisfactory with large samples.

A few milligrams of twice crystallized bovine hemoglobin (Nutritional Biochemicals Corporation) were mixed with each sample. The LD content of this preparation was negligible. This colored protein provided a visual indicator of the progress and sharpness of the electrophoretic migration. It migrated approximately one-half the distance of the rabbit and human serum albumins and served as a convenient control protein for comparing different separations.

Most separations were made in gels 17 × 21 × 0.8 cm. The gel was connected to bridge solutions of barbital buffer, ionic strength = 0.1, pH 8.6, by wads of filter paper saturated with the bridge buffer. Melted white petrolatum at approximately 50° was layered over the gel to prevent evaporation. Electric power was supplied by a Reco D.C. power unit of 750 volts capacity through carbon electrodes to the bridge solutions. A voltage drop across the gel of 3 to 4 volts per cm was used. All separations were made in a refrigerated room at 4°.

After about 18 hours' electrophoresis the power supply was disconnected and the petrolatum removed from the surface of the gel. One strip of gel was cut in the direction of the migration and the distance from the origin to the front of the bovine hemoglobin measured along this cut surface. The remainder of the gel was cut into 0.3-cm strips at right angles to the direction of migration. These strips were placed into numbered test tubes and frozen. The LD isozymes appeared to be stable for several days while frozen in the gel. The gels were thawed as soon as convenient and macerated in an approximately equal volume of a solution of 1.0 mg of α-amylase per ml of 0.067 M phosphate buffer, pH 7.0, which was also 10% saturated with ammonium sulfate. This high salt concentration was used, since the slowest migrating rabbit LD isozyme was relatively unstable in dilute salt solutions. After 30 minutes' incubation at room temperature the residual starch was removed by centrifugation. The LD activity of the clear supernatant fluid in each tube was determined as described above.

Recovery tests on the LD's in a mixture of rabbit liver and heart extracts were performed with the use of the vertical electrophoresis procedure, in which the volume of extract added to the slit was accurately measured. Enzymes recovered in the supernatant fluids after the action of α-amylase on the starch strips accounted for 55% or more of the total enzyme added. When the enzyme remaining in the starch residue was included, total recovery exceeded 85%. It was concluded, therefore, that the procedures used resulted in an approximately correct representation of the relative proportion of LD isozymes in the various extracts.

RESULTS

The percentage inhibition of the lactic dehydrogenases derived from various rabbit and bovine sources by antilactic dehydrogenases revealed both species and tissue differences in serological specificity of these enzymes (Table I). Antibody produced against rabbit skeletal muscle LD, while strongly inhibitive to its homologous enzyme at a concentration of 2.5 units per cuvette (76% inhibition), caused only a trace of inhibition of the LD

TABLE I

Inhibition of lactic dehydrogenase from various sources by antirabbit skeletal muscle lactic dehydrogenase, antibovine heart muscle lactic dehydrogenase, and normal γ-globulin

Source of LD	Inhibition by:		
	Anti-rabbit skeletal muscle LD*	Anti-bovine heart muscle LD*	Normal γ-globulin
	%	%	%
Rabbit			
Skeletal muscle (purified)	75.7	53.3	0.5
Skeletal muscle (crude extract)	77.8		0.1
Erythrocytes	4.3	51.5	−1.7
Leukocytes	8.2	51.2	2.1
Plasma	34.4	37.7	0.0
Carcinoma (Vx-2)	53.4		−1.1
Cow			
Heart muscle (purified)	−5.5	66.3	−1.9
Erythrocytes	5.0	70.7	−2.5
Plasma	2.8	67.1	0.0

* Means of three or more determinations. Standard deviations at <30% inhibition, ±3.8%; at 30 to 60% inhibition, ±3.0%; at >60% inhibition, ±2.1%.

from rabbit erythrocytes and leukocytes. The rabbit plasma LD was inhibited to an intermediate degree, as was the LD in an extract from the transplantable Vx-2 tumor. The fact that the LD in a crude extract of rabbit skeletal muscle was inhibited as strongly as was the purified muscle LD showed that the presence of other proteins in the crude extracts was not responsible for the lower inhibition levels observed with the LD from some sources. None of the LD's from bovine sources was markedly inhibited by 2.5 units of this anti-LD preparation per cuvette. In fact, purified bovine heart muscle showed slightly increased activity in the presence of this anti-LD γ-globulin.

The antibovine LD preparation similarly demonstrated some, but considerably less, species specificity of LD since equal concentrations inhibited the LD from rabbit sources less than the LD from bovine sources, although the former enzyme was inhibited to an appreciable extent. This anti-LD did not appear to show tissue specificity of LD's except that a lower per cent inhibition was obtained with the LD from rabbit plasma than from other rabbit sources. It had previously been shown that when this enzyme was combined with its coenzyme (DPNH) before the addition of anti-LD, the equilibration of LD and anti-LD was greatly delayed (16). In the possibility that sufficient coenzyme may have been present in the plasma to lower the percentage inhibition obtained in these tests the determinations were repeated with plasma dialyzed against 1.8% NaCl. This dialysis increased the inhibition level to approximately 50%, suggesting that coenzyme protection of the LD was responsible for the lower inhibition values obtained. Dialysis of the other crude samples did not result in an altered percentage inhibition by anti-LD.

Extracts obtained from various rabbit and human tissues differed widely in their total LD content. Table II shows the amount of LD extracted from various rabbit tissues. Similar data from human tissues are not included, since the interval between time of death and excision of tissues may have rendered

TABLE II

Total lactic dehydrogenase activity in extracts of rabbit tissues

Tissue	Units of LD per ml of extract	Units of LD per mg of N in extract
Skeletal muscle	900,000	330,000
Liver	410,000	55,000
Heart	41,000	49,000
Brain	41,000	30,000
Kidney	19,000	20,000
Tumor (Vx-2)	12,000	18,000
Lung	8,600	14,000
Spleen	20,000	10,000
Erythrocytes	24,000	1,500
Plasma (Vx-2-bearing animal)	190	13
Plasma (normal)	34	3.1

such quantitative comparisons inaccurate. It will be noted that the enzymatic activity of various solid tissues ranged from 10,000 to 330,000 units of LD per mg extract N, a 33-fold variation. It is apparent that rabbit erythrocytes, although a convenient source of LD since these cells may be easily and quantitatively lysed to release their enzymes, are not richly endowed with this enzyme in comparison to other tissues.

The results of typical electrophoretic separations of LD isozymes from rabbit tissues are shown in Fig. 1. Although replicate determinations revealed minor quantitative variations in the proportions of various electrophoretically distinct LD's, each type of tissue was found to have a typical pattern of these isozymes. A total of five LD isozymes was identified. In order to facilitate the description of results these isozymes are designated, from slowest to fastest migrating forms, as LD_1 to LD_5. In Fig. 1 the graphs have been arranged in a series from the tissue containing only the slowest migrating isozyme (skeletal muscle) to the tissues containing only the fastest migrating isozyme (erythrocytes and heart muscle). Liver, the Vx-2 tumor, plasma, lung, and brain contained all five isozymes but in different proportions. In some electrophoretic separations of the LD isozymes from Vx-2 tumors the amount of LD_2 exceeded the amount of LD_3, whereas in other samples the relative proportion of these forms was reversed. The low LD levels characteristic of the plasma from normal mature rabbits (Table II) resulted in poor electrophoretic separation of the isozymes from this source. Better results were obtained with the plasma from rabbits bearing the Vx-2 tumor. Preliminary results indicated that the distribution of LD isozymes in the plasma of rabbits bearing this tumor showed an increase in the proportion of LD_2 and LD_3 isozymes over the proportion found in plasma from normal animals.

In some separations, with the use of horizontal starch gel electrophoresis of liver extracts from rabbits bearing the Vx-2 tumor, the LD_1 isozyme appeared to split into two components. When the same extracts were separated by the vertical electrophoresis procedure, the LD_1 isozyme moved as a single entity.

When the distances of migration of the five isozymes were compared relative to the migration front of bovine hemoglobin (R_{BH} value) it was found that each homologous isozyme migrated in the same position regardless of tissue of origin. These R_{BH} values, which may therefore be used to characterize and identify the isozymes, are listed in Table III. It will be noted from the R_{BH} values that the isozymes were uniformly spaced in the starch gel after electrophoresis, with the exception of a somewhat greater than average distance between LD_1 and LD_2.

Fig. 2 shows the results of typical electrophoretic separations of LD isozymes derived from human tissues. The distribution of these isozymes resembled the distribution of the isozymes from rabbit tissues in several respects. A total of five isozymes was found in each species. Human skeletal muscle yielded only one isozyme, as with rabbits, although the isozyme moved slightly towards the cathode, whereas the comparable rabbit isozyme moved slightly towards the anode. When the human tissues were arranged in order of an increasing content of fast migrating isozymes, they fell into the same sequence as did the rabbit tissues. The R_{BH} values of the human isozymes (Table III) showed that these LD forms were also uniformly spaced in the starch gel, except for a greater spread between the first two isozymes. The human isozymes were all more widely spaced than the rabbit LD isozymes, permitting a sharper separation of the former.

Some notable differences between the distribution of LD isozymes in the human and rabbit tissues were also apparent. Only four of the five LD isozymes were detected in human plasma, whereas all five LD isozymes were found in rabbit plasma. Human erythrocytes and heart muscle contained the three fastest migrating isozymes; these same tissues from the rabbit contained just the fastest migrating form. Human heart muscle contained a quantitatively predominant amount of LD_5.

DISCUSSION

The data presented here confirm the reports that electrophoretically (4–14) and serologically (1, 2) distinct forms of lactic dehydrogenase occur in mammalian tissues. The electrophoretic separations indicated that the distribution of isozymes in different tissues varied quantitatively as well as qualitatively. For example, skeletal muscle and heart muscle, both human and rabbit, contained qualitatively distinct isozymes. On the other hand, although human heart muscle contained the same three LD isozymes as did human erythrocytes it had a much greater relative amount of LD_5 than did the erythrocytes. This high proportion of LD_5 in human heart muscle may explain the observation by Vesell and Bearn (9) that sera from patients with myocardial infarction showed a selective elevation of the fastest migrating LD component as separated by zone electrophoresis in a starch block. The results reported here for human erythrocytes agree with the separations Vesell and Bearn (9) reported, but these workers did not observe the presence of the LD_1 isozyme in their serum samples. This isozyme appears to be less stable than the faster migrating forms, which may account for their failure to detect it.

Serological differences between the LD's from rabbit tissues were clearly detected with the antirabbit muscle LD. The failure of antibovine heart muscle LD to differentiate between LD's derived from various tissues of a single species may have resulted from the presence of more than one LD isozyme in the heart muscle LD preparation used for the production of antibody (5, 7). Thus the antibovine LD may have been polyvalent. Kubowitz and Ott (20) found no serological differences between purified lactic dehydrogenases derived from a rat sarcoma and normal rat muscle.

A comparison of data on the inhibition by antibody of the lactic dehydrogenases in crude extracts of rabbit tissues (Table I) with the patterns of LD isozymes obtained by electrophoresis

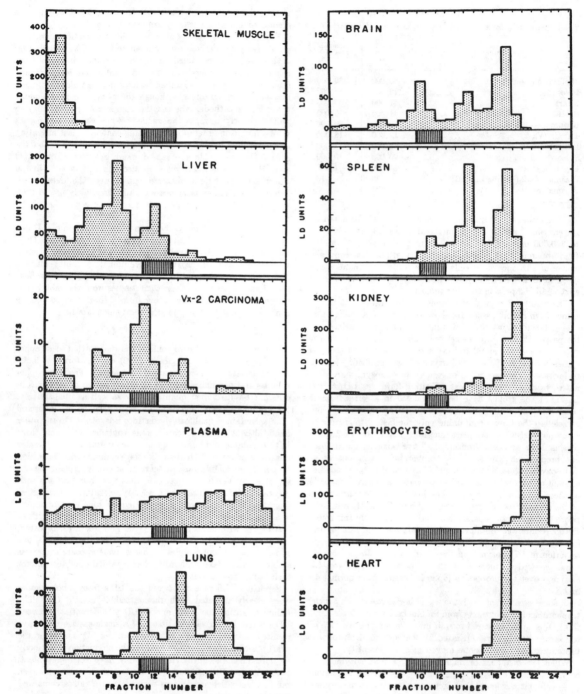

Fɪɢ. 1. Distribution of lactic dehydrogenase isozymes in rabbit tissues as separated by starch gel electrophoresis. Position of the reference protein, bovine hemoglobin, is shown below each graph.

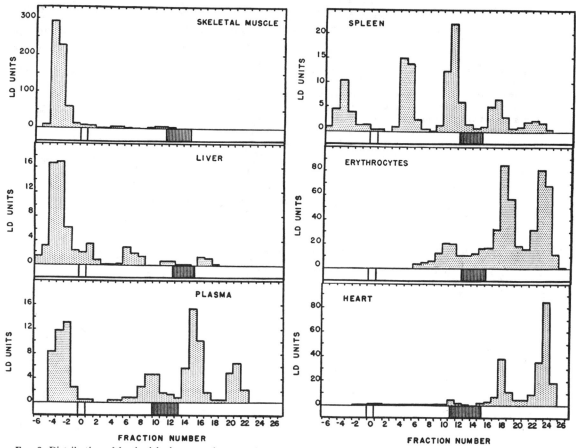

FIG. 2. Distribution of lactic dehydrogenase isozymes in human tissues as separated by starch gel electrophoresis. Positions of the origin and the reference protein, bovine hemoglobin, are shown below each graph.

TABLE III

Electrophoretic migration* of rabbit and human lactic dehydrogenases relative to the migration front of purified bovine hemoglobin (R_{BH})

LD number	Source of enzyme	
	Rabbit	Human
	R_{BH}	R_{BH}
1	0.13 ± 0.05	−0.21 ± 0.02
2	0.54 ± 0.05	0.39 ± 0.03
3	0.85 ± 0.03	0.75 ± 0.02
4	1.18 ± 0.03	1.14 ± 0.05
5	1.51 ± 0.04	1.53 ± 0.05

* In starch gel containing barbital buffer, ionic strength = 0.05, pH 8.6.

(Fig. 1) shows that, at the concentrations used, antibody to rabbit LD_1 (skeletal muscle LD) inhibited only a trace amount of LD_5 (erythrocyte LD). The fact that the same concentration of this anti-LD gave an intermediate level of inhibition of the

LD from the Vx-2 tumor extract and rabbit plasma, agrees with the electrophoretic findings that these samples contained a mixture of isozyme forms and suggests that the isozymes intermediate between the slow and fast migrating forms were inhibited to an intermediate degree by the anti-LD. Similarly, Nisselbaum and Bodansky (2) found that an antirabbit muscle lactic dehydrogenase preparation which inhibited the LD from rabbit skeletal muscle 80% inhibited the LD's from liver, 70%; spleen, 43%; kidney, 25%; and heart, 9%. These data correlate with the LD isozyme patterns found in these tissues.

The data suggest that it should be possible to identify the origin of LD causing elevated serum LD levels observed in certain disease states (15, 21), by determining the proportion of LD isozymes in the serum, or to detect specific changes in these proportions in the absence of an elevation of the total serum LD level. The apparent increase in the proportion of LD_2 and LD_3 isozymes in the plasma of rabbits bearing the Vx-2 tumor is pertinent, since these are the two isozymes present in greatest concentrations in this tumor. Immunochemical procedures have been studied for the determination of the tissue of origin of human serum alkaline phosphatase (22) and rabbit serum LD (2).

Studies on the properties and interrelationships of the LD isozymes described here are presented in Paper II of this series.

SUMMARY

Lactic dehydrogenase has been shown to occur in serologically distinct forms in different rabbit tissues. Five electrophoretically distinct forms (isozymes) of lactic dehydrogenase have been isolated from both rabbit and human tissues. Each tissue was found to have a characteristic distribution of these isozymes and quantitative isozyme patterns for nine rabbit tissues and plasma and five human tissues and plasma have been presented. Analogous rabbit and human tissues were found to have similar but not identical isozyme patterns.

REFERENCES

1. GREGORY, K. F., AND WRÓBLEWSKI, F., *Clin. Research*, **7**, 295 (1959).
2. NISSELBAUM, J. S., AND BODANSKY, O., *J. Biol. Chem.*, **234**, 3276 (1959).
3. KAPLAN, N. O., CIOTTI, M. M., HAMOLSKY, M., AND BIEBER, R. E., *Science*, **131**, 392 (1960).
4. SAYRE, F. W., AND HILL, B. R., *Proc. Soc. Exptl. Biol. Med.* **96**, 695 (1957).
5. NEILANDS, J. B., *Science*, **115**, 143 (1952).
6. WIELAND, T., AND PFLEIDERER, G., *Angew. Chem.*, **69**, 199 (1957).
7. WIELAND, T., AND PFLEIDERER, G., *Biochem. Z.*, **329**, 112 (1957).
8. HAUPT, I., AND GIERSBERG, H., *Naturwissenschaften*, **45**, 268 (1958).
9. VESELL, E. S., AND BEARN, A. G., *Proc. Soc. Exptl. Biol. Med.*, **94**, 96 (1957).
10. VESELL, E. S., AND BEARN, A. G., *J. Clin. Invest.*, **37**, 672 (1958).
11. VESELL, E. S., AND BEARN, A. G., *Ann. N. Y. Acad. Sci.*, **75**, 286 (1958).
12. HESS, B., *Ann. N. Y. Acad. Sci.*, **75**, 292 (1958).
13. MARKERT, C. L., AND MØLLER, F., *Proc. Natl. Acad. Sci. U.S.*, **45**, 753 (1959).
14. FUTTERMAN, S., AND KINOSHITA, J. H., *J. Biol. Chem.*, **234**, 3174 (1959).
15. WRÓBLEWSKI, F., AND LADUE, J. S., *Proc. Soc. Exptl. Biol. Med.*, **90**, 210 (1955).
16. GREGORY, K. F., AND WRÓBLEWSKI, F., *J. Immunol.*, **81**, 359 (1958).
17. CAMPBELL, W. R., AND HANNA, M. I., *J. Biol. Chem.*, **119**, 1 (1937).
18. SMITHIES, O., *Biochem. J.*, **61**, 629 (1955).
19. SMITHIES, O., *Biochem. J.*, **71**, 585 (1959).
20. KUBOWITZ, F., AND OTT, P., *Biochem. Z.*, **314**, 94 (1943).
21. WRÓBLEWSKI, F., *Cancer*, **12**, 27 (1959).
22. SCHLAMOWITZ, M., AND BODANSKY, O., *J. Biol. Chem.*, **234**, 1433 (1959).

Reprinted from *J. Mol. Biol.* (1967) **23**, 577–585

Protein Synthesis in Embryonic Chick Lens Cells

Ronald Reeder† and Eugene Bell

*Department of Biology, Massachusetts Institute of Technology, Cambridge
Massachusetts 02139, U.S.A.*

(*Received 30 June 1966, and in revised form 7 October 1966*)

In the chick lens at 12 days of incubation, there are cells in all stages of differentiation from the cuboidal, stem cells of the germinal zone of the anterior epithelium to the differentiated, non-dividing fiber cells of the lens body to which they give rise. The electrophoretic pattern of ^{14}C pulse-labeled protein from different parts of the lens and the stability of the messenger RNA utilized has been examined. Cells throughout the lens epithelium synthesize a number of proteins, at least one of which may be made on relatively short-lived messenger RNA. As epithelial cells enter the body region and begin to elongate, they suppress the synthesis of all proteins except two. In the body these two proteins are made on long-lived messenger RNA.

1. Introduction

The optical lens of the chick embryo arises at about 2·5 days of incubation, when the optic cup approaches the overlying head ectoderm and induces it to form the lens placode. Subsequent changes in the morphology of the lens up to 12 days are shown in Fig. 1. The lens placode bulges inward to form a sac which in turn separates from the epidermis to become a hollow ball of cells. Between the third and fourth day of incubation, the cells in the posterior of this hollow ball undergo a striking elongation, pushing forward until they have filled the lenticular space. By eight days of incubation, these elongated primary fiber cells have stopped growing. All further growth comes from divisions of stem cells, which occupy a narrow ring in the anterior lens epithelium. As stem cells divide, their progeny are displaced posteriorly, pass through a transition zone in the epithelium called the annulus, then enter the lens body, where they elongate to form secondary lens fiber cells wrapped in concentric layers around the primary fiber cells.

Thus, from the eighth day on, the chick lens contains cells in three principal stages of differentiation: the stem cells in the anterior lens epithelium; the non-dividing transitional cells in the lens annulus; and the highly differentiated non-dividing fiber cells in the body. This arrangement provides opportunity for studying changes which a cell undergoes during differentiation, particularly since the three components can be separated from one another.

There is already evidence that some proteins of the epithelium differ from proteins of the body. In the newt lens, fluorescent antibody analysis has shown that an antigen present in fiber cells cannot be detected in epithelial cells (Takata, Albright & Yamada,

† Present address: Department of Medical Chemistry, Kyoto University Faculty of Medicine, Sakyo-ku, Kyoto, Japan. Please send reprint requests to the Massachusetts Institute of Technology.

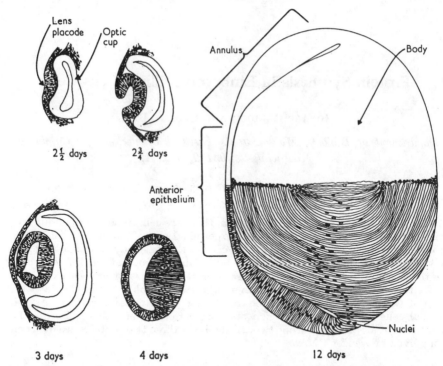

FIG. 1. Morphology of the chick lens at various stages of development.

Note that the epithelium consists of two regions, the anterior epithelium and the annulus. (Redrawn in part from Rabl, 1899).

1965). Papaconstantinou, Kochn & Stewart (1964) have demonstrated that protein from the epithelium of the bovine lens gives a more complex elution pattern from DEAE-cellulose than does protein from the body of the bovine lens. These experiments suggest that the synthesis of some protein stops as a lens cell enters the body, while some new proteins may begin to be synthesized for the first time.

Both long- and short-lived messenger RNA's are present in the developing chick lens (Scott & Bell, 1965). Autoradiographic evidence suggests that protein synthesis in chick lens stem cells in the epithelium of the organ occurs on short-lived messenger RNA, while protein synthesis in the lens body occurs on long-lived messenger RNA (Reeder & Bell, 1965).

In this paper evidence is presented that chick lens cells change their pattern of protein synthesis as they move from the epithelium into the body. While in the epithelium, the cells synthesize many proteins. At least one of these, the major epithelial protein, and possibly most proteins, are made on short-lived messenger RNA templates. As the cells enter the body and begin to elongate, protein synthesis is restricted to only two proteins and these are made on relatively stable messenger RNA.

2. Materials and Methods

Lenses were from White Leghorn embryos incubated at 38·5°C; staging was by days of incubation. Watchmaker's forceps were used to remove the cornea, and to press down on either side of the eyeball, thus causing the vitreous humour to be extruded. The lens thus pushed out of the eyeball could be plucked free. The lens capsule remained intact and virtually no vitreous humour or ciliary body adhered to the lens. Lenses were kept in cold Tyrode's solution (Parker, 1954) until use.

Radioactive precursors were administered by incubating lenses with precursor in about 1 ml. of CW medium (Charity Weymouth medium, MB 752/1; Parker, 1954) containing penicillin and streptomycin, phenol red indicator, and in some cases 30 μg actinomycin D/ml. Incubation was in a 5% CO_2 humidity-controlled atmosphere at 37·5°C. ^{14}C-labeled algal protein hydrolysate was used to label protein and [^{14}C]uridine was used to label RNA. After a 1-hr warm-up period, lens protein synthesis continues at a constant rate for at least 6 hr, since the same amount of radioactivity is incorporated during a 1-hr pulse-label with ^{14}C-labeled algal hydrolysate at any time during this 6-hr period (see results, Fig. 4). Also, during a continuous label with [^{14}C]uridine, uptake of isotope is linear for at least 3 hr. By these criteria, lenses appear to survive *in vitro* culture well for at least 6 hr.

Acid-insoluble radioactive material was assayed by precipitating samples with an equal volume of cold 10% trichloroacetic acid and collecting the precipitate on a Millipore filter, washing thoroughly with cold 5% trichloroacetic acid, and counting the filter in a Tracerlab low-background gas-flow counter. Self-absorption was negligible. Protein was determined by the method of Lowry, Rosebrough, Farr & Randall (1951).

Lens epithelia were separated from lens bodies after labeling with ^{14}C-labeled algal protein hydrolysate. For some experiments a brief exposure to ultrasound was used to loosen the epithelium from the lens body (Bell, 1959). With lenses older than 12 days, this treatment was not necessary. Lenses were placed in cold Tyrode's solution under a dissecting microscope and the capsule torn off with watchmaker's forceps. The epithelium sticks to the capsule and comes off the body cleanly, except for a collar of cells from the annulus which adheres to the lens equator. This collar was trimmed away with iridectomy scissors and discarded. The "epithelial fraction" contained the acellular lens capsules and approximately 75% of the lens epithelium which adheres to the capsule. The "body fraction" contained lens bodies after capsule and adherent epithelium had been removed and the collar of remaining annular epithelium trimmed away.

Protein for electrophoresis was homogenized in electrophoresis buffer (0·038 M-glycine, 0·005 M-Tris (pH 8·3)) by rapidly forcing the whole lenses or lens fractions through a 25-gauge hypodermic needle several times. This disrupts all cells but leaves nuclei intact. The homogenate was spun at 20,000 g for 30 min to pellet cell membranes, nuclei and lens capsules. Samples of the supernatant fraction containing about 0·5 mg of protein were lyophylized. About 85% of the insoluble radioactive material is extracted into the supernatant fraction by this procedure. The lyophylized fractions were dissolved in 8 M-urea for electrophoresis.

Electrophoresis was done essentially as described by Davis (1964). His recipe was used for the alkaline standard gel, except that the acrylamide concentration in the lower gel was reduced to 4·5%. All stock solutions with the exception of the electrode reservoir

TABLE 1

Recovery of acid-precipitable ^{14}C-labeled protein after electrophoresis in acrylamide gel

Exp.	Acid-precipitable radioactive material put on gel (calc.) (decays/min)	Radioactivity of stacking gel (decays/min)	Radioactivity of lower gel (decays/min)	% recovery of acid-precipitable radioactive material in lower gel (decays/min)
1	54,945	1264	51,079	93·4
2	54,945	1238	53,677	97·7
3	54,945	1234	52,664	95·9
Averages	54,945	1245	52,473	95·7

Electrophoresis was at pH 9·5 in a 4·5% acrylamide gel made up in 8 M-urea.

buffer were made up in 8 M-urea instead of water. As shown in Table 1, when ^{14}C-labeled lens protein is electrophoresed on such a gel, at least 96% of the acid-insoluble radio-active material migrates into the lower gel.

The radioactivity of stained gels was measured either autoradiographically (Fairbanks, Levinthal & Reeder, 1965), or by dissolving the gel in H_2O_2 and counting it in a scintillation counter (Moss & Ingram, 1965). The optical densities of stained gels and exposed X-ray film were measured with a Joyce–Loebl recording microdensitometer with a white light source, and the areas under the various peaks measured with a planimeter.

Fig. 2 shows that the amount of blackening of the X-ray film is directly proportional to the amount of radioactive protein applied to the gel.

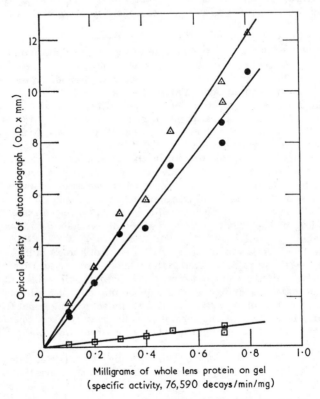

FIG. 2. Calibration curve showing film density (o.d. mm) associated with X-ray film autoradiographs of the whole gel (—△—△—), bands 1 and 2 (—●—●—), and band 3 (—□—□—) when increasing amounts of ^{14}C-labeled whole-lens proteins are subjected to electrophoresis on urea-acrylamide gels.

The gels were dried and autoradiographed for 72 hr. Film density was measured from the area under a densitometer trace of the autoradiograph and is recorded as optical density units × milli-meters (o.d. mm). One o.d. mm equals a segment of the autoradiograph 1 mm in length having a density of 1 o.d. unit.

3. Results

(a) Electrophoresis of lens proteins

(i) Whole lens

Proteins of the whole 12-day chick lens pulse-labeled with ^{14}C-labelled algal hydrolysate are shown in Plate I(a) as stained bands after electrophoresis on acryl-amide gel; underneath is the autoradiograph of the dried gel. Among the bands,

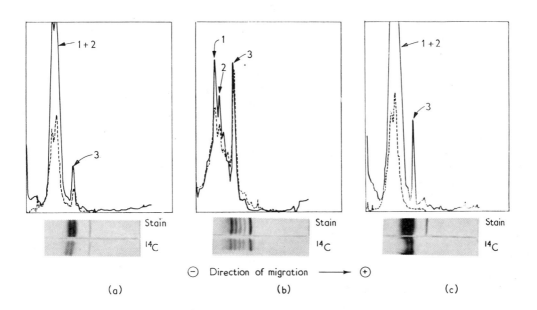

PLATE I. Stain and autoradiograph patterns obtained from electrophoresis of protein from various parts of the 12-day chick lens.

Lens protein was pulse-labeled for 1 hr with ^{14}C-labeled algal protein hydrolysate. Approximately 1 mg of protein was applied to each gel.

(a) Whole lens; (b) lens epithelium; (c) lens body. —————, Densitometer trace of stained gel; −−−−−−−, densitometer trace of ^{14}C-autoradiograph.

[facing p. 580

three predominate and are arbitrarily designated bands 1, 2 and 3. (In the following discussion, protein bands have been identified solely by their mobility upon electrophoresis under conditions described in Materials and Methods; i.e., band 3 from whole lens extracts has the same mobility under standard conditions as does band 3 from epithelial or body extracts.) Together these three components account for at least 90% of the stainable material and at least 83% of the radioactivity in the gel. In addition to the major bands, about eight minor bands are visible in the stained gel; they are too faint to measure quantitatively or reproduce well in the Plate.

(ii) *Epithelium*

All the components visible in both stain and autoradiograph patterns of the whole lens are also present when epithelial protein is subjected to electrophoresis alone (Plate I(b)). However, the relative proportion of the various proteins is changed. Band 3 now contains about 25% of the radioactivity in the gel and bands 1 and 2 together account for another 25% of the radioactivity. The remaining 50% is distributed among a number of smaller bands which are not sufficiently resolved by the densitometer to be measured individually.

Since the chick lens epithelium has two distinct regions, the anterior epithelium and the annulus (see Fig. 1), attempts were made to separate these regions by dissection and to determine their electrophoretic patterns. On four separate occasions electrophoresis of protein from isolated anterior epithelia gave essentially the same pattern as those obtained from whole epithelia. There was no evidence that the pattern of protein synthesis changes as the cells move from the anterior epithelium into the annulus.

(iii) *Body*

The stain pattern obtained from lens body protein (Plate I(c)) shows all the components seen with whole lens protein. In the body, however, bands 1 and 2 are now much larger in comparison to band 3. Also, in the autoradiograph, bands 1 and 2 contain at least 95% of the total radioactivity in the gel.

These results indicate that cells throughout the lens epithelium are synthesizing essentially the same set of proteins in about the same proportions. In the epithelium, bands 1 and 2 contain about 25% of the total radioactivity in the gel. In the body, bands 1 and 2 account for at least 95% of the radioactivity in the gel. This implies that as cells leave the epithelium and enter the body, they repress the synthesis of nearly all proteins except those of bands 1 and 2. Some of the proteins the synthesis of which is repressed as cells leave the epithelium (such as band 3, Plate I(c)) do not appear to be degraded but are carried into the body by cells which have lost the capacity to synthesize them.

(b) *Effect of actinomycin D on protein synthesis*

The effect of actinomycin D on whole lens protein synthesis during *in vitro* organ culture is shown in Fig. 3. After a one-hour warm-up period, the rate of amino acid incorporation in the untreated controls is nearly constant for at least six hours. In contrast, the presence of actinomycin D causes the rate of protein synthesis to decline with a half-life of about six hours.

In order to follow the rate of synthesis of individual lens proteins in the absence of RNA synthesis, samples of soluble protein from each group of pulse-labeled lenses (prepared for the experiment shown in Fig. 3) were subjected to electrophoresis on

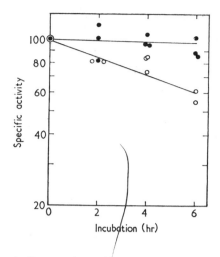

FIG. 3. Effect of actinomycin D on amino acid incorporation into whole lens soluble protein.

40 lenses were placed in each of two flasks with 20 ml. of CW medium. One flask contained 30 μg/ml. actinomycin D. After a 1-hr warm-up incubation, 10 lenses were removed from each flask in 0·5 ml. of medium and added to separate vials containing 0·5 ml. warmed medium plus 10 μc of ^{14}C-labeled algal protein hydrolysate. After a 1-hr incubation with the latter, the lenses were homogenized and soluble protein extracted to determine its specific activity (cts/min/mg protein). This operation was repeated on two more groups of 10 lenses every 2 hr for 6 hr. Specific activity is plotted as percentage of the initial (zero-time) value. Results from three separate experiments are summarized in this Figure.

—●—●—, Without actinomycin D; —○—○—, with actinomycin D.

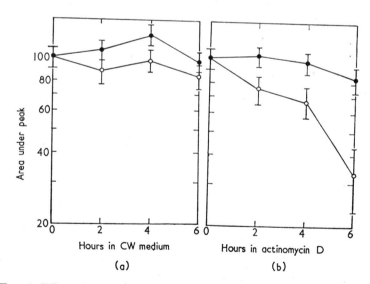

FIG. 4. Effect of actinomycin D on synthesis of bands 1 and 2 and band 3.

Lenses were pulse-labeled for 1 hr at intervals after being in culture with and without actinomycin D, as described in Fig. 3. Soluble protein from lenses was electrophoresed and the specific activity of each band determined by autoradiography of the dried gel. Specific activities are plotted as percentage of the initial (zero-time) value. Brackets indicate ± 10% experimental error.
(a) Without actinomycin D; (b) with actinomycin D.

—●—●—, Bands 1 and 2; —○—○—, band 3.

urea–acrylamide gels. To permit comparison among gels, equal amounts of protein were put on each gel; all gels were electrophoresed, dried together and autoradiographed for the same length of time. It has been shown (Fairbanks *et al.*, 1965) that in autoradiographs prepared as above, the area under a densitometer trace of any exposed band in the autoradiograph is directly proportional to the rate of synthesis of the protein responsible for that band. In Fig. 4 the areas under various bands are plotted against time in culture. In the absence of actinomycin D, the protein of band number 3 is synthesized at a constant rate for six hours. After actinomycin D treatment, the rate of synthesis of this protein decays with a half-life of about three hours. In contrast, the synthesis of the proteins of bands 1 and 2 are unaffected by *in vitro* culture for six hours, whether actinomycin D is present or not.

These results indicate that the bulk of bands 1 and 2 is synthesized on relatively stable messenger RNA. It is also possible that band 3 is synthesized on a relatively short-lived template. However, in view of the known toxicity of actinomycin D, the latter conclusion should be accepted with some caution.

(c) *Effect of actinomycin D on lens RNA synthesis*

Two experiments were designed to determine what effect actinomycin D has on lens RNA synthesis. In the first experiment, recorded in Fig. 5, the rate of incorporation of [14C]uridine into acid-insoluble material was followed before and after addition of actinomycin D. Following a lag period of about ten minutes, [14C]uridine was incorporated at a linear rate for the duration of the experiment in the control lenses. In the experimental lenses, addition of actinomycin D caused an abrupt cessation of [14C]uridine incorporation. In fact, lenses treated with actinomycin D immediately began to lose acid-precipitable radioactive material. This loss of radioactivity is a finding which is in agreement with results obtained by other workers studying RNA synthesis in HeLa cells. Harris (1963) has shown that most of the decay induced by actinomycin D occurs in the nucleus. Girard, Penman & Darnell (1964) attribute this to enzymic destruction of ribosomal precursors which have

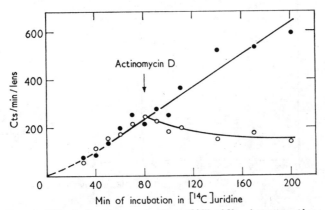

FIG. 5. Effect of actinomycin D on [14C]uridine incorporation.

Two groups of lenses were incubated in separate vials containing 1 ml. of CW medium plus 100 μc [14C]uridine. Vials were incubated at 37°C, and at intervals one lens was removed from each vial to assay for acid-insoluble radioactive material. At 80 min 1 ml. of warmed medium containing 60 μg actinomycin D/ml. and 100 μc [14C]uridine was added to the experimental vial. The control vial received 1 ml. of warmed medium and 100 μc [14C]uridine with no actinomycin D.
●—●—, Without actinomycin D; —○—○—, with actinomycin D.

been prevented from forming stable ribosomes by the action of actinomycin D. Due to the breakdown, it is difficult to tell from an experiment of this design how completely actinomycin D has suppressed RNA synthesis.

To determine this a second experiment was performed, in which the actinomycin D was added simultaneously with the [^{14}C]uridine. After two hours incubation, total RNA was extracted and its specific activity determined. The results are summarized in Table 2. After two hours, the lenses treated with actinomycin D had incorporated only 1·9% as much [^{14}C]uridine as the controls. Similar results for lenses of other ages have been reported elsewhere (Scott & Bell, 1965). The experiments show that 30 μg actinomycin D/ml. acts to suppress RNA synthesis almost instantly and to a level less than 2% of the control level.

TABLE 2

Effect of actinomycin D on [^{14}C]uridine incorporation

Exp.	Actinomycin D-treated (cts/min/o.d.)	Control (cts/min/o.d.)	% remaining RNA synthesis
1	41·6	2454	1·7
2	52·5	2522	2·1
		Average	1·9%

25 lenses were added to each of two vials containing 1 ml. of CW medium plus 20 μc of [^{14}C]-uridine. One vial also contained 30 μg actinomycin D/ml. After 2 hr incubation at 37°C, RNA was extracted from both sets of lenses by shaking twice with phenol, and its specific activity determined (cts/min/o.d. unit).

4. Discussion

As a lens cell differentiates and passes from the epithelium into the body, its pattern of protein synthesis changes markedly. In the epithelium, bands 1 and 2 incorporate about 25% of the total radioactive material in soluble protein. The other 75% is incorporated by several other bands, of which band 3 is the most predominant. In the body, however, at least 95% of the total radioactive material in soluble protein is associated with peaks 1 and 2, implying that the synthesis of the other proteins has been drastically curtailed or terminated altogether. Even though band 3 does not appear to be synthesized in the body, it is still quite evident in the stain pattern from body extracts. This suggests that the protein of band 3 is not degraded, but is carried from the epithelium into the body by cells which have lost the capacity to synthesize it.

In the body cells, at least, the synthesis of the proteins of bands 1 and 2 is directed by relatively stable messenger RNA. This conclusion is also consistent with previous autoradiographic evidence (Reeder & Bell, 1965). Possibly band 3 is made on unstable messenger RNA, but due to the high toxicity of actinomycin D this conclusion is much less certain. Whether or not the templates for bands 1 and 2 are also stable in the epithelium cannot be determined from these data. The interesting possibility remains that both long- and short-lived messenger RNA may co-exist in lens epithelial cells.

The present data appear to be consistent with the results of Papaconstantinou *et al.* (1964), who demonstrated that protein from the epithelium of the bovine lens gives a more complex elution pattern from DEAE-cellulose than does protein from the body of the bovine lens. Our results do not agree with those of Takata *et al.* (1965), who detected a major antigen in the bodies of newt lenses which was not detectable in newt lens epithelia. Their results suggest that some new protein arises as a lens cell enters the body, but we have found no evidence for this in the chick lens. Whether this reflects a species difference or is due to different experimental technique is not known at present.

This work was supported by a grant, GB3537, from the National Science Foundation to one of us (E. B.). The other author (R. R.) was the recipient of fellowships from the National Science Foundation and the National Institutes of Health during the period of this work.

REFERENCES

Bell, E. (1959). In *Proceedings of the First National Biophysics Conference*, ed. by H. Quastler & H. J. Morowitz, p. 674. New Haven: Yale University Press.

Davis, B. J. (1964). *Ann. N. Y. Acad. Sci.* **121**, Art. 2, 404.

Fairbanks, G., Levinthal, C. & Reeder, R. H. (1965). *Biochem. Biophys. Res. Comm.* **20**, 393.

Girard, M. S., Penman, S. & Darnell, J. E. (1964). *Proc. Nat. Acad. Sci., Wash.* **51**, 205.

Harris, H. (1963). *Nature*, **198**, 184.

Lowry, O. H., Rosebrough, N. J., Farr, A. L. & Randall, R. J. (1951). *J. Biol. Chem.* **193**, 265.

Moss, B. & Ingram, V. M. (1965). *Proc. Nat. Acad. Sci., Wash.* **54**, 967.

Papaconstantinou, J., Koehn, P. V. & Stewart, J. A. (1964). *Amer. Zool.* **4**, 321.

Parker, R. C. (1954). *Methods of Tissue Culture*. New York: Harper.

Rabl, C. (1899). *Zeit. Wiss Zool.* **65**, 304.

Reeder, R. H. & Bell, E. (1965). *Science*, **150**, 71.

Scott, R. B. & Bell, E. (1965). *Science*, **147**, 405.

Takata, C., Albright, J. F. & Yamada, T. (1965). *Science*, **147**, 1299.

Reprinted from *J. Mol. Biol.* (1967) **29**, 357–370

Stabilization of mRNA Templates
in Bovine Lens Epithelial Cells

JAMES A. STEWART†

Department of Zoology, University of Connecticut, Storrs, Connecticut, U.S.A.

AND

JOHN PAPACONSTANTINOU

Biology Division, Oak Ridge National Laboratory, Oak Ridge, Tennessee 37830, U.S.A.

(*Received 1 May 1967*)

Through the use of actinomycin D, it has been shown that the half-life of α-, β- and γ-crystallin mRNA in bovine lens epithelium increases with lens age. Crystallin synthesis in epithelial cells from embryonic lenses was potently inhibited by actinomycin D; the synthesis of these same proteins in adult lens epithelial cells was not affected. In both cases, all RNA synthesis was completely turned off by the antibiotic. Since the mitotic index of epithelial cells in embryonic lenses is much greater than that of the adult epithelial cells, our results indicate that stabilization of the protein-synthesizing templates found in adult epithelial cells may be related to the decreased replicative activity of these cells.

1. Introduction

The lens is composed of an outer single layer of epithelial cells completely covering its anterior surface and extending to the peripheral area. Beneath this layer are found fiber cells which make up the bulk of the lens. Epithelial cells in the peripheral area (lens equator) undergo cellular differentiation and elongation to form the lens fiber cells. This entire tissue is enclosed by an outer collagenous capsule. Thus the lens is composed of a single cell type in its various differentiated forms and is one of the few tissues (vertebrate) that is made up of a pure line of cells (Papaconstantinou, 1967).

The differentiation of a lens epithelial cell to a fiber cell represents the terminal stage of cellular differentiation in this tissue. One of the characteristics associated with the maturation of the lens fiber cell is its loss of mitotic activity. The fiber cell is, therefore, in a permanent stationary phase.

Studies on the mitotic activity of the epithelial cells in embryonic, early post-natal, and adult lenses have shown that the cells of the embryonic lens have a high mitotic index and, as the lens reaches its maximal size in the adult, that the mitotic index is negligible (Hanna & O'Brien, 1961; Cotlier, 1962; Mikulicich & Young, 1963; Hanna, 1965). The epithelial cells in the adult are stationary and will remain in this extended G_1 phase of the cell cycle indefinitely. However, the stationary phase is

---

† Present address: Biology Division, Oak Ridge National Laboratory, Oak Ridge, Tennessee 37830, U.S.A.

reversible, and the cells can be stimulated out of the G_1 phase into DNA synthesis (S phase) and mitosis (M phase), by physical or chemical means. Thus, the epithelial cells of the adult resemble the fiber cells in that both are in a stationary phase. The epithelial cells are in a reversible stationary phase, whereas the fiber cells are in an irreversible stationary phase.

In our studies it became apparent that adult lens epithelial cells have properties more similar to fiber cells than to the epithelial cells of either young lenses or to actively dividing cells in culture (Stewart & Papaconstantinou, 1966,1967a). During fiber cell formation, stabilization of RNA templates takes place (Papaconstantinou, Stewart & Koehn, 1966; Stewart & Papaconstantinou, 1967b), and the question arises as to whether this phenomenon is characteristic of cells in the stationary phase, regardless of whether or not they have lost the ability to divide. To study this question, we used epithelial cells of the adult lens to determine whether protein synthesis by cells in the stationary phase of extended G_1 occurs on stable templates, and whether the degree of stability of RNA templates in these cells is greater than that of actively dividing cells. A preliminary report has already appeared (Stewart & Papaconstantinou, 1967a).

2. Materials and Methods

(a) Radioactive labeling of lens proteins and RNA

Calf eyes were removed from animals within 10 min after death and placed in ice for transport to the laboratory. The lenses were removed with their capsules intact and placed in ice-cold Hanks salts solution. After all the lenses had been collected, and equally distributed into two beakers, the medium containing radioactive precursors ([^{14}C]amino acids and/or [^{3}H]uridine) with and without actinomycin D (30 μg/ml.) was added. After incubation for 4 hr at 37°C, the radioactive medium was poured off, and the lenses rinsed with ice-cold Hanks salts to remove the isotopes and stop further incorporation. The epithelial cells and fiber cells were separated manually and frozen at −20°C until needed.

In the experiments reported here, simultaneous labeling of proteins and nucleic acids was performed (with ^{14}C-labeled reconstituted amino acid mixture and [^{3}H]uridine, New England Nuclear) to measure in the same group of lenses the effect of actinomycin D on nucleic acid and protein synthesis.

(b) RNA isolation

Epithelial cells or fiber cells were homogenized in 0·01 M-Tris–HCl buffer (pH 7·4) containing 0·01 M-KCl, 0·0015 M-MgCl$_2$, 5 μg polyvinyl sulfate/ml. and 1% sodium dodecyl sulfate. After homogenization, an equal volume of 90% (w/v) phenol was added, and the preparation was shaken in the cold (0 to 4°C) for 1 hr (Kirby, 1956; Devi, 1962). The emulsion was then broken by centrifugation for 30 min at 12,000 g. The top aqueous phase was removed, and the interface was combined with an equal volume of 0·02 M-potassium acetate buffer (pH 5·0) containing 0·003 M-MgCl$_2$, 0·28 M-LiCl and 1·0% sodium dodecyl sulfate; to this was added an equal volume of 90% phenol (w/v), the temperature was brought to 60°C, and the material continuously mixed at this temperature for 5 min (McCarthy & Hoyer, 1964). The suspension was then cooled and centrifuged at 12,000 g for 30 min. The aqueous phase was removed and combined with the aqueous phase from the cold phenol extraction. The pH of the combined material was adjusted to 5·2 with 0·2 N-HCl, and potassium acetate added to a final concentration of 2%. Following this, 2·5 vol. of cold ethanol were added, and the mixture left overnight at 0°C. The precipitated RNA was collected by low-speed centrifugation, dissolved in 1 to 5 ml. of buffer (0·01 M-Tris–HCl, 0·01 M-KCl, 0·0015 M-MgCl$_2$ and 5 μg PVS/ml.) and dialyzed to removed phenol and ethanol before being analyzed by sucrose density-gradient centrifugation.

(c) *Sucrose density-gradient analyses*

Resolution of the phenol-extracted RNA was accomplished by using 26 ml. of a linear (5 to 20%) sucrose gradient, layered over a 2-ml. cushion of 60% sucrose. The gradients were prepared in the Tris buffer (pH 7·4) described in (b). The RNA sample was layered over the sucrose and centrifuged at 24,000 rev./min for 16 hr at 5°C in a Spinco model L-2 preparative ultracentrifuge with the SW25·1 rotor. After centrifugation, 1-ml. fractions were collected from the bottom of the tube. The absorbancy at 260 mμ of each fraction was measured in a Zeiss PMQII spectrophotometer and corrected for the absorbance of sucrose by using fractions from a sample-free gradient as blanks. The radioactivity in the RNA fractions was assayed by one of two methods. Either 0·5 ml. of each fraction was pipetted directly into a hyamine–toluene–Fluors mixture and counted, or 1 mg of bovine serum albumin followed by 1·25 ml. of 10% trichloroacetic acid was added to each 0·5-ml. sample. The trichloroacetic acid precipitates were collected by centrifugation, washed with 10% trichloroacetic acid, and then dissolved in the hyamine–toluene–Fluors solution. The method used is noted in each Figure.

·Since [^{14}C]amino acids and [^{3}H]uridine were added simultaneously, the amount of protein contaminant in the RNA preparation after one phenol extraction could be tested. Some ^{14}C-labeled material was found in the top ten fractions of the sucrose gradients when the fractions were added directly to the hyamine–toluene–Fluors system. If the gradient fractions were precipitated with trichloroacetic acid before being counted, then no protein contaminant could be detected. Similarly, after trichloroacetic acid precipitation, some of the [^{3}H]uridine was lost, indicating the presence of some acid-soluble material in the preparations.

(d) *Homogenization*

Unless otherwise noted, all homogenizations were done in 0·005 M-sodium phosphate buffer (pH 7·0), by using 5 ml./lens cortex and 1 ml./lens capsule. Prior to fractionation of the lens proteins, homogenates were dialyzed against 3 to 4 liters of the same buffer for 16 to 24 hr with one or two volume changes.

(e) *DEAE cellulose column chromatography*

The procedure for fractionation and identification of the bovine lens proteins has been described (Papaconstantinou, 1965). A column of 1·5 cm inside diameter and a length of 45 cm was used; the height of DEAE cellulose was approximately 10 cm. The flow rate of the column effluent was 1 ml./min, and was kept constant by the use of a peristaltic pump. 3-ml. fractions were collected. DEAE cellulose, type 20, was obtained from the Carl Schleicher & Schuell Co., Keene, N.H. Step-wise elution is obtained with the following sodium phosphate buffers: (I) 50 ml. of 0·005 M-phosphate, pH 7·0; (II) 50 ml. of 0·0075 M-phosphate, pH 6·5; (III) 50 ml. of 0·01 M-phosphate, pH 6·0; (IV) 75 ml. of 0·02 M-phosphate, pH 5·7; (V) 50 ml. of 0·02 M-phosphate (pH 5·7) containing 0·1 M-NaCl; (VI) 50 ml. of 0·10 M-phosphate (pH 5·7) containing 0·1 M-NaCl; (VII) 50 ml. of 0·1 M-phosphate (pH 5·7) containing 0·3 M-NaCl.

Protein concentrations were estimated spectrophotometrically (Warburg & Christian, 1941). In experiments where incorporation of radioactive material into protein was being studied, 0·5 ml. of each column fraction was counted in a liquid-scintillation counter.

(f) *Scintillation counting*

Radioactivity was determined in a Nuclear Chicago Mark II scintillation counter. The same toluene and Fluors solvent system was used to count both protein and RNA fractions. This solvent consisted of 13 ml. of toluene and Fluors plus 2 ml. of 1·5 M-Hyamine 10X. The toluene and Fluors solution alone consisted of 4 g PPO (2,5-diphenyloxazole) and 0·05 g POPOP (*p*-bis-(5-phenyloxazolyl-2-)-benzene) dissolved in 1 liter of reagent grade toluene. The hyamine solution consisted of 75 g of Hyamine 10X (Rohm & Haas) added to 33 ml. of methanol (Meade & Stiglitz, 1962), then filtered to remove gross impurities. The above solution would hold 0·5 ml. of an aqueous solution without separation occurring, or trichloroacetic acid precipitates could be dissolved directly in it, then quantitatively transferred to scintillation vials.

24

3. Results

(a) *Effect of actinomycin D on protein synthesis in embryonic, calf and adult lens cells*

A series of experiments was carried out to determine the concentration of actinomycin D necessary to inhibit protein synthesis in *calf* lens epithelial cells. Figures 1 and 2 show the effect of 20 and 30 μg of actinomycin D/ml., respectively. In the epithelial cells (Figs 1(a) and 2(a)). protein synthesis is significantly inhibited after three hours of incubation in actinomycin D at both concentrations used; 30 μg/ml. is somewhat more effective than 20 μg/ml. The fiber cells (Figs 1(b) and 2(b)) are not affected by either concentration of actinomycin D for as long as six hours. On the basis of these results, incubation for 4 hr with 30 μg of actinomycin D/ml. was chosen for all subsequent experiments.

The effect of actinomycin D on total protein synthesis in *adult* lenses, was studied at concentrations of 10, 20 and 30 μg/ml. Table 1 shows that none of these concentrations inhibited protein synthesis either in the epithelial cells or fiber cells. In fact, protein synthesis in the fiber cells seems to be slightly stimulated by the antibiotic.

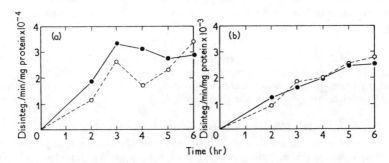

FIG. 1. Effect of 20 μg of actinomycin D/ml. on protein synthesis in calf lens epithelial cells (a) and fiber cells (b).
—●—●—, Protein in control cells (disinteg./min/mg protein); --○--○--, protein in actinomycin D-treated cells (disinteg./min/mg protein). Protein concentrations were determined by the biuret method.

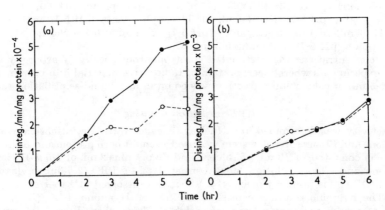

FIG. 2. Effect of 30 μg of actinomycin D/ml. on protein synthesis in calf lens epithelial cells (a) and fiber cells (b).
—●—●—, Protein in control cells (disinteg./min/mg protein); --○--○--, protein in actinomycin D-treated cells (disinteg./min/mg protein).

TABLE 1

Effect of various concentrations of actinomycin D on protein synthesis in adult lens

	Concn actinomycin D (μg/ml.)	Disinteg./min/ mg protein
Epithelial cell	0 (control)	16,500
	10	20,400
	20	16,950
	30	20,500
Fiber cell	0 (control)	694
	10	739
	20	835
	30	866

Protein concentrations were determined by the biuret method.

It is possible that, in the lens, the synthesis of some proteins may be inhibited, whereas that of others may not be affected, or perhaps even stimulated. To determine whether actinomycin D exerts a differential effect (either inhibition or stimulation) on the synthesis of the individual crystallins, the α-, β- and γ-crystallins from *adult* lens epithelial cells were analyzed. Figure 3 shows that there is essentially no effect of actinomycin D on protein synthesis in these epithelial cells. The specific activities of the α-, β- and γ-crystallins from control and actinomycin D-treated lenses are shown in Table 2; both α- and γ-crystallin syntheses are inhibited by 7%, but β-crystallin synthesis is not affected at all. Similar analyses were carried out with the crystallins of the *adult* fiber cells (see Fig. 4). Again, actinomycin D does not inhibit protein synthesis; in fact, protein synthesis is slightly stimulated as can be seen from the specific activities in Table 2.

Similar experiments were done with *calf* lenses and with *embryonic* lenses to compare the effects of actinomycin D on protein synthesis in lens cells of different ages. The effect of actinomycin D on protein synthesis in *calf epithelial* cells is shown in Fig. 5. Protein synthesis in these cells is significantly inhibited, whereas the effect in the *calf fiber* cells is less pronounced (Fig. 6 and Table 3). A comparison between Tables 2 and 3 clearly shows the difference in sensitivity to actinomycin D, between the *adult* and the *calf* epithelial cells on one hand and the greater resistance to the antibiotic by the fiber cells on the other hand.

Finally, experiments similar to those described above were performed with *embryonic* lenses. Because of the limited amount of material available, carrier protein had to be added for the fractionation of the crystallins on DEAE cellulose. The incorporation of amino acids into *fetal epithelial* cell proteins (Fig. 7) was potently inhibited by actinomycin D. Furthermore, the *fetal* epithelial cells were more sensitive to actinomycin D than were the *calf* epithelial cells, indicating progressive stabilization of the protein-synthesizing templates with cell age.

107

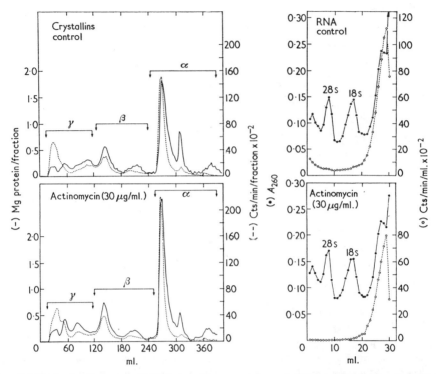

Fig. 3. Effect of actinomycin D (30 μg/ml.) on protein and RNA synthesis in adult lens epithelial cells.

Lenses were incubated for 4 hr in the presence of ^{14}C-labeled reconstituted amino acid mixture (1 μc/ml.) and [^{3}H]uridine (2 μc/ml.). The crystallins were fractionated on DEAE cellulose columns; 39 mg protein from control cells were placed on the column, with a final recovery of 91%; 40 mg protein from actinomycin D-treated cells were placed on the column with a final recovery of 100%. The sucrose gradients were layered with 240 μg RNA from control cells and 230 μg RNA from actinomycin D-treated cells. Each 1-ml. fraction was added directly to 15 ml. of the hyamine–toluene–Fluors mixture for liquid-scintillation counting.

TABLE 2

Effect of actinomycin D on protein synthesis in adult lens

		Cts/min/mg protein in		
		α-	β-	γ-
Epithelial cell	Control	4827	5123	8816
	Actinomycin D (30 μg/ml.)	4508	5136	8172
	% Inhibition	7	0	7
Fiber cell	Control	131	84	428
	Actinomycin D (30 μg/ml.)	198	120	482
	% Stimulation	51	43	13

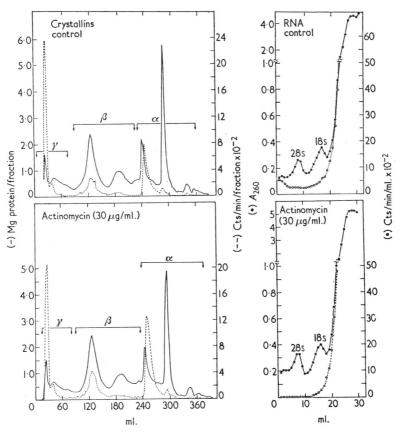

FIG. 4. Effect of actinomycin D (30 μg/ml.) on protein and RNA synthesis in adult lens fibre cells.

All experimental procedures are described in Fig. 3. 100 mg protein from control and from actinomycin D-treated cells were placed on the column with a final recovery of 90% for each. The sucrose gradients were layered with 1·6 mg RNA from control cells and 1·9 mg RNA from actinomycin D-treated cells.

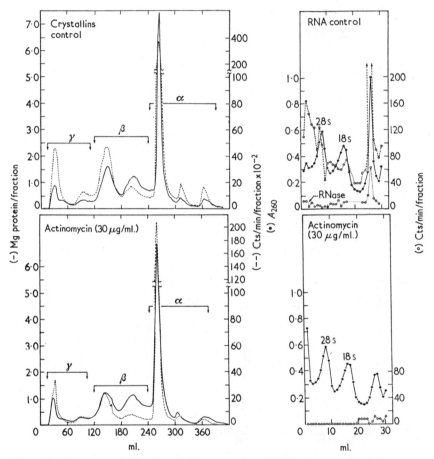

FIG. 5. Effect of actinomycin D (30 μg/ml.) on protein and RNA synthesis in calf lens epithelial cells.

Lenses were incubated for 4 hr in the presence of ^{14}C-labeled reconstituted amino acid mixture (1 μc/ml.) and [^{3}H]uridine (2·6 μc/ml.). 100 mg protein from control and actinomycin D-treated cells were placed on the DEAE cellulose columns with final recoveries of 92 and 91%, respectively. The sucrose gradients were layered with 500 μg RNA from control cells and 500 μg RNA from actinomycin D-treated cells. A 0·5-ml. portion was precipitated with 10% trichloroacetic acid prior to counting, as described in the Materials and Methods section. The remainder of the fraction (0·5 ml.) was treated with ribonuclease (10 μg/ml., 30 min, 22°C) prior to precipitation and **counting.**

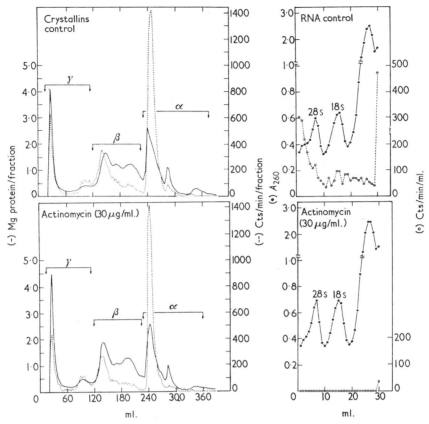

Fig. 6. Effect of actinomycin D (30 μg/ml.) on protein and RNA synthesis in calf lens fiber cells. The conditions are described in Fig. 5. 100 mg protein from control and 103 mg from actinomycin D-treated cells were placed on the columns with 93% and 90% recoveries, respectively. The sucrose gradients were layered with 1·25 mg RNA from control cells and 1·25 mg RNA from actinomycin D-treated cells.

TABLE 3

Effect of actinomycin D on protein synthesis in calf lens

		\multicolumn{3}{c}{Cts/min/mg protein in}		
		α-	β-	γ-
Epithelial cell	Control	3796	2046	3896
	Actinomycin D (30 μg/ml.)	1948	1123	2340
	% Inhibition	49	45	40
Fiber cell	Control	275	119	164
	Actinomycin D (30 μg/ml.)	239	88	130
	% Inhibition	13	26	21

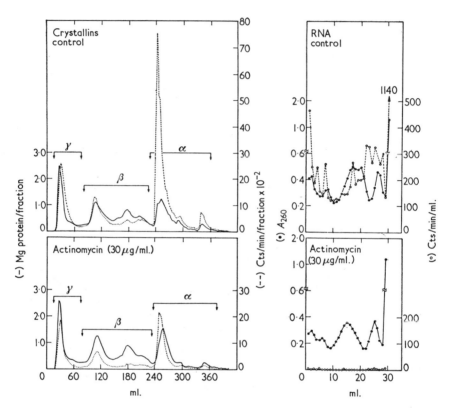

Fig. 7. Effect of actinomycin D (30 μg/ml.) on protein and RNA synthesis in fetal lens epithelial cells.

The lenses were incubated for 4 hr in the presence of ^{14}C-labeled reconstituted amino acid mixture (1 μc/ml.) and [3H]uridine (5 μc/ml.). For protein fractionation, 4·7 mg protein from control and from actinomycin D-treated cells were mixed with 60 mg of unlabeled protein from calf cortex fiber cells. For RNA extraction, 30 unlabeled calf lens capsules (epithelial cells) were used as a source of carrier RNA and extracted together with five control capsules or five actinomycin D-treated capsules. All RNA recovered from the phenol extraction was placed on the sucrose gradients in a volume of 1 ml. Each gradient fraction was precipitated with trichloroacetic acid prior to counting.

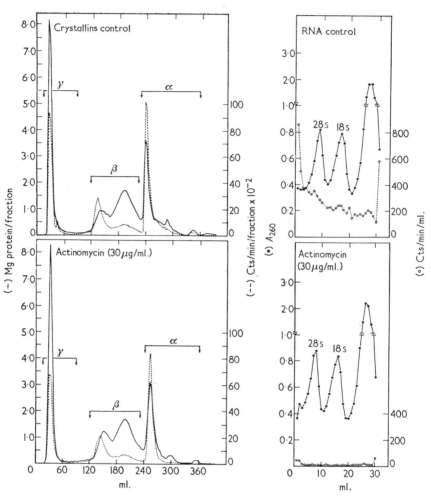

Fig. 8. Effect of actinomycin D (30 μg/ml.) on protein and RNA synthesis in fetal lens fiber cells.

The experimental conditions are described in Fig. 7. 100 mg protein from control and from actinomycin D-treated cells were placed on the column, with 92% recovery in both cases. The sucrose gradients were layered with 1·16 mg RNA from the control fiber cells and 1·19 mg RNA from the actinomycin D-treated fiber cells.

In the *fetal fiber* cells, protein synthesis was sensitive to the antibiotic (Fig. 8) to about the same extent as in the fiber cells of the *calf* cortex. The specific activities of the α-, β- and γ-crystallins from control and actinomycin D-treated embryonic lenses are shown in Table 4.

TABLE 4

Effect of actinomycin D on protein synthesis in fetal lens

		Cts/min		
		α-	β-	γ-
Epithelial cell	Control	46,262	22,326	17,060
	Actinomycin D (30 μg/ml.)	15,590	10,168	9884
	% Inhibition	65	54	42
		Cts/min/mg protein in		
		α-	β-	γ-
Fiber cell	Control	2098	949	1232
	Actinomycin D (30 μg/ml.)	1631	767	1038
	% Inhibition	22	19	16

(b) *Effect of actinomycin D on RNA synthesis in embryonic, calf and adult lens cells*

Since the synthesis of the lens crystallins is affected by actinomycin D to different degrees in cells from animals of different ages, the effect of this antibiotic on RNA synthesis was determined by sucrose density-gradient analyses of phenol-extracted labeled RNA from epithelial cells and fiber cells, from adults, calves and embryos, respectively. The incorporation of [³H]uridine into the RNA from *adult* epithelial cells and fiber cells may be seen in Figs 3 and 4; the radioactive material in tubes 19 to 30 could be shown to be soluble in 10% trichloroacetic acid. This was the only experiment performed in this manner; i.e. the remaining gradient analyses were done by trichloroacetic acid precipitation before counting. Therefore, these data show that actinomycin D, at a concentration of 30 μg/ml., inhibits RNA synthesis in both cell types by about 99%. Thus, under conditions in which RNA synthesis has been essentially stopped, the synthesis of the lens crystallins is unchanged in the epithelial cells and slightly stimulated in the fiber cells.

In *calf* lens cells, actinomycin D completely inhibited RNA synthesis in epithelial as well as in fiber cells (Figs 5 and 6). At this cell age, however, inhibition of RNA synthesis resulted in a marked inhibition of crystallin synthesis in the epithelial cells and a slight inhibition in the fiber cells. Finally, with *embryonic* cell material, actinomycin D potently inhibits both RNA and protein synthesis in epithelial cells. The response of embryonic fiber cells was similar to that of calf lens fiber cells (Figs 7 and 8). Thus, 30 μg of actinomycin D/ml. stops RNA synthesis in epithelial and in fiber cells of adults, calves and embryos; and this inhibition produces a differential response in terms of protein synthesis.

4. Discussion

One of the characteristics of cellular differentiation is the increase in the half-life of mRNA. This has been shown to be the case in fibrogenesis in the vertebrate lens (Papaconstantinou, Koehn & Stewart, 1964; Reeder & Bell, 1965); in the maturation of the reticulocyte (Reich, Acs, Mack & Tatum, 1962; Marks, Burka & Schlessinger, 1962); in the differentiation of pancreas epithelium (Wessells & Wilt, 1965); in myogenesis (Yaffe & Feldman, 1964); and in differentiated chick neural retina cells (Moscona & Kirk, 1965). In several of the cases mentioned here, the stabilization of mRNA occurs at a time during cellular differentiation when nuclear RNA and DNA synthesis decreases, e.g. during the maturation of the reticulocyte or the lens fiber cell. Therefore, the stabilization of mRNA appears to be associated with the loss of mitotic activity.

The epithelial cells of the embryonic lens are actively dividing, and the mitotic index of these cells progressively decreases as the lens grows to its adult size. Thus, a major difference between the epithelial cells of the embryonic and adult lens is their replicative activity. Our data show that these cells also differ significantly with respect to their regulation of RNA and protein synthesis.

The experiments reported in this paper show that stabilization of mRNA is not limited to the terminal stage of cellular differentiation in the vertebrate cell, and that it may be a characteristic of the lack of mitotic activity. Thus, the epithelial cells of the adult bovine lens contain protein-synthesizing templates that are more stable than the templates found in the actively dividing epithelial cells of the embryonic lens. The adult lens epithelial cells have not lost their ability to divide; but, at this age, they are in an extended G_1 phase of the cell cycle and will proceed into the S phase and into mitosis only after they have been stimulated by physical or chemical injury (Srinivasan & Harding, 1965). The stabilization of mRNA may therefore be related to the replicative activity of the cell.

A comparison may also be made between the effect of actinomycin D on RNA and protein synthesis in the epithelial cells and fiber cells of the embryonic, calf and adult lens. Here it can be seen that at all ages the synthesis of α-, β- and γ-crystallins by fiber cells is relatively insensitive to actinomycin D. This indicates that fiber cell formation throughout the growth of the lens is associated with the stabilization of mRNA. This has been reported in detail from our laboratory (Papaconstantinou et al., 1966; Stewart & Papaconstantinou, 1967b) and from others (Reeder & Bell, 1965).

The RNA analyses show a significant decrease in RNA synthesis when the epithelial cell has differentiated to a fiber cell. This has also been shown in the maturation of the reticulocyte. This decrease of RNA synthesis, during cellular maturation, appears to be characteristic of cellular differentiation and may be associated with the stabilization of mRNA. The sucrose gradient analyses for RNA synthesis in adult epithelial cells, where stable templates are also found, are very similar to those observed for the fiber cell. Thus, the stabilization of mRNA appears to occur at a time when RNA synthesis is decreased. This should be a reversible type of regulation in cells which exhibit this phenomenon without having lost their ability to divide. In fact, preliminary experiments in which adult lenses were placed in organ culture to stimulate mitosis have shown that actinomycin D will inhibit total protein synthesis to the same degree as observed for the embryonic lens epithelial cells.

This research sponsored by the U.S. Atomic Energy Commission under contract with the Union Carbide Corporation.

One of us (J. A. S.) was supported in part by a Public Health Service Fellowship (1-F1-GM-30,907-02) from the National Institute of General Medical Sciences, the National Institutes of Health.

REFERENCES

Cotlier, E. (1962). *Arch. Ophthal.* **68**, 80.

Devi, A. (1962). *Canad. J. Biochem. Physiol.* **40**, 41.

Hanna, C. (1965). *Invest. Ophthal.* **4**, 480.

Hanna, C. & O'Brien, J. E. (1961). *Arch. Ophthal.* **66**, 103.

Kirby, K. S. (1956). *Biochem. J.* **64**, 405.

Marks, P. A., Burka, E. R. & Schlessinger, D. (1962). *Proc. Nat. Acad. Sci., Wash.* **48**, 2163.

McCarthy, B. J. & Hoyer, B. H. (1964). *Proc. Nat. Acad. Sci., Wash.* **52**, 915.

Meade, R. C. & Stiglitz, R. A. (1962). *Int. J. Appl. Radiat. Isotopes*, **13**, 11.

Mikulicich, A. G. & Young, R. W. (1963). *Invest. Ophthal.* **2**, 344.

Moscona, A. A. & Kirk, D. L. (1965). *Science*, **148**, 519.

Papaconstantinou, J. (1965). *Biochim. biophys. Acta*, **107**, 81.

Papaconstantinou, J. (1967). *Science*, **156**, 338.

Papaconstantinou, J., Koehn, P. V. & Stewart, J. A. (1964). *Amer. Zool.* **4**, 321.

Papaconstantinou, J., Stewart, J. A. & Koehn, P. V. (1966). *Biochim. biophys. Acta*, **114**, 428.

Reeder, R. & Bell, E. (1965). *Science*, **150**, 71.

Reich, E., Acs, G., Mack, B. & Tatum, E. L. (1962). In *Informational Macromolecules*, ed. by H. J. Vogel, V. Bryson and J. O. Lampen, pp. 317–333. New York: Academic Press.

Srinivasan, B. D. & Harding, C. V. (1965). *Invest. Ophthal.* **4**, 452.

Stewart, J. A. & Papaconstantinou, J. (1966). *Biochim. biophys. Acta*, **121**, 69.

Stewart, J. A. & Papaconstantinou, J. (1967a). *Fed. Proc.* **26**, 604.

Stewart, J. A. & Papaconstantinou, J. (1967b). *Proc. Nat. Acad. Sci., Wash.* **58**, 95.

Warburg, O. & Christian, W. (1941). *Biochem. Z.* **310**, 384.

Wessels, N. F. & Wilt, F. H. (1965). *J. Mol. Biol.* **13**, 767.

Yaffe, D. & Feldman, M. (1964). *Develop. Biol.* **9**, 347.

Reprinted from Science, August 14, 1964, Vol. 145, No. 3633, pages 711-714. Copyright © 1964 by the American Association for the Advancement of Science

Protein Synthesis During Development: Control through Messenger RNA

ROBERT B. SCOTT
EUGENE BELL
Department of Biology, Massachusetts Institute of Technology, Cambridge

Abstract. *Utilization of long-lived messenger RNA appears to be the exception rather than the rule in cells which are differentiating and synthesizing large amounts of specialized product at the same time. The fact that polyribosomes synthesize protein after RNA synthesis is turned off by actinomycin D is used to demonstrate messenger RNA of long half-life. The data suggest that most tissues examined have short-lived messenger RNA's, but the ocular lens can synthesize protein after an incubation of 24 hours in 40 μg of actinomycin D per milliliter. A common basis for the presence of long-lived messenger RNA in the cells of the lens, the feather, and in reticulocytes is discussed.*

A mark of the differentiated cell is its capacity to synthesize structural or enzymatic cell specific proteins. Some cells, such as skin, liver, muscle, connective tissue, reticulocyte, pancreas, and thyroid, produce large amounts of one or a few kinds of protein. We have asked whether all or only some differentiating cells synthesize their specialized product on messenger RNA which has a long half-life. It has already been shown that hemoglobin (1) and feather

117

proteins (2, 3) are synthesized on messenger RNA which has a long life span. In bacteria the half-life of messenger RNA is about 2 minutes (4), while in HeLa cells the half-life of messenger RNA is about 3 hours (5). In some, if not all, cells of the down feather some messenger RNA's have a half-life which is longer than 24 hours (3).

Polyribosomal protein synthesis can be demonstrated as early as the first day of incubation (6) in the chick embryo, although, apart from blood cells, the earliest actual demonstration of messenger RNA of long half-life has been in the 9-day skin. The earliest chick blood cells in which hemoglobin can be detected have been shown to contain messenger RNA of long half-life (7). In sea urchin embryos it has been shown that immediately after fertilization proteins can be synthesized without production of new RNA (8). This condition appears to persist throughout cleavage and implies that stable messenger is present in the ovum and is put to use for a limited time after fertilization. Similar data on chick embryos of comparable age are not available.

There are at least two ways by which differentiating cells can make large amounts of one or a few characteristic

Table 1. Results of 2-hour labeling period with uridine-2-C¹⁴ after 23 hours incubation of 14-day-old embryonic lenses (72 lenses in each sample) in 25 ml of Charity Waymouth medium. Experimental reaction mixtures contained 40 μg of actinomycin D per milliliter, and each contained penicillin and streptomycin. After dividing each group into two parts, RNA was extracted according to the method of Scherrer and Darnell (13).

Flask	Treatment	RNA (OD 260 mμ units)	Count/min
Control 1	None	0.395	548
Control 2	None	.598	809
Expt. 1	Actinomycin	.627	8.6
Expt. 2	Actinomycin	.560	15.8

$$\frac{\text{Experimental average (count/min per OD)}}{\text{Control average (count/min per OD)}} \times 100 = 1.55 \text{ percent}$$

proteins. The first is through the repeated use of limited amounts of long-lived specific messenger RNA's. The second is to make the specific protein through the continued synthesis of short-lived messenger RNA's. To determine which of these alternatives can best describe the use of messenger RNA in different cell types, a variety of embryonic and adult chicken tissues have been examined for long-lived polyribosomes. Long-lived polyribosomes are defined as those which will function to

produce new protein for long periods after RNA synthesis has been reduced to less than 2 percent of controls by treating tissues (in vitro) with actinomycin D for varying periods. It is assumed that polyribosomes which function under the foregoing conditions provide a measure of the stability of messenger RNA.

Protein synthesis on polyribosomes in ocular lenses from embryos 13, 14, 15, or 20 days old was not abolished after tissues were incubated for 21 to 24 hours in 40 μg of actinomycin D per milliliter (Fig. 1). Treatment of the labeled homogenate with ribonuclease at 4°C for 10 minutes moves all of the radioactivity measured in the polysome region to the 74S peak. The incorporation of uridine-2-C¹⁴ into 14-day lenses during a 2-hour period of labeling was 1.5 percent of controls after 22 hours in 40 μg of actinomycin D per milliliter as judged by radioactivity of RNA extracted by a hot-phenol procedure (Table 1). Incorporation of amino acid into protein on polyribosomes in lenses treated with actinomycin D ranged from 4 to 16 percent of controls. It is clear from these data that there are some messenger RNA's in the ocular lens which have a life span comparable to the long-lived messenger RNA in feather cells (2, 3).

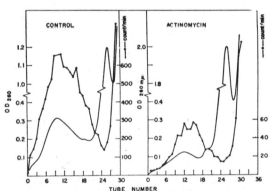
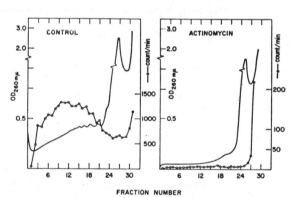

Fig. 1 (left). Fourteen-day embryonic lenses. Two groups of lenses (approximately 12 dozen) were removed aseptically, cut, and then incubated for 23 hours (with agitation) at 37°C in 25 ml Charity Waymouth medium (14) with 4 mg penicillin, 2.5 mg streptomycin, and phenol red indicator. The experimental flask also contained 40 μg of actinomycin D per milliliter (15). The medium was then removed, and tissues were labeled for 3 minutes at 37°C in buffered saline with 20 μc of C¹⁴-labeled algal hydrolysate per milliliter but no actinomycin. The reaction was stopped with ice-cold saline, and the tissues were washed three times before suspending them in four volumes of cold hypotonic buffer (0.01M tris, pH 7.4; 0.0015M Mg⁺⁺; 0.01M KCl) for 30 minutes. Samples were homogenized gently with three to six strokes of a tightly fitting Dounce homogenizer. Nuclei were sedimented at 600g for 10 minutes, and sodium deoxycholate was added to the supernatant to give a concentration of 0.5 percent prior to layering on a linear 25-ml sucrose gradient (15 to 30 percent by weight) in the same buffer. Gradients were centrifuged at 24,000 rev/min in an SW-25 rotor of a Spinco model L centrifuge for 2 hours at the −9°C setting. Twenty (drop) fractions were collected and the optical density at 260 mμ was recorded continuously on a Gilford spectrophotometer. To each fraction 0.5 ml of 2N NaOH was added. Protein was precipitated with trichloracetic acid at a final concentration of 5 percent, and the precipitate was collected on Millipore filters. The radioactivity was counted on aluminum planchets in a low background gas flow counter. Fig. 2 (right). Optical density profile of polyribosomes of whole 3½-day chick embryo showing radioactivity of nascent protein in the control and the effect of actinomycin D (10 μg/ml). The peak at fraction 25 represents single ribosomes.

SCIENCE, VOL. 145

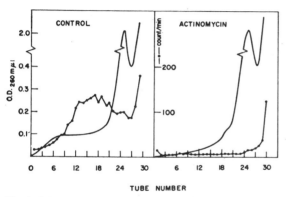
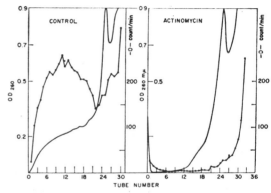

Fig. 3 (left). Polyribosomal protein synthesis in the smooth muscle of the proventriculus of 15-day chick embryos and the effect of actinomycin (20 μg/ml). Fig. 4 (right). Polyribosomal protein synthesis in the brain of 9-day chick embryos showing inhibition by actinomycin (20 μg/ml).

In contrast to the foregoing results, in studying the sedimentation in a sucrose density gradient of the polyribosomes from 3½-day-old chick embryos it is seen that no labeled amino acids were incorporated into proteins on polyribosomes after tissues were incubated for 21 hours with actinomycin D (10 μg/ml). In fact, by 6 hours in 6-day-old whole embryos treated with actinomycin D, protein synthesis on polyribosomes is already less than 10 percent of that on polyribosomes of untreated controls. Examination of 3-, 4-, 5-, or 6-day-old embryos shows the same absence of long-lived messenger RNA after actinomycin treatment. After 5 days of incubation many organs of the embryo are morphologically well differentiated; these include liver, brain, and skeletal and smooth muscle. However, the skin is poorly developed, and feather primordia have not yet appeared. It should be pointed out that there is essentially no contribution to the polyribosome profile from circulating blood cells because the tissues are washed free of blood during preparation.

Some older embryonic tissues were similarly treated with actinomycin, and homogenates were studied for persistence of polyribosomes (Figs. 3 and 4). Protein synthesis on polyribosomes in 15-day liver and smooth muscle (proventriculus), 14- and 16-day skeletal muscle, and 9-day brain was completely inhibited by treatment with 20 μg of actinomycin per milliliter.

In order to obtain adequate samples of adrenal, pancreas, and spleen, pullet tissues were used, and the ovary was studied in adult hens. Only that portion of the ovary containing the relatively immature ova was selected for incubation. Satisfactory polysome profiles were difficult to obtain in some of these older tissues, but, in homogenates not

treated with deoxycholate, radioactivity incorporated into the membrane-bound ribosomes (9) could be compared with and without actinomycin treatment. Long-lived messenger RNA was found in none of these tissues. It is possible that some tissues are more adversely affected by actinomycin D than others and that our failure to demonstrate long-lived messenger RNA's in some reflects this. However, in tissues such as the pancreas or adrenal, protein synthesis (greater than 10 percent of control levels) can still be measured after incubation of 17 or 15 hours, respectively, in actinomycin D. By 24 hours, protein synthesis in both is brought to a halt.

From our data and previous data, it is now evident that large fractions of relatively stabilized protein-forming complexes (messenger RNA and ribosomes) can be demonstrated in some but not all highly specialized cells which produce large amounts of a limited variety of specific protein. It has been reported that lamb thyroid (10) and adult rat liver (11) continue to synthesize protein after treatment with actinomycin D.

Cells which clearly have long-lived messenger RNA, namely lens, down feather, and reticulocyte, share a number of features. Each type makes large quantities of a limited number of proteins (crystallins, keratins, and hemoglobin, respectively), and in each case long-lived messenger RNA is found during periods of intense protein synthesis and cell differentiation. Also common to these cell types, which convert virtually their entire substance into a single product, is early cell death or loss of the nucleus shortly after a spurt of intense protein synthesis which occurs, at least in part, through the repeated use of long-lived messenger

molecules. In the differentiation of mammalian erythrocytes, the nucleus is lost and the cytoplasm then functions independently for a limited period. The fate of nuclei in the feather cells and in cells of the lens is not clear, although it has been shown that in the central, more differentiated, portions of the lens no DNA can be detected (12). In feather cells, however, the nucleus along with the cytoplasm seems to "keratinize." We have no information on the fate of the DNA. In all three cell types the nucleus is effectively "turned off" as differentiation of the cell progresses towards its terminal state. By the time this occurs, differentiation of these cell types is a one way street paved with messenger RNA molecules which have a long half-life.

References and Notes

1. E. Reich, R. M. Franklin, A. J. Shatkin, E. L. Tatum, Proc. Natl. Acad. Sci. U.S. 48, 1238 (1962).
2. E. Bell, in Symposium on Metabolic Control Mechanisms in Animal Cells, W. Rudder, Ed. (National Cancer Institute Monograph No. 13, 1964), p. 1.
3. T. Humphreys, S. Penman, E. Bell, Biophysical Society Abstracts, 8th Annual Meeting, 26 February 1964.
4. C. Levinthal, A. Keynan, A. Higa, Proc. Natl. Acad. Sci. U.S. 48, 1631 (1962).
5. S. Penman, K. Scherrer, Y. Becker, J. E. Darnell, ibid. 49, 654 (1963).
6. R. B. Scott and E. Bell, unpublished observations.
7. F. Wilt, personal communication.
8. P. R. Gross, L. A. Malkin, W. A. Moyer, Proc. Natl. Acad. Sci. U.S. 51, 407 (1964).
9. E. C. Henshaw and H. H. Hiatt, J. Mol. Biol. 7, 122 (1963).
10. R. W. Seed and I. Goldberg, Proc. Natl. Acad. Sci. U.S. 50, 275 (1963).
11. G. Giudice and G. D. Novelli, Biochem. Biophys. Res. Commun. 12, 383 (1963); M. Revel and H. H. Hiatt, Proc. Natl. Acad. Sci. U.S., in press.
12. P. Mandel and M. L. Schmitt, Compt. Rend. Soc. Biol. 151, 368 (1957).
13. K. Scherrer and J. E. Darnell, Biochem. Biophys. Res. Commun. 7, 486 (1962).
14. J. Paul, Cell and Tissue Culture (Livingstone, Edinburgh, 1959), pp. 78–79.
15. Actinomycin D was a gift from Merck Sharp and Dohme, Inc., Rahway, N.J.
16. Supported by NSF grant GB-614. Robert B. Scott was aided by a postdoctoral research scholarship of the American Cancer Society.

19 June 1964

Reprinted from DEVELOPMENTAL BIOLOGY, Volume 8, Number 3, December 1963
Copyright © 1963 by Academic Press Inc. *Printed in U.S.A.*

DEVELOPMENTAL BIOLOGY, **8**, 341–357 (1963)

Synthesis of Experimentally Induced Glutamine Synthetase (Glutamotransferase Activity) in Embryonic Chick Retina *in Vitro*[1]

DAVID L. KIRK AND A. A. MOSCONA

With the technical assistance of Nilda Saenz

Department of Zoology, University of Chicago, Chicago, Illinois

Accepted October 9, 1963

INTRODUCTION

Detailed studies on mechanisms controlling differentiation in embryonic cells and tissues require, in our opinion, experimental systems in which the appearance and activity of characteristic enzyme patterns can be manipulated and effectively modified. A particularly desirable situation would be one in which it would be possible to cause a precocious appearance in a tissue of an enzyme system that is normally associated with the onset of functional differentiation at a later stage of development. It has been recently found (Moscona and Hubby, 1963) that when the neural retina of the early chick embryo is isolated and cultivated *in vitro* there is a precocious appearance and a very rapid increase of glutamotransferase activity in this tissue. The data suggested that this striking increase in enzyme activity, days in advance of normal ontogeny, was not a nonspecific response to tissue transplantation, but that it represented a modification or acceleration of an aspect of the developmental pattern typical to the retina. The possibilities of a precocious induction, derepression, or stimulation of the enzyme-forming system at the level of genomic or cytoplasmic controls were raised, but the information available did not suffice for further consideration of the mechanisms that might be involved. Since this experimental system appeared highly suitable (both as a specific case and possibly as a model of more general significance) for detailed

[1] Supported by grants from the National Science Foundation (G-23852), National Cancer Institute (C-4272), and the Dr. Wallace C. and Clara A. Abbott Fund of the University of Chicago.

investigation of mechanisms involved in controlling tissue-specific enzymatic patterns, it has been further studied with particular reference to: (1) functional identity of the enzyme, (2) whether the experimentally induced increase in its activity represented new synthesis or an activation of preexisting enzyme, independent of biosynthetic processes, and (3) factors affecting level of enzyme activity in cultured tissue. It will be noted that the enzyme assay method outlined here is a modification of previous ones; detailed discussion of these modifications will be made elsewhere together with a report of some further improvements which have subsequently been made (Kirk, 1963).

Some of the advantages of chick neural retina for studies on the molecular aspects of differentiation were listed previously (Moscona and Hubby, 1963). It can be isolated readily and cleanly in relatively large quantities from embryos of different ages and lends itself well to studies *in vitro* at both tissue and cellular levels. In the embryo, active cell proliferation in this tissue is greatly reduced past the tenth day of incubation (Coulombre, 1961), and thus the phenomena that accompany further growth and differentiation are not as complicated by extensive cell replication as in some other embryonic systems. In addition to its homogeneous developmental origin, the retina appears also to be relatively homogeneous with respect to presence of glutamotransferase in its different layers (Rudnick, 1963); thus for purposes of studying this enzymatic activity it can be treated, tentatively, as a uniform cell population.

A more satisfactory definition of the actual functional identity of the retinal enzyme detectable by its glutamotransferase activity was sought, and the evidence suggests that it is a glutamine synthetase. Although the precise metabolic role of retinal glutamotransferase (or glutamine synthetase) is uncertain, its relevance to retinal function can be inferred from the following lines of information. The *in vivo* appearance and accumulation of retinal glutamotransferase in the last few days of embryonic life is temporally correlated with functional maturation of the retina as indicated by appearance of both visual pigments and the electroretinogram (Rudnick and Waelsch, 1955; Wald and Zussman, 1938). Secondly, neural tissues in general are characterized by high levels of glutamine synthetase (Meister, 1962; Wu, 1963) and by highly active metabolic pools of glutamate, glutamine, and associated metabolites (Garfinkel, 1962); neural retina is no exception to this pattern (Pirie, 1956). Last, it appears that the retina depends upon synthesis of glutamine for maintenance of electrolyte balance, a phenomenon as yet incompletely explained (Pirie, 1956). All these facts contributed to our interest in this system and stimulated a series of improvements in both the culture and assay procedures previously used (Moscona and Hubby, 1963) resulting in increased precision of the system and, thus, increased usefulness as a model for studying this sort of enzymatic differentiation.

The previous report (Moscona and Hubby, 1963) discussed only the appearance of enzymatic *activity* and offered no information concerning synthesis of enzyme molecules. This communication deals more directly with this problem. Since no quantitative technique for isolation of this enzyme yet exists (Meister, 1962; Pamiljans *et al.*, 1962), direct evidence of *de novo* synthesis was not feasible and less direct methods were used: a systematic search for enzyme activators or inhibitors at various developmental stages and a determination of the sensitivity of the appearance of activity *in vitro* to the inhibitor of protein synthesis, puromycin. Furthermore, the recent demonstration (Davidson *et al.*, 1963) that continued synthesis of a product characteristic of a differentiated cell line was dependent upon an actinomycin D-sensitive process (presumably DNA-primed synthesis of messenger RNA) raised the question to what extent appearance and maintenance of retinal glutamotransferase activity was under control of an actinomycin-sensitive mechanism.

Finally, investigation was also made of the influence of the substrate and end product of the enzyme (i.e., glutamate and glutamine), glucose, other ocular tissues and extracts of young embryos upon the *in vitro* appearance of glutamotransferase activity.

MATERIAL AND METHODS

Retinal Cultures

Organ cultures of embryonic chick neural retina were established as previously described (Moscona and Hubby, 1963). Two retinas, each cut in two pieces, were suspended in 24 ml of culture medium in a 125-ml Erlenmeyer flask; the flasks were then gassed with a mixture of 5% CO_2 in air, sealed and placed on a gyratory shaker rotating at 85 rpm (diameter of rotation $\frac{3}{4}$ inch) at 38°C for 12, 24, or 48 hours. Random variability was minimized by distributing pieces of tissue from each pair of retinas through control and experimental flasks. Thus, while each culture contained the equivalent of two retinas, in no case was all the tissue in one culture flask derived from a single embryo. Unless otherwise mentioned all studies were performed on retinas from embryos of 10 days' incubation. A minimal maintenance medium was routinely used; it consisted of 100 parts Tyrode's solution, 10 parts horse serum, and 1 part of a penicillin-streptomycin mixture (Microbiological Associates). Additions to the medium were made in sterile, neutral, Tyrode's-based solutions at the expense of the basal Tyrode's solution. Whenever experimental protocol called for a change of medium, part of the control cultures were simultaneously changed to fresh medium. A thorough investigation of the effect of light upon retinal cultures indicated a slightly higher rate of enzymatic growth in the dark, so that in the routine procedure retinas were isolated under normal illumination but cultured in a darkened incubation room.

At the conclusion of the culture period, tissues were sampled for routine histological examination, harvested, washed quickly three times in cold Tyrode's solution by decantation, collected by mild centrifugation, and lyophilized immediately in the plastic centrifuge tubes. Just prior to analysis, tissues were suspended in 2.5 ml of cold phosphate buffer (0.01 M, pH 7.1), packed in ice, and submitted to about three 5-second bursts of ultrasound (20 Kcps) from the probe of a Branson model 75 sonifier tuned to maximum output. Such ultrasonic treatment yielded a lightly opalescent, homogeneous suspension and released significantly more activity than Potter-Elvejhem glass grinding.

Enzyme Assays

Glutamotransferase was determined by the following modification (Kirk, 1963) of standard procedures (Moscona and Hubby, 1963; Rudnick and Waelsch, 1955). To 0.35 ml of cold sonicate (diluted with phosphate buffer when necessary) was added 0.50 ml of a fresh pH 5.4 solution containing: L-glutamine, 120 μmoles; acetate buffer, 50 μmoles; NaH_2PO_4, 5 μmoles; ATP, 0.05 μmole. This mixture was preincubated 10 minutes at 38°C, whereupon 0.15 ml of a solution (pH 5.4) containing 30 μmoles hydroxylamine and 5 μmoles $MnCl_2$ was added to start the reaction. Each assay was run in triplicate, one tube receiving all but the hydroxylamine and serving as the blank. The reaction was stopped with the standard ferric chloride reagent (Moscona and Hubby, 1963) after an incubation time estimated to produce approximately 0.3–0.6 μmole of product. Absorbance was determined on a Zeiss PMQII spectrophotometer at 500 mμ and related to a succinohydroxamate standard and a biologic standard (see Kirk, 1963). Glutamine synthetase was determined by the method of Levintow *et al.* (1955). Protein was determined by the method of Lowry *et al.* (1951), and specific activity was defined as micromoles of glutamohydroxamate formed per hour per milligram of protein.

Materials

Puromycin, adenine nucleotides, and all amino acids employed (except hydroxylysine and methionine sulfoximine) were obtained from Nutritional Biochemicals Corporation. DL-*allo*-δ-hydroxylysine was obtained from Sigma Chemical Company. DL-methionine-*dl*-sulfoximine was obtained from California Biochemical Corporation. Actinomycin D was generously supplied by Merck, Sharp, & Dohme Inc.

RESULTS

Properties of Retinal Glutamotransferase

At least two discrete enzymes with glutamotransferase activity are known: glutamine synthetase and glutaminase (Meister, 1962). The enzyme most studied in neural tissue is glutamine synthetase. Among its characteristic properties are an absolute divalent cation requirement (Mn^{++} effective at lower levels than Mg^{++}), an inverse shift in pH optimum with Mn^{++} concentration (for the transferase reaction at least), a ratio of transferase to synthetase between 2 and 15 depending on tissue source and preparative methods (cf. Meister, 1962; Pamiljans *et al.*, 1962), a noncompetitive inhibition by DL-*allo*-δ-hydroxylysine (Wu, 1963), and methionine-insensitive inhibition by methionine sulfoximine (Tower, 1960).

Using these properties, preparations of retinal tissue from 20-day embryos and/or retinal cultures were tested to determine whether embryonic retinal glutamotransferase activity is due to a glutamine synthetase (Table 1). It was found that in all cases there was indeed an absolute requirement for a divalent cation: in the absence of added Mn^{++} ion the transferase activity was less than 1% that obtained

TABLE 1

PROPERTIES OF EMBRYONIC RETINAL GLUTAMOTRANSFERASE (20-DAY EMBRYOS)

Assay conditions	Relative activity	pH Optimum
Standard (see text)	100	5.4
Decreased Mn^{++}		
2.5 μmoles	92	6.3
1 μmole	87	6.8
0	<1	?
Hydroxylysine added		
5 μmoles	39	—
50 μmoles	11	—
Methionine sulfoximine added		
2.5 μmoles	31	—
5 μmoles	18	—
5 μmoles plus 10 μmoles methionine	13	—
Synthetase (by the method of Levintow *et al.*, 1955)	20–35	—

in the presence of 5 μmoles/ml. Furthermore, as the Mn^{++} level was lowered from 5 to 2.5 to 1 μmole/ml, the pH optimum of the transferase reaction catalyzed by embryonic retina shifted from 5.4 to 6.3 to 6.8. Preliminary assays of synthetase activity of crude sonicates yielded transferase:synthetase ratios between 3:1 and 5:1. DL-*allo*-δ-Hydroxylysine added to the assay mixture at the level of 5 μmoles/ml inhibited the transferase activity of 20-day retina by 61%; at 50 μmoles the degree of inhibition was about 90%. DL-methionine-*dl*-sulfoximine also was a definite inhibitor of the reaction: 2.5 μmoles/ml gave 70% inhibition, 5.0 μmoles/ml resulted in 80% inhibition. The effect of the sulfoximine could not be reversed by methionine. It is particularly important that by no test yet performed has it been possible to differentiate (qualitatively) between the properties of the enzyme which develops in the retina of late embryos and that which can be caused experimentally to develop several days precociously in the retina in culture. On the basis of these data and in the absence of any data to the contrary, it must be assumed (1) that the enzyme being investigated here is a *glutamine synthetase;* (2) that it is identical in retina in the embryo and in culture; (3) that its precocious appearance under the experimental conditions described represents, indeed, an acceleration of a developmental trait characteristic of retinal differentiation.

Evidence for Synthesis of Enzyme

1. Absence of detectable inhibitors or activators. As noted above, the previous report discussed only changes in specific activity of the retina and made no attempt to answer the question of *de novo* synthesis versus activation of preexisting molecules or removal of a specific enzyme inhibitor (Moscona and Hubby, 1963). According to preliminary data (Hubby, Moscona, and Saenz, unpublished) the activities of retinas from early and late embryos were additive, suggesting the absence of any change in concentration of either a competitive inhibitor or a hitherto-unidentified activator. Such mixed assays have been repeated and some representative data are given in Table 2. The precisely additive nature of these results indicates the

TABLE 2

PRODUCTION OF GLUTAMOHYDROXAMATE (GHA) FROM GLUTAMINE BY
RETINAS OF DIFFERENT AGES, ASSAYED SEPARATELY AND COMBINED

Age[a]	Volume[b]	Retinal equivalent[c]	μmoles GHA/hr	Predicted value
7	0.35	1.7	0.061	—
10	0.35	1.1	0.280	—
18	0.20	0.16	0.276	—
7	0.25	1.2 }	0.184	0.182
18	0.10	0.08 }		
10	0.25	0.79 }	0.340	0.338
18	0.10	0.08 }		

[a] Days of incubation of donor embryo.

[b] Ml of sonicate used per assay.

[c] Number of retinas represented by the volume of sonicate used.

absence of detectable change in concentration of any activators or competitive inhibitors during this period (from 7 to 18 days of incubation) when retina is undergoing marked escalation of glutamotransferase activity. Similar additive data have been obtained in mixed assays of cultured and freshly isolated retinas. The second classical approach to this problem—varying dilution and incubation time inversely—has been applied to many stages of *in ovo* and *in vitro* retinal development. In all cases there is a slight departure (10–15%) from first-order kinetics with respect to enzyme (cf. Kirk, 1963). This appears, however, to be a result of inherent instability of the enzyme at prolonged incubation times since it is more dependent upon time of incubation than upon degree of dilution. In any case, no significant difference has yet been observed in this departure from linearity with age or history of the retina.

2. *Inhibition by puromycin of the normal glutamine synthetase increase.* While the above studies preclude a major participation of variation in competitive inhibitors or activators in the apparent enzymatic growth of the retina, they do not exclude the possibility that removal of *noncompetitive* inhibitors or modification of inactive but preexisting enzyme molecules is involved. In an attempt to answer this question, puromycin, an inhibitor of protein synthesis, was used. It was applied in varying concentrations to 10-day retinas, either at the time of explantation into the medium or after a precultivation period of 12 or 24 hours (by which time the tissues had developed readily detectable levels of enzymatic activity). As can be seen from Fig. 1A, there is a definite dose-dependent depression exerted by puromycin on the normal rate of increase in glutamotransferase

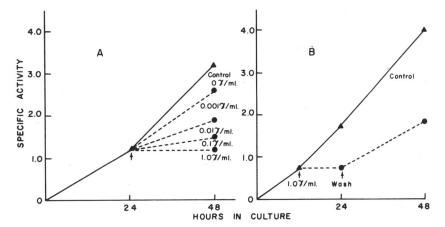

FIG. 1. The effect of puromycin upon the glutamine synthetase (glutamo-transferase activity) of 10-day chick neural retinal cultures. Specific activity is defined as micromoles of glutamohydroxamic acid produced per hour per milligram of protein. (A) Concentration-dependent effect of puromycin. Puromycin was supplied to retinas precultured for 24 hours in control medium, and the cultures were maintained for an additional 24 hours. (B) Partial reversibility of the puromycin effect. Puromycin was added to 12-hour cultures and left in 12 hours. The cultures were then washed and transferred to fresh puromycin-free medium for the remainder of the cultivation period.

activity. Puromycin at a level of 1.0 μg per milliliter of culture medium prevented, consistently and completely, any increase in specific activity of the cultures for as long as it was present, whether added after zero, 12, or 24 hours of culture. Levels as high as 10 μg/ml caused no statistically significant decrease in enzymatic activity from the values existing prior to treatment (at least during the following 24 hours). That the retinal cells had not been irreversibly damaged by such puromycin treatment is demonstrated by the reversibility data plotted in Fig. 1B. The cultures from which the data in Fig. 1B were obtained were washed three times in Tyrode's solution, cultured 20 minutes in puromycin-free medium, and then transferred to fresh medium, where they remained for the rest of the cultivation period. The degree of reversibility was very variable—sometimes nil—but with vigorous washing, after exposure to puromycin, reversibility could be demonstrated. Histologic examination of puromycin-treated retinas confirmed the opinion that levels of puromycin which completely blocked enzymatic growth were not grossly cytotoxic. From these data it can be concluded that at least one step in the appearance of glutamotransferase activity *in vitro* is puromycin sensitive; in the absence of any contrary data, this can be taken as strong presumptive evidence for *de novo* synthesis of the enzyme under culture conditions.

3. *Inhibition by actinomycin of the normal glutamine synthetase increase.* Since the experimentally induced appearance of glutamine synthetase involves protein synthesis, it is of interest to determine to what extent this synthetic process is under continuous nuclear control. As an initial approach to this problem retinal cultures were briefly exposed to low concentrations of actinomycin D, an inhibitor of DNA-dependent RNA synthesis (Hurwitz *et al.*, 1962). As seen in Fig. 2, a 20-minute exposure to 1.0 μg of this antibiotic per milliliter was sufficient to block completely and irreversibly further increase in the enzyme in cultures previously undergoing a high rate of enzymatic growth. This finding, coupled with the puromycin effect, indicates that the increase in the appearance of glutamine synthetase in cultured retina depends upon biosynthetic activities which appear to be under rather direct and continuous control by DNA. Furthermore, attention is drawn to the fact that both puromycin and actinomycin at the appropriate levels completely blocked further increase in enzymatic activity, without ever causing any significant reduction from preexisting enzymatic levels even when administered at tenfold blocking concen-

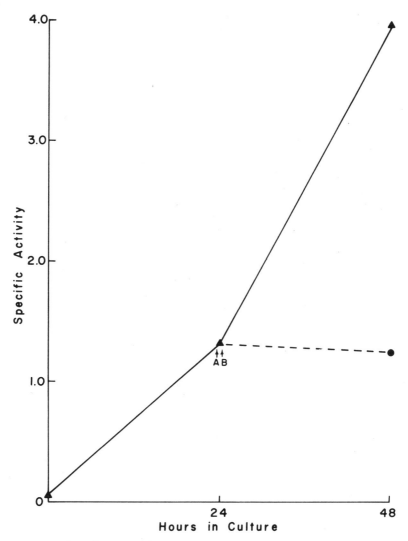

FIG. 2. The effect of a brief exposure to actinomycin D on the glutamine synthetase (glutamotransferase activity) of organ cultures of neural retinas of 10-day chick embryos. Actinomycin D (1 μg/ml) was added to the cultures at A; at B (20 minutes) the cultures were washed and transferred to fresh medium for the remainder of the cultivation period.

trations; this clearly suggests that the enzyme itself is relatively stable, but that the RNA involved in its production is, under the conditions of these experiments, of low stability. Proof of such suppositions rests, of course, upon demonstration that these metabolic inhibitors are exerting their generally accepted effects upon the retina; hence, studies of the synthetic and turnover rates of retinal proteins and nucleic acids (via labeled precursors) have been commenced at this writing.

Absence of Detectable Control Factors in Ocular Tissues and Embryo Extracts

Since the enhancement in rate of enzyme production commences practically immediately upon isolation of the retina from the embryo, the possible role of systemic suppressors in controlling the level of enzyme in the retina *in situ* must be considered. The possibility was tested by culturing 10-day neural retina in the presence of pigmented epithelium (tapetum) or vitreous humor from the same embryos, and by culturing retina in medium supplemented with saline extracts of 7- or 10-day whole chick embryos. In none of these cultures was there any significant effect upon the rate of enzyme synthesis in the explanted retinas. While these results do not preclude the existence of such systemic control factors, they indicate that if such occur their demonstration will require a more subtle approach. Such work is in progress.

The Partial Suppressing Effect of Glutamine and Glutamate

Having tentatively established the occurrence of *de novo* synthesis of glutamine synthetase in the explanted retina, a prime consideration is the mechanism whereby this synthesis is normally repressed for several additional days in the embryo and derepressed or stimulated in culture. In the light of current theories of control over gene expression (Jacob and Monod, 1961), the reports that in HeLa cells (DeMars, 1958) and L cells (Paul and Fottrell, 1963) glutamo-transferase activity is depressed when glutamine is added to the culture medium were of particular interest. In this context it was postulated that perhaps isolation to culture effected rapid enzymatic growth by exposing the retina to sub-repressing levels of glutamine or inducing levels of glutamate. Earlier data demonstrating a partial repressing effect of glutamine in culture (Hubby, Moscona, and Saenz, unpublished) had supported this possibility. Thus it was of obvious

interest to determine whether, and to exactly what extent, the glutamine synthetase level of explanted retinas could be controlled by
varying the concentrations of glutamine or glutamate in the culture
medium.

Retinas from 10-day embryos were isolated and grown for 48 hours
in the standard Tyrode's-horse serum culture medium supplemented
with glutamine or glutamate at various concentrations. The results
are presented graphically in Fig. 3. It can be seen that *both* glutamine

$$\frac{\text{control activity-experimental activity}}{\text{control activity}} \times 100$$

and glutamate were effective in partially depressing enzymatic growth
in the explanted retina. Whether this partial repressing effect of
glutamate represents a significant difference between the response of
this tissue and that of HeLa (DeMars, 1958) and L cells (Paul and
Fottrell, 1963) is as yet unknown, since the effect of glutamate was
not tested with either of those cell lines. However, it is quite clear
that under our experimental conditions, neither glutamate nor glutamine depressed enzymatic growth completely: the glutamate curve
plateaus at less than 20% repression and the glutamine curve appears
to be plateauing at something less than 70% repression. In an attempt
to further examine the specificity and significance of these inhibitory
effects, analogous studies were made employing γ-aminobutyric acid,
glutathione (both oxidized and reduced), asparagine, and aspartic
acid. These substances were chosen for their known metabolic and
chemical similarity to glutamate and glutamine. Although γ-aminobutyric acid proved to be more effective than either glutamine or
glutamate (Fig. 3), even this curve, if extrapolated at constant slope,
would not reach 100% repression until the concentration reached approximately 100 μmoles/ml—a grossly unphysiologic level. Even the
cultures which were grown in the presence of 16 μmoles of γ-aminobutyric acid per milliliter and which demonstrated 80% repression
relative to control cultures were synthesizing new enzyme at ten times
the rate of retinas of similar chronologic age *in situ*. Neither glutathione (reduced or oxidized), asparagine, nor aspartate had any
detectable effect upon the enzymatic growth. These data suggest that
glutamate, glutamine, and γ-aminobutyrate may have a rather specific
role in quantitatively modifying the amount of glutamine synthetase
produced by this tissue; however, this is far from the qualitative sort of

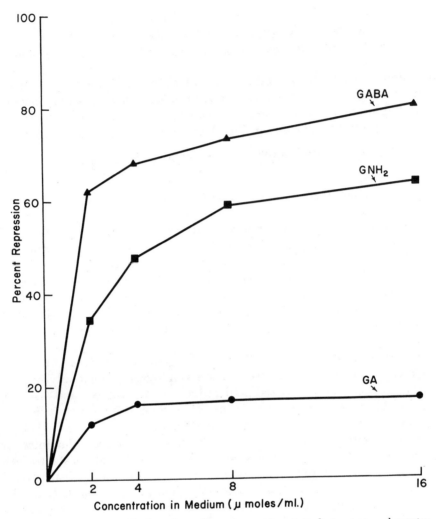

Fig. 3. The effect of glutamate, glutamine, and γ-aminobutyrate on glutamine synthetase (glutamotransferase activity) of 10-day chick neural retina in culture for 48 hours. GA, glutamic acid; GNH₂, glutamine; GABA, γ-aminobutyric acid. Per cent repression is defined as:

control expected of a Jacob-Monod type of repressor substance, and it is inadequate to explain the difference in response to *in ovo* and *in vitro* conditions. While this in no way detracts from the possible applicability of the Jacob-Monod model to this aspect of retinal differentiation, it does indicate that the mechanism controlling glutamine synthetase synthesis in the differentiating retina is not by simple and reversible end-product inhibition or substrate stimulation. Whether the three amino acids which partially suppress formation of glutamine synthetase in retinal cultures function strictly by a simple negative-feedback control on the already derepressed enzyme-forming system or whether they are converted very slowly and at different rates to a common metabolite which functions as a repressor substance is as yet undetermined.

The Absence of an Effect of Elevated Glucose

The results obtained with γ-aminobutyrate prompted an examination of the effect of glucose content of the medium, since the role of this amino acid in energy metabolism of neural tissue is well established (Albers, 1960; Tower, 1960). It was postulated that the effect of explantation upon glutamotransferase activity of the retina might be part of a general compensatory stimulation of glutamate metabolism resulting from an energy deficiency of the Tyrode's-horse serum medium. If this were true, not only would the observed effects of glutamate, glutamine, and γ-aminobutyrate be expected, but glucose enrichment of the medium should markedly repress formation of the enzyme. Experimental enrichment of the medium up to eight times the control level, however, yielded no statistically significant effect upon glutamine synthetase production.

DISCUSSION

The findings presented in this paper raise a number of points for discussion; however, the somewhat exploratory and novel nature of some of the findings reported calls for postponement of detailed consideration and discussion of their implications. The present results justify further interest in embryonic retinal glutamine synthetase as a system for studying mechanisms that control the appearance and activity of tissue-characteristic enzymatic patterns. The demonstration that the glutamotransferase activity of the retina both in the embryo and in culture is attributable to a glutamine synthetase places the phenomenon in a more meaningful physiologic context. By all available indications, *de novo* synthesis of the enzyme appears to be involved in both the normal development and the precocious development in culture; the evidence appears to exclude the possibility that the precocious increase in enzyme activity of the cultured retina is due to purely trivial causes such as dilution of an enzyme inhibitor.

The suggestion, from studies with actinomycin, that genomic control is exerted directly and continuously over the synthesis of the enzyme during its early ontogenesis broadens the relevance of the problem since it may ultimately provide insight into the nature of differential gene expressions in differentiating vertebrate cells. It should be restated here that in this system an actinomycin-sensitive process (presumably nuclear synthesis of RNA) appears essential to new synthesis of the enzyme, but not to maintenance of preexisting activity. This suggests that the enzyme protein is relatively stable, but that its synthesis is dependent on a relatively labile RNA messenger. If tracer studies substantiate this impression, the immediacy of nuclear control over retinal glutamine synthetase will be demonstrated to be intermediate to that proposed by Davidson *et al.* (1963) for control of polysaccharide (AMPS) synthesis in cultured fibroblasts and that demonstrated by Reich *et al.* (1962) for control of hemoglobin synthesis. In the former case an actinomycin-sensitive process appears to be essential for maintenance of preexisting levels of enzyme activity (suggesting lability of both the enzyme and the enzyme-forming system); in the latter case *de novo* synthesis of the tissue-specific protein proceeds uninterrupted in the presence of actinomycin (demonstrating the stability of the corresponding messenger). It is conceivable that an entire spectrum of such relationships will occur, wherein the apparent immediacy of nuclear control over differentiated processes will be predicated by the stability of the characteristic protein and the corresponding RNA.

SUMMARY

The phenomenon of precocious appearance and rapid enhancement of glutamotransferase activity of embryonic chick neural retina in response to explanation *in vitro* has been subjected to more detailed scrutiny. On the basis of cofactor requirements, pH optima, response to specific inhibitors, and ratio of transferase to synthetase activity, the enzyme undergoing change was classified as a glutamine synthetase.

Tests for the presence of enzyme activators and/or inhibitors undergoing change during increase in enzyme activity were negative, suggesting that increase in activity was due to synthesis of new enzyme. This was substantiated by the finding that low levels of puromycin blocked completely and reversibly increases in enzyme activity under culture conditions; and that actinomycin D similarly blocked such increases irreversibly. Preexisting levels of activity appeared stable in the presence of either inhibitor. These data were interpreted to mean that enhancement of glutamotransferase activity which occurs in culture is due to synthesis of new enzyme; it also suggested a lability of the RNA involved and consequently a rather direct genomic control over the rate of synthesis of the enzyme in early ontogenesis.

Pigmented epithelium of embryonic eye, vitreous humor, and embryo extract showed no effect on the increase in glutamine synthetase activity in the explanted retina; this was interpreted as diminishing but not excluding the possibility that a stable, diffusible systemic factor is responsible for control of early ontogenesis of this enzyme in the embryo.

Glutamine, glutamate, and γ-aminobutyrate were found to lower synthesis of the enzyme in culture when added to the medium, but none of these amino acids appeared capable of total repression at concentrations approaching physiological values. Glutathione (oxidized and reduced), asparagine, aspartate, and glucose all had no demonstrable affect upon the growth of the enzyme in culture.

REFERENCES

ALBERS, R. W. (1960). Gamma-amino butyric acid. In "The Neurochemistry of Nucleotides and Amino Acids" (R. O. Brady and D. B. Tower, eds.), pp. 146–158. Wiley, New York.

COULOMBRE, A. J. (1961). Cytology of the developing eye. Intern. Rev. Cytol. 11, 161–194.

DAVIDSON, E. H., ALLFREY, V. G., and MIRSKY, A. E. (1963). Gene expression in differentiated cells. Proc. Natl. Acad. Sci. U.S. 49, 53–60.

DEMARS, R. (1958). The inhibition by glutamine of glutamyl transferase formation in cultures of human cells. Biochim. Biophys. Acta 27, 435–436.

GARFINKEL, D. (1962). Computer simulation of steady state glutamate metabolism in rat brain. J. Theoret. Biol. 3, 412–422.

HURWITZ, J., FURTH, J. J., MALANY, M., and ALEXANDER, M. (1962). The role of deoxyribonucleic acid in ribonucleic acid synthesis. III. The inhibition of the enzymatic synthesis of ribonucleic acid and deoxyribonucleic acid by actinomycin D and proflavin. Proc. Natl. Acad. Sci. U.S. 48, 1222–1229.

JACOB, F., and MONOD, J. (1961). Genetic regulatory mechanisms in the synthesis of proteins. J. Mol. Biol. 3, 318–356.

KIRK, D. L. (1963). In preparation.

LEVINTOW, L., MEISTER, A., KUFF, E., and HOGEBOOM, G. H. (1955). Studies on the relationship between the enzymatic synthesis of glutamine and the glutamyl transfer reaction. J. Am. Chem. Soc. 77, 5304–5308.

LOWRY, O. H., ROSEBROUGH, N. J., FARR, A. L., and RANDALL, R. J. (1951). Protein measurement with the Folin phenol reagent. *J. Biol. Chem.* **193**, 265–275.

MEISTER, A. (1962). Glutamine synthesis. *In* "The Enzymes" (P. D. Boyer, H. Lardy, and K. Myrbäck, eds.), Vol. 6, pp. 443–468. Academic Press, New York.

MOSCONA, A. A., and HUBBY, J. L. (1963). Experimentally induced changes in glutamotransferase activity in embryonic tissue. *Develop. Biol.* **7**, 192–206.

PAMILJANS, V., KRISHNASWAMY, P. R., DUMVILLE, G. D., and MEISTER, A. (1962). Studies on the mechanism of glutamine synthesis; isolation and properties of the enzyme from sheep brain. *Biochemistry* **1**, 153–158.

PAUL, J., and FOTTRELL, P. F. (1963). Mechanism of D-glutamyl transferase repression in mammalian cells. *Biochim. Biophys. Acta* **67**, 334–336.

PIRIE, A. (1956). "Biochemistry of the Eye," pp. 205–231. Blackwell, Oxford.

REICH, E., FRANKLIN, R. M., SHATKIN, A. J., and TATUM, E. L. (1962). Action of actinomycin D on animal cells and viruses. *Proc. Natl. Acad. Sci. U.S.* **48**, 1238–1244.

RUDNICK, D. (1963). Distribution of glutamotransferase activity in the chick retina. *Develop. Biol.* **7**, 94–102.

RUDNICK, D., and WAELSCH, H. (1955). Development of glutamotransferase and glutamine synthetase in the nervous system of the chick. *J. Exptl. Zool.* **129**, 309–326.

TOWER, D. B. (1960). The neurochemistry of asparagine and glutamine. *In* "The Neurochemistry of Nucleotides and Amino Acids" (R. O. Brady and D. B. Tower, eds.), pp. 173–204. Wiley, New York.

WALD, G., and ZUSSMAN, H. (1938). Carotenoids of the chicken retina. *J. Biol. Chem.* **122**, 449–460.

WU, C. (1963). Glutamine synthetase. I. A comparative study of its distribution in animals and its inhibition by DL-*allo*-δ-hydroxylysine. *Comp. Biochem. Physiol.* **8**, 335–351.

Reprinted from SCIENCE, 27 October 1967
Volume 158, pages 496-497

Enzyme Induction by Corticosteroids in Embryonic Cells: Steroid Structure and Inductive Effect

A. A. Moscona
R. Piddington

Abstract. *Glutamine synthetase in the developing retina of the chick embryo can be induced to increase by certain corticosteroids. The inductive effectiveness of various natural corticosteroids has been examined in organ cultures of embryonic retina and correlated with specific groupings on the steroid molecules.*

Glutamine synthetase in the neural retina of the chick has a characteristic and unique developmental pattern that coincides with other aspects of retinal development and provides a quantitative marker of differentiation in this tissue (*1*). This pattern and other aspects of retinal development can be modified by corticosteroids (*2*). In normal embryonic development, glutamine synthetase in the retina begins to increase at a very sharp rate after the 16th day of incubation, during the period of final differentiation and maturation of this tissue; however, glutamine synthetase can be induced to rise at a sharp rate several days ahead of time, in cultures of retina tissue and in the retina in the embryo by treatment with hydrocortisone (*2, 3*). This precocious induction of glutamine synthetase is accompanied by acceleration of other developmental features in the retina; it requires RNA and protein synthesis (*4*) and appears to be specific for this embryonic tissue. Exploratory tests indicated that, in addition to hydrocortisone, other corticosteroids had an inductive effect in this system. We have, therefore, examined the correlations between the molecular structure of various natural adrenal steroids and their effectiveness as inducers of glutamine synthetase in organ cultures of embryonic retina in vitro.

Single, whole retinas from 12-day chick embryos were explanted and cultured in 3 ml of medium in 25-ml erlenmeyer flasks. The culture medium consisted of 20 percent fetal bovine serum in Tyrode's solution, 1 percent penicillin-streptomycin mixture (Microbiological Associates), and 10^{-8} g of steroid per milliliter. Stock suspensions of the steroids were prepared in 1 ml of Tyrode's solution with 0.04 ml of Tween 80; controls did not contain the steroid. A mixture of 5 percent CO_2 in air was passed through the cultures which were then incubated at 38°C on a rotary shaker (70 rev/min). The retinas were harvested after 24 hours in culture and assayed for glutamine synthetase activity (*4*).

The results (Table 1) show that, at the concentration tested, hydrocortisone, corticosterone, and aldosterone are the strongest inducers of glutamine synthetase in the embryonic retina. These three steroids have in common the 11β-hydroxyl group and the 17β-side chain with the 20-ketone and the 21-hydroxyl groups. The activity of the strongest inducers was not appreciably lowered by esterification of the 21-hydroxyl group with phosphoric acid. Molecules with a methyl group in the 21-position (11β-hydroxyprogesterone and 11β,17α-dihydroxyprogesterone)

had intermediate activities. On the other hand, molecules without hydroxyl on carbon 11 or with the 11-hydroxyl in the α-configuration had only a very slight or no effect. In addition to the steroids listed in Table 1, 11α-hydrocortisone was also tested (10^{-8} g per ml) and was essentially ineffective (5 percent increase in glutamine synthetase activity); this is in marked contrast to the high effectiveness of the natural, 11β-hydrocortisone. All of this suggests that the 11β-position is of primary significance in the activity of these molecules in inducing retinal glutamine synthetase in this system. This conclusion is further supported by the fact that cortisone, which has a ketone group in the 11-position, had no effect under these conditions.

While the detailed mechanisms whereby these corticosteroids exert an inductive effect on glutamine synthetase in the embryonic retina and enhance the developmental program of this tissue remain to be determined, it is of interest that the steroid molecules which are strong inducers in this system also have a high glucocorticoid activity (*5*). The significance of this remarkably close correlation to the differential effects of these steroids on protein synthesis in various embryonic and adult tissues (*6*) is unknown. Evidence from other systems (*7*) suggests that the function of these molecules involves their association with specific receptors on or in the target cells, and subsequent effects on translative and transcriptive processes (*6*). If the specific inductive effect of the corticosteroids on the glu-

Table 1. Effect of different adrenal steroids on glutamine synthetase (GS) activities in cultured embryonic retina. Numbers in parentheses indicate the number of assays.

Structural formula	Steroid (10^{-8} g/ml)	Specific activity (12-day retina cultured for 24 hr)	Increase in GS activity (%)
	Control	$0.95 \pm .28$ (12)	
	Cholesterol	$0.84 \pm .05$ (2)	
	Pregnenolone	$0.86 \pm .03$ (2)	
	Progesterone	$0.97 \pm .12$ (4)	2.0
	Deoxycorticosterone	$1.22 \pm .28$ (4)	28.4
	11-Deoxycortisol	$1.16 \pm .15$ (4)	22.1
	17α-Hydroxyprogesterone	$0.84 \pm .19$ (4)	
	11α-Hydroxyprogesterone	$1.39 \pm .14$ (4)	46.3
	11β-Hydroxyprogesterone	$2.62 \pm .10$ (3)	175.7
	11β,17α-Dihydroxy-progesterone	$3.59 \pm .16$ (3)	277.8
	Aldosterone	$4.34 \pm .08$ (2)	356.8
	Corticosterone	$4.36 \pm .30$ (4)	358.9
	Hydrocortisone	$5.06 \pm .89$ (4)	432.6
	Cortisone	$0.94 \pm .18$ (4)	

tamine synthetase system in the embryonic retina depends initially on specific interactions with retinal receptors, our data suggest that the position and orientation of the 11β-hydroxyl group is critical for the specificity of these interactions and that the 21-position has a secondary role in this sequence. However, the possibility also exists that one of these positions is more important for interactions with receptors, while the other is more closely involved in the regulation of biosynthetic processes relevant to the sequence of induction in these cells (4).

The present system lends itself well to detailed studies of these problems with respect to the mechanism of induction in embryonic cells. It provides a rather unique correlation between the structural, chemical, and physiological properties of an inducer molecule and its effect on the development of an enzyme characteristic of differentiation in a well-defined population of embryonic cells. Of added interest is the possibility that induction in vitro of glutamine synthetase in the embryonic retina may offer a sensitive and practical bioassay system for testing glucocorticoid activity of various steroids (8).

A. A. MOSCONA
R. PIDDINGTON
Department of Zoology, University of Chicago, Chicago, Illinois

References and Notes

1. A. A. Moscona and J. L. Hubby, *Develop. Biol.* **7**, 192 (1963); R. Piddington and A. A. Moscona, *J. Cell Biol.* **27**, 246 (1965).
2. A. A. Moscona and R. Piddington, *Biochim. Biophys. Acta* **121**, 409 (1966); R. Piddington, *Develop. Biol.*, in press.
3. R. Piddington and A. A. Moscona, *Biochim. Biophys. Acta*, in press.
4. D. L. Kirk and A. A. Moscona, *Develop. Biol.* **8**, 341 (1963); A. A. Moscona and D. L. Kirk, *Science* **148**, 519 (1965); D. L. Kirk, *Proc. Nat. Acad. Sci. U.S.* **54**, 1345 (1965).
5. J. Fried and A. Borman, *Vitamins and Hormones* **16**, 303 (1958).
6. F. Moog, in *The Biochemistry of Animal Development*, R. Weber, Ed. (Academic Press, New York, 1965), vol. 1, p. 307; P. Feigelson, M. Feigelson, O. Greengard, *Recent Prog. Hormone Res.* **18**, 491 (1962); L. D. Garren, R. R. Howell, G. M. Tomkins, R. M. Crocco, *Proc. Nat. Acad. Sci. U.S.* **52**, 1124 (1964); E. H. Davidson, *Sci. Amer.* **212**, 36 (1965); C. Kidson, *Biochem. Biophys. Res. Commun.* **21**, 283 (1965); E. B. Thompson, G. M. Tomkins, J. F. Curren, *Proc. Nat. Acad. Sci. U.S.* **56**, 296 (1966)
7. I. E. Bush, *Pharmacol. Rev.* **14**, 317 (1962).
8. Research supported by grants from USPHS, Institute for Child Health and Human Development (HD-01253), and from NSF (G-23852). We acknowledge the assistance of N. Saenz and M. Gundersen. We thank Dr. W. J. Cole, Abbott Laboratories, and Dr. P. W. O'Connell, Upjohn Company, for gifts of steroids, and Dr J. Fried of the University of Chicago for counsel and discussion.

7 August 1967

Reprinted from the Proceedings of the National Academy of Sciences
Vol. 61, No. 1, pp. 160–167, September, 1968.

ENZYME INDUCTION IN EMBRYONIC RETINA: THE ROLE OF TRANSCRIPTION AND TRANSLATION*

By A. A. Moscona, M. H. Moscona, and N. Saenz

DEPARTMENT OF BIOLOGY, UNIVERSITY OF CHICAGO

Communicated by Dwight J. Ingle, June 21, 1968

The mechanisms of induction in embryonic cells and of the timing and stability of phenotypic changes are of major importance to the understanding of differentiation. Detailed studies of these problems have been hindered by the scarcity of suitable experimental systems. What is required is an embryonic tissue in which a chemically defined inducer promptly elicits a specific, measurable response characteristic of differentiation. The induction of glutamine synthetase in embryonic neural retina meets these requirements. The normal developmental pattern of this enzyme is representative of the progress of retinal differentiation and provides a quantitative indicator of this process; moreover, this pattern can be significantly modified by defined experimental conditions.

Glutamine synthetase activity (GS) in the embryonic chick neural retina follows a characteristic developmental pattern that is typical for this tissue and is temporally and spatially correlated with other aspects of retinal development.[1-4] During early embryonic development, GS activity in the retina increases at a slow rate, then rises very sharply after the sixteenth day during the period of rapid functional differentiation and maturation of the retina. Particularly important is the fact that the rapid rise of GS activity can be induced precociously, several days before the normal time, in cultures of embryonic retina with 11β-hydroxycorticosteroids (hydrocortisone, aldosterone, or corticosterone).[5, 6] A similar precocious induction of retinal GS can be elicited also in embryos by injecting one of these steroids. Induction of GS by steroids is specific for the embryonic neural retina; it does not involve cell proliferation and therefore is not due to differential growth. The induced rise in GS activity is accompanied or followed by additional developmental changes which normally occur later in development;[2, 7, 8] thus, it is not an isolated response but one of a number of phenotypic changes accelerated by the steroid inducer. Since changes in retinal GS activity are an essential aspect of differentiation, the mode of regulation of GS activity is relevant to the mechanisms that control differentiation in this tissue.

Previous work on control mechanisms in this system was limited to long-term cultures of the retina;[4, 9-12] however, the enzyme begins to rise very shortly after exposure of the tissue to the inducer.[13] The present report is concerned with an analysis of the processes that control the early phases of the induction of retinal GS by steroid (hydrocortisone).

Materials and Methods.—Organ cultures of retina: Standard procedures for the isolation and cultivation of embryonic chick neural retina in flask organ cultures were described before.[3-7] In this study, retina tissue from 12-day chick embryos was used. Each culture contained one whole retina (approximately 10^8 cells; 2.5 mg protein) in 3 ml of culture medium in a 25-ml Erlenmeyer flask; the flasks were rotated (70 rpm) at 38°C on a gyratory shaker. The cultures were maintained for various times, as described, up to 24 hr. The medium was 80% Eagle's medium (without glutamine) with 20% fetal bovine serum and 1% penicillin-streptomycin mixture (5000 units each/ml) (Microbiological Associates). To induce retinal GS, 3×10^{-6} gm/flask hydrocortisone (free alcohol) in Tyrode's solution was added to the culture medium.[5, 6]   Radioactive materials were added in sterile, neutral salt solution.   All the cultures were gassed with 5% CO_2-air mixture.

Enzyme assay: The activity of glutamine synthetase was determined by a modified glutamyl-transferase reaction[14] described in detail previously.[1, 3, 4]   Tissue samples were sonicated in 0.01 M phosphate buffer (pH 7.1) and frozen or lyophilized, then stored at $-20°$ or assayed immediately.   Protein was determined by the method of Lowry *et al.*[15] GS specific activity was calculated as micromoles of glutamylhydroxamate formed per hour per milligram of tissue protein.   Since the total protein content of the retina in culture did not change appreciably in 24 hr, changes in the specific activity of the enzyme are a measure of changes in total GS activity.

Radioactive tracer methods: The concentration of H^3-uridine (25,500 mC/mM) was 1 μc/3 ml of culture medium.   After incubation the tissue was washed three times with Tyrode's solution and sonicated in 0.01 M phosphate buffer, pH 7.1 (1–2 ml/retina).   Portions of the sonicate (0.05–0.1 ml) were placed on 25 mm Whatman GF/A glass fiber disks, dried, and counted (see below) to determine the total uptake of the label into the tissue.   To measure the incorporation of this label, the dried disks were treated with cold 10% trichloroacetic acid (TCA) and then washed with 5% TCA, ethanol-ether, and ether, according to standard procedure.   The dry disks were placed in vials with a mixture of PPO-POPOP (Spectrafluor; Nuclear-Chicago) in toluene and counted in a Nuclear-Chicago Mark I liquid scintillation counter.   Other portions of the same sample (0.1–0.2 ml) were used for protein and GS activity determinations.

For measuring amino acid incorporation 1 or 2 μc of a mixture of 15 amino acids (~1 mc/mg; New England Nuclear) was added to 3 ml of culture medium.   The cultures were harvested and sonicated, and portions of the sonicate were placed on disks, as described above.   After treatment with cold TCA, the disks were heated in 5% TCA for 30 min at 90°C and then washed, dried, and counted as above.   Other portions of the same sample were used for measurements of the total uptake of the label into the tissue and for protein and GS determinations.

Results.—Induction of GS in organ cultures of embryonic retina: When retina tissue from 12-day chick embryos was cultured at 37°C in medium with hydrocortisone, there was a 1.5–2-hour "lag period," after which GS activity increased rapidly[13] (Fig. 1).   In the absence of the steroid there was only a slight increase of GS activity in 24 hours, similar to that which takes place normally in embryonic retina during the corresponding period.   The retina of the 12-day embryo con-

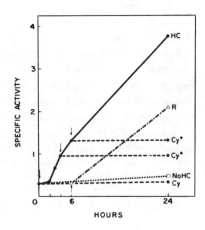

Fig. 1.—Kinetics of induction of GS activity in cultures of embryonic retina tissue by *HC* (hydrocortisone; 8.2×10^{-7} M) and its inhibition by cycloheximide. All cultures were with inducer except the one marked *NoHC*. Arrows pointing down mark the addition times of cycloheximide (*Cy*) (2 μg/ml) to cultures with inducer. Arrow pointing up marks transfer of tissue from medium with inducer and cycloheximide to inducing medium without the inhibitor (*R*). Similar effects were obtained with puromycin. These data represent averages from one set of experiments; the absolute values varied somewhat in different experiments. Star indicates that the same values were obtained when cultures were transferred from medium with inducer to inducer-free medium with cycloheximide.

tains very few dividing cells, and there was no measurable increase in cell number either in induced or in control cultures. Hydrocortisone did not change the total uptake or incorporation into proteins of C^{14}-amino acids. Therefore, induction by the steroid is not accompanied by any gross changes in the cellular composition of this tissue or in its over-all protein synthesis.

Requirement for protein synthesis: The induction of retinal GS was blocked by inhibiting protein synthesis. Cycloheximide, 2–5 μg/ml, added to the culture medium at the beginning of incubation inhibited 90–100 per cent of the incorporation of C^{14}-amino acids; these concentrations of the inhibitor also completely prevented GS induction (Fig. 1). Similar effects were obtained with puromycin (2–5 μg/ml). Furthermore, addition of cycloheximide at any time after GS activity began to rise stopped further increases (Fig. 1). These inhibitions could be partially reversed by washing the tissue and transferring it into inducing medium without the inhibitor. Cycloheximide caused no decrease in incorporation of H^3-uridine into RNA. Therefore, protein synthesis is essential for the initial and the continued increase in GS activity. These results and conclusion agree with findings obtained in long-term cultures of the retina[4, 9, 10, 12, 13] and suggest that the induced increase in GS activity is the result of synthesis of enzyme protein; however, other possibilities are not excluded, for example, the synthesis of proteins which regulate GS synthesis or activity.

The level of GS activity attained at the time of cycloheximide addition did not decrease rapidly in the presence of the inhibitor (Fig. 1) and, under these conditions the enzyme had a half life longer than 20 hours. The stability of GS in the presence of cycloheximide was not dependent on the simultaneous presence of the steroid inducer in the culture medium; in cultures transferred after four or six hours from inducing medium into inducer-free medium with cycloheximide, GS activity leveled off but did not decline appreciably (Fig. 1). It remains to be determined if the stability of GS under these conditions depends on the intracellular pool of inducer that might have accumulated in the cells in the first four hours.[13]

RNA synthesis and GS induction: Actinomycin D (Act D) added at the beginning of incubation to cultures in inducing medium at concentrations from 0.2 to 10 μg/ml blocked H^3-uridine incorporation into RNA by 75–99 per cent and completely prevented GS induction (Fig. 2); 0.2 μg/ml Act D was a borderline concentration that occasionally allowed some increase in GS activity. Therefore, RNA synthesis is essential for the induction of GS by hydrocortisone. We next sought to determine whether the increase in GS activity was continuously dependent on new RNA synthesis. Act D (10 μg/ml) was added to cultures at various times between zero and six hours; enzyme activities were measured over a period of 24 hours. The results (Fig. 2) showed that in the first three to four hours of cultivation the induction of GS became progressively less dependent on new RNA synthesis; if RNA synthesis was blocked after four hours, GS activity continued to rise to values close to those of the controls. Act D (10 μg/ml) added at four hours blocked H^3-uridine incorporation as efficiently as at zero hours (Table 1). Thus, the later Act D was added between zero and four hours, the greater was the subsequent increase of GS activity; this suggests that in the first

Fig. 2.—Effects of Act D (10 μg/ml) added at various times on the induced increase in GS specific activity. All cultures (except control—*No HC*) were with the inducer (*HC*). Act D was added at the times listed on the right, next to the specific activity values at 24 hr. In this series of experiments, the results for 3, 4, 5, and 6 hr were below the control (*HC*) average but fell within the general range of control values. The absolute values varied somewhat in different experiments.

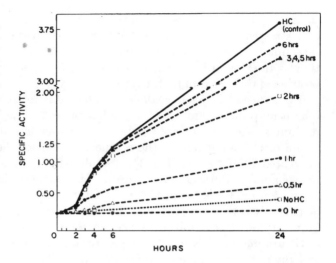

four hours of induction there is an accumulation in the cells of relatively stable RNA which mediates the increase of GS activity either directly, as templates for enzyme synthesis, or indirectly by controlling the rate of translational processes. If the increase in GS activity is the result of enzyme synthesis, then the RNA templates for this enzyme are relatively stable and after four hours of induction can continue to function under these conditions for at least 20 hours independently of further transcription.

Transcription-independent increase of GS activity requires protein synthesis: Actinomycin D (10 μg/ml) added to cultures after four hours of induction inhibited incorporation of amino acid into protein during the first hour by approximately 20 per cent, compared with controls without the antibiotic (findings to be published); thus, protein synthesis continues in these cultures in the absence of RNA synthesis, presumably on stable messenger RNA. We sought to determine whether the continued increase of GS activity in the absence of RNA synthesis required protein synthesis. Cycloheximide (2 μg/ml) and Act D (10 μg/ml) were added after four hours to cultures in medium with the steroid inducer. The effect of cycloheximide was monitored by measuring the incorporation of C^{14}-amino acids into proteins and by determinations of GS activity at the end of the 24-hour culture period. There was no increase in GS activity in cultures with cycloheximide (Fig. 3). Thus, at the time when transcription was no longer required for the increase in GS activity, protein synthesis continued to be essential. This supports the possibility that the accumulation of GS activity in the absence of transcription may also be due to enzyme synthesis or require the synthesis of other proteins involved in this process, or both.

Transition to independence from transcription does not require protein synthesis: As shown above, RNA synthesis is essential in the initial phases of GS induction, but after four hours GS activity can continue to increase in the absence of further transcription. We next sought to determine whether during those first four hours continuous protein synthesis was required in order that the increase might become independent of RNA synthesis. Cycloheximide (2 μg/ml) was added at the beginning of incubation to cultures in medium with the steroid inducers. After four hours the tissues were washed free of cycloheximide, transferred to new medium with inducer and with Act D (10 μg/ml), and incubated for the remainder of the 24-hour culture period. Controls were without Act D. The results (Fig. 3) showed that GS activity increased in each case after removal of cycloheximide. Therefore, continuous protein synthesis during the first four hours of induction is not essential for causing the rise in GS activity to become potentially independent of further transcription. Since RNA synthesis is essential, the conclusion that this independence is due to accumulation of stable RNA during the first four hours of induction seems inevitable. Furthermore, these results indicate that the function of the steroid inducer in this system is not dependent on continuous protein synthesis and that it affects, directly or indirectly, transcriptional processes.

The increase of GS activity after four hours of induction in the absence of transcription does not depend on the presence of the steroid inducer in the culture medium. Retinas maintained for four hours in medium with hydrocortisone were washed as much as possible to reduce the external pool of the steroid; they were divided into two groups and transferred to the following media: (1) with inducer and Act D (10 μg/ml); (2) without inducer, with Act D. At the end of the 24-hour culture period, GS activity was measured (Fig. 3). GS activity continued to rise in the absence, as well as in the presence, of the inducer in the culture medium. Therefore, the transcription-independent increase in GS activity in the presence of Act D does not require a continuous supply of exogenous inducer and is, therefore, due to the internal pool of steroid that accumulates earlier in the cells, to the effects of the steroid during the initial phases of induction, or to Act D which at this concentration may exert effects that in their final outcome equal those of the inducer.

Effect of a low dose of Act D at four hours: Act D (0.2 μg/ml) was added to cultures in medium with the steroid inducer four hours after the start of incubation;

TABLE 1. *Effect of different concentrations of Act D* on incorporation of H^3-uridine into RNA and on the increase of GS specific activity.*

Act D added at:	Dose of Act D (μg/ml)	Dpm/mg protein	Inhibition of H^3-uridine incorporation (%)	GS specific activity at 24 hr
—	—	72,573	—	3.84–5.14
0 hr	10.0	660	99.10	0.28–0.30
"	2.0	2,040	97.19	0.23–0.32
"	0.6	15,200	79.06	0.27–0.55
"	0.2	18,420	74.62	0.48–1.00
—	—	65,473	—	4.00–6.00
4 hr	10.0	433	99.34	3.00–6.14
"	2.0	4,406	93.28	2.05–2.00
"	0.6	14,720	77.52	1.79–2.21
"	0.2	27,113	58.59	1.03–2.20

H^3-uridine (1 μc/3 ml medium) was added 0.5 hr after addition of Act D; the cultures were harvested and processed 1 hr later. The range of GS specific activities at 0 hr is 0.21–0.34; after 4 hr in inducing medium, the range is 0.80–1.21.
   * Added at 0 or 4 hr to cultures with inducer.

GS activity was assayed at the end of the 24-hour culture period (Fig. 4). In marked contrast to the noninhibitory effect of the higher concentration of Act D added at the same time, 0.2 µg/ml suppressed further increase in GS activity by 70–90 per cent. Measurements of uridine incorporation showed that 0.2 µg of Act D/ml was less effective in inhibiting RNA synthesis than 10 µg/ml was (Table 1). Therefore, after four hours of induction complete inhibition of transcription does not interfere with the continued increase in GS activity, whereas partial inhibition of RNA synthesis does. An explanation for these seemingly paradoxical results is suggested below.

Discussion and Summary.—A simple explanation of these findings requires the assumption that the induced increase in GS activity is the result of enzyme synthesis and accumulation; it applies to the possibilities that the induction involves either an increase in the rate of GS synthesis or a decrease in its rate of degradation. This assumption is supported by the observations that the increase in GS activity requires at all times continuous protein synthesis; however, its confirmation must await data from immunological precipitation of radioactively labeled enzyme. Granted the assumption of enzyme synthesis, we suggest that the following sequence of events may be involved in the induction of retinal GS:

(a) Synthesis of RNA is required for GS induction by the steroid. Tran-

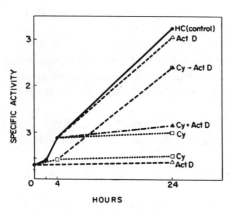

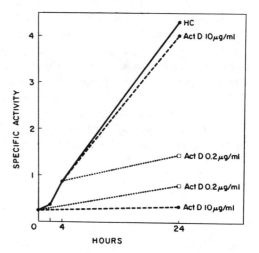

FIG. 3.—Summary of results showing that (1) after 4 hr of induction GS activity continues to increase although RNA synthesis is halted (10 µg/ml Act D); (2) inhibition of protein synthesis by cycloheximide (2 µg/ml) during the first 4 hr of induction does not prevent the subsequent transcription-independent rise in GS activity; (3) protein synthesis is essential for the transcription-independent increase of GS activity after 4 hr. All cultures were in medium with inducer. *HC* (*control*), cycloheximide (*Cy*) was added at 0 or 4 hr, as indicated. *Cy → Act D*, GS activity in cultures transferred after 4 hr in cycloheximide into medium with Act D.

FIG. 4.—Reverse effects of high and low doses of Act D on the increase of GS activity when the inhibitors were added to cultures at 0 or 4 hr. All cultures were in medium with the steroid inducer. (Table 1 shows the inhibition of H³-uridine incorporation under these conditions.) Added to the cultures at 0 hr, both doses of Act D inhibited GS induction; the lower dose sometimes inhibited incompletely, as in the experiments represented here. Added at 4 hr, the high dose was not inhibitory, whereas the low dose suppressed approximately 70–90% of GS increase, compared with control cultures.

scription in the initial phases of induction leads to the accumulation of stable RNA that is essential for the increase of GS. The evidence suggests that the steroid affects, directly or indirectly, transcriptive processes; it may initiate the synthesis of new transcripts or modify the rate of existing transcription.

(b)   The effects of the high and low concentrations of Act D suggest that the synthesis of GS after four hours of induction (and possibly earlier) is subject to control by two endogenous regulators, both of which are RNA or require RNA synthesis and have different susceptibilities to Act D: (1) A translational *repressor* of GS synthesis (or degrader of GS, if GS induction is due to a decrease in its rate of degradation) with its formation blocked by a high, but not by a low, concentration of Act D; and (2) a *derepressor*, which counteracts the translational repressor, with its formation suppressed by a low dose of Act D. Thus, the blocking of all RNA synthesis in four-hour cultures by a high dose of Act D stops also the transcription of the repressor (degrader) RNA and allows the continued increase of GS because by that time the RNA species directly involved in enzyme synthesis has already accumulated and can function in the absence of further transcription. On the other hand, a low dose of Act D does not stop the synthesis of the repressor (degrader) RNA but blocks the synthesis of the derepressor RNA and thus decreases the accumulation of GS. Thus, the persistent need for the derepressor RNA under normal conditions is masked by the repressor RNA-blocking effect of the high dose of Act D.

The continued increase of the induced GS when all transcription is stopped recalls similar observations in other eukaryont cells in which protein synthesis can go on after arrest of RNA synthesis.[10, 12, 16-23] However, the significant and distinct point that emerges from our data is that, under normal conditions the GS system does not actually cease to be under genomic control, in that the continued increase in GS activity after four hours remains dependent on transcription of the postulated derepressor RNA. Thus, in reality, the accumulation of GS appears to be continuously controlled through transcription-dependent processes. Whether this control circuitry persists in later stages of retinal development remains to be determined.

It was suggested above that the steroid inducer may be directly or indirectly responsible, during the initial four hours, for the formation of RNA required for the increase of GS. This may be messenger RNA (mRNA) for GS, as suggested by Reif-Lehrer and Amos.[12] However, there are other possibilities. For example, mRNA for GS may be present in these cells at the time of induction, but it may not be active or it may function at a low rate; thus, induction could be primarily an increase in the translational efficiency of pre-existing GS templates through provision of RNA species that are limiting (transfer or ribosomal RNA). In the first four hours of induction, sufficient GS templates become activated or accumulate *de novo*, and GS formation can then continue without further transcription of the RNA species that function directly in the synthesis of the enzyme; however, its rate of synthesis or accumulation remains indirectly subject to genomic control through the dual effects of the translational controllers, as discussed above.

The above interpretation is, in general, consistent with the original models of

Jacob and Monod in which translational as well as transcriptional controls were envisaged.[24]   The possible role of translational repressors in the control of inducible enzymes has been postulated for tryptophan pyrrolase and tyrosine transaminase in rat liver[19] and for tyrosine transaminase in cultured Morris hepatoma cells.[20]   Control at the level of translation and the activation of pre-existing RNA templates have been suggested for postfertilization protein synthesis in sea-urchin eggs,[25–27] for hemoglobin synthesis,[28] for the increased protein synthesis by ribosomes from insulin-treated muscle,[29] and for other systems.[30]   We are aware of alternative interpretations for the facts described here, possibly along the concepts proposed for other systems by Monod *et al.*[31]   Our present interpretations are intended primarily as working guidelines; their testing should help in clarifying further the regulatory events involved in the induction of GS in the embryonic retina and might provide more detailed insights into the mechanisms of differentiation in other embryonic cells.

We thank Dr. D. L. Kirk for advice in technical matters, and Mrs. M. Gundersen for competent and invaluable assistance.   We also thank Drs. Ira Wool and E. Goldwasser for reviewing the manuscript.

* This investigation was supported by research grants from the National Science Foundation (G-23852) and Institute of Child Health and Human Development, USPHS (HD-01253).

[1] Rudnick, D., and H. Waelsch, *J. Exptl. Zool.*, **129**, 309 (1955).
[2] Piddington, R., and A. A. Moscona, *J. Cell Biol.*, **27**, 247 (1965).
[3] Moscona, A. A., and J. L. Hubby, *Develop. Biol.*, **7**, 192 (1963).
[4] Kirk, D. L., and A. A. Moscona, *Develop. Biol.*, **8**, 341 (1963).
[5] Moscona, A. A., and R. Piddington, *Biochim. Biophys. Acta*, **121**, 409 (1966).
[6] Moscona, A. A., and R. Piddington, *Science*, **158**, 496 (1967).
[7] Piddington, R., *Develop. Biol.*, **16**, 168 (1967).
[8] Piddington, R., and A. A. Moscona, *Biochim. Biophys. Acta*, **141**, 429 (1967).
[9] Moscona, A. A., and D. L. Kirk, *Science*, **148**, 519 (1965).
[10] Kirk, D. L., these PROCEEDINGS, **54**, 1345 (1965).
[11] Reif, L., and H. Amos, *Biochem. Biophys. Res. Commun.*, **23**, 39 (1966).
[12] Reif-Lehrer, L., and H. Amos, *Biochem. J.*, **106**, 425 (1968).
[13] Moscona, A. A., N. Saenz, and M. H. Moscona, *Exptl. Cell Res.*, **48**, 646 (1967).
[14] Meister, A., *The Enzymes*, **6**, 443 (1962).
[15] Lowry, O. H., N. J. Rosebrough, A. L. Farr, and R. J. Randall, *J. Biol. Chem.*, **193**, 265 (1951).
[16] Reich, E., R. M. Franklin, A. J. Shatkin, and E. L. Tatum, these PROCEEDINGS, **48**, 1238 (1962).
[17] Scott, R. B., and E. Bell, *Science*, **145**, 711 (1964).
[18] Brachet, J., H. Denis, and F. de Vitry, *Develop. Biol.*, **9**, 398 (1964).
[19] Garren, L. D., R. R. Howell, G. M. Tomkins, and R. M. Crocco, these PROCEEDINGS, **52**, 1121 (1964).
[20] Tomkins, G. M., E. B. Thompson, S. Hayashi, T. Gelehrter, D. Granner, and B. Peterkofsky, in *Cold Spring Harbor Symposia on Quantitative Biology*, vol. 31 (1966), p. 349.
[21] Sussman, M., *Current Topics Develop. Biol.*, **1**, 61 (1966).
[22] Eliasson, E. E., *Biochem. Biophys. Res. Commun.*, **27**, 661 (1967).
[23] Gross, P. R., *Current Topics Develop. Biol.*, **2**, 1 (1967).
[24] Jacob, F., and J. Monod, *J. Mol. Biol.*, **3**, 318 (1961).
[25] Monroy, A., R. Maggio, and A. M. Rinaldi, these PROCEEDINGS, **54**, 107 (1965).
[26] Slater, D. W., and S. Spiegelman, these PROCEEDINGS, **56**, 164 (1966).
[27] Spirin, A. S., *Current Topics Develop. Biol.*, **1**, 2 (1966).
[28] Colombo, B., and C. Baglioni, *J. Mol. Biol.*, **16**, 51 (1966).
[29] Wool, I. G., and K. Kurihara, these PROCEEDINGS, **58**, 2401 (1967).
[30] Cline, A. L., and R. M. Bock, in *Cold Spring Harbor Symposia on Quantitative Biology*, vol. 31 (1966), p. 321.
[31] Monod, J., J. Wyman, and J.-P. Changeux, *J. Mol. Biol.*, **12**, 88 (1965).

HORMONAL CONTROL OF ENZYME SYNTHESIS
IN BARLEY ENDOSPERM*

BY J. E. VARNER AND G. RAM CHANDRA

RIAS, BALTIMORE

Communicated by James Bonner, May 4, 1964

The activities of several enzymes of isolated barley endosperm increase markedly in response to added gibberellic acid.[1-6] In the normal, intact germinating seed, evocation of these same enzymatic activities in the endosperm is caused by the embryo which is known to produce gibberellic acid.[7,8] We have, in the present case then, an example of hormonally regulated enzymatic activity and one with which it is particularly convenient to work since the principle enzyme involved is α-amylase. We shall show below that the gibberellic acid-dependent increase in α-amylase activity in barley endosperm is due to *de novo* synthesis of the enzyme. Thus, when isolated barley endosperm is treated with gibberellic acid in the presence of C^{14}-labeled amino acids and the α-amylase subsequently isolated, it is found to contain label.

We shall further show that the α-amylase produced in response to application of gibberellic acid is identical with that synthesized by the normally germinating seedling. Finally, we shall show that the gibberellic acid-induced synthesis of α-amylase is suppressed in the presence of actinomycin D, and that the effect of gibberellic acid is therefore upon the expression of the genetic information which controls α-amylase production.

Materials and Methods.—Dry barley seeds (*Hordeum vulgare*, var. Himalaya) were cut in half along their equatorial axes and the embryo halves discarded.   The endosperm halves were soaked in 1% sodium hypochlorite for 15–20 min, rinsed in sterile distilled water, and transferred aseptically to sterile moist sand contained in Petri dishes.   After incubation for 3 days at 17–23°, ten

Reprinted by permission of the authors and the National Academy of Sciences from PROCEEDINGS OF THE NATIONAL ACADEMY OF SCIENCES, 52, 100–106 (1964).

half-seeds were transferred to an aseptic 25-ml Erlenmeyer flask containing 2.0 ml of 0.001 M sodium acetate buffer (pH 4.8) and the appropriate treatment solution. Such flasks were shaken at top speed at 25° on a Dubnoff metabolic shaker during the incubation period. The medium was then poured off, and the half-seeds were rinsed once with 3.0 ml distilled water. They were next ground in a mortar with sand and 5.0 ml 0.001 M acetate buffer (pH 4.8). The homogenate was then centrifuged at 1000 × g. The resultant supernatant (extract) and the incubation medium were next assayed separately for α-amylase activity by the method of Shuster and Gifford.[9] The assay was calibrated by use of crystalline α-amylase prepared according to Schwimmer and Balls.[10]

Labeled, gibberellic acid-induced α-amylase for fingerprinting was prepared as follows: twenty preincubated half-seeds were aseptically transferred to an aseptic 25-ml Erlenmeyer flask which contained 1.0 ml of 0.001 M acetate buffer (pH 4.8), 10^{-6} M gibberellic acid, and 20 μc of L-threonine-C[14]. After 24 hr incubation at 25°, the medium contained 400 μg of α-amylase. The medium was poured off, and the half-seeds were rinsed twice with 1.0-ml portions of water. Authentic carrier α-amylase (4.5 mg) was added to the combined medium and washings.

Calcium chloride was added to a final concentration of 0.003 M and the solution adjusted to pH 7.0. The solution was then heated at 70° for 20 min, centrifuged, and the precipitate discarded. Carrier L-threonine (0.01 M) was added and enough absolute alcohol added to make the solution 40% with respect to ethanol. After 10 min the solution was centrifuged and the precipitate discarded. Glycogen (0.2 ml of a 1.6% solution[11]) was added and after 10 min the precipitate recovered by centrifugation. The glycogen-α-amylase precipitate was washed once with 2.0 ml of 40% ethanol and taken up in 1.0 ml of H_2O. The solution of the glycogen-α-amylase complex was incubated at 25° for 1 hr to digest the glycogen then dialyzed overnight against 0.01 M L-threonine.

The labeled α-amylase preparation was heated to 95° for 5 min and ammonium carbonate added to a final concentration of 0.01 M, and incubated at 20° for 18 hr with 20 μg of trypsin. After freeze-drying and sublimation of the ammonium carbonate, the hydrolysate was separated into its component peptides by chromatography and electrophoresis.[14]

The α-amylase is produced by the aleurone layer of the seed. Dissection of half-seeds into aleurone layers (plus testa-pericarp) and starchy endosperm was performed after the 3-day preincubation period.

Labeled amino acids (L-threonine-u-C[14] and L-phenylalanine-u-C[14]) were purchased from the New England Nuclear Corporation, Boston. The actinomycin D was a gift from Dr. Clement A. Stone of the Merck Institute for Therapeutic Research, West Point, Pa. The 5-bromouracil, 6-azaguanine, and 8-azaadenine were purchased from California Corporation for Biochemical Research, Bethesda, Md.

Crystalline trypsin was obtained from the Worthington Biochemical Corporation, Freehold, N. J.

The rabbit liver glycogen was purchased from Nutritional Biochemicals, Cleveland, Ohio, and further purified as described by Loyter and Schramm.[11] Barley malt α-amylase for use as standard and carrier was purified and crystallized by the method of Loyter and Schramm[11] and of Schwimmer and Balls.[10] The two methods yielded α-amylase of identical specific (enzymatic) activities. The incorporation of labeled amino acids into protein was determined by addition to the extract of 10% trichloroacetic acid containing 0.01 M carrier amino acid. The precipitate was filtered on a membrane filter (Schleicher and Shuell, B-6) and washed with 10% trichloroacetic acid. Radioactivity was measured with a Nuclear-Chicago gas-flow (D-47) detector.

Results.—The time course of the development of α-amylase activity in half-seeds and in isolated aleurone layers in response to added gibberellic acid is given in Figure 1. There is a lag period of 9–15 hr after addition of gibberellic acid before the maximum rate of production of α-amylase is attained. Production of the enzyme ceases suddenly about 33 hr after addition of the hormone. The bulk of the α-amylase produced is released into the medium surrounding the tissue. Although isolated aleurone layers do not produce as much α-amylase as intact half-seeds, we believe that this is a matter of nutrition. The addition of phosphate ions, calcium ions, magnesium ions and glucose, and amino acids increases the quantity of α-amylase produced by isolated aleurone layers.

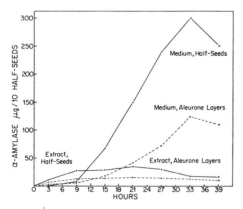

FIG. 1.—Time course for the development of α-amylase activity in half-seeds and in isolated aleurone layers. The fresh weight of ten half-aleurone layers (plus testa-pericarp) is 168 mg. The gibberellic acid ($10^{-6}\,M$) was added at 0 time.

It is clear that the aleurone cells are able to incorporate labeled amino acids into protein in the absence of added gibberellic acid (Table 1). This fact, together with the knowledge that there is no increase in respiration preceding or paralleling α-amylase formation,[12] and that there is no qualitative change in the pattern of $P^{32}O_4$ incorporation into acid-soluble compounds[12] following the addition of gibberellic acid, allows us to conclude that the energy apparatus and the materials for protein synthesis are at hand before the addition of gibberellic acid. It is, therefore, the function of gibberellic acid to influence the synthesis of certain specific proteins. A further examination of Table 1 shows that the total label of amino acid incorporated into protein decreased in half-seeds incubated with gibberellic acid. This is the result of a gibberellic acid-dependent increase in proteolytic activity[13] which causes the release within the tissue of relatively large quantities of free amino acids.[4] The increase in level of free amino acids in turn dilutes out the label added and makes it impossible to determine readily the amount of protein synthesized in the gibberellic acid-treated half-seeds. Inhibitors of protein synthesis prevent the gibberellic acid-induced increase in proteolytic activity.[12] It is, therefore, likely that the protease is also produced by *de novo* synthesis. For the present discussion, it is sufficient to observe (Table 1) the marked difference in the distribution of the labeled protein between medium and extract in the gibberellic acid-treated and -untreated half-seeds, and the rough parallel between the release of α-amylase into the medium and the release of labeled proteins into the medium. In the absence of gibberellic acid, about 5 per cent of the newly synthesized, i.e., labeled, protein is released into the medium during a 30-hr incubation period. In the presence of gibberellic acid, about 50 per cent of the newly synthesized protein is released into the medium.

TABLE 1

L-PHENYLALANINE-C14 INCORPORATION INTO PROTEIN *in vivo*

Hours		——Minus Gibberellic Acid——			—— Plus Gibberellic Acid ——		
		Radioactivity, in protein, cpm	% Labeled protein precipitated by heating	α-Amylase, μg	Radioactivity in protein, cpm	% Labeled protein precipitated by heating	α-Amylase, μg
10	Medium	16	0	3	41	0	19
	Extract	640	74	<20	480	79	28
20	Medium	92	2	7	287	37	276
	Extract	2200	75	<20	588	74	31
30	Medium	176	23	12	480	40	440
	Extract	2760	75	<20	465	76	15

Each flask contained ten half-seeds, $10^{-3}\,M$ acetate buffer, and 1.0 μc of L-phenylalanine-C14. The counts shown were for 0.10-ml aliquots of a total of 5.0 ml.

The physical properties of the labeled proteins formed undergo a dramatic qualitative transformation in the presence of gibberellic acid (Table 1). Of the proteins labeled in the absence of gibberellic acid, about 75 per cent are precipitated by heating to 70° for 20 min. Only 0–40 per cent of the labeled proteins released into the medium in the presence of GA are thus precipitated (Table 1). Addition of carrier extract to the labeled medium does not carry down any more of the labeled proteins during the heating of the medium, nor does the medium stabilize the labeled proteins in the extract. It is, of course, well known that α-amylase is heat-stable. So also is the endo-β-glucanase which increases as does α-amylase in response to added gibberellic acid.[4] The α-amylase recovered by the ethanol-glycogen procedure[11] contains about 12 per cent of the total counts incorporated into protein and about 35 per cent of the heat-stable labeled proteins (Table 2). Thus, α-amylase accounts for a large fraction of the total protein synthesis triggered by gibberellic acid.

TABLE 2

PHYSICAL PROPERTIES OF LABELED PROTEINS

Fraction	Radioactivity, cpm	Heat-precipitable, per cent
Extract	34,000	80
Medium	29,200	15
Ethanol PPT	7,000	0
Glycogen S.F.	8,000	0
α-Amylase	8,000	0

The numbers shown indicate the total number of counts incorporated into protein during incubation of ten half-seeds in acetate buffer, 10^{-6} M gibberellic acid, and 1 μc of L-leucine-C[14]. The ethanol precipitate, glycogen supernatant fraction, and α-amylase fraction refer to the fractions produced during the purification procedure.[11]

Labeled leucine, alanine, proline, and threonine were all shown, in separate experiments, to be incorporated into the purified α-amylase. Each of these labeled samples of α-amylase was digested with trypsin and "fingerprinted".[14] Of a total of 31 ninhydrin spots, 20 were labeled with proline, 26 with alanine, 30 with leucine, and 25 with threonine. Only 2 of the 31 ninhydrin spots contained none of the above labeled amino acids. The fingerprint obtained with labeled threonine is shown in Figure 2. We experienced some difficulty in obtaining complete digestion of the α-amylase with trypsin. The rate of digestion is slow and variable. This is probably due to the presence of limit dextrins and traces of calcium ions which may serve to protect the α-amylase against tryptic attack. It appears from the information of Figure 2 as well as from the similar fingerprints of α-amylase labeled with other amino acids that the entire α-amylase molecule is synthesized in response to the addition of gibberellic acid.

We turn next to the question of how gibberellic acid causes the production of α-amylase. It could, in principle, be through derepression of the previously repressed gene for α-amylase synthesis with consequent production of appropriate messenger RNA. We approach this problem by finding out whether inhibitors of RNA synthesis inhibit the gibberellic acid-dependent synthesis of α-amylase.

Of the RNA synthesis inhibitors used, 5-bromouracil, 8-azaadenine, and actinomycin D caused some inhibition of α-amylase formation (Table 3). Application of 100 μg/ml of actinomycin D completely inhibits the formation of α-amylase (Table 3), although 10 μg/ml is almost without effect. We suspect that actinomycin D is

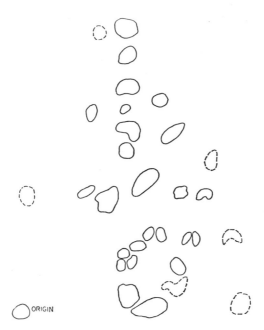

Fig. 2.—Autoradiograph of a fingerprint of α-amylase obtained by tryptic digestion of threonine-C[14] labeled α-amylase. The solid lines show the position of ninhydrin-positive spots which coincide with the exposed spot on the film. The dotted lines are ninhydrin-positive spots which were not labeled.

partially destroyed by the proteases of barley because addition of 10^{-3} M potassium bromate (which inhibits the protease action without preventing α-amylase synthesis)[12] to the medium together with gibberellic acid and actinomycin D increases the inhibition caused by 10–50 μg/ml of actinomycin D. Evidence that actinomycin D, even at these high concentrations, is, in fact, selective is shown in Table 4.

TABLE 3
THE EFFECT OF RNA SYNTHESIS INHIBITORS ON α-AMYLASE FORMATION BY ISOLATED ALEURONE LAYERS

Treatment	Extract	α-Amylase, μg Medium	Total
− GA	9.4	5.8	15.2
Control	12	53	65
5-Bromouracil	10	26	36
6-Azaguanine	14	43	57
8-Azaadenine	10	33	43
Actinomycin D	10	4.3	14.3

For each sample, ten half-aleurone layers were incubated with buffer, 10^{-4} M gibberellic acid, and 10^{-4} M inhibitor—except the actinomycin D which was 100 μg/ml—for 30 hrs at 25°.

TABLE 4
AMINO ACID INCORPORATION *in vivo* BY ALEURONE LAYERS

Treatment GA	Act D	Radioactivity Extract	Medium	α-Amylase, μg Extract	Medium
−	−	72,600	18,900	22	11
+	−	21,300	25,500	12	55
−	+	69,900	12,700	4	0.5
+	+	74,000	18,000	26	12

The numbers shown indicate total c/m incorporated into protein during a 30-hr incubation of ten half-aleurone layers with buffer, 1 μc L-phenylalanine-C[14], 10^{-6} M gibberellic acid, and 100 μg/ml actinomycin D where indicated.

In the presence of gibberellic acid and actinomycin D, the small amount of α-amylase formed and the distribution of labeled proteins are characteristic of the untreated aleurone layers.   However, actinomycin D has little effect on the rate of the gibberellic acid-independent incorporation of labeled phenylalanine into proteins.   The obvious and most attractive conclusion is that the labeled heat-stable proteins synthesized and released into the medium after the addition of gibberellic acid require DNA-dependent synthesis of RNA.   That incorporation which occurs without added gibberellic acid could use messenger RNA formed during the preincubation period or perhaps even during the maturation of the developing seed.

The formation of α-amylase by the isolated aleurone layers is sensitive to actinomycin D only during the first few hours after addition of gibberellic acid (Table 5).

TABLE 5

TIME COURSE OF SENSITIVITY TO INHIBITORS

Conditions	α-Amylase, μg
$-$GA	13
$+$GA	66
$+$GA $+$ Act D	24
$+$GA $+$ Act D (after 7 hr)	55
$+$GA $+$ pFϕ Ala	12
$+$GA $+$ pFϕ Ala (after 7 hr)	12

For each sample, ten half-aleurone layers were incubated with buffer, and 10^{-6} M gibberellic acid added at the beginning of the incubation.   The actinomycin D (100 μg/ml) and p-fluorophenylalanine (10^{-3} M) were added either at the same time as the gibberellic acid or after 7 hr.

Actinomycin D added 7 hr after the addition of gibberellic acid has little effect. However, p-fluorophenylalanine added at this time is still effective.   These results are consistent with the postulate that the addition of gibberellic acid causes the formation of a specific messenger RNA which directs the *de novo* synthesis of α-amylase.   Within a few hours after the addition of gibberellic acid, the quantity of messenger RNA is no longer rate-limiting in α-amylase synthesis.   From this time on, the formation of α-amylase would not be susceptible to inhibition by actinomycin D but would, of course, still be susceptible to protein synthesis inhibitors.

Discussion.—Simple dissection experiments have shown that only the aleurone layer cells are capable of respiration and amino acid incorporation.[6]   The QO_2 (μl $\cdot$ O_2 $\cdot$ hr^{-1} $\cdot$ 100 mg fresh wt^{-1}) for the aleurone layers at 25° is 15–30.   The aleurone layers consist of a single cell type derived from the triple fusion nucleus. Aside from the possibility that a layer of living cells surrounding the dead starchy endosperm may provide protection against attack by microorganisms, the only obvious function of the aleurone cells is to produce and secrete hydrolytic enzymes for the digestion of the reserves of the dead starchy endosperm cells.   It is a delightful nicety that the key to these reserves is kept by the embryo—the only tissue capable of growth.

The simplest possible way to explain the data in this paper is to postulate that gibberellic acid exerts its control at the level of the gene to bring about the synthesis of messenger RNA's specific for the proteins being synthesized.   It appears that this hypothesis can be checked experimentally by the techniques developed for assessing those DNA sites available in chromatin for transcription into messenger RNA by RNA polymerase.[15]

Summary.—The development of α-amylase activity by isolated aleurone layers of barley endosperm is completely dependent upon added gibberellic acid and is a result of the *de novo* synthesis of the α-amylase molecule.   The synthesis of α-amylase and of other heat-stable proteins is prevented by actinomycin D.   It is therefore postulated that gibberellic acid controls the synthesis of α-amylase and of other heat-stable proteins in aleurone cells by causing the production of specific messenger RNA's.

The authors gratefully acknowledge the technical assistance of Miss Nancy Joseph and Miss Anne Wiley. We wish to thank Dr. H. Yomo for supplying translations of his papers, and Professor R. A. Nilan for supplying the Himalaya variety of barley.

* This research was supported by research contract AT(30-1)-3232 with the Atomic Energy Commission.

[1] Yomo, H., and H. Iinuma, *Agri. Biol. Chem. (Tokyo)*, **26**, 201 (1962).

[2] Paleg, L., *Plant Physiol.*, **36**, 829 (1961).

[3] MacLeod, A. M., and A. S. Millar, *J. Inst. Brewing*, **68**, 322 (1962).

[4] Briggs, D. E., *J. Inst. Brewing*, **69**, 13 (1963).

[5] Varner, J. E., and G. Schidlovsky, in *Proceedings of the International Seed Protein Conference*, New Orleans, USDA (1963).

[6] Varner, J. E., *Plant Physiol.*, **39**, 413 (1964).

[7] Yomo, H., *Hakko Kyokaishi*, **18**, 603 (1960).

[8] Paleg, L. G., *Plant Physiol.*, **35**, 902 (1960).

[9] Shuster, L., and R. H. Gifford. *Arch. Biochem. Biophys.*, **96**, 534 (1962).

[10] Schwimmer, S., and A. K. Balls, *J. Biol. Chem.*, **179**, 1063 (1949).

[11] Loyter, A., and M. Schramm, *Biochim. Biophys. Acta*, **65**, 200 (1962).

[12] Ram Chandra, G., and J. E. Varner, unpublished.

[13] Yomo, H., *Hakko Kyokaishi*, **19**, 284 (1961); *Chem. Abstracts*, **57**, 11544 (1961).

[14] Katz, A. M., W. J. Dreyer, and C. B. Anfinsen, *J. Biol. Chem.*, **234**, 2897 (1959).

[15] Bonner, J., R. C. Huang, and R. O. Gilden, these Proceedings, **50**, 793 (1963).

Reprinted from PLANT PHYSIOLOGY, Vol. 42, No. 7, July, 1967, pages 1008–1016.

(PRINTED IN U.S.A.)

Hormonal Control of Enzyme Synthesis: On the Mode of Action of Gibberellic Acid and Abscisin in Aleurone Layers of Barley[1]

Maarten J. Chrispeels[2] and J. E. Varner

**MSU/AEC Plant Research Laboratory, Michigan State University
East Lansing, Michigan 48823**

Received March 31, 1967.

Summary. Gibberellic acid (GA) enhances the synthesis of α-amylase and ribonuclease in isolated aleurone layers and this process is inhibited by abscisin. Removal of gibberellic acid in mid-course of α-amylase production results in a slowing down of α-amylase synthesis, suggesting a continued requirement of GA for enzyme synthesis. This is paralleled by a continuous requirement for RNA synthesis. Addition of 6-methylpurine or 8-azaguanine in mid-course results in an inhibition of α-amylase synthesis within 3 to 4 hours. However, actinomycin D added in mid-course is almost without effect. This is not due to its failure to enter the cells, because it does inhibit ^{14}C-uridine incorporation at this stage. Addition of abscisin to aleurone layers which are synthesizing α-amylase results in an inhibition of this synthesis within 2 to 3 hours. Cycloheximide on the other hand inhibits enzyme synthesis immediately upon its addition. These data are consistent with the hypothesis that the expression of the GA effect requires the synthesis of enzyme-specific RNA molecules. The similarity in the kinetics of inhibition between abscisin on the one hand and 8-azaguanine or 6-methylpurine on the other suggests that abscisin may exert its action by inhibiting the synthesis of these enzyme-specific RNA molecules or by preventing their incorporation into an active enzyme-synthesising unit.

Gibberellic acid greatly enhances the synthesis of amylolytic enzymes (and several other hydrolytic enzymes) in aleurone cells of barley (20, 23, 27), wild oats (16), and rice (19). We have studied in detail the GA-enhanced synthesis and release of α-amylase and ribonuclease (4) and of protease (Jacobsen and Varner, in preparation) by isolated aleurone layers. The manifestation of this action of gibberellic acid is inhibited by inhibitors of protein synthesis (*p*-fluorophenylalanine and cycloheximide) and of ribonucleic acid synthesis (actinomycin D and 8-azaguanine). Evidence obtained by a new method indicates that the appearance of α-amylase (6) and protease (Jacobsen and Varner, in preparation) is due to the de novo synthesis of all the enzyme which is produced. This de novo synthesis is dependent on the synthesis of one or more species of ribonucleic acid.

Recently we reported that abscisin (abscisin II or dormin) inhibits the GA-enhanced synthesis of α-amylase and the release of free amino acids by aleurone layers (3). The inhibition of enzyme synthesis by abscisin can be partially overcome by the addition of a larger amount of GA. The kinetics of this interaction are neither competitive, nor non-competitive. The complexity of the system makes an interpretation of the kinetics data impossible. The inhibition of enzyme synthesis by abscisin is different from, and much more specific than, that obtained by metabolic inhibitors. Indeed, abscisin does not affect respiration or phosphorylation; neither does it inhibit the incorporation of radioactive precursors into protein (other than the hydrolases) and RNA (3).

An interaction between GA and abscisin has been reported in several systems. Abscisin inhibits the expansive growth of leaf sections of corn and this inhibition is reversed by GA (21). It also inhibits the GA-enhanced elongation of normal and dwarf peas (21). The elongation (normal and GA-enhanced) of lentil epicotyls is accompanied by DNA synthesis (16); both elongation and DNA synthesis are inhibited by abscisin and this inhibition can be partially reversed by the addition of GA (Chrispeels, unpublished).

We have studied in greater detail the effect of GA and abscisin on barley aleurone layers, as well as the effect of RNA-synthesis-inhibitors on α-amylase synthesis in order to learn more about the mode of action of the 2 hormones.

[1] This work was supported by the United States Atomic Energy Commission under contract No. AT (11-1) 1338.
[2] Present address: John Muir College, Department of Biology, UCSD, La Jolla, California 92307.

Materials and Methods

Most of the materials and methods used in these experiments have been described in detail in our previous paper (4). Synthetic d,l-abscisin, a gift from Dr. J. van Overbeek (Shell), was used in all the experiments reported here. A stock solution of 0.2 mM abscisin in water was kept frozen or in the refrigerator.

The incorporation of ^{14}C-leucine and ^{14}C-uridine was measured in the following way: Aleurone layers were incubated as usual and 1 μc of ^{14}C-leucine (200 mc/mmole) or of ^{14}C-uridine (25 mc/mmole) (both purchased from Schwarz Bio-research, Inc.) was added, and incorporation was allowed to proceed for the appropriate period of time. The aleurone layers were then rinsed 3 times with 1 mM cold, carrier leucine or uridine. When ^{14}C-leucine was used the aleurone layers were homogenized in the cold in 5 ml of 0.2 N NaCl in the usual way, and the extracts were centrifuged for 10 minutes at 2000 $\times$ g. An aliquot of 0.2 ml of the supernatant was plated on a glass planchet to determine the total uptake. Another aliquot of 0.25 ml of the salt soluble proteins was mixed with an equal volume of 10 mM leucine and precipitated with 2 volumes of 15 % trichloroacetic acid. The precipitated proteins were collected by filtration on Millipore filters and washed with 5 % trichloroacetic acid. The filters were dried and counted in a gas flow counter. When ^{14}C-uridine was used the aleurone layers were homogenized in the cold in 5 ml of 1 M NaCl with 5 mg of carrier RNA. Incorporation of the precursor into the salt-soluble nucleoproteins was determined as described above, except that carrier uridine was used. This method gives results similar to those obtained with more elaborate extraction procedures for nucleic acids.

Results

Removal of Gibberellic Acid in Midcourse of α-Amylase Production. The addition of GA to isolated aleurone layers of barley results in a linear synthesis of α-amylase after a lag-period of 7 to 9 hours. When aleurone layers are incubated in 0.05 μM GA for 11 hours, frequent rinsing over a period of 1 hour to remove as much GA as possible results in a substantial reduction of the α-amylase synthesized in the next 12 hour period (4). Gibberellic acid can therefore not be considered as a trigger because its presence is required during the lag-period as well as during the period of α-amylase synthesis, if maximal enzyme synthesis is to be obtained. In the present experiments the removal of GA was improved by rinsing the aleurone layers 4 times at half-hour intervals with a medium containing 10 mM CaCl$_2$ and 1 mM sodium acetate buffer pH 8. At the end of the rinsing period 1 set of aleurone layers was further incubated with GA and without GA. The results of such an experiment are shown in figure 1. It is apparent that α-amylase synthesis is severely inhibited within a few hours, if GA is not added again after it has been removed.

When aleurone layers are incubated without GA for 10 hours, and 0.1 μM GA is added, no α-amylase is produced in the first 5 to 7 hours indicating that GA is required to overcome the lag-period. The lag-period can be shortened, but not abolished by first incubating the aleurone layers in a low concentration of GA (2.5 mμM) and adding a higher amount of GA (0.5 μM) after 10 hours (fig 2). After such an increase in GA concentration there is a lag-period of 3 to 4 hours before the aleurone layers synthesize α-amylase at a rate equivalent to the one obtained with the higher GA concentration.

Once the lag-period has been overcome it cannot be reintroduced by a prolonged incubation of the aleurone layers in the absence of GA. Aleurone layers were incubated for 8 hours in 0.05 μM GA, and GA was removed as described above. The aleurone layers were further incubated without GA for 6 hours. The rate of enzyme synthesis had slowed down considerably at this time. Subsequent addition of GA resulted in an immediate resumption of α-amylase synthesis at the control rate (fig 3).

Inhibition of GA Enhanced Synthesis of α-Amylase and Ribonuclease by Abscisin. The GA-enhanced production of α-amylase by aleurone layers is inhibited by abscisin (table I). When aleurone layers are incubated with 0.1 μM GA and 1 μM abscisin, very little enzyme is synthesized. Abscisin also inhibits the small amount of α-amylase synthesis which occurs in the absence of GA. Addition of a larger amount of GA reverses this inhibition by abscisin, as shown earlier (3) and as demonstrated in a different way in table II. Aleurone layers were incubated with increasing amount of GA (from 0.1 mμM to 0.1 mM) and either without abscisin or with 0.05 μM or 5 μM abscisin. The inhibitory effect of 0.05 μM abscisin is almost completely reversed by 1 μM GA. When 5 μM abscisin are used reversal by GA never exceeds 30 % regardless of the amount of GA used. This demonstrates that reversal is not merely a matter of the molar ratio of GA and abscisin.

Abscisin inhibits the GA enhanced production of ribonuclease in a similar fashion (table III). The

Table I. *Inhibition of α-Amylase Synthesis by Abscisin*

Ten aleurone layers were incubated with buffer, 20 mM of CaCl$_2$ and with or without 0.1 μM GA and the concentrations of abscisin indicated.

Treatment	α-Amylase per 10 aleurone layers
	μg
Control	40
Control + 0.5 μM abscisin	8
GA	475
GA + 1 μM abscisin	67

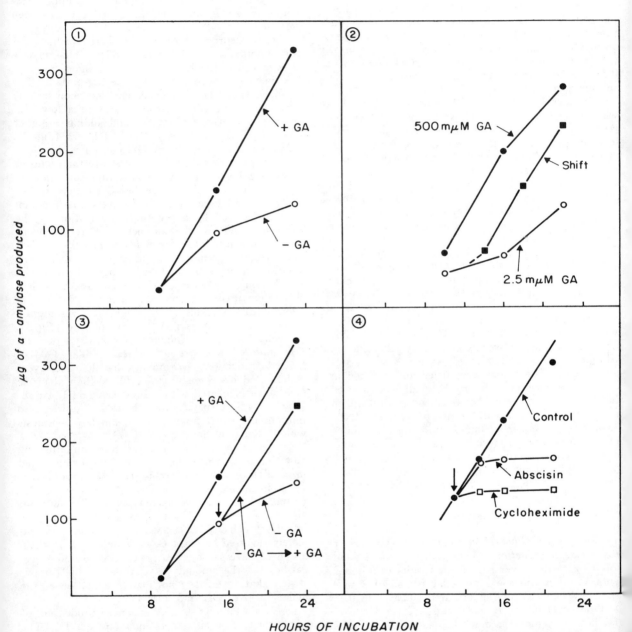

HOURS OF INCUBATION

FIG. 1. Effect of removing GA at the end of the lag-period. Aleurone layers were incubated for 7 hours in 0.5 μM GA. GA was then removed by 4 consecutive one-half-hour rinses. The aleurone layers were further incubated either with GA, or without GA, and α-amylase synthesis was measured 6 and 14 hours later.

FIG. 2. Shift from a low to a high concentration of GA. Aleurone layers were incubated in 2.5 mμM GA or in 500 mμM GA and α-amylase synthesis was measured after 10, 16 and 22 hours. To 1 set of flasks the GA concentration was increased to 500 mμM after the aleurone layers had been in 2.5 mμM GA for 10 hours (Shift).

FIG. 3. Effect of adding GA after it has been withheld for 6 hours. All conditions as in figure 1, except that GA was added again at 15 hours to aleurone layers from which it had been withheld at 9 hours. Total α-amylase synthesis was measured 15 and 23 hours after the start of the incubation.

FIG. 4. Mid-course inhibition of α-amylase synthesis by abscisin and cycloheximide. Aleurone layers were incubated in 0.1 μM for 11 hours. At this time abscisin (5μM) or cycloheximide (10 μg/ml) was added and α-amylase synthesis was measured 2 and one-half, 5 and 10 hours later.

Table II. *Reversal by Gibberellic Acid of the Abscisin Inhibition of α-Amylase Synthesis*

Ten half aleurone layers were incubated in buffer with 20 mM $CaCl_2$ and the concentrations of GA and abscisin indicated. Activity of α-amylase was measured in the medium and a tissue-extract after 24 hours.

GA concentration	α-Amylase per 10 aleurone layers Abscisin concentration		
	0	0.05 μM	5 μM
	μg	μg	μg
0.1 mμM	73	10	…
1 mμM	248	71	…
10 mμM	522	280	22
0.1 μM	638	525	101
1 μM	662	584	189
10 μM	692	…	185
0.1 mM	580	…	113

increase in ribonuclease which takes place in isolated aleurone layers in the absence of added GA, or in half seeds preincubating on moist sand (4) is also inhibited by abscisin.

In the experiments discussed above the 2 hormones, GA and abscisin, were added simultaneously. However, abscisin is also effective as an inhibitor of α-amylase synthesis if it is added in mid-course, while enzyme synthesis is in progress (fig 4). Aleurone layers were incubated for 11 hours in 0.1 μM GA and 5 μM abscisin was added at that time. Further synthesis of α-amylase was inhibited completely after a delay of 2 to 3 hours. If both hormones had been added at these concentrations, at the same time, at the beginning of the incubation, α-amylase synthesis would have been inhibited completely. Addition of cycloheximide (10 μg/ml) at this time results in an immediate inhibition of enzyme synthesis. It was also found that both the production and the release of ribonuclease can be inhibited by the addition of abscisin in mid-course (20–24 hrs after GA).

Requirement for RNA Synthesis. Actinomycin D and various base analogues which inhibit RNA

Table III. *Inhibition of Ribonuclease Production by Abscisin*

Ten aleurone layers were incubated in buffer, 20 mM of $CaCl_2$ and with or without 2 mμM GA and the concentrations of abscisin indicated. Ribonuclease activity was measured after 48 hours in the medium and in extract of the tissue. Initial refers to the amount of ribonuclease present in the aleurone layers at the start of incubation.

Treatment	Units of ribonuclease per 10 aleurone layers
Initial	29
Control	108
Control + 0.5 μM abscisin	61
GA	256
GA + 5 μM abscisin	53

synthesis prevent α-amylase formation if they are added at the same time as the hormone (4, 23, 24). The synthesis of α-amylase is inhibited to a much lesser extent if actinomycin D is added 4 hours after GA, and is almost unaffected if the antibiotic is added 8 hours after the hormone (table IV). A different effect is observed with 6-methyl-purine, a potent inhibitor of all RNA synthesis (11). When aleurone layers are incubated with 1 μM

Table IV. *Inhibition of α-Amylase Synthesis and ^{14}C-Uridine Incorporation by Actinomycin D Added 4 and 8 Hours After GA*

Ten aleurone layers were incubated in 0.1 μM GA and after 4 or 8 hours actinomycin D (100 μg/ml) was added. Enzyme synthesis was measured at the end of the 24 hour incubation period. ^{14}C-Uridine (1 μc/flask) was added 4 hours after actinomycin D and incorporation was allowed to proceed over a 4 hour period.

Treatment	α-Amylase per 10 aleurone layers	^{14}C-Uridine incorporated
	μg	cpm
GA	359	1380
GA + Act. D after 4 hrs	212	
GA + Act. D after 8 hrs	325	466

Table V. *Inhibition of α-Amylase Synthesis by 6-Methylpurine*

Ten aleurone layers were incubated in buffer, 20 mM, $CaCl_2$ and 0.5 μM GA. 6-Methylpurine was added at the same time as GA or 4 or 8 hours later and total α-amylase production was measured after 24 hours incubation.

Treatment	α-Amylase per 10 aleurone layers	
Time of addition of 6-methylpurine	0.1 mM Of 6-methylpurine	1.0 mM Of 6-methylpurine
	μg	μg
0 hrs	38	9
4 hrs	115	55
8 hrs	208	140
Control	384	426

GA and 0.1 mM 6-methylpurine α-amylase synthesis is inhibited by 90 %. However, if the analogue is added 4 or 8 hours after the hormone enzyme synthesis is inhibited by only 70 % and 45 % respectively (table V). Larger inhibitions are obtained with 1 mM 6-methylpurine, and α-amylase synthesis is still inhibited by 66 % if this concentration of the analogue is added 8 hours after GA.

The failure of actinomycin D to inhibit α-amylase synthesis if the antibiotic is added 8 hours after the hormone could be due to its inability to inhibit RNA synthesis in general at this stage or to its inability to inhibit the RNA fraction which is required for α-amylase synthesis. To test the first possibility aleurone layers were incubated in 0.1 μM GA, and 100 μg/ml of actinomycin D were added after 8 hours. After 4 more hours 1 μc of ^{14}C-uridine was added to each flask containing 10 aleurone layers and incorporation was allowed to proceed for 4 hours. During this period actinomycin D inhibited the incorporation of ^{14}C-uridine by 66 % (table IV). We can assume that the inhibition of RNA synthesis was even greater because some of the incorporation represents turnover of the terminal ends of the transfer RNA molecules. (It was shown by Chandra and Varner (2) that there is a rapid conversion of uridine to cytidine in this tissue). It appears then that actinomycin D is a good inhibitor of ^{14}C-uridine incorporation whether it is added at the same time as GA (4) or 8 hours after the hormone. This leads to the conclusion that the inability of actinomycin D to inhibit α-amylase synthesis must be due to its inability to prevent the synthesis of the specific RNA fraction which is required for continued α-amylase synthesis.

Table VI. *Sensitivity of α-Amylase Synthesis to Actinomycin D and 6-Methylpurine After Removal of GA*

Ten aleurone layers were incubated in buffer, 20 mM CaCl$_2$ and 0.5 μM GA for 9 hours. GA was removed by 4 subsequent one-half-hour rinsings in a medium without GA. The aleurone layers were further incubated for 11 hours without GA or with 0.5 μM GA and actinomycin D (100 μg/ml) or 6-methylpurine (0.2 mM). Initial refers to the amount of α-amylase present in the aleurone layers after the removal of GA (at the end of the washing out procedure).

Treatment	α-Amylase per 10 aleurone layers
	μg
Initial	61
—GA	128
+GA	285
+GA + actinomycin D	221
+GA + 6-methylpurine	153

We have shown above that GA is not a trigger, but is required continuously for maximal α-amylase synthesis. The following experiment was done to test whether the α-amylase synthesis which is dependent on the second addition of GA also requires continued RNA synthesis. Aleurone layers were incubated for 10 hours in 0.05 μM GA and the GA was removed by 4 successive one-half-hour rinses. The aleurone layers were then further incubated without GA, or with GA and with actinomycin D (100 μg/ml) or 6-methylpurine (0.2 mM). The results show (table VI) that the α-amylase synthesis which is dependent on the second addition of GA is not very sensitive to actinomycin D but is very strongly inhibited by 6-methylpurine. Synthesis of α-amylase under these circumstances proceeds without delay upon the addition of GA, even if GA has been withheld for many hours (fig 3). This indicates that the aleurone layers are capable of a rapid synthesis of the RNA fraction necessary for α-amylase synthesis. When aleurone layers are incubated with GA there is normally a 7 to 9 hour lag before α-amylase synthesis begins.

The observations discussed above suggest that this lag is not necessitated by the requirement for the synthesis of the metabolically unstable RNA fraction, the synthesis of which must accompany α-amylase synthesis and can be inhibited by 6-methylpurine. It seems likely that other biochemical processes are associated with the lag-period and must occur before α-amylase synthesis can start. The possibility that a more stable RNA needs to be synthesized during the lag-period can, of course, not be ruled out.

To test whether the requirement for RNA synthesis can be satisfied by incubating for a long time with a small amount of GA, half seeds were preincubated for 3 days on sterile sand moistened with GA (0.01 or 0.1 μM) instead of water. The aleurone layers were removed from the starchy endosperm and further incubated with GA (1 μM) or with GA and actinomycin D (50 μg/ml). The data show (table VII) that actinomycin D inhibits enzyme synthesis to approximately the same extent whether the half seeds were preincubated in water

Table VII. *Inhibition of α-Amylase Synthesis by Actinomycin D After Preincubation of Half Seeds in Gibberellic Acid*

Half seeds were preincubated in water or in GA (0.01 μM or 0.1 μM) for 3 days. The aleurone layers were removed and further incubated in buffer, 20 mM, CaCl$_2$ and 1 μM GA, and with or without actinomycin D (50 μg/ml) 0 hours refers to the amount of α-amylase present in the aleurone layers at the start of the incubation.

	α-Amylase per 10 aleurone layers		
Treatment and time	Preincubation in water	Preincubation in 0.01 μM GA	Preincubation in 0.1 μM GA
	μg	μg	μg
0 hrs GA	11	22	64
8 hrs GA	35	64	136
24 hrs GA	408	445	505
24 hrs GA + actinomycin D	240	270	278

or in GA. As a result of preincubation in 0.1 μM GA α-amylase synthesis is initiated at a slow rate (compare α-amylase synthesis at 0 and 8 hrs after preincubation in 0.1 μM GA with preincubation in water), but this does not obviate the necessity for the initiation of more RNA synthesis if a higher concentration of GA is added.

Comparison of the Effect of Abscisin and Inhibitors of RNA Synthesis. We have shown that the addition of cycloheximide, a potent inhibitor of protein synthesis at the level of translation, to aleurone layers results in an immediate cessation of α-amylase synthesis and also of the incorporation of ^{14}C-leucine into the cellular proteins of aleurone layers (Varner, unpublished). Abscisin, on the other hand, inhibits enzyme synthesis after a lag of 2 and one-half to 3 hours. Experiments with 6-methylpurine show a continuous requirement for RNA synthesis during the period of α-amylase synthesis. It seemed, therefore, of interest to study the mid-course inhibition of α-amylase synthesis by abscisin and base analogues and compare their kinetics.

Aleurone layers were incubated in 0.5 μM GA for 11 hours to induce the GA enhanced synthesis of α-amylase. At this stage the medium was withdrawn, the aleurone layers were rinsed and further incubated for 12 hours in a medium containing GA (0.5 μM) or GA and various inhibitors (10·μM abscisin, 0.5 or 5 mM 6-methylpurine, 5 mM 8-azaguanine and 5 mM 5-azacytidine). The results in table VIII indicate that abscisin and 5 mM 6-methylpurine give the same amount of inhibition (74%) while 0.5 mM 6-methylpurine and 5 mM 8-azaguanine or 5-azacytidine are less inhibitory (58–39%). The kinetics of inhibition of α-amylase synthesis by abscisin and the base analogues are very similar (fig 6). Abscisin inhibits α-amylase synthesis completely within 2 and one-half to 3 hours, as shown earlier (fig 4). The base analogues also

Table VIII. *Mid-course Inhibition of α-Amylase by Abscisin and Base Analogues*

Aleurone layers were incubated in buffer, 20 mM CaCl$_2$ and 0.5 μM GA for 11 hours. The medium was drawn off and the aleurone layers were rinsed. The aleurone layers were further incubated for 12 hours in 5 μM GA together with the inhibitors, as indicated. The figures represent the amount of α-amylase produced in the 12 hour incubation.

Treatment	α-Amylase per 10 aleurone layers
	μg
Control	317
Abscisin (10 μM)	82
Methylpurine (0.5 mM)	156
Methylpurine (5 mM)	84
Azacytidine (5 mM)	194
Azaguanine (5 mM)	132

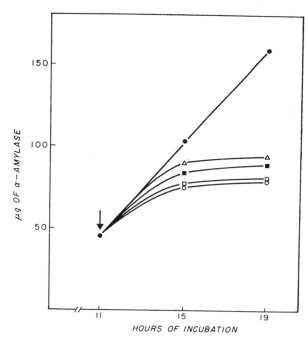

FIG. 5. Mid-course inhibition of α-amylase synthesis by abscisin, 6-methylpurine and 8-azaguanine. Aleurone layers were incubated in 0.05 μM GA for 11 hours. At this time the medium was removed, the aleurone layers were rinsed, and they were further incubated with 0.05 μM GA (●—●), or with GA and 10 μM abscisin (○—○), 5 mM 6-methylpurine (□—□), 0.5 μM 6-methylpurine (■—■), or 5 mM 8-azaguanine (△—△).

inhibit α-amylase synthesis completely within 2 and one-half to 4 hours depending on the concentration used. The incorporation of ^{14}C-uridine by the aleurone layers is inhibited by 1 mM 6-methylpurine in the following way: 30 to 35% within 2 and one-half hours of its addition and 65 to 70% after 4 hours of its addition. However, if the 6-methylpurine concentration is increased to 5 mM the inhibition of ^{14}C-uridine incorporation is 65 to 70% within 2 and one-half hours. This may account for the shorter lag time in the inhibition of α-amylase synthesis observed with the higher concentration of 6-methylpurine. The incorporation of ^{14}C-leucine by the aleurone layers into the cellular proteins is inhibited by only 30%, 4 hours after the addition of 1 mM 6-methylpurine. This is probably an indirect effect mediated through its inhibition of RNA synthesis. We therefore conclude that the rapid inhibition of α-amylase synthesis caused by 6-methylpurine is not due to a direct inhibition of protein synthesis.

Discussion

It is not yet possible to decide whether these hormones work at the level of transcription or at the level of translation. The data presented here, as well as the earlier results obtained by Varner and coworkers (4, 22, 23, 24), are consistent with the hypothesis that GA exerts its control at the level of the gene, to bring about the synthesis of an RNA fraction specific for the proteins being synthesized. The similarity in kinetics for the inhibition of α-amylase synthesis by abscisin and 6-methylpurine or 8-azaguanine suggests that abscisin exerts its control by inhibiting the synthesis of such a specific RNA fraction. However, much caution must be used in basing a model on the mode of action of the hormones on a study of the effect of inhibitors alone. The data are equally consistent with a control mechanism at the level of translation with a requirement for continued RNA synthesis.

Many hormonal effects are inhibited by actinomycin D (1, 9, 13, 17, 20, 25), and this has often been interpreted as evidence that the hormones affect the synthesis of messenger RNA in a direct way while all that can be concluded with certainty is, that some kind of DNA directed RNA synthesis must be allowed to go on before the hormonal effect can express itself at the level of protein synthesis or of morphogenesis. Hybridization experiments with bacterial nucleic acids have shown regions of complementarity between DNA and messenger RNA, ribosomal RNA, and transfer RNA suggesting that the synthesis of all 3 major classes of cytoplasmic RNA is DNA directed. The synthesis of any or all of these 3 may be required for the hormonal effect to become evident.

A second reason for caution is that the hormone-enhanced enzyme synthesis may result in a more rapid turnover of one of the RNA's involved in the synthesis of these enzymes (e.g. messenger RNA or a particular transfer RNA). This would result in a requirement for RNA synthesis, and such a process would be inhibited by actinomycin D or by base analogues, even though the initial effect of the hormone is not at the level of transcription.

The principal, easily observed effect of GA on the aleurone layers is the enhancement of the synthesis of several hydrolytic enzymes. RNA synthesis must be allowed to occur in order to obtain this effect. A control mechanism at either transcription or translation would probably involve the synthesis of a new RNA. There does not appear to exist a great reserve of this critical RNA fraction. Indeed, base analogues inhibit α-amylase synthesis within 2 and one-half to 4 hours and continued RNA synthesis must accompany enzyme synthesis. We can also conclude that this RNA fraction is synthesized very rapidly since addition of GA to aleurone layers from which this hormone has been withheld for several hours results in an immediate resumption of α-amylase synthesis which is completely dependent on continued RNA synthesis.

The principal, easily observed effect of abscisin is the inhibition of hydrolase synthesis (both normal and GA-enhanced). The kinetics of this inhibition resemble those obtained with the base analogues 6-methylpurine and 8-azaguanine. In the presence of 10 μM abscisin or 5 mM 6-methylpurine, at this concentration the base analogue inhibits ^{14}C-uridine incorporation by 70 % within 2 and one-half hours, α-amylase synthesis is completely inhibited within 2 to 3 hours. With 0.5 mM 6-methylpurine or 5 mM 8-azaguanine it takes somewhat longer before inhibition is complete. The incorporation of ^{14}C-leucine is inhibited to a much smaller extent (30 %) than the incorporation of ^{14}C-uridine (70 %) when aleurone layers are incubated for 4 hours in 1 mM 6-methylpurine. This suggests that the inhibition of protein synthesis is a result of the inhibition of RNA synthesis, brought about by the decay of short-lived messengers. This was confirmed by A. Morris (private communication) who showed that 10 mM 6-methylpurine has no effect on the incorporation of ^{14}C-valine into the proteins of rabbit reticulocytes, indicating that the analogue has no direct effect on protein synthesis in this system. (Reticulocytes have no nucleus and protein synthesis is independent of continued RNA synthesis). The 2 and one-half to 3 hour delay in the inhibition of α-amylase synthesis which is observed with abscisin as well as with the base analogues could be due to the presence of a sufficient amount of the critical RNA fraction necessary to sustain enzyme synthesis for this period of time.

However, similar kinetics might be expected if abscisin exerted its action at the level of translation by inhibiting the incorporation of this RNA into an active enzyme-synthesizing unit. In this case the delay would reflect the half-life of this active complex.

The inhibition of α-amylase synthesis by abscisin can be overcome, at least partially, by the addition of a larger amount of GA. However, if too high a concentration of abscisin is used, no reversal is obtained. Similar observations were made by J van Overbeek (personal communication) who studied the inhibition of growth of *Lemna minor* by abscisin and the reversal of this inhibition by benzyladenine. Reversal by benzyladenine only takes place if growth has not been completely inhibited by abscisin.

A large number of studies indicate that plant hormones increase the rate of protein and RNA synthesis in the tissues to which they are applied. In some systems this can be measured by an increase in the total amount of protein and RNA while in others there is only an increase in the rate of incorporation of radioactive precursors into these macromolecules. Hormone application always results in a general derepression of RNA synthesis and in no instance has a system been found in which the hormone preferentially increases the synthesis of 1 particular RNA fraction.

Gibberellic acid does not enhance the incorporation of ^{14}C-uridine into the RNA[3] or of ^{14}C-leucine into the cellular proteins of isolated aleurone layers, dissected from the half seeds after the customary 3-day preincubation period (Chandra, Chrispeels and Varner, unpublished); neither does abscisin inhibit these processes (3). Although the hormones appear to have no effect on protein synthesis as measured by precursor incorporation, they do affect the synthesis of specific enzymes. This observation has not been matched at the RNA level, and we have been unable to find a specific RNA fraction (after extraction of the RNA and chromatography on methylated albumen kieselguhr columns), the synthesis of which is evoked by GA and inhibited by abscisin. Recent improvements in the methods used to extract nucleic acids from animal tissues (12) and to separate the various RNA's (5, 14) will be applied in our search for such an RNA fraction. The possibility that GA and abscisin exert their control at the level of translation can be checked by studying the effect which these hormones have on the in vitro synthesis of α-amylase by a subcellular fraction isolated from aleurone layers.

Acknowledgments

We acknowledge with pleasure the skillful technical assistance of Miss Nancy Joseph. We thank R. A. Nilan for supplying the Himalaya variety of barley, and A. Morris for determining the effect of 6-methylpurine on amino acid incorporation in rabbit reticulocytes. The actinomycin D was a gift from Merck, Inc.

Literature Cited

1. ABELES, F. B. AND R. E. HOLM. 1966. Enhancement of RNA synthesis, protein synthesis, and abscision by ethylene. Plant Physiol. 41: 1337–42.

2. CHANDRA, G. R. AND J. E. VARNER. 1965. Gibberellic acid controlled metabolism of RNA in aleurone cells of barley. Biochim. Biophys. Acta 180: 583–92.

3. CHRISPEELS, M. J. AND J. E. VARNER. 1966. Inhibition of gibberellic acid induced formation of α-amylase by abscision II. Nature 212: 1066–67.

4. CHRISPEELS, M. J. AND J. E. VARNER. 1967. Gibberellic acid-enhanced synthesis and release of amylase and ribonuclease by isolated barley aleurone layers. Plant Physiol. 42: In press.

5. ELLEM, K. A. O. 1966. Some properties of mammalian DNA-like RNA isolated by chromatography on methylated bovine serum albumin-kieselguhr columns. J. Mol. Biol. 20: 283–305.

6. FILNER, P. AND J. E. VARNER. A simple and unequivocal test for de novo synthesis of enzymes: density labeling of barley α-amylase with H_2O^{18}. Proc. Natl. Acad. In press.

7. FLETCHER, R. A. AND D. J. OSBORNE. 1966. Gibberellin, as a regulator of protein and ribonucleic acid synthesis during senescence in leaf cells of Taraxacum officinale. Can. J. Botany 44: 739–45.

8. HAMILTON, T. H., R. J. MOORE, A. F. RUMSEY, A. R. MEANS, AND A. R. SCHRANK. 1965. Stimulation of synthesis of ribonucleic acid in subapical sections of Avena coleoptile by indolyl-3-acetic acid. Nature 208: 1180–83.

9. KEY, J. L. 1964. Ribonucleic acid and protein synthesis as essential processes for cell elongation. Plant Physiol. 39: 365–70.

10. KEY, J. L. 1966. Effect of purine and pyrimidine analogues on growth and RNA metabolism in the soybean hypocotyl, the selective action of 5-fluorouracil. Plant Physiol. 41: 1257–64.

11. KEY, J. L. AND J. SHANNON. 1964. Enhancement by auxin of ribonucleic acid synthesis in excised soybean hypocotyl tissue. Plant Physiol. 39: 360–64.

12. KIRBY, K. S. 1965. Isolation and characterization of ribosomal ribonucleic acid. Biochem. J. 96: 266–69.

13. LEAVER, C. J. AND J. EDELMAN. 1965. Nucleic acid synthesis in carrot tissue slices. Biochem. J. 95: 27 p.

14. LOENING, V. E. 1967. The fractionation of high-molecular-weight ribonucleic acid by polyacrylamide-gel electrophoresis. Biochem. J. 102: 251–57.

15. NAYLOR, J. M. 1966. Dormancy studies in seed of Avena fatua. 5. On the response of aleurone cells to gibberellic acid. Can. J. Botany 44: 19–32.

16. NITSAN, J. AND A. LANG. 1966. DNA synthesis in the elongating nondividing cells of the lentil epicotyl and its promotion by gibberellin. Plant Physiol. 41: 965–70.

17. NOODÉN, L. D. AND K. V. THIMANN. 1963. Evidence for a requirement for protein synthesis for auxin-induced cell enlargement. Proc. Natl. Acad. Sci. 50: 194–200.

18. OGAWA, Y. AND S. IMAMURA. 1965. Effect of plant extracts and gibberellin A_3 on α-amylase production in embryoless rice endosperm in relation to growth promoting activity. Proc. Japan Acad. 41: 842–45.

19. PALEG, L. 1960. Physiological effects of gibberellic acid. I. On carbohydrate metabolism and amylase activity of barley endosperm. Plant Physiol. 35: 293–99.

20. ROYCHOUDHURY, R. AND S. P. SEN. 1964. Studies on the mechanism of auxin action: auxin regulation of nucleic acid metabolism in pea internodes and coconut milk nuclei. Physiol. Plantarum 17: 352–62.

[3] Chandra and Varner (2) and Varner et al. (24) reported a GA-enhanced incorporation of radioactive precursors into the RNA of aleurone layers 8 to 24 hours after the start of imbibition of half seeds. Naylor (15) observed a GA-enhanced incorporation of ^{3}H-cytidine into the nuclei of aleurone cells from wild oats, 24 hours after the start of imbibition. It seems likely that in these cases GA is accelerating processes which are associated with inhibition or with biochemical changes which follow It is exactly for this reason, to avoid all biochemical changes associated with imbibition, that half seeds are preincubated for 3 days before we study the effects of A and abscisin on aleurone layers.

21. THOMAS, T. H., P. F. WAREING, AND P. M. ROB-INSON. 1965. Action of the sycamore 'Dormin' as a gibberellin antagonist. Nature 205: 1270–72.

22. VARNER, J. E. 1964. Gibberellic acid controlled synthesis of α-amylase in barley endosperm. Plant Physiol. 39: 413–15.

23. VARNER, J. E. AND G. R. CHANDRA. 1964. Hormonal control of enzyme synthesis in barley endosperm. Proc. Natl. Acad. Sci. U. S. 52: 100–06.

24. VARNER, J. E., G. R. CHANDRA, AND M. J. CHRIS-PEELS. 1965. Gibberellic acid-controlled synthesis of α-amylase in barley endosperm. J. Cellular Comp. Physiol. 66, suppl. 1: 55–68.

25. VENIS, M. A. 1964. Induction of enzymatic activity of indolyl-3-acetic acid and its dependence on synthesis of ribonucleic acid. Nature 202: 900–01.

26. YOMO, H. 1960. Studies on the α-amylase activating substances. IV. On the amylase activating action of gibberellin. Hakko Kyokaishi, 18: 600–02 (C.A. 55: 26145, 1961).

Reprinted from the Proceedings of the National Academy of Sciences
Vol. 59, No. 2, pp. 590–597. February, 1968.

IN VITRO SYNTHESIS OF NATIVE MYOSIN, ACTIN, AND TROPOMYOSIN FROM EMBRYONIC CHICK POLYRIBOSOMES*

By Stuart M. Heywood† and Alexander Rich

DEPARTMENT OF BIOLOGY, MASSACHUSETTS INSTITUTE OF TECHNOLOGY, CAMBRIDGE

Communicated by Paul Doty, October 27, 1967

There is a low level of free ribonuclease present in embryonic chick muscle, and the ribosomes are not attached to an endoplasmic reticulum. Thus, it is easy to isolate the polyribosomes (polysomes) in a relatively undegraded fashion. In a previous study we have shown that it is possible to use the undegraded polysomes isolated from embryonic chick leg muscle to form a highly active cell-free protein synthetic system.[1] A class of large polysomes containing 50–60 ribosomes was shown to be active in the synthesis of myosin. In the present communication we identify the polysomes which carry out the synthesis of actin and tropomyosin—the other major fibrous proteins of muscle tissue. It is further shown that these proteins synthesized *in vitro* have the same chemical properties as those seen in native preparations. From the size of the polysomes and the size of the polypeptide chains, we conclude that all three of these fibrous proteins are being synthesized with monocistronic messenger RNA's. By observing changes in the polysomal pattern during different stages of embryonic development, it is inferred that actin-synthesizing polysomes are formed in large numbers initially, followed by myosin and, finally, tropomyosin polysomes at later stages of embryogenesis.

Materials and Methods.—Methods for preparing the tissue homogenate from leg muscles of 14-day-old chick embryos were described previously.[1] Four polysome fractions, *A–D*, were isolated and pooled from six sucrose gradients. The polysomes from fractions *A* through *D* were sedimented and gently resuspended in buffer. Fraction *A* had 0.1 mg of ribosomes, *B* and *C* each had 0.2 mg, and *D* had 0.35 mg. An energy-generating system, radioactive amino acids, and a pH-5 enzyme fraction were added as described previously to make a total incubation volume of 1.0 ml for each of the four fractions.[1] Incubation was carried out at 37°C for 1 hr, 50 γ of ribonuclease was then added, and the incubation mixtures cooled to 0°. The products of the incubation mixture were analyzed both by acrylamide gel electrophoresis[1] and by protein purification procedures. Myosin was prepared both from adult chicken pectoral muscle and from embryonic leg muscle.[2] After incubation, mixtures *A–D* were each added to 4 ml of a solution containing 10 mg of purified myosin in KCl buffer: 0.5 M KCl, 0.01 M tris buffer (pH 7.4), and 0.001 M ethylenediaminetetraacetate (EDTA). The radioactive products of the cell-free incorporation were analyzed by carrying out a series of purification steps for isolating myosin at 3°C. At each step the radioactivity per milligram of protein was measured. An aliquot of protein was precipitated in 5% trichloroacetic acid and the precipitate collected on Millipore filters for radioactive counting. Protein content was determined by the method of Lowry.[3] The specific activity of the initial mixture is plotted as step 1. The solution was diluted with water to lower the ionic strength to 0.03 M KCl to precipitate myosin. After centrifugation at 10,000 $\times$ g for 10 min, the supernatant was decanted and the precipitate redissolved in 0.5 M KCl buffer. Step 2 is the specific activity of the redissolved material. The ionic strength was then lowered to 0.28 M KCl to precipitate actomyosin. The solution was spun at 20,000 $\times$ g for 20 min, the supernatant decanted, and its specific activity is step 3. The ionic strength of the solution was next reduced to 0.03 by the addition of water and the precipitate was again centrifuged. After decanting, the precipitate was dissolved in 0.5 M KCl buffer for step 4. Saturated NH₄SO₄ was added to the solution and the precipitate obtained between 40 and 47% saturation was collected by low-speed centrifugation. This material was dissolved in the 0.5 M KCl buffer and then dialyzed against this buffer for 18 hr for step 5. The measurements for steps 6, 7, 8, and 9 were repetitions of steps 2, 3, 4, and 5 above. At the end of these procedures, the myosin migrated as a single band on the acrylamide gel.

Tropomyosin was prepared from chicken pectoral muscle by the method of Kay and Bailey.[4] The four incubation tubes, *A–D*, were dialyzed against 1 M KCl for 20 hr at room temperature followed by 4 hr against H_2O at 5°. The reaction mixtures were then added to 5 ml of a solution containing 10 mg of tropomyosin in 0.001 M Tris (pH 7.0). Step 1 represents the specific activity of this material. One M HCl was slowly added to the stirred solution until the pH dropped to 4.6. The precipitate was centrifuged at 10,000 × g for 5 min and the supernatant decanted. The precipitate was then dissolved in 5 ml H_2O and brought to pH 7 by the slow addition of 1 M NaOH. This material was centrifuged at 100,000 × g for 1 hr. The supernatant is step 2. This procedure was repeated again for steps 3 and 4 in the purification sequence. The resultant solution at pH 7 then had solid NH_4SO_4 added to it, and the precipitate which formed between 46 and 70% saturation was collected by slow-speed centrifugation. The precipitate was dissolved in water and dialyzed against a large volume of distilled water for 18 hr for step 5. Steps 6, 7, and 8 in the purification procedure were repetitions of the isoelectric precipitation at pH 4.6, and step 9 was a repetition of step 5. At the end of the tropomyosin purification, the material migrated on acrylamide gel electrophoresis as a single band. Actin was prepared from chicken pectoral muscles by the method of Dowben *et al.*[5] At the end of the incubation, 7 vol of cold acetone were added to the four fractions, the solutions were centrifuged at low speed, and the precipitate dried to form an acetone dry powder. The powder was extracted with 5 ml of actin buffer (0.001 M Tris(pH 7.8), 0.002 M ATP, 0.0002 M ascorbic acid) for 1 hr at 3°. The insoluble residue was centrifuged out at low speed and the supernatant solution had added to it 3 ml of a solution containing 8 mg of actin in buffer. The specific activity of the resultant solution represented the first step in actin purification. The purification was carried out by successively converting actin from the soluble globular to the insoluble fibrous form. KCl was added to a concentration of 0.001 M, and the solution stood overnight. The F actin precipitate was centrifuged at 60,000 × g for 1 hr. After decanting, the precipitate was resuspended in 3 ml of actin buffer and the specific activity measured for step 2. This material dialyzed overnight against actin buffer, then $MgCl_2$ was added to 0.7 mM $MgCl_2$, and it was then allowed to stand for 12 hr. The resultant turbid solution was again centrifuged. This partial polymerization resulted in smaller aggregation and therefore has less trapped impurity. The precipitate was redissolved again in actin solution and its specific activity represents step 3 in the purification. Steps 2, 3, and 2 were repeated to produce steps 4, 5, and 6 in the purification.

Results.—The polysomes obtained from the chick muscle lysate were collected in four separate fractions, *A* through *D*, as shown in Figure 1. Fraction *A* has the largest polysomes with 50–60 ribosomes. These were previously identified as being active in myosin synthesis.[1] Fraction *B* contains polysomes with 15–25 ribosomes as shown by carrying out ribosomal counts in electron microscopic preparations. Fraction *C* has polysomes containing 5–9 ribosomes, while fraction *D* consists mostly of single ribosomes and a small number of ribosomal dimers. Portions of the gradient between the fractions were omitted from the incubation in order to characterize more clearly the material made in these different portions of the gradient. Polysomes from fractions *A–D* were used to prepare systems for cell-free amino acid incorporation as described in *Methods.* Fractions *A–C* were very active in protein synthesis. Fraction *D* had only 6 per cent of the protein synthetic activity of fraction *A*. After 60 minutes of incubation, fraction

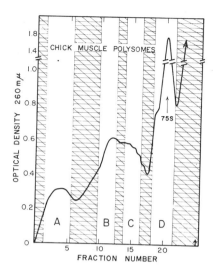

Fig. 1.—Sucrose gradient analysis of cytoplasmic extract from 0.7 gm of 14-day-old embryonic chick leg muscles. The arrow at the lower right represents the position of the last fraction; 75*S* indicates the peak due to single ribosomes. Fractions *A* through *D* were prepared for cell-free protein synthesis, while fractions in the cross-hatched areas were not used.

A had synthesized radioactive protein with 35,000 cpm, or approximately 1 mμ *M* of amino acids, per milligram of ribosomes. At the end of the incubation, 50 γ of ribonuclease were added to each tube and the incubation mixture was cooled and dialyzed against the electrophoresis buffer. The protein was analyzed on acrylamide gels in 12 *M* urea at 45°C to ensure complete denaturation of the fibrous proteins. Purified myosin, actin, and tropomyosin were run under the same conditions in parallel tubes. The results of a typical gel analysis are shown in Figure 2. Fraction *A* shows one major peak which penetrates a short distance into the gel with the same mobility as myosin. These results are similar to those observed previously.[1] The remaining radioactivity in fraction *A* migrates more rapidly than myosin but fails to form well-defined peaks. The total protein was included in all of these preparations, including the radioactive nascent polypeptide chains on polysomes. These smaller peptides would tend to migrate more rapidly than the completed protein in a more or less continuous distribution. Some of this material may account for the more rapidly migrating radioactivity ahead of the main peak in fraction *A*. Fraction *B* has two or three major peaks. The slowest one migrates with the same mobility as actin. In some preparations, the two closely spaced peaks migrating more rapidly than actin did not resolve into two separate components. Fraction *C* has two major peaks, the more rapid of which moves with a mobility equal to that of tropomyosin. The more slowly migrating peak moves with the same speed as one of the components of *B*. The radioactive material formed in fraction *D* never migrates as a single component but rather forms a broad distribution spread along the gel.

The results of the gel analysis suggested that fractions *A*, *B*, and *C* were active in the synthesis of myosin, actin, and tropomyosin, respectively, because one of the products of the cell-free synthesis co-electrophoresed with marker preparations of proteins in the denatured state. In the previous work,[1] myosin could be identified because its polypeptide chain was so large that no other molecules migrated so slowly in the acrylamide gel. However, many proteins migrate at the same speed as actin and tropomyosin. Accordingly, it was necessary to utilize an alternative method to identify the products of cell-free synthesis. This was accomplished by adding small quantities of unlabeled native actin, myosin, or tropomyosin to incubations *A* through *D* and then re-isolating the proteins. If the native protein can be continually re-isolated at constant specific activity, it would indicate that that particular protein had been synthesized in that fraction. This procedure is based on the fact that nonspecific adsorption of contaminating molecules is gradually eliminated through a series of preparative isolations which utilize different chemical properties of the molecules.

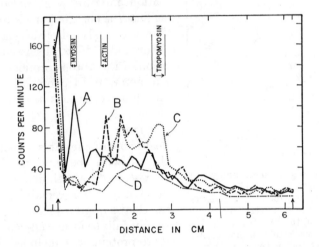

FIG. 2.—Distribution of radioactive proteins on acrylamide gel electrophoresis. The electrophoresis was performed as described previously[1] except that a 0.5-cm 3% spacer gel at pH 7.2 was used on top of a 6-cm 7% running gel at pH 8.6. The electrode buffer was at pH 8.6. A 0.2-ml sample in 12 M urea, 0.1% 2-mercaptoethanol, and 50% sucrose was layered on the 12 M urea gel. Gels were run at 4 ma per tube for 5 hr at 45°C. Direction of migration is to the right.

Radioactivity was measured by freezing and slicing the gel in pieces 0.47-mm thick and counting them in groups of three.

Parallel runs were made with purified preparations of myosin, actin, and tropomyosin, and the position and widths of their peaks are indicated by horizontal arrows at the top.

At each purification step in Figure 3, the radioactivity and the amount of protein were measured so that the specific activity is plotted as a function of purification. Myosin purification utilized the peculiar properties of the native molecule which makes it soluble in high ionic strength KCl but insoluble when the ionic strength is lowered. In addition, myosin precipitates over a narrow concentration range of NH_4SO_4. It can be seen in Figure 3a that the specific activities of fractions B, C, and D decrease at a rapid rate. The NH_4SO_4 precipitation in step 5 eliminated most of the remaining radioactivity in fractions B, C, and D, but the specific activity in A remained near 50 per cent of its initial value and did not decrease further. The tropomyosin purification shown in Figure 3b utilized both isoeletric precipitation of tropomyosin at pH 4.6 as well as NH_4SO_4 precipitation. The results show that almost 40 per cent of the radioactivity in fraction C could be isolated to a constant specific activity of tropomyosin. Fraction B appears to have a small amount of material isolatable as tropomyosin, while fractions A and D have none at all. Figure 3c shows the results when actin is isolated from the

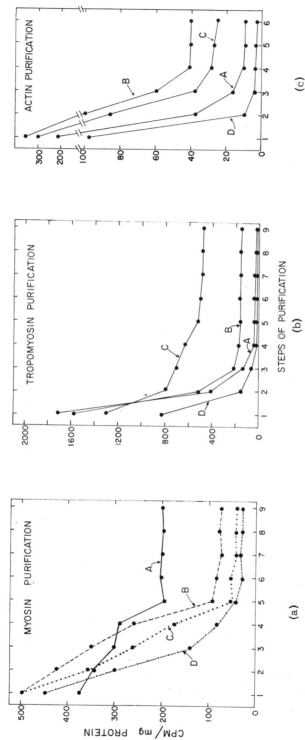

FIG. 3.—Specific radioactivity of proteins synthesized in the cell-free system as a function of purification procedures. At the end of the incubation period, unlabeled protein, myosin, tropomyosin, or actin was added to the incubations A through D. Following this, a series of purification procedures was carried out for the protein which had been added, and the radioactivity was measured per milligram of protein at each step. A–D refer to the four incubation mixtures obtained from the polysomes illustrated in Fig. 1. The isolation procedures are described in *Methods*.

reaction mixtures.   Approximately 12 per cent of the radioactive protein in fraction *B* was isolatable as actin at specific constant activity; slightly more than half of this amount was found in fraction *C*, although the specific activity in that fraction was decreasing during the last three steps of the isolation procedure.

The results of these isolation procedures indicate that fraction *A* has a sizeable component of its radioactive protein with chemical properties identical to those of native myosin molecules, while fraction *C* has a substantial amount which has the properties of tropomyosin.   Actin synthesis appears to be largely in fraction *B*, although some of the actin may also be found in fraction *C*.   This is consistent with the gel electrophoresis pattern which shows a shoulder of one of the migrating peaks in fraction *C* which has the same electrophoretic mobility as purified actin.   Thus there appears to be more actin contaminating fraction *C* than tropomyosin contaminating fraction *B*.   This is probably related to the fact that large polysomes can assume a variety of configurations in solution and consequently sediment in a broader envelope than is found with polysomes containing a smaller number of ribosomes.

The polysomal pattern of chick embryo muscle tissue is characteristic and quite distinct from that found in other tissues.   However, this pattern varies as a function of the developmental age of the embryo.   Figure 4 shows the sucrose gradi-

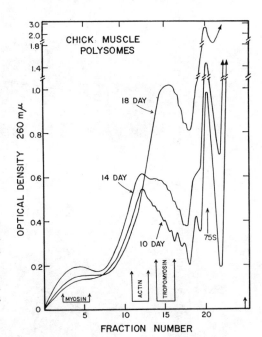

Fig. 4.—Sucrose gradient analyses of cytoplasmic extracts from 0.7 gm of embryonic chick leg muscle at different ages of embryological development.

Single ribosomes are labeled 75*S*.

The positions labeled with myosin, actin and tropomyosin correspond to fractions *A–C* in Fig. 1.

ent analysis of chick embryo muscle polysomes at three different developmental stages.   Each curve represents material from 0.7 gm of embryonic muscle tissue. There is a gradual increase in the number of ribosomes in the tissue as development proceeds.   Seventy per cent of the ribosomes are found in polysomes in the 10-day-old embryo, while 80 per cent are found in polysomes at 18 days.   In the ten day embryo, there is a sharp peak in the polysome region associated with actin synthesis, while the rapidly sedimenting peak of myosin polysomes is relatively small at this early stage. By 14 days there has been a significant increase in the number of myosin polysomes with very little change in the number of polysomes in the region synthesizing actin. A rise of polysomal material is seen at this time in the region where tropomyosin synthesis occurs. By 18 days the pattern has changed appreciably largely due to a great increase in the number of polysomes containing four to eight ribosomes.

Discussion.—The formation of myofilaments in the developing leg muscle of chick embryos has been studied in the electron microscope.[6-8] Two varieties of myofilaments have been seen, actin filaments 60–70 Å in diameter, and thicker myosin filaments, 160–170 Å in diameter. In the early development of chick embryos, the thin actin filaments appear first. At 12 days, the thin filaments still outnumber thick filaments by a ratio of 7:1.[6] These results are in agreement with the polysomal patterns described above. In the electron microscope studies, the actin and myosin filaments are seen to associate together in a hexagonal array before the characteristic appearance of tropomyosin Z band material. These observations are also in agreement with our findings that a prominence in the part of the polysomal peak associated with tropomyosin synthesis appears later in development than that associated with actin or myosin. The marked change in the polysome pattern between 14 and 18 days is due to the emergence of a polysome containing 4–8 ribosomes. We do not know which new protein is being synthesized during this period, although the leg muscles redden between 14 and 18 days. This may be associated with the accumulation of myoglobin.

In hemoglobin synthesis, a ribosomal pentamer is the predominant polysomal species active in synthesizing a polypeptide chain of molecular weight 17,000.[9] In the previous paper[1] identifying the polysomes active in myosin synthesis, it was pointed out that polysomes with 50–60 ribosomes would be capable of synthesizing a polypeptide chain of molecular weight 170,000–200,000 if the ribosomal loading on messenger RNA were similar to that found in hemoglobin synthesis. This is the molecular weight range estimated by physical-chemical techniques for the subunit of myosin.[10, 11] It was concluded that myosin is synthesized on a monocistronic messenger RNA. This analysis can now be extended to actin and tropomyosin. Actin has a molecular weight which has been reported at 60,000–70,000,[12, 13] and it is synthesized predominantly in fraction *B* which contains polysomes with 15–25 ribosomes. If the messenger loading were similar to that seen in the synthesis of hemoglobin, we would expect polysomes containing from 17 to 21 ribosomes to be active in the synthesis of actin. This agreement leads us to infer that the messenger RNA for actin synthesis is monocistronic. Tropomyosin is a molecule made of two identical subunits which have a reported molecular weight of 30,000–35,000.[14] This is synthesized largely in fraction *C* which has polysomes containing five to nine ribosomes. The larger of these covers the size range of polysomes which would be estimated to be active in synthesizing a polypeptide chain of this size if the loading were similar to that seen in hemoglobin synthesis. From this we infer that tropomyosin is also synthesized by monocistronic messenger RNA.

In the present experiments the basis for believing that native molecules of myosin, actin, and tropomyosin were synthesized *in vitro* is the fact that continual re-isolation of these proteins led to a constant specific activity. This implies that the newly synthesized protein has the same chemical properties as the unlabeled carrier protein which was added to the system. These chemical manipulations were sufficiently varied so that it is reasonable to conclude that native molecules had been manufactured in the cell-free system. This implies that the polypeptide chains were assembled and then assumed native configurations, including subunit associations, since the subunits do not have the same chemical properties as the native molecule. However, it is clear that this conclusion must rest ultimately upon a more detailed characterization including fingerprinting techniques.

Summary.—Three groups of different-size polysomes obtained from a sucrose gradient analysis of embryonic chick muscle lysate were used as a basis for a cell-free system of protein synthesis. Incubation and characterization of these three fractions showed that they were synthesizing myosin, actin, and tropomyosin. Isolation and purification of these molecules indicated that they had been formed in a native configuration. From an analysis of the size of the polysomes and the size of the polypeptide chains in the proteins, it was inferred that all of them are synthesized on monocistronic messenger RNA molecules. Changes in the polysomal pattern during embryonic differentiation suggest that actin synthesis is somewhat more predominant initially than myosin synthesis, and that tropomyosin synthesis increases at a later stage than the others.

We wish to thank Professors M. Young and R. M. Dowben for helpful suggestions.

* This research work was supported by grants from the National Institutes of Health and the National Science Foundation.
† National Institute of Health postdoctoral fellow. Present address: Department of Biology, University of Connecticut, Storrs, Connecticut.

[1] Heywood, S. M., R. M. Dowben, and A. Rich, these Proceedings, **57**, 1002 (1967).
[2] Finck, H., *Biochim, Biophys. Acta,* **111**, 208 (1965).
[3] Lowry, O. H., N. Rosebrough, A. L. Farr, and R. J. Randall, *J. Biol. Chem.,* **193**, 265 (1951).
[4] Kay, C. M., and K. Bailey, *Biochim. Biophys. Acta,* **40**, 141 (1960).
[5] Dowben, R. M., W. M. Curry, K. M. Anderson, and R. Zak, *Biochemistry,* **4**, 1264 (1965).
[6] Fischman, D. A., *J. Cell Biol.,* **32**, 557 (1967).
[7] Allen, E. R., and F. A. Pepe, *Am. J. Anat.,* **116**, 115 (1965).
[8] Obinata, T., M. Yamamoto, and K. Maruyama, *Develop. Biol.,* **14**, 192 (1966).
[9] Warren, J. R., A. Rich, and C. E. Hall, *Science,* **138**, 1399 (1962).
[10] Kielly, W. W., and W. F. Hanington, *Biochim. Biophys. Acta,* **41**, 401 (1960).
[11] Driezen, P., D. J. Hartshorne, and A. Stracher, *J. Biol. Chem.,* **241**, 443 (1966).
[12] Hanson, J., and J. Lowy, *J. Mol. Biol.,* **6**, 46 (1963).
[13] Lewis, M. S., K. Maruyama, W. R. Carroll, D. R. Kominz, and K. Laki, *Biochemistry,* **2**, 34 (1963).
[14] Woods, E. F., *J. Mol. Biol.,* **16**, 581 (1966).

Reprinted from the Proceedings of the National Academy of Sciences
Vol. 60, No. 1, pp. 229–234.   May, 1968.

DE NOVO SYNTHESIS OF MYOSIN IN A CELL-FREE SYSTEM*

By Stuart M. Heywood and Mark Nwagwu

INSTITUTE OF CELLULAR BIOLOGY, UNIVERSITY OF CONNECTICUT, STORRS

Communicated by Fritz Lipmann, March 12, 1968

There have been a number of successful attempts to direct protein synthesis in cell-free systems by adding natural messenger RNA (mRNA).[1-3] Some success has been achieved using reticulocyte RNA for programming the synthesis of hemoglobin.[4] However, Hunt and Wilkinson[5] recently pointed out that high-molecular-weight RNA from a variety of sources can stimulate the synthesis of hemoglobin in reticulocyte systems presumably by the stimulation of protection of endogenous RNA on the ribosomes.

Polyribosomes from embryonic chick muscle are a good source of mRNA for *in vitro* protein synthesis. Intact polysomes are obtainable and may be separated into different size classes that synthesize different cell-specific proteins.[6, 7] Using this system, we found that the RNA extracted from myosin-synthesizing polysomes directed the *de novo* synthesis of myosin. RNA from other polysomes or single ribosomes was not effective in promoting myosin synthesis.

Materials and Methods.—We have previously described a method for preparing polysomes from embryonic chick muscle.[6] In the present study, polysomes were obtained from 14- and 15-day-old chick embryo leg muscles. Polysomes of two size classes (*A* and *B*, Fig. 1) as well as single ribosomes (*C*, Fig. 1) were collected from six sucrose gradients. The pelleted ribosomes were stored at $-20°C$ until used.

RNA used to program the *in vitro* synthesis of proteins was prepared as follows: the pelleted polysomes (*A*, *B*) and ribosomes (*C*) were gently resuspended in 0.02 M sodium acetate, and 0.002 M ethylenediaminetetraacetate (EDTA), 0.04 M tris(hydroxymethyl)-aminomethane (Tris) (pH 7.8), and 0.5% Na dodecyl sulfate. The suspension was extracted with 1 vol of buffer-saturated phenol for 4 min at 55°C. The aqueous phase was extracted with phenol a second time for 2 min at 55°C, and the RNA was precipitated by the addition of 2 vol of ethanol at $-20°C$. After 10 hr, the RNA was centrifuged from the ethanol and the tube allowed to drain at 2°C for 1 hr. The RNA was then dissolved in 0.2 ml of 0.15 M KCl, 0.008 M $MgCl_2$, and 0.02 M Tris (pH 7.6).

The enzymes for *in vitro* amino acid incorporation were prepared in 0.15 M KCl, 0.008 M $MgCl_2$, 0.02 M Tris (pH 7.6), and 10% glycerol in the following manner: the lower two thirds of the 150,000 $\times$ g (2 hr) supernatant from 14-day embryonic muscle was dialyzed for 12 hr against glycerol buffer containing 0.003 M 2-mercaptoethanol. The resulting S-150 fraction was stored in 50% glycerol at $-20°C$.

In vitro amino acid incorporation was carried out with 0.2 mg ribosomes (*C*, Fig. 1) suspended in 0.7 ml incubation buffer containing the following: 0.15 M KCl, 0.008 M $MgCl_2$, 0.0025 M dithiothreitol, 0.02 M Tris (pH 7.6), 1.0 μM each of 20 amino acids, and 0.6 mg S-150 enzyme preparation. This mixture was preincubated for 20 min at 37°C in order to reduce endogenous incorporation. A longer preincubation period or addition of an energy source did not further decrease the endogenous incorporation. After preincubation, 2 μmoles adenosine 5′-triphosphate (ATP), 10 μmoles phosphoenolpyruvate, 0.5 μmole guanosine triphosphate (GTP), 50 μg pyruvate kinase, 1 μc of a uniformly labeled C^{14}-amino acid mixture (0.5 mμmole each), and 100 μg RNA from fraction *A*, *B*, or *C* (Fig. 1) were added to the reaction mixtures in a final volume of 1 ml. After incubation for 1 hr at 37°C, KCl was added to a final concentration of 0.5 M, and the mixtures were centrifuged at 150,000 $\times$ g for 2 hr.

The products of amino acid incorporation were analyzed both by acrylamide gel electro-

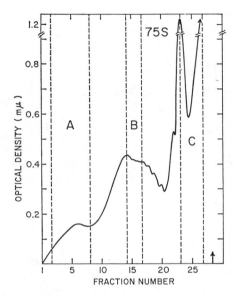

Fig. 1.—Sucrose gradient patterns of cytoplasmic extracts from embryonic chick muscle. The arrow at the lower right indicates the last fraction at top of tube; 75S indicates peak of single ribosomes. Material from fractions A, B, and C were pooled from six sucrose gradients and centrifuged at 150,000 × g for 3 hr. RNA was extracted from the pelleted fractions as described in *Materials and Methods*. Ribosomes and ribosomal subunits for *in vitro* amino acid incorporation were obtained from fraction C.

phoresis as described previously[6] and by O-(diethylaminoethyl)cellulose (DEAE-cellulose) chromatography. Myosin used as a marker was prepared from chick leg muscles by the method of Baril *et al.*[8] Radioactivity was measured with a Nuclear-Chicago liquid scintillation counter after hot trichloroacetic acid (TCA) and ethanol-chloroform extractions. In the case of electrophoretic and chromatographic analysis, radioactivity was measured with a Nuclear-Chicago low-background counter. Chemicals were purchased from Sigma Chemical Co. and radioactive amino acids from New England Nuclear Corp.

Results.—The addition of polysomal RNA to muscle ribosomes in a cell-free system resulted in a marked increase in the incorporation of C[14]-amino acids into TCA-precipitable material (Fig. 2). When ribosomes were incubated without the addition of RNA, only a slight increase in radioactivity occurred. The RNA extracted from fraction B polysomes stimulated incorporation to proceed at a faster rate and the radioactivity to reach a higher maximum than did RNA extracted from fraction A polysomes. Presumably this is due to the greater susceptibility to damage of the larger mRNA associated with fraction A polysomes.

The amount of radioactivity released from the ribosomes during incubation was determined. Without the addition of RNA to the incubation mixtures, most of the radioactivity remained associated with the ribosomes (Table 1). With the addition of RNA from fraction C, there was only a slight increase in total radioactivity with an accompanying increase in the amount of released radioactivity. However, with RNA from either fraction A or B, a large increase in total radioactivity occurred, and 70–80 per cent of this radioactivity was released from the ribosomes during incubation. Normally, RNA from fractions A and B produced a 5- to 15-fold stimulation over the background with no added RNA.

The products of the RNA-directed amino acid incorporation were examined by acrylamide gel electrophoresis. It has been shown previously that myosin will migrate in 12 M urea at 45°C, as a monodisperse, single peak.[7, 9] The

Vol. 60, 1968

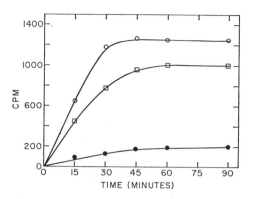

Fig. 2.—Time course of *in vitro* incorporation. Duplicate 0.05-ml samples were withdrawn at intervals during incubation and the radioactivity was determined. Conditions for *in vitro* amino acid incorporation are described in *Materials and Methods*. (●—●) Complete system without added RNA; (□—□) complete system plus 100 μg of RNA from fraction *A;* (○—○) complete system plus 100 μg of RNA from fraction *B*.

150,000 × *g* supernatant of the incubation mixture was therefore analyzed by acrylamide gel electrophoresis. A myosin marker was run concurrently on a separate gel. The results of the gel analysis are shown in Figure 3. The curves labeled *A* through *C* represent the radioactivity associated with the proteins programmed by RNA extracted from polysomes (*A, B*) and ribosomes (*C*). The dotted line represents ribosomes incubated without the addition of RNA. In this case, virtually no radioactivity was found on the gel. Addition of RNA from fraction *C* to the incubation mixture caused only a slight increase in radioactivity with no well-defined peaks. The stimulatory activity of the RNA from fraction *C* may be a nonspecific effect such as that observed by Hunt and Wilkinson[5] in the reticulocyte cell-free systems. The ribosomal RNA from fraction *C* may therefore be used to measure background incorporation.

RNA extracted from fraction *A* and *B* polysomes caused a significant increase in radioactivity, which migrated in a characteristic manner during electrophoresis (Fig. 3). Protein programmed by RNA from polysome fraction *A* migrated in a well-defined peak, which could be superimposed on the myosin marker. It has been shown that large polysomes from embryonic muscle, forming a characteristic shoulder near the bottom of sucrose density gradients, are responsible for myosin synthesis.[6, 7] The results reported here further support this conclusion. Furthermore, virtually all of the radioactivity released from the ribosomes incubated with RNA from fraction *A* can be accounted for in the myosin peak. The small peak at the beginning of the gel is tentatively identified as a

TABLE 1. *Relationship between stimulation of amino acid incorporation by RNA and amount of radioactivity released from ribosomes during incubation.*

Incubation medium	Total cpm	Percentage cpm released
Complete minus RNA	200	<0.5
Complete plus RNA (*A*)	1800	70.0
Complete plus RNA (*B*)	2000	78.0
Complete plus RNA (*C*)	250	20.0

After preincubation, 100 μg RNA from fractions *A–C* (Fig. 1) was added to the complete reaction mixture. Incubations were carried out as described in *Materials and Methods*. After incubation, the reaction mixtures were centrifuged at 150,000 × *g* for 2 hr. The amount of radioactivity of the supernatant was taken as a measure of the released protein.

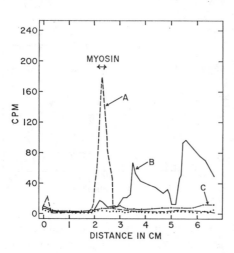

Fig. 3.—Acrylamide gel electrophoresis of radioactive proteins from *in vitro* incorporation directed by RNA from fractions *A–C* (Fig. 1). Dotted line represents the complete system without added RNA. After centrifuging the incubation mixtures, the supernatants were dialyzed for 8 hr against electrode buffer (pH 8.6), 70% glycerol, and 0.1% 2-mercaptoethanol. A 0.2-ml sample was layered on the 3.75% acrylamide, 12 M urea gel and run at 4 ma per tube for 2.5 hr at 45°C. Direction of migration is to the right. A myosin marker was run concurrently in a separate gel. Its position and width of peak is indicated by horizontal arrow at top. Radioactivity was measured by freezing and sectioning the gel in 1-mm slices and counting each slice with a low-background counter.

myosin aggregate (*A*, Fig. 3). It is therefore likely that the polysomes found in fraction *A* are a single population of myosin-synthesizing polysomes.

When RNA extracted from fraction *B* polysomes was added to the incubation mixture, radioactive proteins that migrated more rapidly than myosin were synthesized (*B*, Fig. 3). Although the peaks of radioactivity in curve *B* are more poorly defined, it is apparent that RNA from fraction *B* polysomes directed the synthesis of proteins other than myosin. A reproducible but small peak of radioactivity in curve *B* was found to migrate with the myosin marker. The radioactivity found in this peak amounted to only 5 per cent of the radioactivity migrating as myosin in curve *A* (Fig. 3). It is likely that the presence of the small myosin-like peak in curve *B* is related to the broad sedimentation of large polysomes which assume a variety of configurations in solution.

The synthesis of a radioactive protein, electrophoretically identified as myosin, by RNA from fraction *A* polysomes cannot be attributed to a general nonspecific stimulation of amino acid incorporation (see ref. 5) because: (1) RNA from fraction *A* polysomes programs the synthesis essentially of only this protein; (2) RNA from fraction *B* polysomes directs the synthesis of a number of radioactive proteins electrophoretically distinct from myosin; (3) radioactivity incorporated in the presence of RNA from fraction *C* ribosomes, containing little, if any, mRNA, forms no well-defined peaks. Therefore, it is concluded that fraction *A* RNA specifically directs the *de novo* synthesis of a protein electrophoretically identified as myosin.

The conditions under which acrylamide gel electrophoresis was run allowed only for the analysis of the synthesis of myosin subunits. Accordingly, an alternative procedure was used to test for the *in vitro* synthesis of native myosin. Chromatographically pure myosin can be obtained on DEAE-cellulose.[9, 11] Therefore, in order to determine if the myosin subunits synthesized under the direction of fraction *A* RNA would assemble into native myosin molecules during the incubation, the reaction mixtures were cochromatographed with myosin on DEAE-cellulose. The 150,000 × *g* supernatants from the incubation mixtures were dialyzed against 0.02 M $K_4P_2O_7$ (pH 8.5) containing an excess of C^{12}-

FIG. 4.—DEAE-cellulose cochromatography of radioactive products of RNA (fractions *A–C*, Fig. 1) directed synthesis. The complete system without added RNA (not shown) is identical to *C*. After the reaction mixtures had been centrifuged, the supernatants were dialyzed for 2 hr against 0.02 *M* $K_4P_2O_7$ (pH 8.5) containing an excess of C^{12}-amino acids. Then, 100 μg of myosin was added to each sample. Chromatography was accomplished by eluting the soluble proteins with 120 ml 0.02 *M* $K_4P_2O_7$ (pH 8.5). Myosin was then eluted with 0.36 *M* KCl, 0.02 *M* $K_4P_2O_7$ (pH 8.5). The elution of myosin was followed by absorbance at 280 mμ (fractions 26–28). Finally, 5-ml fractions were collected and assayed for radioactivity. For details of chromatography see Baril *et al.* (1966).

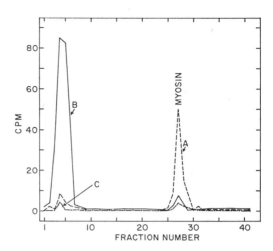

amino acids. Prior to elution, 100 μg of myosin was added to each sample. With the first elution buffer, 0.02 *M* $K_4P_2O_7$ (pH 8.5), all of the soluble proteins were eluted. These appear in fractions 2–7 in Figure 4. The myosin was then eluted with 0.36 *M* KCl, 0.02 *M* $K_4P_2O_7$ (pH 8.5) buffer, which was added after fraction 23 had been collected. Myosin was found in fractions 26–28. The curves *A–C* (Fig. 4) represent the radioactivity associated with proteins synthesized under the direction of RNA from fractions *A–C* (Fig. 1). RNA extracted from fraction *C*, and incubated in the cell-free system, resulted in a low level of radioactive products which eluted with both the soluble proteins and myosin. This level of radioactivity was not measurably different from that observed when ribosomes were incubated without added RNA (not shown in Fig. 4). When RNA from fraction *A* polysomes was incubated in the cell-free system, the radioactive protein that was synthesized cochromatographed with myosin (fractions 26–29). A small amount of radioactivity was eluted with the soluble proteins. This may be accounted for either by the elution of individual myosin subunits or by the synthesis of radioactive proteins by smaller polysomes which had sedimented in a broad envelope contaminating fraction *A* with nonmyosin mRNA. RNA from fraction *B* polysomes directed the synthesis of radioactive proteins which chromatographed with the soluble proteins (fractions 2–7, Fig. 4). As in the case of acrylamide gel electrophoresis, a small amount of radioactivity was found to elute with myosin. Again, this may be a result of the diffuse sedimentation pattern of large polysomes. Nevertheless, the chromatographic analysis of the products of the cell-free system indicates not only that myosin subunits are synthesized *de novo* under the direction of RNA from fraction *A*, but also that they are assembled into the native myosin molecule.

Discussion.—The basis for the success of the experiments reported here lies in the fact that a unique population of large, intact polysomes can be obtained from embryonic muscle tissue. These polysomes, composed of 55–65 ribosomes, have been shown to be responsible for myosin synthesis.[6, 7] The RNA extracted from this specific class of polysomes may be used in directing the synthesis of myosin, whereas RNA from other polysomes of the same tissue may be used as an experimental control. Furthermore, since myosin is composed largely of subunits of molecular weight of approximately 200,000,[10, 12] a relatively small number of initiations will result in the incorporation of measurable amounts of radioactivity.

In order to establish that the stimulatory effect of added RNA in a cell-free amino acid incorporating system is due to the presence of mRNA, two criteria must be met: (1) the synthesis of a specific protein must be dependent upon the addition of RNA; and (2) it must be shown that the RNA does not nonspecifically stimulate or protect endogenous mRNA associated with the ribosomes. In the results reported here, the endogenous activity was lowered by preincubating the ribosomes. Furthermore, the RNA extracted from single ribosomes or polysomes from a different area of the sucrose gradient was not effective in directing myosin synthesis. On the contrary, RNA extracted from nonmyosin-synthesizing polysomes directed the synthesis of proteins other than myosin, while RNA extracted from single ribosomes could only be shown to cause a small nonspecific response. Therefore, it cannot be argued that RNA from the myosin-synthesizing polysomes acts in a nonspecific manner. It is clear that RNA extracted from these large polysomes contains a single population of mRNA which programs the *de novo* synthesis of myosin subunits. These subunits assemble into the native myosin molecule, a protein having a molecular weight of over 500,000.[10, 12]

Preliminary analysis of the proteins synthesized under the direction of RNA from fraction *B* polysomes suggests that actin may also be synthesized under the conditions reported here. This system, then, may allow for the combined study of both the synthesis and interaction of myosin and actin molecules.

The authors thank Drs. H. Herrmann, A. Wachtel, and J. Speyer for their helpful advice in the preparation of the manuscript.

* Contribution no. 158 from the Institute of Cellular Biology, University of Connecticut, Storrs, Connecticut. This investigation was supported by grant HD-00203 from the National Institute of Child Health and Human Development, and by the Research Foundation of the University of Connecticut.
[1] Salser, W., R. F. Gesteland, and A. Bolle, *Nature*, 215, 588 (1967).
[2] Ohtaka, Y., and S. Speigelman, *Science*, 142, 493 (1963).
[3] Van Ravenswaay Claasen, J. C., A. B. J. Van Leeuwen, A. H. Duijts, and L. Bosch, *J. Mol. Biol.*, 23, 535 (1967).
[4] Weisberger, A. S., and S. A. Armentrout, these PROCEEDINGS, 56, 1612 (1966).
[5] Hunt, J. A., and B. R. Wilkinson, *Biochemistry*, 6, 1688 (1967).
[6] Heywood, S. M., R. Dowben, and A. Rich, these PROCEEDINGS, 57, 1002 (1967).
[7] Heywood, S. M., and A. Rich, these PROCEEDINGS, 59, 590 (1968).
[8] Baril, E. F., D. S. Love, and H. Herrmann, *J. Biol. Chem.*, 241, 822 (1966).
[9] Small, P. A., W. F. Harrington, and W. W. Kielley, *Biochim. Biophys. Acta*, 49, 462 (1961).
[10] Dreizen, P., D. J. Hartshorne, and A. Stracher, *J. Biol. Chem.*, 241, 443 (1966).
[11] Harris, M., and C. H. Suelter, *Biochim. Biophys. Acta*, 133, 393 (1967).
[12] Kielley, W. W., and W. F. Harrington, *Biochim. Biophys. Acta*, 41, 401 (1960).

Section III

CHROMOSOMAL DIFFERENTIATION

LYON, M. F., 1961.   Nature *190,* 372. Gene action in the *X*-chromosome of the mouse (*Mus musculus* L.) .

DAVIDSON, R. G., H. M. NITOWSKY, and B. CHILDS, 1963.   Proc. Nat'l Acad. Sci. *50,* 481. Demonstration of two populations of cells in the human female heterozygous for glucose-6-phosphate dehydrogenase variants.

SALZMANN, J., R. DEMARS, and P. BENKE, 1968.   Proc. Nat'l Acad. Sci. *60,* 545. Single-allele expression at an x-linked hyperuricemia locus in heterozygous human cells.

GANDINI, E., S. M. GARTLER, G. ANGIONI, N. ARGIOLAS, and G. DELL'-ACQUA, 1968.   Proc. Nat'l Acad. Sci. *61,* 945. Developmental implications of multiple tissue studies in glucose-6-phosphate dehydrogenase-deficient heterozygotes.

BROWN, D. D., and I. B. DAWID, 1968.   Science *160,* 272. Specific gene amplification in oocytes.

GALL, J. G., 1968.   Proc. Nat'l Acad. Sci. *60,* 553. Differential synthesis of the genes for ribosomal RNA during amphibian oögenesis.

Cells of female mammals carry two copies of each gene on the X (sex) chromosome, while cells of males contain only a single copy. Yet cells of males and females are metabolically identical except in a few specialized tissues. How do the cells correct for this difference in gene dosage?

The genetic studies of Lyon (p. 181) and others gave rise to the theory that only a single X chromosome may be functional in a given cell. It is thought that the other X chromosome of females is condensed and forms the observed "Barr body" (Barr, 1966). Biochemical evidence in support of the theory has been derived from studies on the products of two X-chromosome genes, glucose-6-phosphate dehydrogenase, and hypoxanthine-guanine-phosphoribosyl transferase (pp. 184, 189).

The total shutdown of a complete chromosome may be too crude for differential regulation of most genes; however, the correlation of genetic activity with a cytologically observable differentiation of the X chromosome gives encouragement to similar studies on selective gene regulation on other chromosomes.

Since the choice of which member of a pair of X chromosomes will form the hereditarily stable active chromosome appears to be random, one can estimate the number and distribution of cells at the time of developmental commitment to a particular path of differentiation. An analysis of the development of blood cells by this method is included in this collection (p. 197). There is no apparent reason that the technique cannot be applied to the development of many different tissues.

For many years it has been observed that the number of nucleoli often increases during the differentiation of germ cells into eggs. The site of ribosomal RNA synthesis has been shown to lie in the nucleoli (Penman et al., 1966). The studies of Evans and Birnstiel (1968), Brown and Dawid (p. 201), and Gall (p. 210) have shown that the genes for ribosomal RNA are located in the nucleoli and are found in much larger numbers in developing eggs than in somatic cells. Thus, a selective increase in gene number appears to be one of the mechanisms by which a cell can alter the rate of accumulation of a specific gene product. At present, this mechanism has only been studied in the control of rRNA and tRNA genes because of the difficulty in enriching for other genes by physiochemical techniques.

Barr, M. (1966) Intern. Rev. Cytol. *19,* 35-95. The significance of sex chromatin.

Evans, D., and M. Birnstiel (1968) Biochim. biophys. Acta *166,* 274-276. Localization of amplified ribosomal DNA in the oocyte of *Xenopus laevis.*

Penman, S., I. Smith, and E. Holtzmann (1966) Science *154,* 786-789. Ribosomal RNA synthesis and processing in a particulate site in the HeLa cell.

RELATED READING

Beerman, W. (1966) In "Cell Differentiation and Morphogenesis."
North Holland Publishing Co., pp. 34-54. Differentiation at the level
of the chromosomes.

Gall, J. (1963) In "Cytodifferentiation and Macromolecular Synthesis,"
ed. M. Locke. Acad. Press, pp. 119-143. Chromosomes and cytodifferentiation.

Kiefer, B. (1968) Proc. Nat'l Acad. Sci. *61,* 85-89. Dosage regulation
of ribosomal DNA in *Drosophila melanogaster.*

Ritossa, F., and S. Spiegelman (1965) Proc. Nat'l Acad. Sci. *53,* 737-
745. Localization of DNA complementary to ribosomal RNA in the
nucleolus organizer region in *Drosophila melanogaster.*

(*Reprinted from Nature*, Vol. 190, No. 4773, *pp.* 372–373,
April 22, 1961)

Gene Action in the *X*-chromosome
of the Mouse (*Mus musculus* L.)

Ohno and Hauschka[1] showed that in female mice
one chromosome of mammary carcinoma cells and of
normal diploid cells of the ovary, mammary gland
and liver was heteropyknotic. They interpreted this
chromosome as an *X*-chromosome and suggested
that the so-called sex chromatin was composed of one
heteropyknotic *X*-chromosome. They left open the
question whether the heteropyknosis was shown by
the paternal *X*-chromosome only, or the chromosome
from either parent indifferently.

The present communication suggests that the
evidence of mouse genetics indicates: (1) that the
heteropyknotic *X*-chromosome can be either paternal
or maternal in origin, in different cells of the same
animal; (2) that it is genetically inactivated.

The evidence has two main parts. First, the normal
phenotype of *XO* females in the mouse[2] shows that
only one active *X*-chromosome is necessary for normal
development, including sexual development. The
second piece of evidence concerns the mosaic phenotype of female mice heterozygous for some sex-linked
mutants. All sex-linked mutants so far known
affecting coat colour cause a 'mottled' or 'dappled'
phenotype, with patches of normal and mutant colour,
in females heterozygous for them. At least six mutations to genes of this type have been reported, under
the names mottled[3,4], brindled[3], tortoiseshell[5],
dappled[6], and 26*K* [2]. They have been thought to be
allelic with one another, but since no fertile males
can be obtained from any except, in rare cases,
brindled, direct tests of allelism have usually not
been possible. In addition, a similar phenotype,
described as 'variegated', is seen in females heterozygous for coat colour mutants translocated on to the
X-chromosome[7,8].

It is here suggested that this mosaic phenotype
is due to the inactivation of one or other *X*-chromo-
some early in embryonic development. If this is true,
pigment cells descended from cells in which the
chromosome carrying the mutant gene was inactivated
will give rise to a normal-coloured patch and those in
which the chromosome carrying the normal gene
was inactivated will give rise to a mutant-coloured
patch. There may be patches of intermediate colour

due to cell-mingling in development. The stripes of the coat of female mice heterozygous for the gene tabby, *Ta*, which affects hair structure, would have a similar type of origin. Falconer[9] reported that the black regions of the coat of heterozygotes had a hair structure resembling that of the *Ta* hemizygotes and homozygotes, while the agouti regions had a normal structure.

Thus this hypothesis predicts that for all sex-linked genes of the mouse in which the phenotype is due to localized gene action the heterozygote will have a mosaic appearance, and that there will be a similar effect when autosomal genes are translocated to the *X*-chromosome. When the phenotype is not due to localized gene action various types of result are possible. Unless the gene action is restricted to the descendants of a very small number of cells at the time of inactivation, these original cells will, except in very rare instances, include both types. Therefore, the phenotype may be intermediate between the normal and hemizygote types, or the presence of any normal cells may be enough to ensure a normal phenotype, or the observed expression may vary as the proportion of normal and mutant cells varies, leading to incomplete penetrance in heterozygotes. The gene bent-tail, *Bn* [10], may fit into this category, having 95 per cent penetrance and variable expression in heterozygotes. Jimpy, *jp*, is recessive, suggesting that the presence of some normal cells is enough to ensure a normal phenotype, but Phillips[11] reported one anomalous female which showed the jimpy phenotype. Since it showed the heterozygous phenotype for *Ta* this animal cannot be interpreted as an *XO* female ; it is possible that it represents an example of the rare instance when by chance all the cells responsible for the jimpy phenotype had the normal gene inactivated.

The genetic evidence does not indicate at what stage of embryonic development the inactivation of one *X*-chromosome occurs. In embryos of the cat, monkey and man sex-chromatin is first found in nuclei of the late blastocyst stage[12,13]. Inactivation of one *X* at a similar stage of the mouse embryo would be compatible with the observations. Since an *XO* female is normally fertile it is not necessary to postulate that both *X*-chromosomes remain functional until the formation of the gonads.

The sex-chromatin is thought to be formed from one *X*-chromosome also in the rat, *Rattus norvegicus*[14], and in the opossum, *Didelphis virginiana*[15]. If this should prove to be the case in all mammals, then all female mammals heterozygous for sex-linked mutant genes would be expected to show the same phenomena as those in the mouse. The coat of the tortoiseshell cat, being a mosaic of the black and yellow colours of the two homozygous types, fulfils this expectation.

MARY F. LYON

Medical Research Council
Radiobiological Research Unit,
Harwell, Didcot.

[1] Ohno, S., and Hauschka, T. S., *Cancer Res.*, **20**, 541 (1960).
[2] Welshons, W. J., and Russell, L. B., *Proc. U.S. Nat. Acad. Sci.*, **45**, 560 (1959).
[3] Fraser, A. S., Sobey, S., and Spicer, C. C., *J. Genet.*, **51**, 217 (1953).
[4] Lyon, M. F., *J. Hered.*, **51**, 116 (1960).
[5] Dickie, M. M., *J. Hered.*, **45**, 158 (1954).
[6] Phillips, R. J. S., *Genet. Res.* (in the press).
[7] Russell, L. B., and Bangham, J. W., *Genetics*, **44**, 532 (1959).
[8] Russell, L. B., and Bangham, J. W., *Genetics*, **45**, 1008 (1960).
[9] Falconer, D. S., *Z. indukt. Abstamm. u. Vererblehre*, **85**, 210 (1953).
[10] Garber, E. D., *Proc. U.S. Nat. Acad. Sci.*, **38**, 876 (1952).
[11] Phillips, R. J. S., *Z. indukt. Abstamm. u. Vererblehre*, **86**, 322 (1954).
[12] Austin, C. R., and Amoroso, E. C., *Exp. Cell Res.*, **13**, 419 (1957).
[13] Park, W. W., *J. Anat.*, **91**, 369 (1957).
[14] Ohno, S., Kaplan, W. D., and Kinosita, R., *Exp. Cell Res.*, **18**, 415 (1959).
[15] Ohno, S., Kaplan, W. D., and Kinosita, R., *Exp. Cell Res.*, **19**, 417 (1960).

Printed in Great Britain by Fisher, Knight & Co., Ltd., St. Albans.

Reprinted from the PROCEEDINGS OF THE NATIONAL ACADEMY OF SCIENCES
Vol. 50, No. 3, pp. 481–485. September, 1963.

DEMONSTRATION OF TWO POPULATIONS OF CELLS IN THE HUMAN FEMALE HETEROZYGOUS FOR GLUCOSE-6-PHOSPHATE DEHYDROGENASE VARIANTS*

BY RONALD G. DAVIDSON,[†] HAROLD M. NITOWSKY, AND BARTON CHILDS

DEPARTMENTS OF PEDIATRICS, SINAI HOSPITAL OF BALTIMORE, AND THE
JOHNS HOPKINS UNIVERSITY SCHOOL OF MEDICINE

Communicated by Theodore T. Puck, July 17, 1963

In 1932, Muller coined the term "dosage compensation"[1] to account for the equality of phenotypic expression in males and females for most genes located on the X chromosome. Over the years several explanatory theories for this phenomenon have been considered, and these have been recently reviewed by Stern[2] and by McKusick.[3]

In 1961, a unique hypothesis was developed by Lyon[4] and by Russell.[5] The hypothesis, often referred to as the "Lyon Hypothesis," proposes that in each somatic cell of the female, one of the two X chromosomes is genetically inactive. The inactivation must occur early in development, and it is a matter of chance whether the maternal or paternal X is inactivated. Once an X chromosome is inactivated in a developing cell, all progeny of that cell presumably maintain the same inactive X.

Examination of single cells in a female who is heterozygous for an X-linked gene(s) with a measurable effect would provide direct evidence bearing on the hypothesis. In such a case, the female would be expected to produce a mosaic of X chromosome activity. In some of her cells, one allele would be active; in the remainder, the other allele would function.

The enzyme, glucose-6-phosphate dehydrogenase (G-6-PD), provides both a quantitative and a qualitative tool for testing the hypothesis. It has been shown that in a Caucasian male whose erythrocytes have deficient G-6-PD activity cultured skin cells are also clearly deficient.[6] Our own studies have confirmed this and have shown the ranges of activities for skin cells of the various genotypes.[7] If the "Lyon Hypothesis" holds, the heterozygous Caucasian female should produce two quantitatively different cell populations, one with G-6-PD activity in the mutant range, and one with activity in the normal range.

Starch gel electrophoresis has demonstrated qualitative variants of erythrocyte and leucocyte G-6-PD in the American Negro population, but not among Caucasians.[8, 9] Negro males can have a fast G-6-PD band, A, or a slow one, B. Females can have A, B, or both A and B. These studies have proved that the electrophoretic variants are inherited, and that the responsible genetic locus is on the X chromosome. Thus, if the "Lyon Hypothesis" applies, the female who is heterozygous for the two electrophoretic variants should also be a mosaic—some of her cells producing A type G-6-PD, some the B type, but none producing both.

The quantitative and qualitative variants are genetically related, but the precise relationship is not clear. With rare exceptions, among Negroes, all males with erythrocyte G-6-PD deficiency have the A electrophoretic variant. However, not all males with A variant are enzyme-deficient. To date, all Caucasians have the B electrophoretic band.

This paper reports the results of quantitative and qualitative analyses of clones derived from single cells from females heterozygous for the G-6-PD variants.

Materials and Methods.—Individuals studied: Skin biopsies from 17 Caucasian males and females were obtained in Sardinia, and these were studied for G-6-PD deficiency.[7] The genotype of each individual was designated in a previous family analysis.[10]

The Negro females presumed to be heterozygous for the qualitative electrophoretic variants were selected on the basis of appearance of two electrophoretic G-6-PD bands in extracts of cultured cells. Four of the six women were also studied for erythrocyte G-6-PD deficiency[10] and are heterozygous for the enzyme deficiency as well. Two of the women with the AB phenotype were found among Negro female employees at Sinai hospital.

Experimental procedures: (1) *Skin biopsies:* Biopsies were obtained without anesthesia using a high-speed electric rotating biopsy punch.[11] A core drill of 3 mm in diameter was employed. (2) *Culture technique:* The cores of skin were minced into 20 or 30 tiny fragments and cultured in Eagle's "Minimum Essential Medium" with 20% human AB or B serum and 5% beef embryo extract ultrafiltrate.[12] Plastic culture dishes were used, and the tissue was incubated at 37°C in an atmosphere of 5% CO_2 in air. Clones were developed from single cell platings of cultured cells according to the techniques described by Puck *et al.*[13] (3) *Assay of G-6-PD activity:* Suspensions of cultured cells were disrupted by sonication, and enzyme activities were measured by a modification of the method of Kornberg and Horecker.[14] A Beckman DU spectrophotometer, equipped with a Gilford optical density converter, model 220, was used. G-6-PD activities are expressed as Δ O. D. per mg of protein per hr. (4) *Electrophoresis:* Sonicates of cultured cells were subjected to starch gel electrophoresis, using the Smithies technique.[15] The continuous buffer system of Kirkman[8] was used, substituting 0.02 M sodium barbital for this, and the gels were developed after 15–16 hr using the procedure described by Boyer *et al.*[9]

Results.—Quantitative study: In Table 1, G-6-PD activities are given for two proved heterozygous Caucasian women. Four clones were analyzed from each, and in each case one clone was clearly in the deficient range and three in the normal range. The established ranges of G-6-PD activity in skin cell culture for normal and deficient Caucasians are given below the table.[7]

TABLE 1

CLONE RESULTS—HETEROZYGOUS CAUCASIAN FEMALES (G-6-PD ACTIVITY/MG PROTEIN)

Individual	Original activity*	Clone number	Clone activity
Sardinian #3	6.3	1	12.9
		3	8.7
		5	9.0
		2	1.2
Sardinian #5	2.4	13	2.7
		2	9.7
		15	9.1
		16	10.3

Ranges of G-6-PD activity for cultured Caucasian skin cells
Normal (males and females): 5.2–16.2

Deficient $\Big\langle$ Hemizygous males
               Homozygous females : 0.7–3.4

* Refers to the activity of the cultured cell strain prior to cloning.

In Table 2, original and clonal G-6-PD activities are compared for various genotypes. It is quite evident that deficient individuals produce clones with deficient enzyme activities, and clones derived from normal individuals have normal enzyme activities.

TABLE 2

CLONE RESULTS—NORMAL AND DEFICIENT CAUCASIANS

Individual	Sex	Genotype	Original activity	Clone number	Clone activity
Sardinian #4	Male	Hemizygous mutant	1.8	1	1.3
				2	1.2
				5	2.1
Sardinian #13	Female	Homozygous mutant	2.3	4	1.6
Sardinian #12	Male	Hemizygous normal	10.4	1	13.7
Sardinian #14	Female	Homozygous normal	11.1	4	11.3

Qualitative (electrophoretic) study: Clones have been developed from single cell platings from six Negro women found to have the two G-6-PD electrophoretic bands; that is, they are all presumed heterozygotes for the electrophoretic variants. With no exceptions, the clones have yielded only single bands, some of which are A and some B. Table 3 shows the number of A and B clones for each heterozygote. Figure 1 depicts two heterozygous females (double bands), and three individuals with single bands, 2 A's and 1 B. Figure 2 shows an original double band with nine clones beside it, 3 A's and 6 B's.

Discussion.—Both the quantitative and qualitative clonal data show that, with respect to the G-6-PD locus, there are indeed two distinct populations of cells in the heterozygous female. This is direct evidence in favor of the "Lyon Hypothesis"—in each single cell of the female only one G-6-PD locus is operative. Thus,

TABLE 3

RESULTS OF STARCH GEL ELECTROPHORESIS OF CLONES FROM WOMEN WHO POSSESS THE AB ELECTROPHORETIC G-6-PD PHENOTYPE

	Mrs. Bi.	Mrs. Mi.	Mrs. Wi.	Mrs. Bo.	Mrs. De.	Mrs. Ha.
Type A	8	1	0	8	7	0
Type B	2	8	8	0	7	5
Type AB	0	0	0	0	0	0
Total number of clones	10	9	8	8	14	5

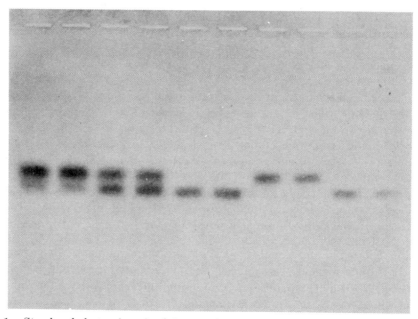

Fig. 1.—Starch gel electrophoresis of G-6-PD from sonicates of cultured skin cells. Samples were run in duplicate, starting from the origin which appears at the top of the figure. From left to right are shown the AB phenotype of 2 Negro females (double bands) and 3 individuals with single bands, 2 A's (fast band) and 1 B (slow band).

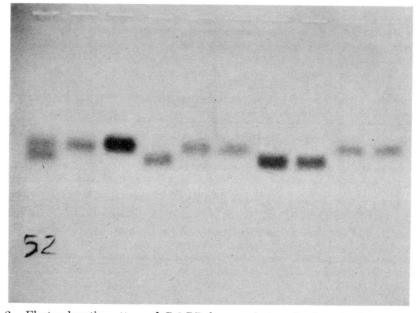

Fig. 2.—Electrophoretic pattern of G-6-PD from sonicates of cultured cells. Samples were run singly, starting from the origin at the top of the figure. From left to right are the AB phenotype of the cell culture from Mrs. De. prior to cloning, and the single bands of nine clones derived from the original cell lines. Variation in intensity of staining is due to inequality of enzyme concentration applied to the starch gel.

the inactivation of one, or at least part of one, X chromosome is most probably the mechanism of dosage compensation.

However, these findings do not imply that an entire X chromosome is inactivated in the female. Recent experiments involving the sex-linked Xg[a] blood group have failed to show mosaicism.[16]

The probable mechanism of inactivation of an X chromosome is its transformation into heterochromatin. This belief is based on the observation that in the female one X chromosome is allocyclic,[17] replicates late,[18, 19] and probably forms the heterochromatic sex chromatin body.[20] However, inactivation of chromosomes by conversion to heterochromatin is not an all or none phenomenon either. In Drosophila, several genes are known to function even though located in the midst of heterochromatin,[21] and in a recent paper, Russell[22] has described experiments using translocations of marked autosomal fragments to the X chromosomes of female mice. It was shown that heterochromatin does not inactivate the entire attached fragment. Instead, there is a gradient of inactivation spreading only over limited distances.

Summary.—The appearance of two distinct populations of cells in the female heterozygous for both quantitative and qualitative G-6-PD variants is direct evidence in favor of the "Lyon Hypothesis." As far as the locus for G-6-PD is concerned, in each single cell only one X chromosome is functional. However, these data do not imply that one entire X chromosome is inactivated.

The authors wish to express their gratitude to Prof. M. Siniscalco and his associates in Italy, under whose auspices the skin biopsies from Sardinia were collected. The technical assistance of Mr. Denis Soderman is gratefully acknowledged.

* This investigation was supported by grants A–494 and GM-05945 from the National Institutes of Health.

† Trainee under Genetics Training Grant 2G–795 of the National Institutes of Health.

[1] Muller, H. J., in *Proceedings of the Sixth International Congress of Genetics*, vol. 1 (1932), p. 213.

[2] Stern, C., *Can. J. Genet. Cytol.*, **2**, 105 (1960).

[3] McKusick, V. A., *Quart. Rev. Biol.*, **37**, 117 (1963).

[4] Lyon, M. F., *Nature*, **190**, 372 (1961).

[5] Russell, L. B., *Science*, **133**, 1795 (1961).

[6] Gartler, S. M., E. Gandini, and R. Ceppellini, *Nature*, **193**, 602 (1962).

[7] Nitowsky, H. M., R. G. Davidson, and B. Childs, in press.

[8] Kirkman, H. N., *Am. J. Human Genet.*, in press.

[9] Boyer, S. H., J. H. Porter, and R. G. Weilbacher, these Proceedings, **48**, 1868 (1962).

[10] Davidson, R. G., M. Siniscalco, and B. Childs, in press.

[11] Davidson, R. G., S. W. Brusilow, and H. M. Nitowsky, *Nature*, **199**, 296 (1963).

[12] Chu, E. H. Y., and N. H. Giles, *Am. J. Human Genet.*, **11**, 63 (1959).

[13] Puck, T. T., P. J. Marcus, and S. J. Cieciura, *J. Exptl. Med.*, **103**, 273 (1956).

[14] Kornberg, A., and B. L. Horecker, in *Methods of Enzymology*, ed. S. P. Colowick and N. O. Kaplan (New York: Academic Press, 1955), vol. 1, p. 323.

[15] Smithies, O., *Biochem. J.*, **71**, 585 (1959).

[16] Gorman, J. G., A. M. Treacy, and A. Cahan, *J. Lab. Clin. Med.*, **61**, 642 (1963).

[17] Ohno, S., and T. S. Hauschka, *Cancer Res.*, **20**, 541 (1960).

[18] Taylor, J. H., *J. Biophys. Biochem. Cytol.*, **7**, 455 (1960).

[19] German, J., Jr., *Trans. N. Y. Acad. Sci.*, Ser. 2, **24**, 395 (1962).

[20] Ohno, S., and S. Makino, *Lancet*, **1**, 78 (1961).

[21] Cooper, K. W., *Chromosoma*, **10**, 535 (1959).

[22] Russell, L. B., *Science*, **140**, 976 (1963).

Reprinted from the Proceedings of the National Academy of Sciences
Vol. 60, No. 2, pp. 545–552. June, 1968.

SINGLE-ALLELE EXPRESSION AT AN X-LINKED HYPERURICEMIA LOCUS IN HETEROZYGOUS HUMAN CELLS*

By Jeanette Salzmann,† Robert DeMars, and Paul Benke‡

GENETICS LABORATORY, UNIVERSITY OF WISCONSIN, MADISON

Communicated by R. A. Brink, April 4, 1968

One type of control over genic expression involves repression of genes on all but one of the X chromosomes in somatic cells of mammals, according to the Lyon hypothesis[1] or a counterpart of this concept termed the single-active-X hypothesis.[2] (See refs. 3–6 for recent reviews.) The differentiation into a single "active" X and additional "inactive" X's (one in normal females) begins during cleavage. The two functional states of the X defined at that time appear to be stable during succeeding cell divisions; active X's replicate as such, and inactive X's produce only inactive replicas. The X that is active can be of maternal origin in some cells and of paternal origin in other cells of an individual. These statements imply that cells heterozygous for X-linked alleles will have the phenotype corresponding to either one allele or the other and that such single-allele expression[7] will be manifested in clones derived from heterozygotes. Tests of this prediction can be made with clones of cultured cells that are heterozygous for X-linked genes having phenotypes which are expressed *in vitro*. This aspect of the single-active-X control scheme has already been demonstrated in clones of cultured human cells that were heterozygous for alleles at the X-linked loci concerned with glucose-6-phosphate dehydrogenase (G6PD)[7, 8] or with Hunter's syndrome.[9] Similar studies of additional genes will be necessary to evaluate the hypotheses correctly and to discover how the control is effected.

Primary hyperuricemia in boys is often the pathological expression of mutant alleles, *jh*, of a normal X-linked gene, *Jh*.[10] The immediate biochemical lesion is a deficiency in the enzyme hypoxanthine-guanine-phosphoribosyl transferase ("PRTase"; E.C. 2.4.2.8[11]), which converts the bases hypoxanthine and guanine into their ribonucleotides.[12, 13] The enzyme can be indirectly demonstrated in cultured fibroblasts by autoradiography of cells grown in a medium containing tritiated hypoxanthine. Fibroblasts grown from mutant individuals incorporate little or none of the radioactive compound into their nucleic acids and have few grains of reduced silver over them in autoradiographs.[14]

The hypothesis of X-linked inheritance of hyperuricemia is supported by the observation of the disease in males only up to the present time and by the data from five published pedigrees[15−17] (and our unpublished pedigree). Additional supporting evidence which suggests linkage of the *Jh* locus to the X-linked locus, Xg_a, is found in one pedigree.[17] Assuming X-linkage of *Jh*, one would expect the locus to exhibit single-allele expression. Rosenbloom *et al.*[14] have described the occurrence of phenotypically normal and phenotypically mutant cells in a culture derived from the skin of a female heterozygous for the mutant *jh* gene. We demonstrate here that clones of cells cultured from such heterozygotes maintain the same discreteness and are of two phenotypic classes, normal and mutant. These data provide additional support for the single-active-X hypothesis by

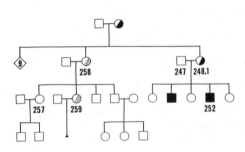

Fig. 1.—Pedigree depicting part of a larger kindred in which the mutant *jh* gene was transmitted through at least four generations. Numbers refer to the strains of cells derived from the indicated donors. Individuals not having a number designation have not yet been studied with cell culture methods. Mutant males are designated by solidly filled squares, and half-filled circles denote obligate heterozygotes. Circles half-filled with dots signify females presumed to be heterozygous on the basis of the present results. The small triangle indicates a spontaneous abortion, and the diamond represents sibships that are not diagrammed in detail here.

showing that one more system, the third in which clones could be tested, yielded the expected result.

Materials and Methods.—Human subjects and cell cultures: Skin fibroblasts were cultivated from members of the pedigree shown in Figure 1 with the use of described methods.[7] No. 252 (and his affected brother) have characteristics conforming to the syndrome described by Lesch and Nyhan.[18] His red cells were deficient in PRTase activity. Since the mother (no. 248.1) had two affected sons but is, herself, phenotypically normal, we assume that she is heterozygous. Cultures 157 and 254 were from normal females unrelated to the kindred. The medium used, referred to as "2:1" below, and consisting of two parts Diploid Medium (Grand Island Biol. Co.) and one part F_4,[19] supplemented with 15% fetal bovine serum, was found to support more rapid growth than either of these media alone.

Autoradiography: (1) *Uncloned populations:* Cells were inoculated onto 22 × 22-mm cover slips in 35-mm-diameter Falcon plastic Petri dishes at about $^1/_{20}$ maximal density. The medium was renewed on the second day after subculture, and radioactive hypoxanthine (see (3) below) was introduced on the third day, when the cell populations were increasing rapidly.

(2) *Clones:* Method I: Trypsinized cell suspensions from nearly confluent monolayer cultures were diluted to contain ten cells per milliliter, and 2-ml aliquots were distributed in 35-mm Petri dishes with 22 × 22-mm cover slips, giving an average of about ten cells per cover slip.

Method II: Aliquots (0.02 ml) of a cell suspension containing 50 cells per milliliter were placed on cover slips (18 mm in diameter) in 35-mm dishes which contained 0.1 ml of 2:1 about their perimeters to reduce evaporation. Two ml of 2:1 were added to each dish after a 3–4-hr attachment period. The medium was replaced twice weekly after the first week until labeling was done 3–4 weeks after inoculation. Clones by method I averaged 5 mm in diameter and contained about 2×10^4 cells, whereas clones by method II averaged about 1.5×10^5 cells.

(3) *Labeling:* Culture medium was replaced with 2 ml of 2:1 containing 5 μc/ml of tritiated hypoxanthine (Tracerlab; sp. act. 6.3 c/mmole) or 25 μc/ml (sp. act. 1.4 c/mmole) in the case of 43 method II clones of no. 248.1. Cover slips were rinsed in 0.9% NaCl after 6 hr of incubation and then fixed in absolute methanol for 10–15 min. They were then air-dried. After a 10–15-minute treatment with ice-cold 5% trichloroacetic acid, cover slips were rinsed in three changes of distilled water, dried, and mounted (cells up) on slides with a drop of Permount. Ilford K.5. emulsion was applied, exposed at −20°C and developed with standard techniques described by Prescott.[20]

Microscopic observations: The unstained cells were first located with phase-contrast optics. If labeled, they remained visible when examined with bright-field optics but became virtually invisible if unlabeled. A standard pattern of fields sampling entire cover slips was used in scoring uncloned populations. Obvious macroscopic differences in grain density were confirmed microscopically, whereas individual cells were scored at 128–640 magnifications. Some slides were mounted in glycerine for detailed study with a $40\times$ oil apochromat objective.

Results.—The phase-contrast and bright-field appearances of normal cells (no. 247) after autoradiography are illustrated in Figure 2A and B. Every cell is clearly visible in uncloned populations when viewed with bright-field illumination; each cell is distinctly labeled, with the densest labeling usually over the nucleus. Densely labeled nuclei remain, but the cytoplasms become unlabeled after RNase treatment.

Mutant cells (no. 252) are almost invisible when viewed with bright-field optics after autoradiography (Fig. 2C and D), although examination with higher magnification reveals a low degree of labeling over the cells.

Cells with the mutant phenotype and normal-appearing cells were both found in uncloned populations of the obligate heterozygote no. 248.1. Figure 2E and F show a sample field in which five of the ten cells visible with phase contrast became almost invisible with bright field. Similar cells were found in uncloned populations of three other females (nos. 257, 258, and 259) from the kindred, each of whom is potentially heterozygous.

The two distinct cell types were used as scoring standards and in discerning a "plus-minus" ($\pm$) category of cells. The $\pm$ cells had an apparent excess of silver grains when compared with standard mutant cells (the grains were numerous

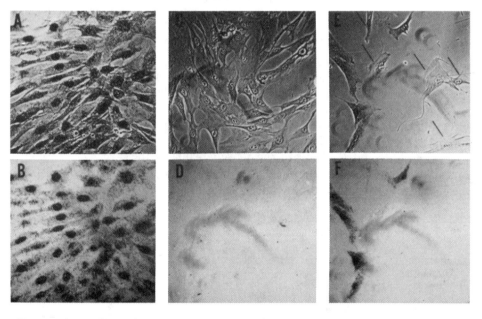

FIG. 2.—Autoradiographic appearance of cultured fibroblasts after growth in the presence of tritiated hypoxanthine. (*A*), (*C*), and (*E*) Phase-contrast views of cells whose bright-field appearances are shown in (*B*), (*D*), and (*F*), respectively. (*A*, *B*) Cell strain 247 (normal); (*C*, *D*) 252 (mutant); (*E*, *F*) 248.1 (heterozygous). Pointers in (*E*) indicate heterozygous cells with the mutant phenotype, which are visible with phase contrast but not with bright field ($111.55\times$.)

Table 1.   *Autoradiographic phenotypes of cells in uncloned populations of fibroblasts grown with H³-hypoxanthine.*

Strain no.	Genotype	(−) Cells	(+) Cells	(±) Cells	Total	(−) Cells (%)
Affected males:						
252	jh/Y	3342	0	0	3342	100
253	jh/Y	2326	0	0	2326	100
255	jh/Y	1711	0	0	1711	100
Heterozygotes:						
248.1	Jh/jh	82	788	46	916	9
257	Jh/jh*	2	1905	9	1916	0.1
258	Jh/jh*	39	941	50	1030	4
259	Jh/jh*	14	943	23	980	1.4
Controls:						
247	Jh/Y	0	2079	0	2079	0
254	Jh/Jh	0	2027	0	2027	0

* These genotypes are assigned because these females could be heterozygous on the basis of their relationships to members of the kindred known to have the mutant gene and because they have − cells.

enough to make the cells visible in bright field but did not define the cell outlines as in standard normal cells).   The frequencies of the three categories of cells in various strains are given in Table 1.   Cells of the ± type occurred only in the four strains derived from proved or potential heterozygotes.   Cultures from controls or mutant males contained only one cell type.

The clonal continuity of phenotypically mutant and of phenotypically normal cells was established by growing clones from one proved and two potentially heterozygous females and from one female control.   The results are presented in Table 2.

Two types of clones were derived from the proved (no. 248.1) and presumptively (nos. 258 and 259) heterozygous strains.   One type of clone was scored minus (−) because all individual cells were so lightly labeled as to place them in the − or ± class; an abundance of cells could be seen in these clones (Fig. 3*A* and *C*), but the same cells were almost invisible when viewed with bright-field illumination (Fig. 3*B* and *D*).   The second type of clone was distinctly plus (+).   Figure 3*E* and *F* illustrate the dense labeling of these + cells.   Macroscopically these + clones are dark gray (Fig. 3*G*), whereas negative clones are transparent when viewed in this manner.

Table 2.   *Autoradiographic phenotypes of clones of fibroblasts cultured from control and experimental females.*

Strain no.	Genotype	(+) Clone	(−) Clone*	Total	(−) Clone (%)
Method I:					
248.1	Jh/jh	78	61	139	44
258	Jh/jh	124	99	223	44
259	Jh/jh	106	72	178	40
157	Jh/Jh	221	0	221	0
Method II:					
248.1	Jh/jh	13	30	43†	69†

* (−) Clones contain mainly − cells and lack + cells, but they do have some ± cells.
† These numbers apply only to cover slips having purely + or − growths. In addition, nine cover slips had growths with + and − sectors (see text).

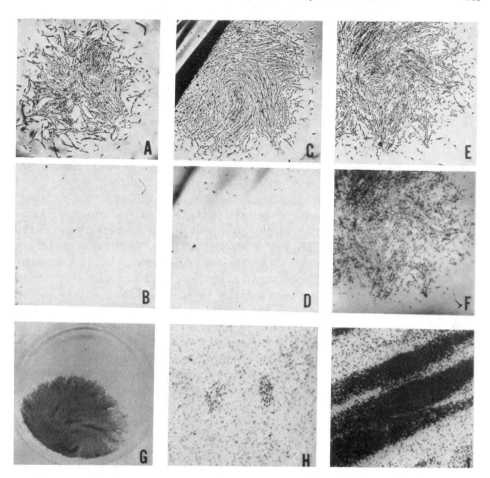

FIG. 3.—Autoradiographic appearance of heterozygous clones after growth in the presence of tritiated hypoxanthine. (*A*), (*C*), and (*E*) Phase-contrast views of clones whose bright-field appearances are shown in (*B*), (*D*), and (*F*), respectively. (*A, B*) − Clone of strain 248.1; (*C, D*) − Clone of strain 258; (*E, F*) + Clone of strain 258. These clones were produced by method I (see text) (*A–F:* 14.55×). (*G*) Macroscopic view of a + clone of strain 248.1 produced with method II(see text) (1.94×). (*H*) Bright-field appearance of cells in a − clone of no. 248.1. Note the concentration of label over the nuclei of two ± cells (496.64). (*I*) Bright-field appearance of cells from a + clone of no. 248.1 (496.64×).

Nine cover slips in the cloning experiment with method II bore cell populations consisting of large + and − sectors that obviously represented clones which had originated from two separate cells and had become confluent.   The number of such cover slips agrees with expectation based on the proportions of purely + and purely − cover slips in the experiment and the probability (Poisson) of drops containing two cells initially.   This implies that some growths scored as being purely + or purely − actually originated from two cells of the same phenotypic class. The proportions of + and − clones given in Table 2 are to be regarded, therefore, as merely reasonably close estimates.

Individual ± and + cells from separate clones of a heterozygote are compared in Figure 3*H* and *I*.   No cell having a degree of labeling approaching that found in standard + cells has yet been found in − clones.

All 221 clones from a control female strain (no. 157) were unmistakably +.

Discussion.—The results demonstrate clonal, single-allele expression at the *Jh* locus in cultured, heterozygous cells.   Similar demonstrations have been made with cells heterozygous for alleles at the loci concerned with G6PD[7, 8] and Hunter's syndrome,[9] the only other genes that have been tested.   These three loci are not functionally related in any obvious way.   Data concerning their linkage relation within the X chromosome are still scanty.[17, 21]   Conceivably, single-allele expression is an attribute of a particular segment of the X containing the three loci, but it cannot be an attribute of only one of them.[22]

The frequency with which activation of the inactive alleles occurs in cultured cells can now be estimated with greater accuracy than previously.   Earlier studies of G6PD in cultured, heterozygous cells utilized alleles causing electrophoretic variation[7, 8] or a deficiency[8] in enzyme activity.   Activation could have been manifested by expression of both alleles in individual cells or by reversal of their roles as expressed and unexpressed alleles.   A 5 per cent admixture of these cells probably could not have been detected in single clones because of the high background activity possessed by the predominant type of cell.   Estimates of activation based on enzyme activities will be more sensitive where the activity of single cells can be evaluated.   A single-cell method capable of detecting + cells in G6PD − clones has been described.[23]   In principle, single mutant cells in initially normal clones of cells heterozygous for the gene causing Hunter's syndrome[9] can also be detected, but heterozygous cells in which both alleles are expressed may have a phenotype that is not distinguishable from normal.   The *Jh* alleles used here seem to be ideal for studying activation at the single-cell level since no clearly + cells have so far been detected in cell populations from mutant males.   Should any + cells be found in such cultures, they will provide an estimate of the fraction of + cells in − heterozygous clones that can be attributed to mutational changes of the *jh* allele on the active X.   Any significant excess of + cells above this mutational background in clonal cultures from heterozygous females could then be attributed to activation of the *Jh* allele.   No clearly + cells have been found in 30 − clones of a proved heterozygote.   The estimated average number of cells in these clones is about 1.5×10^5, which suggests an upper limit of less than 10^{-6} per cell division for the activation rate.   This stability in the functional differentiation of the respective active and inactive X's will be a favorable factor in experimental attempts at activation.

Our results suggest that, by observing uncloned cultures, it will be possible to identify heterozygous females who may produce affected sons and (through their daughters) affected grandsons.   Caution must be exercised, however, since the incidence of − and ± cells in heterozygous cell populations is much less than the incidence of − clones.   This discrepancy cannot be accounted for solely by selection during cloning.   The cloning efficiency of strain no. 248.1 with method II is estimated at 0.52.   The summed proportion of − and ± cells in the population from which the clones were derived was 0.14.   No more than 17 cover slips should have had − clones if the cloning efficiency was one.   Instead, at least 39 cells formed — clones on 39 different cover slips. Similar arguments apply to clones derived by method I, where the cloning efficiencies ranged between 0.35 and 0.60.

The phenotype studied here may not be completely cell-limited under our conditions. Phenotypically + cells in heterozygous populations may convert hypoxanthine into forms that can be incorporated by — cells. Such cross-feeding would not be possible with single clones developing in isolation and would be less efficient even where several clones develop in the same dish.

Cross-feeding also may have contributed to the difference between the low incidence of — cells that we found in heterozygous cell populations and the 50–60 per cent incidence reported by Rosenbloom et al.[14] Although a large variance in the proportions of the two phenotypic classes of cells in different heterozygotes is expected because of the apparently random nature of the initial events in X-chromosome differentiation (e.g., see refs. 7 and 24), this does not appear to be the correct explanation for the difference noted here. Our work with clones indicates that the heterozygous cultures studied by us and by Rosenbloom et al. probably have similar frequencies of intrinsically — cells. The difference in the observed frequencies of — cells probably results from differences in the techniques used in the two laboratories. Our cell populations were deliberately grown so as to be in rapid, log-phase growth when labeled. This was reflected in the high proportion of nuclei that retained label after treatment with RNase. Rosenbloom et al. labeled their cells about 12 hours after subculture, before rapid cell increase had begun. RNase removed almost all label from their cells. Cross-feeding may have been minimized under their conditions. It should be possible to standardize the labeling conditions with the use of cells from obligate heterozygotes so that uncloned populations could be used for detecting heterozygosis. There will remain the chance that a very low incidence of — cells will not constitute reliable enough evidence of heterozygosity (e.g. no. 257 in Table 1); in such cases, cloning studies may be needed.

A low but definite degree of labeling occurs in cells from mutant males and — clones derived from heterozygous females. This might be the result of a utilizable radioactive contaminant in the hypoxanthine. Alternatively, such cells may have small amounts of PRTase. Comparisons of the enzyme activities of — clones derived from mutant males and from heterozygous females will provide an opportunity to detect limited expression of the allele on the inactive X. Perhaps such partial activation is already evident in the ± cells that we have observed in — clones under conditions where cross-feeding by + cells could not have occurred. These cells, two of which are illustrated in Figure 3*H*, may reflect either transient expression that can occur in every cell of a heterozygous — clone, perhaps at a particular part of the cell cycle,[6] or more regular expression in a minority component of the cell population in which the functional differentiation between the X's has been partially reversed. If the reversal is stable, it may be possible to demonstrate a clonal distribution of ± cells in heterozygous — clones.

Summary.—Cultured clones of human cells that were heterozygous at an X-linked hyperuricemia locus had either the normal phenotype or the phenotype corresponding to the recessive mutant allele. These results support the single-active-X hypothesis by showing that a third gene on the human X chromosome (in addition to those conditioning Hunter's syndrome and G6PD) manifests clonal, single-allele expression.

* Paper 1204 from the Genetics Laboratory. Supported by U.S. Public Health Service research grants GM06983 and GM08217 from the National Institute of General Medical Sciences.

† Predoctoral trainee supported by training grant GM0398 from the National Institutes of Health.

‡ Postdoctoral fellow of the USPHS.

[1] Lyon, M. F., *Nature*, **190**, 372 (1961).

[2] Russell, L. B., *Science*, **140**, 976 (1963).

[3] Lyon, M. F., *Advan. Teratol.*, **1**, 25 (1966).

[4] Barr, M. L., *Intern. Rev. Cytol.*, **19**, 35 (1966).

[5] *The Sex Chromatin*, ed. K. L. Moore (Philadelphia: W. B. Saunders Co., 1966).

[6] DeMars, R., *Natl. Cancer Inst. Monograph*, **26**, 327 (1967).

[7] DeMars, R., and W. E. Nance, *Wistar Inst. Monograph*, **1**, 35 (1964).

[8] Davidson, R. G., H. M. Nitowsky, and B. Childs, these Proceedings, **50**, 481 (1963).

[9] Danes, B. S., and A. G. Bearn, *J. Exptl. Med.*, **126**, 509 (1967).

[10] We do not know of a generally accepted symbol for this locus. The symbol *jh*, signifying juvenile hyperuricemia, is used here for the recessive mutant alleles of a dominant, normal gene, denoted by *Jh*.

[11] *Enzyme Nomenclature: Recommendations (1964) of the International Union of Biochemistry* (Amsterdam: Elsevier Publishing Co., 1965).

[12] Kelley, W. N., F. N. Rosenbloom, J. F. Henderson, and J. E. Seegmiller, these Proceedings, **57**, 1735 (1967).

[13] Seegmiller, J. E., F. M. Rosenbloom, and W. N. Kelley, *Science*, **155**, 1682 (1967).

[14] Rosenbloom, F. M., W. N. Kelley, J. F. Henderson, and J. E. Seegmiller, *Lancet*, **II**, 305 (1967).

[15] Hoefnagel, D., E. D. Andrew, N. G. Mireault, and W. O. Berndt, *New Engl. J. Med.*, **273**, 130 (1965).

[16] Shapiro, S. L., G. L. Sheppard, Jr., F. E. Dreifuss, and D. S. Newcombe, *Proc. Soc. Exptl. Biol. Med.*, **122**, 609 (1966).

[17] Nyhan, W. L., J. Pesek, L. Sweetman, D. G. Carpenter, and C. H. Carter, *Pediat. Res.*, **1**, 5 (1967).

[18] Lesch, M., and W. L. Nyhan, *Am. J. Med.*, **36**, 561 (1964).

[19] Ham, R., and T. T. Puck, in *Methods in Enzymology* (New York: Academic Press, 1961), vol. 5.

[20] Prescott, D. M., in *Methods in Cell Physiology* (New York: Academic Press, 1964), vol. 1, p. 365.

[21] Adam, A., *et al.*, *Ann. Hum. Genet. (London)*, **26**, 187 (1963).

[22] Grüneberg, H., *Ann. Hum. Genet. (London)*, **30**, 239 (1967).

[23] Wajntal, A., and R. DeMars, *Biochem. Genet.*, **1**, 61 (1967).

[24] Nance, W. E., in *Cold Spring Harbor Symposia on Quantitative Biology*, vol. 29 (1965), p. 415.

Reprinted from the PROCEEDINGS OF THE NATIONAL ACADEMY OF SCIENCES
Vol. 61, No. 3, pp. 945–948. November, 1968.

DEVELOPMENTAL IMPLICATIONS OF MULTIPLE TISSUE STUDIES IN GLUCOSE-6-PHOSPHATE DEHYDROGENASE-DEFICIENT HETEROZYGOTES*

BY E. GANDINI,† S. M. GARTLER,‡ G. ANGIONI,§ N. ARGIOLAS,**
AND G. DELL'ACQUA†

UNIVERSITY OF FERRARA, ITALY; UNIVERSITY OF WASHINGTON, SEATTLE;
UNIVERSITY OF CAGLIARI, ITALY; AND OSPEDALE SS. TRINITÁ, CAGLIARI, ITALY

Communicated by Curt Stern, September 6, 1968

The mosaic cell populations that result from mammalian X-chromosome inactivation reproduce true to type throughout somatic growth and form a natural system of cell markers for use in developmental studies.[1-5] The sex-linked glucose-6-phosphate dehydrogenase (G-6-PD) variants have already been used in attempts to estimate the size of the embryonic cell population at the time of inactivation, in studies of the growth characteristics of different tissues, and in research into the origin of abnormal growths later in life.[6-11] The basic approach in such studies is to estimate the variance of cell types among heterozygotes or among the tissues or tumors of a heterozygote: the greater the variance, the smaller the number of cells at the time of inactivation or at the formation of a tissue or tumor. Most heterozygotes for G-6-PD deficiency express intermediate phenotypes, and it is difficult to determine accurately the relative proportions of the two cell types in these individuals. On the other hand, those heterozygotes who express one or the other of the hemizygous phenotypes can be classified simply, and it is this part of the heterozygote distribution that we have utilized in the present study.

Several workers have now reported cases of proved heterozygotes for G-6-PD variants who appear to exhibit a single hemizygous phenotype in their red blood cells.[7, 12, 13] The frequency of these exceptional cases seems to be greater than 1 per cent. Assuming random inactivation and no differential growth of cell types during development, this frequency leads to an estimate of no more than eight cells for the embryonic cell population at inactivation. (On the basis of the above assumptions with eight cells, the chance that in a heterozygous embryo all cells will express either one or the other of the two possible phenotypes is $2(^1/_2)$,[8] or less than 1%.) As pointed out by Nance,[7] such an estimate could reflect either the embryonic cell population at inactivation or the red cell population at differentiation. These alternatives can be distinguished by multiple tissue studies in heterozygotes with hemizygous phenotypes. If the variation in red blood cell G-6-PD types among heterozygotes reflects the total embryonic cell population at inactivation, heterozygotes selected for a single red cell phenotype should show only one and the same phenotype in all tissues. If the variation in red cell G-6-PD types among heterozygotes reflects only the primordial red cell population at inactivation, then other tissues should, in some cases, show G-6-PD values differing from that of the red cell phenotype.

The present investigation was designed to study multiple tissues in a number of proved heterozygotes with a single red cell phenotype. Such a project requires a population where the G-6-PD variant is polymorphic, and where family studies can be easily carried out. The population of the island of Sardinia, Italy, in which the Mediterranean variant has a high frequency, meets these requirements.[14]

Materials and Methods.—950 women, primarily hospitalized in Cagliari and selected for having a father and/or one or more sons available for study, were screened for red-blood cell G-6-PD activity by the Brilliant Cresyl Blue discoloration technique.[15] Family studies were conducted on those individuals who had a discoloration time of more than 90 min. This cut-off point included individuals with enzyme levels ranging from the deficiency phenotype to about 25% of normal. Sixty-four individuals of this type were found, and 49 family studies were carried out. Eleven of the females were proved to be heterozygous by the fact that either their father and/or a son had a normal red blood cell G-6-PD level. Quantitative red blood cell studies were carried out in these 11 cases, and 4 had enzyme levels indistinguishable from those of hemizygous-affected males. None of these four subjects had neoplastic disease.

We considered these four cases as representing proved heterozygotes with a single red cell phenotype. Studies were performed on granulocytes and lymphocytes in all cases, and on solid tissues in two cases. Separation of red cells, granulocytes, and lymphocytes was carried out by a combination of differential centrifugation and absorption on cotton after red cell sedimentation in gelatin.[16] In all cases the preparations were checked by morphological study, and all were above 90% in purity. Crude enzyme extracts from red blood cells, granulocytes, and lymphocytes were made by repeated freezing and thawing, followed by centrifugation. Crude extracts from skin biopsies were obtained by grinding in a Potter homogenizer.

Enzymatic activity was analyzed by following the reduction of nicotinamide-adenine dinucleotide phosphate at 340 mμ, and was expressed in units of change of optical density/min/gm. of Hb for red cells, by cell number in the case of granulocytes and lymphocytes, and by soluble protein in the case of solid tissues. Protein was estimated by the Lowry technique.[17]

Results.—The evidence of heterozygosity in the four cases was as follows: cases 1, 2, and 3 had a son with normal G-6-PD activity in the red blood cells. Case 4 had a father with normal enzyme activity.

The results of the quantitative analyses are presented in Table 1.

The granulocytic activity in all four cases is within the range of deficient males. Lymphocytic activity is within the deficient range for three cases, while in one case, it falls within the low end of the intermediate values.

The skin G-6-PD level in case 1 is approximately twice the mean value for deficients, while in case 3, the skin G-6-PD is more than four times this value. Although the data on normal and deficient skin values are limited, studies in our laboratory on fibroblast cultures derived from skin biopsies consistently show deficient cultures ranging from 10 per cent to 15 per cent of normal values. Thus we are positive that the skin biopsy analyzed in case 3 represents a mixture of normal and mutant cells (possibly 1:1), while the skin biopsy in case 1 very likely contains normal cells, though considerably less than 50 per cent. The subcutaneous fat value for case 3 is higher than our normal values and suggests that this biopsy contains a high proportion of normal cells.

Discussion.—As was mentioned earlier, the frequency of heterozygotes for G-6-PD variation expressing a single phenotype appears to be greater than 1 per cent. The population we have examined is heterogeneous and represents a mixture of people living in Cagliari and coming to the Cagliari hospitals from the surrounding towns. From the data on frequency available to us, we estimate

Table 1. *G-6-PD Activity in different cells and tissues of heterozygous, deficient, and normal subjects.*

	Erythro-cytes (gm Hb)	Granulo-cytes (10^9 cells)	Lympho-cytes (10^9 cells)	Skin (mg. prot.)	Subcutaneous fat (mg. prot.)
Genotype					
Heterozygotes					
Case 1	<1	11.5	<1	0.048	—
" 2	<1	9.0	<1	—.	—
" 3	<1	9.5	5.2	0.116	0.311
" 4	<1	13.0	2.3	—	—
Normals ♀ ♀	$\bar{X} = 40.9^*$ (25.7–70.0)	$\bar{X} = 41.4^*$ (26.5–75.2)	$\bar{X} = 21.5^*$ (7.6–34.0)	0.240, 0.305, 0.298	0.171, 0.170
Deficients ♂ ♂	$\bar{X} < 1\dagger$	$\bar{X} = 10.75\dagger$ (5–17)	$\bar{X} = 1.15\dagger$ (0–2)	0.023, 0.020, 0.018	

Change in Optical Density/Min/Gm

$*\bar{X}$, normal mean values estimated from 52 subjects.
$\dagger\bar{X}$, deficient mean values estimated from 8 subjects.

that the number of heterozygotes in our sample is approximately 300. Our four cases of heterozygotes with a deficient red cell phenotype represent a minimal estimate of such cases, since some cases will have a "deficient" father or a "deficient" son and not be detected. Therefore, in our population, a minimal estimate of heterozygotes with a deficient red blood cell phenotype is 1.3 per cent, and could be twice as high.

The frequency with which exceptional heterozygotes occur leads to an estimation of the embryonic cell population at inactivation of less than eight cells. Our data strongly suggest that this estimate represents only the primordial cells destined to form the erythroid series; otherwise, all the skin and lymphocytic values should have been in the deficient range. The fact that all the granulocytic values are in the deficient range suggests that this line is also derived from the erythroid pool or primordial embryonic cells. This is in complete agreement with other work arguing for a common stem cell for granulocytes and red cells.[11, 18]

The lymphocytic value in one case is at the low end of the intermediate range, which suggests that lymphocytes may be derived from a different primordial cell pool. The absence of the Ph1 chromosome in lymphocytes, and its presence in bone marrow cells, leads to the same suggestion.[18] Furthermore, data to be published on heterozygotes with intermediate red cell values show less correlation between lymphocytic and granulocytic or erythrocytic values than the erythrocytic and granulocytic correlation. This finding is in agreement with the view that lymphocytes derive from different cell precursors than those of the granulocytes and erythrocytes.

The results of this study suggest that by determining the frequency with which G-6-PD heterozygotes express hemizygous phenotypes in different tissues, one may quantitatively map the embryo in terms of its primordial cell pools.

Summary.—Four known heterozygotes for G-6-PD deficiency, exhibiting a deficient phenotype in their red blood cells, were found among 950 women in Sardinia screened for G-6-PD deficiency. It was estimated that the frequency of such heterozygotes was more than 1 per cent, which is in general agreement with the data of other workers. From the data on the frequency of exceptional heterozygotes, it has been estimated that the size of the embryonic cell population at inactivation is of the order of eight cells or less.

Multiple tissue studies of these individuals, showing differences between tissues in the same individual, suggest that this cell number does not represent the total embryo at that time, but only a pool of primordial cells destined to form the hematopoietic system.

* This work has been supported by grants from NATO [SA. 5-2-05 (333) 1909 (67)], and from the NIH (GM 15253).

† Instituto di Genetica Medica, Universita di Ferrara, Ferrara, Italy.
‡ Departments of Medicine and Genetics, University of Washington, Seattle, Washington.
§ Clinica Ostetrica e Ginecologica, Università of Cagliari, Cagliari, Italy.
** Reparto Malattie Infettive, Ospedale SS. Trinità, Cagliari, Italy.

[1] Lyon, M. F., *Am. J. Human Genet.*, 14, 135 (1962).
[2] Davidson, R. G., H. N. Nitowsky, and B. Childs, these PROCEEDINGS, 50, 481 (1963).
[3] Danes, B. S., and A. G. Bearn, *J. Exptl. Med.*, 126, 509 (1967).
[4] Rosenbloom, F. M., W. N. Kelley, J. F. Henderson, and J. E. Seegmiller, *Lancet*, II, 305 (1967).
[5] McKusick, V. A., *Quart. Rev. Biol.*, 37, 69 (1962).
[6] Gartler, S. M., and D. Linder, in *Cold Spring Harbor Symposia on Quantitative Biology*, vol. 29 (1964), p. 253.
[7] Nance, E. W., in *Cold Spring Harbor Symposia on Quantitatve Biology*, vol. 29 (1964), p. 475.
[8] Linder, D., and S. M. Gartler, *Science*, 150, 67 (1965).
[9] Gartler, S. M., L. Ziprkowski, E. R. Krakowski, A. Szeinberg, and A. Adam, *Am. J. Human Genet.*, 18, 282 (1966).
[10] Beutler, E., Z. Collins, and L. E. Irwin, *New Engl. J. Med.*, 276, 389 (1967).
[11] Fialkow, P. J., S. M. Gartler, and A. Yoshida, these PROCEEDINGS, 58, 1468 (1967).
[12] Davidson, R. G., B. Childs, and M. Siniscalco, *Ann. Human Genet.*, 28, 61 (1964).
[13] Stamatoyannopoulos, G., personal communication.
[14] Siniscalco, M., L. Bernini, G. Filippi, B. Latte, K. P. Melra, S. Pionelli, and M. Rattazzi, *Bull. World Health Org.*, 34, 379 (1966).
[15] Motulsky, A. G., and J. M. Campbell-Kraut, in *Proceedings of the Conference on Genetic Polymorphism and Geographic Variations in Disease*, ed. B. S. Blumberg (New York: Grune & Stratton, 1961), p. 159.
[16] Yam, T. L., G. L. Castoldi, and W. J. Mitus, *J. Lab. Clin. Med.*, 70, 699 (1967).
[17] Lowry, O. H., W. J. Rosebrough, A. L. Farr, and R. J. Randall, *J. Biol. Chem.*, 193, 265 (1951).
[18] Whang, J., E. Frei, J. H. Tjio, P. P. Carbone, and G. Brecher, *Blood*, 22, 664 (1963).

Reprinted from Science
April 19, 1968, Vol. 160, pages 272-280

Specific Gene Amplification in Oocytes

Oocyte nuclei contain extrachromosomal replicas of the genes for ribosomal RNA.

Donald D. Brown and Igor B. Dawid

So little is known about developmental mechanisms that the broadest questions are unanswered. For example, it is generally believed that "differential gene action" rather than any change in the genes themselves leads to the different phenotypes of cells in multicellular organisms. According to this hypothesis all types of cells within a single organism contain the same genes in equal number. Cells of one tissue would differ from those of another tissue according to which group of genes was expressed. The alternative hypothesis to that of "differential gene action" is that of "differential gene alteration" which proposes that one cell type differs from another because of a modification of the genes themselves [1]. This "alteration" could result from a change in the DNA by base substitution or from a modification of bases by such reactions as methylation [2] or glucosylation [3]. It could also be a deletion or replication of a specific region of the DNA. Hypermutation, recombination, and translocation of genes for antibodies have been considered to account for the variability of these proteins [4]. Several lines of evidence have made the hypothesis of "differential gene action" attractive. The first cause of its acceptance has been the repeated demonstration that the size and number of chromosomes, as well as the quantity of DNA per diploid chromosome set, are constant in different cell types of a single organism [5, 6]. Chromosome diminution and chromosome loss which occur in somatic cells of some insects, worms, and crustaceans appear to be restricted to a few organisms [6]. The second, more sensitive comparison of genes present in different cell types has been made by DNA-DNA hybridization studies [7]. McCarthy and Hoyer tested the DNA's from different mouse tissues for their abilities to compete with labeled DNA from cultured mouse cells in the hybridization reaction; they detected no differences. The sensitivity of this method is not adequate since DNA's from species as different as higher apes and man can hardly be distinguished by it. Nuclear transplantation is a more stringent test for nuclear changes during differentiation. Nuclei from differentiated tissues of frogs, toads, and salamanders [8] have been transplanted into homologous enucleated eggs as a test of their ability to support development, and some nuclei from the intestinal epithelium of swimming tadpoles of *Xenopus laevis* can support normal development [9]. Furthermore, whole plants have been reared from single somatic cells [10]. However, these examples do not prove that the genetic material of the differentiated cell is unchanged, but rather that it has not been irreversibly altered.

We will discuss a case of reversible gene alteration in which the DNA specifying the sequences for 28S and 18S ribosomal RNA's (rRNA) [11] has been selectively replicated. This specific amplification of genes [12, 13] for ribosomal RNA (termed rDNA) [11] occurs in one cell type—the oocyte; this amplification has been demonstrated in the oocytes of several amphibians, an echiuroid worm, and the surf clam.

The Extra Nucleoli in Amphibian Oocytes

The first suggestion that extra copies of rDNA are present in oocytes came from cytological observations of the large nuclei ("germinal vesicles") of amphibian oocytes [6, 14]. Somatic cells of amphibia usually contain one nucleolus for each haploid set of chromosomes [15]. Each nucleolus appears to be derived from a "nucleolar organizer" region which frequently can be seen as a secondary constriction on one autosome at metaphase [16]. Since the growing oocyte persists in the first meiotic prophase for an extended period [17], the cell is tetraploid and therefore would be expected to contain four nucleoli in its germinal vesicle. However, counts by MacGregor [18] for different species of *Triturus*, by Callan [19] for *Siredon mexicanum*, and by Miller [20] for *X. laevis* have shown approximately 600, 1000, and 1000 nucleoli per germinal vesicle, respectively. These nucleoli are not attached to the chromosomes in the germinal vesicle. There is now considerable evidence that these multiple nucleoli in the oocyte are analogous to the nucleoli in somatic cells and that each is an autonomous site for the synthesis of rRNA [21]. Miller and Peacock [22] demonstrated that DNA-containing cores could be isolated from nucleoli of germinal vesicles of the newt *Triturus pyrrhogaster*, salamanders, and Plethodontids. They showed furthermore that each core contains a circular structure whose axis is DNA and which may be regarded as a "chromosome."

With molecular hybridization methods, it is possible to test the hypothesis that these multiple nucleolar "chromosomes" contain nucleotide sequences homologous to rRNA. Before presenting experiments which support this hypothesis, we will discuss some of the facts known about the DNA which is homologous to rRNA in *X. laevis* and the methods for its analysis.

Ribosomal Genes and Their Measurement

Ribosomal genes [11] are measured by their complementarity with rRNA, the product made on these genes [23]. The most recent data for *X. laevis* show that 0.057 percent of the DNA of somatic cells is complementary to rRNA (0.114 percent of the base pairs) [24]. Since a haploid chromosome set of *X. laevis* contains 3 picograms of DNA [25] and since the molecular weights of the 18S and 28S rRNA components are known, it can be calculated that

The authors are staff members of the department of embryology, Carnegie Institution of Washington, Baltimore, Maryland 21210.

each chromosome set contains about 450 of the 18S genes and an equal number of 28S genes (24).

Wallace and Birnstiel (26) predicted from the base composition of rRNA that its complementary DNA (rDNA) should have a higher content of guanylic and cytidylic acid (about 63 percent) than the bulk DNA (40 percent) and that it should therefore have a higher buoyant density in CsCl. They fractionated X. laevis DNA by equilibrium centrifugation in CsCl and showed that a high-density fraction hybridized with radioactive rRNA. This minor high-density DNA fraction was also detected by its optical density in analytical CsCl gradient centrifugation. When the DNA was hybridized with rRNA before centrifugation in the CsCl, the density of the hybrid was substantially higher than that of the rDNA itself. Since RNA has a much higher density than DNA, this large increase in the density of the hybrid suggests that a considerable proportion of each rDNA molecule was duplexed with rRNA. Since the DNA molecules were much longer than rRNA molecules, a high proportion of rRNA in the hybrid indicates that the rRNA genes are clustered, that is, that several of these genes are present on each fragment of DNA. Clustering of the 450 genes for rRNA was proved when these methods were applied to the DNA isolated from mutant embryos of X. laevis.

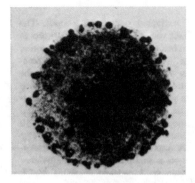

Fig. 1. Photomicrograph of an isolated germinal vesicle of X. laevis. The germinal vesicle was dissected from a mature oocyte in 0.01M MgCl₂, 0.02M tris, pH 7.4. It was then flooded with cresyl violet stain and photographed. Its diameter is about 400 μm. The deeply stained spots are some of the hundreds of nucleoli.

Embryos carrying this mutation in the homozygous form are anucleolate (0-nu) (27), and these embryos do not synthesize any rRNA during their limited life-span (28). The 0-nu embryos are devoid of the "nuclear organizer" constriction on both allelic autosomes which normally carry it (29), and their DNA does not hybridize with rRNA (26). Since this deletion removes more than 99 percent of the DNA homologous to 28S and 18S rRNA (24), the 450 rRNA genes

must be clustered on one part of a single chromosome, most likely the autosome containing the "nucleolar organizer" constriction.

The high buoyant density of rDNA in CsCl facilitates its visualization and measurement in the analytical ultracentrifuge as well as its separation from bulk DNA by preparatory centrifugation in CsCl prior to hybridization with radioactive rRNA.

The DNA of Amphibian Germinal Vesicles

If the amount of rDNA in a germinal vesicle is increased relative to the amount present in a single somatic cell, is the increase a specific enrichment of ribosomal genes or does it reflect a proportional increase of the entire DNA in the germinal vesicle? Haggis (30) reported that the DNA content of germinal vesicles isolated from Rana pipiens (the leopard frog) is over a hundred times higher than the amount predicted for a tetraploid nucleus (4C), whereas Izawa et al. (31) found about four times the tetraploid complement in Triturus viridescens germinal vesicles. To reinvestigate this problem, we isolated germinal vesicles from oocytes of three genera of amphibia known to have widely different amounts of DNA per nucleus—Necturus maculosus (the mudpuppy), Siredon mexicanum (an axolotl), and Xenopus laevis (the South African clawed toad) (Table 1). The correlation of genome size with the DNA content in the germinal vesicle for each species should establish whether amphibian oocyte nuclei actually contain a large excess of chromosomal DNA.

Germinal vesicles were collected by hand from mature oocytes under a dissecting microscope, with particular care being taken to remove the nucleated blood cells and the cellular ovarian tissue. Because it was important to retain all of the nuclear contents, germinal vesicles (Fig. 1) were isolated in 0.01M MgCl₂ which causes the nucleoplasm to gel. These nuclei have a diameter of about 400 μm in mature oocytes compared to approximately 5 to 10 μm for most somatic nuclei of X. laevis.

The method used for the determination of DNA in germinal vesicles was designed to measure very small quantities of DNA and then to recover it for subsequent hybridization studies. DNA was prepared from 10,000, 6,000, and 3,000 germinal vesicles of X. laevis,

Table 1. The content of "chromosomal" and "nucleolar" DNA in somatic nuclei and germinal vesicles of four amphibia.

Species	DNA (pg)					
	"Chromosomal" (low density)		"Nucleolar" (high density)			
	4C *	Germinal vesicle †	4C Total	4C rDNA ‡	Germinal vesicle † total	Germinal-vesicle § rDNA
X. laevis	12.6	70	0.02||	0.014	25	5.3
S. mexicanum	140	170	0.16	0.16	13	5.5
N. maculosus	380	500	0.08	0.08	30	5.3
T. viridescens	178			0.16		8.5

* The value for N. maculosus was determined by the diphenylamine reaction in a sample of counted erythrocytes. Literature citations for the other values are: X. laevis (25), S. mexicanum and T. viridescens (49). † Calculated from the band areas in the experiment shown in Fig. 2 and corrected for losses during purification by comparison with the band area of a known amount of dAT as described in the text (see also 51). ‡ These values have been calculated from the 4C complement of DNA for each species (see first column) and from the percentage of the genome homologous to X. laevis ³H-rRNA. The percentage of the genome that is homologous to X. laevis rRNA in X. laevis, S. mexicanum, N. maculosus, and T. viridescens is 0.057, 0.05, 0.01, and 0.05, respectively. The homology of X. laevis rRNA with these heterologous DNA's is extensive; if it is not 100 percent, then rDNA complements are underestimated. In calculating the amount of rDNA, we assumed that only one strand of DNA is homologous to rRNA and therefore doubled each value. § The amount of rRNA homologous to germinal-vesicle DNA was determined from the extent of hybridization found in the experiments recorded in Fig. 3. The hybridization in each sample was compared to that of a known amount of somatic DNA. Since there is a direct relationship between the amount of DNA on filters and the radioactive RNA hybridized, even at the subsaturating concentration of ³H-rRNA used in these experiments, the amount of rDNA can be calculated for each unknown preparation (24). Since losses of rDNA may have occurred during the hybridization steps, the rDNA values are minimum. Once again it is assumed that only one strand of the DNA is homologous to rRNA and therefore each value has been doubled. \|\| Estimated from experiments of Birnstiel et al. (26) in which the proportion of high-density DNA in somatic DNA was directly measured by CsCl centrifugation in an analytical ultracentrifuge and found to be between 0.15 and 0.2 percent of the total DNA.

S. mexicanum, and *N. maculosus*, respectively. Deoxyadenylate-deoxythymidylate copolymer (2.8 μg) was added to each preparation; the germinal vesicles were lysed with 0.5 percent sodium lauryl sulfate, digested for 2 hours with 1 mg of pronase per milliliter at 37°C,

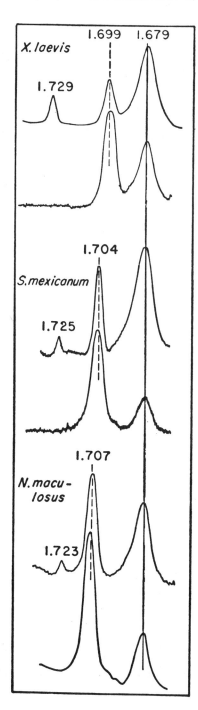

Fig. 2. Tracings of germinal-vesicle and somatic-cell DNA centrifuged to equilibrium in CsCl in the analytical centrifuge. For each species the germinal-vesicle DNA is traced on the top, and the somatic DNA is traced below. The band at the density of 1.679 is the deoxyadenylate-deoxythymidylate copolymer (dAT) carrier added at the beginning of the isolation. The density of the DNA in the main band is the same in germinal-vesicle and somatic-cell DNA in all cases; in addition to this band the germinal-vesicle preparations show a high-density component which contains sequences complementary to rRNA.

and extracted once with phenol. The extract was dialyzed and centrifuged to equilibrium in CsCl in a horizontal rotor. The refractive index of the fractions was measured to determine the location of the DNA. These fractions were pooled, dialyzed, treated with pancreatic ribonuclease (0.1 mg/ml) and ribonuclease T_1 (50 unit/ml) for 30 minutes at 37°C, and dialyzed. The DNA was purified further by adsorption on a small column of methylated albumin on kieselguhr in 0.3M NaCl, and eluted with 0.8M NaCl. After dialysis and concentration in vacuum the samples were centrifuged in CsCl in an analytical ultracentrifuge for 20 hours at 44,000 rev/min (32) (Fig. 2). The amount of DNA at each buoyant density was measured by comparison of its band area with the band area of the dAT, thereby correcting for losses of DNA during purification.

In addition to the major band of DNA at the buoyant density characteristic of somatic-cell DNA, the preparations of germinal-vesicle DNA from all three species contained additional DNA at a higher buoyant density (Fig. 2). At these concentrations, somatic-cell DNA does not have a visible high-density component. The corrected amount of DNA per germinal vesicle at each buoyant density is given in Table 1. The quantity of DNA in the main (low-density) band was close to the expected tetraploid amount (4C) in the case of *S. mexicanum* and *N. maculosus*. The amount in excess of the 4C complement in the preparations of germinal vesicles from *X. laevis* might be a result of contamination by a small portion of the cell's mitochondria. The total amount of mitochondrial DNA present in mature *X. laevis* eggs is about 200 times the 4C value, and the densities of nuclear and mitochondrial DNA's in *X. laevis* are so similar that distinction between them is difficult

Table 2. Relative abundance of sequences homologous to 28S and 18S RNA in the somatic and egg DNA's of *X. laevis*. Nine micrograms of each DNA were fractionated in CsCl, and the DNA in each fraction was immobilized on a Millipore filter (Fig. 3). The filters were split, and half-filter sets of egg and somatic-cell DNA were hybridized together with either 28S or 18S ³H-RNA (1.5 μg of ³H-RNA at 10⁵ count min⁻¹ μg⁻¹ in 5 ml of 0.6M NaCl). Only radioactive material that hybridized with high-density DNA was scored. Since hybridization was not performed with saturating concentrations of radioactive RNA, the absolute 28S and 18S ratios are not significant, only the comparative ratios between the two DNA preparations (24).

Source of DNA	Count/min		28S:18S
	28S	18S	
Somatic cells	178	68	2.6
Eggs	640	262	2.4

(33). If only 2.5 percent of the oocyte's mitochondria contaminated the germinal vesicle during its isolation, it would account for the 60 pg of DNA in excess of the 4C amount. Since the chromosomal DNA complement is much higher in the two urodele species than it is in *X. laevis*, a comparable amount of mitochondrial contamination of these germinal vesicles would not be expected to alter substantially the apparent DNA content of the germinal vesicles. These considerations suggest that individual germinal vesicles contain about a 4C complement of chromosomal DNA, in agreement with their tetraploidy.

To measure the homology of the high-density DNA of germinal vesicles with rRNA, the three preparations of germinal vesicle DNA recovered from the experiments shown in Fig. 2, as well as 40 μg of somatic DNA of each of the three species, were denatured with alkali, and each of the six DNA samples was divided in half. One half was first hybridized in 0.6M NaCl and 0.06M sodium citrate for 1 hour at 70°C in a final volume of 1.5 ml with 20 μg of nonradioactive rRNA isolated from adult liver of the homologous species. The other half was incubated under identical conditions but without the addition of unlabeled RNA. All preparations were then diluted with an equal volume of water and treated with pancreatic ribonuclease (10 μg/ml) for 10 minutes at room temperature. Cesium chloride was added to a final density of 1.72 g/cm³ and a final volume of 3.5 ml, and each preparation was centrifuged for 64 hours in the Spinco SW-39 rotor at 33,000 rev/min with a temperature setting of 15°C. Each gradient was fractionated, and the DNA was denatured with alkali to liberate the bound RNA. The solutions were neutralized and diluted with 0.6M NaCl and 0.06M sodium citrate, and the DNA in each sample was trapped on a Millipore filter (23). The filters were then baked overnight at 70°C and stacked together in vials; the material was allowed to hybridize overnight at 70°C in 0.6M NaCl with 0.06M sodium citrate containing ^{3}H-rRNA (0.5 μg/ ml, 4 × 10[5] count min[−1] μg[−1]). This concentration of RNA hybridizes with about 40 percent of the total rDNA sites. The radioactive RNA was isolated from cultured cells of *X. laevis* labeled with ^{3}H-uridine (24). The rRNA from *X. laevis* hybridizes well with the heterologous DNA's used here (unpublished observations). The filters were then washed with 0.3M NaCl, treated with ribonuclease, dried, and counted (Fig. 3). The amounts of rDNA in each preparation of germinal vesicles were calculated by comparison with the degree of hybridization obtained with somatic-cell DNA (24); the fraction of rDNA in somatic DNA had previously been measured by hybridization to saturation. The results (Table 1) demonstrate that, as determined by direct measurement of the high-density DNA component and its hybridization with radioactive rRNA, the ratio of rDNA to main-band chromosomal DNA is increased enormously in germinal vesicles. Similar results were obtained in hybridization experiments with germinal vesicles of *Triturus viridescens*. Furthermore, the hybridization studies show that the extra rDNA in germinal vesicles resembles the rDNA of somatic cells in three ways: (i) it has a high buoyant density in CsCl; (ii) hybridization of the DNA with rRNA before centrifugation in CsCl greatly increases the buoyant density of the rDNA (Fig. 3); and (iii) the ratio of DNA sequences homologous to 28*S* RNA to those homologous to 18*S* RNA is the same in germinal-vesicle and somatic-cell DNA (Table 2). The nucleotide sequences in germinal-vesicle DNA which are homologous to 28*S* and 18*S* RNA band at the same buoyant density and therefore are located on the same DNA molecules. The same is true of the sequences homologous to 28*S* and 18*S* RNA in somatic-cell rDNA (24).

Despite these general similarities between somatic-cell and germinal-vesicle rDNA's, their buoyant densities in CsCl

are different. Somatic-cell rDNA was purified from *X. laevis* erythrocyte DNA by two cycles of centrifugation in CsCl in a fixed-angle rotor. The buoyant density of the somatic-cell rDNA satellite was 5 mg/cm[3] lower than the buoyant density of the germinal-vesicle rDNA (Fig. 4). This difference was confirmed by hybridization with rRNA after preparative CsCl centrifugation of the native DNA (Fig. 5). Inclusion of a bacterial DNA as a density marker and collection of a large number of fractions from the preparatory CsCl centrifugation permitted a precise localization of the rDNA in both samples. The good agreement between the density measured by analytical centrifugation and that determined by specific RNA hybridization clearly establishes that the two different techniques measure the same DNA component. The high-density DNA components of the somatic cells and the germinal vesicles from *S. mexicanum* have an analogous difference in their densities, which are 1.718 and 1.725 g/cm[3], respectively. We do not know

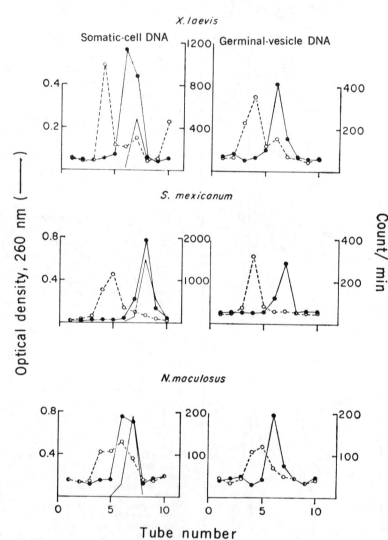

Fig. 3. Hybridization of germinal-vesicle and somatic-cell DNA with and without previous hybridization with homologous rRNA. Results were plotted without subtraction of background, which was about 50 count/min per filter without DNA. The optical densities at 260 nm were only plotted for somatic DNA because preparations of germinal vesicles contained no measurable optical density under conditions of these experiments. (●), Without previous hybridization; (○), with previous hybridization.

the reason for this difference in buoyant density, but several considerations are pertinent. There is no detectable difference between the base composition of rRNA synthesized during oogenesis of *X. laevis* (presumably under the direction of the higher-density germinal-vesicle DNA) and the rRNA made during development (transcribed from the lower-density somatic rDNA) (*34*). Furthermore, hybridization of either rDNA with rRNA causes a large shift in their buoyant densities (Fig. 3). This latter experiment suggests that the ratio of RNA to DNA in hybrids formed with either egg or somatic-cell rDNA is high, but the method has not been calibrated to measure small differences in the ratio of RNA to DNA. Even though the hybridization values are minimal for that portion of the high-density DNA complementary to rRNA, it is almost certain that nucleotide sequences are present in both high-density DNA's which are not homologous to rRNA (Table 1) (*24*). The suggested presence of nonhomologous nucleotide sequences intermingled with the sequences homologous to 28*S* and 18*S* RNA agrees with recent studies on rRNA metabolism in HeLa cells (*35*). The polycistronic rRNA precursor molecules of 28*S* RNA and 18*S* RNA have a much higher content of guanylic and cytidylic acids than either mature rRNA molecule, and about half of this precursor appears to be discarded during the maturation process. Whether the difference between the buoyant densities of the somatic-cell and germinal-vesicle rDNA's reflects a difference in nucleotide composition or a more subtle alteration in the DNA remains to be determined.

Selective Amplification of rDNA Relative to 4S DNA and 5S DNA

Whole unfertilized eggs are a more convenient source of DNA than are germinal vesicles. Therefore, egg DNA has been used to show the specific enrichment of rDNA relative to the DNA homologous to 4*S* RNA (a class of RNA including transfer RNA) and 5*S* RNA [a third structural RNA component of ribosomes (*36*, *37*)]. Egg DNA was isolated from *X. laevis* as described previously (*25*). Since most egg DNA is mitochondrial (*33*), it was necessary to test whether the mitochondrial DNA can hybridize with these radioactive RNA preparations. There is no specific hybridization of purified mi-

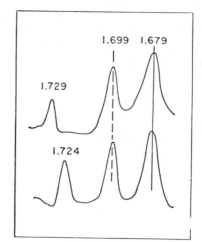

Fig. 4. Tracings of CsCl density-gradient experiments comparing the high-density components of germinal-vesicle DNA (top) and somatic-cell DNA (bottom) of *X. laevis*. Nuclear DNA from *X. laevis* (density 1.699) and dAT (density 1.679) were added to the purified somatic component to provide the same markers present in the samples of germinal vesicles. The density obtained for the high-density somatic-cell DNA agrees well with that reported earlier by Birnstiel *et al.* (*26*).

tochondrial DNA with ³H-rRNA, whereas total egg DNA hybridizes extensively with rRNA (Fig. 6). The small amount of radioactive material which binds to the mitochondrial DNA is not due to sequences homologous to rRNA because this material binds to DNA fragments of average rather than high buoyant density, and because this low level of hybridization cannot be reduced by competition with an excess of unlabeled egg rRNA. Purified mitochondrial DNA has no detectable homology with either 4*S* ³H-RNA or 5*S* ³H-RNA, nor does its presence interfere with the analysis of rDNA when the DNA is fractionated in CsCl before its hybridization. An unfertilized egg contains about the same amount of rDNA as does an individual germinal vesicle.

The ratio of rDNA to 4*S* DNA and 5*S* DNA (*11*) has been compared in preparations of egg and somatic DNA's. The 4*S* DNA and 5*S* DNA can be separated from rDNA because they have different buoyant densities in CsCl; the 4*S* DNA has a buoyant density lighter than that of rDNA but slightly heavier than that of the bulk DNA, whereas 5*S* DNA has a density lighter than that of the bulk DNA (*24*). The abundance of rDNA relative to that of 5*S* DNA is the same in different somatic tissues (*24*) but very different from that found in

egg DNA (Fig. 7). Egg DNA hybridizes well with rRNA, but there is no detectable hybridization with 5*S* RNA; the amount of 5*S* DNA of chromosomal origin is below the limit that this experiment could detect. The relative abundance of 4*S* DNA and rDNA has been compared in egg and somatic-cell DNA's (Fig. 8) with similar results. Therefore, we conclude that eggs are greatly enriched for DNA homologous to 28*S* and 18*S* rRNA relative to the bulk of nuclear DNA as well as to the DNA homologous to 4*S* RNA and 5*S* RNA.

Extra Copies of Ribosomal DNA in Oocytes of Other Animals

Do oocytes of animals other than amphibia contain extra copies of rDNA? The presence of multiple nucleoli in amphibian germinal vesicles is exceptional, since individual oocytes of most animals contain a single, prominent nucleolus. However, despite this difference, the patterns of oocyte maturation in widely different species are remarkably similar (*6*, *17*). In an analysis of DNA from sea urchin eggs by analytical centrifugation in CsCl, Pikó *et al.* (*38*) found a DNA of high density which was not present in sperm DNA. It remains to be shown whether this DNA, which is equivalent in amount to a 1C (haploid) complement of sea-urchin DNA, contains extra replicas of rDNA.

We have purified total DNA from eggs of the echiuroid worm *Urechis caupo*, and the surf clam, *Spisula solidissima*. In experiments similar to that described in Fig. 8, the ratio of rDNA to 4*S* DNA was at least five times higher in egg DNA preparations than in sperm DNA of the same species. From this we conclude that these oocytes which contain only a single nucleolus also have extra copies of rDNA.

The Life History of Extra rDNA

The life history of the additional rDNA in amphibian oocytes can be reconstructed in the following way. During an early period of oogenesis, even before the oocyte chromosomes have extended to their specialized configuration termed "lampbrush," the extra copies of high-density rDNA are synthesized, and extra nucleoli appear in the germinal vesicle (*13*, *18*, *19*). Ovaries of young *X. laevis* actively incorporate

³H-thymidine into the high-density DNA about 2 to 4 weeks after metamorphosis, and Feulgen-positive deposits become visible in the germinal vesicle at this stage (13). Formation of new nucleoli (18–20) and rDNA replication (13) do not occur in later stages of oogenesis.

Ribosomes are synthesized and accumulate in oocytes throughout "lampbrush" chromosome stages (39). Later, during yolk deposition, the lampbrush loops contract and stop functioning, but rRNA synthesis in the nucleoli continues throughout this period. When the egg is mature and ready for ovulation, all RNA synthesis stops. The germinal vesicle breaks down at the first meiotic reduction division, and the multiple nucleoli disappear and do not reappear when the nuclear membrane reforms (21). After meiosis the extra rDNA never functions again; there is no rRNA synthesis in eggs or embryos until the onset of gastrulation (34). At this stage, the expected diploid number of two nucleoli appears for the first time during embryogenesis (21), and they are undoubtedly the sites of the new rRNA synthesis (40). Although the extra rDNA is still present in unfertilized eggs, it is not replicated during cleavage. This fact is deduced from hybridization experiments which show that DNA from gastrula embryos, which are composed of about 30,000 cells, contains the same proportion of rDNA and 5S DNA as does adult somatic DNA (24). Thus, the extra rDNA either is diluted out by extensive nuclear replication or has been degraded. These extrachromosomal copies of rDNA are used for rRNA synthesis only during oogenesis and are subsequently rendered nonfunctional and discarded into the cytoplasm at the first meiotic reduction division.

Control of rDNA Replication
in Oocytes

The amount of rDNA clustered within a single somatic-cell nucleolus in *X. laevis* is about 0.0035 pg (the haploid amount of rDNA calculated from values in Table 1). The minimum amount of rDNA in a germinal vesicle of *X. laevis* as determined by hybridization is 5.3 pg (1500 times the haploid amount); the total amount of high-density DNA is 25 pg, or 5000 times the haploid amount. Miller has found about 1000 nucleoli in a *X. laevis* germinal vesicle (20), and if each contained a single continuous DNA molecule, the average

length of these molecules would be equivalent to or larger than one cluster of rDNA on the nucleolar organizer region of the chromosome. However, Miller (22) found that the circular structures ("chromosomes") from nucleoli of *T. pyrrhogaster* were not of equal length. If this is true for the nucleolar "chromosomes" in *X. laevis* oocytes, then at least some of them must contain DNA molecules that are either larger or smaller than the entire rDNA cluster at the nucleolar organizer region of the master chromosome. Furthermore, there is considerable variation in the number of nucleoli in each germinal vesicle (18–20) and presumably in the number of nucleolar "chromosomes" as well. If neither the length nor the number of these extra "chromosomes" is strictly determined in each oocyte, what are the important factors which govern the replication? Two observations that we have made are germane to this problem. First, the four amphibia analyzed in these studies

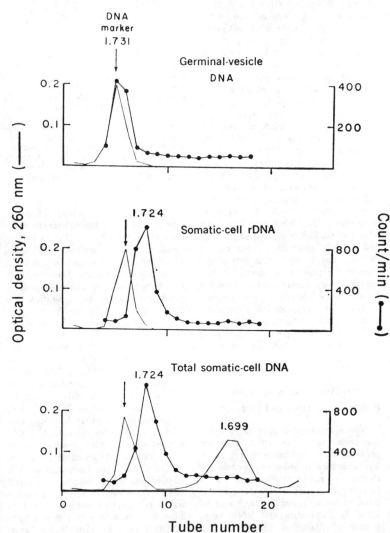

Fig. 5. Demonstration of the difference in buoyant density of germinal-vesicle and somatic-cell rDNA by hybridization with ³H-rRNA. Samples of *X. laevis* germinal-vesicle DNA (0.2 μg), purified high-density somatic-cell DNA (0.07 μg), and total somatic-cell DNA (20 μg), each containing 20 μg of native *Micrococcus lysodeikticus* DNA (density 1.731) were centrifuged in CsCl gradients in the 65-fixed-angle rotor of a Spinco centrifuge at 33,000 rev/min for 64 hours at 25°C. The initial density of the solution was 1.70 g/cm³. Each fraction was denatured with alkali, and the DNA was trapped on filters and hybridized with ³H-rRNA as described in the text.

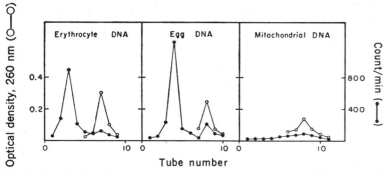

Fig. 6. Hybridization of somatic-cell (erythrocyte), egg, and mitochondrial DNA's of *X. laevis* with ³H-rRNA. About 10 μg of each DNA were fractionated in CsCl in a fixed-angle rotor and hybridized according to the method described in the text. The background binding was not subtracted.

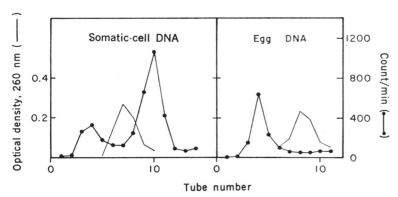

Fig. 7. Relative abundance of 5S DNA and rDNA in somatic-cell and egg DNA's of *X. laevis*. About 15 μg of each DNA was denatured and fractionated in CsCl, and the DNA from each fraction was immobilized on a filter and hybridized with a mixture of 0.02 μg of ³H-rRNA and 0.2 μg of 5S ³H-RNA in 3 ml of the salt solution. It has been demonstrated that 5S RNA hybridizes with DNA molecules of lower buoyant density than that of bulk DNA (24).

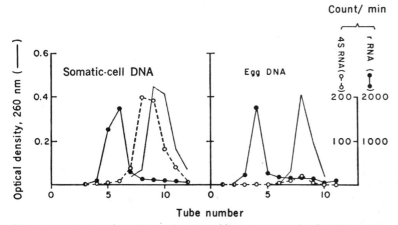

Fig. 8. Hybridization of 4S RNA and rRNA with egg and somatic-cell DNA's. About 60 μg of native somatic-cell DNA and 36 μg of egg DNA of *X. laevis* were fractionated in CsCl in a 65-fixed-angle rotor, and the DNA from each fraction was immobilized on a filter. Each filter was split in half, and material on one set of half filters was hybridized with 1.8 μg of ³H-rRNA (●——●); the other set was hybridized with 1.2 μg of 4S ³H-rRNA (○——○) in 4 ml of salt solution.

(Table 1) have widely different contents of DNA per cell and widely different numbers of rDNA replicas in their somatic genomes. Nevertheless, they have accumulated about the same amount of extra rDNA per germinal vesicle, and germinal vesicles from those species studied contain about the same number of nucleoli. Second, the rDNA content in germinal vesicles isolated from heterozygous (1-*nu*) females is the same as that found in the wild-type (2-*nu*) germinal vesicles (Table 3), although the somatic nuclei of the heterozygous animals have lost half their rDNA complement (26). Therefore, the control of this DNA replication is sensitive in some way to the final content of rDNA in a germinal vesicle rather than to the individual size, or total number of the replicas, or to the number of 28S and 18S genes clustered at the nucleolar organizer.

Necessity for Extra Copies of rDNA in Oocytes

Why do oocytes need copies of rDNA in excess of the 4C complement present on their "master" chromosomes? Two possible answers have occurred to us. The most obvious explanation is that they are needed to support the high rates of rRNA synthesis characteristic of oocytes. We have estimated that an immature oocyte of *X. laevis* can synthesize rRNA at a rate comparable to that of an equal weight of liver tissue, which comprises about 200,000 cells (21). However, since the maximum rate of rRNA synthesis that each gene can support is unknown, this interpretation remains conjecture. In this context it is of interest that the third type of RNA found in ribosomes —5S RNA—is accumulated coordinately with 28S and 18S RNA in oocytes (37), as in somatic tissues, but the DNA for 5S RNA is not amplified (Fig. 7). Perhaps the extreme redundancy of 5S DNA in the somatic-cell DNA of *X. laevis*, which amounts to more than 20,000 copies of the 5S sequences per haploid complement compared to 450 genes for rRNA (24), permits 5S RNA synthesis to keep pace with 28S and 18S RNA synthesis in oogenesis. The rate at which 5S RNA accumulates apparently is regulated by the rate of synthesis of 28S and 18S RNA both in oogenesis and embryogenesis. The latter control is exemplified by anucleolate embryos, which during their life-span do not accumulate detectable amounts

Table 3. Content of rDNA in germinal vesicles of heterozygote (1-*nu*) and wild type (2-*nu*) *X. laevis*. The total amounts of high-density DNA were calculated from band areas in analytical CsCl centrifugation according to the methods described in Fig. 2 and Table 1; 2000 germinal vesicles were isolated for each determination. The amount of rDNA was calculated by hybridization with ^{3}H-rRNA according to methods described in Fig. 3 and Table 1. The results of two separate hybridization experiments are given for 1-*nu* and 2-*nu* germinal vesicles (*51*).

Genotype	Amount (pg per germinal vesicle)	
	Total high-density DNA	rDNA
1-*nu*	25	4.0, 4.4
2-*nu*	25	5.6, 4.4

of new 5*S* RNA (*41*) even though they contain normal DNA complementary to 5*S* RNA (*24*).

A second hypothesis to explain the need for additional rRNA genes during oogenesis attempts to account for the difference between the ways in which rRNA synthesis is regulated in oocytes and in somatic cells. It has been shown in bacteria that the number of ribosomes produced is a direct function of the rate of protein synthesis (*42*). Changes in the rate of protein synthesis are accompanied by changes in the number of ribosomes, the majority of which enter polysomal aggregates; inactive monosomes do not accumulate (*43*). Somatic cells of higher organisms appear to regulate ribosome synthesis in a similar way. A good example is the response of some tissues to hormones. The small cells of the rat ventral prostate before puberty or after castration contain few ribosomes. In response to testosterone the cells enlarge rapidly and synthesize ribosomes at a high rate which results in a large net increase in their total ribosome content (*44*). We have investigated whether this rapid increase in ribosome synthesis results from a specific replication of the ribosomal RNA genes. We found that the prostates of castrated rats and of those injected with hormone had the same fraction of their DNA homologous to rRNA (*45*).

In contrast to somatic tissues such as the prostate gland, oocytes synthesize ribosomes primarily as a storage product to be used months later during embryogenesis. At all stages of oogenesis in *X. laevis* more than 60 percent of the ribosomes sediment as single ribosomes in sucrose and do not appear to be engaged in protein synthesis (*46*). With this proportion of monosomes, somatic tissues and bacteria would be expected to shut off synthesis of ribosomes.

However, oocytes are unique in that they synthesize ribosomes for storage and for this reason might be independent of the functional regulation imposed upon somatic cells. Perhaps the extra replicas of rRNA genes, functioning as "episomes" in extrachromosomal nuclear organelles, can escape the control mechanisms which function in somatic cells.

Specific Gene Replication: A Mechanism in Differentiation

Oocytes of four amphibians as well as those of an echiuroid worm and the surf clam contain many extra copies of the genes for 28*S* and 18*S* ribosomal RNA. The oocytes of these animals synthesize large quantities of ribosomes for storage, and the extra gene copies clearly act as templates in this synthesis. The extra genes are active only during oogenesis and cease to function when the oocyte reaches maturation.

The products elaborated by cells can be divided into two general classes: those made for their own maintenance and those produced as specialized "differentiated" products. One property of a "differentiated" product is that it is not generally required for the metabolism of the cell in which it is formed. In this context somatic cells synthesize rRNA for their own "maintenance" and do so most actively when they are growing and dividing, whereas the vast majority of ribosomes synthesized by the nondividing oocytes is stored for future use during embryogenesis. The change from synthesis of substances for the cell's own maintenance to synthesis of their differentiated products often is accompanied by the slowing or cessation of cell division (*47*). Likewise, oocytes synthesize and accumulate ribosomes during their long maturation period in the absence of cell division. The selective replication of genes is a mechanism best suited for nondividing cells; continued mitosis would not only dilute out the extrachromosomal genes but probably would also render them nonfunctional by relocating them into the cytoplasm.

Ribosome synthesis by somatic cells is a "maintenance" function which appears to be controlled without change in the number of rRNA genes (*24, 48*). In contrast, synthesis of ribosomes by oocytes appears to be a "differentiated" function involving the specific replication of the structural genes for two of the ribosome components.

There is no evidence that "specific gene amplification" is involved in the differentiated function of other cells. However, techniques are now available to begin an assessment of the relative importance of "differential gene action" and "differential gene alteration" in developmental phenomena.

Note added in proof: Perkowska, MacGregor, and Birnstiel (*51*) report that oocytes from 1-*nu* and 2-*nu* female *X. laevis* contain similar numbers of nuclei and similar amounts of germinal-vesicle DNA as measured cytochemically. They also reported that *X. laevis* germinal vesicles contain 30 pg of DNA in excess of the 4C complement. Both of these findings agree with our results.

References and Notes

1. For a review of this subject, see J. Schultz, in *Genetic Control of Differentiation* (Brookhaven National Laboratory, Upton, N.J., 1965), pp. 116–147.
2. M. Gold and J. Hurwitz, *J. Biol. Chem.* **239**, 3858 (1964).
3. S. R. Kornberg, S. B. Zimmerman, A. Kornberg, *ibid.* **236**, 1487 (1961).
4. For a review of this subject, see E. S. Lennox and M. Cohn, *Annu. Rev. Biochem.* **36**, 365 (1967).
5. A. Boivin, R. Vendrely, C. Vendrely, *Compt. Rend. Acad. Sci.* **226**, 106 (1948); A. E. Mirsky and H. Ris, *Nature* **163**, 666 (1949).
6. E. B. Wilson, *The Cell in Development and Heredity* (Macmillan, New York, 1928).
7. B. J. McCarthy and B. H. Hoyer, *Proc. Nat. Acad. Sci. U.S.* **52**, 915 (1964); B. H. Hoyer, B. J. McCarthy, E. T. Bolton, *Science* **144**, 959 (1964).
8. R. Briggs and T. J. King, *Proc. Nat. Acad. Sci. U.S.* **38**, 455 (1952); T. R. Elsdale, J. B. Gurdon, M. Fischberg, *J. Embryol. Exp. Morphol.* **8**, 437 (1960); J. Signoret, R. Briggs, R. R. Humphrey, *Develop. Biol.* **4**, 134 (1962).
9. J. B. Gurdon, *J. Embryol. Exp. Morphol.* **8**, 505 (1960).
10. F. C. Steward, A. E. Kent, M. O. Mapes, in *Current Topics of Development*, A. Monroy and A. A. Moscona, Eds. (Academic Press, New York, 1966), vol. 1, pp. 113–154.
11. Abbreviations: rRNA is a collective term for the 28*S* and 18*S* RNA molecules which are two of the structural RNA components of the ribosome. The term "rDNA" has been used interchangeably with the term "genes for rRNA" and refers to the DNA homologous to 28*S* RNA and 18*S* RNA as judged by molecular hybridization. The use of "gene" when referring to results of molecular hybridization is validated by the results obtained with the nucleolar mutant of *X. laevis*. In this case, deletion of the homologous DNA (*26*) results in no synthesis of the product in vivo (*28*). Since no such correlation has been made for the DNA homologous to 4*S* or 5*S* RNA, the terms 4*S* DNA and 5*S* DNA are used exclusively.
12. D. D. Brown and C. S. Weber, *Proc. Int. Congr. Biochem. 7th* **2**, 385 (1967); D. D. Brown, C. S. Weber, J. H. Sinclair, *Carnegie Inst. Wash. Year Book* **66**, 8 (1967).
13. J. G. Gall, *Proc. Nat. Acad. Sci. U.S.*, in press.
14. T. S. Painter and A. N. Taylor, *ibid.* **28**, 311 (1942).
15. G. Fankhauser, in *Analysis of Development*, B. H. Willier, P. A. Weiss, V. Hamburger, Eds. (Saunders, Philadelphia, 1955), pp. 126–150.
16. B. McClintock, *Z. Zellforsch. Mikroskop. Anat.* **21**, 294 (1934).
17. C. P. Raven, *Oogenesis: The Storage of Developmental Information* (Pergamon Press, New York, 1962).
18. H. C. MacGregor, *Quart. J. Microscop. Sci.* **106**, 215 (1965).
19. H. G. Callan, *J. Cell Sci.* **1**, 85 (1966).

20. O. L. Miller, personal communication.
21. For a review of this evidence, see D. D. Brown, *Nat. Cancer Inst. Monogr.* **23**, 297 (1966).
22. O. L. Miller, *ibid.*, p. 53; W. J. Peacock, *ibid.* **18**, 101 (1965).
23. S. Spiegelman and S. A. Yankofsky, in *Evolving Genes and Proteins*, V. Bryson and H. J. Vogel, Eds. (Academic Press, New York, 1965), pp. 537–579.
24. D. D. Brown and C. S. Weber, *J. Mol. Biol.*, in press.
25. I. B. Dawid, *ibid.* **12**, 581 (1965).
26. H. Wallace and M. L. Birnstiel, *Biochim. Biophys. Acta* **114**, 296 (1966); M. L. Birnstiel, H. Wallace, J. Sirlin, M. Fischberg, *Nat. Cancer Inst. Monogr.* **23**, 431 (1966).
27. T. R. Elsdale, M. Fischberg, S. Smith, *Exp. Cell Res.* **14**, 642 (1958).
28. D. D. Brown and J. B. Gurdon, *Proc. Nat. Acad. Sci. U.S.* **51**, 139 (1964).
29. J. Kahn, *Quart. J. Microscop. Sci.* **103**, 407 (1962).
30. A. Haggis, *Science* **154**, 670 (1966).
31. M. Izawa, V. G. Allfrey, A. E. Mirsky, *Proc. Nat. Acad. Sci. U.S.* **50**, 811 (1963).
32. M. Meselsohn, F. W. Stahl, J. Vinograd, *ibid.* **43**, 581 (1957).

33. I. B. Dawid, *ibid.* **56**, 269 (1966).
34. D. D. Brown and E. Littna, *J. Mol. Biol.* **8**, 669 (1964).
35. R. A. Weinberg, U. Loening, M. Willems, S. Penman, *Proc. Nat. Acad. Sci. U.S.* **58**, 1088 (1967); G. Attardi, personal communication.
36. R. Rosset, R. Monier, J. Julien, *Bull. Soc. Chim. Biol.* **46**, 87 (1964); F. Galibert, C. J. Larsen, J. C. Lelong, M. Boiron, *Nature* **207**, 1039 (1965).
37. D. D. Brown and E. Littna, *J. Mol. Biol.* **20**, 95 (1966).
38. I. Pikó, A. Tyler, J. Vinograd, *Biol. Bull.* **132**, 68 (1967).
39. D. D. Brown and E. Littna, *J. Mol. Biol.* **8**, 688 (1964); E. H. Davidson, V. G. Allfrey, A. E. Mirsky, *Proc. Nat. Acad. Sci. U.S.* **52**, 501 (1964).
40. S. Karasaki, *J. Cell Biol.* **26**, 937 (1965).
41. D. D. Brown, in *Current Topics in Developmental Biology*, A. Monroy and A. A. Moscona, Eds. (Academic Press, New York, 1967), vol. 2, pp. 47–73.
42. F. C. Neidhardt, *Progr. Nucleic Acid Res.* **3**, 145 (1964).
43. D. W. Morris and J. A. DeMoss, *Proc. Nat. Acad. Sci. U.S.* **56**, 262 (1966); E. Z. Ron, R. E. Kohler, B. D. Davis, *ibid.*, p. 471.
44. H. G. Williams-Ashman, S. Liao, R. L. Hancock, L. Jurkowitz, D. A. Silverman, *Rec. Progr. Hormone Res.* **20**, 247 (1964).
45. D. D. Brown, H. G. Williams-Ashman, D. S. Coffey, unpublished.
46. D. D. Brown, in *Developmental and Metabolic Control Mechanisms and Neoplasia*, D. N. Ward, Ed. (Williams and Wilkins, Baltimore, 1965), pp. 219–234.
47. For a review of this subject, see J. D. Ebert and M. E. Kaighn, in *Major Problems in Developmental Biology*, M. Locke, Ed. (Academic Press, New York, 1966), pp. 29–84.
48. F. M. Ritossa, K. C. Atwood, D. L. Lindsley, S. Spiegelman, *Nat. Cancer Inst. Monogr.* **23**, 449 (1966).
49. J. E. Edström, *Biochim. Biophys. Acta* **80**, 399 (1964); ———— and J. G. Gall, *J. Cell Biol.* **19**, 279 (1963).
50. We thank Mrs. E. Jordan and E. Hallberg for expert technical assistance; Drs. Briggs, DeLanney, and Humphrey for gifts of axolotl; and Drs. Ebert, Kasinsky, Reeder, and Sinclair, Mrs. Schwartz, and Mr. Hallberg for their critical appraisal of the manuscript.
51. E. Perkowska, H. C. MacGregor, M. L. Birnstiel, *Nature* **217**, 650 (1968).

Reprinted from the PROCEEDINGS OF THE NATIONAL ACADEMY OF SCIENCES
Vol. 60, No. 2, pp. 553–560. June, 1968.

DIFFERENTIAL SYNTHESIS OF THE GENES FOR RIBOSOMAL RNA DURING AMPHIBIAN OÖGENESIS

By Joseph G. Gall

DEPARTMENT OF BIOLOGY, KLINE BIOLOGY TOWER, YALE UNIVERSITY

Communicated by Norman H. Giles, November 7, 1967

Molecular hybridization experiments have shown that the genes for ribosomal RNA are located in or near the nucleolus organizer in *Drosophila melanogaster*[1, 2] and in the toad *Xenopus laevis*.[3, 4] Under normal circumstances the number of organizers per genome will be characteristic of the organism, and DNA from various tissues should contain the same proportion of ribosomal genes. This conclusion has been confirmed for several tissues of the chicken.[2] However, cytological evidence has long suggested that the nucleolus organizer undergoes a differential replication in oöcytes of certain animals. Data supporting this view will be summarized later in this article. If such a differential replication occurs, oöcyte DNA should be enriched with respect to the ribosomal genes. The cytological picture is particularly striking in ovaries of the toads *Bufo* and *Xenopus*, in which the differential synthesis occurs during pachytene. In recently metamorphosed toads the ovary contains a sufficiently high proportion of pachytene oöcytes to permit detection of the differential synthesis by biochemical means.[5] This communication describes the ovarian DNA of *Xenopus* and demonstrates that it contains an excess of sequences coding for rRNA. Recently Brown and co-workers[6, 7] have studied the DNA from older oöcytes of *Xenopus* and have reached similar conclusions.

Materials and Methods.—(1) *Animals:* Tadpoles of the African clawed toad *Xenopus laevis* were grown in the laboratory. During the second and through the fourth weeks after metamorphosis, a large number of oöcytes are in the pachytene stage. At this time the testes and ovaries can be distinguished by gross inspection (cf. Figs. A and B in Blackler[8]). When the oöcytes pass into diplotene and begin their growth phase, they have completed the differential DNA synthesis. If individual oöcytes are detectable with the dissecting microscope (10×–20×), the ovary will show little incorporation into the nucleolar DNA.

(2) *DNA extraction:* Ovaries from 8–10 toads were dissected under sterile conditions and cultured 20–60 hr in a medium containing 9 μc thymidine-C^{14} (47 mc/mM) or 100 μc thymidine-H^3 (14 c/mM). The ovaries were rinsed in SSC and homogenized in 2 ml tris-EDTA-sucrose solution. Predigested pronase (100 μg) and SDS (0.2%) were added and the mixture incubated several hours at 37°C. The solution was mixed with phenol and centrifuged, after which the aqueous layer was extracted three times with ether and finally bubbled with air. Previously boiled RNase (100 μg) was added and allowed to act 1–2 hr. Pronase (100 μg) was added and digestion continued for 1–2 hr. The solution was next mixed with 2 vol of ethanol and held in the freezer for 3 hr or longer. No precipitate was visible, but the DNA could be deposited on the walls of the test tube by centrifuging at 10,000 *g* for 30 min. The DNA was redissolved in 1 ml 0.1 × SSC. Denaturing was accomplished by heating 10 min in a boiling water bath or by adding NaOH and neutralizing with HCl. Samples labeled with C^{14} had a specific activity of 500–1500 cpm/μg; those with H^3 had about 10,000 cpm/μg. A total of 1.5–3.0 μg of DNA was recovered per pair of ovaries.

(3) *RNA:* Radioactive RNA was prepared from immature ovaries of *Xenopus* cultured 3–4 days in a medium containing 300–600 μc uridine-H^3 (25 c/mM). Labeled mouse RNA was obtained from cultured L cells. In both cases the RNA was prepared essentially

as recommended by Brown and Littna.[9] Purification was carried out on sucrose gradients, and the 28*S*, 18*S*, and 4*S* fractions were collected separately. The specific activity of *Xenopus* RNA samples varied between 10,000 and 30,000 cpm/μg, the mouse RNA between 50,000 and 140,000 cpm/μg.

(4) *Centrifugation:* Density equilibrium centrifugation was performed in the Spinco No. 50 angle-head rotor.[10] Samples of 4.5 ml were placed in polyallomer tubes, covered with mineral oil, and spun for 20–24 hr at 42,000 rpm and 20°C. Fractions were collected by puncturing the bottom of the tube. All samples were filtered onto nitrocellulose membranes. Denatured DNA was collected in 6 × SSC and filtered immediately. Native DNA was either collected in 5% TCA and filtered after chilling 1–3 hr, or was denatured with alkali and filtered in 6 × SSC.

(5) *Annealing:* The filter technique described by Gillespie and Spiegelman[11] was used for forming molecular hybrids between RNA and DNA. Annealing was routinely carried out at 66°C for 16–20 hr.

(6) *Counting procedure:* All radioactive samples were deposited on nitrocellulose membrane filters and counted in toluene-PPO-POPOP. For double-labeling experiments representative H^3 and C^{14} spectra were measured *on filters* and appropriate channels chosen for minimizing spillage of C^{14} counts into the H^3 channel. In annealing experiments the filters which contained C^{14}-labeled DNA were counted both before and after hybridization. In this way the fraction of C^{14} counts in the H^3 channel was directly determined, and the retention of DNA during the hybridization step was monitored.

(7) *Abbreviations:* rRNA, ribosomal RNA; rDNA, the DNA sequences coding for rRNA; SDS, sodium dodecyl sulfate; SSC, 0.15 *M* NaCl, 0.015 *M* Na citrate, pH 7.0; toluene-PPO-POPOP, 4 gm 2,5 diphenyloxazole and 50 mg 1,4 bis [2-(4-methyl-5-phenyl-oxazolyl)]-benzene in 1 liter toluene; tris-EDTA-sucrose, 0.05 *M* tris-(hydroxymethyl)-amino methane, 0.1 *M* ethylenediaminetetraacetate, 27% w/v sucrose, pH 8.4; TCA, trichloroacetic acid.

Results.—As used here the term *ovarian DNA* refers to unfractionated DNA from the whole ovary. It is derived primarily from follicle cells and oöcytes, but contains contributions from primordial germ cells, oögonia, erythrocytes, and connective tissue cells.

Buoyant density of ovarian DNA: Labeled DNA from young ovaries of *Xenopus* separates into two bands of radioactivity when centrifuged to equilib-

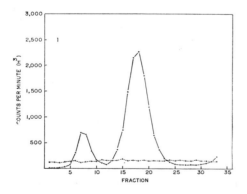 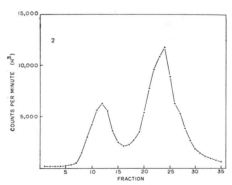

Fig. 1.—Separation of labeled ovarian DNA into two bands after equilibrium centrifugation in CsCl. (· — ·) Native DNA; (· - - · - - ·) sample treated with DNase before centrifugation.

Fig. 2.—Ovarian DNA of *Xenopus* denatured by boiling and centrifuged to equilibrium in CsCl. Major and minor peaks retained their relative heights and positions in the gradient, although both are denser than in native sample. The minor peak contained 30% of the radioactivity.

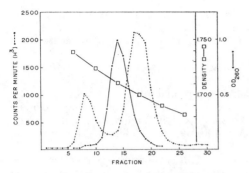

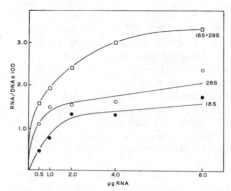

Fig. 3.—Labeled ovarian DNA of *Xenopus* (·-----·) and unlabeled *E. coli* DNA (·——·) centrifuged together in CsCl. The density scale was determined from refractive index measurements on a second CsCl gradient run simultaneously; the absolute values were adjusted to give $\rho = 1.710$ at the *coli* peak. Main *Xenopus* peak, $\rho = 1.700$; minor *Xenopus* peak, $\rho = 1.729$.

Fig. 4.—Saturation curves for annealing of *Xenopus* ribosomal RNA with *Xenopus* ovarian DNA. The plateau levels were much higher than with *Xenopus* somatic DNA. See Table 1 for further details.

rium in CsCl. Both bands are eliminated by prior treatment with DNase (Fig. 1). The majority of the radioactivity is in the lighter band, which has the same buoyant density as DNA derived from liver and other somatic tissues of *Xenopus*. The minor, more dense band is seen only when ovaries of the appropriate age are labeled; detectable radioactivity is not found in this part of the gradient when labeled DNA is isolated from older ovaries or from liver. During the second and through the fourth weeks after metamorphosis, up to 30 per cent of the total radioactivity may be found in the minor peak (Fig. 2); after this time, labeling of the minor peak drops off rapidly as many oöcytes pass into the diplotene stage of meiosis. The minor peak can be detected in older ovaries by optical density measurements (Fig. 7).

The buoyant density of the peaks was estimated by centrifuging radioactive ovarian DNA with unlabeled *E. coli* DNA as a density standard (Fig. 3). The densities of the major and minor peaks are 1.700 and 1.729, corresponding to guanine + cytosine contents of 41 per cent and 70 per cent, respectively.[12] When ovarian DNA is boiled or treated with strong alkali before centrifugation both peaks increase in density, while retaining the same relative heights and positions in the gradient (Fig. 2). In one experiment the new densities were determined as 1.714 and 1.746. These observations suggest that the minor peak, like the major, contains double-stranded DNA that is denatured in the usual way by alkali.[12]

Annealing of ovarian DNA: If the minor peak represents nucleolar DNA in whole or in part, then we should expect ovarian DNA to be enriched in the cistrons for rRNA. This has been tested by means of annealing experiments utilizing ovarian DNA and several RNA samples.

Wallace and Birnstiel[3, 4] showed that somatic DNA of *Xenopus* hybridizes with about 0.1 per cent of its weight of rRNA; the saturation levels for 28*S* and 18*S* rRNA being, respectively, 0.04–0.09 per cent and 0.025–0.04 per cent.

TABLE 1.   *Details of an annealing experiment between Xenopus ovarian DNA and Xenopus rRNA (mixed 28S and 18S).*

DNA on Filter Before Annealing		DNA on Filter after Annealing		RNA used for annealing	RNA in RNase-Resistant Hybrid		RNA/ DNA
(cpm)	(μg)	(cpm)	(μg)	(μg)	(cpm)	(μg)	(%)
574	0.845	430	0.633	0.5	112	0.0100	1.58
555	0.817	416	0.613	1	133	0.0119	1.94
558	0.822	403	0.594	2	161	0.0144	2.42
559	0.823	407	0.599	4	202	0.0180	3.01
562	0.828	392	0.577	8	217	0.0193	3.34
35 μg E. coli unlabeled		Not determined		2	2	—	—

C[14]-labeled ovarian DNA (679 cpm/μg) was boiled and placed on nitrocellulose filters. The filters were annealed with the indicated amounts of H[3]-labeled rRNA (11,200 cpm/μg) for 16 hr at 66°C. After treatment with RNase (20 μg/ml in 2 × SSC) for 1 hr at room temperature the filters were washed in 6 × SSC and the radioactivity determined in a liquid scintillation counter. The counts of hybrid were made at restricted channel settings to minimize spillage of C[14] into the H[3] channel. All values are corrected for spillage (10%) and are adjusted to full channel.

Their values were obtained by annealing in solution.   In the present experiments the filter technique of Gillespie and Spiegelman[11] was used.   DNA from *Xenopus* liver gave a saturation value of 0.10–0.15 per cent when annealed with a mixture of 28S and 18S rRNA.   The saturation levels for 28S and 18S separately were about 0.09 per cent and 0.05 per cent.   Thus there is reasonable agreement between the two techniques.

When unfractionated DNA from early ovaries was annealed with rRNA much higher saturation levels were found.   Although only very small amounts of ovarian DNA were available, the annealing could be studied with no more than 0.5–1.0 μg DNA on each filter.   The results with one sample of ovarian DNA are shown in Table 1 and Figure 4.   In this sample the saturation levels for 18S and 28S rRNA are about 1.5 per cent and 2.0 per cent, respectively, and about 3.2 per cent for the mixture.   A second DNA sample saturated at 0.8 per cent and 2.0 per cent with 18S and 28S rRNA, and a third at 2.8 per cent with 28S rRNA. These values correspond to a 20- to 30-fold enrichment of the ribosomal genes in ovarian DNA as compared to somatic DNA.   Since the oöcytes constitute a minority of the cells in the ovary, their specific enrichment must be considerably higher than this figure.

Annealing of gradient fractions: Wallace and Birnstiel[3, 4] demonstrated that the sequences in somatic DNA which hybridize with 28S rRNA are denser than the bulk of the DNA.   This they did by separately hybridizing the fractions from a CsCl gradient.   A repetition of their experiment is shown in Figure 5, where *Xenopus* liver DNA was fractionated and hybridized with a mixture of 28S and 18S rRNA.   Annealing experiments were next carried out with fractions from CsCl gradients of ovarian DNA.   In Figures 6 and 7 one can see that nearly all of the hybridization takes place in the heavy peak.   In Figure 7 the DNA was derived from ovaries with diplotene oöcytes, and the DNA of the minor peak did not label; however, it was detectable by optical density measurements.   A saturation value has not been determined for the heavy peak alone.   Since it represents only a small fraction of the total DNA (Fig. 7), its saturation level must be well above the 3 per cent found for unfractionated ovarian DNA.

Discussion.—The experiments reported here demonstrate a differential synthesis of rDNA in ovaries of recently metamorphosed *Xenopus*. The rDNA has a buoyant density of 1.729, corresponding to a G + C content of 70 per cent. This value is somewhat higher than that reported for the rDNA of *Xenopus* somatic tissues, namely 1.723.[4] A direct comparison of ovary and somatic DNA must be made before this difference can be considered significant. However, it seems possible that the G + C content of the ovary rDNA exceeds the G + C content of *Xenopus* rRNA (about 60%[7, 9]). Perhaps certain high G + C regions in the rDNA are not transcribed, or, if transcribed, are eliminated in the transformation from precursor 45S rRNA to definitive 28S and 18S rRNA. Alternatively, the buoyant density of the rDNA may be unusual for its base composition.

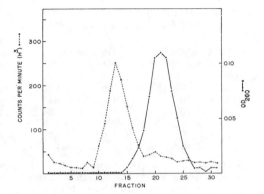

Fig. 5.—An experiment to demonstrate the ribosomal complements in somatic DNA. *Xenopus* liver DNA (200 μg) was boiled and then centrifuged to equilibrium in CsCl ($\cdot$———$\cdot$). Each gradient fraction was placed on a nitrocellulose filter and annealed with 1 μg of mouse ribosomal RNA. The RNase-resistant hybrid ($\cdot$-----$\cdot$) was formed with DNA sequences of high density. Mouse rRNA anneals well with amphibian DNA,[7] and was available at the high specific activity needed for this experiment (60,000 cpm/μg).

There is compelling cytological evidence that the excess rDNA is made in the oöcytes and that it is involved in the formation of the multiple nucleoli characteristic of these cells. The cytological features will be briefly summarized. In many Amphibia the oöcyte nucleus reaches a diameter of over 0.5 mm and contains 1000 or more nucleoli.[13, 14] Oöcyte nucleoli are similar to somatic nucleoli in most respects,[15] including fine structure,[16-18] but they are not attached to the chromosomes; during most of oögenesis they are situated just inside the nuclear envelope. They incorporate uridine and other RNA precursors rapidly,[17, 18] and the incorporation is actinomycin-sensitive.[19] In the newt *Triturus*, the RNA of the oöcyte nucleoli has a base composition similar to that of rRNA.[20]

Each of the multiple nucleoli contains a small amount of DNA, which is frequently, though not invariably, demonstrable as a Feulgen-positive granule.[21-23] During part of oögenesis the nucleoli take the form of beaded circles or necklaces, and these are fragmented by DNase.[24, 25] Finally the nucleolar DNA has been demonstrated by the specific binding of actinomycin.[26] Electron micrographs suggest that the DNA may exist as circles of several sizes.[24]

The origin of the nucleolar DNA was first studied by King in 1908.[27] She showed that extra "chromatin" arises in the oöcytes of the toad *Bufo* during pachytene, and that this "chromatin" is associated with the forming nucleoli. Later Painter and Taylor[22] used the Feulgen reaction to demonstrate that the material observed by King was in fact DNA. Photometric measurements show that in *Bufo* the synthesis of nucleolar DNA results in a two to threefold increase

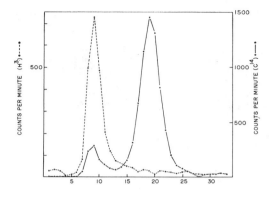

Fig. 6.—An experiment to demonstrate the ribosomal complements in ovarian DNA. *Xenopus* ovarian DNA (12 μg) was centrifuged to equilibrium in CsCl (·———·). Each gradient fraction was denatured, placed on a nitrocellulose filter, and annealed with 1 μg of mouse ribosomal RNA (120,000 cpm/μg). As in somatic DNA (Fig. 5), the DNA sequences complementary to rRNA occurred at a high density, coincident with the minor DNA peak.

in nuclear DNA content.[28] Early meiotic nuclei contain the expected 4C amount of DNA, but by late pachytene this has increased to more than 10C. Macgregor[29] has found that in *Xenopus* the DNA content during pachytene rises from 4C to about 14C. Thus in these two species most of the DNA in the late pachytene nucleus is newly synthesized nucleolar DNA. The extra DNA is in the form of minute granules or fibers separate from the chromosomes (Fig. 8). During the period of DNA increase the oöcyte nuclei exhibit a marked uptake of thymidine-H[3] into the nucleolar granules, while the chromosomes remain unlabeled.[28,29]

The biochemical and cytological data taken together suggest the following sequence of events. During pachytene, specific replication of the nucleolus organizer region takes place; this involves the genes for both 18S and 28S rRNA. The extra organizers, possibly in the form of circular DNA molecules, migrate to the nuclear envelope, where they serve as the templates for the synthesis of rRNA precursors. The formation of the multiple nucleoli is the cytological expression of these events. The synthesis of the extra DNA is limited to the pachytene stage, but the DNA itself is metabolically stable and persists throughout oögenesis in association with the nucleoli.

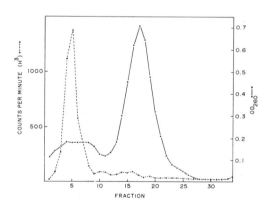

Fig. 7.—*Xenopus* ovarian DNA (40 μg) was boiled and centrifuged to equilibrium (·———·) Each fraction was then annealed with 1 μg of mouse ribosomal RNA. This DNA sample was derived from older ovaries in which the minor peak did not label with thymidine; the minor peak was nevertheless demonstrable by optical density measurements.

The phenomenon described here is of widespread occurrence in animal oögenesis. DNA granules associated with the multiple nucleoli can be demonstrated in many amphibians, both urodele and anuran.[30] The nucleoli of grasshopper oöcytes occur as long strands which are disrupted by DNase,[31] while in the cricket they are small circles which arise in association with Feulgen-positive material.[32] In the fly *Tipula*, excess DNA occurs in the oöcyte along with

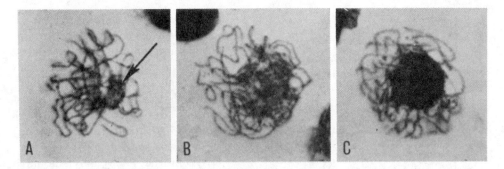

F<small>IG</small>. 8.—*Xenopus* oöcyte nuclei during the period of nucle·lar DNA synthesis. Feulgen stain, ×1700.

(*A*) Very early stage containing normal pachytene chromosomes with the 4C amount of DNA. Arrow indicates nucleolus.

(*B*) Excess DNA begins to accumulate as granules around the nucleolus. Such nuclei show intense thymidine incorporation.

(*C*) After synthesis the nuclear DNA content has more than tripled and the excess DNA appears as a compact mass. Subsequently the mass will break up into hundreds of granules which become associated with the multiple nucleoli.

nucleolar material,[33-35] and the same has been shown in several other insects,[33] including a number of beetles.[36]   Among the latter, "Giardina's ring" in oöcytes of *Dytiscus* is particularly striking.

The synthesis of extra rDNA is related to the extreme demand for rRNA which arises during oögenesis.   The oöcyte faces a unique problem: its single nucleus must supply RNA to a mass of cytoplasm which in other tissues would contain several thousand nuclei.   Polyploidy or polyteny as mechanisms for the increase of DNA templates are ruled out by the need for an orderly meiosis.   Differential replication provides a genetically "acceptable" mechanism whereby those templates in demand, namely the rDNA, can be produced in abundance.   Painter and Taylor[22] recognized the essential features when they concluded, "If these nucleolar organizers are genetically the same as those which form nucleoli in ordinary somatic cells, then we may say that the germinal vesicle of the toad is highly polyploid in nucleolar organizers, but otherwise lampbrush chromosomes are normal meiotic structures."

Summary.—The DNA synthesized in ovaries of recently metamorphosed toads (*Xenopus laevis*) consists of two fractions, one of which has the same buoyant density as somatic DNA ($\rho = 1.700$).   The other is a double-stranded DNA of unusually high buoyant density ($\rho = 1.729$) which contains up to 30 per cent of the thymidine incorporated by the ovary.   Molecular hybridization experiments demonstrate that unfractionated ovarian DNA is enriched 20–30 times over somatic DNA in the genes for rRNA.   The extra genes are located in the heavy DNA fraction.   The differential synthesis of the genes for ribosomal RNA is correlated with the appearance of hundreds of nucleolus organizers during the pachytene stage of meiosis.   The multiple nucleoli of the oöcyte later arise in association with these organizers, which provide extra templates for the massive synthesis of rRNA that occurs during oögenesis.

This study was aided by a U.S. Public Health Service grant from the National Institute of General Medical Sciences (GM 12427). The technical assistance of Miss Carolyn Staehly is gratefully acknowledged.

[1] Ritossa, F. M., and S. Spiegelman, these PROCEEDINGS, **53**, 737 (1965).

[2] Ritossa, F. M., K. C. Atwood, D. L. Lindsley, and S. Spiegelman, *Natl. Cancer Inst. Monograph*, **23**, 449 (1966).

[3] Wallace, H., and M. L. Birnstiel, *Biochim. Biophys. Acta*, **114**, 296 (1966).

[4] Birnstiel, M. L., H. Wallace, J. Sirlin, and M. Fischberg, *Natl. Cancer Inst. Monograph*, **23**, 431 (1966).

[5] Gall, J. G., *J. Cell Biol.*, **35**, 43A (1967).

[6] Brown, D. D., and I. B. Dawid, *Science*, **160**, 272 (1968).

[7] Brown, D. D., C. S. Weber, and J. H. Sinclair, in *Carnegie Institution of Washington Year Book 66* (1967).

[8] Blackler, A. W., *J. Embryol. Exptl. Morphol.*, **13**, 51 (1965).

[9] Brown, D. D., and E. Littna, *J. Mol. Biol.*, **8**, 669 (1964).

[10] Flamm, W. G., H. E. Bond, and H. E. Burr, *Biochim. Biophys. Acta*, **129**, 310 (1966).

[11] Gillespie, D., and S. Spiegelman, *J. Mol. Biol.*, **12**, 829 (1965).

[12] Schildkraut, C. L., J. Marmur, and P. Doty, *J. Mol. Biol.*, **4**, 430 (1962).

[13] Wilson, E. B., *The Cell in Development and Heredity* (New York: Macmillan, 1925).

[14] Macgregor, H. C., *Quart. J. Microscop. Sci.*, **106**, 215 (1965).

[15] Gall, J. G., *J. Morphol.*, **94**, 283 (1954).

[16] Miller, O. L., in *Proc. Intern. Congr. Electron Micr., 5th*, **2**, NN8 (1962).

[17] Macgregor, H. C., *J. Cell Sci.*, **2**, 145 (1967).

[18] Lane, N. J., *J. Cell Biol.*, **35**, 421 (1967).

[19] Izawa, M., V. G. Allfrey, and A. E. Mirsky, these PROCEEDINGS, **49**, 544 (1963).

[20] Edström, J. E., and J. G. Gall, *J. Cell Biol.*, **19**, 279 (1963).

[21] Brachet, J., *Arch. Biol.*, **51**, 151 (1940).

[22] Painter, T. S., and A. N. Taylor, these PROCEEDINGS, **28**, 311 (1942).

[23] Guyénot, E., and M. Danon, *Rev. Suisse Zool.*, **60**, 1 (1953).

[24] Miller, O. L., *Natl. Cancer Inst., Monograph*, **23**, 53 (1966).

[25] Kezer, J., cited in W. J. Peacock, *Natl. Cancer Inst. Monograph*, **18**, 101 (1965).

[26] Ebstein, B. S., *J. Cell Biol.*, **35**, 709 (1967).

[27] King, H. D., *J. Morphol.*, **19**, 369 (1908).

[28] Gall, J. G., unpublished observations.

[29] Macgregor, H. C., *J. Cell Sci.*, in press.

[30] The author and H. C. Macgregor have seen granules in the following species: *Bufo bufo*, *B. terrestris*, *B. americanus*, *B. marinus*, *Xenopus laevis*, *Rana clamitans*, *Eleutherodactylus johnstonii*, *Triturus viridescens*, *T. cristatus*. The situation in *Triturus* and *Rana* needs further study. Biochemical analysis of isolated germinal vesicles has yielded values of 36C for *Triturus viridescens* (Izawa, M., V. G. Allfrey, and A. E. Mirsky, these PROCEEDINGS, **50**, 811 (1963) and over 500C for *Rana pipiens* (Finamore, F., D. Thomas, G. Crouse, and B. Lloyd, *Arch. Biochem. Biophys.*, **88**, 10 (1960); Haggis, A., *Science*, **154**, 670 (1966)). Feulgen preparations of early oöcytes give little indication that such large amounts of DNA are present, at least in pachytene and early diplotene, although some Feulgen-positive material is associated with the nucleoli.

[31] Kunz, W., *Chromosoma*, **20**, 332 (1967).

[32] *Ibid.*, **21**, 446 (1967).

[33] Bauer, H., *Z. Zellforsch. Mikr. Anat.*, **18**, 254 (1933).

[34] Bayreuther, K., *Chromosoma*, **7**, 508 (1956).

[35] Lima-de-Faria, A., *Chromosoma*, **13**, 47 (1962).

[36] Urbani, E., and S. Russo-Caia, *Rend. Ist. Sci. Univ. Camerino*, **5**, 19 (1964).

Section IV

CONTROL OF ENZYME CONTENT IN LIVER CELLS

SCHIMKE, R. T., 1961. Cold Spring Harbor Symp. Quant. Biol. *26*, 363-366. Studies on adaptation of urea cycle enzymes in the rat.

SCHIMKE, R. T., M. B. BROWN, and E. T. SMALLMAN, 1962. Ann. N. Y. Acad. Sci. *102*, 587. Turnover of rat liver arginase.

SCHIMKE, R. T., 1964. Nat'l Canc. Instit. *13*, 197-217. Enzymes of arginine metabolism in cell cultures: studies on enzyme induction and repression.

SCHIMKE, R. T., E. W. SWEENEY, and C. M. BERLIN, 1965. J. Biol. Chem. *240*, 322-331. The roles of synthesis and degradation in the control of rat liver tryptophan pyrrolase.

PIRAS, M. M., and W. E. KNOX, 1967. J. Biol. Chem. *242*, 2952-2958. Tryptophan pyrrolase of liver. II.

KNOX, W. E., and M. M. PIRAS, 1967. J. Biol. Chem. *242*, 2959-2965. Tryptophan pyrrolase of liver, III.

LIN, E. C. C., and W. E. KNOX, 1957. Biochim. biophys. Acta, *26*, 85. Adaptation of the rat liver tyrosine-α-ketoglutarate transaminase.

KENNEY, F. T., 1962. J. Biol. Chem. *237*, 1610. Induction of tyrosine-α-ketoglutarate transaminase in rat liver.

HAGER, C. B., and F. T. KENNEY, 1968. J. Biol. Chem. *243*, 3296. Regulation of tyrosine-α-ketoglutarate transaminase in rat liver.

CIVEN, M., R. ULRICH, B. M. TRIMMER, C. B. BROWN, 1967. Science *157*, 1563. Circadian rhythms of liver enzymes and their relationship to enzyme induction.

TOMKINS, G. M., E. B. Thompson, S. HAYASHI, T. GELEHRTER, D. GRANNER, and B. PETERKOFSKY, 1966. Cold Spring Harbor Symp. Quant. Biol. *31*, 349-360. Tyrosine transaminase induction to mammalian cells in tissue culture.

REEL, J. R., and F. T. KENNEY, 1968. Proc. Nat'l Acad. Sci. *61*, 200. "Superinduction" of tyrosine transaminase in hepatoma cell cultures.

Changes in the chemical environment of mammalian cells normally occur following changes in diet and changes in hormonal levels. Since the products of intestinal absorption are carried directly to the liver via the portal vein, cells of this tissue are subject to frequent chemical changes. Thus, it seemed logical to look for cases of substrate stimulation of enzyme synthesis in liver cells. Early studies of arginase, tryptophan pyrrolase, and tyrosine transaminase indicated that the respective substrates increased the specific activity of these enzymes in liver cells (pp. 223, 279, Knox and Mehler, 1950). However, further work indicated that the increases in specific activity are not the result of substrate stimulation of the rate of synthesis of these enzymes, but rather result from preferential stabilization of the enzymes or hormonal involvement (pp. 227, 242, 262, 272, and 286). These studies pointed out the dynamic state of most proteins in liver cells in which a given concentration of a specific enzyme is the result of a balance between the rate of synthesis and the rate of inactivation. The importance of directly studying the rate of synthesis of a protein rather than the level of enzyme activity became apparent from these studies.

Hormonal "induction" of tyrosine transaminase in liver cells, on the other hand, does appear to be similar to bacterial inductions in that steroids increase the rate of synthesis of this enzyme (pp. 286, 290). Further analysis of this control mechanism in whole animals was hampered by the multiple effects of several hormones on the specific activity of tyrosine transaminase (Holten and Kenney, 1967; Kenney, 1967; p. 295). Experimental procedures often elicited uncontrolled changes in hormonal levels which then affected the rate of synthesis or degradation of the enzyme. Superimposed on these complications is a circadian change in the specific activity (p. 300). Thus, it is exceedingly difficult to analyze the regulatory effects of chemical treatment of whole animals. This problem is overcome by utilizing liver cells in tissue culture (p. 302).

Since the chemical environment of cells in culture is strictly controlled, the steps in the regulation of tyrosine transaminase could be clearly delineated. The use of drugs which preferentially inhibit RNA or protein synthesis indicated that hormonal induction affects the rate of synthesis by increasing mRNA for the enzyme. However, certain paradoxical results occurred when actinomycin D was added several hours after addition of the hormone. Reel and Kenney (p. 314) were able to show that the observed "superinduction" could be explained by effects of the drug on the stability of the enzyme. The danger of relying too strongly on chemical inhibition of macromolecular synthesis in the analysis of the biochemical steps involved in an "induction" is emphasized by these studies. However, present techniques for direct analysis of single proteins cannot be applied in many developing systems.

Holten, D., and F. Kenney (1967) J. Biol. Chem. *242,* 4372. Regulation of tyrosine-α-ketoglutarate transaminase in rat liver. VI. Induction by pancreatic hormones.

Kenney, F. (1967) J. Biol. Chem. *242,* 4367. Regulation of tyrosine-α-ketoglutarate transaminase in rat liver. V. Repression in growth hormone-treated rats.

Knox, W., and A. Mehler (1950)   J. Biol. Chem. *187*, 419. The conversion of tryptophan to kynurenine in liver. I. The coupled tryptophan peroxidase-oxidase system forming formylkynurenine.

RELATED READING

DeMars, R. (1958)   Biochim. biophys. Acta *27*, 435. The inhibition by glutamine of glutamyl transferase formation in cultures of human cells.

Ennis, M., and M. Lubin (1963)   Biochim. biophys. Acta *68*, 78. Capacity for synthesis of a pyrimidine biosynthetic enzyme in mammalian cells.

Nierlich, D., and E. McFall (1963)   Biochim. biophys. Acta *76*, 469. Repression of an enzyme of purine biosynthesis in L-cells.

Peraino, C., C. Lomar, and H. Pitot (1966)   J. Biol. Chem. *241*, 2944. Studies on the induction and repression of enzymes in rat liver. IV. Effects of cortisone and phenobarbital.

Reprinted from COLD SPRING HARBOR SYMPOSIA ON QUANTITATIVE BIOLOGY
Volume XXVI, 1961
Printed in U.S.A.

Studies on Adaptation of Urea Cycle Enzymes in the Rat

ROBERT T. SCHIMKE

National Institutes of Health, Bethesda, Maryland

Previous papers in this Symposium have been devoted to a biochemical and genetic analysis of control mechanisms involved in the biosynthesis of arginine in *Escherichia coli*. I should like to report on some studies involving a group of enzymes catalyzing many of the same chemical reactions in rat liver, namely those concerned with the synthesis of urea: carbamyl phosphate synthetase, ornithine transcarbamylase, argininosuccinate synthetase, argininosuccinate cleavage enzyme, and arginase (for discussions of the enzymatic steps of urea synthesis and general problems of urea synthesis see Ratner [1955] and Cohen and Brown 1960]). This sequence of enzymes serves both biosynthetic and degradative functions in the rat, i.e., the synthesis of arginine, and the formation of urea, in which form amino nitrogen is excreted in mammals. It is the latter function with which I shall deal.

The basis of these studies is the well-known fact that urea excretion can be altered by varying the dietary protein intake. By growing rats on diets containing from 15 to 60% casein, under which conditions growth rates and daily caloric intakes are essentially similar, the relationships shown in Fig. 1 were established (Schimke, to be published). It can be seen that there is a direct relationship between the hepatic content of each of the urea cycle enzymes and the daily intake of dietary protein. This relationship holds for each of the enzymes, and not only for the one present in least abundance, i.e., argininosuccinate synthetase. Various investigators have previously indicated a relationship between rat liver arginase and dietary protein (Lightbody and Kleinman, 1939; Mandelstam and Yudkin, 1952; Ashida and Harper, 1961). Under similar dietary conditions the hepatic contents of glutamic and malic dehydrogenases were unchanged, whereas the content of lactic dehydrogenase showed an inverse relationship to dietary protein intake. Glutamic-pyruvic and glutamic-oxaloacetic transaminases showed relationships to dietary protein similar to those of the urea cycle enzymes.

Alterations in the levels of the urea cycle enzymes were not produced by any one of a number of amino acids administered individually in concentrations present in a 60% casein diet when added to a 15% casein diet, including arginine, ornithine, citrulline, glycine, alanine, glutamic or aspartic acids, or tryptophan, as well as urea itself. Furthermore, administrations of glucocorticoids in doses known to affect the level of

tryptophan pyrrolase (Knox and Auerbach, 1955) and tyrosine alpha-ketoglutarate transaminase (Lin and Knox, 1957) had no significant effects on the levels of urea cycle enzymes. On the other hand, any change in diet which resulted in a change in the rate of urea excretion would result in proportional changes in the levels of each of the urea cycle enzymes. These included starvation, variations in dietary casein from 0 to 60%, and the use of diets containing various concentrations of a nutritionally incomplete protein (gelatin).

The increased activities of the urea cycle enzymes observed in crude homogenates could result from a number of alterations in the tissue, including changes in the concentrations of activators or inhibitors, changes in the kinetic properties of the enzymes, or actual changes in the content of specific enzyme protein. Various mixing experiments with crude extracts, subcellular fractions, and purified enzymes from rat liver with high or low activities have failed to demonstrate the presence of inhibitors or activators. When arginase was purified in parallel steps from livers of rats grown on either a 15 or 60% protein diet, the enzyme preparations behaved in a similar manner during purification with similar yields at each step. A similar phenomenon was found during purification of ornithine transcarbamylase. The final preparations of both enzymes were homogeneous by starch gel electrophoresis. Kinetic studies on the enzyme preparations revealed no differences in pH optima, K_s values, temperature coefficients, and molecular weights estimated by sucrose density gradient centrifugation in the case of both arginase and ornithine transcarbamylase. The only differences found in the preparations were the manifest differences in the amounts of homogeneous protein that were isolated. Thus it is apparent that, at least for arginase and ornithine transcarbamylase, differences in activities observed in crude homogenates were indeed due to differences in the net content of specific enzyme protein.

Under present study is the question of the process whereby the levels of the urea cycle enzymes are altered under conditions of abruptly varying the casein content of the diet. As has become evident from the presentation of Dr. Potter, the levels of an enzyme activity in rat liver can undergo rapid changes in either direction. Increases and decreases in the hepatic contents of each of the urea cycle enzymes can also be

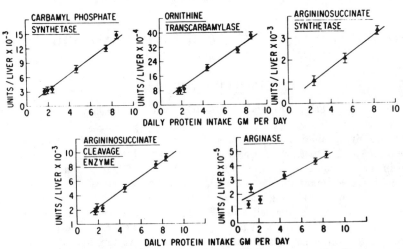

FIGURE 1. Relationships of total hepatic content of each urea cycle enzyme to the dietary protein intake. Enzyme activity is expressed in units, defined as micromoles of product formed per 60 minutes incubation at 37°. Each value represents the mean of 6 animals ±4 standard errors. Squares indicate animals of 6 weeks age, and circles and triangles indicate separate groups of rats 4 months old.

demonstrated, but the changes occur more slowly than those demonstrated by Dr. Potter. Thus, increases in the hepatic contents of carbamyl phosphate synthetase, ornithine transcarbamylase, and argininosuccinate cleavage enzyme are completed in 4 days after increase from a 15 to 60% protein diet, while arginase contents attain maximal levels only after 8 days. Decreases in the contents of the urea cycle enzymes after change from 60 to 15% dietary protein are completed in 6–12 days. Such findings suggest that the levels of an enzyme may be controlled not only by the rate of synthesis, but also by the rate of degradation. Initial attempts to determine the half-life of liver arginase, using tritium labeled DL lysine, have resulted in apparent values of 6.0 to 6.8 days irrespective of the level of arginase activity, whereas apparent half-lives of crude liver protein are of the order of 4 to 4.5 days. These findings suggest that breakdown and synthesis of arginase are active and continuous processes. In an attempt to evaluate the relative roles of synthesis and degradation during periods of active changes in levels of one of the urea cycle enzymes, namely arginase, a series of experiments was undertaken to study the incorporation and loss of labeled amino acids from arginase during periods when the levels of this enzyme were in active flux.

Groups of 3 rats were maintained under dietary conditions resulting in constant high or low levels of arginase, or under conditions resulting in increasing or decreasing arginase levels, as shown in Fig. 2. At specified times, again shown in Fig. 2, each rat was given a single intraperitoneal injection of tritium labeled DL lysine (25 microcuries [16 µg] per g of dietary protein consumed in the previous 24 hours). Either 12 hours or 6½ days after injection, the animals were killed and arginase was purified from the

pooled livers of each group. Specific activities of purified enzyme and crude liver protein (cpm/mg protein) were determined in a Packard Tri-Carb Liquid Scintillation Spectrometer. The 12 hour incorporation

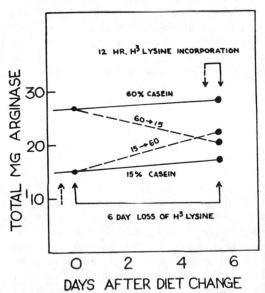

FIGURE 2. Time course of labeled amino acid administration in relation to changes in levels of rat liver arginase. Groups of male, Osborne-Mendel rats, weighing 10 110 g each were placed on diets containing either 15 60% casein for 14 days prior to the experimental period. Solid lines indicate the change in total liver content arginase from three, pooled livers from rats maintain on their original diet. Dotted lines indicate the course change in contents of arginase following change of d from 15 to 60% casein and vice versa. Dotted arrows dicate the time of injection of tritium labeled DL lysi (Volk Radiochemical Corp., specific activity 309 mi curies/mmole). Solid arrows indicate times at which a mals were sacrificed for purification of liver arginase.

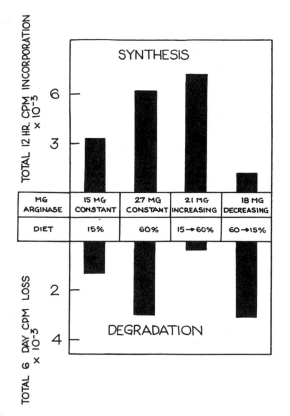

FIGURE 3. Contributions of synthesis and degradation of rat liver arginase during periods of constant, increasing, and decreasing enzyme levels. The experimental conditions are described in the text and Fig. 2. The diets, total content of arginase (3 livers), and direction in which the enzyme level is changing are shown in the middle of the diagram. Results are expressed in total counts incorporated or lost, rather than as specific activities, because of the differences in the size of the arginase pool.

labeled amino acid was considered to be a reflection of the rate of synthesis of the enzyme, as at this time the maximal extent of incorporation of counts into both total liver protein and arginase had occurred. As an indication of the rate of degradation, the 6 day loss of counts was determined under conditions similar to those used for the incorporation studies, as depicted in the lower part of Fig. 2. The changes in the hepatic contents of arginase shown in Fig. 2 represent the total content of enzyme, expressed in mg, present in the pooled sample of 3 livers, as based on the per cent yields and the mg of purified enzyme. Yields during purification were consistently between 30 to 36% of the initial activity present in the livers. The arginase preparations were electrophoretically homogeneous, and contained at most 10% impurity by ultracentrifuge analysis.

The results for DL lysine experiments with arginase are shown in Fig. 3. Qualitatively similar results have been obtained with tritium labeled DL phenylalanine. When there is no net change in the level of arginase,

the extent of incorporation and loss of label is proportional to the content of enzyme, as would be the case if the half-lives were indeed similar. During a period when the level of arginase is increasing, there is an increased incorporation of labeled amino acid into arginase. Furthermore, it was also found that there was a decreased loss of label. These findings suggest that the increased levels of arginase following change from a low to a high protein diet result from a twofold mechanism, that is, both an increased rate of synthesis, and a decreased rate of degradation. On the other hand, during a period when the level of arginase is decreasing, there is a striking decrease in the incorporation of counts into arginase, while the extent of loss of label remains high. Thus the decreasing levels of arginase can be ascribed to a combination of diminished synthesis and increased degradation. The results for incorporation and loss of label with respect to total liver protein are shown in Fig. 4, where it can be seen that there is essentially equal incorporation and loss of labeled amino acid, irrespective of the change in diet. Thus the differing patterns of labeling of purified arginase are indeed specific, and indicate that changes

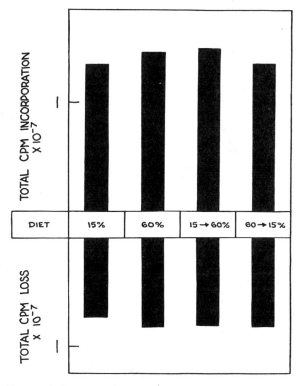

FIGURE 4. Incorporation and loss of tritium labeled DL lysine from crude liver protein. Protein was precipitated from aliquots of homogenized liver used for the purifications of arginase with 8% trichloroacetic acid, containing unlabeled DL lysine. The precipitates were washed with hot 4% trichloroacetic acid containing unlabeled DL lysine, ethanol, ether, and acetone before being dissolved in hydroxide of hyamine (1.0 ml for 2.5 mg protein) for counting.

in levels of this enzyme are not simply a reflection of alterations in the general rate of protein synthesis and degradation as effected by changes in the content of protein in the diet.

The data are incomplete and can be considered at most to demonstrate qualitatively that the rates of synthesis and degradation of a specific liver protein, i.e., arginase, can be either increased or decreased. However, because of the uncertainties resulting from the possible differences in amino acid pool sizes, possible compartmentalization of specific amino acid pools, and the unknown extent to which amino acids are being reutilized under these specific circumstances, quantitative conclusions concerning half-lives of arginase cannot be made with certainty. The demonstration of Steinberg and Vaughan (1956) that protein breakdown in liver is energy dependent indicates that this process is complex. The present studies indicate that protein breakdown is a process that is under some type of control. They further suggest that the rates of synthesis and degradation are both important in controlling the level of a given enzyme in rat liver.

SUMMARY

The level of each of the urea cycle enzymes in the liver of the rat is not fixed, but rather undergoes changes, as produced by a variety of dietary alterations that are proportional to alterations in nitrogen intake or urea excretion. In such a sense these changes can be considered as adaptive. The observed differences in enzyme activity are due to differences in the content of specific enzyme protein in the case of the two urea cycle enzymes studied, ornithine transcarbamylase and arginase. Preliminary data have been presented to suggest that alterations in the levels of one of the urea cycle enzymes, arginase, are not due entirely to changes in the rate of enzyme synthesis, but that alterations in the rate of enzyme degradation are also of importance in determining the eventual level of enzyme.

REFERENCES

ASHIDA, K., and A. E. HARPER. 1961. Metabolic adaptations in higher animals. VI. Liver arginase activity during adaptation to high protein diet. Proc. Soc Exptl. Med Biol., 107: 151–156.

COHEN, P. P., and G. W. BROWN, JR. 1960. Ammonia metabolism and urea biosynthesis. pp. 161–244. Comparative Biochemistry Vol. II, ed. M. Florkin and H. S. Mason. New York: Academic Press Inc.

KNOX, W. E., and V. H. AUERBACH. 1955. The hormonal control of tryptophan peroxidase in the rat. J. Biol. Chem., 214: 307–313.

LIGHTBODY, H. D., and A. KLEINMAN. 1939. Variations produced by food differences in the concentrations of arginase in the livers of white rats. J. Biol. Chem., 129: 71–78.

LIN, E. C. C., and W. E. KNOX. 1957. Adaptation of the rat liver tyrosine alpha-ketoglutarate transaminase. Biochim. Biophys. Acta, 26: 85–88.

MANDELSTAM, J., and J. YUDKIN. 1952. Studies in biochemical adaptation. The effect of variation in dietary

protein upon the hepatic arginase of the rat. Biochem. J., 51: 681–686.

RATNER, S. 1955. Arginine metabolism and interrelationships between the citric acid and urea cycles. A Symposium on Amino Acid Metabolism, ed. W. D. McElroy and H. B. Glass. Baltimore: The Johns Hopkins Press.

STEINBERG, D., and M. VAUGHAN. 1956. Intracellular protein degradation in vitro. Biochim. Biophys. Acta, 19: 584–585.

DISCUSSION

KOCH: The difference in turnover of the enzymes of the urea cycle and most of the liver proteins is much greater than indicated by Dr. Schimke. This is because of the recycling of the lysine or phenylalanine molecules. When a pool exists that serves both as the source and the sink for macromolecular synthesis, a fraction of the molecules liberated from breakdown are reutilized. If the pool is small, its existence will not be detected by complications in the shape of the curve, but the half-life obtained will no longer be the "true" half-life, but rather will be the "true" half-life times the rate at which pool is formed from all sources divided by the rate at which it formed from non-turning-over sources, such as the diet. In fact, it has been found for liver protein (Swick, 1957) that the "true" half-life of liver protein is nearly two days, instead of the apparent four days found here and in many other experiments.

On the other hand, it may readily be shown (Koch, J. Theoretical Biol., in press) that very nearly the "true" half-life will be obtained for proteins which turn over more slowly than average, even when extensive recycling is taking place.

RICKENBERG: I should like to report very briefly some findings we have made recently and which suggest the possible existence of a repressible enzyme forming system in mammalian cells. The cells employed were the L-cell (mouse) fibroblasts grown as suspension cultures. These cells do not require an exogenous supply of proline. We find that cultures of L-cells when grown in a medium not containing added proline produce approximately five times as much Δ'-pyrroline-5 carboxylic acid reductase (p.c. reductase) as do similar cultures grown in the presence of proline. P.c reductase catalyzes the last step in the sequence of reactions leading from glutamic acid to proline and in this particular case is DPNH specific and soluble, i.e., non mitochondrial. The fivefold increase in enzyme activity may well represent a minimal value as our medium (modified Eagle's) contains dialyzed horse serum which presumably releases proline slowly. We shall continue the investigation of p.c. reductase formation in a strain of L-cells able to grow in the absence of added protein and hope to elucidate the mechanism responsible for the increase in p.c. reductase activity. Superficially the process resembles the de-repression of enzyme synthesis as described for microbial systems.

Reprinted from Annals of The New York Academy of Sciences
Volume 102, Article 3, Pages 587-601
January 21, 1963

TURNOVER OF RAT LIVER ARGINASE

Robert T. Schimke, Mary B. Brown,* Elizabeth T. Smallman

Laboratory of Biochemical Pharmacology
National Institute of Arthritis and Metabolic Diseases
National Institutes of Health, Bethesda, Md.

The subject of protein turnover in animal tissues is vast in complexities of subject matter, choices of experimental approach, and problems of interpretation of results. Review papers of Schoenheimer and Rittenberg,[1] Tarver,[2] and Mandelstam[3] have indicated many of the problems encountered in the studies of protein turnover, as well as the results obtained. This paper will not attempt to review the entire subject of protein turnover in animal tissues. We shall, rather, limit the discussion of protein turnover to a single animal tissue, namely the liver of the rat, and—specifically—to a single protein, the enzyme arginase. Evidence will be presented that turnover—that is, a continual synthesis and degradation—of this enzyme exists. We shall also examine several different physiological states in which the level of this enzyme changes and shall demonstrate that the rates of synthesis and degradation of this protein can be altered independently to produce the observed changes in arginase levels.

Following the introduction of radioisotopes into biological research an extensive series of studies was undertaken by many groups,[1,2] which indicated an active uptake and release of various isotopic compounds from liver proteins. Thus the well-known phrase "dynamic state of body constituents" was coined by Schoenheimer and his associates[4] to describe the concept of a continual replacement of protein, among other constituents. Although such studies did indeed indicate replacement of liver protein, the concept of a continual breakdown or turnover of intracellular proteins was questioned by Hogness et al.[5] following the demonstrated lack of protein breakdown or turnover in growing bacteria by Hogness et al.,[5] Koch and Levy,[6] and Rotman and Spiegelman.[7] Thus the uptake and loss of isotope by liver proteins was ascribed to synthesis and secretion of plasma proteins and cell death and replacement, rather than to a true, or intracellular, protein turnover. However, the early studies of Ussing[8] with D_2O, as well as the more recent investigations of Ballou and Thompson[9] also utilizing D_2O, Swick[10] using atmospheric $C^{14}O_2$, and Buchanan[11] who administered a C^{14}-uniformly labeled algae diet, have clearly demonstrated that liver proteins are essentially all undergoing turnover. These studies have employed the theoretically more sound method of continuous administration of isotope,[12,13] which is not subject to the type of criticism of Hogness et al.[5] with turnover experiments that use a single

* Present address: *Department of Radiology, Stanford University School of Medicine, Stanford, Calif.*

isotope administration and determine the decay in radioactivity of the isolated protein with time. Buchanan has in fact found that 95 per cent of the protein of rat liver is replaced every 4½ days.[11] Furthermore, from various estimates of hepatic cell life span of from 160 to 400 days,[11,14,15] it is evident that protein turnover is largely taking place within cells rather than involving death and renewal of entire cells.

Although it is clear that the breakdown and synthesis of liver protein is a continuous and extensive process, the extent and rate at which specific proteins take part in such a process is essentially unknown. The studies to be presented with the enzyme arginase are directed to give this information for one protein. Our interest in the problem of protein turnover arises as part of a continuing investigation of the mechanism of enzyme adaptation in mammalian tissues involving the five enzymes of the Krebs-Henseleit[16] or ornithine-urea cycle in rat liver. In this tissue it can be shown that the specific activities of these enzymes are not constant, but vary under a variety of physiological conditions in a manner such that the rate of urea formation is proportional to the level of each of the five enzymes.[17,18] The choice of arginase, the last of this series of five enzymes, is largely dictated by the ability to purify this enzyme from liver in consistently high yields in a homogeneous state. It has previously been shown that arginase purified from livers with different arginase specific activities is similar in kinetic and physicochemical properties, and that the differences in arginase specific activities in liver extracts can be attributed to differences in the content of a specific enzyme protein.[17] The finding that the administration of ethionine, an inhibitor of protein synthesis, to rats prevents increases in arginase activity[19] would indicate that protein synthesis is concerned with the increased levels of this enzyme. However, if synthesis and breakdown—i.e., turnover—are normal, continuous events, then clearly increased levels of arginase could be due to increased synthesis and/or decreased breakdown of the enzyme.

The method chosen for the study of arginase turnover was to give a single administration of isotopic amino acid at time zero, and to determine the rate of loss of isotope from the labeled, purified arginase as a measure of breakdown of the enzyme. This method has been analyzed by Reiner.[13] The method ideally requires that the incorporation of the administered isotope be of a short duration, i.e., that the administration be essentially a pulse, and that there be no reutilization of the labeled isotope from subsequent degradation of labeled protein. These two requirements can be satisfactorily met by the use of the amino acid arginine labeled with carbon-14 specifically in the guanido grouping. This choice is made on the basis of the continual and rapid hydrolysis of free intracellular arginine to ornithine and urea in the normal functioning of the ornithine-urea cycle. Since the urea contains the isotopic carbon atom and is metabolically inert, there is no effective reutilization. Swick and Handa have in fact estimated that, at most, 2 per cent of the guanido group of arginine derived from liver proteins is reutilized in protein synthesis.[20]

Methods

Animals. Male Osborne-Mendel rats were used in all experiments. The specific conditions for the maintenance of animals are described in the legends to the figures. Diets were prepared as described previously.[17]

Arginase assay. Arginase was assayed as described previously.[17] Activity is expressed in μmoles of urea formed/min./mg. protein at $37°$ C.

Protein. Protein was measured by the method of Lowry *et al.*[21]

Administration of isotope. Guanido-C^{14}-arginine was obtained from ChemTrac Corporation, Cambridge, Mass. (specific activity 5.2 mc./-μmole). The product was dissolved in 0.85 per cent saline to a concentration of 100 microcuries/ml. The arginine was injected intraperitoneally in a single 25 microcurie dose to each animal unless otherwise stated.

Preparation and counting of samples. Protein samples were prepared for counting by the method of Siekevitz[22] with the addition of unlabeled 0.1 M arginine to the trichloroacetic acid and ethanol washes. The protein samples were dissolved in 60 per cent formic acid at a concentration of approximately 4 mg./ml. Protein estimations were made on the samples by the method of Lowry *et al.*,[21] using a sample of the treated liver protein as a standard. Samples were counted to within 5 per cent error in a Nuclear Chicago, windowless gas flow, Geiger counter. Because of wide differences in specific radioactivities of protein samples encountered in these experiments, the use of differing amounts of protein was required to obtain counting accuracy to five per cent. Therefore, within any given experiment similar amounts of arginase protein and total liver protein were counted.

Purification of arginase. TABLE 1 presents the purification procedure used in these experiments that embodies several of the steps utilized by Greenberg[23] and Grassman *et al.*[24] The procedure has been found to be highly reproducible and gives a product of constant specific enzyme activity and uniformly high yield. These studies obviously are dependent on the ability to isolate arginase protein specifically and consistently. Representative preparations of the final product have been subjected to various analyses for homogenity, including ultracentrifugation, electrophoresis on paper at several pH values, electrophoresis in acrylamide gel,[25] and sucrose gradient analysis.[26] Although the enzyme has not been crystalized, it has been found to be homogeneous by all criteria. A complete report of these results is to be published.

Results

Turnover of arginase. The first question to ask is simply, does turnover of arginase occur? If turnover did not occur, one of the following two conditions should be found: (1) there is no incorporation of isotope into arginase, because the enzyme is not being synthesized, or (2) incorporation of isotope occurs to the extent of new cell formation, in which case the label would be retained for the life-span of the cell, *i.e.*, at least 160 days. TABLE 2 shows the result of studies that demonstrate incorporation of isotope into arginase protein. Groups of four rats were killed 15 minutes

TABLE 1

ARGINASE PURIFICATION SCHEME

Step	Specific Activity[°]	Yield (%)
Homogenate	4	100
KCl extract	10	104
Acetone	58	87
Heat	251	96
Ethanol	1012	87
Carboxymethyl cellulose	5520	77

[°] μmoles urea/min./mg. protein.

1. *Homogenate.* Rat liver totaling from 15 to 30 gm. is homogenized in three volumes by weight of Tris-Cl 0.01 M pH 7.5, containing 0.05 M $MnCl_2$, and 0.100 M KCl.

2. *Extract.* The homogenate is centrifuged 15 minutes at 15,000 × g. The supernatant contains all the arginase activity and constitutes the extract.

3. *Acetone.* One and one-half volumes of acetone at −10° C. are added to the extract and centrifuged 5 minutes at 15,000 × g. The precipitate is homogenized in a volume of Tris-Cl 0.01 M, pH 7.5 containing 0.05 M $MnCl_2$ equal to the original liver weight and centrifuged 15 minutes at 15,000 × g. The supernatant is dialyzed 2 hours against the same Tris-$MnCl_2$ solution.

4. *Heat.* The dialyzed solution is made 0.025 M in glycine with stock 1.0 M glycine, pH 7.5, and heated 15 minutes at 60° C. The solution is chilled in an ice bath and the precipitate is removed by centrifugation.

5. *Ethanol.* The centrifuged solution is chilled to 0° C. and an equal volume of absolute ethanol at −10° C. containing 0.05 M $MnCl_2$ is added. The resulting precipitate is removed by centrifugation for 10 minutes at 15,000 × g at −10° C. Two additional volumes of ethanol are added and the resulting precipitate is suspended in a small volume of Tris-Cl 0.01 M, pH 7.5, containing 0.05 M $MnCl_2$ and 0.025 M glycine. The solution is frozen rapidly and lyophilized.

6. *Carboxymethyl cellulose chromatography.* A column 0.5 cm. × 5 cm. is packed with carboxymethyl cellulose equilibrated with 0.01 M Tris-Cl, pH 7.5 at 4° C. The lyophilized sample is dissolved in 5–10 ml. of 0.01 M Tris-Cl, pH 7.5, centrifuged to remove a variable amount of precipitate, and placed on the column. The column is washed with 10 ml. of 0.01 M Tris-Cl, pH 7.5, and then with 5 ml. of 0.01 M Tris Cl, 0.05 M L-arginine, pH 7.5. These fractions contain no arginase. The arginase is eluted with 5–10 ml. of 0.01 M Tris-Cl, 0.20 M L-arginine, pH 7.5. Glycine and $MnCl_2$ are added for 1.0 M stock solutions to concentrations of 0.02 M and 0.05 M respectively.

after an intraperitoneal administration of 50 microcuries of guanido-C^{14}-L-arginine to each animal and the arginase isolated. By the end of 15 minutes the intracellular pool of C^{14}-arginine has been found to decrease to essentially zero (Schimke, Brown, and Smallman, to be published). Arginase from a similar group of animals injected with C^{14}-arginine one hour previously was also isolated as were total protein samples. It can be seen that radioactivity is indeed present in the protein isolated as arginase, and that the specific radioactivity of this protein is different from that found for total liver protein. Furthermore incorporation of isotope into arginase is completed by the end of the C^{14}-arginine pulse, *i.e.*, 15 minutes. A portion of the one-hour arginase sample was further analyzed

TABLE 2

INCORPORATION OF GUANIDO-C[14]-L-ARGININE INTO ARGINASE

Time after C[14]– arginine administration (min.)	Specific radioactivity (CPM/mg. protein)	
	Arginase	Total liver protein
15	40	84
60	38	88

Eight rats, each weighing 140–150 gm., maintained on 30 per cent casein, were given a single intraperitoneal injection of 50 microcuries of guanido-C[14]-L-arginine. Fifteen minutes later, four rats were killed and arginase isolated by the procedure outlined in TABLE 1. The remaining four rats were killed one hour after isotope administration and arginase isolated. Samples of the purified arginase and total liver protein were prepared for counting, as described under *Methods,* and counted to 5 per cent accuracy in a windowless gas-flow counter.

by ultracentrifugation using the separation cell of Yphantis and Waugh.[27] †The protein peak was bisected and specific enzyme activities and specific radioactivities of the top and bottom compartments were found to be similar. The sedimentation coefficient as determined by schlieren optics was found to be similar to that calculated on the basis of either enzyme activity or radioactivity.[27] Thus it is apparent that isotope is incorporated into arginase.

FIGURE 1 presents the results of experiments that determine the time course of the breakdown of the prelabeled arginase, as well as total liver protein. These experiments have been undertaken in animals maintained on diets containing 8, 30, or 70 per cent casein, which are associated with three different steady state levels of arginase, as shown in the parentheses. It can be seen that the specific radioactivity of the prelabeled arginase does fall with time and, in a manner that can be expressed by a first order rate constant, as indicated by the slope of the line. Further, it is of interest that this constant is quite similar in all three dietary conditions, despite different amounts of enzyme present in the sample of pooled livers, as shown in the parentheses. Furthermore, the rate of degradation of arginase is different from that for total liver protein. If expressed in terms of a half life (2, 13), values for liver protein were found to be 3.0, 2.4, and 2.6 days for animals on 8, 30, and 70 per cent casein diet respectively, whereas for arginase the half life values were 5.2, 4.8, and 4.6 days under similar dietary conditions. These data would therefore indicate that the protein isolated as arginase has a significant turnover, that is, it is continually being synthesized and degraded. Furthermore, the rate of turnover is not the same as that for total liver protein.

† The authors are indebted to William Carroll and E. R. Mitchell for assistance with the ultracentrifuge studies.

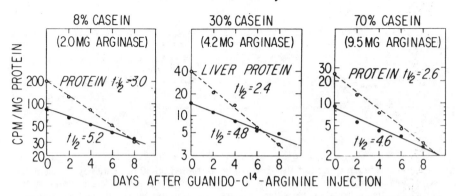

FIGURE 1. Turnover of arginase in rat liver: Animals weighing 110-120 gm. each, maintained for 14 days on either 8 per cent, 30 per cent or 70 per cent casein, were given single intraperitoneal injections of 25 microcuries guanido-C14-L-arginine. Maximal labeling of liver protein occurred in 15 minutes. At one hour, and thereafter at two day intervals, three animals from each group are killed, the livers pooled, and arginase isolated as indicated in TABLE 1. All fractions discarded during the isolation were combined to constitute the total liver protein. All protein samples were prepared for counting by the Siekewitz procedure[22] using 0.1 M unlabeled L-arginine in the trichloroacetic acid and ethanol washes. The final protein preparations were dissolved in 60 percent formic acid, assayed for protein,[21] and counted in a gas-flow counter to 5 percent accuracy, as described in *Methods*. Values for total liver protein and arginase are expressed in counts/min./mg. protein. Value for total arginase content, expressed as mg./pooled liver sample, are based on the final amount of purified enzyme corrected for the yield, *i.e.*,

$$\text{total arginase} = \frac{\text{actual amount isolated}}{\text{per cent}} \times 100.$$

•—•, Arginase; o - - - o, total liver protein.

Arginase degradation during alterations of enzyme levels. A number of investigators have reported altered levels of arginase activity under various conditions of diet or hormonal administrations.[17-19, 28, 29] We have selected two of these conditions for a study of the role of altered rates of degradation in producing observed changes in enzyme levels: (1) starvation, starting from an 8 per cent casein diet, which results in an increased level of arginase and (2) change from a 70 per cent to a 8 per cent casein diet, which results in a decrease in arginase levels. The method used was similar to that used in the experiments of the previous section, that is to prelabel arginase with guanido-C14-arginine and isolate the labeled arginase at specified intervals thereafter. FIGURE 2 shows the results for animals maintained 10 days on 8 per cent casein and subsequently starved up to 6 days. It can be seen that there is a decrease in total liver protein during the first 2 days of starvation, but none thereafter, although total body weight during the entire starvation period continues to fall. The content of arginase, on the other hand, shows a steady increase, such that at the end of 6 days there has been a two-fold increase in total and specific enzyme activity. Total liver protein shows an extensive loss of isotope, indicating a continu-

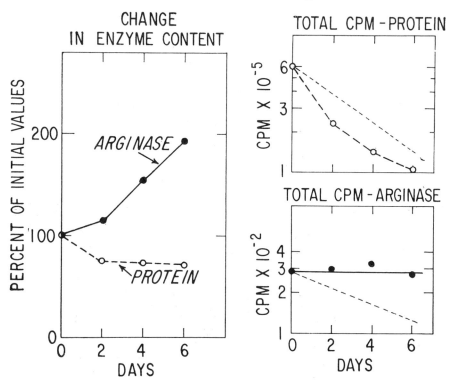

FIGURE 2. Effects of starvation on arginase levels and arginase degradation in rat liver: Rats weighing 120–130 gm. each, maintained on an 8 per cent casein diet, were given single intraperitoneal injections of 25 microcuries of guanido-C¹⁴-arginine. Four rats were used for isolation of arginase one hour later, and the remainder were placed on water only for periods up to 6 days. At two-day intervals, arginase was isolated from the livers of four rats. The change in total arginase activity, and total liver protein are expressed as changes in per cent relative to the values prior to the onset of starvation. Specific activity of the prelabeled protein and arginase are expressed in total CPM/total pooled sample. The theoretical curves for total CPM based on steady-state conditions as found in FIGURE 1 are shown by the thin dotted lines.

ous, active replacement of protein. In contrast to total liver protein, there is virtually no loss of counts from the prelabeled arginase, that is to say, the rate of degradation is zero. The theoretical course for the loss of isotope assuming a first order rate constant for degradation found for the steady-state condition is indicated by the thin, dotted line.

An opposite type of change in arginase is found in FIGURE 3, where animals initially maintained on 70 per cent casein where changed to a diet containing 8 per cent dietary casein. Both total liver protein and arginase decrease under these conditions, but the decrease in arginase is more extensive than that for total protein. The time course of the loss of

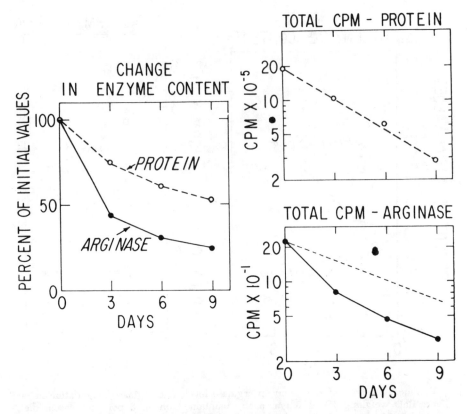

FIGURE 3. Effects of change from 70 per cent casein to 8 per cent dietary casein: Rats weighing 120-130 gm. each, maintained 10 days on a diet containing 70 per cent casein, were given single intraperitoneal administrations of 50 microcuries guanido-C^{14}-arginine. Arginase was isolated from three pooled livers one hour later; the remainder of the rats were placed on an 8 per cent casein diet, and arginase was isolated from three pooled livers at three-day intervals. The changes in total arginase activity and total liver protein are expressed as changes in per cent relative to the values prior to the onset of dietary change. Specific activity of the prelabelled protein and arginase are expressed in total CPM/total pooled sample. The theoretical curves for total CPM based on steady-state conditions as found in FIGURE 1 are shown by the thin dotted lines.

isotope from total liver protein is similar to those shown previously in FIGURES 1 and 2. The slope of the change in total counts in arginase varies with time. It is initially much greater than that found for the steady state, and then decreases to approximate that found in the steady state.

These results, then, indicate that the rate of degradation can be increased or decreased to result in differing enzyme levels.

Discussion

The turnover of liver protein has been shown to be an extensive and continuous process.[8-11] The rate of this turnover approximates the one per cent per hour found by Eagle *et al.*[30] in mammalian cell culture. The turnover of total protein in the intact liver continues at approximately the same rate whether the animals are starved or given diets containing different amounts of total protein. These findings are in contrast to the occurrence of detectible protein turnover in bacteria only in nongrowing cells.[31]

Although one may speak of a turnover rate, or half life for total liver protein, it is apparent from the data presented here that such a value is made up of a large number of rates for individual protein species. Furthermore, significant changes in the rates for individual proteins may well occur without any reflection in the value obtained for total liver protein.

The data presented have shown an incorporation of isotopic arginine into the pool of protein constituting the enzyme arginase and a subsequent loss of that isotope from the same pool. This has been taken to indicate a continual synthesis and degradation of the protein, *i.e.*, turnover. Certain clarifications, however, are necessary in the use of the terms "synthesis" and "degradation" to describe the results of the isotopic experiments. We have defined as arginase that protein from liver that we can isolate by the purification procedure outlined in TABLE 1. In terms of tracer, then, any loss of isotope from the pool of arginase, with time, will constitute degradation of this protein. Synthesis, in the same terms, can be defined as any increase in unlabeled arginase with time. These are clearly descriptive terms and do not in themselves imply anything about the nature of the synthesis or degradation processes. Thus degradation could consist of any process in which arginase is transformed into a molecular species that is not reutilized in the formation of new arginase, whether this be protein, polypeptide, or amino acids. It does not imply that the end-product of all protein breakdown is, in fact, individual amino acid. By the same token, synthesis could result from the utilization of a preformed, unlabeled precursor protein, polypeptides, or the use of unlabeled amino acids. The utilization of a preformed precursor would necessarily imply that such a protein is not turning over, *i.e.*, is not being synthesized. However, the demonstrations that protein turnover involves essentially all liver proteins would make this possibility unlikely. On the other hand, there is some indirect evidence that at least a part of the arginase molecule is formed from amino acids. Thus it has been shown that isotope is incorporated into arginase protein, and that this incorporation is completed by the time the pool of labeled amino acid has disappeared (TABLE 2). This finding indicates a rapid incorporation of label into arginase, and, further, that if amino acids are first incorporated into a precursor, the rate of conversion of the precursor into arginase is as rapid as the incorporation of amino acids into the precursor. The possibility that the incorporation of isotopic arginine into protein is the result of amino acid exchange into a protein, which is not undergoing extensive degradation and resynthesis from constituent amino acids, cannot be excluded. However, this type of mechanism, first suggested by Gale and Folkes[32] has not been found to be a significant mechanism in amino acid incorporation into protein.[33,34] No definitive experiments, however, have thus far been performed with a liver protein that is intracellular, *i.e.*, is not secreted, to determine if the protein is, indeed, formed directly and entirely from amino acids, such have been performed for rat liver ferritin,[35] bovine pancreatic trypsinogen, chymotrypsinogen-A, and ribonuclease,[36] and several rabbit muscle enzymes.[37,38]

With these operational definitions for synthesis and degradation, it is possible to make some estimations on the contributions of synthesis and degradation to the observed changes in enzyme levels during starvation and change from a 70 per cent to 8 per cent protein diet. The content of arginase (A) has been shown to be dependent on the rate of synthesis (K_s), and the rate of degradation (K_d). From the results shown in FIGURE 1, it has been empirically found that K_d can be expressed by a first order rate constant k_d. From the slope of the curves for total arginase counts in FIGURES 2 and 3, we can obtain the value for k_d and can, therefore, solve for the amount of arginase degraded during the observational period (A_d) from the integral:

$$k_d = \frac{2.3}{t} \cdot \log \frac{A_0}{A_t}, \tag{1}$$

where A_0 is the amount of arginase present at the beginning of the experimental period and A_t is the amount at time t, the end of the experimental period. From the formulation

$$\Delta A = A_s - A_d, \tag{2}$$

where ΔA represents the change in enzyme during the experimental period, A_s and A_d are the amounts of arginase synthesized and degraded respectively, and knowing ΔA experimentally and calculating A_d from (1), an estimate of A_s can be obtained. Their values, are expressed as simple zero order rates for each observational period, expressed as mg. arginase/-observational period/gm. liver protein. This formulation is similar to the replacement rate as discussed by Tarver.[2]

The calculated values for synthesis and degradation of arginase are shown in FIGURE 4. As can be seen prior to the onset of starvation, the amount of enzyme is constant and synthesis and degradation are balanced. During the first two days of starvation, there is an initial cessation of degradation, followed by a small increase in rate of synthesis from the second to sixth day. During the change from a high to a low protein diet (as shown on the right of FIGURE 4), there is an initial marked increase in the rate of degradation and synthesis is decreased. By the sixth day, the rate of degradation has decreased, but synthesis has ceased. By the ninth day the rate of degradation has decreased still further, and the rate of synthesis has increased to the point that the level of arginase is approaching a new, and lower, steady-state equilibrium.

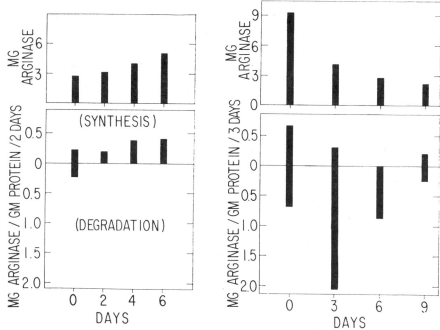

FIGURE 4.   Rates of synthesis and degradation of rat liver arginase during starvation (*left*) and change from 70 per cent to 8 per cent casein diet (*right*): The upper set of bars indicate the total mg. arginase present in the pooled liver samples at the end of the specific experimental periods under study during starvation (*left*) and change from a 70 per cent to 8 per cent casein diet (*right*). Below are shown the rates of synthesis and degradation as calculated on the basis of the considerations indicated in the text. These rates are expressed as mg. arginase synthesized or degraded per gm. total liver protein per observational period.

We have shown that the level of a given enzyme, arginase, is dependent on both the rate of synthesis and the rate of degradation during various physiological conditions resulting in changed enzyme levels. These observations are of general significance for studies on the mechanism of enzymatic adaptation in mammalian tissues, many of which have implicated protein synthesis in the mechanism for the observed changes in enzyme activities.[39,40] The appropriate question is not, however, Is this protein synthesis?, since the very presence of turnover indicates this phenomenon; but rather, does the observed change in enzyme protein result from an increased rate of synthesis or from a decreased rate of degradation? Our studies would indicate that both factors may be important, depending on the conditions studied.

Thus what are observed as increases in enzyme protein in animal tissues may not be strictly analogous to classical bacterial enzyme induction,[34] since the increased enzyme levels in animal tissues may be entirely, or in part, due to a decreased breakdown of enzyme protein that is being synthesized as a constant rate. The general significance of a mechanism of mammalian enzyme "induction" involving decreased rates of breakdown is unknown at present and must await detailed studies of other "adaptive" mammalian enzymes. This type of mechanism has been suggested by Bojarski and Hiatt[41] for the increased levels of thymidylate kinase in rat liver produced by thymidylate administration on the basis of stabilization of the enzyme by thymidylate during purification. Such a mechanism would necessarily require that the time course of induction of enzymes would bear some direct relationship to the half-life of the enzyme. It is therefore significant that liver thyrosine-glutamate transaminase, which increases up to 6–10 fold in 6 hours following adrenocortical administration,[42,43] has recently been shown to have a half life of not more than 4 hours.[44] The stabilization of enzymes by substrates and cofactors during purification procedures is a well-known phenomenon in biochemistry. By analogy, then, a substrate or cofactor may be conceived to combine with an enzyme protein within the cell, changing the confirmation of the protein in a manner such that the protein is more resistant to enzymatic degradation. The phenomenon of increased rates of breakdown of denatured proteins by proteolytic enzymes has been repeatedly demonstrated.[45,46] This phenomenon may be considered as a model for the previously proposed mechanism for changing enzyme stability in the intact liver.

The mechanism for the normal process of protein degradation in animal tissues is unknown. The studies of Simpson[47] and Steinberg and Vaughan[48] indicate that an energy source is required. Several systems for protein breakdown have been described, including the lysosomes of DeDuve[49] and the mitochondrial system for albumin breakdown of Penn,[50] which requires coenzyme A. It remains for further work to determine the relationship of these degradative systems to the process of protein turnover, the differences in rates of turnover of specific proteins, and the differences in rates of degradation of these proteins at different times.

Summary

Turnover of the enzyme arginase has been studied in rat liver. Cellular proteins have been prelabeled with guanido-C^{14}-L-arginine. Arginase has been purified to a homogeneous state and the loss of isotope from this enzyme protein determined as a function of time. Arginase has been found to be continually synthesized and degraded, with a half life of 4.5–5.2 days, compared to a value of 2.4–3.0 days for total liver protein.

During starvation and during change from a high to a low protein diet, the levels of arginase change. These changes in enzyme activity have been shown to result from alterations in rates of both synthesis and degradation. The results confirm that turnover of intracellular proteins in liver does exist. They also suggest that mammalian enzyme adaptation may in some cases result from a decreased rate of enzyme degradation.

Note Added in Proof

Several recent reports have presented estimates of turnover rates for two hepatic enzymes in the rat. Kenny (1962, J. Biol. Chem., 237:496) has estimated the half-life of hepatic tyrosineglutamate transaminase to be three to four hours. Price, Sterling, Tarantola, Hartley, and Rechcigl (1962, J. Biol. Chem., 237:3468) have estimated the half-life of hepatic catalase as one day.

References

1. SCHOENHEIMER, R. & D. RITTENBERG. 1940. The study of intermediary metabolism of animals with the aid of isotopes. Physiol. Rev. **20**: 218.

2. TARVER, H. 1954. Peptide and protein synthesis; protein turnover. *In* The Proteins, vol. 2, part B.: 1199–1296. H. Neurath and K. Bailey, Ed. Academic Press, Inc. New York N. Y.

3. MANDELSTAM, J. 1960. The intracellular turnover of protein and nucleic acids and its role in biochemical differentiation. Bacteriol. Rev. **24**: 289.

4. SCHOENHEIMER, R. 1942. The dynamic state of body constituents. Harvard University Press. Cambridge, Mass.

5. HOGNESS, D. S., M. COHN & J. MONOD. 1955. Studies on the increased synthesis of β-galactosidase: the kinetics and mechanics of sulfur incorporation. Biochem. et Biophys. Acta. **16**: 99.

6. KOCH, A. L. & H. R. LEVY. 1955. Protein turnover in growing cultures of *Escherichia coli*. J. Biol. Chem. **217**: 947.

7. ROTMAN, B. & S. SPEIGELMAN. 1954. On the origin of the carbon in the increased synthesis of β-galactosidase in *Escherichia coli*. J. Bacteriol. **68**: 419.

8. USSING, H. H. 1941. The rate of protein renewal in mice and rats studied by means of heavy hydrogen. Acta Physiol. Scand. **2**: 209.

9. THOMPSON, R. G. & J. R. BALLOU. 1956. Studies of metabolic turnover with tritium as a tracer. V. The predominately non-dynamic state of body constituents in the rat. J. Biol. Chem. **223**: 795.

10. SWICK, R. W. 1958. The measurement of protein turnover in rat liver. J. Biol. Chem. **231**: 751.

11. BUCHANAN, D. L. 1961. Total carbon turnover measured by feeding a uniformly labeled diet. Arch. Biochem. Biophys. **94**: 501.

12. BUCHANAN, D. L. 1961. Analysis of continuous dosage isotope experiments. Arch. Biochem. Biophys. **94**: 489.

13. REINER, J. M. 1953. The study of metabolic turnover rates by means of isotopic tracers. II. Turnover in a simple reaction system. Arch. Biochem. Biophys. **46**: 80.

14. SWICK, R. W., A. L. KOCH & D. T. HANDA. 1956. The measurement of nucleic acid turnover in rat liver. Arch. Biochem. Biophys. **63**: 226.

15. McDONALD, R. A. 1961. "Lifespan" of liver cells. Arch. Internal. Med. **107**: 335.

16. KREBS, H. A. & K. HENSELEIT. 1932. Intersuchungen über des harnstoffbildung im tierkorper. Z. Physiol. Chem. **210**: 33.

17. SCHIMKE, R. T. 1962. Adaptive characteristics of urea cycle enzymes in the rat. J. Biol. Chem. **237**: 459.

18. SCHIMKE, R. T. 1962. Differential effects of fasting and protein free diets on levels of urea cycle enzymes in rat liver. J. Biol. Chem. **237**: 1921.

19. SCHIMKE, R. T. 1963. Studies on factors affecting the levels of urea cycle enzymes in rat liver. J. Biol. Chem. In press.

20. Swick, R. & D. T. Handa. 1956. The distribution of fixed carbon in amino acids. J. Biol. Chem. **218**: 577.

21. Lowry, O. H., N. J. Roseborough, A. L. Farr & R. J. Randall. 1951. Protein measurement with the folin phenol reagent. J. Biol. Chem. **193**: 265.

22. Siekevitz, P. 1952. Uptake of radioactive alanine *in vitro* into the proteins of rat liver fractions. J. Biol. Chem. **195**: 549.

23. Greenberg, D. M. 1955. Arginase. In Methods in Enzymology Vol. II.: 368. S. P. Colowick and N. O. Kaplan, Eds. Academic Press. New York, N. Y.

24. Grassman, W., H. Hörmann & O. Janowsky. 1958. Arginase, I Elektrophoretische reiningung des enzymes. Z. Physiol. Chem. **312**: 273.

25. Raymond, S., M. Nakamicki & B. Aurell. 1962. Acrylamide gel as an electrophoresis medium. Nature. **195**: 697.

26. Martin, R. G. & B. N. Ames. 1961. A method for determining the sedimentation behavior of enzymes. Application to protein mixtures. J. Biol. Chem. **236**: 1372.

27. Yphantis, D. A. & D. F. Waugh. 1956. Ultracentrifugal characterization by direct measurement of activity II. J. Phys. Chem. **60**: 630.

28. Mandelstam, J. & J. Yudkin. 1952. Studies in biochemical adaptation. The effect of variation in dietary protein upon the hepatic arginase of the rat. Biochem. J. **51**: 681.

29. Ashida, K. & A. E. Harper. 1961. Metabolic adaptations in higher animals. VI. Liver arginase activity during adaptation to high protein diet. Proc. Soc. Exptl. Biol. Med. **107**: 151.

30. Eagle, H., K. A. Piez, R. Fleischman & V. I. Oyama. 1958. Protein turnover in mammalian cell cultures. J. Biol. Chem. **233**: 592.

31. Mandelstam, J. 1958. Turnover of protein in growing and non-growing populations of *Escherichia coli*. Biochem. J. **69**: 110.

32. Gale, E. F. & J. P. Folkes. 1953. The incorporation of glutamic acid into the protein fraction of *Staphylococcus aureus*. Biochem. J. **55**: 721.

33. Zamecnik, P. C., E. B. Keller, J. W. Littlefield, M. B. Hoagland & R. B. Loftfield. 1956. Mechanism of incorporation of labelled amino acids into proteins. J. Cellular Comp. Physiol. **47**: Supp. I: 81.

34. Cohn, M. 1957. Contributions of studies on the β-galoctosidase of *Escherichia coli* to our understanding of enzyme synthesis. Bacteriol. Rev. **21**: 140.

35. Loftfield, R. B. & A. Harris. 1956. Participation of free amino acids in protein synthesis. J. Biol. Chem. **219**: 161.

36. Keller, P. J., E. Cohen & H. Neurath. 1959. The proteins of bovine pancreatic juice. II. Rates of synthesis *in vivo* of the cationic proteins. J. Biol. Chem. **234**: 311.

37. Simpson, M. V. & S. F. Velick. 1954. The synthesis of aldolase and glyceraldehyde 3-phosphate dehydrogenase in the rabbit. J. Biol. Chem. **208**: 61.

38. Heimberg, M. & S. F. Velick. 1954. The synthesis of aldolase and phosphorylase in rabbits. J. Biol. Chem. **208**: 725.

39. Kvam, D. C. & R. E. Parks, Jr. 1960. Inhibition of hepatic-induced enzyme formation. J. Biol. Chem. **235**: 2893.

40. Goldstein, L., E. J. Stella & W. E. Knox. 1962. The effect of hydrocortisone on trysosine-α-ketoglutarate transaminase and tryptophan pyrrolase activities in the isolated, perfused liver. J. Biol. Chem. **237**: 1723.

41. Bojarski, T. B. & H. H. Hiatt. 1960. Stabilization of thymidylate kinase activity by thymidylate and by thymidine. Nature. **188**: 112.

42. Lin, E. C. C. & W. E. Knox. 1957. Adaptation of the rat liver trysosine-α-ketoglutarate transaminase. Biochem. et Biophys. Acta. **26**: 85.

43. Kenney, F. T. & R. M. Flora. 1961. Induction of Tyrosine-α-ketoglutarate transaminase in rat liver. I. Hormonal nature. J. Biol. Chem. **236**: 2699.

44. Kenney, F. T. 1962. Induction of tyrosine-α-ketoglutarate transaminase in rat liver. Fed. Proc. **21**: 235.

45. LINDERSTROM-LANG, K. 1950. Structure and enzymatic breakdown of proteins. Cold Spring Harbor Symposium Quant. Biol. **14**: 117.

46. GREEN, N. M. & H. NEURATH. 1954. Proteolytic enzymes. *In* The Proteins Vol. II, Part B.: 1057. H. Neurath and K. Bailey, Eds. Academic Press, Inc. New York, N. Y.

47. SIMPSON, M. V. 1953. The release of labelled amino acids from the proteins of rat liver slices. J. Biol. Chem. **201**: 143.

48. STEINBERG, D. & M. VAUGHAN. 1956. Observations on intracellular protein catabolism studied *in vitro*. Arch. Biochem. Biophys. **65**: 93.

49. DeDUVE, C. 1959. Lysozymes. A new group of cytoplasma particles. *In* Subcellular Particles: 128. T. Hyashi, Ed. The Ronald Press Co. New York, N.Y.

50. PENN, N. W. 1961. Metabolism of the protein molecule in a rat-liver mitochondrial fraction. Biochem. et Biophys. Acta. **53**: 490.

Reprinted by the
U. S. DEPARTMENT OF HEALTH, EDUCATION, AND WELFARE
Public Health Service

ENZYMES OF ARGININE METABOLISM IN CELL CULTURE: STUDIES ON ENZYME INDUCTION AND REPRESSION [1]

ROBERT T. SCHIMKE, Laboratory of Biochemical Pharmacology, National Institute of Arthritis and Metabolic Diseases,[2] Bethesda, Maryland

THE control of metabolic processes by alterations in contents of critical enzymes by the mechanisms of enzyme induction and repression has been well established in various microorganisms (1). Demonstrations of similar control mechanisms in intact mammalian tissues have been hindered by the inherent complexities of the intact animal. The isolated mammalian cell grown in continuous culture, on the other hand, affords a far more simplified system for studies of enzyme induction and repression in mammalian tissues. The studies presented are on the series of enzymes, shown in text-figure 1, which are involved with the synthesis of arginine from citrulline, *i.e.*, argininosuccinate synthetase and argininosuccinase, and with the degradation of arginine, *i.e.*, arginase. The two enzymes involved in arginine biosynthesis are affected by the concentration of arginine in the growth medium, so that when the concentration of arginine in the medium limits growth, the levels of argininosuccinate synthetase and argininosuccinase are from 2-fold to 15-fold greater than when the cells are grown in excess arginine. This phenomenon is similar to arginine repression as demonstrated in *Escherichia coli* (2) and *Bacillus subtilis* (3) and indicates some similarities between control of arginine biosynthesis in microorganisms and higher animals.

The level of arginase has a direct relation to the concentration of arginine in the medium, that is, it is controlled by a substrate inductive effect. A similar effect of arginine has been noted by Klein (4). Further, the addition of manganese to the medium profoundly increases arginase activity of the cells. The mechanisms of these increases in enzyme activity were investigated with a specific antiarginase antibody, and were found to be related not only to the rate of *de novo* synthesis of the arginase, but also to the rate of its turnover, *i.e.*, breakdown.

Although the following observation is unrelated to enzyme induction and repression in mammalian cells, it should be emphasized that in studies of metabolic processes in cell cultures the cell lines used must be rigidly free of contamination by pleuropneumonia-like organisms (PPLO). The

---

[1] Presented at the Symposium on Metabolic Control Mechanisms in Animal Cells, Boston, Mass., May 27–30, 1963.

[2] National Institutes of Health, Public Health Service, U.S. Department of Health, Education, and Welfare.

714–852—64——22

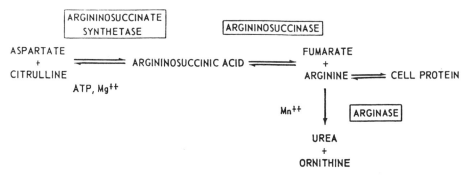

TEXT-FIGURE 1.—Arginine metabolism in cultured mammalian cells.

frequent, unapparent contamination of cell cultures by these organisms may lead to false conclusions. This is particularly true with studies of arginine metabolism since, in the presence of PPLO, arginine is rapidly degraded to ornithine by the pathway shown in text-figure 2. This pathway is present in all PPLO strains isolated from cell culture, and is absent in all PPLO-free cultures (5).

MATERIALS AND METHODS

Cell cultures.—PPLO-free lines of HeLa-S₃, HeLa, KB, and L-929 were grown in suspension culture in Eagle's spinner medium (6) with 5 percent (HeLa-S₃ and L) or 10 percent (HeLa and KB) horse serum filtered through Sephadex G-50 before use. Cells were harvested and resuspended in medium containing specific concentrations of arginine, citrulline, etc., as described elsewhere (7). Growth of the cells was determined by either cell counts with a hemocytometer or by protein determinations on cells washed with serum-free medium (8). Cell populations were routinely maintained from 2 to 6×10^5 cells per ml.

Enzyme assays.—The details of preparation of cells and assays for argininosuccinate synthetase, argininosuccinase, and arginase were presented elsewhere (7). The assays of argininosuccinate synthetase and argininosuccinase utilized C^{14}-labeled amino acid substrates, *i.e.*, ureido-C^{14}-L-citrulline, obtained from the New England Nuclear Corporation (argininosuccinate synthetase), and guanido-C^{14}-L-argininosuccinic acid (argininosuccinase), synthesized according to Ratner (9). The product of the immediate reaction is converted to urea by the addition of excess amounts of ancillary enzymes according to the pathway indicated in

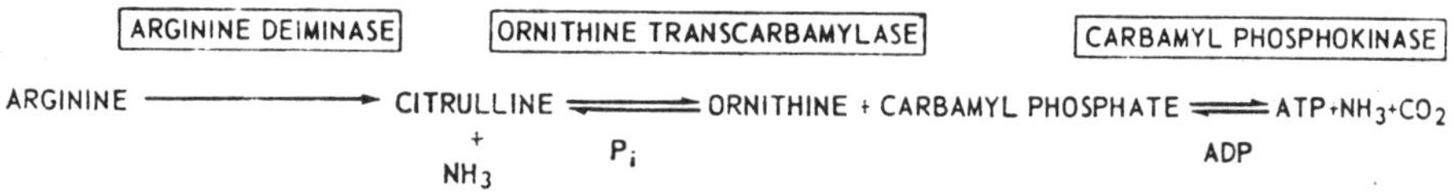

ARGININE DEIMINASE	ORNITHINE TRANSCARBAMYLASE	CARBAMYL PHOSPHOKINASE

ARGININE ⟶ CITRULLINE ⇌ ORNITHINE + CARBAMYL PHOSPHATE ⇌ $ATP + NH_3 + CO_2$
$+$ P_i ADP
NH_3

TEXT-FIGURE 2.—Arginine breakdown in pleuropneumonia-like organisms-contaminated cell cultures.

NATIONAL CANCER INSTITUTE MONOGRAPH NO. 13

text-figure 1. The urea, labeled with C^{14}, was decomposed by urease, and the liberated $C^{14}O_2$ was collected and counted. Results of all assays are linear with respect to time and tissue concentration under the existing conditions.

Immunologic studies.—The details of the preparation of the anti-arginase antibody from rabbits, with the use of purified rat liver arginase and the preparation of HeLa-S_3 extracts for precipitin reactions have been described (*10*).

RESULTS

Repression of Argininosuccinate Synthetase and Argininosuccinase

Repression-derepression, *i.e.*, the ability to alter the rate of synthesis of a series of biosynthetic enzymes by varying the availability or concentration of the end product, has classically been demonstrated to its fullest extent in microorganisms when the specific end product was present in an amount small enough to limit growth (*11*). The repression effect of arginine on levels of the two enzymes involved in its biosynthesis in mammalian cells can also be demonstrated only when the cells are grown under conditions in which arginine limits growth.

Text-figure 3 indicates the range of arginine concentrations which limited growth in HeLa-S_3. Between the arginine concentrations of 0.1 mM and 0.02 mM, there was a direct relationship between growth rate and arginine concentration. Increasing the concentration of arginine

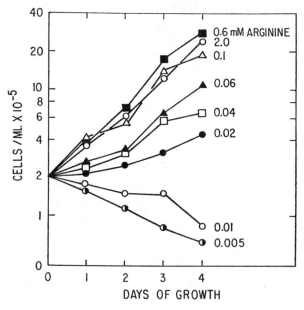

TEXT-FIGURE 3.—Effect of varying arginine concentrations of medium on HeLa-S_3 cells grown for 4 days. Medium was replaced daily without removal of any cells.

METABOLIC CONTROL MECHANISMS
714–852—64——23

above 0.1 mM did not further increase growth rates. Decreasing the concentration of arginine below 0.02 mM did not further decrease growth but resulted in cell lysis and death. These data are similar to those of Eagle et al. (12) with lysine, threonine, and valine.

Text-figure 4 shows the effects in suspension cultures of HeLa-S₃ of varying the concentration of arginine and citrulline in the medium on levels of argininosuccinate synthetase, representing an enzyme of the biosynthetic pathway, and of arginase, as the control enzyme. The level of argininosuccinate synthetase activity was increased threefold to fourfold under conditions in which arginine, at a concentration of 0.02 mM, limited growth. High concentrations of citrulline (2.0 mM) produced maximal growth and had no effect in increasing argininosuccinate synthetase activity. Concentrations of citrulline that supported limited growth also resulted in increased levels of argininosuccinate synthetase, but no higher than those occurring with limiting arginine concentrations. The effects of arginine on the levels of arginase are the opposite of those on argininosuccinate synthetase, the level of arginase increasing with the arginine concentration. High concentrations of citrulline in the medium, however, did not increase levels of arginase activity.

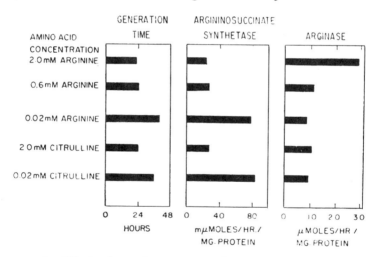

TEXT-FIGURE 4.—Effect of varying concentrations of arginine and citrulline on growth and levels of argininosuccinate synthetase and arginase of HeLa-S₃ cells. Cells were grown for 4 days in medium containing the indicated concentrations of arginine or citrulline before enzyme assays. Medium was replaced every 48 hours.

Text-figure 5 presents the results of an experiment showing that changes in enzyme levels were not simply due to retardation of growth. In this experiment growth was limited by decreasing the concentration of histidine in the medium, but this limitation by histidine in the presence of high arginine concentrations did not alter enzyme levels. Only when the arginine concentration was also diminished was the level of argininosuccinate synthetase increased.

NATIONAL CANCER INSTITUTE MONOGRAPH NO. 13

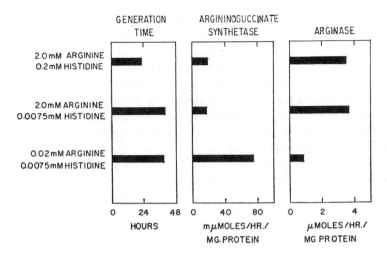

TEXT-FIGURE 5.—Effect of growth limitation by histidine on argininosuccinate synthetase and arginase of HeLa-S₃ cells. Cells were grown for 4 days in medium
containing indicated concentrations of arginine and histidine before harvest and
enzyme assay. Medium was replaced every 48 hours.

Text-figure 6 shows the results of a series of cell lines studied for the
existence of the arginine repression effect. In addition to HeLa-S₃,
lines of HeLa, KB, and L-929 were examined for argininosuccinate
synthetase and argininosuccinase activities under conditions of excess
arginine (2.0 mM) and limiting (0.02 mM or 0.01 mM for the L-929 cell
line) arginine. All cell lines showed an effect that varied in extent.
In the HeLa line, the repression effect was least striking, whereas in KB
and L-929 cells the differences between cells grown in high or low arginine were up 10-fold to 15-fold. There were comparable changes in the
levels of both enzymes involved in arginine biosynthesis, that is, they
were affected in a coordinated manner. As with HeLa-S₃ cells (text-
fig. 4), the substitution of citrulline for arginine gave no higher enzyme
levels than limiting concentrations of arginine, which indicated no "inductive" effect of the citrulline.

Many experiments have failed to demonstrate the presence of activators or inhibitors of argininosuccinate synthetase, argininosuccinase,
or arginase activity in extracts of the cells, or a direct effect of arginine
on the enzyme activities under the assay conditions used. Studies of
apparent Michaelis constants and pH optima of argininosuccinate synthetase and argininosuccinase have also failed to indicate any qualitative
differences in the enzyme activities.

Text-figure 7 shows the results of a typical experiment of the time
course of increase in argininosuccinase produced when cells are changed
from a medium containing excess arginine to one containing a limiting
concentration. The increase in argininosuccinase activity was completed
within one generation of growth. With change back to a medium containing excess arginine, the enzyme activity was stable. In other experi-

METABOLIC CONTROL MECHANISMS

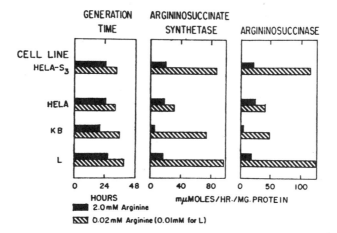

TEXT-FIGURE 6.—Effect of varying arginine concentrations of medium on argininosuccinate synthetase and argininosuccinase. PPLO-free cell lines were grown 4 days in indicated concentrations of arginine before harvest and enzyme assays.

ments in which the cells were maintained in limiting arginine concentrations up to 10 days, a similar time course of increase, decrease, and extent of change in argininosuccinase activity was found. This result excludes the possibility that the arginine effect was due to a selection of cells containing a higher level of the enzyme rather than a change within the cells.

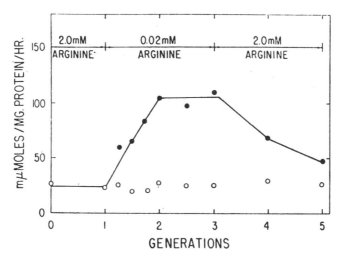

TEXT-FIGURE 7.—Time course of change in argininosuccinase activity of HeLa-S₂ cells produced when the concentration of arginine in the medium was altered. Cells maintained in 2.0 mM L-arginine were transferred to medium containing 0.02 mM arginine (●—●) and assayed daily for argininosuccinase activity for a total of two generations of growth. Medium was replaced daily. Cell concentrations were maintained from 2 to 4 × 10⁵ cells per ml. Cells maintained in 2.0 mM L-arginine (○—○) were assayed daily for control.

NATIONAL CANCER INSTITUTE MONOGRAPH NO. 18

No ornithine transcarbamylase activity (ornithine + carbamyl phosphate→citrulline) was demonstrated under any growth conditions. This finding is in keeping with the fact that ornithine is unable to substitute for the arginine requirement of cultured cells (6), and indicates that the absence of ornithine transcarbamylase is a genetic defect and not simply associated with repression.

Induction of Arginase in HeLa-S₃

Two separate factors involved in the control of levels of arginase activity were found. In addition to the effect of arginine previously described (text-figs. 4 and 5), there was a more profound effect when manganese was added to the medium, and a lesser effect when cobalt and nickel were added. The time course of these separate and additive effects of arginine and manganese is shown in text-figure 8. In these experiments HeLa-S₃ cells originally maintained in 0.1 mM arginine were transferred to medium containing 0.1 mM arginine, 0.1 mM arginine plus 0.1 mM MnCl₂, 4.0 mM arginine, or 4.0 mM arginine plus 0.1 mM MnCl₂.

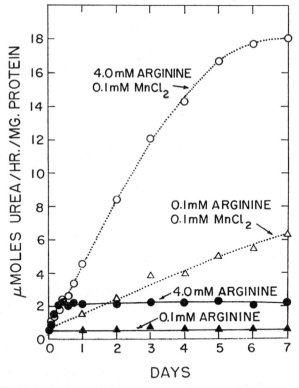

TEXT-FIGURE 8.—Time course of increase in arginase activity produced by addition of high arginine and/or MnCl₂ to medium. HeLa-S₃ cells maintained in 0.1 mM L-arginine were placed in medium containing indicated concentrations of arginine and manganese. Medium was replaced daily. Aliquots were removed daily and the cells assayed for arginase activity.

METABOLIC CONTROL MECHANISMS

Samples were assayed daily for arginase activity. Cell growth rates were similar under all conditions of growth. The arginine effect resulted in a fourfold to fivefold increase in specific enzyme activity (μmoles of urea formed/hour/mg protein). This increase was completed within 12 hours after the change in medium. The manganese effect was strikingly different in time course, with linear increases in enzyme activity for up to 3 to 5 generations of growth. The time course of increases in arginase activity produced by addition of manganese to the medium occurred at two different rates, being 2 to 3 times as rapid in the presence of 4.0 mM arginine as with 0.1 mM arginine.

The changes in enzyme activities indicated in text-figure 8 could result from a number of mechanisms. The presence of activators or inhibitors must always be considered. These were ruled out by various experiments involving the mixing of aliquots of extracts from cells having widely differing specific enzyme activities. Furthermore, the arginase assays were routinely performed under conditions of maximal activation of arginase by manganese, and hence the manganese effect cannot be readily ascribed to a simple activation of the enzyme.

A number of experiments were performed which indicated that the changes in enzyme levels were due to changes in content of enzyme protein, and that increases in content of enzyme protein occurred by de novo protein synthesis. For most of these studies it was necessary to isolate specifically the arginase protein in high purity and high yield. Conventional enzyme purification procedures were totally inadequate because of the small amount of material. The use of an antibody precipitating only arginase protein from cell extracts has proved of inestimable value in elucidating the mechanisms for increased arginase activities produced by arginine and manganese. Figure 1 shows an Ouchterlony gel diffusion plate (13) of a rabbit antiarginase antiserum, a highly purified, homogeneous arginase purified from rat liver (14), the original antigen (well 2), and two extracts of HeLa-S$_3$ with differing specific enzyme activities (wells 1 and 3). The antiserum was placed in the center well. It is evident that similar precipitin reactions have taken place irrespective of the growth conditions of the cells, and that there is virtually complete cross reactivity with this antibody preparation.

It has been possible to demonstrate that the differences in enzyme activity resulted from differing contents of specific enzyme protein rather than the presence of activators, inhibitors, or alterations in the kinetic properties of the arginase protein. Text-figure 9 illustrates a comparison between the measurable enzyme activity as altered by growth for 24 hours in various combinations of arginine and manganese and the amount of antiarginase precipitate. It is apparent that the amount of protein precipitated and the measurable enzyme activity are comparable.

The increased content of arginase protein produced by an increase of arginine concentration in the medium, or the addition of manganese to the medium, could arise from either de novo synthesis from constituent amino acids, or by conversion of a preformed precursor to an enzymatically

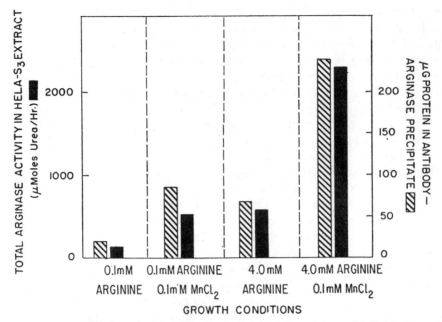

TEXT-FIGURE 9.—Comparison of arginase activity and protein precipitable by anti-arginase in HeLa-S₃ extracts. Cells maintained in 0.1 mM arginine were grown 24 hours in the media. Extracts of cells from each of the flasks (2000 ml of culture fluid) were assayed for arginase activity, after which aliquots were added to the antiarginase and the amount of precipitated protein was compared with the measured enzyme activity. The values for precipitated protein were corrected for a small amount of precipitate present in extracts added to nonimmunized serum. The enzyme activity was quantitatively recovered from the precipitated protein. No enzyme activity was present in the precipitate of the control serum and HeLa-S₃ extract.

and immunologically active protein. Indirect evidence for *de novo* synthesis was obtained from studies in which various means of inhibiting protein synthesis during the "induction" period were used (text-fig. 10). The addition of either puromycin (*15*) or actinomycin D (*16*), or the removal of histidine from the medium abolished the increases in arginase produced by either increased arginine concentrations or the addition of manganese to the medium. Two additional findings were: In the presence of inhibitors of protein synthesis, when the cells were maintained in the basal medium containing 0.1 mM arginine, the specific activity of arginase was consistently diminished 30 to 40 percent of control levels. Furthermore, when manganese was added to the medium this decline in specific activity was prevented. The possible significance of these findings will be discussed later.

A more definitive demonstration of the *de novo* synthesis of arginase was obtained with the use of amino acid-labeling experiments, isolating the arginase protein by means of the antiarginase antisera. Text-figure 11 shows the results of an experiment in which cells grown in 0.1 mM arginine were changed to media containing the indicated concentrations of arginine

METABOLIC CONTROL MECHANISMS

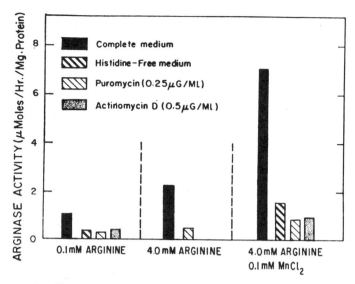

TEXT-FIGURE 10.—Effect of inhibitors of protein synthesis on arginase "induction" by arginine and manganese (24 hours' growth of HeLa-S₃ maintained previously in 0.1 mM arginine). Cells were grown in 0.1 mM L-arginine and then placed in media containing the concentrations of arginine and manganese, plus the additions or deletions indicated. Cells were grown an additional 24 hours, then harvested and assayed for arginase activity.

and manganese and grown in the presence of C^{14}-L-histidine for 24 hours. The cells were then harvested and the counts incorporated into total protein and protein precipitable with the antiarginase antiserum were compared to enzyme activity. The amount of label incorporated into total cell protein was essentially similar under the four conditions. The counts in the antiarginase precipitate, on the other hand, were proportional to the enzyme activity present in the extracts.

In another experiment cells were grown for five generations in medium with 0.1 mM arginine, containing S^{35}-L-cystine, thereby producing a culture with complete and uniform labeling of the protein. At zero time a portion of the cells was harvested, the remaining cells were centrifuged and replaced with medium containing S^{32}-L-cystine, and either 0.1 mM arginine or 4.0 mM arginine plus 0.1 mM manganese, and grown an additional 24 hours before harvest. The results of this experiment are shown in table 1. There was a sixfold increase in arginase activity produced in cells grown in medium containing 4.0 mM arginine plus 0.1 mM manganese. If a preformed, and necessarily labeled, precursor accounted for this increase in enzyme protein, then there should have been a comparable increase in counts found in the antiarginase precipitate. It is evident that there was no increase in counts over those present at the time the labeled cystine was removed from the medium. This experiment indicates conclusively that the precursor hypothesis is untenable and, together with the previous experiment, rules out the possibility that the increased arginine and manganese caused a molecular modification in cellular

NATIONAL CANCER INSTITUTE MONOGRAPH NO. 13

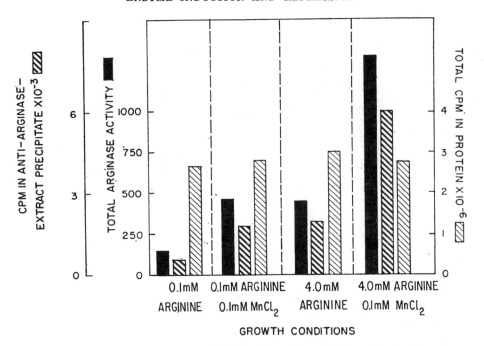

TEXT-FIGURE 11.—Incorporation of C¹⁴-histidine into total protein and arginase during arginase "induction" by arginine and manganese. Cells grown in 0.1 mM L-arginine were placed in the specified media containing 20 μc C¹⁴-L-histidine, total volume of culture 2000 ml for each medium, and grown an additional 24 hours. Cells were harvested and separated into protein precipitable by antiarginase and total cell protein.

protein that resulted in an active protein, both enzymatically and immunologically.

Both the effect of arginine and the effect of manganese can be considered as examples of enzyme induction, that is, they cause an increase in enzyme protein. However, the time course studies shown in text-figure 8 indicate that the effects of arginine and manganese were not similar. Enzyme induction has been generally considered to result in an "increased synthesis of enzyme protein" (17). In growing bacteria, the accumulation of an enzyme can be accomplished only if the rate of synthesis relative to other cell proteins is increased, since there is no demonstrable protein turnover (18). But in mammalian tissues, both in cell culture and the intact animal, protein turnover is a consistent and constant finding (19, 20). Thus, the processes determining the level of a given protein may be depicted as follows:

Amino acids →→→→→→→→→→ (Enzyme) →→→→→→→→→→→ Breakdown products
    Synthesis   Breakdown   (amino acids).

The accumulation of increased amounts of a given enzyme protein may result from increased rates of synthesis and/or decreased rates of breakdown.

METABOLIC CONTROL MECHANISMS

TABLE 1.—Loss of S^{35}-L-cystine label from arginase and total protein of HeLa-S$_3$ during arginase "induction" by arginine and manganese

Growth conditions	0 Time	24 Hours	
	0.1 mM Arginine	0.1 mM Arginine	4.0 mM Arginine plus 0.1 mM MnCl$_2$
Total cell protein (mg)	168	250	241
Total cpm S^{35}-L-cystine $\times$ 10^{-5}	7. 33	5. 35	5. 75
Total arginase (μmoles urea/hr)	126	185	1, 222
Total cpm S^{35}-L-cystine in arginase	1, 020	322	895

HeLa-S$_3$ cells were grown in medium containing 0.1 mM L-arginine and 0.1 mM S^{35}-L-cystine, specific activity 0.3 mc per mM, for a total of five generations. The cells, in a total volume 4500 ml, were divided into three portions. One portion was harvested immediately, and the remainder was washed and replaced with medium containing 0.1 mM S^{32}-L-cystine plus 4.0 mM arginine, 0.1 mM manganese, or 0.1 mM arginine only, and grown for 26 hours. The cells were harvested, and the counts incorporated into total cellular protein and into protein precipitable by antiarginase were determined. These were compared with total cell protein and total arginase activity in the extracts.

A considerable accumulation of data suggests that arginase in HeLa-S$_3$ cells has a significant turnover, and hence the rate of breakdown may well affect the given level of the enzyme. Text-figure 12 shows a part of the experiment illustrated in text-figure 8, in which the cells were returned to a medium containing the basal 0.1 mM arginine. It is apparent that the loss of enzyme activity was far more rapid than can be explained by dilution due to continued cell growth with arginase produced at the level characteristic of growth in 0.1 mM arginine. There is further evidence of a rapid turnover in the experiments in which inhibition of protein synthesis produced a rapid decrease in arginase activity (text-fig. 10).

A labeling experiment to demonstrate turnover is illustrated in text-figure 13. Cells were grown in 2.0 mM arginine. At zero time S^{35}-L-cystine was added to each flask and samples were removed at the indicated intervals. One portion of the cells was grown for five generations in the S^{35}-L-cystine to produce a uniformly labeled culture. The results are expressed as percent of maximal labeling obtained after five generations of growth in S^{35}-L-cystine. If no turnover at all occurred after 24 hours of growth (one generation), the samples of cell protein and arginase should have contained 50 percent of the maximal label, as indicated by the "theoretical" curve. However, it is evident that such was not the case. The protein precipitable with the antiarginase antiserum was maximally labeled within 12 hours, which indicates that the entire content of the enzyme was resynthesized and degraded within the 12-hour period. It is clear that arginase turnover occurred at a relatively rapid rate compared to the turnover of total cell protein.

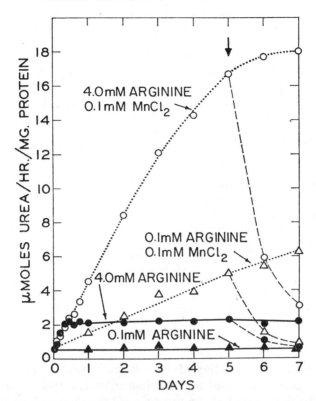

TEXT-FIGURE 12.—Time course of decrease in arginase activity produced by change of HeLa-S₃ to medium containing 0.1 mM arginine. Details of handling of cells are described in text-figure 8. At time indicated by *arrow* a portion of the cells grown in each type of medium was placed in medium containing 0.1 mM L-arginine. Arginase activities were determined daily thereafter for 2 days.

Secretion of arginase by the cells was excluded as the cause of the demonstrated turnover as there was no arginase activity attributable to the cells in the growth medium; arginase of cell lysates incubated in culture medium for 24 hours can be readily detected.

The incorporation of label into total protein was also more than that predicted if no turnover existed. The calculated turnover of total protein based on the results shown in text-figure 13 is 1 percent per hour. This value is similar to that previously reported by Eagle *et al.* (*20*).

It is suggested that the mechanism of manganese effect involves a decrease in the breakdown of the enzyme; *i.e.*, its stabilization. Such a hypothesis would account for the linear increase in specific arginase activity over several generations of growth (text-fig. 8). This hypothesis is supported by the results of the experiment shown in table 2. Cells were grown in 4.0 mM arginine for four generations with S³⁵-L-cystine. At zero time the medium was replaced with medium containing S³²-L-cystine and 4.0 mM arginine with and without 0.1 mM MnCl₂ and grown for 24 hours before harvest. With no manganese there was a rapid loss of total

METABOLIC CONTROL MECHANISMS

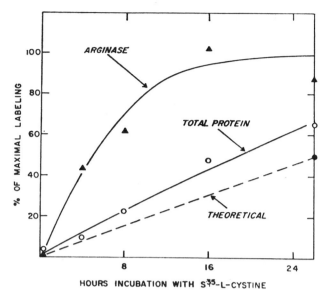

TEXT-FIGURE 13.—Incorporation of S^{35}-L-cystine into cell protein and arginase of HeLa-S₃. HeLa-S₃ were grown, in 5 flasks, in 2.0 mM L-arginine and 0.1 mM S^{35}-L-cystine to a final volume of 10 liters (2.5×10^5 cells/ml). At zero time S^{35}-L-cystine was added to a final specific activity of 0.42 mc per mM. At specified intervals 1500 ml of the culture was harvested and counts incorporated into total cell protein and arginase were determined. A portion of the culture was grown for five generations in S^{35}-L-cystine medium to produce complete labeling of all cell protein. The values obtained are expressed as the percent of specific activity (cpm/mg for total cell protein, and cpm/100 units of arginase for arginase) of that obtained with the maximally labeled cells.

counts precipitable with the antiarginase antibody, which again indicates the rapid turnover of the enzyme. If arginase was stabilized by the presence of manganese, there should have been less loss of label than in its absence. The results indicate that there is, indeed, little loss of label from arginase when manganese is added to the medium and that stabilization of arginase has occurred.

At the present time there is not much available information on the mechanism of the arginine effect. However, the different rates of accumulation of arginase produced when cells are grown in the presence of manganese at two different concentrations of arginine in the medium (text-fig. 8) can best be explained by the assumption that arginine affects the rate of enzyme synthesis by acting as an inducer in the classical bacterial meaning of the concept. However, a separate type of stabilization effect has not been excluded. Further studies on the mechanisms of the separate arginine and manganese effects are in progress.

Conversion of Arginine to Urea and Ornithine by Arginase in the Intact Cell in Culture

The extent to which arginine is converted to urea and ornithine, *i.e.*, by arginase, is dependent as much on the concentration of arginine in the

NATIONAL CANCER INSTITUTE MONOGRAPH NO. 13

TABLE 2.—Loss of S^{35}-L-cystine label from arginase and total protein of HeLa-S_3 cells during arginase "induction" by manganese

	0 Time	24 Hours	
Growth conditions	4.0 mM Arginine	4.0 mM Arginine	4.0 mM Arginine plus 0.1 mM MnCl$_2$
Cell protein (mg)	131	195	205
Total cpm S^{35}-L-cystine $\times$ 10^{-5}	5. 65	4. 10	4. 22
Total arginase (μmoles urea/hr)	310	462	1, 068
Total cpm S^{35}-L-cystine in arginase	2, 540	1, 012	2, 020

HeLa-S_3 were grown in medium containing 4.0 mM L-arginine and S^{35}-L-cystine as indicated in table 1. Conditions of growth and experimental procedures were similar to those given in table 1, except that the cells were grown in medium containing 4.0 mM L-arginine at all times.

medium as on the content of the enzyme arginase. The data in table 3 show the extent (percent) of conversion of arginine to urea, determined in growing cultures of HeLa-S_3 as a function of the arginine concentration. The amount of arginine converted to ornithine and urea, by the arginase reaction, was essentially negligible at concentrations of arginine generally used in culture media, *i.e.*, 0.1 mM. Significant arginine conversion occurred only when the concentration of arginine in the medium was increased to 10 mM, at which 15 percent of the arginine was converted, as compared to 0.01 percent at 0.1 mM arginine. This large difference in extent of conversion was not associated with a comparable increase in enzyme specific activity, as measured under optimal conditions of arginine concentration (250 mM at pH 9.5). Thus the increase in extent to which arginine is metabolized by the arginase reaction is probably because the concentration of arginine required for half-saturation of the arginase in cell extracts, *i.e.*, Michaelis constant, is of the order of 10 to 15 mM arginine (*10*). This point is emphasized because it is often forgotten that the substrate concentration may be equally, or more, important in the determination of the over-all rate of a physiological reaction—such appears to be the case with arginine breakdown by arginase in cell culture.

DISCUSSION

We have demonstrated the presence of argininosuccinate synthetase and argininosuccinase activities in several lines of mammalian cells, thereby accounting for the ability of these cells to utilize citrulline instead of arginine for growth. It has further been demonstrated that the levels of these two enzymes are not constant, but vary inversely with the concentration of arginine in the medium. Examples of enzyme changes

METABOLIC CONTROL MECHANISMS

TABLE 3.—Dependence of the conversion of arginine to ornithine and urea on concentrations of arginine in the growth medium

Arginine in medium (mM)	Total amount of arginase in extracts* (specific activity)	Actual percent of arginine converted to urea in the cells during growth†
0. 1	0. 6	0. 01
1. 0	1. 4	0. 30
10. 0	2. 6	15. 10

HeLa-S₃ cells were grown for four generations in medium containing the specified arginine concentrations. The medium was then replaced with 100 ml of medium (2 × 10⁵ cells/ml) containing guanido-C¹⁴-L-arginine (Chemtrac Corporation, Cambridge, Mass.), specific activity 0.01 mc per mM at the specified concentrations. The cells were grown for an additional 24 hours, removed by centrifugation, an aliquot assayed for arginase as described in the text, and the protein of the medium was precipitated with a final trichloroacetic acid concentration of 10 percent. The protein-free supernatant fluid was extracted with ether to remove the trichloroacetic acid. The pH was adjusted to 6.6 with 1 M potassium phosphate, pH 6.6. A 1 ml aliquot was incubated with 5 mg urease (Sigma Chemical Co., Type V urease) for 60 minutes. The C¹⁴O₂ liberated by the action of urease and collected and counted, as described previously (7), indicated the amount of urea formed from arginine during the growth of the cells.

*Extracts of HeLa-S₃ cells measured under optimal conditions of pH, manganese and L-arginine concentrations, expressed in terms of enzyme specific activity, i.e., μmoles urea formed per hour per mg protein.
†As measured by formation of urea during growth.

in cultured cells indicative of repression phenomena have also been demonstrated for glutamyl transferase by DeMars (21) and for aspartate transcarbamylase by Ennis and Lubin (22). These studies indicate that the potential for repression phenomena exists under certain conditions in mammalian tissues. In the present study the repression phenomenon could be demonstrated only when growth was limited by the specific repressor, i.e., arginine, which indicates that under normal growth conditions argininosuccinate synthetase and argininosuccinase are fully repressed. Ennis and Lubin (22) have come to the same conclusion in their studies with aspartate transcarbamylase. Other examples of repression in mammalian cells may well exist, and will probably be demonstrated only under conditions in which the biosynthetic product can be made to limit growth.

The studies with arginase demonstrated two separate and additive factors that resulted in the accumulation of increased enzyme activity: an effect of the substrate, arginine, and of a metal required for enzyme activity, manganese. The increased enzyme activity resulted from an increased content of enzyme protein caused by de novo protein synthesis. The results indicate that so-called enzyme induction in mammalian systems does not necessarily signify an increased rate of enzyme synthesis. In view of the general phenomenon of protein turnover in animal tissues and cell cultures, the possibility that the induction results from stabilization of the enzyme protein must always be considered. Changes in enzyme levels in mammalian tissues by a mechanism involving stabilization of proteins, *i.e.*, prevention of degradation, may represent a common and significant mechanism for mammalian adaptation in general. Such a stabilization phenomenon has been shown to exist with rat liver arginase (*14*) and has been suggested as the mechanism for the increased activity of thymidylate kinase as produced by thymidine administration (*23*).

These studies also indicate the potential significance of small amounts of metal ions, in establishing the enzymatic properties of cell cultures, which may be introduced into the culture medium in ways unsuspected by the investigator. Thus Klein (*4, 24*) demonstrated a stimulation of arginase activity in several cell lines by yeast ribonucleic acid (RNA). In view of the effects of manganese demonstrated in these studies, and the known contamination of RNA preparations by divalent metals, including manganese (*25*), the RNA effect may well be the result of the contaminating metal present.

SUMMARY

Arginine in cell cultures can be synthesized from citrulline by a two-enzyme pathway, involving argininosuccinate synthetase and argininosuccinase, and can be degraded by arginase, thereby allowing for an evaluation of the existence of repression (biosynthetic pathway) and induction (degradative pathway) as metabolic control mechanisms in mammalian cell cultures.

A phenomenon analogous to classical bacterial repression was demonstrated in several continuous cultures with the arginine biosynthetic pathway. When HeLa, KB, or L-929 cells were grown in concentrations of citrulline or arginine that produced limitation of growth, the specific activities of argininosuccinate synthetase and argininosuccinase were 2-fold to 15-fold greater than when the cells were grown in excess arginine. The extent of change in enzyme levels was similar for both enzymes, *i.e.*, they were coordinated.

The level of arginase activity in HeLa-S_3 cells can be augmented by two separate, additive factors: 1) increase of arginine concentrations in the medium and 2) addition of manganese to the medium. An analysis of the time course of increases in arginase produced by arginine and manganese indicates that the effects are different. With the use of an antibody that specifically precipitates arginase of HeLa-S_3 extracts, both effects have been found to result from *de novo* protein synthesis. Arginase in cell cultures had a more rapid turnover, *i.e.*, degradation, than total cell protein. The addition of manganese to the medium stabilized the arginase molecule, which produced an accumulation of newly synthesized arginase by decreasing enzyme breakdown.

REFERENCES

(*1*) Jacob, F., and Monod, J.: Genetic regulatory mechanisms in the synthesis of proteins. J Molec Biol 3: 318–356, 1961.

METABOLIC CONTROL MECHANISMS

214 SCHIMKE

(2) Vogel, H. J.: Aspects of repression in the regulation of enzyme synthesis: pathway-wide control and enzyme-specific response. Sympos Quant Biol (Cold Spring Harbor) 26: 163–172, 1961.

(3) Lehrer, H. I., and Jones, M. E.: Repression of ornithine transcarbamyl-transferase of *Bacillus subtilis*. Biochim Biophys Acta 65: 360–362, 1963.

(4) Klein, E.: Studies on the substrate-induced arginase synthesis in animal cell strains cultured in vitro. Exp Cell Res 22: 226–232, 1961.

(5) Schimke, R. T., and Barile, M. F.: Arginine metabolism in pleuropneumonia-like organisms isolated from mammalian cell culture. J Bact 86: 195–206, 1963.

(6) Eagle, H.: Amino acid metabolism in mammalian cell cultures. Science 130: 432–437, 1959.

(7) Schimke, R. T.: Enzymes of arginine metabolism in mammalian cell culture. I. Repression of argininosuccinate synthetase and argininosuccinase. J Biol Chem 239: 1964.

(8) Lowry, O. H., Roseborough, N. J., Farr, A. L., and Randall, R. J.: Protein measurement with the Folin phenol reagent. J Biol Chem 193: 265–275, 1951.

(9) Ratner, S.: Preparation and determination of argininosuccinic acid. *In* Methods in Enzymology, vol. 2 (Colowick, S. P., and Kaplan, N. O., eds.). New York, Academic Press Inc., 1955, pp. 643–647.

(10) Schimke, R. T.: Enzymes of arginine metabolism in mammalian cell culture. II. Mechanisms for arginase induction. To be published.

(11) Gorini, L., and Maas, W. K.: The potential for the formation of a biosynthetic enzyme in *Escherichia coli*. Biochim Biophys Acta 25: 208–209, 1957.

(12) Eagle, H., Piez, K. A., and Levy, M.: The intercellular amino acid concentrations required for protein synthesis in cultured human cells. J Biol Chem 236: 2039–2042, 1961.

(13) Ouchterlony, O.: *In vitro* method for testing the toxin-producing capacity of diphtheria bacteria. Acta Path Microbiol Scand 25: 186–191, 1948.

(14) Schimke, R. T., Brown, M. B., and Smallman, E.: Turnover of rat liver arginase. Ann NY Acad Sci 102: 587–601, 1963.

(15) Zamecnik, P. C.: Unsettled questions in the field of protein synthesis. Biochem J 85: 257–264, 1962.

(16) Reich, E., Franklin, R. M., Shatkin, A. J., and Tatum, E. L.: Action of actinomycin D on animal cells and viruses. Proc Nat Acad Sci USA 48: 1238–1245, 1962.

(17) Cohn, M., Monod, J., Pollock, M., Spiegelman, S., and Stanier, R.: Terminology of enzyme formation. Nature (Lond) 172: 1096, 1953.

(18) Mandelstam, J.: The intracellular turnover of protein and nucleic acids and its role in biochemical differentiation. Bact Rev 24: 289–309, 1960.

(19) Swick, R. W.: The measurement of protein turnover in rat liver. J Biol Chem 231: 751–764, 1958.

(20) Eagle, H., Piez, K. A., Fleishman, R., and Oyama, V. I.: Protein turnover in mammalian cell cultures. J Biol Chem 234: 592–597, 1959.

(21) DeMars, R.: The inhibition by glutamine of glutamyl transferase formation in cultures of human cells. Biochim Biophys Acta 27: 435–436, 1958.

(22) Ennis, H. L., and Lubin, M.: Capacity for synthesis of a pyrimidine biosynthetic enzyme in mammalian cells. Biochim Biophys Acta 68: 78–83, 1963.

(23) Bojarski, T. B., and Hiatt, H. H.: Stabilization of thymidylate kinase activity by thymidylate and by thymidine. Nature (Lond) 188: 1112–1114, 1960.

(24) Klein, E.: Formation in animal cells cultured *in vitro* on the substrate induced enzyme. Exp Cell Res 21: 421–429, 1960.

(25) Wacker, W. E. C., and Vallee, B. L.: Nucleic acids and metals. J Biol Chem 234: 3257–3262, 1959.

PLATE 19

FIGURE 1.—Ouchterlony diffusion pattern of antiarginase with rat liver arginase and HeLa-S₃ extracts. HeLa-S₃ extracts were prepared from cells grown in 0.1 mM L-arginine (*well 1*), or 2.0 mM L-arginine and 0.1 mM manganese chloride (*well 3*). *Well 2* contains highly purified rat liver arginase (*14*) similar to that used to immunize the rabbit. *Center well* contains the rabbit antiarginase antiserum. Photograph was made 21 days after introduction of the samples.

HELA-S_3 Extract: Specific Arginase Activity: 47μMoles urea/Hr/Mg Protein

HELA-S_3 EXTRACT: SPECIFIC ARGINASE ACTIVITY: 550μMOLES UREA/MG. PROTEIN

SCHIMKE   217

THE JOURNAL OF BIOLOGICAL CHEMISTRY
Vol. 240, No. 1, January 1965
Printed in U.S.A.

The Roles of Synthesis and Degradation in the Control of Rat Liver Tryptophan Pyrrolase

ROBERT T. SCHIMKE, E. W. SWEENEY, AND C. M. BERLIN

*From the National Institute of Arthritis and Metabolic Diseases, National Institutes of Health,
United States Public Health Service, Bethesda, Maryland 20014*

(Received for publication, July 6, 1964)

It is now well established that in animal tissues a large number of enzyme activities can be increased by the administration of hormones (1–3), by specific substrates (1, 4), or by alterations in the nutritional state of the animal (5–8). In certain of these cases an increased content of newly synthesized enzyme protein has been shown to account for the increases in enzyme activity, as opposed to an activation phenomenon (9–12). Thus such changes in enzyme activity superficially resemble enzyme induction as observed in bacteria, the mechanism of which involves an increase in the differential rate of enzyme synthesis (13). An increased rate of synthesis has been shown to be responsible for the increases in rat liver tyrosine-glutamate transaminase (14) and glutamate-alanine transaminase (15) produced by corticosteroid administration. However, in view of the extensive and rapid replacement of liver proteins, *i.e.* turnover (16–20), a decrease in the rate of enzyme degradation can result equally well in the accumulation of enzyme. Recent studies from this laboratory have, in fact, shown that such a mechanism, *i.e.* enzyme stabilization, is important in regulating the level of arginase in rat liver (12).

In this paper studies on the roles of both synthesis and degradation in controlling enzyme levels have been extended to rat liver tryptophan pyrrolase. Studies from various laboratories have indicated that tryptophan pyrrolase can be increased by the administration of either corticosteroids or tryptophan (1, 11, 21–24). Both agents produce an increased content of protein synthesized *de novo* from amino acids, as indicated by studies with inhibitors of protein synthesis (21, 23, 24) and by specific immunological reactions (11). Nevertheless, certain studies have suggested that the corticosteroid- and the tryptophan-mediated increases in tryptophan pyrrolase result from different mechanisms (22, 25). Inasmuch as tryptophan pyrrolase is rapidly degraded *in vivo* (26, 27), an alteration in the rate of such degradation, as well as in the rate of enzyme synthesis, may be of significance in controlling the level of this enzyme.

In a preliminary communication (27) we presented data suggesting that the administration of hydrocortisone to the intact rat increased the rate of synthesis of tryptophan pyrrolase, and that the administration of tryptophan decreased the rate of degradation of tryptophan pyrrolase. This evidence was based on the finding that the time courses of increase in tryptophan pyrrolase produced by repeated administrations of hydrocortisone or tryptophan, or both, were consistent with the time courses of increase predicted from a theoretical model if hydrocortisone increased the rate of synthesis 5- to 7-fold, and if

tryptophan decreased the rate of enzyme degradation essentially to zero (27).

In the present paper these studies have been extended, and the results of data on the incorporation *in vivo* of isotopic amino acids into, and loss from, tryptophan pyrrolase isolated by precipitation with specific antiserum are presented. These results indicate and confirm (27) that hydrocortisone increases the rate of tryptophan pyrrolase synthesis, and that tryptophan administration prevents the normally occurring, rapid degradation of the enzyme.

EXPERIMENTAL PROCEDURE

Treatment of Animals

Adrenalectomized rats were used in all experiments, so that the nonspecific adrenal response resulting from the injection of amino acids would be abolished. Male Osborne-Mendel rats weighing 150 to 180 g each were used in all experiments. They were maintained on Purina laboratory chow and 0.85% NaCl at all times. Adrenalectomies were performed at least 4 to 5 days before animals were used. The completeness of the adrenalectomies was determined on various occasions by the inability of adrenalectomized animals to survive on salt-free water for more than 5 to 7 days. Hydrocortisone 21-phosphate (Merck Sharp and Dohme), a rapidly active and rapidly excreted hydrocortisone preparation (28), was administered either intraperitoneally or subcutaneously in doses indicated in legends to the figures and tables. L-Tryptophan was administered intraperitoneally as a solution of 15 mg per ml in 0.85% NaCl in doses of 1 mg per g of body weight. Puromycin dihydrochloride (kindly supplied by Dr. A. Stanley, National Cancer Institute) was administered intraperitoneally in a dose of 3 mg/100 g of body weight every 2 hours.

Enzyme Assays

Animals were killed by decapitation, and the livers were either assayed immediately or frozen. In any given experiment, either all livers were assayed immediately or all were stored at −20° for at least 10 hours before assay. No difference in enzyme activity was found between livers assayed immediately or those stored in a frozen state. Tryptophan pyrrolase was assayed by the method of Knox and Mehler (29) as modified by Feigelson and Greengard by the addition of hematin (30). In crude homogenates and extracts containing formylkynurenine formylase, the reaction rate was estimated from the linear portion of the time course of kynurenine formation determined spectro-photometrically. In purified extracts devoid of the formylase, formylkynurenine formation was followed spectrophotometrically at 321 mμ. In supernatant fractions devoid of microsomal particles (105,000 $\times$ g supernatant) and in purified extracts, ascorbate was added to the assay medium as described by Tokuyama and Knox (31) to diminish the lag in onset of formyl-kynurenine formation. The amount of homogenate used in the assays was varied in order to maintain product formation at a measurable, constant rate. Thus, for extracts with very high enzyme activities, as little as one-seventh to one-tenth as much homogenate was used as for control animals. Extracts with high levels of tryptophan pyrrolase nevertheless contained sufficient formylkynurenine formylase to permit measurement of the tryptophan pyrrolase product as kynurenine. Formyl-kynurenine formylase was assayed as described by Knox (32). Arginase was assayed as described previously (5). All enzyme activities were expressed in terms of a unit, defined as the amount of enzyme that catalyzes the formation of 1 μmole of product per hour at 37°.

Protein was assayed by the biuret method (33).

Purification of Tryptophan Pyrrolase

Extract—Thirty male rats, weighing 200 to 250 g each, were given 5 mg of hydrocortisone 21-phosphate and 25 mg of corti-sone acetate intraperitoneally. At 4-hour intervals, 1 mg of L-tryptophan per g of body weight was administered intra-peritoneally. At the end of 16 hours, the animals were killed and livers stored overnight at −20°. All subsequent procedures were performed at 4° unless stated otherwise. The livers were thawed and then homogenized in 3 volumes (by weight) of 0.15 M KCl. The homogenate was centrifuged for 30 minutes at 45,000 $\times$ g. The resulting supernatant fluid (700 ml) was passed through a Sephadex G-25 column (coarse form) (34), 10 $\times$ 60 cm, equilibrated with 0.01 M sodium phosphate, pH 7.0, containing 0.001 M L-tryptophan. This buffer, denoted as phosphate-tryptophan buffer, was used in all purification proce-dures.

DEAE-cellulose Chromatography—The extract was applied to a DEAE-cellulose (35) column, 5 $\times$ 40 cm, equilibrated with phosphate-tryptophan buffer. A large part of the protein (60 to 70%) passed through the column. The column was washed with 500 ml of phosphate-tryptophan buffer to remove all nonabsorbed protein. A linear gradient of 0 to 1.2 M NaCl-phosphate-tryptophan buffer (total volume, 1200 ml) was used to elute the protein. Tryptophan pyrrolase was eluted be-ginning at 0.7 M NaCl in a total volume of 250 to 300 ml. The fractions containing enzyme activity were combined and passed through a Sephadex G-25 column, 4 $\times$ 60 cm, equilibrated with phosphate-tryptophan buffer.

Calcium Phosphate Gel—To the Sephadex-treated solution was added an amount of aged calcium phosphate gel sufficient to remove 90 to 95% of the tryptophan pyrrolase activity from solution (about 15 mg of calcium phosphate gel, dry weight, for each 7 ml of enzyme solution). The gel was then eluted with 200 ml each of 0.10 and 0.15 M sodium phosphate, pH 7.0, con-taining 0.001 M L-tryptophan. These fractions contained the majority of the absorbed protein, but little or no tryptophan pyrrolase activity. The gel was then eluted with 250 ml of 0.5 M sodium phosphate, pH 7.0, containing 0.001 M L-tryptophan. This procedure was quickly performed at room temperature to prevent crystallization of sodium phosphate. The 0.5 M eluate, containing 50 to 65% of the enzyme activity, was rapidly passed through a Sephadex G-25 column, 5 $\times$ 50 cm, equilibrated with phosphate-tryptophan buffer.

Second DEAE-cellulose Chromatography—The Sephadex G-25 fractions containing the protein were applied to a DEAE-cellulose column, 2 $\times$ 5 cm, equilibrated with phosphate-tryptophan buffer. The enzyme was eluted with a linear concentration gradient of NaCl from 0 to 1.0 M, in the above equilibrating solution (total volume, 50 ml). The fractions containing enzyme activity were concentrated by ultrafiltration for 8 to 10 hours.

Ammonium Sulfate—The concentrated enzyme solution (10 mg of protein per ml) was fractionated with saturated ammonium sulfate adjusted to pH 7.0 with concentrated NH$_4$OH. The protein which precipitated between 30 and 36% ammonium sulfate saturation was dissolved in 1 to 5 ml of phosphate-tryptophan buffer and dialyzed for 12 hours against the same solution.

Table I shows a typical purification protocol. The specific activity of the final preparations was 160 to 220 units per mg of protein. This purification represents a 10-fold increase in specific activity over the preparation of Feigelson and Greengard (36). Yields of 50 to 60% of enzyme activity present in the initial extracts were obtained.

Immunological Procedures

Antibody against tryptophan pyrrolase was prepared by injection of 3 to 5 mg of tryptophan pyrrolase (specific activity, 220 units per mg of protein) in complete Freund's adjuvant (Difco) into toe pads of rabbits as described by Leskowitz and Waksman (37). Before use, the enzyme solution used for the immunizations was passed through a Sephadex G-100 column, 0.5 $\times$ 20 cm, equilibrated with phosphate-tryptophan buffer. This procedure removed a small amount of low molecular weight protein present in the preparations. The rabbits were bled at 2-week intervals. The serum was subjected to ammonium sul-fate fractionation; the protein precipitating between 0 and 50% ammonium sulfate saturation was dialyzed against 0.85% NaCl at least 24 hours before use. Control antisera obtained from rabbits receiving injections of Freund's adjuvant only were treated in a similar manner. All sera were stored at −20°.

Ouchterlony double diffusion patterns, equivalence point de-terminations, and quantitative precipitin analyses were per-formed as outlined by Kabat and Mayer (38).

TABLE I

Purification of tryptophan pyrrolase from rat liver

This is a purification from animals receiving repeated adminis-trations of cortisone acetate and tryptophan as outlined under "Experimental Procedure."

Step	Volume	Protein	Specific activity*	Total	Yield
	ml	*mg/ml*	*μmoles/hr/mg*	*μmoles/hr*	*%*
Extract..............	640	31.1	0.46 (K)	91,500	100
DEAE-cellulose.....	300	6.3	4.2 (K)	78,000	85
Calcium phosphate gel................	210	0.5	42.0 (FK)	44,800	49
DEAE-cellulose.....	10	8.2	61.0 (FK)	49,400	54
Ammonium sulfate..	3.2	6.25	200 (FK)	43,900	48

* Assayed as kynurenine (K) or formylkynurenine (FK) forma-tion.

The liver extracts used for immunological analyses were prepared as follows. Livers were homogenized in 3 volumes (by weight) of 0.15 M KCl and were centrifuged for 30 minutes at 45,000 × g and then for 60 minutes at 105,000 × g. The resulting extracts were used directly for equivalence point determinations (Fig. 2). However, because use of such extracts resulted in nonspecific precipitation of protein with control antiserum, further purification was undertaken for all other immunological studies. The 105,000 × g supernatant was passed through a DEAE-cellulose column with a bed volume of 1 ml per ml of applied extract, which was equilibrated with phosphate-tryptophan buffer. The column was washed free of nonabsorbed protein. Tryptophan pyrrolase was eluted with 10 to 20 ml of 1 M NaCl in 0.01 M sodium phosphate-0.001 M tryptophan, pH 7.0. The eluate was further concentrated by ultrafiltration to a final volume 0.05 to 0.025 that of the original extract. The concentrates were dialyzed for 8 to 12 hours against 0.01 M sodium phosphate-0.001 M L-tryptophan, pH 7.0. Such concentrates contained from 50 to 60 mg of protein per ml. This partial purification procedure did not result in any loss of enzyme activity present in the original 105,000 × g supernatant (see Table IV), regardless of the starting specific enzyme activity of the extract. The DEAE-cellulose-treated preparations did not produce nonspecific precipitation, and were used for the quantitative precipitin studies and for isolation of enzyme protein for the isotopic studies.

Isotope Incorporation

Uniformly labeled ^{14}C-L-leucine (specific activity, 120 mc per mmole) and uniformly labeled ^{14}C-L-lysine (specific activity, 80 mc per mmole) were obtained from New England Nuclear Corporation. Samples (20 μc each) were diluted to a volume of 1.0 ml in 0.05 M sodium phosphate (pH 7.4)-0.15 M NaCl, and administered intraperitoneally to each rat. At time intervals specified in the legends to figures and tables, generally 40 minutes, livers were removed and extracts prepared for isolation of tryptophan pyrrolase by use of antibody precipitation. A sample of the high speed 105,000 × g supernatant was also saved for determination of radioactivity present in total supernatant protein. For the precipitation of tryptophan pyrrolase by antibody, each liver extract was divided into two equal portions. To one sample was added sufficient tryptophan pyrrolase antiserum to precipitate all enzyme activity present in the extract. A similar volume of control antiserum was added to the other sample. Since extracts from livers of different animals contained varying amounts of tryptophan pyrrolase activity, varying amounts of an extract with high enzyme activity, prepared from animals that had not received labeled compounds, were added so that an equal amount of total enzyme activity was always precipitated from each sample. This procedure equalized the total precipitate formed, and ensured the presence of sufficient precipitate to minimize errors from losses during washing procedures. After additions of antisera and unlabeled tryptophan pyrrolase extract, all tubes were incubated for 30 minutes at 37° and stored overnight at 4°. Precipitates were collected by centrifugation and washed twice with 0.85% NaCl at 4°. Generally no precipitation was present with control antisera. Following removal of the precipitate from the sample containing the tryptophan pyrrolase antiserum, an amount of extract from animals that did not receive labeled compounds, equal to that which had been originally precipitated,

was added, along with additional antiserum sufficient to precipitate the added enzyme. This sample was again incubated for 30 minutes at 37° and for 16 hours at 4°. The resulting precipitate contained none of the labeled enzyme, since this had been precipitated in the initial reaction. This second precipitate, however, contained any radioactivity trapped in the antigen-antibody complex, and thus served as a control for nonspecific precipitation.

The antigen-antibody precipitates, including the controls, and the supernatant protein samples were prepared for counting as outlined by Siekevitz (39). The entire antibody-antigen precipitate, or a sample of supernatant protein, was dissolved in 60% formic acid, plated on steel planchets, and counted at infinite thinness in an end window gas flow Geiger counter with a background of 15 to 16 c.p.m. to 5% reproducibility.

RESULTS

Time Course of Changing Enzyme Levels

Fig. 1 depicts the increases in tryptophan pyrrolase produced by repeated administrations of hydrocortisone or tryptophan, or both. Tryptophan administration alone results in a virtually linear increase in enzyme activity, reaching levels 5 times those of control animals in 16 hours. Hydrocortisone administration alone results in an exponential increase, reaching a maximum 6 to 7 times control levels. The most extensive increases were found when hydrocortisone and tryptophan were administered simultaneously, resulting in a nearly linear increase in tryptophan pyrrolase activity at a rate 7 times that produced by tryptophan alone, to levels 30 to 40 times greater than those of control animals in 16 hours.

The results of Fig. 1 are consistent with the theoretical model of increasing enzyme levels developed previously (27), in which maximal doses of tryptophan decrease the rate of degradation to zero, and maximal doses of hydrocortisone increase the rate of synthesis 6- to 7-fold without altering the rate of degradation. The greatest increase in enzyme, then, results from *both* an increased rate of synthesis and a cessation of enzyme degradation.

Table II shows the effects of repeated administration of hydrocortisone and tryptophan for 16 hours on liver weight, tryptophan pyrrolase, formylkynurenine formylase, and arginase. It can be seen that the total liver weight and formylkynurenine formylase activity did not change significantly. Arginase, another enzyme concerned with amino acid metabolism, was increased, although not nearly to the same extent as tryptophan pyrrolase.

If stabilization of tryptophan pyrrolase, *i.e.* decrease in rate of degradation, is the basis of the tryptophan effect, tryptophan administration should prevent the rapid loss of enzyme activity (26, 27). Table III shows the effects of various agents on the decay of tryptophan pyrrolase activity. Tryptophan did indeed abolish the loss of enzyme activity, whereas histidine and hydrocortisone did not alter the decay. The possibility that the administered tryptophan has somehow maintained a high level of enzyme synthesis was ruled out by Experiment 2 of Table III. The concomitant administration of an inhibitor of protein synthesis, puromycin, in amounts that abolish the increases in tryptophan pyrrolase activity produced by either tryptophan or hydrocortisone (22), did not alter the effect of tryptophan in preventing the decay of enzyme activity. Hence the tryptophan effect does not appear to be related to a process associated with enzyme synthesis. In other experiments similar to those of Table III with a series of tryptophan analogues, D-tryptophan and α-methyl-DL-tryptophan prevented the rapid fall of tryptophan pyrrolase, whereas 5-methyl-DL-tryptophan, 6-methyl-DL-tryptophan, and tryptophol did not. Inasmuch as the administration to intact animals of only D-tryptophan and α-methyl-DL-tryptophan among this group of tryptophan analogues also results in increases in tryptophan pyrrolase levels (40), it is apparent that only those tryptophan analogues that act as stabilizers *in vivo* also act as inducers.

Immunological Analyses

Immunological analyses of the increase in tryptophan pyrrolase activity were undertaken for two purposes: (*a*) to demon-

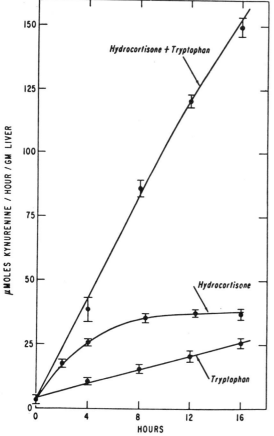

FIG. 1. The time course of increases in tryptophan pyrrolase produced by repeated administrations of hydrocortisone 21-phosphate and tryptophan. Adrenalectomized rats weighing 150 to 170 g each were given injections as follows every 4 hours: 150 mg of L-tryptophan in 12 ml of 0.85% NaCl intraperitoneally and 5 mg of hydrocortisone 21-phosphate subcutaneously. At the onset of the experiment an additional 5 mg of hydrocortisone 21-phosphate were given intraperitoneally. Every 4 hours, the livers of four animals were assayed for tryptophan pyrrolase activity. *Brackets* indicate ±2 standard errors of the mean.

TABLE II

Effect of repeated doses of tryptophan and hydrocortisone on liver weight and tryptophan pyrrolase, formylkynurenine formylase, and arginase of rat liver

Adrenalectomized rats weighing 150 to 180 g were treated by intraperitoneal injection with hydrocortisone 21-phosphate (5 mg) and L-tryptophan (1 mg per g of body weight) at 4-hour intervals for 16 hours. Enzyme assays were performed on 105,000 × *g* supernatant fluids from livers homogenized in 0.15 M KCl.

Treatment	Total liver weight*	Enzyme activity		
		Tryptophan pyrrolase	Formylase	Arginase
	g	*μmoles product/hr/g wet liver*		
NaCl	25.4	3.0	1,800	13,800
Hydrocortisone	27.4	38	1,810	19,740
Tryptophan	28.7	28	2,060	15,200
Hydrocortisone + tryptophan	25.0	116	2,180	20,160

* Combined weight of four animals.

TABLE III

Effect of various agents on loss of tryptophan pyrrolase activity

Tryptophan pyrrolase activity was increased to high levels as described in Table II and Fig. 1. Five hours after the last series of injections ("zero time" in the table), livers of six rats were assayed for enzyme activity and four animals in each group received the following, in 12 ml of 0.85% NaCl intraperitoneally: L-tryptophan, 200 mg; hydrocortisone 21-phosphate, 5 mg; or L-histidine, 200 mg. After 4½ hrs, these livers were assayed for tryptophan pyrrolase activity. In Experiment 2, rats were also given 3.0 mg of puromycin dihydrochloride at 0 and 2 hours and were killed after 4 hours.

Treatment and agent	Tryptophan pyrrolase activity at 4½ hours
	units/g liver
No treatment	3.5 ± 0.5
Pretreatment with hydrocortisone + tryptophan	
Experiment 1	
Zero time assay	97 ± 5
NaCl	25 ± 3
Histidine	25 ± 4
Hydrocortisone	35 ± 3
Tryptophan	96 ± 5
Experiment 2	
Zero time assay	103 ± 3
Tryptophan + puromycin	93 ± 5
NaCl + puromycin	39 ± 5

strate that the increased measurable enzyme activity was associated with an increase in amount of immunologically reactive protein over the entire 30-fold difference in specific enzyme activity produced by hydrocortisone and tryptophan administration (Fig. 1), and (*b*) to establish the specificity of the antibody for the precipitation of tryptophan pyrrolase as is required for its use in studies on isotopic amino acid incorporation. Details of the enzyme purification and immunological procedures are described under "Experimental Procedure."

Fig. 2 shows a titration of the antibody against enzyme

activity in the $100,000 \times g$ liver supernatant of animals receiving a series of four injections each at 4-hour intervals of 0.85% NaCl, tryptophan, hydrocortisone 21-phosphate, or tryptophan + hydrocortisone. The equivalence point, *i.e.* the point at which enzyme activity first appears in the supernatant fluid, was the same for extracts from all treatments when based on the amount of enzyme activity added, although as much as 40 times the amount of extract was added from control animals as from hydrocortisone- and tryptophan-treated animals to provide equal amounts of enzyme activity. This finding shows that the measurable enzyme activity is in fact due to an increased content of immunologically reactive protein. These results confirm those of Feigelson and Greengard (11) over a far greater range of differences in enzyme activity than the 4-fold differences that they reported. It is also to be noted in Fig. 2 that decay of the enzyme activity, after hydrocortisone and tryptophan administration was stopped, *i.e.* from 116 to 64 units per g of liver, was associated with a comparable loss of immunologically reactive protein.

The specificity of the antibody for tryptophan pyrrolase was shown by the presence of a single connecting precipitin band in Ouchterlony double diffusion analysis (Fig. 3) of an extract from control animals (*Well 1*), a partially purified enzyme (*Well 2*), and an extract from hydrocortisone- and tryptophan-treated animals (*Well 3*). Fig. 4 shows a quantitative precipitin analysis with the extracts described in Fig. 3. The protein content of the antigen-antibody precipitates was similar when equivalent

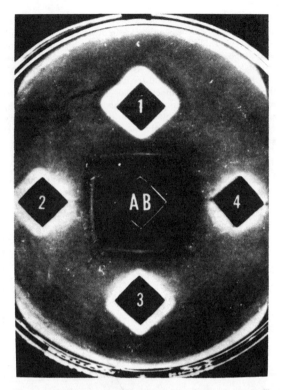

Fig. 3. Ouchterlony double diffusion analysis of tryptophan pyrrolase antibody and liver extracts. The *center well* contained 0.3 ml of tryptophan pyrrolase antibody (*AB*) from rabbit. *Well 1* contained 5 units of tryptophan pyrrolase from untreated rats (specific activity, 0.25 unit per mg of protein); *Well 2* contained 10 units of a partially purified tryptophan pyrrolase (specific activity, 21 units per mg of protein); *Well 3* contained 10 units of enzyme from animals that received repeated administrations of hydrocortisone and tryptophan for 12 hours (specific activity, 4.8 units per mg of protein); and *Well 4* contained control serum. Extracts used were absorbed and eluted from DEAE-cellulose as described under "Experimental Procedure." The patterns were allowed to develop for 1 week before photography.

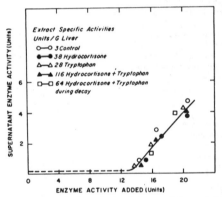

Fig. 2. Immunological analysis of tryptophan pyrrolase activity of rat liver extracts. Adrenalectomized rats weighing 150 to 170 g were given repeated administrations of 0.85% NaCl (control) or either hydrocortisone 21-phosphate, L-tryptophan, or both, as described in Fig. 3. At the end of 16 hours, the livers were removed; $105,000 \times g$ extracts were prepared as described under "Experimental Procedure." In addition, two rats that had received both hydrocortisone and tryptophan were killed 3 hours later, at a time when the enzyme level was falling (26, 27). Specific enzyme activities of the resulting extracts are shown in the figure. To 0.3 ml of tryptophan pyrrolase antiserum or control serum was added an amount of extract containing the enzyme activity indicated. The maximum amount of extract added varied from 0.25 to 10 ml. Following immunological precipitation as described under "Experimental Procedure," the supernatant fluids were assayed for tryptophan pyrrolase activity. With control sera, the results of which are not shown here, enzyme activity was detectable in the supernatant fluid when as little as 0.5 unit of enzyme activity was added. The *dashed line* indicates that no enzyme activity was detectable in the supernatant fluid.

amounts of enzyme activities were added, even though a 16-fold difference in quantity of total liver protein was added to obtain a similar amount of enzyme activity. The fact that identical amounts of protein were precipitated again indicates the specificity of the antibody for tryptophan pyrrolase protein. The equivalence point of the two extracts was similar when based on amount of added enzyme activity, in confirmation of the results of Fig. 2. The suspended antigen-antibody precipitates contained a significant amount of tryptophan pyrrolase activity, amounting to 10 to 15% of that originally precipitated. The lack of complete recovery of activity possibly is due to incomplete or total lack of dissociation of antigen from antibody during the assay or to partial blockage of the active site of the enzyme by the antibody, or to both.

The completeness of connections of the precipitin bands in Ouchterlony double diffusion analysis, and the similarity of the quantitative precipitin reactions, indicate that tryptophan pyrrolase from untreated animals is similar immunologically to that obtained from liver of animals receiving repeated administrations of hydrocortisone and tryptophan.

Isotopic Amino Acid Incorporation Studies

Studies on the incorporation of amino acids into tryptophan pyrrolase were undertaken to obtain direct evidence that hydrocortisone increases the rate of enzyme synthesis and that tryptophan decreases the rate of enzyme degradation. As a measure of the rate of synthesis, the extent of ^{14}C-L-leucine or ^{14}C-L-lysine incorporation in a short time into protein precipitated by the tryptophan pyrrolase antiserum was determined. As a control, Fig. 5 shows that treatment of animals with 0.85% NaCl, hydrocortisone, or tryptophan 3 hours prior to administration of isotopic ^{14}C-leucine did not alter the time course of disappearance of the free amino acid pool (counts soluble in trichloroacetic acid), or counts incorporated into total liver protein. A 40-minute period for isotope incorporation was chosen because at such a time the maximal amount of labeling of protein had occurred, and a minimum of time had elapsed during which enzyme was being synthesized from an amino acid pool with a low or neglible radioactivity.

Table IV shows the results of experiments on the incorporation of ^{14}C-L-lysine into tryptophan pyrrolase of rats that had received hydrocortisone or tryptophan 3 hours previously. In this table also are shown typical data on recovery of enzyme activity during the DEAE-cellulose chromatography step used prior to immunological precipitation, and the magnitude of radioactivity precipitated in the various control tubes. It can be seen that the amount of enzyme activity present in the DEAE-cellulose extract used for the immunological precipita-

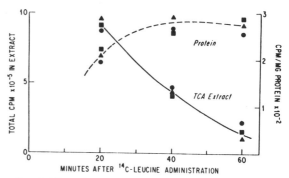

Fig. 5. Effect of hydrocortisone 21-phosphate and tryptophan administration on free pool of administered ^{14}C-L-leucine and its incorporation into liver protein. Adrenalectomized rats weighing 150 to 170 g each, six to each group, were given the following: ●——●, 10 ml of 0.85% NaCl; ■——■, hydrocortisone 21-phosphate, 5 mg subcutaneously and 5 mg intraperitoneally; or ▲——▲, 150 mg of L-tryptophan in 10 ml of 0.85% NaCl-0.05 M sodium phosphate, pH 7.4. At the time intervals specified, the livers of two animals from each group were homogenized in 9 volumes of 10% trichloroacetic acid (*TCA*). Following centrifugation, the trichloroacetic acid was removed by ether extraction, and the samples were counted for total radioactivity at infinite thinness in an end window gas flow Geiger counter. Protein was prepared and counted as described under "Experimental Procedure."

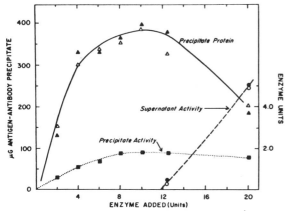

Fig. 4. Quantitative precipitin reactions of tryptophan pyrrolase. The DEAE-cellulose extracts used are described in the legend to Fig. 3. △——△, untreated animals (specific activity, 0.25 unit per mg of protein); ▲——▲, repeated administrations of hydrocortisone and tryptophan (specific activity, 4.8 units per mg of protein). To 0.3 ml of tryptophan pyrrolase antiserum was added an amount of extract containing the enzyme activity indicated. Following completion of precipitation as described under "Experimental Procedure," the supernatant fluids were assayed for enzyme activity. The precipitates were washed twice with chilled 0.85% NaCl. Enzyme activity and protein content were determined on suspensions of the washed precipitates. A similar experiment with nonimmune serum yielded no visible precipitate, and no activity absorbed to the glass.

tions was about 55 to 60% of that present in the crude homogenates. This has been a consistent finding in all preparations, irrespective of the specific enzyme activity. In extracts from control animals, with a total enzyme activity of 41 units, a total of 1406 c.p.m. were specifically precipitated by the antiserum. In extracts from hydrocortisone-treated animals, which have 180 units of enzyme activity, 9466 counts were precipitated. This difference is to be contrasted with the total counts incorporated into supernatant protein of the two extracts, i.e. 883 c.p.m. per mg versus 1120 c.p.m. per mg. These data, then, indicate that hydrocortisone increases the incorporation of radioactivity into tryptophan pyrrolase protein 7-fold. Furthermore, although tryptophan administration increased the total amount of enzyme, it did not appreciably increase the counts incorporated into tryptophan pyrrolase. This finding indicates that no increase in rate of enzyme synthesis took place as a result of tryptophan administration.

If one assumes that the pure enzyme has a specific activity of 220 units per mg of protein, it can be calculated that the specific radioactivity of the enzyme protein synthesized by the control animals would be about 15,000 c.p.m. per mg of protein as compared to 883 c.p.m. per mg in the total supernatant protein. This indicates a more rapid synthesis of tryptophan pyrrolase than of liver protein in general, and supports the concept that tryptophan pyrrolase is being rapidly synthesized and degraded under basal conditions.

Table V shows a more extensive series of studies with ^{14}C-L-leucine incorporation after varying periods of continuous administration of hydrocortisone, tryptophan, or both hydrocortisone and tryptophan, resulting in differences in specific enzyme activity from 3 to 72 units per g of liver, wet weight. Hydrocortisone administration increases isotope incorporation 4- to 5-fold, i.e. 1360 c.p.m. versus 5640 and 6503. Furthermore,

TABLE IV

Immunological precipitation of tryptophan pyrrolase from liver extracts of rats that received ^{14}C-L-lysine

Adrenalectomized rats weighing 150 to 160 g each were given single intraperitoneal injections of 10 ml of 0.85% NaCl, 8.0 mg of hydrocortisone 21-phosphate, or 150 mg of L-tryptophan in 10 ml of 0.85% NaCl. After 3 hours and 20 minutes, each animal was given an intraperitoneal injection of 20 μc of ^{14}C-L-lysine (specific activity, 80 mc per mmole) in 1 ml of 0.85% NaCl. After 40 minutes the animals were killed, and extracts were prepared for immunological precipitation as described in "Experimental Procedure." To extracts adsorbed and eluted from DEAE-cellulose were added 1.5 ml of either tryptophan pyrrolase antiserum or control serum. Procedures for precipitation, washing, and counting of the precipitates are described in "Experimental Procedure."

In all samples, sufficient extract containing a high level of tryptophan pyrrolase activity was added to precipitate 50 units of enzyme in each case. Total volumes for the precipitin reactions varied from 3.0 to 6.0 ml. The following precipitated samples were counted: A, extract plus immune serum; B, extract plus control serum; and C, supernatant from Sample A after initial precipitation, to which additional antiserum and unlabeled extract had been added. The latter two precipitates are controls for nonspecific precipitation with rabbit serum and nonspecific trapping of protein in the antigen-antibody precipitate. The data represent total enzyme activity and radioactivity precipitated in the total extract sample.

Treatment	Total enzyme activity in			^{14}C-L-Lysine incorporation				
	Homogenate	105,000 × g supernatant	DEAE-cellulose eluate	A	B	C	Net, A − (B + C)	Supernatant protein
	units/hr			*total c.p.m.*				*c.p.m./mg*
NaCl	41.1	26.0	23.1	1772	70	196	1406	883
Hydrocortisone	189	118	107	9820	92	250	9466	1120
Tryptophan	80.1	56.7	51.3	2196	108	220	1954	960

TABLE V

Forty-minute incorporation of ^{14}C-leucine into rat liver tryptophan pyrrolase

The experimental procedures are similar to those described in Table IV and "Experimental Procedure." Rats were given repeated doses of hydrocortisone or L-tryptophan, or both, at 4-hour intervals for the times indicated. Each rat was given, 40 minutes before death, a single intraperitoneal injection of 20 μc of ^{14}C-leucine (specific activity, 120 μc per mmole) in 1.0 ml of 0.85% NaCl. Results of ^{14}C-L-leucine incorporation into tryptophan pyrrolase are reported as total net counts per minute present in the precipitate from the total DEAE-cellulose extract. Total yields of enzyme activity and counts precipitated in control tubes were similar to those listed in Table IV.

Treatment	Enzyme activity	^{14}C-Leucine incorporation	
		Tryptophan pyrrolase	Supernatant protein
	units/g liver	*total c.p.m.*	*c.p.m./mg*
None	4.2	1368	1190
Hydrocortisone			
4 hours	13.6	5640	1320
12 hours	31.4	6502	1491
Tryptophan			
4 hours	8.2	1620	1564
12 hours	14.1	1670	1165
Hydrocortisone + tryptophan			
4 hours	28.3	7680	1491
12 hours	72.0	7280	1018

isotope incorporation was the same at 4 and 12 hours of repeated hydrocortisone administrations, although there was a continuing increase in specific enzyme activity, *i.e.* 13.6 and 31.4 units per hour per g of liver, wet weight. The administration of tryptophan did not increase isotope incorporation, although there was an increase in specific enzyme activity to 8.2 and 14.1 units per g at 4 and 12 hours, respectively. The concomitant administration of tryptophan and hydrocortisone increased the incorporation of ^{14}C-leucine to an extent similar to that produced

by hydrocortisone alone. The differences in incorporation of counts into tryptophan pyrrolase are to be contrasted with the similarity of counts incorporated into total supernatant protein. These data are in agreement with the data on ^{14}C-lysine incorporation and indicate that hydrocortisone administration increases the rate of enzyme synthesis whereas tryptophan administration does not.

As a measure of the rate of degradation, the rate of loss of radioactivity from prelabeled enzyme was determined. For this type of experiment, the isotope should be essentially removed from the free amino acid pool so that no more isotope is incorporated into the protein. That this condition was fulfilled is shown by Fig. 5, where it can be seen that by 60 minutes the trichloroacetic acid-soluble counts comprised only 10% of the counts present at 20 minutes after isotope administration. Furthermore, isotope incorporation into protein had been essentially completed, since there was no increase in specific radioactivity of the protein during the period between 40 and 60 minutes after administration. In other experiments, extended to 4 hours, no further incorporation into protein could be demonstrated.

Tryptophan stabilization of tryptophan pyrrolase *in vivo* is shown in the experiment of Fig. 6. In this experiment all animals were given a single intraperitoneal injection of 20 μc of ^{14}C-L-leucine. After 60 minutes, maximal incorporation of isotope into protein had occurred, and the amount of radioactivity in the free amino acid pool was approaching zero (Fig. 5). At this time, designated as zero time in the figure, animals were given intraperitoneal injections of 0.85% NaCl (control) or tryptophan solutions. At 3-hour intervals two animals were killed, and tryptophan pyrrolase protein was precipitated by immunological procedures. The results are presented as total counts precipitable with antibody from the combined extracts of two animals.

In control animals, in which the total amount of enzyme remained constant, there was a rapid loss of total counts precipitable with the antiserum, such that by the end of 9 hours only 7% of the counts present at zero time remained. This finding

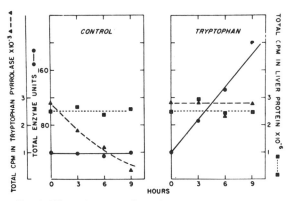

FIG. 6. Effect of L-tryptophan administration on the loss of tryptophan pyrrolase prelabeled with ¹⁴C-L-leucine. A total of 14 adrenalectomized rats weighing 150 to 160 g each were given single injections of 20 μc of ¹⁴C-L-leucine. Sixty minutes later, two animals were killed. The remainder were given 10 ml of 0.85% NaCl or 10 ml of 0.85% NaCl containing 150 mg of L-tryptophan. These injections were repeated in the remaining animals after 4 and 8 hours. At the times specified, the livers of two animals in each group were removed and frozen immediately. At the end of the experiment, extracts of the livers were prepared and the radioactivity incorporated into tryptophan pyrrolase and protein was determined as described under "Experimental Procedure." The values given represent total enzyme activity present in the combined extracts of two animals (●——●). CPM (counts per minute) represents total radioactivity present in protein precipitated by the tryptophan pyrrolase antiserum (▲- - -▲) or in total cellular protein (■-----■) from two livers.

shows that tryptophan pyrrolase is continually being replaced in the normal animal. This loss of total counts is to be contrasted with the loss that occurred when tryptophan was administered to the animals. In this case the enzyme which had been prelabeled remained in the liver, as evidenced by the complete retention of the prelabeled counts in tryptophan pyrrolase. The increase in enzyme activity produced by the tryptophan administration, then, results from a stabilization of the enzyme which accumulates because of continued synthesis at a rate similar to that which occurs in the control animal, as indicated by the incorporation data of Tables IV and V.

It is also of interest that the rate of loss of isotope from prelabeled tryptophan pyrrolase in the control animals (Fig. 6) is very similar to the rate of decay of enzyme activity in animals in which the enzyme level had been increased by administrations of tryptophan and hydrocortisone (26, 27). The similarities of these rates of decay indicate that tryptophan pyrrolase of normal animals has the same stability as that in animals that have received hydrocortisone and tryptophan.

DISCUSSION

The results of two independent experimental approaches have indicated that different mechanisms are involved in the hormonal and substrate-mediated accumulation ("induction") of rat liver tryptophan pyrrolase protein. An increase in the rate of enzyme synthesis accounts for the enzyme increase produced by hydrocortisone administration. A decrease in the rate of enzyme degradation accounts for the enzyme increase produced by tryptophan administration. The term

"induction," then, as applied to the phenomenon of changing enzyme levels in animal tissues, is ambiguous, inasmuch as at least two mechanisms can be involved. The time course of increases in tryptophan pyrrolase produced by the administration of hydrocortisone or tryptophan, or both (Fig. 1), was consistent with a theoretical model in which hydrocortisone increased the rate of enzyme synthesis and tryptophan decreased the rate of enzyme degradation (27). The isotopic amino acid studies have confirmed these conclusions. Hence the 5- to 6-fold increase in isotopic amino acid incorporated into tryptophan pyrrolase following hydrocortisone administration (Table IV and V) indicated the stimulation of enzyme synthesis. The effect of tryptophan in stabilizing tryptophan pyrrolase was shown by Fig. 6, in which radioactivity in prelabeled enzyme was not lost when tryptophan was administered, as opposed to its rapid loss in untreated animals. Although stabilization can account for the increases in tryptophan pyrrolase produced by tryptophan administration in the experiments presented here, a second effect of tryptophan in facilitating the synthesis of the enzyme has not been rigorously excluded. The possibility of such a second effect of tryptophan is being studied.

The existence of enzyme stabilization as a mechanism for the accumulation of enzyme protein is dependent on the occurrence of turnover of the enzyme protein under normal conditions. Evidence for the rapid turnover of tryptophan pyrrolase, i.e. rapid removal and resynthesis, is based on the following findings: (a) an exponential decay of enzyme activity following stimulation of enzyme to high levels (26, 27), (b) a 15-fold greater uptake of isotope into tryptophan pyrrolase protein than into total liver protein within a 40-minute incorporation period, (c) loss of isotope from prelabeled tryptophan pyrrolase protein at a rate similar to the decay of enzyme activity (26, 27), and (d) decay of basal enzyme activity during repeated administrations of inhibitors of protein synthesis (41, 42).

The studies presented indicated that tryptophan administration results in stabilization of the enzyme in vivo, thereby accounting for the accumulation of enzyme by preventing its normal, rapid degradation while synthesis continues at the normal rate. Substrate stabilization of tryptophan pyrrolase was first suggested by Lee in 1956 (43) on the basis of his finding of a linear increase in enzyme activity during a 4-hour period following administration of tryptophan to nonadrenalectomized rats. Dubnoff and Dimick showed that tryptophan protected against inactivation of the enzyme in crude liver homogenates and therefore suggested that stabilization in vivo might be the mechanism of the tryptophan effect (44). Certain findings suggest that the stable form of the enzyme is that in which the iron-porphyrin cofactor (hematin) is bound to it, a binding that is facilitated by the presence of tryptophan (36). Thus, following tryptophan administration, tryptophan pyrrolase continues to accumulate at a time when the level of the substrate has fallen to normal levels (25, 43). This is a time when the enzyme continues to be saturated with respect to hematin (45). The nature of the changes in the enzyme imparted by the presence of hematin or tryptophan, or both, which accounts for resistance to degradation is unknown. In view of the widespread ability of substrates to protect enzymes against various forms of denaturation, and the known ability of proteolytic enzymes to degrade denatured proteins (46), it may be that stabilization involves the maintenance of tryptophan pyrrolase in a conformational state resistant to enzymatic attack. Preliminary studies[1] have indicated that tryptophan indeed protects the purified enzyme from various forms of denaturation and proteolytic attack.

In addition to the effect of corticosteroid administration on the synthesis of tryptophan pyrrolase demonstrated in this paper, corticosteroids have also been shown to increase the rate of synthesis of tyrosine-glutamate transaminase (14) and glutamate-alanine transaminase (15). In both of these cases the data indicate that the rate of enzyme synthesis has been increased about 3- to 4-fold over control rates, an increase approximating the 5- to 6-fold increase found for tryptophan pyrrolase in this paper. The effect of corticosteroids, then, is analogous to enzyme induction in bacteria in that the rate of enzyme synthesis has been increased.

In view of the specificity of enzyme induction in bacteria (13), the question arises whether the effect of corticosteroids in increasing the rate of enzyme synthesis is specific for a group of enzymes of which tryptophan pyrrolase, tyrosine-glutamic transaminase, and glutamic-alanine transaminase are members, or whether corticosteroids increase the rate of synthesis of a large number of liver proteins. The finding that the incorporation of isotope into total cellular protein is increased only 20 to 30% by the administration of corticosteroids (15, 47), as opposed to the 300 to 600% increases for the above enzymes, would suggest a specificity for the corticosteroid response. However, certain other findings suggest that the corticosteroid effect is relatively nonspecific. Continuous corticosteroid administration for 6 days has been found to increase the total nitrogen content per liver cell 100% (48). Furthermore, a large number of enzyme activities are increased by the administration of corticosteroids (1–3, 6, 48, 49). The apparent specificity of corticosteroids in increasing the level of a particular enzyme relative to another enzyme or total liver protein does not necessarily indicate a specificity for increasing the rate of synthesis of that enzyme, but may in fact only reflect a high rate of turnover of the enzyme. For example, increases in tryptophan pyrrolase produced by hydrocortisone would appear to be specific, since another enzyme, arginase, does not change remarkably during the same 16-hour period (Table II). However, if the disparity in rates of turnover is considered, *i.e.* 2 to 3 hours for tryptophan pyrrolase *versus* 5 days for arginase (12), then the time courses of increases are entirely consistent with a comparable increase in the rate of synthesis of both enzymes. In view of the heterogeneity of turnover rates of various enzymes (12, 14, 15, 26, 50), specificity of an effect for a given enzyme cannot be concluded on the basis of differential changes in enzyme levels as studied during the short time periods. Thus it may be that the administration of corticosteroids increases the rate of synthesis of a large number of liver proteins 4- to 6-fold, and that the apparent specificity for a given enzyme is related only to its relatively high rate of turnover.

The ability of rat liver to degrade tryptophan is carefully controlled by a variety of mechanisms: (a) activation of the apoenzyme by combination with an iron-porphyrin cofactor as shown by Greengard and Feigelson (45), (b) accumulation of enzyme as a result of substrate stabilization in the presence of continued enzyme synthesis, and (c) accumulation of enzyme as a result of stimulation of the rate of enzyme synthesis. Any one of these mechanisms may be operational, depending on the immediate demands on the organism. Hence the presence of a

[1] Unpublished observations.

small amount of tryptophan might involve only the activation phenomenon, whereas in the presence of a continual supply of tryptophan, stabilization of enzyme would occur. An increased rate of enzyme synthesis might become operative only under more drastic or stressful conditions in which a rapid increase in enzyme content would be required. In view of the multiplicity of mechanisms for the control of activity of this one enzyme, it is likely that control of enzyme activities in animal tissues exists at any point at which it can be potentially exerted, that is, at the level of genetic expression, polypeptide synthesis, subunit interaction, enzyme-cofactor interaction, and enzyme degradation, as well as on enzyme activation and inhibition.

SUMMARY

The mechanisms for the separate effects of hydrocortisone and tryptophan administration in increasing tryptophan pyrrolase levels of rat liver have been investigated. Alterations in the rates of enzyme synthesis and enzyme degradation are both important in controlling the level of tryptophan pyrrolase. An analysis of the time course of changing enzyme levels and results of isotope incorporation studies indicate that hydrocortisone administration increases the rate of enzyme synthesis, whereas tryptophan administration decreases the rate of degradation of the enzyme.

Two general mechanisms, then, function to result in the accumulation of newly synthesized enzyme protein in animal tissues (enzyme "induction"): (a) an increase in the rate of enzyme synthesis and (b) a decrease in the rate of enzyme degradation. It is suggested that alterations in rates of enzyme synthesis are mediated by hormonal action, whereas substrates or cofactors act by altering the rate of enzyme degradation.

REFERENCES

1. Knox, W. E., and Mehler, A. H., *Science*, **113**, 237 (1951).
2. Lin, E. C. C., and Knox, W. E., *J. Biol. Chem.*, **233**, 1186 (1958).
3. Rosen, F., Roberts, N. F., and Nicol, C. A., *J. Biol. Chem.*, **234**, 476 (1959).
4. Conney, A. H., and Gilman, A. G., *J. Biol. Chem.*, **238**, 3682 (1963).
5. Schimke, R. T., *J. Biol. Chem.*, **237**, 459 (1962).
6. Knox, W. E., Auerbach, V. H., and Lin, E. C. C., *Physiol. Revs.*, **36**, 164 (1956).
7. Freedland, R. A., and Harper, A. E., *J. Biol. Chem.*, **234**, 1350 (1959).
8. Weber, G., and McDonald, A., *Exptl. Cell Research*, **22**, 292 (1961).
9. Kenney, F. T., *J. Biol. Chem.*, **237**, 1610 (1962).
10. Segal, H. L., Rosso, R. G., Hopper, S., and Weber, M. M., *J. Biol. Chem.*, **237**, PC3303 (1962).
11. Feigelson, P., and Greengard, O., *J. Biol. Chem.*, **237**, 3714 (1962).
12. Schimke, R. T., *J. Biol. Chem.*, **239**, 3808 (1964).
13. Jacob, F., and Monod, J., *J. Molecular Biol.*, **3**, 318 (1961).
14. Kenney, F. T., *J. Biol. Chem.*, **237**, 3495 (1962).
15. Segal, H. L., and Kim, Y. S., *Proc. Natl. Acad. Sci. U. S.*, **50**, 912 (1963).
16. Ussing, H. H., *Acta Physiol. Scand.*, **2**, 209 (1941).
17. Thompson, R. G., and Ballou, J. R., *J. Biol. Chem.*, **223**, 795 (1956).
18. Swick, R. W., *J. Biol. Chem.*, **231**, 751 (1959).
19. Buchanan, D. L., *Arch. Biochem. Biophys.*, **94**, 501 (1961).
20. Schoenheimer, R., *The dynamic state of body constituents*, Harvard University Press, Cambridge 1942.
21. Lee, N. D., and Williams, R. H., *Biochim. et Biophys. Acta*, **9**, 698 (1952).

22. GREENGARD, O., SMITH, M. A., AND ACS, G., *J. Biol. Chem.*, **238**, 1548 (1963).
23. KNOX, W. E., AND AUERBACH, V. H., *J. Biol. Chem.*, **214**, 307 (1955).
24. HORTON, H. R., AND FRANZ, J. M., *Endocrinology*, **64**, 258 (1959).
25. CIVEN, M., AND KNOX, W. E., *J. Biol. Chem.*, **234**, 1787 (1959).
26. FEIGELSON, P., DASHMAN, T., AND MARGOLIS, F., *Arch. Biochem. Biophys.*, **85**, 478 (1959).
27. SCHIMKE, R. T., SWEENEY, F. T., AND BERLIN, C. M., *Biochem. and Biophys. Research Communs.*, **15**, 214 (1964).
28. MELBY, J. C., AND ST. CYR, M., *Metabolism, Clin. and Exptl.*, **10**, 75 (1961).
29. KNOX, W. E., AND MEHLER, A. J., *J. Biol. Chem.*, **187**, 419 (1950).
30. FEIGELSON, P., AND GREENGARD, O., *J. Biol. Chem.*, **236**, 153 (1961).
31. TOKUYAMA, K., AND KNOX, W. E., *Biochim. et Biophys. Acta*, **81**, 281 (1964).
32. KNOX, W. E., in S. P. COLOWICK AND N. O. KAPLAN (Editors), *Methods in enzymology, Vol. II*, Academic Press, Inc., New York, 1955, p. 246.
33. GORNALL, A. G., BARDAWILL, C. J., AND DAVID, M. M., *J. Biol. Chem.*, **177**, 751 (1949).
34. PORATH, J., AND FLODIN, P., *Nature*, **183**, 1657 (1959).
35. SOBER, H. A., AND PETERSON, E. A., *J. Am. Chem. Soc.*, **76**, 1711 (1954).
36. FEIGELSON, P., AND GREENGARD, O., *J. Biol. Chem.*, **237**, 1908 (1962).
37. LESKOWITZ, S., AND WAKSMAN, B., *J. Immunol.*, **84**, 58 (1960).
38. KABAT, E. A., AND MAYER, M. M., *Experimental immunochemistry*, Charles C Thomas, Springfield, Illinois, 1961, p. 22.
39. SIEKEVITZ, P., *J. Biol. Chem.*, **195**, 549 (1952).
40. CIVEN, M., AND KNOX, W. E., *J. Biol. Chem.*, **235**, 1716 (1960).
41. NEMETH, A. M., *J. Biol. Chem.*, **237**, 3703 (1962).
42. GOLDSTEIN, L., STELLA, E. J., AND KNOX, W. E., *J. Biol. Chem.*, **237**, 1723 (1962).
43. LEE, N. D., *J. Biol. Chem.*, **219**, 211 (1956).
44. DUBNOFF, J. W., AND DIMICK, M., *Biochim. et Biophys. Acta*, **31**, 541 (1959).
45. GREENGARD, O., AND FEIGELSON, P., *J. Biol. Chem.*, **236**, 158 (1964).
46. LINDERSTRØM-LANG, K., *Cold Spring Harbor symposia on quantitative biology, No. 15*, Long Island Biological Association, Cold Spring Harbor, New York, 1950, p. 117.
47. FEIGELSON, P., AND FEIGELSON, M., *J. Biol. Chem.*, **238**, 1073 (1963).
48. WEBER, G., AND SINGHAL, R. L., *J. Biol. Chem.*, **239**, 521 (1964).
49. SCHIMKE, R. T., *J. Biol. Chem.*, **238**, 1012 (1963).
50. PRICE, V. E., STERLING, W. R., TARANTOLA, V. A., HARTLEY, R. W., JR., AND RECHCIGL, M., *J. Biol. Chem.*, **237**, 3468 (1962).

THE JOURNAL OF BIOLOGICAL CHEMISTRY
Vol. 242, No. 12, Issue of June 25, pp. 2952-2958, 1967
Printed in U.S.A.

Tryptophan Pyrrolase of Liver

II. THE ACTIVATING REACTIONS IN CRUDE PREPARATIONS FROM RAT LIVER*

(Received for publication, February 13, 1967)

MARTA M. PIRAS‡ AND W. EUGENE KNOX

From the Department of Biological Chemistry, Harvard Medical School, and the Cancer Research Institute, New England Deaconess Hospital, Boston, Massachusetts 02215

SUMMARY

The activation of the apoenzyme of tryptophan pyrrolase in preparations from hydrocortisone-induced rats was shown to consist of two separate, sequential steps, only the second of which is necessary to activate preparations from tryptophan-induced rats. These reactions are as follows. (*a*) Conjugation of the apoenzyme to the oxidized holoenzyme with hematin supplied by added methemoglobin, a reaction which requires the presence of L-tryptophan or certain analogues and which is inhibited by thiol reagents as well as by globin. (*b*) Reduction of the oxidized holoenzyme, a reaction which is promoted by L-tryptophan specifically and by ascorbate. It is reversed by oxidation in air in the absence of L-tryptophan.

Conjugation is the more rapid of the two reactions, especially at lower temperatures. The over-all activation is, therefore, limited by the rate of reduction.

The sites on the apoenzyme and the holoenzyme that react with L-tryptophan for conjugation and catalysis, respectively, are different. They are distinguished by the wider specificity and higher affinity of the site on the apoenzyme involved in conjugation.

The tryptophan pyrrolase (L-tryptophan:oxygen oxidoreductase, EC 1.13.1.12, tryptophan oxygenase) in soluble fractions of rat liver is substantially inactive until incubated with tryptophan, methemoglobin, and ascorbate (1). This activation is equally necessary for preparations of the enzyme from rats treated with tryptophan (unless tryptophan is added during the preparation (2, 3)) as well as from rats treated with hydrocortisone. The enzyme as prepared from tryptophan-treated

* This investigation was supported by United States Public Health Service Grant AM 00567, by Research Career Award AM-K6-2018 from the National Institute of Arthritis and Metabolic Diseases of the National Institutes of Health, United States Public Health Service, and by United States Atomic Energy Commission Contract AT(30-1)-901 with the New England Deaconess Hospital.

‡ Present address, Universidad de Buenos Aires, Cátedra de Química Biológica Patológica, Facultad de Farmacia y Bioquímica, Buenos Aires, Argentina.

This is reprint No. 370 of the Cancer Research Institute of the New England Deaconess Hospital.

rats is largely conjugated with its hematin prosthetic group although that from hydrocortisone-treated rats is mostly the apoenzyme, as indicated by the effects on the activities of either omitting methemoglobin (1, 4) or adding globin (3) to prevent the occurrence of conjugation during incubation of the enzyme. These facts indicate that the activation involves a conjugation in the hydrocortisone type of preparation, and also another reaction common to both types of enzyme preparations. This other reaction appears to be a reduction of the oxidized holoenzyme, because ascorbate is needed in the incubation mixture (1, 3) and because the active enzyme is the reduced holoenzyme (ferroporphyrin form) (5). However, it was not established whether the oxidized holoenzyme was a normal intermediate or whether conjugation plus reduction to the reduced holoenzyme occurred in one reaction, because the oxidized holoenzyme could also be formed secondarily by oxidation in air (3). This latter possibility was excluded in the present experiments, and activation was then shown to consist of a separate conjugation reaction involving a thiol group on the protein and forming the oxidized holoenzyme, followed by its reduction to the active reduced holoenzyme.

METHODS

Adult female and male NEDH inbred rats were treated 5 hours before use with 2.5 mg of hydrocortisone acetate or 100 mg of L-tryptophan per 100 g of body weight. The livers were homogenized in 3 volumes of 0.14 M KCl-0.02 M sodium phosphate, pH 7.0, and centrifuged for 1 hour at 78,000 × *g*. The supernatant fraction was used for all experiments. The liver tryptophan pyrrolase averaged 20 and 30 μmoles per hour per g of liver (25°), respectively, in the hydrocortisone- and tryptophan-induced preparations.

The standard assay of tryptophan pyrrolase activity depended upon the increase in absorbance at 360 mμ (kynurenine, $\epsilon = 4530$) in 1-cm cuvettes in a Gilford spectrophotometer at 25°. The mixture contained 0.4 ml of 12.5% liver extract, 0.7 ml of 0.2 M sodium phosphate (pH 7.0), 0.2 mg of methemoglobin, 0.2 ml of 0.05 M L-tryptophan, and 0.1 ml of freshly neutralized 0.3 M ascorbate, in a total volume of 3.0 ml. The activities were calculated from the initial rates during the first 20 min, and expressed as units (micromoles of kynurenine formed per hour) per g of liver (25°).

Prior to assay, incubation of concentrated (12.5%) or dilute (1.7%) liver extracts under a variety of conditions was employed to activate the tryptophan pyrrolase. Incubation of the former for 30 min at 37° in air ("concentrated incubation") provided the standard activating system to which other activating systems were compared. The final concentrations in the concentrated incubation mixture were 12.5% liver extract, 2.5 mM L-tryptophan, 0.5 mg of methemoglobin per ml, and 30 mM freshly neutralized ascorbate. At least 1 ml of this mixture was incubated at a time in test tubes. The same type of incubation was also done in nitrogen and in two stages by use of Thunberg tubes with side arms.

The "diluted incubation" of 1.7% liver extract consisted of the mixture used in the standard assay, placed in evacuated and nitrogen-filled Thunberg tubes when anaerobic, and with necessary additions made from the side arm. L-Tryptophan was present or added for protection of the reduced holoenzyme before the tubes were opened to the air after the incubation period. The mixture was poured into cuvettes and immediately assayed.

The degree of conjugation of a preparation was measured by the fraction of the total activity found when 0.5 mg of globin per ml was added to the concentrated incubation mixture and methemoglobin was omitted. A larger amount of globin, sufficient to prevent further conjugation, was added to the second of two sequential incubations of concentrated (Table IV) and dilute (Tables III and VI, Figs. 3 and 4) mixtures. In this way the conditions for conjugation during the first incubation could be determined separately from the conditions for reduction in the second incubation.

RESULTS

Oxidation of Reduced Holoenzyme—The possibility that the oxidized holoenzyme is an intermediate in the activation of the apotryptophan pyrrolase could not be assessed in the kind of aerobic activations previously used (1), because of the alternative possibility that oxidized holoenzyme could be formed by oxidation in air of the reduced holoenzyme (3). As shown in Table I, aerobic dialysis of the reduced holoenzyme to remove L-tryptophan resulted in the loss of enzyme activity. The inactive, oxidized holoenzyme that was formed was previously identified by its reactivation in the presence of globin (3). The

TABLE I

Preservation of tryptophan pyrrolase activity during aerobic and anaerobic dialyses

Fully activated 12.5% liver fractions (17.6 to 60 units per g of liver) were dialyzed for 4 hours at 5° against 0.14 M KCl-0.02 M sodium phosphate, pH 7.0, in closed bottles with the gas phases and the additions indicated. After the dialyses with N₂ and CO, 5 mM L-tryptophan was added before the admission of air, and the solutions were shaken in O₂ to remove CO (1). The results are the averages from two or three preparations, expressed as percentage of the activity present before dialysis.

Gas phase	Additions to dialysis		
	L-Tryptophan (5 mM)	None	α-Methyltryptophan (5 mM)
	% activity preserved		
Air	81	10	26
N₂		81	
CO		97	

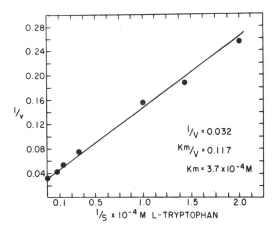

Fig. 1. Concentrations of L-tryptophan preventing oxidation of reduced holoenzyme. Activated tryptophan pyrrolase (24 units per g of liver) freed of L-tryptophan by dialysis under nitrogen (Table I) was added, without prior exposure to air, to the aerobic assay mixtures containing the indicated concentrations of L-tryptophan ($S = 10^{-4}$ M) and the activity was measured for 2 min (v). Excess (1.66 mM) L-tryptophan was then added without change in the activity. The same activities were obtained in the presence of 0.1 mM α-methyltryptophan. The three sets of activity measurements were averaged.

activity loss was prevented by the presence of L-tryptophan, but not by α-methyltryptophan. The loss was also prevented in the absence of L-tryptophan by dialysis under anaerobic conditions with N₂ or CO, which preserved the reduced holoenzyme.

After anaerobic dialysis in the absence of L-tryptophan, the reduced holoenzyme was still oxidized promptly when exposed to air, unless tryptophan had been added for protection, as was done in the experiments of Table I. The rapidity of this aerobic oxidation of the reduced holoenzyme and the concentration of L-tryptophan necessary to prevent this oxidation were measured by adding the dialyzed, reduced holoenzyme to aerobic assay mixtures containing different concentrations of L-tryptophan. The reduced holoenzyme was prepared from a fully activated enzyme dialyzed free of tryptophan under nitrogen as in Table I. It was added to the aerobic assay mixtures without prior exposure to air and promptly assayed. The reactions began immediately at linear rates.

The full activity of the reduced holoenzyme was preserved when it was added to assay mixtures containing more than 1 mM L-tryptophan. With less tryptophan present, there was an immediate loss of activity. The remaining activity for at least 15 min was proportional to the tryptophan concentration present in the assay mixture. The loss was not immediately reversible by tryptophan since excess tryptophan (1.66 mM) added 2 min later did not change the reaction rate for the next 15 min. The inactivation was reversible, but only by excess tryptophan and the removal of oxygen in a short anaerobic incubation. The effect of L-tryptophan concentration on the preservation of the reduced holoenzyme activity under aerobic conditions is shown in Fig. 1 as a double reciprocal plot. The half-maximal protection occurred with 3.7×10^{-4} M L-tryptophan, a value comparable to those previously reported

TABLE II

Relative activation of tryptophan pyrrolase in diluted and concentrated liver extracts with anaerobic and aerobic incubation

Hydrocortisone-induced supernatant fractions kept frozen for several days with activities averaging 20 units per g of liver were incubated for 30 min at 37° in wide test tubes (aerobic) or in evacuated and nitrogen-filled Thunberg tubes (anaerobic) with the quantities of additions described under "Methods." The dilute incubation mixtures were equivalent to the standard assay mixtures (0.2 ml of 25% liver extract in 3 ml). The additions missing from the incubation were added just before assay (in the anaerobic incubations from a side arm before opening the Thunberg tubes to air). Results are the averages of at least four preparations, expressed as the percentage of activity obtained in the complete concentrated system incubated aerobically.

Additions	Condition of incubation at 37° for 30 min			
	Concentrated (12.5%)		Diluted (1.7%)	
	Air	N₂	Air	N₂
	% standard activity		*% standard activity*	
None	12	27		12
Methemoglobin	11	60		13
Methemoglobin + L-tryptophan	57	101		42
Methemoglobin + L-tryptophan + ascorbate	100	110	52	89

as the K_m for the tryptophan pyrrolase reaction (6–8), which presumably also measured the protection of the active form. The presence of α-methyltryptophan in the assay mixtures did not prevent this inactivation, just as it did not protect the reduced holoenzyme during aerobic dialysis (Table I).

Requirements for Activation in Anaerobic, Concentrated and Dilute Systems—The requirements for the activation were restudied with the precautions of anaerobiosis and addition of L-tryptophan before air outlined above. The inadequacy of methemoglobin alone and the need for tryptophan and ascorbate for activation were evident from previous studies in the usual aerobic incubation of concentrated (12.5%) liver extracts (1) (first column of Table II). With anaerobic incubation of the concentrated liver extract, slightly more activity was obtained. However, anaerobiosis decreased the need for L-tryptophan and eliminated the need for ascorbate (second column), making impossible the separation of conjugation from reduction. As seen in the last column, dilute (1.7%) systems were also almost fully activated under anaerobic conditions, and had the advantage of requiring both tryptophan and ascorbate. It was not attempted to show these requirements in the dilute system aerobically, because this system could not be fully activated (third column).

Dissociation of Conjugation from Reduction—In the dilute, anaerobic system of Table II, omission of ascorbate resulted in less than maximal reduction. Anaerobiosis prevented the alternative formation of oxidized holoenzyme from reduced holoenzyme. It was therefore possible in this system to determine whether the oxidized holoenzyme was an intermediate in the activation of the apotryptophan pyrrolase by letting it accumulate in a first incubation in the absence of ascorbate and then determining the conjugated enzyme by the extra

activity obtained after reduction in a second incubation where globin prevented further conjugation.

Added globin can be used to prevent conjugation without resolving the already conjugated enzyme (3). It was only necessary to show that globin, without preventing reduction, would stop conjugation by the amount of methemoglobin added for optimal conjugation in the first incubation. As shown in Fig. 2, quite small concentrations of added methemoglobin (0.1 mg per ml) were sufficient for nearly maximal conjugation of both the hydrocortisone- and tryptophan-induced preparations from perfused livers. The addition of 0.5 mg of globin per ml of the incubation mixture prevented the conjugation by endogenous hematin and also largely prevented the conjugation by added methemoglobin. The globin nearly neutralized the effect of an equal weight of methemoglobin, yet it did not interfere with the reductive activation of the oxidized holoenzyme present in the tryptophan-induced preparations.

The first column in Table III shows the activities obtained after anaerobic incubation of diluted enzyme with different additions, like those in Table II. The second column shows the result of reincubating the same preparations in the presence of ascorbate and tryptophan and with added globin. This second incubation did not change the activity of the already fully supplemented preparations (last line) but increased the activity of all the others. Since globin prevented further conjugation, only reduction could have occurred during the second incubation. The difference between Columns 2 and 1, shown in Column 3, represents that fraction of the enzyme which became conjugated but not reduced during the first incubation. Since it was subsequently activated in the presence of globin and the complete system, this fraction was the oxidized holoenzyme. This fraction was often greater than that which was both conjugated and reduced in the first incubation. In

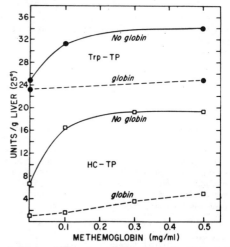

FIG. 2. The activity of tryptophan-induced (*Trp*) (●) and hydrocortisone-induced (*HC*) (□) tryptophan pyrrolase (*TP*) after concentrated, aerobic incubation at 37° for 30 min with increasing concentrations of methemoglobin (——), plus additions of 0.5 mg of globin per ml (– – –). Preparations were made from livers perfused with cold 0.9% NaCl immediately after death to minimize their blood content.

the presence of tryptophan, without ascorbate 61% was only conjugated and later reduced. In the presence of α-methyltryptophan (with or without ascorbate) at least 71% was conjugated and only 22% was conjugated and also reduced.

Inspection of Table III reveals that there was very little activity after the first incubation with α-methyltryptophan, even in the presence of ascorbate, although with L-tryptophan and ascorbate the activation was complete. Yet with α-methyltryptophan, the activation after the second incubation in the presence of globin and L-tryptophan was nearly complete. It is apparent that α-methyltryptophan permitted conjugation but not reduction, and that the second incubation with L-tryptophan and ascorbate was necessary for the reduction. Thus both α-methyltryptophan and L-tryptophan facilitated conjugation, but only L-tryptophan permitted the reduction of the inactive, oxidized holoenzyme formed by the conjugation. Ascorbate was not necessary for the conjugation, but facilitated the reduction. The nature of the measurements made in Table III also established that the conjugation of the apotryptophan pyrrolase in the first incubation preceded the reduction in the second incubation.

Affinities of Tryptophan Analogues for Conjugation and Reduction—α-Methyltryptophan and some other tryptophan analogues did not replace L-tryptophan for the over-all activation in the concentrated, aerobic system (1). Since α-methyltryptophan replaced L-tryptophan for the conjugation, the other compounds were also tested for their ability to permit conjugation. The two-step experiments were like those of Table III but in aerobic, concentrated incubations like the earlier experiments. The tested compounds permitted conjugation. They did not activate because they did not promote reduction. The concentrations of several compounds giving half-maximal conjugation as determined by double reciprocal plots are given in Table IV. L-Tryptophan was effective for conjugation ($K_m = 2.6 \times 10^{-5}$ M) in one-tenth the concentration effective in preventing oxidation of the reduced holoenzyme (apparent $K_m = 3.7 \times 10^{-4}$ M, Fig. 1). The K_m values of D-tryptophan and α-methyltryptophan were twice that for L-tryptophan, suggesting that the D isomers were relatively ineffective and that the L isomers of tryptophan and α-methyltryptophan were equally effective for conjugation. This specificity and affinity distinguishes the site of tryptophan reaction with the enzyme for conjugation from the site for catalysis. D-Tryptophan itself also permitted conjugation, but it was tested only at the high concentration of 5 mM. 5-Methyl-DL-tryptophan also permitted conjugation, but it was also required in a high concentration.

The concentration of L-tryptophan needed for reduction was also determined. Oxidized holoenzyme, prepared by dialysis in air of a fully activated preparation as in Table I, was incubated in nitrogen with ascorbate and L-tryptophan. It was activated with the same small concentrations of L-tryptophan that were effective in conjugation. The results, shown by a double reciprocal graph in Fig. 3, indicate a K_m for reduction of 1.7×10^{-5} M L-tryptophan. This was not significantly different from the value for the over-all activation of conjugation plus reduction in the same experiments, and not different from the observed K_m for conjugation that was also determined in concentrated mixtures (2.6×10^{-5} M, Table IV). Miss Jeanne Li kindly determined the K_m of L-tryptophan for reduction in dilute mixtures, after conjugation with α-methyltryptophan

TABLE III

Conjugation without reduction of tryptophan pyrrolase demonstrated by second incubation in presence of globin

A hydrocortisone-induced preparation (0.2 ml) was first incubated anaerobically for 30 min at 37° with 0.2 mg of methemoglobin and 0.7 ml of 0.02 M sodium phosphate (pH 7.0) in a total volume of 2.7 ml, plus the additions listed in the table (0.2 ml of 0.05 M L-tryptophan or α-methyltryptophan, 0.1 ml of 0.3 M ascorbate). At the end of this incubation 0.3 ml containing 1.5 mg of globin plus the additions omitted during the first incubation period were tipped in from a side arm. The solutions were aerated and immediately assayed (first column). Duplicate tubes with the additions after the first incubation were kept unopened, and were incubated for a second 30-min period at 37°, and then assayed (second column). The results are expressed as percentage of the activity obtained under these conditions with the complete system of methemoglobin, L-tryptophan, and ascorbate (28.8 units per g). The difference (third column) represents the enzyme that was conjugated but not reduced in the first incubation.

Additions	After first incubation	After second incubation (with globin)	Difference
	% activity		
Methemoglobin only	11	39	28
Methemoglobin + ascorbate		43	
Methemoglobin + α-methyltryptophan	11	93	82
Methemoglobin + α-methyltryptophan + ascorbate	22	93	71
Methemoglobin + L-tryptophan	47	108	61
Methemoglobin + L-tryptophan + ascorbate	100	100	0

TABLE IV

Concentrations for half-maximal conjugation of tryptophan pyrrolase

Hydrocortisone-induced preparations (12.5% liver extract) were incubated 30 min at 37° with 0.4 mg of methemoglobin per ml and with methemoglobin plus various concentrations of tryptophan or its analogues. The incubations with L- and DL-tryptophan were anaerobic to avoid loss of substrate. At the end of the incubation, 0.5 mg of globin per ml, excess L-tryptophan, and ascorbate were added and the incubation was continued for 30 min in air. The concentrations of analogues and the activities, less that with methemoglobin alone, were plotted in double reciprocal graphs to determine the K_m values.

Compound	K_m for conjugation
	μM
L-Tryptophan[a]	26
DL-Tryptophan[a]	52
α-Methyl-DL-tryptophan	53
5-Methyl-DL-tryptophan	2500

[a] Anaerobic incubations.

and addition of globin and ascorbate, and this was 7.1×10^{-5} M. Both values were clearly less than the apparent K_m for catalysis and for the prevention of oxidation (3.7×10^{-4} M, Fig. 1) that were determined in dilute solutions.

Kinetics of Activation of Tryptophan Pyrrolase—The soluble liver fractions from 12.5% homogenates incubated in air with

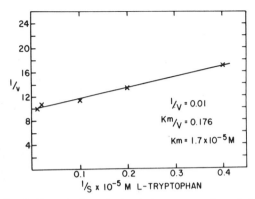

FIG. 3. Concentrations of L-tryptophan necessary for reduction of the oxidized holoenzyme. Three activated preparations, 25 units per g of liver, were dialyzed in air as in Table I. They were incubated at 12.5% concentration in nitrogen for 30 min at 37° with ascorbate and the indicated concentrations of L-tryptophan ($S = 10^{-5}$ M). Excess L-tryptophan was added before admission of air and the activity immediately determined. The activity, less the blank activation in the absence of L-tryptophan of 50 to 60% (Table II), was expressed as the percentage of full activation (v).

tryptophan, methemoglobin, and ascorbic acid at 37° become fully activated in 30 to 60 min (1). In a large number of experiments, the initial rate of the activation during the first 15 min of incubation was found to be proportional to the total enzyme activity formed, and this rate (average 71% of total) was not different for enzymes from tryptophan-treated rats (approximately 80% conjugated) or enzymes from hydrocortisone-treated rats (approximately 10% conjugated). The rates of activation in the concentrated, aerobic incubation for two such enzymes with low and high degrees of conjugation are shown in Fig. 4. Less than 20% increase in activity occurred in the first 5 min, and the *curves* were not significantly different for the two kinds of preparations, indicating that the limiting reaction under these conditions is not the conjugation. These results suggested that the conjugation must precede the rate-limiting step, which is presumably the reduction.

The rates of conjugation and reduction were measured separately in dilute, anaerobic incubations by determining the activation at intervals in two sequential steps like those of Table III. Conjugation in the presence of α-methyltryptophan was interrupted at intervals by the addition of globin from a side arm, followed by treatment with the complete activating system of L-tryptophan and ascorbic acid. To measure the rate of reduction, an enzyme already fully conjugated by anaerobic incubation with α-methyltryptophan and methemoglobin was reduced for various periods of time in the presence of globin and the complete activating system. The results at 37° (Fig. 4) show that conjugation occurred faster (an increase of 62% in 5 min) than the reduction (an increase of 33% in 5 min). This was expected from the earlier observations which indicated that the second step of activation was rate-limiting. Both reactions in the dilute, anaerobic system were somewhat faster than the over-all activation in the concentrated, aerobic system, suggesting that dilution and anaerobiosis accelerated the rate-limiting step.

With incubation at 25°, the rate of conjugation was only

slightly slower than at 37°, but the rate of reduction was considerably less. The initial rates, as the percentage of reaction during the first 5 min for conjugation and reduction, respectively, were 62% and 33% at 37°, and 42% and 12% at 25°. The over-all activation rates in the concentrated, aerobic system at 37° and 25° were in the ratio of 2.0 (1), but in the dilute incubation the ratio of rates at 37° and 25° for conjugation was 1.5 and for reduction 2.8.

Effect of Sulfhydryl Reagents on Conjugation—Certain thiol reagents inhibited the activation of the hydrocortisone-induced tryptophan pyrrolase more than the tryptophan-induced enzyme. The effects of three different reagents were therefore studied on the separate conjugation and reduction reactions. That the reagents could act at one and not the other step in the activation, and not on the catalytic reaction, was evident from comparing the inhibition of the activations of hydrocortisone-induced enzyme with low conjugation and of tryptophan-induced enzyme with high conjugation (Table V). The percentage of inhibition by globin of the two types of enzyme preparations, which measures the percentage of apoenzyme present before activation, is included in Table V for com-

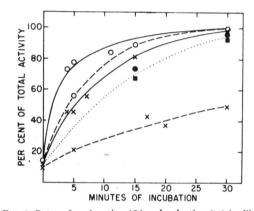

FIG. 4. Rates of conjugation (O) and reduction (X) in dilute, anaerobic incubations at 25° (- - -) and 37° (——). Each *curve* is an average of two or three experiments on hydrocortisone-induced preparations with total activities, determined in the same system after incubation for 60 min at 37°, of 19.6 to 28.0 units per g. The values are expressed as the percentage of the total activity of the preparation. Thunberg tubes contained, in the main vessel, 0.2 ml of 25% liver fraction, 0.7 ml of 0.02 M phosphate (pH 7.0), 0.2 mg of methemoglobin, 0.1 ml of 0.05 M α-methyltryptophan, and 1.2 ml of water; and in the side arm, 0.2 ml of 0.05 M L-tryptophan, 0.3 ml of solution containing 1.5 mg of globin, and 0.1 ml of 0.3 M ascorbate. The tubes at 0° were evacuated and filled with nitrogen then incubated at 37° for two successive periods of up to 30 min. To measure conjugation, the tubes were first incubated for the indicated times, the side arm contents were added, and the incubation was continued for 30 min more. The contents were then quickly equilibrated at 25°, aerated, and assayed. To measure reduction, the tubes were first incubated for 30 min to complete conjugation, then the side arm contents were added, and the incubation was continued for the indicated times. The initial activity of the contents was assayed. After the first 6 to 8 min of the reaction, the rate increased because of increased reduction. For comparison, the rates of over-all activation in concentrated aerobic incubations of a 10% conjugated hydrocortisone-induced (··· ● ···) and a 70% conjugated tryptophan-induced (··· ■ ···) preparation with total activities after 60 min of 22.5 and 28.3 units per g, respectively, are shown at 37°.

TABLE V

Inhibition of activation of hydrocortisone- and tryptophan-induced preparations by globin and thiol reagents

Inhibitors were added to 25% liver extracts at 37°, 5 min before dilution to 12.5% with the components of the complete activating system. The concentrations are those during the aerobic incubation at 37° for 30 min. The results are given as the percentage of inhibition (for the number of preparations indicated in parentheses), compared to the activity of the preparations not treated with the inhibitors.

Preparation	Globin (0.5 mg per ml)	N-Ethyl-maleimide (1 × 10⁻³ M)	Formamidine disulfide (100 μg per ml)
	% inhibition		
Hydrocortisone-induced..	85 (5)	87 (5)	71 (3)
Tryptophan-induced.....	30 (5)	32 (3)	20 (1)

TABLE VI

Inhibition by thiol reagents of catalysis and of conjugation, and reduction in dilute activating system

There were two 30-min incubations at 37° of dilute (1.7%) liver extract in nitrogen. The first (with α-methyltryptophan) conjugated and the second (with L-tryptophan) reduced the apotryptophan pyrrolase of a hydrocortisone-induced preparation (as in Table III); then the solution was assayed. The thiol reagents, in the final concentrations indicated, were added just before the first (conjugation) or second (reduction) incubations or the assay (catalysis). Results are expressed as the percentage of inhibition of activity compared to the preparations treated in the same way without the addition of inhibitors.

Reaction	N-Ethyl-maleimide (3 × 10⁻⁴ M)	Formamidine disulfide (33 μg per ml)	p-Mercuribenzoate (8 × 10⁻⁴ M)
	% inhibition		
Conjugation.......	90	86	80
Reduction........	5	4	60
Catalysis........	0	3	54

[a] The effect of GSH on the inhibition of activation was measured in the concentrated, aerobic system. GSH (3.3 × 10⁻³ M) added 5 min after p-mercuribenzoate reversed all but 6% inhibition of conjugation plus reduction, and all of the inhibition of catalysis.

parison with the effects of N-ethylmaleimide and formamidine disulfide. There is remarkable agreement between the degrees of inhibition by globin and the two reagents. The reagents, like globin, apparently prevented the activation of that fraction present as the apoenzyme, but not that present as the oxidized holoenzyme. The reagents apparently inhibited at the stage of conjugation but not of reduction, and not in the catalytic reaction.

The effects of the same thiol reagents and also p-mercuribenzoate were then tested in two-step activations of apoenzyme like those of Table III and Fig. 4. The presence of the reagents during the first incubation (conjugation) inhibited (Table VI). When present only during the second incubation (reduction), there was very little inhibition except by p-mercuribenzoate. The reagents had the same effects during the assay (catalytic reaction) as on the reduction. Only p-mercuribenzoate inhibited. The inhibitions were equally complete if the reagents were first added to the apoenzyme for 30 min, which was then

dialyzed before the incubation. There was no protection if the reagents were added to the apoenzyme after the additions to it of methemoglobin and tryptophan. Thus two of the reagents inhibited only if added before conjugation had occurred, and independently of the other components.

p-Mercuribenzoate reacted differently. It inhibited each of the reactions of conjugation, reduction, and catalysis to about the same extent at all the concentrations tested. When p-mercuribenzoate was added before activation, its inhibition (after incubation) was overcome by a second incubation with GSH and the necessary components for activation. When p-mercuribenzoate was added to the assay mixture of the fully activated enzyme, its inhibition could be promptly reversed by the addition of GSH or dithiothreitol (9) (Table VI).

DISCUSSION

For routine measurements of the tryptophan pyrrolase activity in crude liver extracts, the prior incubation of concentrated mixtures in air or nitrogen provides the optimal activation (Table II). However, incubation of diluted mixtures in nitrogen was necessary to separate and identify the individual steps of the activation process, the conjugation of the apoenzyme to the oxidized holoenzyme, and its reduction to the active, reduced holoenzyme.

In air, in the absence of tryptophan, the reduced holoenzyme is rapidly oxidized. The concentration of L-tryptophan which prevented half of this oxidative inactivation (3.7×10^{-4} M, Fig. 1) was the same as that previously reported as the apparent K_m of the catalytic reaction (6, 7), and as calculated for this value from the data of Schimke, Sweeney, and Berlin (8). This indicates that in the presence of oxygen the reduced holoenzyme that is combined with L-tryptophan will oxidize it, although that not combined will itself be oxidized. The oxidative inactivation was reversible by addition of tryptophan and removal of oxygen. The two measurements are equivalent ways of determining the affinity of tryptophan for the enzyme in the presence of oxygen. The oxidative formation of the oxidized holoenzyme was easily prevented in nitrogen, so long as L-tryptophan was added before subsequent admission of air (Table I).

Therefore, oxidized holoenzyme formed during anaerobic experiments could not be due to reoxidation, but would prove that conjugation occurred without reduction and that the oxidized holoenzyme was an intermediate in the over-all activation process. The actual separation of these two reactions required not only anaerobiosis, but also incubation of a diluted mixture in which full activation would not occur spontaneously in the absence of tryptophan and ascorbate. Then, by two sequential incubations, the first with limited reduction and the second in the presence of globin to limit conjugation, it was possible to show the occurrence of conjugation as a first step, and reduction as a second (Table III). It was also possible to distinguish between the different requirements for the two steps of the activation; α-methyltryptophan and L-tryptophan promoted conjugation, but only L-tryptophan promoted reduction. Ascorbate promoted reduction but had no function in the conjugation.

Although all of the analogues of tryptophan tested were effective in permitting conjugation, the L isomers of tryptophan and α-methyltryptophan were effective in the lowest concentrations. Half-maximal conjugation occurred with 2.6 ×

10^{-5} M of these compounds (Table IV), one-tenth of the apparent K_m of the catalytic reaction and of the concentration for the prevention of oxidation of the reduced holoenzyme.

Schimke, Sweeney, and Berlin (8) earlier proposed that there was a second site on the enzyme with a greater affinity for L-tryptophan and for α-methyltryptophan than the catalytic site, because of the very low concentrations that protected the apoenzyme against heat and urea, relative to the (apparent) K_m of L-tryptophan (3.2×10^{-4} M) and the K_I of α-methyltryptophan (1×10^{-2} M) in the catalytic reaction. A different site can, in fact, be clearly distinguished on the apoenzyme as the one for conjugation. It has not only a relatively high affinity for L-tryptophan but an equally high affinity for α-methyltryptophan, although the affinity of the catalytic site of the holoenzyme for α-methyltryptophan is very low.

It is possible that combination of tryptophan and its analogues with the site for conjugation does not itself stabilize the enzyme, but that any stabilization results from the conjugation with hematin promoted by tryptophan. The occurrence of conjugation was not determined in the protection studies *in vitro* of Schimke *et al.* (8). *In vivo*, the concentration of free tryptophan in liver (about 5×10^{-5} M (10, 11)) is of the same order of magnitude as that effective for conjugation and reduction *in vitro*, so that increases in the concentration of tryptophan *in vivo* could potentially increase its metabolism by promoting the conjugation and reduction of the tryptophan pyrrolase (12). Both L-tryptophan and α-methyltryptophan administration do induce the accumulation *in vivo* of the conjugated form of tryptophan pyrrolase (1, 13), which correlates with their promotion of conjugation *in vitro*. Since, the conjugation may lead to the accumulation of tryptophan pyrrolase during substrate type induction (4), the promotion of conjugation may be the basis of the inductions that these compounds cause. This possibility is examined in the next paper (14).

The site for reduction has little or no affinity for α-methyltryptophan, and in this, it resembles the catalytic site. Only L-tryptophan promoted reduction, and, even though its K_m for the reductive reaction (in nitrogen) was lower than for catalysis and for preventing the oxidation of the reduced holoenzyme, the difference could be attributed to the competitive effect of oxygen in the latter measurements.

The reduction reaction and the oxidation of the reduced holoenzyme have great similarities. They effectively represent a reversible reaction and may be one. The conditions that promote reduction (anaerobiosis, fresh and concentrated preparation, and L-tryptophan) in their opposite favor the oxidation. Ascorbate also promotes reduction, and it was previously observed to retard the oxidative inactivation during the enzyme reaction (5, 15). It is significant also that the tryptophan analogues do not promote reduction and do not retard oxidation.

The conjugation and reduction reactions occurred in that sequence, even though this was not established as the obligatory order. The possibility of conjugation with ferroporphyrins, for example, was not excluded. In all of the conditions tested in these crude preparations, the rate of the reduction appeared to be limiting. It is therefore probably responsible for the lag in the reaction and for the low activity found in earlier assays of tryptophan pyrrolase without a prior incubation. The large temperature coefficient and the possible acceleration with dilution further distinguish the reduction reaction from the conjugation.

The effects of the thiol reagents suggest that a thiol group on the protein is somehow involved in the activation and catalysis. Each of the reagents used reacts in a different way with thiols, but all three inhibited the conjugation step. Only *p*-mercuribenzoate also inhibited the reduction and catalysis, and only the inhibition of *p*-mercuribenzoate was reversed by GSH, immediately in the catalytic reaction in which the time course could be followed. Thus *p*-mercuribenzoate apparently caused no significant denaturation of the protein. Since it has often been noted that *p*-mercuribenzoate will react with certain thiols not accessible to N-ethylmaleimide (16, 17), it appears that conjugation may have made the thiol group inaccessible to N-ethylmaleimide and formamidine disulfide, while it remained accessible to *p*-mercuribenzoate. It is possible that hematin covers a thiol group, perhaps conjugating through it, or that conjugation with hematin changes the accessibility to the thiol by altering the configuration of the protein. Associated with this change is the transformation of the reactive site for tryptophan from that characteristic of conjugation to that of catalysis.

REFERENCES

1. Knox, W. E., Piras, M. M., and Tokuyama, K., *J. Biol. Chem.*, **241**, 297 (1966).
2. Greengard, O., Mendelsohn, N., and Acs, G., *J. Biol. Chem.*, **241**, 304 (1966).
3. Knox, W. E., and Piras, M. M., *J. Biol. Chem.*, **241**, 764 (1966).
4. Greengard, O., and Feigelson, P., *J. Biol. Chem.*, **236**, 158 (1961).
5. Tanaka, T., and Knox, W. E., *J. Biol. Chem.*, **234**, 1162 (1959).
6. Knox, W. E., and Mehler, A. H., *J. Biol. Chem.*, **187**, 419 (1950).
7. Greengard, O., and Feigelson, P., *J. Biol. Chem.*, **237**, 1903 (1962).
8. Schimke, R. T., Sweeney, E. W., and Berlin, C. M., *J. Biol. Chem.*, **240**, 4609 (1965).
9. Cleland, W. N., *Biochemistry*, **3**, 480 (1964).
10. Civen, M., and Knox, W. E., *J. Biol. Chem.*, **234**, 1787 (1959).
11. Denckla, W. D., and Dewey, H. K., *J. Lab. Clin. Med.*, **69**, 160 (1967).
12. Knox, W. E., *Advance. Enzyme Regulat.*, **4**, 287 (1966).
13. Greengard, O., *Biochim. Biophys. Acta*, **85**, 492 (1964).
14. Knox, W. E., and Piras, M. M., *J. Biol. Chem.*, **242**, 2959 (1967).
15. Knox, W. E., and Ogata, M., *J. Biol. Chem.*, **240**, 2216 (1965).
16. Stoppani, A. O. M., and Milstein, C., *Biochim. Biophys. Acta*, **24**, 655 (1957).
17. Strittmatter, P., *J. Biol. Chem.*, **236**, 2336 (1961).

THE JOURNAL OF BIOLOGICAL CHEMISTRY
Vol. 242, No. 12, Issue of June 25, pp. 2959-2965, 1967
Printed in U.S.A.

Tryptophan Pyrrolase of Liver

III. CONJUGATION *IN VIVO* DURING COFACTOR INDUCTION BY TRYPTOPHAN ANALOGUES*

(Received for publication, February 13, 1967)

W. EUGENE KNOX AND MARTA M. PIRAS‡

From the Department of Biological Chemistry, Harvard Medical School, and the Cancer Research Institute, New England Deaconess Hospital, Boston, Massachusetts 02215

SUMMARY

Tryptophan pyrrolase, measured in an assay where its activity was proportional to its reaction with a specific antiserum, was induced in the liver of adrenalectomized rats by only those tryptophan analogues that also specifically promoted the conjugation of the apotryptophan pyrrolase *in vitro* and *in vivo* whether or not these analogues had affinity for the catalytic site of the tryptophan pyrrolase. The apotryptophan pyrrolase induced by hydrocortisone became conjugated upon injection of these analogues, and the elevated level was maintained *in vivo* as long as sufficient amount of the analogues was present. This action *in vivo* of the inducers with a site on the enzyme different from the catalytic site was associated with a decreased rate of disappearance of the protein and an increased rate of its synthesis.

One kind of induction of the tryptophan pyrrolase (L-tryptophan:oxygen oxidoreductase, EC 1.13.1.12, tryptophan oxygenase) occurs in rats treated with L-tryptophan or some of its analogues. Like many inducers of enzymes, these are substrates or analogues closely related structurally to the substrate of the enzyme they induce. This commonly met steric relationship was accounted for by the almost forgotten "mass action hypothesis of enzymatic adaptation" (1). It attributed induction to the specific combination of enzyme with its substrate, which removed the enzyme from its dynamic equilibrium between formation and degradation. Since then other specifically combining substances, such as coenzymes (2, 3) and inhibitors (4), have been found to induce certain enzymes in animals. These steric relationships cannot be ignored, even when the inducing analogues are not known to combine with the enzyme. Civen and

Knox (5) found that several close analogues of tryptophan with little or no affinity for the catalytic site of the enzyme, either as substrates or inhibitors, were inducers of tryptophan pyrrolase in rat liver. One of these, α-methyltryptophan (6), shared with L-tryptophan the ability to stabilize the enzyme activity during incubation *in vitro*, but the other inducers did not. The stabilization *in vivo* was itself a composite effect eliminated by full activation of the enzyme (7). The several inducing analogues also caused the high level of tryptophan pyrrolase (when previously elevated by hydrocortisone treatment) to persist longer *in vivo*. Schimke, Sweeney, and Berlin (8, 9) therefore concluded that only those analogues that stabilized tryptophan pyrrolase *in vivo* acted as inducers, even though the means of such stabilization *in vivo* remained obscure.

Recently, Piras and Knox (10) showed that the several tryptophan analogues specifically reacted *in vitro* with the apotryptophan pyrrolase to promote its conjugation with hematin. The reactive site on the apoenzyme had broader specificity and higher affinity for the tryptophan analogues than did the catalytic site of the holoenzyme. We have now correlated the ability of these tryptophan analogues to conjugate apotryptophan pyrrolase *in vitro* with their abilities to conjugate and to induce to maintain high levels of tryptophan pyrrolase *in vivo*. Those analogues that induce tryptophan pyrrolase share with L-tryptophan the ability to react with the apoenzyme, not with the holoenzyme, and not as substrates but as specific promoters of its conjugation.

METHODS

Adrenalectomized, adult male NEDH rats were used 5 to 10 days after operation in all experiments to avoid stimulated adrenal secretion and consequent induction of tryptophan pyrrolase by the hormonal mechanism (11, 12). They were given 0.9% NaCl as drinking water. Intact rats, when used, are identified. The rats were treated, as indicated, with 2.5 mg of hydrocortisone acetate or 100 mg of tryptophan or other amino acid analogues per 100 g of body weight, all given intraperitoneally as suspensions in 0.9% NaCl. In the experiments of Fig. 2 and Table VI, the more soluble hydrocortisone phosphate was used in the lower dose of 0.25 mg/100 g of body weight to limit the duration of the induction (13). Unless stated otherwise, the rats were killed 5 hours after treatment. The livers were immediately removed and assayed for tryptophan pyrrolase activity. This consisted of the preparation of a particle-

* This investigation was supported by United States Public Health Service Grant AM 00567 and by Research Career Award AM-K6-2018, both from the National Institute of Arthritis and Metabolic Diseases of the National Institutes of Health, United States Public Health Service, and by United States Atomic Energy Commission Contract AT(30-1)-3779 with the New England Deaconess Hospital.

‡ Present address, Universidad de Buenos Aires, Cátedra de Química Biológica Patológica, Facultad de Farmacia y Bioquímica, Buenos Aires, Argentina.

This is reprint No. 371 of the Cancer Research Institute of the New England Deaconess Hospital.

free supernatant fraction from a 25% homogenate of liver in 0.15 M KCl containing 0.02 M sodium phosphate buffer (pH 7.0), its incubation with an equal volume of a mixture of methemoglobin, L-tryptophan, and ascorbate for 30 min at 37° to activate the total enzyme, and its immediate spectrophotometric assay at 25°. Methemoglobin was omitted and 0.5 mg of globin per ml was added in the incubation prior to assay to activate only the holoenzyme. These procedures have been described in detail (7, 10, 12). The unit of tryptophan pyrrolase activity is 1 μmole of kynurenine formed per hour at 25°, expressed per g of fresh liver.

The tryptophan and α-methyltryptophan in 0.02 ml of plasma withdrawn from the cut tail were quantitatively determined by the fluorometric method of Denckla and Dewey (14). This method gave identical values on a molar basis with these two compounds.

The antiserum was prepared by the injection into the foot pads of a rabbit of 1 ml of purified apotryptophan pyrrolase (6.9 mg of protein, initial activity 18 units per mg of protein) (15). This preparation was put through a Millipore filter (Gelman Type 6M, 0.3-μ pore) and homogenized with equal volumes of adjuvant (Bacto H 37 Ra, Difco). This treatment of the rabbit was repeated with intramuscular injections 3 and 5 weeks later. The precipitin reaction reached a maximum (positive in a serum dilution of 1:64) 1 week after the third treatment and the rabbit was bled. Serum was separated after clotting at 5° for 24 hours, heated at 56° for 30 min, and portions were frozen at −9°. These were used within 1 month for all experiments.

The rabbit antiserum, when added to the incubation mixture used for activation of the soluble liver fractions, caused inhibition of the tryptophan pyrrolase reaction in the subsequent assay. Control serum did not inhibit. The degree of inhibition increased to a maximum after incubation for about half an hour

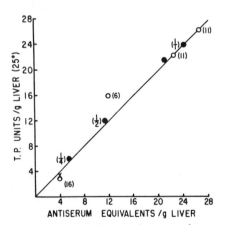

FIG. 1. Antiserum titrations of the tryptophan pyrrolase (*TP*) activity in soluble supernatant fractions from livers of adrenalectomized rats. An equivalent of antiserum (0.004 ml) inhibited 1 unit of tryptophan pyrrolase by 50% during a 45-min incubation period at 37° in the complete activating system. The preparations were from rats that were untreated (×), treated with hydrocortisone acetate (○) (the hours after injections are in parentheses), treated with hydrocortisone, then with tryptophan 11 and 17 hours later, and killed at 24 hours (●) (the dilutions of one of these preparations are indicated in parentheses).

at 37°, with no centrifugation before the assay. Subsequent storage of the mixture at 5° for 24 hours, followed by centrifugation in the cold before the assay, did not significantly increase the inhibition observed. An equivalent of antiserum was defined as the amount that with 45-min incubation in the complete activation system would inhibit by 50%, as determined by a semi-logarithmic plot of inhibition and antiserum, the activity of 1 ml of the mixture containing 1.0 unit of tryptophan pyrrolase when fully activated. An average of 4 eq of antiserum was needed for 90% inhibition of 1 unit of tryptophan pyrrolase activity in all the different types of preparations. An equivalent was present in 0.004 ml of the antiserum used.

RESULTS

Levels of Tryptophan Pyrrolase after Induction Measured by Antibody Titrations—The activity assays used in studying the induced enzyme levels were checked by independent measurements of the specific immunologically reactive protein. Approximate correlations have already been shown between the activities of tryptophan pyrrolase and the amounts of antiserum necessary to inhibit these activities, in preparations from untreated rats and those treated with hydrocortisone and tryptophan (9, 16). Less than the total activities were measured with the assays used in those experiments, and only the early period after the treatment was examined. We repeated such measurements with full activation in the assays, and also measured preparations after the activities had returned to basal levels following hydrocortisone treatment, and preparations with persistent high activity following hydrocortisone and tryptophan treatments.

The antiserum inhibited equally well when added to the tryptophan pyrrolase before and after activation, and did not distinguish between apoenzyme and holoenzyme. The proportionality between the equivalents of antiserum and the units of tryptophan pyrrolase activity is shown in Fig. 1 for three dilutions (1:1, 1:2, and 1:4) of a single enzyme preparation. It was diluted with another preparation of negligible activity from an untreated rat in order to keep the concentration of liver extract constant in the mixtures. Similar proportionality is also shown between the equivalents of antiserum and the units of activity of different preparations covering a 10-fold range of activities. These include preparations from untreated, hydrocortisone-treated, and tryptophan-treated rats. It is noteworthy that the fall in activity 16 hours after treatment with hydrocortisone acetate is associated with a proportionate fall in antiserum equivalents, and that the persistence of high activity beyond 16 hours when the hydrocortisone treatment is followed by repeated tryptophan administration is also associated with a continued high level of the antiserum equivalents that are needed to inhibit the enzyme activity. Thus, before, during, and after both types of induction, the activities as assayed are proportional to the amounts of material reacting specifically with this antiserum.

Form of Tryptophan Pyrrolase in Vivo—The holoenzyme of tryptophan pyrrolase was originally estimated by the activity found in the absence of added hematin (17). However, our soluble liver fractions contained sources of hematin with which some apoenzyme became conjugated during the necessary incubation with tryptophan before assay, and these sources were not completely eliminated by perfusion of the livers to remove blood (7, 10, 18). The addition of globin prevented the conjugation of apoenzyme by the contaminating hematin, even in preparations from poorly perfused livers, and it did not interfere with either the activation or the activity of the holoenzyme (7, 10). Table I compares the two ways of estimating the holoenzyme, by omission of methemoglobin and by addition of globin, in preparations from perfused livers of rats treated in different ways. The activity, and therefore the apparent conjugation, was higher when measured without methemoglobin than when globin was also added. The use of globin provided a lower and more reproducible measure of the degree of conjugation, but both types of measurements show that the tryptophan pyrrolase of untreated and hydrocortisone-induced preparations is largely in the unconjugated, apoenzyme form, while in the tryptophan (and α-methyltryptophan)-induced preparations, with or without hydrocortisone treatment, more than two-thirds of the tryptophan pyrrolase is in the conjugated holoenzyme form.

The highly conjugated enzyme from tryptophan-induced preparations was active at the earliest times after homogenization, but in the absence of added L-tryptophan became inactive within the 2-hour period needed for the usual preparation (7). Since the active, reduced form of holoenzyme (7, 18) could be preserved by strictly anaerobic conditions during dialysis to remove L-tryptophan (7, 10), preparations were made under such anaerobic conditions in order to determine the oxidation state of the holoenzyme in the livers. Table II shows the results obtained when the whole procedure of homogenization and centrifugation of the livers was carried out in nitrogen. The poorly conjugated, hydrocortisone-induced preparations had negligible activity without incubation, whether prepared in N_2 or air. But preparations induced by tryptophan or α-methyltryptophan were already active without incubation when prepared in N_2. They were nearly inactive without incubation when prepared in air. Reduction of the holoenzyme, even that induced by α-methyltryptophan, must have already occurred in the intact

TABLE I

Conjugation of tryptophan pyrrolase in preparations from treated rats determined by omission of methemoglobin or addition of globin

Treatments of intact or adrenalectomized rats with hydrocortisone acetate, tryptophan, or α-methyltryptophan were given 5 to 11 hours earlier. The livers were perfused with 0.9% cold NaCl to remove blood. The percentage of conjugation represents the percentage of the total activity that was found when methemoglobin was omitted from the incubation or when methemoglobin was omitted and 0.5 mg of globin per ml was added. The numbers of preparations are indicated in parentheses.

Treatment of rats	Total activity[a]	Conjugation	
		No Met-hemoglobin	Plus globin
	μmoles/hr/g liver	%	%
Control	3.6 (2)	33.0 (2)	12.0 (2)
Hydrocortisone acetate[b]	16.0–38.4	40.7 (18)	5.9 (9)
L-Tryptophan, 5 hours[c]	29.6 (7)	82.0 (5)	66.5 (3)
L-Tryptophan, 5 hours[d]	11.0 (4)	90.0 (4)	76.5 (2)
α-Methyltryptophan, 8 hours[d]	14.2 (2)	90.0 (2)	69.0 (2)

[a] At 25°.

[b] Adrenalectomized and intact.

[c] Intact.

[d] Adrenalectomized.

TABLE II

Effect of anaerobiosis during enzyme preparation

Intact male rats, 3 months old, were injected with 2.5 mg of hydrocortisone phosphate, 100 mg of L-tryptophan, or α-methyltryptophan per 100 g of body weight. The rats were sacrificed 5 hours after treatment. The livers were immediately removed, halved, and soluble fractions prepared from each half. One was made as usual in air and the other inside a bag filled with nitrogen. The sealed tubes of the latter were opened under nitrogen after centrifugation and an aliquot of the supernatant was immediately assayed without incubation. The preparation in air was also assayed without incubation. Both preparations had the same activity after the standard aerobic incubation (total activity).

Treatment of intact rats	No incubation prepared in		Total activity (incubated)
	Air	N_2	
	μmoles/hr/g liver[a]		
Hydrocortisone phosphate	0.8	1.0	17.6
L-Tryptophan	4.0	26.4	26.0
α-Methyltryptophan	3.6	31.2	32.0

[a] At 25°.

TABLE III

Promotion of conjugation of tryptophan pyrrolase by tryptophan analogues

Apoenzyme preparations from hydrocortisone-treated intact rats were conjugated during a 30-min incubation at 37° of 0.5 ml of 25% liver extract, 0.3 ml of 0.02 M sodium phosphate (pH 7.0), 0.2 mg of methemoglobin in 0.1 ml, and 0.1 ml of 0.04 M L-tryptophan or the listed analogues (final concentration 0.004 M), and then assayed (first activity). Duplicates were then incubated a second time, after addition of 1.0 mg of globin, 30 mM ascorbate, and 5 mM L-tryptophan, for reduction of the already conjugated enzyme (total activity). The activities are given as percentage of the total found after both incubations with L-tryptophan present. The total activities represent the amounts conjugated during the first incubation. Each value represents the average of three or four measurements.

Analogue in first incubation	First activity	Total activity (after reduction plus globin)
	%	%
L-Tryptophan	100	100
α-Methyltryptophan	12	76
5-Methyl-DL-tryptophan	21	65
D-Tryptophan	11	55
N-Acetyl-DL-tryptophan	6	39
None	11	33

liver. Thus the enzyme in liver, if conjugated, is also reduced unless oxidized during its preparation.

Facilitation of Conjugation of Tryptophan Pyrrolase by Tryptophan and Its Analogues in Vitro and Their Conjugation and Induction in Vivo—Several tryptophan analogues did not replace tryptophan for the over-all activation *in vitro* of the enzyme (12), but did promote its conjugation (10). In Table III, the activation with these analogues was carried out in two steps, the first permitting conjugation. In the second step, further conjugation was prevented with added globin, and reduction was promoted by added ascorbate and L-tryptophan. The activity after the

TABLE IV

Induction and conjugation of tryptophan pyrrolase in vivo by tryptophan analogues

Adrenalectomized male rats received 100 mg of the indicated analogues per 100 g of body weight intraperitoneally and were killed 5 hours later. The total activities and the percentage of holoenzyme, measured by the activity after incubation with globin and no added methemoglobin, are given as the averages ($\pm \sigma$) from four rats.

Inducer	Total activity	Holoenzyme
	units/g liver[a]	%
None	3.6	12.2
L-Tryptophan	13.4 ± 2.9	73.0 ± 3.6
α-Methyl-DL-tryptophan	13.4 ± 3.4	74.0 ± 9.9
D-Tryptophan	8.2 ± 2.3	51.0 ± 5.7
5-Methyl-DL-tryptophan[b]	3.2 ± 0.5	53.0 ± 27.0

[a] At 25°.

[b] Rats died between 3 and 5 hours after treatment with 5-methyltryptophan. They were assayed at the time of death.

second incubation with ascorbate was low unless L-tryptophan was present, indicating that the analogues themselves did not allow the reduced holoenzyme to accumulate. The activity formed (in the presence of globin, ascorbate, and L-tryptophan) in the second incubation indicated the extent of conjugation that occurred in the first incubation. All of the analogues of L-tryptophan tested, except *N*-acetyltryptophan, gave more conjugation during the first incubation than the control values with methemoglobin alone. Even D-tryptophan and 5-methyltryptophan, which were required in relatively high concentrations for conjugation (10), promoted conjugation in the 4 mM concentrations tested. The analogues are not oxidized by the enzyme, and in the concentrations present they do not significantly inhibit it (5).

Table IV shows that L-tryptophan, D-tryptophan, and α-methyl-DL-tryptophan, which conjugated the enzyme *in vitro* (Table III), also induced tryptophan pyrrolase when administered to adrenalectomized rats. 5-Methyltryptophan did not. These results confirm those of Civen and Knox (5), Greengard (19), and Schimke, Sweeney, and Berlin (8). Table IV also shows that the compounds caused increased conjugation of tryptophan pyrrolase *in vivo*, as they did *in vitro* (Table III), including 5-methyltryptophan which did not induce the enzyme.

With the exception of 5-methyltryptophan, the extent of induction by the analogues was roughly proportional to the degree of conjugation they produced *in vivo* and *in vitro*. 5-Methyltryptophan in some systems inhibits protein synthesis, an effect reversed by L-tryptophan (20). It also inhibits the hydrocortisone induction of tryptophan pyrrolase, as if it inhibited protein synthesis. The administration of 5-methyltryptophan together with hydrocortisone to two adrenalectomized rats halved the tryptophan pyrrolase level 5 hours later, from the 22 units per g expected with the hydrocortisone alone to 11.8 units per g. Of this, 40% was conjugated.

Schimke, Sweeney, and Berlin (8) reported that administration of L-tryptophan markedly enhanced the induction of tryptophan pyrrolase activity by hydrocortisone, as if L-tryptophan multiplied the accumulation of the extra enzyme that was synthesized under the influence of hydrocortisone. No more than additive effects were seen with such combined inductions by

tryptophan plus hydrocortisone in short term experiments with the improved assay (12), but two longer term experiments were also done. The conditions of the experiments differed slightly as described in Table V. Repeated doses of L-tryptophan were given after a dose of the long acting hydrocortisone acetate (which elevated the tryptophan pyrrolase for 14 hours (13)), or a single dose of the long acting α-methyltryptophan (persisting in plasma more than 12 hours, Fig. 2) was given with repeated doses of the short acting hydrocortisone phosphate. Neither regimen produced the marked synergism that Schimke, Sweeney, and Berlin (8) obtained with repeated doses of both L-tryptophan and hydrocortisone phosphate. The accumulated tryptophan pyrrolase level after combined hydrocortisone phosphate and α-methyltryptophan treatments was more than the sum of the two inductions separately. However, the enhancement was not sufficiently great for comparison of this property in the other analogues.

Persistence of Hydrocortisone-induced Tryptophan Pyrrolase in Vivo after Treatment with Tryptophan—As previously described by Schimke, Sweeney, and Berlin, treatments with L-tryptophan (8) or α-methyltryptophan (9) made the tryptophan pyrrolase, previously elevated by hydrocortisone, persist longer than it would after hydrocortisone alone. The time course of this effect after single doses of L-tryptophan or α-methyltryptophan is shown in Fig. 2. The enzyme previously induced by a minimal dose of hydrocortisone phosphate was present largely as the apoenzyme. Without further treatment, it returned to the basal level within 3 hours. The administration of tryptophan at the peak of hydrocortisone induction caused a rapid conversion of the apoenzyme to holoenzyme, and the total enzyme persisted more than 6 hours after the time in which it would normally disappear. In addition, 3 hours after tryptophan, the tryptophan pyrrolase level was higher than at the peak of the hydrocortisone induction. The excess corresponded to the amount induced by tryptophan alone (Table IV). This increase indicated that tryptophan administration had not only preserved, in conjugated form, the enzyme induced by hydrocortisone, but had itself induced additional enzyme.

Measurements of the tryptophan levels in plasma during this experiment showed that the elevated amounts of holoenzyme and of total enzyme persisted only as long as the tryptophan. When the tryptophan in plasma fell below 100 μg per ml, the amounts of total enzyme and holoenzyme suddenly fell (Fig. 2). The percentage of conjugation remained approximately constant as the total enzyme decreased, so it was not apparent if either the holoenzyme or apoenzyme were preferentially preserved.

A single dose of α-methyltryptophan persisted in the plasma for a much longer time than tryptophan (Fig. 2). It also caused a rapid conjugation and an increase of the enzyme above the initial level induced earlier by hydrocortisone. Paralleling the persistent level of α-methyltryptophan in plasma, the level of conjugated tryptophan pyrrolase remained elevated throughout the experimental period, for a much longer time than after the same dose of L-tryptophan. With repeated administration of tryptophan to maintain an elevated level in plasma, a high level of conjugated tryptophan pyrrolase was made to persist for as long as 24 hours (Fig. 1) (21). It was therefore apparent that so long as tryptophan or its effective analogues were present in sufficiently high concentration in plasma, the tryptophan pyrrolase in liver remained conjugated and undiminished in amount.

Similar experiments to those in Fig. 2 but with additional

TABLE V

Combined inductions of tryptophan pyrrolase by hydrocortisone and tryptophan analogues

Inductions in adrenalectomized rats with hydrocortisone and with L-tryptophan or α-methyltryptophan, separately and combined, are shown during 4-hour (A) and 12-hour (B and C) periods, in comparison with similar 4-hour (D) and 12-hour (E) inductions reported by Schimke, Sweeney, and Berlin (8). In Experiments A, B, and C, the rats were adult males, given doses of 2.5 mg of hydrocortisone and 100 mg of tryptophan, or its analogue, per 100 g of body weight. Those in Experiment B were pretreated with 0.25 mg of deoxy-corticosterone acetate on each of the 3 days before use. Those in Experiments A and B received single doses of hydrocortisone acetate at zero time, and those in Experiment C received repeated doses of hydrocortisone phosphate every 4 hours. They received a single dose of tryptophan (A) or α-methyltryptophan (C) or repeated doses of tryptophan every 4 hours (B). The results are given as the means ± σ for the number of rats in parentheses. The results of Schimke, Sweeney, and Berlin (8) are the means from slightly younger animals with similar doses of hydrocortisone phosphate and tryptophan repeated every 4 hours, but with the enzyme assays at 37°. The combined induction (last line), given as the percentage of the sum of the separate inductions, is a measure of the synergy of the inducers in combination.

Treatment	4 hours, Experiment A (Reference 12)	12 hours		Schimke *et al.* (8) (37°)	
		Experiment B	Experiment C	4 hours, Experiment D	12 hours, Experiment E
	μmoles/hr/g liver	*μmoles/hr/g liver*		*μmoles/hr/g liver*	
1. None....................	2.6 ± 0.6 (8)	2.7 ± 0.6 (7)	3.6 (2)	3	3
2. Hydrocortisone..........	15.4 ± 3.2 (7)	39.2 ± 17.0 (20)	40.1 ± 1.4 (8)	25	38
3. Tryptophan analogue.....	14.8 (3)	12.8 ± 3.6 (7)[a]	10.8 (2)[b]	11	21
4. Hydrocortisone and tryptophan analogue................	28.9 ± 0.9 (5)	44.9 ± 4.4 (5)	66.9 ± 5.9 (8)	40	121
$\dfrac{\text{Combination (4)}}{\text{Sum (2) + (3) − basal (1)}} \times 100$......	105%	91%	142%	121%	216%

[a] Values 6 hours after treatment with L-tryptophan alone. Most adrenalectomized rats died within 8 hours after this treatment.

[b] α-Methyltryptophan was used in Experiment C and L-tryptophan in all others.

compounds are shown in Table VI. At the peak of the hydrocortisone induction, 5 hours after its administration, various compounds were given and the enzyme present in the liver measured 4 or 5 hours later. By then, the enzyme had fallen to the basal level in rats receiving only hydrocortisone, while the enzyme still remained elevated in rats given tryptophan. L-Tyrosine, as was also reported for L-histidine (8), did not maintain the tryptophan pyrrolase level above that of the controls. It also did not significantly increase the degree of conjugation. 5-Methyltryptophan, which conjugated the enzyme *in vitro* (Table III), and conjugated but did not induce the enzyme *in vivo* (Table IV), in the present experiment both conjugated the tryptophan pyrrolase and maintained its level significantly above that of the controls. D-Tryptophan was even more effective. It caused similar conjugation and maintained most of the initial tryptophan pyrrolase level. L-Tryptophan and α-methyltryptophan not only maintained the initial hydrocortisone-induced level, but, as already seen, caused accumulations of extra enzyme.

Of the tryptophan pyrrolase present after L-tryptophan or α-methyltryptophan administration, one part equal to that initially induced by hydrocortisone, could represent preformed enzyme that was preserved. Another part, at least equal to the excess accumulated above the initial level induced by hydrocortisone, represented newly formed enzyme. To distinguish between these amounts, the experiments with L-tryptophan were repeated with administration of puromycin to prevent new protein synthesis (Table VI). The disappearance of the enzyme in the hydrocortisone-treated controls was unchanged by puromycin alone, and the enzyme remained relatively unconjugated. Puromycin given together with tryptophan did not prevent the usual conjugation, but puromycin eliminated the accumulation of the ex-

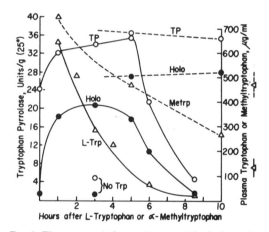

FIG. 2. Time curve of the persistence of the hydrocortisone-induced tryptophan pyrrolase levels in rats treated with L-tryptophan or α-methyltryptophan. The enzyme at zero time in the figure was at the peak of induction by previously administered hydrocortisone. All received 0.25 mg of hydrocortisone phosphate per 100 g of body weight 5 hours before the zero time. Bracketed values at 3 hours (*No Trp*) are rats that received no further treatment. The others received L-tryptophan (*L-Trp*) or α-methyltryptophan (*Metrp*) at zero time. Total tryptophan pyrrolase (*TP*) (○), holoenzyme (*Holo*) (●), and plasma levels (△) of L-tryptophan or α-methyltryptophan were determined in three or more rats per point at intervals after injection of 100 mg of L-tryptophan (——) or α-methyltryptophan (- - -) per 100 g of body weight. All rats were adrenalectomized adult males.

TABLE VI

Preservation of tryptophan pyrrolase in hydrocortisone-treated rats

Adrenalectomized, adult male rats were treated with 0.25 mg of hydrocortisone phosphate per 100 g of body weight 5 hours before zero time. They then received the substances listed in 100-mg doses per 100 g of body weight, except puromycin which was given in doses of 10 mg at zero time, immediately before the tryptophan, and 5 mg at 1½ hours. The rats were killed 4 to 5 hours after zero time, as indicated (time of assay). Means, standard deviations, and the number of rats (in parentheses) are given.

Treatment after hydrocortisone	Time of assay	Total enzyme	Holo-enzyme	Enzyme at zero time
	hrs	*units/g liver[a]*	%	%
None	0	24.4 ± 5.1 (4)	6	(100)
None	4	5.1 ± 1.0 (9)	13	21
L-Tyrosine	5	6.1 ± 1.2 (3)	26	25
5-Methyl-DL-tryptophan	5	9.0 ± 2.0 (4)[b]	47	37
D-Tryptophan	5	17.9 ± 3.3 (9)[b]	41	73
α-Methyl-DL-tryptophan	5	36.5 ± 1.8 (3)[b]	74	149
L-Tryptophan	5	37.6 ± 6.6 (5)[b]	53	154
Puromycin	4	4.0 (2)	22	16
L-Tryptophan + puromycin	4	16.1 ± 2.1 (4)[b, c]	54	66

[a] At 25°.

[b] The differences from the value at 4 hours without treatment (5.1 units per g) are highly significant ($p \ll 0.01$).

[c] The difference from the value at 5 hours with tryptophan (37.6 units per g) is highly significant ($p \ll 0.01$).

tra tryptophan pyrrolase. The difference between the levels with tryptophan, with and without puromycin, were highly significant, indicating that the protein synthesis inhibited by puromycin was responsible for part (about half) of the enzyme that was found after the treatment with tryptophan. On the other hand part (also about half) of the enzyme that was found after treatment with tryptophan still persisted after treatment with tryptophan plus puromycin. The difference between the latter enzyme level and that in the hydrocortisone-induced controls was also highly significant. Thus, half of the enzyme persisted after treatment with tryptophan in the apparent absence of protein synthesis. The amount so preserved represented two-thirds of the initial level of hydrocortisone-induced enzyme. Both the tryptophan pyrrolase induced by hydrocortisone and maintained by tryptophan, as well as the extra tryptophan pyrrolase newly formed, was highly conjugated.

DISCUSSION

The most significant conclusion from these studies is that a series of inducers related structurally to the substrate of tryptophan pyrrolase, including some with little or no affinity for the catalytic site, still interact specifically with the apoenzyme. They react at a site having high affinities for both L-tryptophan and α-methyltryptophan (2×10^{-5} M), where they promote the conjugation of the apoenzyme by hematin (10). By contrast, the catalytic site of the enzyme has less affinity for L-tryptophan (apparent K_m, 3×10^{-4} M) and very much less for α-methyltryptophan (K_I, 1×10^{-2} M (9)). Those compounds that induced tryptophan pyrrolase were those that promoted conjugation of tryptophan pyrrolase *in vitro* and *in vivo*. No such correlation was observed between the induction and the effects of these com-

pounds on the catalytic reaction (5). Besides the qualitative correlation between those compounds that promoted conjugation and those that induced the enzyme, there was also an approximate quantitative correlation. The compounds that promoted conjugation in the lowest concentration and caused the most conjugation *in vivo* (L-tryptophan and α-methyltryptophan) were also the most effective inducers.

These correlations were established by the use of an assay that measured activities proportional to the amounts of the specific, immunologically reactive protein (Fig. 1), and by measurements of conjugation (with globin) that were not affected by the hemoglobin content of the preparations. The results therefore indicate that those compounds that specifically promote the conjugation of tryptophan pyrrolase are those that can induce it by the substrate ("co-factor" (3)) type of mechanism. The results also suggest that the compounds may both conjugate and induce by this same direct action upon the enzyme protein.

5-Methyltryptophan constituted an exception. It conjugated the tryptophan pyrrolase *in vitro* and *in vivo* (Table IV), but, in agreement with earlier studies (5, 9, 19), it did not induce the tryptophan pyrrolase. Since only half the expected rise of tryptophan pyrrolase with hydrocortisone occurred in rats that were treated at the same time with 5-methyltryptophan, it is possible that 5-methyltryptophan inhibits the protein synthesis necessary for tryptophan pyrrolase induction, as it does in microorganisms (20). In contrast to the effective compounds tested, N-acetyltryptophan did not conjugate the enzyme *in vitro* (Table III), and produced little or no induction (5, 9, 19) or conjugation (19) *in vivo*. L-Tyrosine also did not cause conjugation *in vivo* (Table IV) or induction (11). These compounds provided the correlation of negative effects, the lack of conjugation with no induction.

A sensitive test of the conjugation by the compounds *in vivo* was their effect in rats with high levels of the apotryptophan pyrrolase previously induced by hydrocortisone. The tryptophan pyrrolase levels persisted to a striking degree, as reported (8), when the effective inducing compounds were administered (Fig. 2 and Table VI). This maintenance of the elevated tryptophan pyrrolase level by the compounds was associated with a high degree of conjugation of the enzyme. The maintenance and conjugation lasted as long as a significant concentration of the inducer was present in the plasma, and longer if the compound itself persisted (α-methyltryptophan) (Fig. 2), or if L-tryptophan was repeatedly administered (21). This result depended in part upon new synthesis of the enzyme and in part upon the maintenance of preformed tryptophan pyrrolase, because L-tryptophan administration was still partially effective when given with puromycin to inhibit new protein synthesis. Schimke, Sweeney, and Berlin (8) also observed that the level of the enzyme was maintained by tryptophan in the presence of puromycin.

5-Methyltryptophan, which appeared to inhibit protein synthesis and which conjugated tryptophan pyrrolase *in vitro* and *in vivo* without inducing it, was effective here. When given after hydrocortisone, 5-methyltryptophan significantly maintained the elevated level of tryptophan pyrrolase, although less effectively than the combination of L-tryptophan and puromycin (Table VI). This result would be expected of an inhibitor of protein synthesis that also caused conjugation, if maintenance of the level of tryptophan pyrrolase depended upon its conjugation.

Besides maintaining the level of preformed tryptophan pyrrolase that was previously elevated by hydrocortisone, L-tryptophan and α-methyltryptophan caused the accumulation of additional enzyme. This extra enzyme accumulated during the first 5 hours after L-tryptophan administration and was present for a longer period after α-methyltryptophan administration. The extra amount was equal to that induced by these compounds when given alone (Fig. 2 and Table IV). The extra tryptophan pyrrolase appeared to accumulate by synthesis of new protein, and this after the effect of hydrocortisone was spent, since it was eliminated by the puromycin treatment. The tryptophan analogues therefore apparently increase (induce) the tryptophan pyrrolase level both by increasing its synthesis and by slowing its disappearance, and both occur in association with conjugation of the enzyme.

The lack of synergism between the combined inductions by hydrocortisone and tryptophan in short term experiments, and the small synergism in long term experiments (Table V), also indicated that slowing of degradation could not be the only mechanism by which tryptophan induced. Furthermore, these results suggested that tryptophan did not always slow degradation to the same extent. The two mechanisms of slowed degradation and increased synthesis probably operated to different extents in the different physiological situations.

The term "induction" is used here to mean only what has actually been observed here and in most other studies of enzyme induction in animals, *i.e.* the accumulation of more enzyme in cells as a consequence of some altered physiological state. It is not restricted to a particular hypothetical mechanism for the accumulation. In consequence of the turnover of proteins in animal cells, an enzyme can accumulate (be induced) by synthesis of more, or by degradation of less (with continuing synthesis). The induction of tryptophan pyrrolase described here apparently involves both of these means. The slowing of tryptophan pyrrolase degradation by tryptophan analogues is also supported by the data of Schimke, Sweeney, and Berlin (8). They did not exclude the additional possibility of increased synthesis, which apparently also occurs.

The results are compatible with the hypothetical mechanism for enzymatic induction proposed by Yudkin (1) in which more enzyme accumulates (by more synthesis, less degradation, or both) when it is specifically bound with substrate and in this way removed from the (effective) equilibrium with its precursors and degradation products. Other substances combining specifically with enzymes, including coenzymes (2, 3) and inhibitors (4), have since been found to induce certain animal enzymes. These are examples of "induction by cofactors," to which belong that kind of induction of tryptophan pyrrolase discussed here. It is possible that combination of the apotryptophan pyrrolase with the analogues prior to conjugation, the conjugation, the reduction of the enzyme after conjugation, or all of these changes in sequence, act to remove the enzyme from its dynamic equilibrium so that it accumulates. Of these reactions, only the conjugation has not yet proved to be rapidly reversible in crude preparations *in vitro*. Only the purified enzyme under specialized circumstances becomes unconjugated (9, 15). The poor reversibility of conjugation may confer a relative stability on the holoenzyme, and in this way account for the association found between conjugation and induction.

Specific interactions between inducers and some form of the enzymes induced may be more common than appears from the

few examples now known in animals. A very large number of substrate-like compounds induce related enzymes in microorganisms. In explanation of this common steric relationship between inducer and enzyme, and for the reason of economy of hypotheses, Gruber and Campagne (22, 23) proposed that the illusive "repressor," with which the inducer is often thought to combine, is the nascent enzyme itself. Consistent with this view is the observation that thiomethyl β-D-galactoside, whose apparent lack of affinity for β-galactosidase (24) provided the basis for a model of induction at a distance from the enzyme (25), does in fact have equal affinities in whole cells as inhibitor of the enzyme and as inducer of the enzyme (26). The increased synthesis of hemoglobin in isolated systems caused by added hematin (27–29) offers an even closer parallel to the type of effects of conjugation on the accumulation of tryptophan pyrrolase described here.

REFERENCES

1. YUDKIN, J., *Biol. Rev. Cambridge Phil. Soc.*, **13**, 93 (1938).
2. GREENGARD, O., AND GORDON, M., *J. Biol. Chem.*, **238**, 3708 (1963).
3. GREENGARD, O., *Advance. Enzyme Regulat.*, **5**, 14 (1967).
4. BERTINO, J. R., CASHMORE, A., FINK, M., CALABRESI, P., AND LEFKOWITZ, E., *Clin. Pharmacol. Therap.*, **6**, 763 (1965).
5. CIVEN, M., AND KNOX, W. E., *J. Biol. Chem.*, **235**, 1716 (1960).
6. SOURKES, T. L., AND TOWNSEND, E., *Can. J. Biochem. Physiol.*, **33**, 735 (1955).
7. KNOX, W. E., AND PIRAS, M. M., *J. Biol. Chem.*, **241**, 764 (1966).
8. SCHIMKE, R. T., SWEENEY, E. W., AND BERLIN, C. M., *J. Biol. Chem.*, **240**, 322 (1965).
9. SCHIMKE, R. T., SWEENEY, E. W., AND BERLIN, C. M., *J. Biol. Chem.*, **240**, 4609 (1965).
10. PIRAS, M. M., AND KNOX, W. E., *J. Biol. Chem.*, **242**, 2952 (1967).
11. KNOX, W. E., *Brit. J. Exp. Pathol.*, **32**, 462 (1951).
12. KNOX, W. E., PIRAS, M. M., AND TOKUYAMA, K., *J. Biol. Chem.*, **241**, 297 (1966).
13. KNOX, W. E., PIRAS, M. M., AND TOKUYAMA, K., *Enzymol. Biol. Clin.*, **7**, 1 (1966).
14. DENCKLA, W. D., AND DEWEY, H. K., *J. Lab. Clin. Med.*, **69**, 160 (1967).
15. TOKUYAMA, K., AND KNOX, W. E., *Biochim. Biophys. Acta*, **81**, 201 (1964).
16. FEIGELSON, P., AND GREENGARD, O., *J. Biol. Chem.*, **237**, 3714 (1962).
17. GREENGARD, O., AND FEIGELSON, P., *J. Biol. Chem.*, **236**, 158 (1961).
18. KNOX, W. E., AND OGATA, M., *J. Biol. Chem.*, **240**, 2216 (1965).
19. GREENGARD, O., *Biochim. Biophys. Acta*, **85**, 492 (1964).
20. MECKE, D., AND HOLZER, H., *Biochim. Biophys. Acta*, **122**, 341 (1966).
21. KNOX, W. E., *Advance. Enzyme Regulat.*, **4**, 287 (1966).
22. GRUBER, M., AND CAMPAGNE, R. N., *Koniklijke Ned. Akad. Wetensch., Proc., Ser. C*, **68**, 1 (1965).
23. GRUBER, M., AND CAMPAGNE, R. N., *Perspect. Biol. Med.*, **10**, 125 (1966).
24. MONOD, J., COHEN-BAZIVE, G., AND COHN, M., *Biochim. Biophys. Acta*, **7**, 585 (1951).
25. JACOB, F., AND MONOD, J., *J. Mol. Biol.*, **3**, 318 (1961).
26. RICKENBERG, H. V., *Nature*, **185**, 240 (1960).
27. HAMMEL, C. L., AND BESSMAN, S. P., *Arch. Biochem. Biophys.*, **110**, 622 (1965).
28. SADDI, R., AND VON DER DECKEN, A., *Biochim. Biophys. Acta*, **111**, 124 (1965).
29. GRAYZEL, A. I., HÖRCHNER, P., AND LONDON, I. M., *Proc. Nat. Acad. Sci. U. S. A.*, **55**, 650 (1966).

Reprinted from Biochim. Biophys. Acta, Vol. 26 (1957)

ADAPTATION OF THE RAT LIVER
TYROSINE-α-KETOGLUTARATE TRANSAMINASE[*]

EDMUND C. C. LIN[**] AND W. EUGENE KNOX

Department of Biological Chemistry, Harvard Medical School and the
Cancer Research Institute of the New England Deaconess Hospital, Boston, Mass. (U.S.A.).

Numerous adaptive increases in the activity of enzymes in animal tissues are known[1], but in few instances have the stimuli producing these changes been analyzed to determine the physiological mechanisms concerned. Adaptive increases of threonine dehydrase occurred in response to elevation of the substrate concentration in intact

* This work was supported by research grant A-567 from the Institute of Arthritis and Metabolic Diseases, United States Public Health Service, and by United States Atomic Energy Commission Contract No. AT (30-1)-901 with the New England Deaconess Hospital.
** F. M. Shu Scientific Fellow (1953–56).

References p. 88.

animals and in perfused livers[2]. Tryptophan peroxidase[3] and xanthine oxidase[4] both adapted by two separate mechanisms: in response to increases of the concentration of the substrate or of adrenal corticoids. Another pattern of response was shown by the tyrosine-α-ketoglutarate transaminase of rat liver described here. This enzyme increased in activity many-fold in 5 hours in response to hydrocortisone injection. A similar response to injection of the substrate tyrosine occurred, but only if adrenal hormones were also present.

METHODS

The tyrosine-α-ketoglutarate transaminase has been purified and characterized as a specific enzyme distinct from the other known transaminating activities of liver[5]. A new assay was used which depended upon the continuous spectrophotometric measurement of the p-hydroxyphenyl-pyruvate formed from tyrosine. p-Hydroxyphenylpyruvate was trapped as its intensely absorbing enol-borate complex by carrying out the reaction in the presence of borate buffer and an excess of transaminase-free keto-enol tautomerase[6]. Oxidative removal of p-hydroxyphenylpyruvate was prevented by diethyldithiocarbamate[7]. The concentration of borate and diethyldithiocarbamate used did not adversely affect the reaction rate. The conditions chosen (Fig. 1) were optimal for the reaction with respect to pH and concentration of coenzyme and substrates, and the reaction rates were higher than those found with a different assay[5]. Under these conditions the formation of p-hydroxyphenylpyruvate followed zero order kinetics at rates proportional to the amount of liver extract employed (Fig. 1). Since no uncontrolled factors were known to alter the activity, the activities measured were assumed to be proportional to enzyme concentrations in the livers.

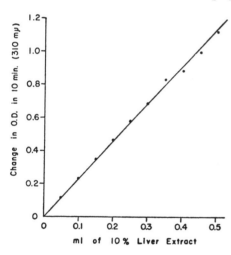

Fig. 1. The activity-concentration curve of rat liver tyrosine-α-ketoglutarate transaminase measured by the accumulation of the enol–borate complex of p-hydroxyphenylpyruvate. The enzyme was assayed at $25° \pm 1°C$ in a 1 cm quartz cell containing 30 μg of pyridoxal phosphate, an excess of a preparation of kidney keto-enol tautomerase ($k = 0.5$) free of the transaminase, 12 μmoles of L-tyrosine, 0.57 M borate, pH 8.0, 0.003 M diethyldithiocarbamate, and 0.3 ml of liver extract in a final volume of 3.5 ml. The reaction was initiated by the addition of 80 μmoles of α-ketoglutarate. The formation of p-hydroxyphenylpyruvate ($\varepsilon_{310} = 9.85 \cdot 10^{13}$) was followed for 10 minutes by readings of optical density at 310 mμ, against a blank containing all components of the reaction mixture except tyrosine.

The enzyme level was determined in the fresh supernatant fraction of 10% liver homogenates from individual adult male Slonaker rats, all of approximately the same age. When adrenalectomized, the rats were given 1% sodium chloride as drinking water and were used 2 to 8 days after the operation. Groups of animals were given the compounds listed in Table I by intraperitoneal injection in 2 to 5 ml of saline, 5 hours before sacrifice and removal of the liver for the enzyme assay. Aliquots of the homogenates were dried for 3 to 5 hours at 110°C and weighed. The enzyme activity was expressed as μmoles of p-hydroxyphenylpyruvate formed per gram dry weight of liver in 1 hour.

RESULTS

The mean activities of the enzyme found in some of the groups of animals investigated are given in Table I. Injection of L-tyrosine increased the enzyme level in the intact

References p. 88.

animals seven-fold in the 5-hour test period. Injection of similar amounts of L-phenylalanine or L-glutamate produced definite increases about one-third as great as did tyrosine, and only in intact animals. Adrenalectomy alone did not significantly alter the level of the enzyme, yet when tyrosine was injected into the adrenalectomized rats, no change in the transaminase level was produced. Tyrosine was also administered for several weeks to intact rats as 5% of their diet, to avoid the stress of injection. Tyrosine given under these conditions did not elevate the level of the enzyme in the liver.

TABLE I

TYROSINE TRANSAMINASE ACTIVITY IN LIVERS OF RATS FIVE HOURS AFTER TREATMENT

| Treatment | No. of animals | Enzyme activity* | | P value (compared with untreated) |
		Mean ± S.E.	% Difference from untreated	
Intact rats				
Untreated	23	159 ± 21	—	—
L-Tyrosine, 1 mmole/300 g	8	1370 ± 168	+760	< 0.001
Hydrocortisone, 10 mg/kg	3	308 ± 9	+94	< 0.05
Hydrocortisone, 30 mg/kg	7	934 ± 84	+490	< 0.001
Adrenalectomized				
Untreated	13	175 ± 21	—	—
L-Tyrosine, 1 mmole/300 g	7	166 ± 73	—5	> 0.5
Hydrocortisone, 10 mg/kg	8	1110 ± 163	+530	< 0.001
Hydrocortisone, 10 mg/kg and L-tyrosine, 1 mmole/300 g	8	2050 ± 151	+1070	< 0.001

* Expressed as μmoles of p-hydroxyphenylpyruvate formed at 25°C per gram dry liver per hour.

Homogentisate was excreted by these animals, indicating that the extra tyrosine was metabolized[8]. It therefore appeared possible that tyrosine administration must be accompanied by release of adrenal cortical hormones from the stress of injection in order to elevate the level of liver tyrosine transaminase.

Hydrocortisone by itself was found to be a sufficient stimulus to elevate the enzyme level in both intact and adrenalectomized rats. Adrenalectomized rats showed larger increases with less hydrocortisone than the intact rats. At least a part of the increase in enzyme level produced by tyrosine and the other amino acids given to intact animals could therefore be attributed to the adrenal cortical hormones released nonspecifically by the stress of injection of the amino acids. The enzyme level was not changed in saline-injected control animals. Such adrenal cortical hormone release was observed after tyrosine or histidine injections and caused increases in the tryptophan peroxidase level[9].

Tyrosine injection appeared also to exert a specific effect on the enzyme level, in addition to its possible release of cortical hormones, since it produced a greater increase in enzyme level in the intact animals than did the other amino acids. This specific effect was demonstrated more clearly by injection of tyrosine together with hydrocortisone to rats two days after adrenalectomy. Although tyrosine alone caused no change in the adrenalectomized rats, when it was given with hydrocortisone the two together produced twice the enzyme level as that obtained by hydrocortisone alone.

References p. 88.

Tyrosine, therefore, exerted a specific substrate-inducing effect, but only in the presence of adrenal cortical hormone released in the intact animal by stress or separately administered to adrenalectomized animals.

DISCUSSION

Adaptive changes have been found in the first one of the series of enzymes leading to the degradation of either tyrosine or of tryptophan, but so far adaptation has not been found in subsequent reactions in these pathways. The rates of metabolism of these amino acids may be effectively controlled by regulation of only the initial reaction in each series. Both enzymes were increased to about the same extent in about the same length of time by hydrocortisone and by injection of their respective substrates to intact animals. The adaptive responses of these two enzymes differed when the substrates were administered to adrenalectomized animals. The tryptophan peroxidase level was increased in adrenalectomized rats by injection of the substrate, tryptophan. Tyrosine transaminase level was affected by tyrosine administration to adrenalectomized animals only if adrenal hormone was also given. While the tryptophan peroxidase level was controlled independently by hormone or substrate concentration, the tyrosine transaminase level appeared to be controlled primarily by adrenal hormones, and upon this mechanism was superimposed an additional control by the substrate concentration.

The major control of tyrosine transaminase level by adrenal corticoids offers an explanation for the alteration in activity of this enzyme known to occur in newborn animals. The activity of the enzyme is absent from liver of rats and human at birth, but appears within hours after birth[10]. Hydrocortisone is also released shortly after birth and is present in adult levels after a few days[11].

SUMMARY

Adaptive increase of the tyrosine-α-ketoglutarate transaminase occurred in the livers of rats following injections of tyrosine or of hydrocortisone. The increases were as great as 10-fold and occurred in 5 hours. Analysis showed that hydrocortisone itself was a sufficient inducing stimulus. Tyrosine was an effective inducing stimulus only if the adrenal glands or hydrocortisone also were present.

REFERENCES

[1] W. E. KNOX, V. H. AUERBACH AND E. C. C. LIN, *Physiol. Revs.*, 36 (1956) 164.
[2] F. W. SAYRE, D. JENSEN AND D. M. GREENBERG, *J. Biol. Chem.*, 219 (1956) 111.
[3] W. E. KNOX AND V. H. AUERBACH, *J. Biol. Chem.*, 214 (1955) 307.
[4] L. S. DIETRICH, *J. Biol. Chem.*, 211 (1954) 79.
[5] Z. N. CANELLAKIS AND P. P. COHEN, *J. Biol. Chem.*, 222 (1956) 53.
[6] W. E. KNOX AND B. M. PITT, *J. Biol. Chem.*, 225 (1957) 675.
[7] S. E. HAGER, R. I. GREGERMAN AND W. E. KNOX, *J. Biol. Chem.*, 225 (1957) 935.
[8] E. PAPAGEORGE AND H. B. LEWIS, *J. Biol. Chem.*, 123 (1938) 211.
[9] W. E. KNOX, *Brit. J. Exptl. Pathol.*, 22 (1951) 462.
[10] N. KRETCHMER, S. Z. LEVINE, H. MCNAMARA AND H. L. BARNETT, *J. Clin. Invest.*, 35 (1956) 236.
[11] R. KLEIN, J. FORTUNATO AND C. PAPADATOS, *J. Clin. Invest.*, 33 (1954) 35.

Received May 10th, 1957

THE JOURNAL OF BIOLOGICAL CHEMISTRY
Vol. 237, No. 5, May 1962
Printed in U.S.A.

Induction of Tyrosine-α-ketoglutarate Transaminase in Rat Liver

III. IMMUNOCHEMICAL ANALYSIS

FRANCIS T. KENNEY

From the Biology Division, Oak Ridge National Laboratory,* Oak Ridge, Tennessee

(Received for publication, January 4, 1962)

Previous papers of this series have demonstrated that induction of tyrosine α-ketoglutarate transaminase of rat liver can be attributed to adrenocortical hormone (1) and described extensive purification of the transaminase from normal and induced livers (2). The present report describes experiments in which the induction phenomenon was analyzed with a highly specific antiserum prepared against the enzyme purified from induced livers. Analysis was directed toward determining whether the increase in activity observed on induction reflects a hormonal stimulation of specific enzyme synthesis or some other mechanism. In a preliminary report (3), the results of precipitin and labeling experiments were interpreted as suggesting the existence of an inactive precursor to the enzyme in the noninduced state. The present experiments, in which a more specific antiserum and techniques for ensuring specificity in immunological assays have been used, confirm the preliminary observations reported, insofar as they demonstrate that enzyme labeling is independent of induction. However, the data also demonstrate that a simple precursor-enzyme interconversion is not involved.

EXPERIMENTAL PROCEDURE

Transaminase activity measurements were as described previously (2, 4). Male Sprague-Dawley rats weighing 250 to 350 g were used in all experiments and, when adrenalectomized, were used 24 to 48 hours after surgery. Tyrosine transaminase induction was accomplished by intraperitoneal administration of hydrocortisone, 10 mg per 100 g of body weight. This dose induces the transaminase to the fullest extent observed (1), and the animals were killed after maximal induction had been attained, between 4 and 5 hours after injection (5).

Liver soluble fractions were obtained from homogenates prepared in 0.15 M KCl-10^{-3} M EDTA by centrifugation at 105,000 × g for 60 minutes. Nuclear, mitochondrial, and lysosomal fractions were isolated from homogenates prepared in 0.25 M sucrose by centrifugation at 600 × g for 5 minutes, 5,000 × g for 10 minutes, and 20,000 × g for 15 minutes, respectively. Each fraction was washed once by resuspension in 0.25 M sucrose and recentrifugation. Microsomes from the livers of rats that had been deprived of food were prepared in a medium containing Mg^{++} as described by Zamecnik and Keller (6). The microsome fraction was subfractionated into ribonucleoprotein particles (ribosomes) and membranous components by treatment with

* Operated by Union Carbide Corporation for the United States Atomic Energy Commission.

deoxycholate according to the method of Palade and Siekevitz (7). All preparative procedures were carried out at 0–3°.

In labeling experiments, C^{14}-amino acids were administered intraperitoneally in three doses 1½ hours apart, induced animals receiving hydrocortisone with the first injection of isotope. Aliquots of liver fractions and of dissolved antigen-antibody complexes were pipetted onto filter paper disks, then freed from nonprotein contaminants, and counted as described by Mans and Novelli (8). Replicate radioactivity determinations agreed to within ±2% and have been averaged in the data presented. Separate aliquots of the preparations counted were analyzed for protein (9).

Antigen-antibody interactions wherein the protein content or the radioactivity of the precipitated complex was to be determined were carried out in either NaCl or KCl solutions at 0.15 M. Both the enzyme and the antibody preparation were centrifuged at 10,000 × g for 10 minutes just before initiation of reaction in order to insure removal of insoluble protein. After mixing, the solutions were left at 23° for approximately 30 minutes and then at 3° for 12 to 36 hours. Precipitates were collected by centrifugation, washed three times with 0.15 M NaCl, and then dissolved in 0.5 N NaOH. This procedure yielded satisfactory duplicate protein assays, and no precipitate was formed if either antigen or antibody was omitted, except when crude liver soluble fractions were analyzed. Nonspecific precipitation from soluble fractions was overcome by first removing the unstable liver proteins by incubating soluble fractions at 37° for 30 minutes before the "clearing" centrifugation. Addition of α-ketoglutarate (10^{-2} M) during this incubation protected the transaminase from thermal denaturation but did not interfere with reaction with antibody (2).

Immunochemical assays in which enzyme inactivation by antibody was the parameter measured were used with several modifications. These assays were all designed to detect and measure enzymically inactive liver components which react specifically with antitransaminase; the measurements depend on the ability of such cross-reactive materials to compete with enzyme in its reaction with antibody. The antibody unit was defined as the amount that inactivates 1 enzyme unit (2); the antibody preparation was standardized by titration with the highly purified enzyme used to stimulate its formation. The antigen unit is here defined as the amount of antigen reacting with 1 antibody unit. In liver preparations which do not contain cross-reactive materials, antigen units (immunological assay) should equal enzyme units (activity assay). The modifications employed were the following.

1. Titration Assay—Antigen content of liver fractions that contain substantial amounts of enzyme activity was determined by direct titration of a known amount of antibody. Enzyme and antibody solutions were mixed and incubated as described above. After centrifugation, the precipitated complex was discarded and residual transaminase activity in the supernatant liquids was determined. This procedure yields a sharp equivalence point at which soluble enzyme can be detected (*cf.* Fig. 1). Cross-reactive material would be detected as saturation of added antibody with less enzyme than predicted from the activity assay. Enzyme inhibition by antibody is rapid, and for some purposes extended incubations could be omitted. However, since the antigen-antibody complex retains some enzyme activity (2), precise determinations of the amount of enzyme bound could not be obtained until the complex was allowed to aggregate and was removed as a precipitate.

2. Antibody Fixation—Liver fractions containing little enzyme activity were assayed by addition of graded aliquots to a constant amount of antibody. The mixtures were incubated at 0–3° for periods of 15 minutes to 12 hours. Enzyme was then added in excess. Inhibition is essentially complete within 10 minutes, and aliquots were taken for activity assay 15 minutes after enzyme addition. Controls in which no liver fraction was added to antibody in the first incubation were routinely included. Material reacting with antibody is reflected in the final assay as a greater recovery of enzyme activity than found in the control.

3. Kinetic Assay—Both antigen assays described are based on the assumption that the cross-reactive material sought is fully competitive, *i.e.* equivalent to active enzyme in capacity for interaction with antibody. Antigen that lacks some antibody-binding sites and is thereby unable to compete with enzyme, or that competes poorly, would not be detected. Hence a kinetic assay was also used in which the rate of enzyme inhibition by antibody was measured. Antibody was incubated with the fractions to be tested as in the competition assay described above. Then a known quantity of enzyme was added, and aliquots of the mixture were taken for activity assay at 0.5- or 1-minute intervals. The activity assay was shortened from 10 to 2 minutes in order to decrease the extent of interaction further. Under these conditions, even a poorly competitive cross-reactive material present in the unknown fraction should effect a decrease in the rate of enzyme inhibition, since its replacement by enzyme on the antibody can be assumed to be time-dependent. Rate measurements were converted to antigen units by standardizing the assay with an enzyme preparation assayed by titration.

Titration assays could be made with precision equal to that of enzyme activity measurements, provided that the partially active antigen-antibody complex was removed by centrifugation. However, the particulate nature of the fractions tested in antibody fixation assays precluded removal of this precipitate, and, similarly, it could not be removed in kinetic assays. For this reason these assays are only semiquantitative, and the results reported should be regarded as approximations.

Diffusion analyses in agar gel were carried out essentially as described by Oudin (10). The low level of essential reacting components in crude liver preparations resulted in precipitation bands too weak for photographic reproduction, and representative drawings were therefore substituted.

RESULTS

Antigen Assays—The possibility that a preformed enzyme precursor is present in noninduced livers, as suggested by earlier experiments (3), was reinvestigated with the specific competition techniques described. The reaction of transaminase and antitransaminase is not dependent on enzymic activity (2), and it is therefore reasonable to assume that such a precursor would be detected immunochemically. However, the results shown in Table I indicate conclusively that a precursor cannot, in fact, be detected. Increased soluble activity after induction is associated with an equivalent increase in soluble antigen. Further, although the results of antigen assays of particulate fractions were somewhat erratic, it is apparent that none of these fractions contains antigenic material in marked excess of the active enzyme present. The results with nuclei, mitochondria, and lysosomes were essentially unchanged when these particles were disrupted by repetitive freezing and thawing, detergent treatment, or sonic oscillation or when they were assayed by the kinetic method.

Deoxycholate treatment of the microsome fraction, however, did reveal more antigen bound to the ribosomes than could be accounted for as active enzyme (Table II). Although this material remained insoluble through detergent treatment and a

TABLE I

Enzyme and antigen activities in subcellular fractions of liver

The data are expressed as units per g of liver. Soluble fractions were analyzed for antigen by titration, and the other fractions by antibody fixation assay. All assays were carried out after overnight storage at −15°. Enzyme and antigen activities of nuclear fractions were exceptionally high in this experiment and were reduced to the level of the mitochondrial fractions when homogenates were filtered through cheesecloth before fractionation.

Fraction	Enzyme		Antigen	
	Control	Induced	Control	Induced
Nuclear	500	2,400	450	2,500
Mitochondrial	80	160	100	230
Lysosomal	<5	100	<5	120
Microsomal	20	470	50	270
Soluble	4400	46,600	4500	47,000

TABLE II

Ribosome-bound cross-reactive material

The data are expressed as units per g of liver. Antigen assays were by the kinetic competition method described in the text. The soluble fraction is the supernatant fluid obtained by centrifugation of liver homogenates at 105,000 × *g* for 60 minutes. Ribosomes were prepared from microsomes and washed once with water and then extracted with 0.05 M PP$_i$, pH 7.5. at 37° for 30 minutes, followed by centrifugation at 105,000 × *g* to remove the insoluble residue.

Fraction	Enzyme		Antigen	
	Control	Induced	Control	Induced
Soluble	3270	41,800	2570	44,300
Ribosomes	<5	20	190	230
Ribosomal extract	<5	30	600	960

subsequent water wash, it could be released by treatment with metal-binding reagents, and antigen activity was appreciably increased by solubilization. EDTA, ATP, and PP_i were tested under a variety of incubation conditions, and optimal extraction conditions were used in the experiment reported. These results were obtained with the kinetic assay designed to detect poorly competitive cross-reactive material. Ribosomal extracts tested in the antibody fixation assay failed to exhibit antigen activity, suggesting that the cross-reactive material may lack some antigenic sites.

Antibody Specificity—Validity of the results of labeling experiments to be presented depends in large part on the specificity with which enzyme can be precipitated from crude liver extracts

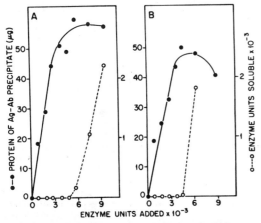

FIG. 1. Antibody titration with purified and crude enzyme preparations. *A*, Purified enzyme. Each tube contained 5500 antibody units; enzyme with a specific activity of 25,000 units per mg of protein, in varying amounts as indicated; and 0.15 M NaCl to a final 2.0-ml volume. The enzyme preparation had been purified through hydroxylapatite chromatography (2). *B*, Crude enzyme. Each tube contained 4400 antibody units. The enzyme preparation (specific activity, 595 units per mg of protein) was the soluble fraction of liver from an induced rat.

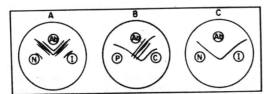

FIG. 2. Agar-gel diffusion (Ouchterlony) analyses of enzyme-antibody interaction. *A*, Comparison of crude induced and non-induced liver preparations. The well marked *N* contained 1.42 mg of a noninduced liver preparation with a specific activity of 106 units per mg of protein; that marked *I* contained 1.34 mg of an induced preparation with a specific activity of 1026 units per mg of protein. *B*, Comparison of crude induced and purified enzyme. The well marked *C* was loaded exactly as was that marked *I* in part *A*; that marked *P* contained 250 μg of purified enzyme with a specific activity of 18,050 units per mg of protein. *C*, Comparison of partially purified induced and noninduced preparations. The preparations tested in part *A* were purified further as described in the text. Each test well contained 190 μg of protein, with specific activity as follows: noninduced, 2100; induced, 18,400 units per mg of protein.

by addition of antibody. A discussion of experimental results bearing on the question of specificity is therefore appropriate here.

Titration of antibody with a partially purified enzyme preparation yields a typical precipitin curve in which antigen excess is indicated by a decrease in the amount of precipitable antigen-antibody complex (Fig. 1*A*). Assay of the supernatants of these mixtures for enzyme activity provides an equivalence point for transaminase-antitransaminase interaction. This equivalence point is identical, within the limits of experimental error, with that of the precipitin assay, in which any reacting components would contribute to the protein precipitated. This identity indicates that the transaminase is the only component reacting with antibody. Thus, with purified enzyme preparations antibody can be considered to be a specific reagent for transaminase, a conclusion which is substantiated by the production of a single precipitation band when these preparations are analyzed by double diffusion in agar gel (2).

Antibody titration with a crude soluble fraction from the livers of induced rats yields the same result (Fig. 1*B*). Under the conditions used, equivalence points of the transaminase-antitransaminase reaction and of the total protein precipitated are again identical within the limits of experimental error. Further, the quantity of protein precipitated per unit of enzyme added is essentially the same whether enzyme is added as a purified preparation or a crude liver fraction. This result, indicating specificity in crude as well as purified enzyme preparations, would appear to be at variance with the results of double diffusion analysis of crude preparations. When soluble fractions of liver were concentrated and partially purified by ammonium sulfate fractionation and heating (2), the product yielded several bands of precipitation (Fig. 2*A*). Most of the bands appear the same whether formed from induced or noninduced liver preparations, but the minor band nearest the antigen well was much more intense with induced livers. The conclusion that this minor band is formed by the transaminase was substantiated by a reaction suggesting identity with the band formed by a purified enzyme preparation (Fig. 2*B*). When the crude preparations were purified further by stepwise elution from DEAE-cellulose columns, each yielded a single band, with intensity proportional to specific activity (Fig. 2*C*). These results indicate that in liver preparations more crude than those analyzed in Fig. 2*C*, there are several components, unrelated to tyrosine transaminase, that react with the antibody preparation.

The apparent discrepancy between the results of titration and diffusion analyses can be resolved by a consideration of the relative levels of antibody and antigen in the gel medium used in diffusion analysis. Antibody level is highest at the antibody well and decreases continuously in the direction of the antigen well; the reverse holds for antigen level. The heavy bands due to contaminants are situated in zones where the antibody to antigen ratio is high. In contrast, the enzyme band lies close to the antigen well, a zone of high antigen and low antibody levels. Thus, under conditions wherein a large amount of the liver fraction reacts with a small amount of antibody, equivalence for the transaminase-antitransaminase reaction can be realized with little or no reaction of the contaminants. These conditions are met in the titration assays described. It can then be concluded that at enzymic equivalence, the antibody preparation is highly specific in its reaction with the transaminase in crude as well as purified liver fractions.

Enzyme Labeling and Induction—The results presented above

made it apparent that previous C^{14} incorporation studies, described in a preliminary report (3), were carried out under conditions wherein immunochemical specificity was not obtained. In the present experiments, a volume of each labeled liver fraction was chosen that would yield sufficient antigen-antibody precipitate (300 to 500 μg) for duplicate radioactivity analyses, and an exact equivalent of antibody units was added.

Labeling of transaminase during induction was compared with that of the total liver soluble proteins, with a variety of C^{14}-amino acids used as precursors (Table III). Hydrocortisone effected a 12- to 14-fold increase in transaminase activity during the experimental period. Radioactivity was incorporated into the soluble proteins of liver to an extent somewhat dependent on the labeled amino acid employed. In each experiment, the specific radioactivity of the transaminase-antitransaminase complex was from 2 to 2.4 times greater than that of the average soluble protein. It should be noted that, owing to the inclusion of unlabeled antibody in the precipitated complex, the full extent of transaminase labeling is not indicated. Corrections cannot be rigorously applied, as the antigen to antibody ratio in the precipitated complex is not known.

To ascertain whether extensive enzyme labeling is dependent on induction, a second type of experiment was carried out, which included control animals that were given radioactive amino acids but not hydrocortisone. The rats used here had been adrenalectomized in order to avoid the possibility of induction in controls as a result of repeated injections. As noted, controls were given somewhat greater amounts of isotope during the experimental period, since previous experiments had indicated that incorporation of labeled amino acids into liver proteins was rather poor after adrenalectomy (3). Results are summarized in Table IV. The low transaminase activity in the pooled soluble fractions from control animals is evidence that no increase in enzyme occurred in these animals during the experimental period, whereas a 25-fold increase occurred in induced animals. Transaminase activity in control soluble fractions was too low to permit specific precipitation of enzyme by antibody, and hence both prepara-

TABLE III

Transaminase labeling during induction

In each experiment a single rat was given 15 μc of the labeled amino acid noted; the mixture used in Experiment 4 contained roughly equivalent amounts of C^{14}-labeled-L-alanine, phenylalanine, valine, glycine, lysine, and leucine. The extent of transaminase induction was calculated by comparison of the specific transaminase activity of these soluble fractions with the average specific activity found in noninduced animals (45 units per mg of protein). By the addition of an equivalent amount of antibody, 50,000 enzyme units were precipitated from each soluble fraction.

Experiment No.	C¹⁴-amino acid given	Percentage of increase in transaminase induction	Radioactivity	
			Total soluble protein	Ag-Ab* protein
			c.p.m./mg	
1	Leucine	1253	189	461
2	Isoleucine	1210	237	535
3	Methionine	1445	344	684
4	Mixture	1375	245	588

* The abbreviation used is: Ag-Ab, the complex formed between enzyme (antigen) and antibody.

TABLE IV

Enzyme labeling in induced and noninduced animals

All animals had been bilaterally adrenalectomized 24 to 48 hours before the experiment. The isotope administered contained equal amounts of uniformly labeled L-leucine and methyl-labeled DL-methionine; six controls were each given 16.5 μc, and two induced animals each received 11.6 μc. Livers from control and induced animals, respectively, were pooled and fractionated as described in the text. By the addition of an equivalent amount of antibody, 31,500 enzyme units were precipitated from each DEAE-cellulose fraction.

Fraction	Treatment	Enzyme specific activity	Radioactivity
		units/mg protein	*c.p.m./mg protein*
Soluble	Control	23	398
	Induced	576	287
DEAE-cellulose	Control	1,100	540
	Induced	18,050	468
Ag-Ab* precipitate	Control		862
	Induced		677

* The abbreviation used is: Ag-Ab, the complex formed between enzyme (antigen) and antibody.

tions were purified and concentrated by ammonium sulfate precipitation, heating, and stepwise elution from DEAE-cellulose before enzyme precipitation. These procedures resulted in a 30- to 50-fold enrichment in enzyme, and a slight increase in specific radioactivity of both preparations was also found. When the enzyme from the DEAE-cellulose eluates was precipitated by antibody and the antigen-antibody complex washed and counted, it was found that the precipitates from both preparations were extensively labeled. Thus, in noninduced controls, specific radioactivity of the precipitated antigen-antibody complex was 2.2 times greater than that of the total soluble proteins, and in induced animals this ratio was 2.4. The small difference observed here is within experimental variation and cannot be considered meaningful. As in the experiments presented in Table III, the inclusion of unlabeled antibody in these precipitates masks the true extent of enzyme labeling. However, it is apparent that this labeling is independent of the process of induction, as shown previously (3).

DISCUSSION

Induction of a hepatic enzyme by hydrocortisone provides an excellent model system in which several key parameters of metabolic control can be analyzed: (a) the cellular mechanism responsible for increased enzyme, (b) the locus and mechanism of control of this process, and (c) the mode of action of adrenal corticosteroids in this control. The present studies lead to conclusions regarding the first of these, but as yet the latter two remain conjectural.

Increased soluble transaminase activity after induction is matched by an equivalent increase in soluble transaminase protein, determined immunochemically. De Duve and coworkers have demonstrated that several hepatic enzymes appear partially inactive under ordinary assay conditions, inactivity being due to their being bound in such subcellular particulate fractions as lysosomes (11) and mitochondria (12). Release into the soluble phase of such a bound enzyme could result in increases in both soluble activity and soluble antigen. However, direct analysis of liver particulate fractions failed to show any antigenic activity in amounts even approaching that required to account for the increase in soluble antigen observed. The conclusion derived from these analyses, that a preformed precursor does not exist, is definitively established by the results of labeling experiments.

When transaminase was induced in the presence of C^{14}-labeled amino acids, extensive incorporation into the enzyme was observed. The data provide a measure of only the lower limit of the extent of transaminase labeling, since radioactivity must be determined in a complex with unlabeled antibody. As yet a reliable estimate of the ratio of transaminase to antibody in this complex is not available. In a recent report concerning studies of repression of enzyme synthesis in *Escherichia coli*, Rogers has found an enzyme to antibody ratio of 0.24:1 in the precipitate formed by the interaction of ornithine transcarbamylase and its antibody (13). If a ratio of this magnitude were to exist for the liver transaminase-antitransaminase complex, appropriate corrections of the data of Tables III and IV would yield results indicating that the enzyme labeling is 12 to 13 times greater than that of the bulk of the soluble proteins. Whatever the true extent of enzyme labeling may be, it is apparent that the transaminase has been synthesized from amino acids during induction, and the possibility of a preformed, unlabeled precursor is thus excluded.

Although the data indicate that transaminase is synthesized during its induction, it cannot be rigorously concluded that enzyme synthesis is due to induction. An exceptionally rapid turnover of this enzyme is reflected in the extensive labeling of transaminase in noninduced livers. The half-life of induced tyrosine transaminase has been estimated at less than 3 hours (14), and that of another inducible hepatic enzyme at 2.3 hours (15). Both of these estimates were presumably based on measurements of the rate of decay of enzyme activity in the postinduction phase and may not have been valid for the noninduced steady state condition. Nevertheless, these estimates are not contradicted by the measurements reported here of incorporation of radioactive amino acids into transaminase under conditions wherein no net increase in enzyme occurred. During a $4\frac{1}{2}$-hour labeling period, enzyme in the livers of noninduced controls was labeled to the same extent as when enzyme increased 25-fold. This result indicates that although no net increase in enzyme took place, the enzyme in control livers was nevertheless newly synthesized within the experimental period. We must conclude, then, that transaminase synthesis is rapid in both the induced and the noninduced conditions. Although stimulation of specific enzyme synthesis is not incompatible with the observations made, alternative mechanisms not directly involving the pathway of protein synthesis as the point of hormonal control are not excluded. Thus, a mechanism whereby induction simply permits the accumulation of the synthesized product would also yield the results observed here.

Such an alternative mechanism would appear to be improbable, however, in view of the 25-fold increase in the amount of enzyme during $4\frac{1}{2}$ hours' induction. If this reflects the true rate of enzyme synthesis, unobscured by concurrent degradation, maintenance of the steady state level in the noninduced condition would require that all of the enzyme be renewed approximately each 11 minutes. Isotopic measurement of the rate of transaminase synthesis should resolve this question conclusively, and such measurements are now in progress.

Immunochemical competition techniques have detected a ribosome-bound component that is enzymically inactive but reacts with antitransaminase. The amount detected is small in relation to the total active enzyme, and there is some suggestion that the material may lack some antigenic sites. These results, together with its origin and the treatment effective in release, could be interpreted as indicating that the antigen detected represents template-bound enzyme in partially completed form. Further study will be required before this can be established, as well as to delineate the possible relations between this ribosomal antigen and the enzymic, energy-requiring activation of microsomal enzyme recently reported[1] by Pitot and Cho (16).

SUMMARY

Induction *in vivo* of rat liver tyrosine α-ketoglutarate transaminase by hydrocortisone was studied with specific immunochemical techniques. Increased enzyme activity is associated with an equivalent increase in enzyme antigen, and a cross-reactive precursor could not be detected in any of the subcellular fractions of liver. Induction in the presence of C^{14}-labeled amino acids results in extensive labeling of the transaminase, but the enzyme is equally labeled in noninduced controls. It is concluded that increased enzyme activity after induction reflects newly synthesized enzyme, but that hydrocortisone may or may not stimulate specific enzyme synthesis. A small amount of enzymically inactive but immunologically active material was detected in isolated ribosomes from both induced and noninduced livers. This material could be released in soluble form by treatment of ribosomes with metal-binding reagents.

Acknowledgments—I am indebted to Drs. C. J. Wust and T. Makinodan for their aid and advice in the immunological aspects of this work, and to Dr. G. David Novelli for his continued interest in these investigations.

REFERENCES

1. Kenney, F. T., and Flora, R. M., *J. Biol. Chem.*, **236**, 2699 (1961).
2. Kenney, F. T., *J. Biol. Chem.*, **237**, 1605 (1962).
3. Kenney, F. T., *Biochem. and Biophys. Research Communs.*, **2**, 333 (1960).
4. Kenney, F. T., *J. Biol. Chem.*, **234**, 2707 (1959).
5. Lin, E. C. C., and Knox, W. E., *Biochim. et Biophys. Acta*, **26**, 85 (1957).
6. Zamecnik, P. C., and Keller, E. B., *J. Biol. Chem.*, **209**, 337 (1954).
7. Palade, G. E., and Siekevitz, P., *J. Biophys. Biochem. Cytol.*, **2**, 171 (1956).
8. Mans, R. J., and Novelli, G. D., *Arch. Biochem. Biophys.*, **94**, 48 (1961).
9. Lowry, O. H., Rosebrough, N. J., Farr, A. L., and Randall, R. J., *J. Biol. Chem.*, **193**, 265 (1951).
10. Oudin, J., in A. C. Corcoran (Editor), *Methods in medical research*, Vol. 5, Year Book Publishers, Chicago, 1952, p. 335.
11. DeDuve, C., in T. Hayashi (Editor), *Subcellular particles*, Ronald Press Co., New York, 1959, p. 128.
12. Bendall, D. S., and DeDuve, C., *Biochem. J.*, **74**, 444 (1960).
13. Rogers, P., *Science*, **134**, 737 (1961).
14. Lin, E. C. C., and Knox, W. E., *J. Biol. Chem.*, **233**, 1186 (1958).
15. Feigelson, P., Dashman, T., and Margolis, F., *Arch. Biochem. Biophys.*, **85**, 478 (1959).
16. Pitot, H. C., and Cho, Y. S., *Biochim. et Biophys. Acta*, **50**, 197 (1961).

[1] The reference cited describes experiments on activation of microsome-bound tryptophan pyrrolase. A similar activation of tyrosine α-ketoglutarate transaminase can also be detected (H. C. Pitot, personal communication).

The Journal of Biological Chemistry
Vol. 243, No. 12, Issue of June 25, pp. 3296–3300, 1968
Printed in U.S.A.

Regulation of Tyrosine-α-Ketoglutarate Transaminase in Rat Liver

VII. HORMONAL EFFECTS ON SYNTHESIS IN THE ISOLATED, PERFUSED LIVER*

(Received for publication, January 12, 1968)

C. Bradley Hager‡ and Francis T. Kenney

From the Biology Division, National Cancer Institute-Atomic Energy Commission Carcinogenesis Program, Oak Ridge National Laboratory, Oak Ridge, Tennessee 37830

SUMMARY

Hormonal regulation of the synthesis of hepatic tyrosine transaminase (L-tyrosine:2-oxoglutarate aminotransferase, EC 2.6.1.5) was studied in the isolated, perfused rat liver. Hydrocortisone, insulin, and glucagon, each of which increases the rate of synthesis of tyrosine transaminase when administered *in vivo*, were all found to do so by direct action on the liver. Induction by continuous infusion of hydrocortisone continued throughout the time course of the experiments (9 to 11 hours). Infusion of either insulin or glucagon initiated a rapid but limited increase in tyrosine transaminase synthesis, the maximum activity being attained 2½ to 3 hours after the initial addition of these hormones. The hormonal inductions of this enzyme were all sensitive to actinomycin D. Growth hormone, which mediates a selective repression of tyrosine transaminase when administered to adrenalectomized rats *in vivo*, did not alter the level of this enzyme in the isolated, perfused rat liver, suggesting that this hormone acts indirectly.

The preceding papers of this series (1, 2) described the effects on synthesis of rat liver tyrosine transaminase (L-tyrosine:2-oxoglutarate aminotransferase, EC 2.6.1.5) brought about by insulin, glucagon, and growth hormone *in vivo*. Administration of either insulin or glucagon to adrenalectomized rats increased the rate of synthesis of hepatic tyrosine transaminase, whereas growth hormone brought about a selective repression[1] of this enzyme. The approach *in vivo* is complicated by the fact that it

* This research was jointly sponsored by the National Cancer Institute and the United States Atomic Energy Commission under contract with Union Carbide Corporation.
‡ Postdoctoral Fellow of the American Cancer Society.
[1] The terms "induction" and "repression" are used here to mean a selective stimulation and inhibition, respectively, of the rate of enzyme synthesis; no genetic or other mechanism is implied.

is impossible to determine whether an observed induction or repression occurs as a result of direct participation of the administered hormone at the tissue level. In the present work the effect of each of the hormones known to alter the rate of hepatic tyrosine transaminase synthesis *in vivo* was studied in the isolated, perfused rat liver by the techniques of Miller *et al.* (3) and Miller, Burke, and Haft (4). Induction by hydrocortisone of tyrosine transaminase in the isolated liver has been previously reported by Barnabei and Sereni (5) and by Goldstein, Stella, and Knox (6). In the present study, hydrocortisone, insulin, and glucagon were all found to induce tyrosine transaminase in the isolated, perfused rat liver. Under the conditions used, the response to each of these hormones was essentially identical with that observed in experiments *in vivo*. However, growth hormone did not alter tyrosine transaminase activity in this system.

EXPERIMENTAL PROCEDURE

Animals—Male rats obtained from Charles River Breeding Laboratories were bilaterally adrenalectomized at least 18 hours before use. After adrenalectomy the rats were continued on a diet of Purina Chow Checkers but were given 1% NaCl as drinking water. Livers were obtained from rats weighting 450 to 650 g, whereas blood was drawn from rats weighing 500 to 700 g. Blood donors were lightly anesthetized with ether and were exsanguinated from the abdominal aorta with a syringe moistened with heparin. Livers for perfusion were taken from rats which were also under ether anesthesia.

Materials—Hydrocortisone (cortisol 21-hemisuccinate) was from Mann. Crystalline insulin and glucagon were from Sigma. In some experiments, preparations of each of these pancreatic hormones were used that were specially treated to remove traces of the other; these were gifts from Dr. Otto Behrens of Eli Lilly Company. Adenosine-3′,5′-cyclic monophosphoric acid was from Sigma. Actinomycin D was a gift from Merck, Sharp, and Dohme. All hormone preparations were used as solutions in 0.15 M NaCl, sometimes made slightly alkaline to facilitate solubilization. Actinomycin D was dissolved in a minimal volume of acetone, then diluted extensively with 0.15 M NaCl.

Liver Perfusion Methods—Liver perfusion was performed according to the technique of Miller *et al.* (3, 4). After hepatectomy by an operation involving cannulation of the portal vein, thoracic vena cava, and bile duct, the liver and the attached diaphragm were placed in a perfusion apparatus (Metaloglass, Inc., Boston, Massachusetts) maintained at 37–39° (3). The livers were perfused with a medium consisting of heparinized rat blood (50 ml) diluted with an equal volume of Krebs-Ringer bicarbonate solution containing enzymatic casein hydrolysate (667 mg), glucose (250 mg), penicillin G (50,000 units), and streptomycin sulfate (80 mg). The blood was oxygenated throughout the perfusion with a gas mixture of 95% oxygen and 5% carbon dioxide.

Before addition of hormones, the liver was allowed to equilibrate with the perfusion medium for 30 min after the start of perfusion. In experiments involving the use of actinomycin D, the antibiotic was injected into the inflow cannula at the start of perfusion and thus was present in the medium during the 30-min equilibration period. In most experiments, a small lobe of liver was ligated at its fundus and excised immediately before addition of hormones. This lobe was used for estimation of the basal hepatic tyrosine transaminase activity. In experiments involving the use of actinomycin D, this lobe was taken during hepatectomy and,

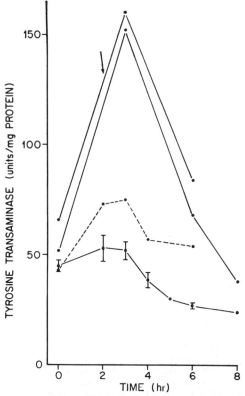

FIG. 2. Induction by insulin in the isolated, perfused liver. ●——●, 0.8 unit of insulin/100 g was added at zero time, and 1 unit per hour was infused thereafter. In the experiment designated by the *arrow* a special lot of insulin containing less than 0.005% glucagon was used. ●- - -●, insulin as above, starting ½ hour after addition of actinomycin (100 μg/100 g). O——O, control curve, as in Fig. 1.

consequently, prior to perfusion. The hormones studied were injected via the inflow cannula following equilibration of the liver with the medium and were then infused into the medium at a lower dosage and at a constant rate throughout the perfusion.

Liver perfusion was continued for a period of 4 to 11 hours, depending upon the activity of the liver as determined by measuring the rate of bile production. A bile flow (through a polyethylene cannula, inside diameter, 0.011 inch) of 1 drop every 20 to 100 sec was generally maintained. The blood flow was between 25 and 35 ml per min in every experiment. Minor hepatic lobes were ligated and excised at various time intervals during the perfusion. Once excised, liver lobes were blotted, weighed, and homogenized in 5 volumes of cold 0.15 M KCl-0.001 M EDTA (pH 8.0). The homogenates were centrifuged at 5° and 105,000 × *g* for 30 min. The supernatant fractions were decanted and stored at −20° for 24 to 48 hours before being assayed for tyrosine transaminase activity and protein content. This storage has been found to have no effect on either of these parameters.

Analytical Methods—Tyrosine transaminase activity was assayed as previously described (7). The unit of activity is the amount required to form 1 μg of *p*-hydroxyphenylpyruvate in

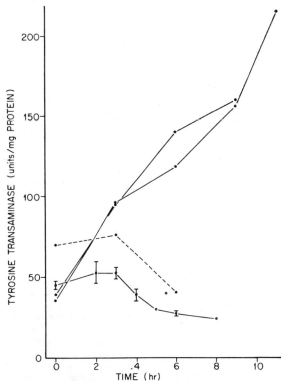

FIG. 1. Induction by hydrocortisone in the isolated, perfused liver. ●——●, 2 mg of hydrocortisone/100 g of body weight of the liver donor were added at zero time, and an additional 1 mg per hour was continuously infused thereafter. ●- - -●, hydrocortisone as above, starting ½ hour after addition of actinomycin (100 μg/100 g of body weight of liver donor). O——O, pooled data from six control experiments with no hormone added; the *vertical bars* indicate standard errors of the mean.

the 10-min assay used. Protein concentration of the supernatant fractions was estimated by the biuret procedure (8).

Induction by Hydrocortisone—The effect of hydrocortisone on synthesis of tyrosine transaminase in the isolated, perfused liver is shown in Fig. 1. An initial dose of 2.0 mg of the steroid per 100 g of body weight of the liver donor was injected into the perfusion medium, and 1.0 mg of hydrocortisone per hour was continuously infused thereafter. In this and subsequent figures, representative results of hormone treatment are presented, while the data for controls are the pooled data from six individual experiments in which no hormone was added to the medium. The adrenal steroid produced a marked elevation in the tyrosine transaminase level, which continued to increase throughout the duration of the experiment, reaching a level as great as 6 times the basal level after 11 hours. When no hormone was added, there was usually a slight increase in the enzyme level during the first 2 to 3 hours, and then a slow decline to below basal levels. Pretreatment with actinomycin D prevented the induction by hydrocortisone and yielded a pattern of activity change much like that seen in control experiments.

Induction by Pancreatic Hormones—Both insulin and glucagon also produced a marked increase in the tyrosine transaminase

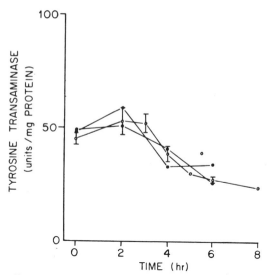

Fig. 4. Perfusion with added growth hormone. ●, 180 μg of growth hormone/100 g were added at zero time, and 100 μg per hour were infused thereafter. ○, control curve, as in Fig. 1.

activity of perfused rat livers. An insulin dose of 0.8 i.u./100 g of liver donor weight added at the end of the equilibration period with 1.0 i.u. infused per hour brought about a 2.5- to 3-fold increase in the level of tyrosine transaminase activity (Fig. 2). Both crystalline insulin and "glucagon-free" insulin preparations were effective. Glucagon addition to the perfusion medium elicited an entirely comparable elevation of tyrosine transaminase activity (Fig. 3). An initial addition of 300 μg of glucagon per 100 g of liver donor weight and the infusion of 125 μg per hour were used in these experiments, and "insulin-free" glucagon was fully effective. A similar pattern of increase in enzyme activity was mediated by insulin and glucagon, and the initial increase was greater with these hormones than when hydrocortisone was added to the perfusion medium. Actinomycin D inhibited the stimulatory effect of either pancreatic hormone on tyrosine transaminase synthesis. Unlike the elevation of tyrosine transaminase initiated by hydrocortisone, that brought about by either insulin or glucagon did not continue throughout perfusion; the enzyme level reached a peak 2 to 3 hours after addition of the pancreatic hormones and then declined rapidly thereafter, despite the continued presence of the hormones.

Glucagon has been shown to elevate the level of cyclic 3',5'-AMP in liver preparations (9, 10). In fact, the glycogenolytic effect of both glucagon and epinephrine (11), as well as effects of several other hormones (12–14), appears to be exerted by way of cyclic 3',5'-AMP. In recent experiments in this laboratory Wicks[2] found that the tyrosine transaminase of cultured explants of the livers of fetal rats is induced by supplementation of the medium with either epinephrine or cyclic-AMP. To examine the possibility that the effects of either or both of the pancreatic hormones in these perfusion experiments may be mediated by cyclic-AMP, a series of perfusions were done in which either this nucleotide, its dibutyryl derivative, or epinephrine was added to the circulating blood. Epinephrine (10

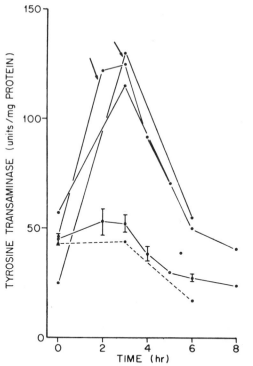

Fig. 3. Induction by glucagon in the isolated, perfused liver. ●——●, 300 μg of glucagon/100 g were added at zero time, and 125 μg per hour were infused thereafter. In the experiments designated by *arrows*, a special lot of glucagon containing 0.01% insulin-like activity was used. ●- - -●, glucagon as above, starting ½ hour after addition of actinomycin (100 μg/100 g). ○, control curve, as in Fig. 1.

[2] W. D. Wicks, personal communication.

μg per ml initially and 1 mg per hour) had no significant effect on the transaminase level, but the evident vasoconstrictive effect of this catecholamine made it impossible to attribute any significance to this negative result. Levels of cyclic-AMP up to 10^{-3} M in the perfusion medium were ineffective, whether added alone or in combination with theophylline, a potent inhibitor of the diesterase which inactivates the cyclic nucleotide (11). Northrop and Parks found that the classical hyperglycemic effect of cyclic-AMP could be observed in liver perfusions at concentrations as low as 6×10^{-5} M (15). Addition of the dibutyryl derivative of cyclic-AMP at 10^{-4} M elicited a slight increase in tyrosine transaminase (maximal, 63%) that was kinetically similar to the response to either insulin or glucagon. However the significance of this result is questionable, as the maximum increase observed was not markedly different from that found in several control experiments. We cannot, therefore, reach a meaningful conclusion at this time on the possibility that the response to either or both of the pancreatic hormones is mediated by cyclic-AMP.

Growth Hormone—Addition of growth hormone (180 μg/100 g of liver donor weight plus 100 μg infused per hour) did not affect the tyrosine transaminase activity in the isolated, perfused rat liver (Fig. 4).

DISCUSSION

These results indicate that each of the hormones which induces tyrosine transaminase *in vivo* does so by direct action on hepatic cells, and support the conclusion (2) that two independent mechanisms of induction are involved.

In confirmation of previous experiments by Barnabei and Sereni (5) and Goldstein *et al.* (6), perfusion of the isolated liver with hydrocortisone added to the blood results in a marked induction. Our results indicate that elevated enzyme synthesis continued as long as the steroid is present. Kenney has noted (16), as have others (17, 18), that tyrosine transaminase induction by hydrocortisone in cell cultures of minimal deviation hepatomas continues until the steroid-containing medium is replaced by fresh hormone-free medium. Similar results have been found in organ cultures of fetal rat liver supplemented with hydrocortisone (19). Since synthesis of tyrosine transaminase is accelerated as long as the steroid hormone is present, we shall term the steroid hormone a "primary" inducer.

Addition of either glucagon or insulin to the perfusing blood causes an induction response that is virtually identical with that observed in previous experimentation *in vivo* with these hormones (2). These results exclude the possibility discussed earlier (2) that only one of these hormones is actually effective, the other acting indirectly by promoting release of the active one. The response to each of the pancreatic hormones is similar, but this differs from the response to hydrocortisone. Thus, the results of these perfusion analyses are consistent with the previous conclusion from experiments *in vivo* that there exist two induction mechanisms, one responsive to the steroid and the other to either of the pancreatic hormones (2). That such different hormones as insulin and glucagon should each promote an identical induction of enzyme synthesis in the liver suggests that they do not directly affect any of the components involved in protein synthesis. Further support for this conclusion comes from the nature of the induction response to these hormones, for elevated enzyme synthesis ceases after 2 or 3 hours, regardless of the continual presence of the protein hormones. This is in sharp contrast to the continuous induction elicited by hydrocortisone;

that the steroid-mediated induction is maintained as long as 11 hours is evidence of the continued capacity of the isolated liver for a high rate of transaminase synthesis. Response to the protein hormones is thus temporary and not linked in an obligatory fashion to the presence of these hormones. We interpret these results as an indication that the pancreatic hormones act as "secondary" inducers, the term being chosen to indicate that, in all probability, the induction response is an indirect result of the primary intrahepatic action of these hormones.

Both the "primary" and "secondary" induction mechanisms are blocked by actinomycin, which would appear to implicate transcriptional events in each type of induction. Hydrocortisone, when administered *in vivo* (20, 21), promotes a large increase in the rate of synthesis of all types of RNA in the liver. However, this nonspecific burst in RNA synthesis is not necessary to the induction of hepatic enzymes, for Tomkins *et al.* have shown that glucocorticoids effect an induction of tyrosine transaminase in hepatoma cultures without a detectable change in general RNA synthesis (22). This result has been confirmed in this laboratory in cultures of similar, but not identical, hepatoma cells,[3] as well as in organ cultures of fetal rat liver (19). Using competitive hybridization techniques, Drews and Brawerman have reported the detection of qualitative changes in the readily hybridizable fraction of nuclear RNA after hydrocortisone administration *in vivo* (23). This implies that the steroid hormone alters transcription to bring about a shift in the spectrum of mRNA being synthesized. Such a shift could be undetectable in assays of general RNA synthesis, and thus the available data are consistent with, but do not prove, the view that the primary inducer, hydrocortisone, acts to promote synthesis of specific enzymes by promoting synthesis of their respective mRNA.

Induction of tyrosine transaminase by the secondary inducers is also blocked by actinomycin. If we interpret this to mean that the secondary type of induction also involves gene activation, we must conclude that the genetic site being activated differs from that activated by hydrocortisone, for the two types of induction are additive (2). These considerations lead to the possibility that multiple genetic sites are operative in the regulation of enzyme synthesis in mammalian cells. This mode of regulation is, of course, well established in microbial systems, as envisioned in the classical model of Jacob and Monod (24); but alternative explanations for two discrete induction mechanisms, both of which require that transcriptional processes be intact, cannot be excluded. For example, the transport of preformed messenger from nucleus to cytoplasm may require that nuclear activity remain unimpeded (25). If the secondary inducers altered nuclear permeability to permit passage of a nuclear store of transaminase messenger, a temporary induction could occur. Elevated enzyme synthesis would continue only for the lifetime of the stored messenger and could not be maintained by continuous exposure to these inducers. This potential mechanism has the distinct advantage of being testable with techniques currently available.

Supplementation of the perfusing blood with growth hormone had no discernible effect on transaminase synthesis in the isolated liver. This negative result gains validity from the fact that the inducing hormones are all effective in this system, and thus it appears that the repression of transaminase synthesis that occurs *in vivo* (1) is mediated by some extrahepatic factor.

[3] J. R. Reel and F. T. Kenney, unpublished observations.

The repression response is thus clearly a secondary one in the sense that this term is used above, *i.e.* the selective shutdown of transaminase synthesis cannot be due to a direct action of growth hormone on any component of the hepatic protein-synthesizing machinery. Like induction by the pancreatic hormones, the repression response to growth hormone *in vivo* is temporary, *i.e.* enzyme synthesis ultimately returns to the normal, basal level, even when growth hormone is given repeatedly. This repression may then reflect the operation in reverse of whatever intracellular mechanism is responsive to the secondary inducing hormones.

In previous reports the repression response has been characterized as being due to a shutdown of the translational phase of transaminase synthesis (26, 27). This conclusion was based on the assumption that the failure of actinomycin to reduce the basal enzyme level could be interpreted to mean that transaminase synthesis occurs on stable templates. This assumption may be invalid. If protein synthesis is blocked (by cycloheximide or puromycin), the enzyme level is maintained by a simultaneous inhibition of both synthesis and turnover (28). If actinomycin has the same effect (a possibility which is currently being studied), the transaminase template is probably not stable, and the argument for a translational level control mechanism cannot be maintained. Indeed, if transaminase synthesis is blocked by treatment with actinomycin, the hormonal effects on synthesis would necessarily be obliterated by the antibiotic, and its effect would be meaningless in attempts to discern the locus of the hormones' actions. These considerations point to the necessity of obtaining much more fundamental information on the effects of inhibitors if these effects are to be accepted as a means of interpreting hormonal regulation of enzyme synthesis.

Acknowledgments—We thank Dr. L. L. Miller of the Department of Radiation Biology, University of Rochester, and Dr. Fabio Sereni of the University of Milan for their guidance in the use of the isolated, perfused rat liver. We also thank Mr. J. Kendrick and Mr. G. R. Holloway for their skilled assistance; Merck, Sharp, and Dohme Research Laboratories for gifts of actinomycin D; Dr. A. E. Wilhelmi and the Endocrinology Study Section, National Institutes of Health, for purified growth hormone; and Dr. Otto Behrens and Eli Lilly Company for specially treated preparations of insulin and glucagon.

REFERENCES

1. KENNEY, F. T., *J. Biol. Chem.*, **242**, 4367 (1967).
2. HOLTEN, D., AND KENNEY, F. T., *J. Biol. Chem.*, **242**, 4372 (1967).
3. MILLER, L. L., BLY, C. G., WATSON, M. L., AND BALE, W. F., *J. Exp. Med.*, **94**, 431 (1951).
4. MILLER, L. L., BURKE, W. T., AND HAFT, D. E., *Fed. Proc.*, **14**, 707 (1955).
5. BARNABEI, O., AND SERENI, F., *Boll. Soc. Ital. Biol. Sper.*, **36**, 1656 (1960).
6. GOLDSTEIN, L., STELLA, E. J., AND KNOX, W. E., *J. Biol. Chem.*, **237**, 1723 (1962).
7. KENNEY, F. T., *J. Biol. Chem.*, **234**, 2707 (1959).
8. GORNALL, A. G., BARDAWILL, C. J., AND DAVID, M. M., *J. Biol. Chem.*, **177**, 751 (1949).
9. RALL, T. W., SUTHERLAND, E. W., AND BERTHET, J., *J. Biol. Chem.*, **224**, 463 (1957).
10. RALL, T. W., AND SUTHERLAND, E. W., *J. Biol. Chem.*, **232**, 1065 (1958).
11. SUTHERLAND, E. W., ØYE, I., AND BUTCHER, R. W., *Recent Progr. Hormone Res.*, **21**, 623 (1965).
12. HAYNES, R. C., JR., *J. Biol. Chem.*, **233**, 1220 (1958).
13. TARUI, S., NONAKA, K., IKURA, Y., AND SHIMA, K., *Biochem. Biophys. Res. Commun.*, **13**, 329 (1963).
14. MARSH, J. M., BUTCHER, R. W., SAVARD, K., AND SUTHERLAND, E. W., *J. Biol. Chem.*, **241**, 5436 (1966).
15. NORTHROP, G., AND PARKS, R. E., JR., *J. Pharmacol. Exp. Therap.*, **145**, 135 (1964).
16. KENNEY, F. T., *J. Cell. Comp. Physiol.*, **66**, 141 (1965).
17. THOMPSON, E. B., TOMKINS, G. M., AND CURRAN, J. I., *Proc. Nat. Acad. Sci. U. S. A.*, **56**, 296 (1966).
18. PITOT, H. C., PERAINO, C., MORSE, P. A., JR., AND POTTER, V. R., *Nat. Cancer Inst. Monogr.*, **13**, 229 (1964).
19. WICKS, W. D., *J. Biol. Chem.*, **243**, 900 (1968).
20. GREENMAN, D. L., WICKS, W. D., AND KENNEY, F. T., *J. Biol. Chem.*, **240**, 4420 (1965).
21. WICKS, W. D., GREENMAN, D. L., AND KENNEY, F. T., *J. Biol. Chem.*, **240**, 4414 (1965).
22. TOMKINS, G. M., THOMPSON, E. B., HAYASHI, S., GELEHRTER, T., GRANNER, D., AND PETERKOFSKY, B., *Cold Spring Harbor Symp. Quant. Biol.*, **31**, 349 (1966).
23. DREWS, J., AND BRAWERMAN, G., *J. Biol. Chem.*, **242**, 801 (1967).
24. JACOB, F., AND MONOD, J., *J. Mol. Biol.*, **3**, 318 (1961).
25. GEORGIEV, G. P., SAMARINA, O. P., LERMAN, M. I., SMIRNOV, M. N., AND SEVERTZOV, A. N., *Nature*, **200**, 1291 (1963).
26. KENNEY, F. T., AND ALBRITTON, W. L., *Proc. Nat. Acad. Sci. U. S. A.*, **54**, 1693 (1965).
27. KENNEY, F. T., HOLTEN, D., AND ALBRITTON, W. L., *Nat. Cancer Inst. Monogr.*, **27**, 315 (1967).
28. KENNEY, F. T., *Science*, **156**, 525 (1967).

Reprinted from Science, September 29, 1967, Vol. 157, No. 3796, pages 1563-1564

Circadian Rhythms of Liver Enzymes and Their Relationship to Enzyme Induction

Abstract. Tyrosine alpha ketoglutarate transaminase, which is rapidly induced by various agents, shows circadian rhythmicity in the intact rat. This rhythmicity is only slightly altered after adrenalectomy, indicating that adrenal hormones do not play a major role in the metabolic control of the activity of tyrosine alpha ketoglutarate transaminase. On the other hand, phenylalaninepyruvate transaminase, which is not inducible over the same time period, does not show circadian variation. The results suggest that the sensitivity of an enzyme's regulating system to inducing agents may be related to the inherent circadian rhythm of the enzyme.

The detection of great circadian changes in the activities of several liver enzymes that metabolize amino acids (1) has shown the necessity for controlling the time factor in the study of the physiology of enzyme regulation. These enzymes have also been shown to be inducible within a few hours when treated with glucocorticoids, glucagon, and casein hydrolyzate (2). However, there is still the question of whether these compounds, at physiological concentrations, are active as inducers of enzyme. In the case of the inducible enzyme mouse liver tryptophan pyrrolase (TP), Rapoport et al. (3) found a relation between the circadian changes in plasma corticosterone and liver TP activity. Furthermore, they reported that adrenalectomy abolishes the very pronounced circadian rhythm of this enzyme, indicating that changes in the endogenous glucocorticoids might play a major role in the physiological induction of TP. Thus, circadian changes in enzyme activity have proved useful in the identification of endogenous inducers of an enzyme.

Another question of interest is the actual physiological significance of enzyme induction and its relation to circadian changes in enzyme activity. Are these rapid changes which occur after administration of various inducing agents simply a reflection of an enzyme's tendency to undergo circadian changes? Thus, the sensitivity of an enzyme's regulatory system to inducing agents would be a reflection of the basal circadian rhythm of the enzyme. If so, an enzyme with a marked circadian rhythm should be inducible in a short period of time (a few hours), whereas one which has no circadian rhythm would not be inducible in this time period.

We looked for circadian changes in two liver enzymes, tyrosine α-ketoglutarate transaminase (TKT) and phenylalanine-pyruvate transaminase (PPT). The former is inducible by glucocorticoids and glucagon, and it reaches maximum activity 4 to 6 hours after glucocorticoid treatment (2) and 2 to 4 hours after glucagon (4). On the other hand, PPT activity changes only slightly after repeated injections of glucocorticoids. Although its activity shows a small increase (30 percent) 6 hours after glucagon treatment, it only reaches a maximum of a threefold increase 24 hours after glucagon induction (4).

Male Sprague-Dawley rats (Berkeley-Pacific Laboratories), weighing 250 to 300 g, were used. The animals were housed in individual cages in an isolated room with controlled temperature (25° ± 1°C) and illumination (5 a.m. to 5 p.m.) and were freely given Purina Lab Chow. To establish a regular rhythmic change in the concentrations of plasma corticosterone, they were placed in their cages for a period of 2 weeks before being killed. Adrenalectomized animals were given 0.9 percent saline and were used 2 weeks after surgery. The rats were killed by guillotine, and the blood was collected in heparinized beakers. The blood was chilled and centrifuged in the cold, and the plasma was removed and frozen for later determination of corticosterone (5). These results are expressed as micrograms of corticosterone per 100 ml of plasma. The livers were rapidly removed and chilled on ice. The finely minced liver tissue was homogenized in Krebs-Ringer bicarbonate medium (Na:K, 1:1, pH 7.4) at 2°C in eight strokes in a glass homogenizer with a Teflon pestle driven by a constant torque motor (400 rev/min). The final homogenate concentration was 10 percent (weight per volume). The homogenates were centrifuged at 13,000g for 30 minutes; the lipid layer was re-

moved, and the clear supernatant was used for the assay of TKT and PPT by the continuous spectrophotometric method of Lin et al. (6). The results are expressed as micromoles of product formed per milligram of protein per hour at 37° ± 0.1°C and represent the averages of 8 to 12 animals for each time period.

The TKT activity at various times of the 24-hour period in intact rats is shown in Fig. 1A. In the intact animal, TKT undergoes a 387 percent change, with minimum TKT activity at 11 a.m. and maximum activity at 9 p.m. The plasma corticosterone rises from its minimum level at 6 a.m. to its maximum at 6 p.m., with an increase of 1870 percent. The peak TKT activity occurs 3 hours after the maximum corticosterone level. Rapoport et al. (3) found that the peak activity in liver TP in the mouse occurred about 7 hours after maximum corticosterone levels. The circadian variation of TP in the rat should be compared with that in the mouse to see whether the

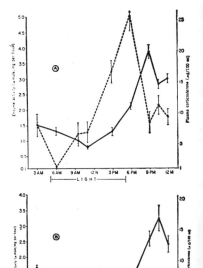

Fig. 1. Relation in normal male rats (A) and in adrenalectomized rats (B) of TKT activity and plasma corticosterone concentrations over a 24-hour period. Each point represents mean ± standard error. Solid lines represent TKT activity; dashed lines represent plasma corticosterone concentrations.

time relation in fluctuations of corticosterone and TP would coincide.

Figure 1B shows that the circadian rhythm of TKT is not appreciably altered after adrenalectomy. There appears to be a lowering of both the maximum and minimum points in the curve; however, this is not statistically significant. Our experiments indicate that adrenal hormones do not play a major role in determining the circadian rhythmic pattern of TKT. Our results are in agreement with the findings of Wurtman and Axelrod (7) who also studied the circadian variation of rat liver TKT. Our findings imply that caution is necessary before assuming that a hormone, capable of inducing an enzyme when administered in pharmacological amounts, is the primary physiological inducer of the enzyme. The natural inducer or inducers of TKT remain to be determined.

It has been shown that TKT activity is increased after starvation, whereas TP activity is decreased (8). In man, starvation produces significant increases in glucagon (9). Studies in this laboratory have shown that glucagon can act as an inducer of TKT activity, but not as an inducer of TP activity, independently of the pituitary adrenal axis (4). Thus, it is possible that glucagon may be one of the hormones involved in the control of the circadian rhythm of TKT.

The other liver transaminase studied, PPT, does not show any circadian variation. This enzyme is not significantly changed in 4 to 6 hours after glucocorticoids and glucagon (4), the period at which the maximum increase in both TP and TKT activities is obtained. Thus, there appears to be a relation between an enzyme's short-term inducibility by exogenous inducing agents and its natural circadian variation.

MORTON CIVEN, RENE ULRICH
BETTY M. TRIMMER
CHARLESTA B. BROWN
Radioisotope Service,
Veterans Administration Hospital,
Long Beach, California, and
Department of Biochemistry,
University of Southern
California, Los Angeles

References and Notes

1. V. R. Potter, R. A. Gebert, H. C. Pitot, *Advances Enzyme Regulat.* 4, 247 (1966).
2. W. E. Knox and V. H. Auerbach, *J. Biol. Chem.* 214, 307 (1955); E. C. C. Lin and W. E. Knox, *Biochim. Biophys. Acta* 26, 85 (1957); C. Peraino, C. Lamar, Jr., H. C. Pitot, *Advances Enzyme Regulat.* 4, 199 (1966).
3. M. I. Rapoport, R. D. Feigin, J. Bruton, W. R. Beisel, *Science* 153, 1642 (1966).
4. M. Civen, B. M. Trimmer, C. B. Brown, *Life Sci.* 6, 1331 (1967).
5. R. Guillemin, G. W. Clayton, H. S. Lipscomb, J. D. Smith, *J. Lab. Clin. Med.* 53, 830 (1959); R. Richard, *Proc. Soc. Exp. Biol. Med.* 124, 276 (1967).
6. E. C. C. Lin, B. M. Pitt, M. Civen, W. E. Knox, *J. Biol Chem.* 233, 668 (1958).
7. R. J. Wurtman and J. Axelrod, *Proc. Nat. Acad. Sci. U.S.* 57, 1594 (1967).
8. O. Greengard, G. T. Baker, M. L. Horowitz, W. E. Knox, *ibid.* 56, 1303 (1966).
9. R. H. Unger, A. M. Eisentraut, M. S. McCall, L. L. Madison, *J. Clin. Invest.* 41, 682 (1962)
10. Supported in part by PHS grant AM 08338.

17 August 1967

Reprinted from Cold Spring Harbor Symposia on Quantitative Biology, Volume XXXI, 1966

Tyrosine Transaminase Induction in Mammalian Cells in Tissue Culture

G. M. Tomkins, E. B. Thompson, S. Hayashi, T. Gelehrter, D. Granner, and B. Peterkofsky

*Laboratory of Molecular Biology, National Institute of Arthritis and Metabolic Diseases,
National Institutes of Health, Bethesda, Maryland*

Enzyme induction is known to occur in mammalian systems. Many in vivo studies have provided suggestive evidence of the phenomenon, and in a few cases true induced synthesis of specific enzymes has been shown. One of the best examples has been the induction of liver gluconeogenic enzymes by steroid hormones. (See reviews by Feigelson and Feigelson, 1964, and Nichol and Rosen, 1964, and references therein.) It has been difficult, however, to probe very deeply into the chemical control mechanisms involved while limited to whole animal or perfused organ experiments. Interpretation of such experiments has had to depend heavily on analogy with work done on microorganisms, since there the cell environment is relatively easily controlled and mutations specifically affecting regulatory function can be obtained readily. Obviously it would be desirable to study mammalian control of enzyme synthesis directly in cell culture, but to date only a few systems in which such work appears feasible have been described (Cox and MacLeod, 1964; Pitot, et al., 1964; Granick, 1963.) The present report describes a new line of tissue culture cells developed by Thompson, Tomkins, and Curran (1966), in which glucocorticoid hormones induce the synthesis of tyrosine-α-ketoglutarate-transaminase. In this system our experiments indicate that control of induction occurs both at the cytoplasmic and at the nuclear level.

Cell Growth and Morphology

The cells (designated HTC for hepatoma tissue culture) were derived from the ascites form of a rat-carried Morris hepatoma (Odashima and Morris, 1965). The primary explant of tumor cells was made in October, 1964, and they have been propagated in culture ever since. HTC cells can be grown in Swim's S-77 medium supplemented with fetal and adult bovine serum and will grow either as a confluent layer attached to glass or in suspension culture. In either case their generation time is approximately 24 hr, as illustrated in Fig. 1. Cell samples which have been frozen in medium containing 5–10% glycerol, stored for as much as a year and then thawed, exhibit the same growth rate and induction characteristics as continuously

grown, unfrozen cells. Full details of the culture methods used have been published (Thompson, Tomkins, and Curran, 1966).

Morphologically, HTC cells are typical epithelioid cells (Fig. 2) and chromosome studies have shown that the majority are hypotetraploid with an irregular distribution around a mode of about 65. Five per cent of the population contained approximately twice that number. In preliminary studies with cloned cells, the distribution was closer to the mode, and in four of five clones studied the mode was about 4N. (N for the rat = 21).

Steroids are known to slow the growth rate and increase the cell size of some lines of tissue culture cells (Cox and MacLeod, 1962); therefore these parameters were examined in HTC cells. The

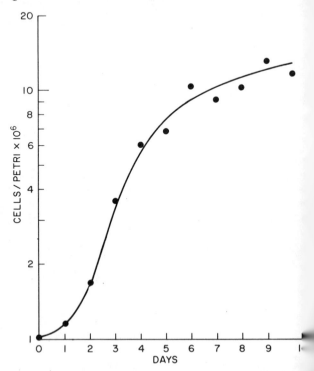

Figure 1. Growth curve of uncloned HTC cells. Replicate petri dishes were inoculated with 10^6 cells and fed daily by replacing half the medium. Each day the cells in one petri dish were removed by trypsinization and counted in a hemocytometer. At least two counts of ≥ 200 cells were done for each point.

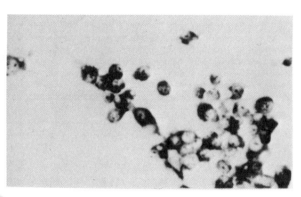

FIGURE 2. HTC cells grown on a coverslip and stained *in situ*. Giemsa stain, ×260 magnification.

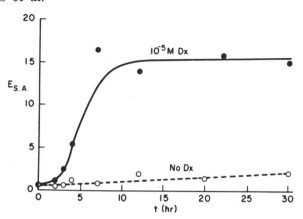

FIGURE 3. Induction of tyrosine transaminase in HTC cells. At 0 time pooled cells were divided into two petri dishes, one of which contained 10^{-5} M Dx. At various times aliquots were removed and washed twice with 0.15 M sodium phosphate buffer, pH 7.9. The cells were then suspended in 0.5–1.0 ml of buffer and broken with a probe sonicator in an ice bath using two 2 amp bursts of 10 sec each. The unbroken cells, nuclei, etc. were removed by centrifugation at 20,000 *g* for 10 min. Aliquots of the supernatant fraction were assayed for tyrosine transaminase activity by the following modification of the method of Lin and Knox (1957): A total volume of 1.0 ml contained 0.5 mmoles of borate as its sodium salt, pH 7.8; 0–0.25 ml cell extract, 5×10^{-3} mmoles of tyrosine, 0.01 ml porcine p-hydroxyphenylpyruvate-enol-ketotautomerase, 2×10^{-4} mmoles of pyridoxal phosphate, 0.01 mmoles of α-ketoglutarate, and 0.15 M sodium phosphate, pH 7.8; to volume. Absorption of light at 310 mμ was followed with a Gilford recording spectrophotometer. Other aliquots were assayed for protein by the method of Lowry et al. (1951). Enzyme specific activity (E_{sa}) is expressed as mμ moles of p-hydroxyphenylpyruvate-enol borate complex formed/min/mg protein with the molar absorbancy of the complex taken to be 10,700, after Jacoby and LaDu (1964). This assay method and manner of expressing transaminase activity is used throughout this paper.

presence of the synthetic glucocorticoid, dexamethasone phosphate (Dx), at 10^{-5}M did not significantly inhibit the exponential growth of HTC cells when included in the growth medium, nor did the hormone cause gross morphological changes in the cells.

In summary, it can be said that as regards growth and morphology, HTC cells are analogous to other epithelial cell lines from neoplastic sources. They possess the interesting feature, however, of rapid enzyme induction in response to steroid hormones.

INDUCTION OF TYROSINE-α-KETOGLUTARATE TRANSAMINASE

A typical example of the steroidal induction of tyrosine-α-ketoglutarate transaminase is the experiment illustrated in Fig. 3. Here 10^{-5} M Dx caused a 15-fold increase in the activity of the enzyme about 6–8 hr after its addition. (For this study and in all the induction experiments to follow except where noted otherwise, cells which had been propagated in serum-containing growth medium were transferred to "induction medium" consisting only of the defined medium, serum-free S-77. In S-77, HTC cells do not grow, but on readdition of serum after as long as 4 days, they resume growth. Tyrosine transaminase is inducible in HTC cells either during exponential growth or in the resting phase.) Baseline levels of tyrosine transaminase in HTC cells are found to be between 1 and 4 units per mg protein. Induced levels vary between 7 and 30 units.

The time course of transaminase induction illustrated in Fig. 3 should be noted. There is a gradually increasing rate of rise in enzyme level followed by a plateau which is maintained as long as the hormone is present. However, if the cells are washed and resuspended in inducer-free medium, the enzyme returns to its basal activity as is shown in Fig. 4. In the experiment illustrated, induced

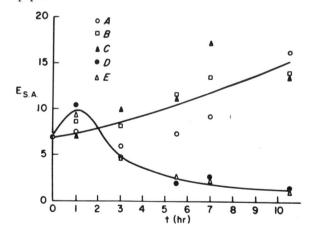

FIGURE 4. Effect of removing Dx on tyrosine transaminase specific activity (E_{sa}). HTC cells induced in 10^{-5} M Dx for 16 hr were collected at zero time, washed twice with steroid-free S-77, and reincubated in various solutions: ○ = fresh S-77 with 10^{-5} M Dx, □ = the original induction medium, ▲ = conditioned medium with 10^{-5} M Dx, ● = conditioned medium with no Dx, and △ = fresh S-77 with no Dx. Conditioned medium was S-77 left in contact with uninduced HTC cells for 16 hr preceding the experiment.

cells were washed and returned to medium S-77 under several conditions. Regardless of other variables, in each medium containing hormone enzyme activity was not only maintained, but continued to rise somewhat. In those media lacking hormone, enzyme activity after a brief period of adjustment fell to basal levels. The two curves are drawn to indicate this general behavior, and are not intended to represent the precise kinetics of each condition. Furthermore, if cycloheximide or puromycin is added during the course of induction, the activity falls to the uninduced level at about the same rate. The significance of these kinetics will be considered below.

In addition to Dx, a number of other steroid and nonsteroid hormones were investigated as possible inducers of tyrosine transaminase. The results of some of these studies are shown in Table 1. The only effective compounds among those tested were steroids with the adrenal corticoid side chain at position 17.

To ascertain whether the increase in transaminase activity was due to net enzyme synthesis rather than activation of a pre-existing precursor, puromycin or cycloheximide was given together with the inducer. This completely blocked the rise in transaminase activity, suggesting that protein synthesis

FIGURE 5. Crystalline tyrosine-α-ketoglutarate transaminase. Phase contrast microscopy, ×970 magnification.

TABLE 1. RESPONSE OF TYROSINE TRANSAMINASE ACTIVITY IN HTC CELLS TO VARIOUS STEROID HORMONES

Treatment	Tyrosine transaminase spec. act., U/mg protein
Zero time, uninduced	2.8
No additions	1.6
0.1% ethanol (95%)	2.4
Dx, 10^{-5} M	15.0
Dx, 10^{-5} M + 0.1% ethanol	12.8
Triamcinolone, 10^{-5} M + 0.1% ethanol	10.5
Hydrocortisone hemisuccinate, 10^{-5} M + 0.1% ethanol	14.3
Deoxycorticosterone, 10^{-5} M + 0.1% ethanol	7.7
Aldosterone, 10^{-5} M + 0.1% ethanol	6.7
Aldosterone, 3×10^{-8} M + 0.1% ethanol	1.8
Stilbesterol diphosphate, 10^{-5} M + 0.1% ethanol	1.4
17 β-estradiol, 10^{-5} M + 0.1% ethanol	2.2
Testosterone, 10^{-5} M + 0.1% ethanol	2.4
Progesterone, 10^{-5} M + 0.1% ethanol	3.6

After sampling in duplicate for zero-time, uninduced enzyme, a pool of cells was distributed into petri dishes with 10 ml S77 prewarmed to 37°. To duplicate petri dishes, steroid and/or ethanol was added to give the final concentrations indicated. After 15 hr in the CO_2 incubator cells were harvested, washed, and assayed for enzyme as before. Tyrosine transaminase specific activity expressed as in Fig. 3. Figures given represent the average of duplicate samples.

was required for induction. For further clarification immunochemical techniques were used. Tyrosine-α-ketoglutarate transaminase was crystallized from the livers of rats which previously had been injected with the glucocorticoid triamcinolone. Crystals were obtained after about 600-fold purification of the enzyme, with a 20% yield (Hayashi, Granner, and Tomkins, in prep.). Figure 5 illustrates the crystalline preparation, the specific activity of which is 1.2×10^5 mμ moles product formed/min/mg protein at 37°. To establish the purity of the enzyme, sedimentation velocity experiments were carried out in the analytical ultracentrifuge (Fig. 6). The $S_{20,w}$ value of the peak was calculated to be 5.9. Sedimentation equilibrium experiments (Yphantis, 1964) revealed a linear log C vs. X^2 plot, also consistent with a homogeneous preparation, from which the molecular weight of the enzyme was calculated to be 91,000. In addition the purified protein chromatographed as a single peak on DEAE cellulose.

With the most purified enzyme as antigen, rabbit antiserum to tyrosine transaminase was prepared and used in Ouchterlony double diffusion experiments as described in Kabat and Mayer (1964).

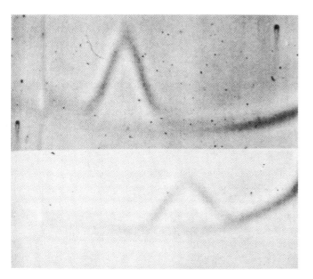

FIGURE 6. Schlieren patterns from sedimentation velocity centrifugation study of crystalline tyrosine transaminase. Protein concentration, 4 mg/ml in 0.02 M potassium phosphate buffer, pH 7.0, containing potassium chloride 0.15 M, EDTA 10^{-3} M, α-ketoglutarate 2×10^{-3} M, pyridoxal phosphate 10^{-5} M, and dithiothreitol 10^{-3} M. Run at 20°C and 59,780 rev/min.

These showed a reaction of identity between the purified tyrosine transaminase and crude extracts from steroid induced and uninduced HTC cells and liver. Furthermore, precipitin experiments showed that the equivalence zone of precipitation with the rabbit anti-transaminase serum was identical for extracts of induced or uninduced cells or liver (Fig. 7). These experiments not only indicate that the tyrosine transaminase in HTC cells is immunologically identical to that in rat liver, but also that upon induction of transaminase activity by steroid hormone in either liver or HTC cells, there is a concomitant increase in immunologically identical protein. It could still be argued that steroid acts only to prevent the breakdown of the enzyme. However, studies following isotopic amino acid incorporation into induced cells show that the transaminase-antitransaminase precipitate has a higher specific activity than does general cell protein (Fig. 16, Table 2). This is strong evidence that the enzyme turns over, and that it is synthesized at a faster rate than general cell protein when induced by Dx.

Our kinetic results can be described approximately by the kinetic model scheme suggested for other inducible enzymes in animal cells (Segal and Kim, 1965; Schimke, Sweeney, and Berlin, 1964). In this scheme, the enzyme in question is synthesized by a zero-order process and inactivated by a first-order reaction as follows:

$$\text{precursors} \xrightarrow{S} \text{tyrosine transaminase (TT)}$$
$$\xrightarrow{k} \text{inactive product.}$$

The rate of transaminase formation is then given by $d(\text{TT})/dt = S - k(\text{TT})$. When integrated, this expression describes an increase in enzyme activity with time which occurs on induction due to an increase in the rate constant for enzyme synthesis (S) caused by the hormone, if degradation (k) is constant. Our preliminary studies indicate that there is probably no change in the first-order inactivation constant (k) during the course of induction, unlike the situation described for liver pyruvate-oxaloacetate transaminase (Schimke, Sweeney, and Berlin, 1964). If it is assumed that the rate constant for synthesis (S) is abruptly changed on induction to a new higher value, S^i, however, integration of the above differential rate expression does not generate the lag in the rate of transaminase synthesis shown in Fig. 3.

It seems reasonable to suppose, therefore, that there is a gradual increase in S for several hours following addition of the inducer. As will be shown below, this may correlate with an apparent increase in transaminase mRNA.

THE INFLUENCE OF Dx ON GENERAL PROTEIN SYNTHESIS

The next question investigated was whether Dx at concentrations at which it induced transaminase synthesis stimulated a general increase in the rate of protein synthesis. This did not seem likely in view of the lack of effect of the hormone on the growth of the cells at these concentrations. First, experiments were done comparing the rate of C^{14} phenylalanine incorporation into total cell protein in the presence and absence of inducer and, as Fig. 8 illustrates, no significant effect of the hormone was found during the first four hours of induction. In other experiments, incorporation has been followed as long as 24 hours and no steroid effect has been found.

To try to determine whether the synthesis of specific proteins other than the transaminase was affected by the inducer, the following double labeling experiment was performed. A low inoculum of HTC cells was grown for 4 days (approximately 4 doubling times) in the presence of 10^{-5} M Dx as inducer, and tritiated phenylalanine. Identical batches of cells taken from the same original stock were grown in inducer-free medium with H^3 phenylalanine or with C^{14} phenylalanine. For the control experiment (Fig. 9A) the uninduced H^3-labeled cells were mixed with the uninduced C^{14}-labeled cells and an extract was prepared by sonic oscillation. The combined extracts were centrifuged, and the $105,000 \times g$ supernatant material passed through a Sephadex G-25 column, and chromatographed on DEAE cellulose. The fractionated eluate from the column was counted simultaneously

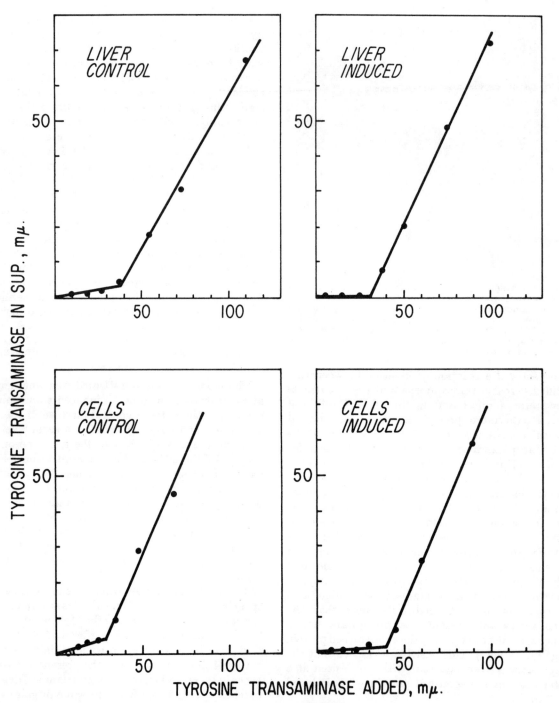

FIGURE 7. Precipitin equivalence curves of liver and HTC cell extracts, both steroid-induced and uninduced, with rabbit antiserum to purified tyrosine transaminase. To a series of tubes containing equal volumes of antiserum, increasing amount of extract were added. The precipitate forming after 15 hr at 4°C was removed by centrifugation, and the supernatant solution assayed for tyrosine transaminase activity. The abbreviation mμ refers to mμ moles product formed/min/m protein.

for C14 and H3. As can be seen, about 5 distinct peaks were eluted but no significant differences in the C14/H3 ratio were noted in any part of the effluent when neither group of cells was induced. This experiment shows that the eluate pattern

does not vary detectably from one batch of cel to another when they are grown under the sam conditions. Hence it is concluded that protei synthesis does not vary under these circumstance However, when the identical procedure wa

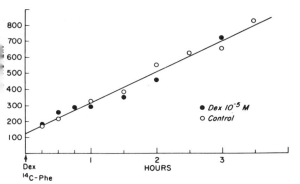

increase in total RNA in target organs, and in the rate of synthesis of RNA as measured by the incorporation of radioactive precursors (Garren et al., 1964b, Korner, 1965; Williams-Ashman, 1965; Kenney et al., 1965; Gorski et al., 1965). On the basis of such studies it has been argued that hormones may affect protein synthesis by acting at the level of DNA, stimulating the transcription of specific genes into messenger RNA (Karlson, 1963; Davidson, 1965). The stimulation of RNA synthesis observed in these studies, however, affects all classes of RNA, rather than a messenger fraction specifically.

FIGURE 8. C^{14} phenylalanine (C^{14} phe) incorporation into protein of HTC cells during induction. To a batch of cells C^{14} phe was added and zero time samples were taken. Then the cells were divided, 10^{-5} M dexamethasone phosphate (Dex) added to one-half, and serial aliquots taken for incorporation into hot TCA insoluble material.

followed, comparing tritiated cells grown with Dx to control cells labeled with C^{14}, as shown in Fig. 9B, small differences were noted in the C^{14}/H^3 ratios of several of the peaks, one of which contains tyrosine transaminase activity. We conclude from these experiments that exposure of the HTC cells to Dx for a considerable length of time probably induces a small number of proteins in addition to tyrosine transaminase, while overall protein synthesis is not affected.

THE EFFECT OF INDUCERS ON RNA METABOLISM

Numerous studies have reported that the administration of hormones to animals results in an

In contrast to these findings in intact animals, no increase in total RNA was observed in the HTC cells during dexamethasone-mediated enzyme induction. Furthermore, no difference between induced and control cells was observed in the rate of incorporation of uridine into either whole-cell, nuclear, or cytoplasmic RNA (Fig. 10). Other experiments utilizing brief pulses of C^{14}-uridine also failed to demonstrate any differences (Fig. 11). Similar results were obtained using a purine (adenosine-8-C^{14}) precursor of RNA.

Although these data failed to demonstrate any gross changes in RNA synthesis accompanying enzyme induction, they did not rule out stimulation of a small RNA fraction. More sensitive double-labeling experiments were carried out to test this possibility. HTC cells were incubated with Dx and tritiated uridine. Control cells were incubated with C^{14}-uridine. At the end of the incubation, both

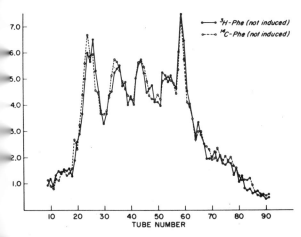

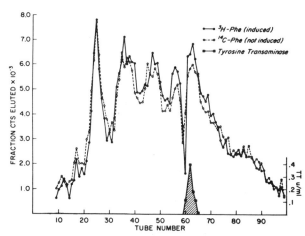

FIGURE 9. Soluble proteins of HTC cells, induced and uninduced. A stock of HTC cells was divided in thirds, diluted in growth medium (S-77 plus serum) and allowed to grow either in the presence of C^{14} phenylalanine or in the presence of H^3 phenylalanine without Dx, 10^{-5} M. After 4 days, the cells were harvested and washed twice. C^{14}-labeled, uninduced cells were mixed with H^3-labeled cells, induced or uninduced, and cell extracts prepared as usual, except that an additional centrifugation at $105,000 \times g$ for 90 min was performed. After passage through a Sephadex G 25 column, aliquots were placed on a 1×23 cm DEAE cellulose column equilibrated with buffer I (0.005 M potassium phosphate, pH 7.8, dithiothreitol 10^{-4} M, EDTA 10^{-3} M). Those proteins adsorbed were eluted by a linear gradient established between buffer I and buffer II (0.005 M potassium phosphate, pH 7.0, dithiothreitol 10^{-4} M, EDTA 10^{-3} M, KCl 0.5 M). Flow rate was 0.8–1 ml/min. Small fractions were collected and aliquots counted for radioactivity in Bray's solution in a Nuclear-Chicago scintillation counter. Activity is expressed as fraction of the total counts eluted $\times 10^{-3}$. Figure 9A shows the elution pattern from induced cells containing the two labels, and Fig. 9B compares induced with uninduced cells. In 9B, tyrosine transaminase activity was located by the standard assay (see Fig. 3).

EFFECT OF DEXAMETHASONE ON ^{14}C-URIDINE
INCORPORATION IN HTC CELLS

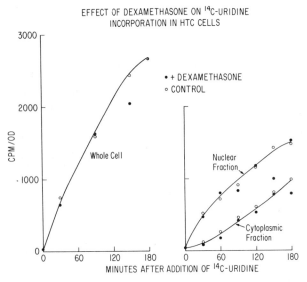

FIGURE 10. HTC cells were incubated in S-77 with C^{14}-uridine, with and without Dexamethasone at 10^{-5} M and samples were taken at times indicated. Fractionation was performed by homogenization in hypotonic buffer (Girard et al., 1965), and separation of nuclei by centrifugation. All samples were collected as TCA-precipitates on millipore filters, and counted on a scintillation counter in PPO-POPOP-Toluene. Counts are corrected for differing cell densities, measured as OD$_{650}$, of the samples.

EFFECT OF DEXAMETHASONE ON RAPIDLY LABELLED RNA
IN HTC CELLS, 15-MINUTE – ^{14}C–URIDINE PULSE

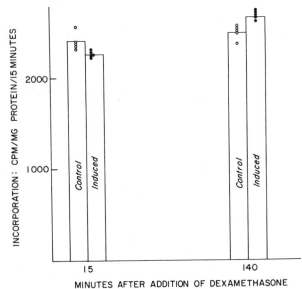

FIGURE 11. HTC cells were incubated in S-77 with and without dexamethasone at 10^{-5} M. At times indicated, C^{14}-uridine was added to each culture, and the reaction stopped after 15 min by chilling. Samples were sonicated and aliquots spotted onto Whatman 3 MM filter paper discs. Nucleic acid was precipitated on the disc by immersion in cold 0.5 N perchloric acid. After washing in acid, alcohol, and ether, the discs were counted in PPO-POPOP-Toluene. Incorporation is expressed per mg protein in each aliquot. The bar graphs represent average values; the points, individual determinations.

EFFECT OF DEXAMETHASONE ON RNA-LABELLING IN HTC
CELLS: 15 MINUTE URIDINE PULSE

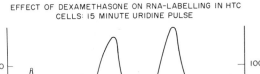

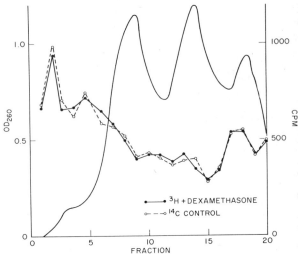

FIGURE 12. HTC cells were incubated in S-77 with and without dexamethasone at 10^{-5} M for 60 min. Isotope was added as described in the text. After 15 min incubation, the reaction was stopped by chilling and the cells pooled. RNA was extracted with hot-phenol-SDS (Scherrer et al., 1963), and examined on 4.6 ml, 5–20% sucrose gradients in 0.01 M acetate buffer, pH 5.1, centrifuged at 39,000 rev/min for 3 hr. The contents of the gradient were continuously analyzed for UV absorbance at 260 mμ using a Gilford recorder. Radioactivity was measured by scintillation counting in Bray's solution, and the counts normalized for comparison of the curves.

batches of cells were pooled, their RNA extracted and various fractions were examined by sucrose density gradient centrifugation. Particular attention was paid to those fractions thought to carry mRNA: rapidly-labeled RNA (Scherrer et al., 1963), polysomal RNA (Penman et al., 1963) and 45 S RNA-protein particles (Girard et al., 1965; Henshaw et al., 1965). As shown in Figs. 12–14, any differences between induced and control cells in the pattern of uridine incorporation into RNA are not large, though preliminary studies do show a small increase in pulse-labeled RNA associated with the microsomal fraction in induced cells. These studies suggest that the impressive changes in RNA metabolism associated with hormone administration to animals are not an essential part of the Dx stimulated enzyme induction in HTC cells.

Despite the absence of gross changes in RNA synthesis in HTC cells on induction, experiments with inhibitors suggest that there is a net increase in RNA during induction, and that the increase in the rate of enzyme synthesis is proportional to the amount of RNA accumulated. For example, the experiment illustrated in Fig. 15 shows that when 0.25 μg/ml actinomycin D is given together with the inducer there is almost complete inhibition of enzyme induction. (Actinomycin D at concentration

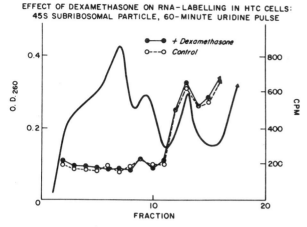

EFFECT OF DEXAMETHASONE ON RNA-LABELLING IN HTC CELLS: 45S SUBRIBOSOMAL PARTICLE, 60-MINUTE URIDINE PULSE

FIGURE 13. HTC cells were incubated as in the previous figure except that the reaction was allowed to continue for 60 min. The pooled cells were fractionated as in Fig. 10, and a post-mitochondrial supernatant fraction prepared. This was analyzed on a 15–30% sucrose gradient in 0.01 M Tris-HCl, 0.01 M KCl, 0.0015 M Mg Cl₂, pH 7.4, centrifuged at 39,000 rev/min for 2 hr to display the 45 S particle. The gradient was analyzed as in Fig. 12.

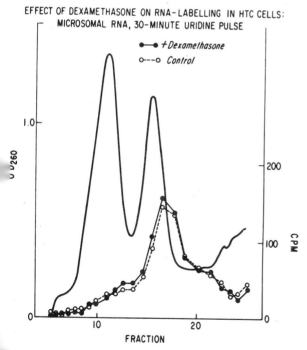

EFFECT OF DEXAMETHASONE ON RNA-LABELLING IN HTC CELLS: MICROSOMAL RNA, 30-MINUTE URIDINE PULSE

FIGURE 14. HTC cells were incubated with and without dexamethasone for 90 min; labeled uridine was then added as in Figs. 12 and 13, and the reaction stopped after 30 min. A post-mitochondrial supernatant was prepared, made 0.5% with sodium deoxycholate, and centrifuged for 60 min at 40,000 rev/min. RNA was released by suspending the pellet in 0.5% SDS at 37°C, and examined on 5–20% sucrose gradients in 0.005 M Tris buffer, pH 7.2, centrifuged at 39,000 rev/min for 3½ hr. Gradients were analyzed as in Fig. 12 except that radioactivity was measured by spotting on filters, as described in Fig. 11.

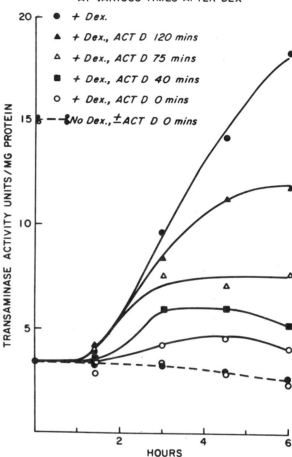

EFFECT OF ACTINOMYCIN D (0.25 γ/ml) ADDED AT VARIOUS TIMES AFTER DEX

● + Dex.
▲ + Dex., ACT D 120 mins
△ + Dex., ACT D 75 mins
■ + Dex., ACT D 40 mins
○ + Dex., ACT D 0 mins
- - ○ No Dex., ±ACT D 0 mins

FIGURE 15. Effect of actinomycin added at various times after dexamethasone: Cells were incubated overnight in S-77 medium in culture bottles. They were then resuspended in fresh S-77 medium to give a concentration of approximately 10⁶ cells/ml. Ten ml aliquots of cell suspension were incubated with or without 10⁻⁵ M dexamethasone (Dex) and actinomycin D was added at the intervals indicated in the figure. The final concentration of actinomycin was 0.25 μg/ml. The incubations were carried out in a Dubinoff shaker under 95% O₂/5% CO₂ at 37% in 50 ml Erlenmeyer flasks. At intervals, aliquots were removed and assayed for tyrosine transaminase activity as described in the legend to Fig. 3.

as low as 0.1 μg/ml given together with Dx is sufficient to inhibit uridine incorporation into RNA by 90%.) When the same concentration of inhibitor was given at various times after Dx, induction occurred but enzyme was synthesized at a lower rate, and the plateau value of transaminase synthesis was lower than the control and depended on the time of addition of the inhibitor.

As discussed earlier, we assume that there is turnover of the transaminase. If we further suppose that there is no significant change in the rate constant for enzyme degradation upon induction, then the plateau level of enzyme activity would depend solely on the magnitude of the rate constant for enzyme synthesis. The data (Fig. 15) would then indicate a progressive increase in the magnitude of this constant, starting from the time of inducer addition. Since actinomycin D inhibits the increase in enzyme synthesis, we presume than an increase in transaminase mRNA is responsible for the increase in the rate constant of synthesis. The data in Fig. 15 also suggest that the messenger, once formed, is relatively stable since enzyme synthesis continues for some hours after messenger formation has been blocked by actinomycin D.

STUDIES ON THE MECHANISM OF INDUCER ACTION

It must be recalled at this time that tyrosine transaminase synthesis stops when the inducer is removed (Fig. 4). Furthermore, as noted in the preceding section the transaminase messenger appears to be stable. Taken together, these two observations suggest that the mechanism of Dx action in HTC cells is not analogous to the action proposed for inducers of enzyme synthesis in bacteria (Jacob and Monod, 1961). In the latter case, there is also a requirement for the continuous presence of the inducer, but this requirement is thought to stem from *rapid* turnover of mRNA which must be continually replenished under the influence of inducer. In the present case, however, the inducer is required even in the presence of a stable messenger. This fact, together with the results of the experiments to be described below, suggest that the inducer is required for the *translation* of the tyrosine transaminase messenger. At the present time we do not know whether the apparent increase in the concentration of transaminase mRNA noted above is a secondary result of the action of Dx on translation or whether there is a direct action of the hormone on the transcription process as well.

In any event, to investigate the mechanism of induction further, we began by analogy with the earlier finding by Garren et al. (1964a) that large doses of actinomycin or 5-fluorouracil, when given to rats which had previously received hydrocortisone, increase the rate of synthesis of induced tyrosine transaminase or tryptophan pyrrolase in the liver. A similar phenomenon occurs in HTC cells, as illustrated in Fig. 16. Tyrosine transaminase was induced for 40 hr, at which time the cells were divided into 2 pairs. The addition of 5 μg/ml actinomycin D to one pair of samples caused a prompt increase in the level of tyrosine transaminase activity. Control cells which did not receive actinomycin showed no such increase. To verify that the actinomycin-induced increase in transaminase level represented the synthesis of new enzyme molecules, C14-labeled amino acids

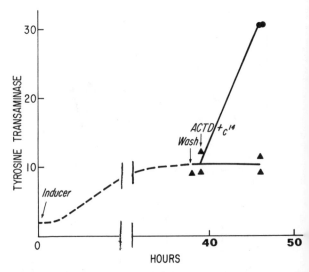

FIGURE 16. Superinduction of tyrosine transaminase by actinomycin D. HTC cells were induced with 2×10^{-5} M Dx for 40 hr, washed twice with steroid-free S-77, suspended in S-77, and C14-labeled yeast protein hydrolysate added. Duplicate samples were then incubated with and without actinomycin D, 5 μg/ml, for 6½ hr. Enzyme was assayed at the beginning and at the end of the washes, and 6½ hr after adding actinomycin D. ▲ = control. ● = act. D treated.

were administered to both the control and antibiotic treated cells. Several hours later, when cell extracts were prepared for enzyme assay, aliquots of the extracts were treated with rabbit antitransaminase and the immune precipitates collected, washed, and their radioactivity determined. The data are shown in Table 2, where the specific radioactivity of the total cell protein is compared with the specific radioactivity of the tyrosine transaminase. Evidently, both in the cells receiving the actinomycin D, and in the control cells, the specific radioactivity of the transaminase was higher than the specific activity of the total cell protein, indicating that in both cases the enzyme was synthesized more rapidly than was general cell protein. Moreover, the specific radioactivity of the transaminase from the actinomycin D-treated cells was significantly higher than the specific radioactivity of the enzyme from cells not receiving the inhibitor, showing that the rate of transaminase synthesis was faster in the former group than in the latter. We conclude that actinomycin D stimulates the synthesis of the transaminase.

Similar increases in transaminase activity could be produced by other inhibitors of RNA synthesis as well: 5-fluorouracil, 5-fluorouridine, or mitomycin C when given under the same conditions. Incidentally, it can also be seen from the data in Table 2 that the overall rate of amino acid incorporation was not stimulated by actinomycin but was, in fact, slightly inhibited.

358 TOMKINS et al.

TABLE 2. SUPERINDUCTION OF TYROSINE TRANSAMINASE BY ACTINOMYCIN D: INCREASED SPECIFIC RADIOACTIVITY IN IMMUNE PRECIPITATES

	Protein (mg/ml)	(a) Specific Radioactivity in Total Protein (count/min × 10³/mg)	+Antiserum count/min	+control serum count/min	(b) Specific Radioactivity in TT (count/min × 10³/mgTT)	(b)/(a)
Control	11.2	172	368	59	1100	6.4
	13.6	183	593	86	1200	6.6
Actinomycin D	11.5	144	1575	80	1720	12.0
	11.5	143	1732	72	1900	13.3

The 6½ hr extracts from the experiment described in Fig. 16 were reacted with antiserum to highly purified tyrosine transaminase, the precipitates collected and their radioactivity determined by scintillation counting. Aliquots were also taken for total protein by the method of Lowry et al. (1951), and for radioactivity in total protein as found in the hot 5% TCA precipitate. Tyrosine transaminase protein was calculated from the specific activity of the purified enzyme, 120 μmoles product formed/min/mg protein.

Since inhibitors of RNA synthesis can stimulate transaminase formation both in intact animals and in tissue culture, we propose that the rate of translation of the transaminase messenger is normally limited by a labile substance which we have referred to as a "cytoplasmic repressor" (Garren et al., 1964a; Tomkins et al., 1965). It is proposed that the mRNA for transaminase is stable, and the mRNA for the repressor as well as the repressor itself must turn over rapidly. The stimulation of tyrosine transaminase synthesis by inhibitors of RNA synthesis would, therefore, result from inhibition of repressor mRNA formation followed by rapid degradation of the remaining repressor messenger as well as the repressor itself. The translation of the stable transaminase messenger would consequently be derepressed.

Earlier in this paper the suggestion was made that Dx exerted an action on the translation of transaminase mRNA. With the evidence just given that translation is inhibited by a cytoplasmic repressor, we considered whether Dx acted to antagonize the repressor, or whether the steroid was involved in another step in the translation process. The experiment illustrated in Fig. 17 favors the possibility that inducer neutralizes repressor by showing that the stimulation of transaminase synthesis by actinomycin does not require inducer. If, as we suggest, actinomycin acts by blocking repressor formation and allowing pre-existing repressor to be degraded, then the inducer is no longer required if the repressor is absent.

Therefore, Dx appears to inhibit either the formation of or the action of the cytoplasmic repressor. This scheme is depicted in Fig. 18 which shows the mRNA for tyrosine transaminase as relatively stable, and the cytoplasmic repressor as well as its messenger as labile. The repressor inhibits the translation of the tyrosine transaminase messenger. In the presence of inducer, the repressor no longer functions and tyrosine transaminase synthesis is stimulated.

As noted earlier, the concentration of tyrosine transaminase message probably also increases on induction, and this increase is not accounted for in the scheme illustrated. At least two possibilities are: 1) the inducer independently stimulates the

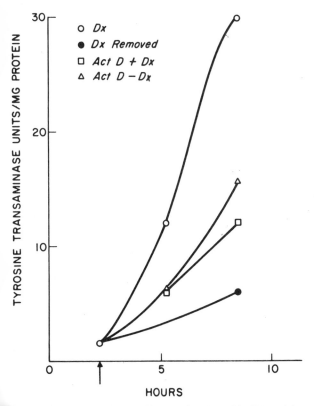

FIGURE 17. Pooled HTC cells were incubated in S-77 with Dx, 10⁻⁵ M. After 2¼ hr, the cells were washed twice with steroid-free S-77 and duplicate samples were then reincubated in steroid-free S-77 with or without actinomycin D, 5 μg/ml, or in the original steroid-containing induction medium, with or without actinomycin D.

311

Mechanism of Inducer Action

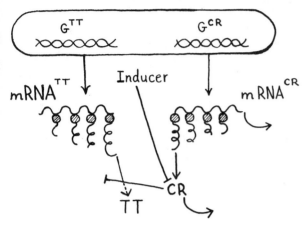

FIGURE 18. Proposed model for control of protein synthesis by steroids at the level of mRNA translation.

production of transaminase mRNA by direct gene activation, or 2) as a secondary consequence of the increased rate of mRNA translation stimulated by the inducer, the level of mRNA is increased. Obviously, further experiments are required to clarify these complicated relationships; however, we feel that HTC cells provide an excellent mammalian model system with which to work.

SUMMARY

1. A newly established line of cells in tissue culture, derived from a rat hepatoma, is described.

2. Glucocorticoid hormones stimulate a 5- to 15-fold increase in the activity of tyrosine-α-ketoglutarate transaminase in either resting or dividing cells.

3. Inhibitor and immunochemical experiments indicate that the steroids cause an increase in the number of enzyme protein molecules rather than the activation of a precursor. The steroids probably act by increasing the rate of enzyme synthesis.

4. The enzyme-inducing steroids do not cause a general increase in the rate of protein or RNA synthesis in these cells, although indirect evidence is presented that they induce an increase in the level of tyrosine transaminase mRNA.

5. Physiological experiments suggest that the hormones exert some control at the level of translation of the transaminase messenger by antagonizing a repressor of messenger function.

6. It cannot yet be determined whether the presumed increase in messenger concentration occurs as a secondary response to the stimulation of translation, or whether there is a direct effect of the hormone on gene transcription.

REFERENCES

COX, R. P. and C. M. MACLEOD. 1962. Alkaline phosphatase content and the effects of prednisolone on mammalian cells in culture. J. Gen. Physiol. 45: 439.

——, ——. 1964. Regulation of alkaline phosphatase in human cell cultures. Cold Spring Harbor Symp. Quant. Biol. 29: 233.

DAVIDSON, E. H., 1965. Hormones and genes. Sci. Amer. 212: 36.

FEIGELSON, P., and M. FEIGELSON. 1964. Studies on the mechanism of cortisone action, Chap. 8, p. 218–233. In G. Litwack and D. Kritchevsky [ed.], Actions of hormones on molecular processes. J. Wiley, New York.

GARREN, L. R., R. R. HOWELL, and G. M. TOMKINS. 1964b. Mammalian enzyme induction by hydrocortisone: The Possible Role of RNA. J. Mol. Biol. 9: 100.

GARREN, L. D., R. R. HOWELL, G. M. TOMKINS, and R. M. CROCCO. 1964a. A paradoxical effect of actinomycin D: The mechanism of regulation of enzyme synthesis by hydrocortisone. Proc. Natl. Acad. Sci. 52(4): 1121.

GIRARD, M., H. LATHAM, S. PENMAN, and J. E. DARNELL. 1965. Entrance of newly formed messenger-RNA and ribosomes into HeLa cell cytoplasm, J. Mol. Biol. 11: 187.

GORSKI, J., W. NOTEBOOM, and J. NICOLETTE. 1965. Estrogen control of the synthesis of RNA and protein in the uterus. J. Cell and Comp. Physiol. 66 Suppl. 1: 91.

GRANICK, S. 1963. Induction of synthesis of δ-aminolevulinic acid synthetase in liver parenchymal cells in culture by chemicals that induce acute porphyria. J. Biol. Chem. 238: PC 2247.

HENSHAW, E. C., M. REVEL, and H. H. HIATT. 1965. A cytoplasmic particle bearing messenger ribonucleic acid in rat liver. J. Mol. Biol. 14: 241.

JACOB, F., and J. MONOD. 1961. On the regulation of gene activity. Cold Spring Harbor Symp. Quant. Biol. 26: 193.

JACOBY, G. A., and B. N. LADU. 1964. Studies on the specificity of tyrosine α-ketoglutarate transaminase. J. Biol. Chem. 239: 419.

KABAT, E. A., and M. M. MAYER. 1964. Experimental immunochemistry, p. 85–90. C. C. Thomas, Springfield, Ill.

KARLSON, P., 1963. New Concepts on the Mode of Action of Hormones. Perspectives in Biol. and Med. 6: 203.

KENNEY, F. T., W. WICK, and D. GREENMAN. 1965. Hydrocortisone Stimulation of RNA synthesis in induction of hepatic enzymes. J. Cell. and Comp. Physiol. 66: Suppl. 1: 125.

KORNER, A. 1965. Growth hormone effects on RNA and protein synthesis in liver. J. Cell. Comp. Physiol. 66: Suppl. 1: 153.

LIN, E. C. C., and W. E. KNOX. 1957. Adaptation of rat liver tyrosine-α-ketoglutarate transaminase. Biochem. Biophys. Acta 26: 85.

LOWRY, O. H., N. J. ROSEBROUGH, A. L. FARR, and R. J. RANDALL. 1951. Protein measurement with the folin phenol reagent. J. Biol. Chem. 193: 265.

NICHOL, C. A., and F. ROSEN. 1964. Adaptive changes in enzymatic activity induced by glucocorticoids, Chap. 9, p. 234–256. In G. Litwack and D. Kritchevsky [ed.], Actions of hormones on molecular processes. J. Wiley, New York.

ODASHIMA, S., and H. P. MORRIS. 1965. Studies on the conversion of Morris' transplantable hepatomas into ascitic form. Gann (Jap. J. Cancer Res.) in press.

PENMAN, S., K. SCHERRER, Y. BECKER, and J. E. DARNELL. 1963. Polyribosomes in normal and poliovirus-infected Hela cells and their relationship to messenger-RNA. Proc. Natl. Acad. Sci. *49:* 654.

PITOT, H. C., C. PERAINO, P. A. MORSE, Jr., and V. R. POTTER. 1964. Hepatomas in tissue culture compared with adapting liver in vivo. Natl. Cancer Inst. Monograph *13:* 229.

SCHERRER, K., H. LATHAM, and J. E. DARNELL. 1963. Demonstration of an unstable RNA and of a precursor to ribosomal RNA in Hela cells. Proc. Natl. Acad. Sci. *49:* 240.

SCHIMKE, R. T., E. W. SWEENEY, and C. M. BERLIN. 1964. An analysis of the kinetics of rat liver tryptophan pyrrolase induction: the significance of both enzyme synthesis and degradation. Biochem. Biophys. Res. Commun. *15*(3): 214.

SEGAL, H. L., and Y. S. KIM. 1965. Environmental control of enzyme synthesis and degradation. J. Cell. and Comp. Physiol. *66 Suppl. 1:* 11.

THOMPSON, E. B., G. M. TOMKINS, and J. F. CURRAN. 1966. Induction of tyrosine-α-ketoglutarate transaminase by steroid hormones in a newly established tissue culture cell line. Proc. Natl. Acad. Sci. *56:* 296.

TOMKINS, G. M., L. D. GARREN, R. R. HOWELL, and B. PETERKOFSKY. 1965. The regulation of enzyme synthesis by steroid hormones: The role of translation. J. Cell. and Comp. Physiol. *66 Suppl. 1:* 137.

WILLIAMS-ASHMAN, H. G. 1965. Androgenic control of nucleic acid and protein synthesis in male accessory genital organs. J. Cell. Comp. Physiol. *66 Suppl. 1:* 111.

YPHANTIS, D. A. 1964. Equilibrium ultracentrifugation of dilute solutions. Biochemistry *3*(3): 297.

Reprinted from the Proceedings of the National Academy of Sciences
Vol. 61, No. 1, pp. 200–206, September, 1968.

"SUPERINDUCTION" OF TYROSINE TRANSAMINASE IN HEPATOMA CELL CULTURES: DIFFERENTIAL INHIBITION OF SYNTHESIS AND TURNOVER BY ACTINOMYCIN D*

By Jerry R. Reel† and Francis T. Kenney

NCI-AEC CARCINOGENESIS PROGRAM, BIOLOGY DIVISION, OAK RIDGE NATIONAL LABORATORY, OAK RIDGE, TENNESSEE

Communicated by William A. Arnold, July 12, 1968

Continuous breakdown and replenishment of the macromolecular constituents of animal cells was recognized some time ago in the pioneering experiments of Schoenheimer and his colleagues,[1] but the significance of degradative processes in regulation of metabolism has become apparent only recently. Schimke, Sweeney, and Berlin have demonstrated[2] that the physiological level of the enzyme tryptophan pyrrolase can be elevated either by stimulation of its synthesis or by inhibition of its degradation, the former process being initiated by glucocorticoid hormones and the latter by the substrate of the enzyme, tryptophan. In a recent report[3] from our laboratory, it was shown that degradation of the tyrosine transaminase of liver was blocked when protein synthesis was inhibited by agents such as cycloheximide or puromycin; under these conditions, the transaminase level was stabilized by concomitant inhibition of both synthesis and degradation of the enzyme. At that time it was suggested[3] that certain "paradoxical" effects of inhibitors of RNA or protein synthesis on enzyme levels might result from differential inhibition of the cellular processes involved in forming an enzyme and of those required for its removal. In the present study, we have analyzed the roles of synthesis and degradation in the elevation of tyrosine transaminase, which follows the addition of actinomycin D to hormonally induced cell cultures. We find that transaminase synthesis, initially high due to induction by hydrocortisone, is progressively inhibited by the antibiotic. That the transaminase level rises during this interval, despite inhibition of its synthesis, reflects a marked inhibition of degradation of the enzyme.

Materials and Methods.—Hepatoma cultures of the Reuber H-35[4] and hepatoma tissue culture (HTC)[5] cell lines were grown in monolayer in 250-ml Falcon plastic flasks containing 10 ml of Eagle's basal medium (BME) enriched fourfold with amino acids and vitamins and supplemented with 20% fetal calf serum and 5% calf serum. Penicillin G (100 units/ml) and streptomycin sulfate (100 µg/ml) were added for routine culturing. Occasionally, antibiotics have been omitted for several passages and the medium cultured for bacterial contamination. Checks for pleuropneumonia-like (PPLO) contamination also have been carried out using the method of Barile, Yaguchi, and Eveland[6] but with horse serum in place of whole blood in the plating agar. No contamination by bacteria or mycoplasmas has been detected. All tissue culture materials were purchased from Grand Island Biological, Co. except penicillin G and streptomycin sulfate, which were obtained from Squibb.

During logarithmic growth, both cell lines had a doubling time of approximately 24 hr. Inoculation of cells at a concentration of 1.3×10^5 cells/ml resulted in cultures which enter stationary phase on about day 9. All experiments were performed using 9- to 12-day (stationary phase) monolayer cultures in serum-free 1X BME (i.e., unenriched). Reuber H-35 and HTC cells do not grow in serum-free BME, but will resume growth on readdition of serum after as long as 6 days in its absence.

Hydrocortisone (Calbiochem) was dissolved in a minimal volume of ethanol and diluted

100-fold with Hanks' balanced salt solution (HBSS) to give a final stock concentration of 10^{-4} M. A medium concentration of 10^{-6} M hydrocortisone was employed to preinduce tyrosine transaminase, since this concentration was found to be the optimal inducing level in these cultures[7] as well as in organ cultures of fetal liver.[8] Actinomycin D, a generous gift from Merck and Co., was dissolved in a minimal volume of acetone and brought to 0.5 mg/ml with HBSS. Aliquots of a freshly prepared actinomycin D solution were added to the culture medium, as required, in each experiment.

Enzyme assays: Hepatoma cells were lysed in 0.15 M KCl–0.001 M ethylenediaminetetraacetate (EDTA), pH 8.0, containing 0.038 mM pyridoxal phosphate and 5.0 mM α-ketoglutarate, pH 7.6. Cell lysis was achieved by alternately freeze-thawing three times in liquid nitrogen and 37°C, respectively. The 105,000 g supernatant fraction of the lysates was assayed directly for tyrosine transaminase activity by a combination of the methods of Kenney[9] and Diamondstone.[10] The unit of activity is defined as that amount required to form 1 μg of p-hydroxyphenyl pyruvate during a 10-min incubation period. Protein was estimated by the procedure of Lowry et al.[11]

Immunochemical analysis: The rates of enzyme synthesis and degradation were measured immunochemically by a combination of the methods employed by Kenney,[12] Segal and Kim,[13] and Schimke, Sweeney, and Berlin.[2] In experiments measuring rates of synthesis, monolayer cultures were exposed to 5.0 μc or 7.5 μc of 4,5-H³-leucine (specific radioactivity 5045 mc/mole) per ml of BME during the final 15 min of the treatment period. Since this labeling time is short relative to the half life of the enzyme, the contribution of turnover is negligible, and the extent of isotope incorporation into the enzyme is a measure of its rate of synthesis. The rate of degradation was measured by following the "chase" of H³-leucine or C¹⁴-leucine from the prelabeled enzyme. Monolayer cultures were exposed either to 5.0 μc of H³-leucine or to 0.5 μc of U-C¹⁴-leucine (specific radioactivity 273 mc/mmole) per ml of BME during the final hour of the 24-hr preinduction period. At the end of the 1-hr labeling period, the H³- or C¹⁴-leucine-containing medium was decanted, the monolayers were washed with HBSS, and then fresh BME medium containing unlabeled leucine and other appropriate treatments was added ("chase" medium). At the end of the pulse label, or "chase" periods, groups of monolayer cultures were scraped, pooled, and collected by centrifugation. The pelleted cells were washed with cold 0.15 M NaCl, lysed by freeze-thawing, and the lysates centrifuged at 105,000 g for 1 hr. Aliquots of the 105,000 g supernatant fraction were assayed for enzyme activity, soluble protein, and radioactivity in the soluble protein. The remainder of the 105,000 g supernatant fraction was rapidly heated to 60°C in the presence of 0.038 mM pyridoxal phosphate and 5.0 mM α-ketoglutarate, coenzyme and substrate, respectively, which stabilize tyrosine transaminase to heat. After being heated, supernatant fractions were rapidly cooled to 0°C and centrifuged at 20,000 g for 30 min. The supernatant enzyme was precipitated with antiserum prepared against a highly purified transaminase preparation.[12] The protein content of the 20,000 g supernatant fraction was essentially constant, but the enzyme content varied according to the treatment given (100–2000 units). Unlabeled carrier enzyme from induced rat livers (spec. act. 12,500 units/mg protein, purified through the $(NH_4)_2SO_4$ [II] step in the scheme described previously[12]) was added to each to bring the enzyme level to a constant value (25,000 units). A slight excess of antibody was added and the mixture incubated at 3°C overnight. Precipitates were collected, washed, and counted as described previously.[12] After removal of the precipitate, the supernatant fractions contained less than 2% of the original enzyme activity. To correct for nonspecific precipitation of radioactivity,[14] a second incubation was carried out in which the enzyme level of the same supernatant fraction was again brought to 25,000 units by addition of unlabeled carrier enzyme. After precipitation with antibody as before, the precipitate was collected and its radioactivity was determined. Radioactivity of the second precipitate was subtracted from the value obtained in the first precipitation, the difference being the actual extent of transaminase labeling. Labeling of the total soluble proteins was assessed by counting an aliquot that was pipetted onto filter paper disks and washed as described before.[15]

Results.—Effect of actinomycin D on the tyrosine transaminase level and its rate of synthesis and degradation: Figure 1 shows the time course of actinomycin D effects on the enzyme level and the rate of enzyme synthesis in preinduced monolayer cultures of the Reuber H-35 hepatoma.   In cultures receiving hydrocortisone plus actinomycin D, the enzyme level began to rise after one hour, reached a peak at three hours, and thereafter fell slightly.   During this interval, actinomycin D treatment resulted in an exponentially *decreasing* rate of enzyme synthesis, presumably reflecting the functional decay of the messenger RNA (mRNA) for tyrosine transminase ($t_{1/2}$ about 3 hr).

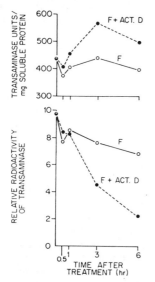

FIG. 1.—Effect of actinomycin D on the time course of transaminase synthesis in preinduced Reuber H-35 cultures in stationary phase. Medium containing hydrocortisone (10^{-6} M) was placed on the monolayers 24 hr before the treatments shown were begun.   At zero time, the hydrocortisone-containing medium (preinduction medium) was decanted, the monolayers washed with HBSS, and medium containing the treatments shown placed on the monolayer cultures.   For measurements of the rate of enzyme synthesis, 5.0 μc of H³-leucine/-ml was added 15 min before collection of cells. Analyses were carried out as indicated in *Materials and Methods*.   The rate of enzyme synthesis is expressed as relative radioactivity, which is defined as cpm in the isolated transaminase $\times$ 10^3/cpm per mg total soluble protein.

The observation that the induced enzyme level increased while the rate of enzyme synthesis decreased following actinomycin D exposure suggested that this antibiotic might be inhibiting processes involved in enzyme degradation. Figure 2 depicts the results of an experiment designed to examine this possibility. As in the previous experiment (Fig. 1), the enzyme level was elevated following actinomycin D addition to preinduced cultures.   Actinomycin D had little or no effect on "chase" of H³-leucine from the total prelabeled soluble proteins.   Actinomycin D markedly inhibited the "chase" of H³ from the prelabeled enzyme, whereas in cells not exposed to this inhibitor, the enzyme was found to undergo turnover with a half life of about three hours.   Thus the elevation of enzyme activity following actinomycin D treatment of induced cells is the resultant of differential inhibitory effects on the rate of enzyme synthesis and degradation (cf. Figs. 1 and 2).   As would be predicted, the enzyme level rises as a consequence of continued synthesis (although at a steadily lower rate) coupled with a marked and apparently immediate inhibition of degradation.

To ascertain whether this effect of actinomycin D was unique to the Reuber H-35 hepatoma, the HTC cell line was employed to carry out similar experiments. Figure 3 illustrates the time course of actinomycin D effects on the enzyme level and the rates of enzyme synthesis and degradation in preinduced HTC cells in

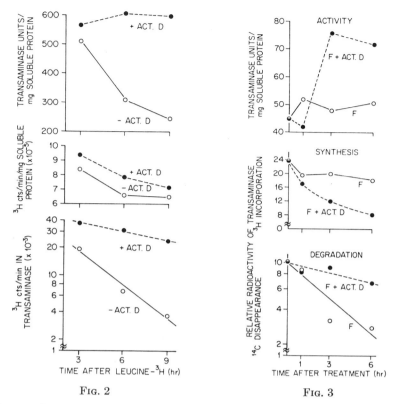

Fig. 2   Fig. 3

Fig. 2.—Effect of actinomycin D on transaminase degradation in preinduced Reuber H-35 cultures in stationary phase. Hydrocortisone (10^{-6} M) was added to monolayer cultures 24 hr before, and H³-leucine (5.0 μc/ml) was present during the final hour of this preinduction period. At the end of this 1-hr labeling period, the "H³ medium" was decanted, the monolayers were washed with HBSS, and fresh medium was added without actinomycin D (*open circles*) or together with 5 μg of actinomycin D/ml (*solid circles*). Analyses were performed as described in *Materials and Methods*.

Fig. 3.—Effect of actinomycin D on transaminase synthesis and degradation in pre-induced HTC cultures in stationary phase. Hydrocortisone (10^{-6} M) was added to monolayer cultures 24 hr before and C¹⁴-leucine (0.5 μc/ml) 1 hr before these measurements were begun. Immediately preceding the zero time the "C¹⁴ medium" was decanted, the monolayers were washed with HBSS, and at zero time fresh medium was added containing hydrocortisone (10^{-6} M) alone (*open circles*) or together with 5 μg of actinomycin D/ml (*solid circles*). For rate of synthesis measurements, 7.5 μc of H³-leucine/ml was added 15 min before collection of cells for analyses. Analyses were carried out as described in *Materials and Methods*.

monolayer culture. In this experiment, a dual isotope technique was employed to permit simultaneous measurement of both synthesis and degradation. The induced level of tyrosine transaminase in the HTC cell line is considerably lower than in the Reuber H-35 cells; however, the extent of hormonal induction in these two cell lines is quite similar (8- to 10-fold). The difference in the induced level of the enzyme is probably attributable to the fact that the basal enzyme level is markedly lower in HTC as compared with Reuber H-35 cells. Hydrocortisone plus actinomycin D brought about a maximum elevation of enzyme activity by three hours, and this persisted for an additional three hours.   During this interval, the rate of enzyme synthesis fell exponentially, again implying a functional half life of three hours for the transaminase mRNA.   As in Reuber H-35 cells, the elevation of enzyme activity was explicable by the finding that the rate of enzyme degradation was rapidly and markedly inhibited by actinomycin D.   The half life of transaminase following actinomycin D was 11.7 hours as compared with 3.0 hours in the control cells.

From the theoretical considerations set forth by Berlin and Schimke,[16] it would be predicted that the differential inhibitory effect of actinomycin D on the rates of transaminase synthesis and degradation would result in the observed elevation of the enzyme level (Fig. 3).   At steady state, the enzyme level (E_{ss}) is equal to the rate constant of synthesis (k_1) over the rate constant of degradation (k_2), i.e.,

$$E_{ss} = k_1/k_2.$$

Therefore, if steady-state conditions are assumed for both the initial preinduced enzyme level and the approximate plateau level after actinomycin D, the relative change in any one of these three parameters should be predictable from the observed changes in the other two.   Using the foregoing steady-state equation, the experimental data of Figure 3 have been found to conform well with theoretical results.   This is demonstrated as follows: the preinduced enzyme level changed from 45 to 73 by 4.5 hours after actinomycin D, whereas the *relative* rate of enzyme synthesis decreased from 23.8 to 10 during this time.   In order to calculate the expected *relative* change in the rate constant of degradation (k_2), the following steady-state equations may be written:

$$\text{at } t = 0 \text{ hours, } k_2 = \frac{23.8}{45} = 0.528, \qquad (1)$$

$$\text{at } t = 4.5 \text{ hours, } k_2' = \frac{10}{73} = 0.137, \qquad (2)$$

thus

$$k_2'/k_2 = \frac{0.137}{0.528} = 0.26.$$

It is apparent that the changes in the enzyme level and in the rate of synthesis at 4.5 hours after actinomycin D require that the rate of degradation (k_2) be decreased to one fourth of its initial value.   The least-squares calculation of k_2 from the control curve and of k_2' from the data for the actinomycin-treated cells gave 0.100 hour^{-1} and 0.026 hour^{-1}, respectively.   Thus the relative change in the experimentally determined k_2 agreed with the theoretical result.

Discussion.—The steady-state level of tyrosine transaminase (and other enzyme proteins) represents a balance between continual synthesis and degradation.   Mechanisms for changing this level are now known to involve alterations in the rate of both synthesis and degradation.   Data previously presented[17, 18] have shown that tyrosine transaminase induction by glucocorticoids in hepatoma cell culture is the result of an increased rate of enzyme synthesis. However, the rise in tyrosine transaminase levels which follows the addition of actinomycin D to preinduced hepatoma cultures is primarily the result of a marked decrease in the rate of enzyme degradation. Synthesis of the enzyme is also inhibited by the antibiotic, but relatively slowly. Thus there occurs a period of time during which synthesis proceeds at a moderate rate while degradation is severely impaired, and as a consequence the enzyme level rises.

These findings are not in accord with those of Tomkins et al.,[19] who reported that actinomycin D increased the rate of transaminase synthesis after addition to preinduced HTC cultures. The discrepancy between these results and ours probably results from the fact that these investigators employed a 6.5-hour labeling period in the presence of actinomycin D in order to determine the rate of transaminase synthesis; the effects of actinomycin D on enzyme degradation were not studied. It is obvious from the half-life data we have presented that an interval of 6.5 hours encompasses approximately two half lives of the enzyme. During this interval, labeling of the enzyme can be increased due to the labeled amino acid's being incorporated into the enzyme and then retained as a result of blockage of degradation by actinomycin D.

Earlier results from our laboratory have demonstrated that inhibitors of protein synthesis (cycloheximide, puromycin) also interfere with tyrosine transaminase degradation.[3] It was suggested that certain protein(s) which turn over rapidly might be required for the degradative process. The results presented here further require, if this interpretation is to be maintained, that the half lives of the mRNA's for these degradative protein(s) be extremely short. A more likely explanation for the effects of inhibitors of protein and RNA synthesis can be proposed on the basis of the results of Mandelstam.[20] He suggested that inhibition by chloramphenicol of protein degradation in *E. coli* cultures in stationary phase results from the accumulation of compounds of small molecular weight that inhibit the degradative process. A similar mechanism may well be operative in the present case.

Summary.—With an isotopic-immunochemical procedure, the "superinduction" of tyrosine transaminase which occurs in preinduced hepatoma cells following the addition of actinomycin D was shown to be due to a differential inhibitory effect on the rate of transaminase synthesis and degradation. Following the addition of actinomycin D, the transaminase level rises as a result of a marked decrease in the rate of enzyme degradation combined with a steadily decreasing rate of synthesis.

We are pleased to acknowledge the kind assistance of Dr. Alfred Hellman, who tested our tissue cultures for bacterial and PPLO contamination, and Mrs. Joan Reel, who aided in the routine farming of the cultures. Special thanks are also due to Mr. Joseph Kendrick and Mr. Larry Roberson for their helpful assistance in certain phases of these experiments, and to Dr. Carl Wust for his aid in the preparation of antiserum. The cell lines used in this study were made available to us through the courtesy of Drs. Paul Morse and Van R. Potter (H35) and Drs. E. Brad Thompson and Gordon M. Tomkins (HTC).

* This research was supported jointly by the National Cancer Institute and by the U.S Atomic Energy Commission under contract with Union Carbide Corporation.

† American Cancer Society postdoctoral fellow.

[1] Schoenheimer, R., *The Dynamic State of Body Constituents* (Cambridge, Mass.: Harvard University Press, 1942).

[2] Schimke, R. T., E. M. Sweeney, and C. M. Berlin, *J. Biol. Chem.*, **240**, 322 (1965).

[3] Kenney, F. T., *Science*, **156**, 525 (1967).

[4] Pitot, H. C., C. Peraino, P. A. Morse, Jr., and V. R. Potter, *Natl. Cancer Inst. Monograph*, **13**, 229 (1964).

[5] Thompson, E. B., G. M. Tomkins, and J. F. Curran, these PROCEEDINGS, **56**, 296 (1966).

[6] Barile, M. F., R. Yaguchi, and W. C. Eveland, *Am. J. Clin. Pathol.*, **30**, 171 (1958).

[7] Reel, J. R., and F. T. Kenney, unpublished results.

[8] Wicks, W. D., *J. Biol. Chem.*, **243**, 900 (1968).

[9] Kenney, F. T., *J. Biol. Chem.*, **234**, 2707 (1959).

[10] Diamondstone, T. I., *Anal. Biochem.*, **16**, 395 (1966).

[11] Lowry, O. H., N. J. Rosebrough, A. L. Farr, and R. J. Randall, *J. Biol. Chem.*, **193**, 265 (1951).

[12] Kenney, F. T., *J. Biol. Chem.*, **237**, 3495 (1962).

[13] Segal, H. L., and Y. S. Kim, these PROCEEDINGS, **50**, 912 (1963).

[14] Schimke, R. T., *Bull. Soc. Chim. Biol.*, **48**, 1009 (1966).

[15] Kenney, F. T., *J. Biol. Chem.*, **237**, 1610 (1962).

[16] Berlin, C. M., and R. T. Schimke, *Mol. Pharmacol.*, **1**, 149 (1965).

[17] Reel, J. R., and F. T. Kenney, *Federation Proc.*, **27**, 641 (1968).

[18] Granner, D. K., B. Thompson, and G. M. Tomkins, *Federation Proc.*, **27**, 641 (1968).

[19] Tomkins, G. M., E. B. Thompson, S. Hayashi, T. Gelehrter, D. Granner, and B. Peterkofsky, in *Cold Spring Harbor Symposia on Quantitative Biology*, vol. 31 (1966), p. 349.

[20] Mandelstam, J., *Biochem. J.*, **69**, 110 (1958).

Section V

HEMOPOESIS

BURNHAM, B. F., and J. LASCELLES, 1963. Biochem. J. *87*, 462. Control of porphyrin biosynthesis through a negative-feedback mechanism.

KARIBIAN, D., and I. M. LONDON, 1965. Biochem. Biophys. Res. Comm. *18*, 243. Control of heme synthesis by feedback inhibition.

LEVERE, R. D., and S. GRANICK, 1967. J. Biol. Chem. *242*, 1903. Control of hemoglobin synthesis in the cultured chick blastoderm.

KAPPAS, A., C. S., SONG, R. D. LEVERE, R. A. SACHSON, and S. GRANICK, 1968. Proc. Nat'l Acad. Sci. *61*, 509-513. The induction of δ-aminolevulinic acid synthetase *in vivo* in chick embryo liver by natural steroids.

GRIBBLE, T. J., and H. C. SCHWARTZ, 1965. Biochim. biophys. Acta *103*, 333. Effect of protoporphyrin on hemoglobin synthesis.

ZUCKER, W. V., and H. M. SCHULMAN, 1968. Proc. Nat'l Acad Sci. *59*, 582. Stimulation of globin-chain initiation by hemin in the reticulocyte cell-free system.

BAGLIONI, C., and T. CAMPANA, 1967. European J. Biochem. *2*, 480-492. α-chain and globin: intermediates in the synthesis of rabbit hemoglobin.

WILT, F. H., 1965. J. Mol. Biol. *12*, 331. Regulation of the initiation of chick embryo hemoglobin synthesis.

FANTONI, A., A. DE LA CHAPELLE, and P. A. MARKS, 1969. J. Biol. Chem. *244*, 675-681. Synthesis of embryonic hemoglobins during erythroid cell development in fetal mice.

MOSS, B., and V. M., INGRAM, 1968. J. Mol. Biol. *32*, 481. Hemoglobin synthesis during amphibian metamorphosis. I. Chemical studies on the hemoglobins from the larval and adult stages of *Rana catesbeiana*.

MOSS, B., and V. M. INGRAM, 1968. J. Mol. Biol. *32*, 493. Hemoglobin synthesis during amphibian metamorphosis. II. Synthesis of adult hemoglobin following thyroxine administration.

LEE, J. C., and V. M. INGRAM, 1967. Science *158*, 1330. Erythrocyte transfer RNA: change during chick development.

An average man forms approximately 10^{11} red blood cells each day. An equal number are destroyed. The new red blood cells are derived from "stem" cells located in the marrow of the long bones which proliferate and differentiate into several blood cell types (Till et al., 1964). The morphological stages in the process of differentiation of a stem cell to a red blood cell have been described in detail. The first cells in which hemoglobin synthesis can be detected are termed basophilic erythroblasts. These are nucleated marrow cells which are recognized by their high content of ribosomes. Hemoglobin accumulates in these cells over a period of several cell divisions until the orthochromatic erythroblast stage is reached. The nucleus is then extruded to form a reticulocyte. These enucleate cells continue to synthesize hemoglobin but do not synthesize DNA, RNA, or other proteins in significant amounts (Fantoni et al., 1968). The last stage in red blood cell development is marked by cessation of hemoglobin synthesis and loss of ribosomes and mitochondria.

The obvious importance of red blood cells to vertebrate life has naturally led to curiosity concerning the formation of these cells. Moreover, the fact that hemoglobin makes up more than 98 percent of the total protein of a red blood cell makes these cells especially suitable for the study of the regulation of gene activity.

Hemoglobin is a fairly large molecule (molecular weight 65,000) consisting of a pair of heterodimers resulting from the association of α and β polypeptide chains. A heme group is bound to each subunit. The synthesis of heme from products of intermediary metabolism requires a series of enzymes, the first of which is δ-aminolevulinic synthetase. The activity of this enzyme is inhibited by heme (pp. 325, 336). Thus, the concentration of free heme is controlled by feedback inhibition. The results of several studies included in this collection indicate that the rate of hemoglobin synthesis is regulated by the amount of heme present (pp. 343, 357, 363, 371). Therefore, it seems possible that the rate of hemoglobin synthesis depends on the activity of δ-aminolevulinic synthetase. The synthesis of this enzyme, in turn, seems to be controlled by steroid hormones (p. 352).

The physiological steps in the stimulation of the synthesis of hemoglobin in hemopoetic cells may involve (1) induction of δ-aminolevulinic synthetase, (2) synthesis of heme, (3) heme stimulation of globin synthesis, and (4) association of heme with globin chains and formation of hemoglobin.

An increase in the rate of hemoglobin synthesis occurs not only during stem cell differentiation but also during embryogenesis. Hemoglobin can be observed in specialized cells within 38 hours of incubation of fertilized chick eggs. The relation of hemoglobin accumulation to protein and RNA synthesis in these embryos has been studied by Wilt (p. 384) and others.

Different globin chains are synthesized at different periods of development (Schroeder and Matsuda, 1958; Baglioni et al., 1961). The regulation of embryonic hemoglobin synthesis in fetal mice has been investigated by Marks and his collaborators (p. 396). Their results indicate that the pattern of synthesis is controlled at steps which occur after transcription of the globin genes. A similar change in the pattern of globin synthesis has been observed during metamorphosis of amphibians by Moss and Ingram (pp. 403, 421). The mechanism which elicits this change is unknown, but the observation that the protein synthetic specificity also changes during development suggests possible models which can be tested *in vitro* (p. 441).

Baglioni, C., V. Ingram, and E. Sullivan (1961)   Nature *189,* 467-469. Genetic control of fetal and adult human hemoglobin.

Fantoni, A., A. de la Chapelle, R. Rifkind, and P. Marks (1968)   J. Mol. Biol. *33,* 79. Erythroid cell development in fetal mice; synthetic capacity for different proteins.

Schroeder, W., and G. Matsuda (1958)   Am. Chem. Soc. J. *80,* 1521. N-terminal residues of human fetal hemoglobin.

Till, J., E. McCulloch, and L. Simminovich (1964)   Proc. Nat'l Acad. Sci. *51,* 29-37. A stochastic model of stem cell proliferation based on the growth of spleen colony-forming cells.

RELATED READING

Ingram, V. (1963)   Columbia Univ. Press, N.Y. The hemoglobins in genetics and evolution.

Shubert, D., and M. Cohn (1968)   J. Mol. Biol. *38,* 273-288. Immunoglobin biosynthesis. III. Blocks in defective synthesis.

Reprinted from *Biochemical Journal*, vol. 87.

Control of Porphyrin Biosynthesis through a Negative-Feedback Mechanism

STUDIES WITH PREPARATIONS OF δ-AMINOLAEVULATE SYNTHETASE AND δ-AMINOLAEVULATE DEHYDRATASE FROM *RHODOPSEUDOMONAS SPHEROIDES*

By B. F. BURNHAM* AND JUNE LASCELLES

Microbiology Unit, Department of Biochemistry, University of Oxford

(*Received 5 November 1962*)

The photosynthetic bacterium *Rhodopseudomonas spheroides*, like many other micro-organisms, accumulates porphyrins in the medium when cultured under iron-deficient conditions (Lascelles, 1961). The addition of small amounts of iron (2 μm-moles/ml.) to suspensions of iron-deficient *R. spheroides* causes a large decrease (up to 100 μm-moles/ml.) in the quantity of porphyrin produced by the organism. Iron cannot therefore be acting solely by diverting porphyrins (or precursors) to iron porphyrins since the quantity of porphyrin that fails to accumulate in the presence of iron is about 100 times more than the amount of iron required to suppress the excretion (Lascelles, 1956).

Iron may act catalytically on porphyrin excretion by promoting the synthesis of a haem compound that in turn controls the activity of an enzyme concerned in porphyrin synthesis through a negative-feedback mechanism. In other negative-feedback systems the final product in a metabolic sequence inhibits the first enzymic step that leads directly to that end product (Umbarger, 1961). In porphyrin synthesis the enzyme that fills this position is δ-aminolaevulate synthetase, which catalyses the formation of δ-aminolaevulate from glycine and succinyl-CoA (Kikuchi, Kumar, Talmage & Shemin, 1958; Gibson, 1958).

* Present address: C.F. Kettering Research Laboratory, Yellow Springs, Ohio, U.S.A.

Previous work has shown that haemin represses the formation of δ-aminolaevulate synthetase in *R. spheroides* (Lascelles, 1960) and that haemin inhibits the action of the enzyme in crude cell extracts (Gibson, Matthew, Neuberger & Tait, 1961). In the present investigation the possibility that haemin exerts a negative-feedback type of control on δ-aminolaevulate synthetase has been examined by studying its action on partially purified preparations of the enzyme from *R. spheroides*. Evidence consistent with such a controlling function has also been shown with suspensions of the organism that produce porphyrins. Preliminary accounts of this work have appeared (Burnham, 1962 a, b). The purification of succinyl-coenzyme A thiokinase (used in the assay for δ-aminolaevulate synthetase) and of δ-aminolaevulate dehydratase from *R. spheroides* is also described.

EXPERIMENTAL

Chemicals

CoA (75%), ATP, pyridoxal phosphate, horse-heart cytochrome *c* and twice-recrystallized bovine haemoglobin were obtained from the Sigma Chemical Co., St Louis, Mo., U.S.A.

Succinyl-CoA was prepared by the method of Simon & Shemin (1953) and was used immediately. The values quoted for succinyl-CoA are based on the amount of CoA (assumed to be 75% pure) used. Alternatively, succinyl-CoA was generated in the reaction mixture from succinate, ATP and CoA by succinyl-coenzyme A thiokinase.

Phosphate buffers were made from KH_2PO_4 and K_2HPO_4. Tris buffers were prepared according to Gomori (1955). Other buffers were prepared by adjusting the pH of 0·2M solutions with N-KOH or N-HCl.

Protohaemin IX was obtained from Schuchardt G.m.b.H., Munich, Germany. A portion of this haemin was recrystallized three times before being used in inhibition studies. The results obtained were indistinguishable from those obtained when the haemin was used without this precautionary purification.

Coproporphyrin III was obtained from culture supernatants of iron-deficient R. spheroides (Lascelles, 1956).

Protoporphyrin and deuteroporphyrin were prepared by the method of Fischer & Putzer (1926) and Fischer, Treibs & Zeile (1931). Haematoporphyrin was purchased from the California Corp. for Biochemical Research, Los Angeles, Calif., U.S.A.

All these porphyrins were converted into their methyl esters, and were chromatographed on $CaCO_3$ with benzene and chloroform (Falk, 1961). Melting points (uncorrected) of the crystalline fractions after chromatography were (with melting points given in the literature in parentheses): haematoporphyrin dimethyl ester, 209° (212°); deuteroporphyrin dimethyl ester, 220° (224°); protoporphyrin dimethyl ester, 220° (225–230°); coproporphyrin tetramethyl ester, 122° (130–158°) and 160° (150–179°). Before use, the esters were hydrolysed in 6N-HCl and subsequently twice evaporated to dryness in vacuo over solid KOH.

Metals were incorporated into the porphyrins as the corresponding acetates (Schwartz, Berg, Bossenmaier & Dinsmore, 1960). Within 1 hr. before use, mM stock solutions were prepared as follows. The crystalline iron porphyrin was dissolved in 0·5 ml. of N-KOH and diluted to 5·5 ml. with freshly boiled water and 0·5 ml. of M-tris buffer, pH 7·8. The solution was gently mixed while 0·4 ml. of N-HCl was slowly added, and the volume was made up to 10 ml. with freshly boiled water. The solutions to be used in the experiments were then prepared from this stock solution by using freshly boiled water.

Crystalline bacteriochlorophyll and bacteriochlorophyllide were prepared from R. spheroides by a method based on that of Jacobs, Vatter & Holt (1954). These were dissolved in 50% (v/v) methanol. Magnesium protoporphyrin was prepared by the method of Granick (1948). Crystalline horse-liver catalase was prepared by the method of Bonnichsen (1947). Crystalline horse myoglobin was generously supplied by Å. Åkeson of the Nobel Medical Institute, Stockholm, Sweden. Native globin was prepared from bovine haemoglobin by the method of Rossi-Fanelli, Antonini & Caputo (1958).

Organism

The strain of R. spheroides used (N.C.I.B. 8253, from the National Collection of Industrial Bacteria) was that described by Lascelles (1956).

Growth and harvesting

The culture medium ('medium MS') was that described by Lascelles (1959). The organisms were grown photosynthetically, harvested by centrifuging at the end of the logarithmic phase of growth (14–20 hr.) and were washed once with 0·1 M-tris buffer, pH 7·8. They were finally suspended at the required concentration in 0·1 M-tris buffer, pH 7·8, and either stored at −20° or used directly. In one phase of the investigation cells were grown by Mr R. Elsworth of the Microbiological Research Establishment, Porton, Wilts. These cells were grown aerobically under low aeration on medium MS supplemented with acetate.

Preparation of cell-free extracts

Suspensions containing 10–50 mg. dry wt. of organisms/ml. were disrupted by ultrasonic vibration for 5 min. at 25 kcyc./sec. with a Mullard ultrasonic generator type E 7590 B (Mullard Ltd., London, W.C. 1), cooled by a rapidly flowing current of cold water. Whole cells and cell debris were removed by centrifuging for 10 min. at 34 000g at 2° in a Servall centrifuge.

Determinations

Dry weight of organisms. The extinction of suspensions was measured at 680 mμ and the dry weight calculated from a calibration curve; the absorption due to photosynthetic pigments is minimal at this wavelength (Cohen-Bazire, Sistrom & Stanier, 1957).

Protein. The concentration of protein in extracts was determined by the method of Lowry, Rosebrough, Farr & Randall (1951). Crystalline bovine plasma albumin (Armour Laboratories, Sussex) was used as the standard.

Bacteriochlorophyll and porphyrins. The bacteriochlorophyll concentration in whole cells was determined by the method of Cohen-Bazire et al. (1957); porphyrins accumulated in the medium were determined as described by Lascelles (1956).

Assay of enzymic activities

δ-Aminolaevulate synthetase. δ-Aminolaevulate-synthetase activity was measured in a standard assay mixture containing: glycine, 100 μmoles; sodium succinate, 100 μmoles; CoA, 0·58 μmole; pyridoxal phosphate, 0·25 μmole; ATP, 7·5 μmoles; $MgCl_2$, 10 μmoles; tris buffer, pH 7·8, 50 μmoles; EDTA, 1·0 μmole; β-mercaptoethanol, 1·0 μmole; succinyl-coenzyme A thiokinase, 0·1 ml. (specific activity 520 μmoles of succinyl-CoA/hr./mg.); inhibitors as indicated; partially purified δ-aminolaevulate synthetase, 0·1 ml. (about 4 mg. of protein); water to give a final volume of 1·0 ml. Incubation was at 37° for 30 min. in 13 mm. tubes. The reaction was terminated by adding 1 ml. of 10% (w/v) trichloroacetic acid and the protein was removed by centrifuging. The δ-aminolaevulate in a sample of the supernatant was determined by the method of Mauzerall & Granick (1956). In experiments with the more highly purified preparations of enzyme there was no advantage in adding either EDTA or β-mercaptoethanol, and they were usually omitted.

δ-Aminolaevulate dehydratase. This enzyme was assayed by a slightly modified version of the method of Gibson, Neuberger & Scott (1955). The system contained: potassium phosphate buffer, pH 7·5, 125 μmoles; $MgCl_2$, 5 μmoles; L-cysteine, 25 μmoles; δ-aminolaevulate, 5 μmoles; inhibitors, as indicated; enzyme, as indicated; water to give a final volume of 2·5 ml. The enzyme was preincubated in the reaction mixture for 10 min. before the addition of δ-aminolaevulate. Incubation was at 37° for

30 min. The reaction was stopped by the addition of 0·1 ml. of 25% (w/v) $CuSO_4,5H_2O$, the precipitated material was centrifuged and porphobilinogen was determined in the supernatant by the method of Mauzerall & Granick (1956).

Succinyl-coenzyme A thiokinase. This enzyme was assayed by a method similar to that of Kaufman & Alivisatos (1955). The system contained: sodium succinate, 100 μmoles; CoA, 0·58 μmole; ATP, 7·5 μmoles; L-cysteine or β-mercaptoethanol, 10 μmoles; hydroxylamine (added as hydroxylamine hydrochloride–KOH mixture, pH 7·4) 800 μmoles; enzyme; water to give a final volume of 1·0 ml. Incubation was at 37° for 30 min. in 13 mm. tubes. Succinohydroxamate was determined by the method of Lipmann & Tuttle (1945).

Purification of succinyl-coenzyme A thiokinase

A suspension (200 ml.) of *R. spheroides* containing 50 mg. dry wt. of organisms/ml. was used as the starting material. All operations were carried out at 2° unless stated otherwise.

Step 1. Preparation of extract. Samples (20 ml.) of cells were disrupted by ultrasonic treatment and centrifuged for 20 min. at 34 000g.

Step 2. Preliminary ammonium sulphate fractionation. The crude supernatant from step 1 was collected and solid $(NH_4)_2SO_4$ was added to give 25% saturation. After equilibration for 30 min., the precipitate was removed by centrifuging and discarded. Solid $(NH_4)_2SO_4$ was slowly added to the supernatant to give 65% saturation. After equilibration for 30 min., the precipitate was removed by centrifuging and the supernatant discarded.

Step 3. Protamine sulphate fractionation. The precipitate from step 2 was dissolved in 50 ml. of 0·2 M-potassium phosphate buffer, pH 6·8, and dialysed against two changes of water for 24 hr. at 2°. After dialysis, the solution was centrifuged to remove insoluble matter, and the pH of the supernatant adjusted to 6·0 with M-acetate buffer. A solution of protamine sulphate (20 mg./ml.) was added slowly with mixing until a total of 40 ml. had been added. The solution was equilibrated at 2° for 1 hr., with occasional stirring, before the copious precipitate was removed by centrifuging.

Step 4. Removal of excess of protamine sulphate. Solid $(NH_4)_2SO_4$ was added to the supernatant to give 60% saturation and the mixture equilibrated for 30 min. before centrifuging. The supernatant containing excess of prot-

amine sulphate was discarded, and the precipitate was dissolved in 10 ml. of 0·1 M-tris buffer, pH 7·8. This solution was chilled to −3°, and was kept at this temperature for 10 min., then centrifuged for 10 min. at −3° at 17 000g. The supernatant was immediately decanted.

Step 5. Final ammonium sulphate fractionation. The supernatant was adjusted to 30% saturation with solid $(NH_4)_2SO_4$. The precipitate was collected by centrifuging and dissolved in 5 ml. of 0·1 M-tris buffer, pH 7·8. This preparation could be kept at 1° for at least 15 days with essentially no loss in activity

Further purification by chromatography on diethylaminoethylcellulose. Further purification of succinyl-coenzyme A thiokinase could be achieved by chromatography on diethylaminoethylcellulose (DEAE-cellulose). The enzyme extract was adsorbed on a column (1·8 cm. × 18 cm.) at pH 7·9 in mM-tris buffer. Elution was carried out by increasing the ionic strength with KCl, either stepwise or with a linear gradient. The enzyme was eluted with approx. 0·3 M-KCl. Difficulty was occasionally encountered in adsorbing the enzyme on the DEAE-cellulose. However, successful runs yielded an enzyme with a specific activity of up to 520 μmoles of succinyl-CoA/hr./mg. of protein. After DEAE-cellulose chromatography the enzyme could be stored at −20° with little loss in activity over several months. The purification procedure is summarized in Table 1.

Preparation of δ-aminolaevulate synthetase

Suspensions of *R. spheroides* containing 50 mg. dry wt. of cells/ml. in 0·04 M-tris buffer, pH 7·8, were divided into 20 ml. samples, frozen and stored at −20°. Such preparations provided a relatively stable and uniform starting material for the purification experiments. All operations were carried out at 2° unless stated otherwise.

Step 1. Preparation of crude enzyme extract. After the ultrasonic treatment, 15 ml. of the broken-cell suspension was centrifuged at 2° for 30 min. at 34 000g. The precipitated cell debris was discarded and 2 ml. of 5 mM-o-phenanthroline, 0·1 ml. of 0·1 M-β-mercaptoethanol and 1 ml. of 0·1 M-$MgCl_2$ were added to 10 ml. of the supernatant.

Step 2. Acetone precipitation. The extract from step 1 was slowly added to 70 ml. of acetone that had been cooled in solid CO_2 to −40°. The mixture was left for 10 min. before centrifuging. The precipitate was resuspended in 20 ml. of acetone at −40° and was centrifuged again, this time the precipitate being collected in a single centrifuge tube.

Table 1. *Purification of succinyl-coenzyme A thiokinase*

Experimental details are given in the text.

Fraction	Volume (ml.)	Concn. of protein (mg./ml.)	Specific activity (μmoles of succinohydroxamate/hr./mg. of protein)
Crude ultrasonically-treated extract	200	26	2·9
Redissolved precipitate from treatment with 65% saturated $(NH_4)_2SO_4$, after dialysis	92	15	4·2
Supernatant from treatment with protamine sulphate	130	3	16
Redissolved precipitate from treatment with 60% saturated $(NH_4)_2SO_4$	10	24	17·9
Redissolved precipitate from treatment with 30% saturated $(NH_4)_2SO_4$	5	10·2	28·9
Eluate from DEAE-cellulose column	—	0·49	520

Table 2. *Purification of δ-aminolaevulate synthetase*

Experimental details are given in the text.

Expt. no.	Preparation	Volume (ml.)	Concn. of protein (mg./ml.)	Specific activity (μm-moles of δ-aminolaevulate/hr./mg. of protein)
1	Crude ultrasonically-treated extract	15	24	205
	Redissolved precipitate from treatment with acetone	10	10	460
	Redissolved precipitate from treatment with 50% saturated $(NH_4)_2SO_4$	8	1·9	2000
2	Crude ultrasonically-treated extract	20	17·8	170
	Redissolved precipitate from treatment with acetone	10	6·4	680
	Redissolved precipitate from treatment with 50% saturated $(NH_4)_2SO_4$	5	4·4	1625

Step 3. Ammonium sulphate precipitation. The precipitate from step 2 was resuspended in 10 ml. of 0·1 M-tris buffer, pH 7·8, containing β-mercaptoethanol (2 mM) and EDTA (2 mM). After being mixed for 15 min. the suspension was centrifuged and the precipitate discarded. To 8 ml. of this supernatant, 0·2 ml. of 0·1 M-β-mercaptoethanol, 0·8 ml. of 5 mM-*o*-phenanthroline, 0·4 ml. of 0·1 M-$MgCl_2$ and 0·2 ml. of 0·1 M-EDTA were added. An equal volume of saturated $(NH_4)_2SO_4$ (at room temperature) was added slowly to this mixture, which was held in an ice bath to keep the temperature below 5°. After equilibration for 20 min. the precipitate was collected by centrifuging, and the supernatant discarded. The precipitate was redissolved in 8 ml. of 0·1 M-tris buffer, pH 7·8, and was then dialysed against 0·01 M-tris for several hours.

The partially purified δ-aminolaevulate synthetase had a specific activity of about 1800 μm-moles of δ-aminolaevulate/hr./mg. of protein. The yield and activity did not generally vary by more than a few per cent. The results obtained in two such preparations are summarized in Table 2. The stability of the different preparations, however, did vary somewhat, though preparations retained about 80% of their activity for about 5 days when stored at 1°.

Repeated attempts to effect further purification of the enzyme with DEAE-cellulose were disappointing: whereas the behaviour of the enzyme in the early stages of purification seemed predictable, it became increasingly erratic with further purification. Likewise, when the described purification procedure was carried out with 5 or 10 times the amounts of materials, it proved to be less reliable.

Purification of δ-aminolaevulate dehydratase

Cells used for the purification of this enzyme were grown at the Microbiological Research Establishment, Porton, Wilts. All fractionations were carried out at 2° unless stated otherwise.

Step 1. Preparation of crude enzyme extract. A thick cell paste containing 77 g. wet wt. of cells was mixed with enough 0·1 M-tris buffer, pH 7·8, to give a mixture just thin enough to be poured. This material was passed once through a French Pressure Cell (American Instrument Co., Silver Spring, Md., U.S.A.). The crushed preparation was treated ultrasonically for 3 min. in 20 ml. portions to denature the nucleic acid released from the disrupted cells. After the ultrasonic treatment there was a large decrease in viscosity. The ultrasonically treated extract was diluted to 300 ml. with 0·1 M-tris buffer, pH 7·8, containing EDTA

(mM) and β-mercaptoethanol (mM). This extract was centrifuged for 90 min. in a Spinco model L ultracentrifuge at 78 400*g*.

Step 2. Acetone precipitation. The supernatants from step 1 were combined and 10 ml. of 0·1 M-$MgCl_2$ plus 1 ml. of 0·01 M-β-mercaptoethanol were added. After being mixed, the extract was slowly added to 1 l. of acetone at −20°. The precipitate was removed by centrifuging at −10°, and was washed once with an additional 200 ml. of cold acetone. The washed acetone precipitate was redissolved in 60 ml. of 0·1 M-tris buffer, pH 7·8, containing EDTA (mM) and β-mercaptoethanol (mM). The mixture was dialysed for 20 hr. against changes of 0·01 M-tris buffer, pH 7·8, containing EDTA (mM) and β-mercaptoethanol (mM). After dialysis, the insoluble residue was removed by centrifuging.

Step 3. Ammonium sulphate fractionation. Solid $(NH_4)_2SO_4$ was added to the supernatant to give increments of 10% saturation. After each addition, the solution was equilibrated for 30 min. before centrifuging. Each precipitate collected during this treatment was redissolved in 10 ml. of 0·1 M-tris buffer, pH 7·8, and was dialysed overnight against the same buffer. The fraction that was precipitated at 40% saturation contained essentially all the δ-aminolaevulate-dehydratase activity.

Step 4. Chromatography on diethylaminoethylcellulose. The active fraction from step 3 was further dialysed against 2 mM-tris buffer, pH 7·8, containing EDTA (mM) and β-mercaptoethanol (mM). After dialysis, this partially purified enzyme extract was placed on a column (1·2 cm. × 20 cm.) of DEAE-cellulose equilibrated with the same buffer. Protein was eluted from the column by increasing the ionic strength of the eluting buffer with M-KCl in a stepwise manner. The δ-aminolaevulate dehydratase was eluted in the presence of about 0·18 M-KCl.

The results obtained with this procedure are summarized in Table 3.

RESULTS

Properties of δ-aminolaevulate synthetase

Under standard assay conditions, the amount of δ-aminolaevulate formed was linear with protein concentration up to 0·8 mg./ml. and with time for at least 50 min.

Effect of pH on enzyme activity. Although there was no apparent sharp optimum pH, maximal activity was observed between pH 7·8 and pH 8·0

(Fig. 1). The activity in tris, glycylglycine and triethanolamine buffers was essentially the same, but in phosphate buffer it was between 50 and 60 % of that in the first group.

Michaelis constant. A Michaelis constant, K_m, of 280 μM for glycine was calculated from a Lineweaver & Burk (1934) plot (Fig. 2).

It was not possible to obtain a satisfactory plot of enzyme activity as a function of pyridoxal phosphate concentration, owing to difficulties in resolving this cofactor and the enzyme. However, several attempts indicated that K_m for this cofactor was about 4 μM.

With chemically prepared succinyl-CoA as the substrate for δ-aminolaevulate synthetase, in the place of succinate, ATP and succinyl-CoA thiokinase, the formation of δ-aminolaevulate as a function of enzyme concentration remained linear

Table 3. *Purification of δ-aminolaevulate dehydratase*

Experimental details are given in the text.

Fraction	Protein concn. (mg./ml.)	Specific activity (μm-moles of porphobilinogen/ hr./mg. of protein)
Supernatant obtained from centrifuging at 78 400g.	16·6	89·5
Redissolved precipitate obtained from treatment with 40 % saturated (NH$_4$)$_2$SO$_4$	9·7	520
Eluate from DEAE-cellulose column	0·43	6000

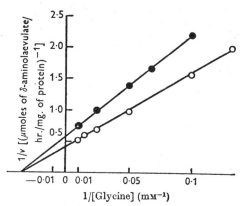

Fig. 2. Michaelis constant for δ-aminolaevulate synthetase. The glycine concentration was varied while the other reaction components were held constant as described in the experimental sections. $\bigcirc$, Reaction without inhibitor; $\bullet$, reaction in the presence of μM-haemin.

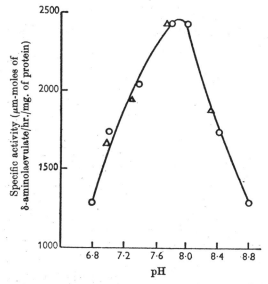

Fig. 1. δ-Aminolaevulate-synthetase activity as a function of pH. The incubation mixture contained: glycine (100 μ-moles), sodium succinate (100 μmoles), CoA (0·58 μmole), pyridoxal phosphate (0·25 μmole), ATP (7·5 μmoles), MgCl$_2$ (10 μmoles), buffer (50 μmoles), succinyl-coenzyme A thiokinase (0·1 ml.), enzyme (0·1 ml.) and water to give a final volume of 1·0 ml. The buffers used were: $\triangle$, tris; $\bigcirc$, triethanolamine. Incubations were at 37° for 30 min. The reaction was stopped with trichloroacetic acid, and δ-aminolaevulate was determined.

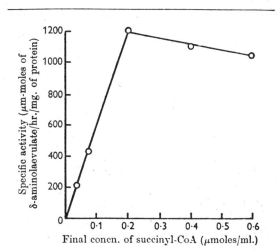

Fig. 3. Synthesis of δ-aminolaevulate as a function of succinyl-CoA concentration. The incubation mixture contained: glycine (100 μmoles), CoA (0·58 μmole), pyridoxal phosphate (0·25 μmole), tris buffer, pH 7·8 (50 μmoles), succinyl-CoA (as shown), enzyme (0·1 ml.) and water to give a final volume of 1·0 ml. Incubations were at 37° for 30 min. The reaction was stopped with trichloroacetic acid, and δ-aminolaevulate was determined.

Table 4. *Effect of metal ions and general enzyme inhibitors on δ-aminolaevulate synthetase*

The incubation mixtures contained: glycine (100 μmoles), sodium succinate (100 μmoles), CoA (0·58 μmole), pyridoxal phosphate (0·25 μmole), ATP (7·5 μmoles), MgCl₂ (10 μmoles), tris buffer, pH 7·8 (50 μmoles), succinyl-coenzyme A thiokinase (0·1 ml.), enzyme (0·1 ml.) and other additions (final concentrations given in parentheses) to 1·0 ml. were incubated at 37° for 30 min. The reaction was stopped with trichloroacetic acid, and δ-aminolaevulate was determined.

Additions	Specific activity (μm-moles of δ-aminolaevulate/ hr./mg. of protein)
Expt. 1	
None	1620
ZnSO₄ (0·1 mM)	1170
MnCl₂ (0·1 mM)	1530
CuSO₄ (0·1 mM)	494
MgCl₂ (0·1 mM)	1550
FeSO₄ (0·1 mM)	730
FeCl₃ (0·1 mM)	1570
KF (0·1 mM)	1390
NaSCN (0·1 mM)	1530
K₃Fe(CN)₆ (0·1 mM)	1550
NaN₃ (0·1 mM)	1390
Expt. 2	
None	1850
FeCl₃ (0·1 mM)	1800
FeCl₃ (0·01 mM)	1820
FeSO₄ (0·1 mM)	845
FeSO₄ (0·01 mM)	1840
FeSO₄ (0·1 mM) + pyridoxal phosphate (mM)	1810

Table 5. *Effects of haemin on δ-aminolaevulate synthetase*

The incubation conditions were as indicated in Table 4. The final concentrations of the additions are given in parentheses.

Additions	Specific activity (μm-moles of δ-aminolaevulate/ hr./mg. of protein)
Expt. 1	
None (control, no haemin)	1700
Haemin (0·1 μM)	1050
Haemin (1·0 μM)	890
Haemin (10 μM)	760
Haemin (100 μM)	304
Haemin (200 μM)	220
Expt. 2	
Haem control*	990
Haemin control*	930
Haem (100 μM)	210
Haemin (100 μM)	290
Haem (25 μM)	440
Haemin (25 μM)	450

* In these controls a mixture of KOH, HCl and β-mercaptoethanol was added to give the same final concentration as that in the experimental tubes containing the highest concentration of haem or haemin.

and the time-course of formation of δ-aminolaevulate was linear up to 40 min. It was not possible to obtain K_m for this substrate since succinyl-CoA was inhibitory even at comparatively low concentrations (Fig. 3).

Inhibition of δ-aminolaevulate synthetase. The effect of several inhibitors and metal ions on the enzymic formation of δ-aminolaevulate are shown in Table 4. In these experiments EDTA and β-mercaptoethanol were omitted from the reaction mixture.

Special attention was paid to the possible effect of iron on the enzyme, as there is evidence that iron may participate with the enzyme from chicken erythrocytes (Brown, 1958a, b; Vogel, Richert, Pixley & Schulman, 1960). Ferrous iron was a relatively potent inhibitor of the enzyme prepared from *R. spheroides*, but ferric iron at the same concentration did not have any effect (Table 4). Inhibition by ferrous iron was prevented by adding o-phenanthroline or pyridoxal phosphate. Although this indicates that the inhibition was overcome by chelation of the metal, it does not indicate whether the inhibition was initially due to a reaction between iron and pyridoxal phosphate, or whether iron reacted with the protein itself.

Effect of tetrapyrrole derivatives on δ-aminolaevulate synthetase

Protohaemin IX was a relatively potent inhibitor of δ-aminolaevulate synthetase (Table 5). Although the inhibition was pronounced even at very low concentrations of haemin, it was never complete even at the highest concentration examined.

Relative effects of haem and haemin on δ-aminolaevulate-synthetase activity. In most of the experiments on haemin inhibition no attempt was made to control the state of oxidation of the iron atom in the tetrapyrrole nucleus. In all cases haemin (i.e. ferric protoporphyrin) was the compound added to the reaction mixture. However, since β-mercaptoethanol, sometimes present in the reaction mixture, can reduce haemin to haem (ferrous protoporphyrin), it was not clear which of these forms was present in the enzyme reaction mixture. To determine this, haemin was prepared in the usual manner to give a mM stock solution and haem was prepared by reducing the ferric iron in this solution by the addition of a tenfold molar excess of β-mercaptoethanol. All dilutions were made with freshly-boiled double-distilled water and incubation was in sealed tubes under nitrogen. After incubation, pyridine was added to a test sample and a haemochromogen absorption band was observed visually with a hand spectroscope. The results indicate that haemin and haem are essentially equal in their inhibitory power (Table 5).

Table 6. *Haemin inhibition of δ-aminolaevulate synthetase with various concentrations of succinyl-coenzyme A and pyridoxal phosphate*

In Expt. 1 the reaction mixture contained: glycine (100 μmoles), tris buffer, pH 7·8 (50 μmoles), pyridoxal phosphate (0·25 μmole), succinyl-CoA (as shown), haemin (0·01 μmole), enzyme and water to give a final volume of 1·0 ml. In Expt. 2 the reaction mixture contained: glycine (100 μmoles), sodium succinate (100 μmoles), CoA (0·58 μmole), ATP (7·5 μmoles), MgCl$_2$ (10 μmoles), tris buffer, pH 7·8 (50 μmoles), β-mercaptoethanol (1 μmole), EDTA (0·2 μmole), pyridoxal phosphate (as shown), haemin (0·01 μmole, where shown), succinyl-coenzyme A thiokinase (0·1 ml.), enzyme and water to give a final volume of 1·0 ml. In both experiments incubation was for 30 min. at 37°.

Expt. 1			Expt. 2		
	Specific activity (μm-moles of δ-aminolaevulate/ hr./mg. of protein)			Specific activity (μm-moles of δ-aminolaevulate/ hr./mg. of protein)	
Succinyl-CoA (μmole)	Without haemin	With haemin	Pyridoxal phosphate (μm-moles)	Without haemin	With haemin
0·4	1290	615	360	1445	536
0·2	1390	610	25	1060	490
0·08	627	577	3	635	297

Table 7. *Reversibility of haemin inhibition of δ-aminolaevulate synthetase*

δ-Aminolaevulate synthetase was pretreated for 5 min. at 1° with haemin as shown. The enzyme was then added to the reaction mixture described in Table 4 and incubated for 30 min. at 37°.

Concn. of haemin preincubated with enzyme (μM)	Final concn. of haemin in assay mixture (μM)	Specific activity (μm-moles of δ-aminolaevulate/ hr./mg. of protein)
0	0	1800
0	10	910
0	2	1370
10	2	1320
10	1	1640

Table 8. *Effect of various metal complexes of porphyrins on δ-aminolaevulate synthetase*

The incubation conditions were as indicated in Table 4. Each compound was tested at a final concentration of 20 μM. Since the results are from several experiments, results are expressed as percentages of the appropriate control without inhibitor.

Additions to standard assay mixture	Relative enzyme activity (%)
None	100
Protoporphyrin	75
Cobalt–protoporphyrin complex	60
Copper–protoporphyrin complex	66
Zinc–protoporphyrin complex	63
Manganese–protoporphyrin complex	60
Magnesium–protoporphyrin complex	66
Iron–protoporphyrin complex (haemin)	47
Iron–deuteroporphyrin complex	42
Iron–haematoporphyrin complex	46
Iron–coproporphyrin complex	58

Nature of the inhibition by haemin. The inhibition by haemin was examined as a function of substrate concentration to determine whether it was com-petitive or non-competitive. The inhibition is non-competitive with glycine (Fig. 2). Chemically-prepared succinyl-CoA was used for the examina-tion of inhibition by haemin as a function of succinyl-CoA concentration. There was no com-petition between haemin and this substrate (Table 6).

The inhibition by haemin was also not influenced by the concentration of pyridoxal phosphate (Table 6).

Reversibility of inhibition by haemin. Enzyme was preincubated for 5 min. at 1° with 10 μM-haemin, then diluted fivefold on addition to the assay mixture. The activity corresponded to that in systems in which 2 μM-haemin had been added directly to the reaction mixture, indicating that the inhibition caused by haemin was reversible (Table 7).

Effect of other tetrapyrroles. The specificity of the inhibition by haemin was examined with proto-porphyrin and various metal complexes of por-phyrins (Table 8).

Protoporphyrin caused a significant inhibition but the concentration necessary to cause 50 % inhibition of the activity was about ten times the haemin concentration required for the same degree of inhibition. The copper complexes and manganese complexes of protoporphyrin inhibited by approxi-mately the same extent as the free tetrapyrrole. The iron complexes of haematoporphyrin, deutero-porphyrin and coproporphyrin all inhibited to a similar extent to haemin. The inhibition caused by iron haematoporphyrin was considerably greater than that found by Burnham (1962a). This dis-crepancy may have been due to variations in the purity of the different batches of haematopor-phyrin used to prepare the iron complex; Granick, Bogorad & Jaffe (1953) found it difficult to prepare pure haematoporphyrin free of other porphyrins.

Since the major tetrapyrrole derivative in *R. spheroides* is bacteriochlorophyll this compound, as well as related compounds, was tested. The following were without effect when tested at concentrations between 10 and 100 μM: bacteriochlorophyll, bacteriochlorophyllide, a mixture of chlorophyll *a* and chlorophyll *b*, and a mixture of the corresponding chlorophyllides. Vitamin B_{12} (40 μmM) also had no effect.

Effect of protein-bound haemin. Though there is some evidence that haemin exists to a small extent in the free form, there is little doubt that the greatest part of the haemin within the cell is protein-bound. The effect of some haemoproteins on the activity of δ-aminolaevulate synthetase was therefore examined. Native globin prepared by the method of Rossi-Fanelli *et al.* (1958) was used as a control. Haemoglobin and myoglobin inhibited δ-aminolaevulate synthetase significantly but catalase and cytochrome *c* had no effect (Table 9).

Experiments with δ-aminolaevulate dehydratase

The experiments were with the fraction (from the DEAE-cellulose column) that had been purified about 60-fold (Table 3). Under standard assay conditions the amount of porphobilinogen formed was linear with protein between 0·01 and 0·09 mg./ml., and with time for at least 60 min.

Effect of pH on enzyme activity. The optimum pH was 7·8 to 8·0 in potassium phosphate buffer, or in tris buffer containing potassium sulphate (40 mM) (Fig. 4).

Requirement for potassium ions. Preliminary experiments with δ-aminolaevulate dehydratase showed that the enzyme was not active in tris buffer. It was active, however, in mixtures of tris and phosphate, indicating that tris was not inhibitory, and suggesting at first a requirement for phosphate. Similar observations were made with the ox-liver enzyme (Gibson *et al.* 1955). Further investigations revealed that the required ion was K^+. This could be provided as the phosphate, sulphate or chloride salt. Sodium sulphate and disodium hydrogen phosphate were without activity (Table 10).

Inhibition studies with δ-aminolaevulate dehydratase. Haemin (20 μM) inhibited the enzyme by only about 23 % if added after the enzyme had been preincubated with cysteine (Table 11). If added before preincubation, it inhibited completely.

Previously it has been demonstrated that δ-aminolaevulate dehydratase from ox liver was in-

Table 9. *Effect of haemoproteins on δ-aminolaevulate synthetase*

The incubation conditions were as indicated in Table 4. The final concentrations of the additions are given in parentheses.

Additions to standard assay mixture	Specific activity (μm-moles of δ-aminolaevulate/ hr./mg. of protein)
None (control)	1090
Haemin (20 μM)	535
Haemoglobin (32 μM)*	760
Haemoglobin (0·64 μM)*	900
Myoglobin (2·7 μM)*	712
Myoglobin (0·68 μM)*	835
Catalase (0·7 μM)*	1020
Cytochrome *c* (50 μM)*	1060
Globin (60 μM)	1000

* Final concentration in terms of haemin content.

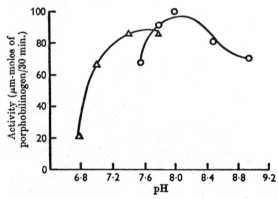

Fig. 4. δ-Aminolaevulate-dehydratase activity as a function of pH. The incubation mixture contained: δ-aminolaevulate (5 μmoles), $MgCl_2$ (5 μmoles), L-cysteine (25 μ-moles), buffer (125 μmoles), enzyme (0·1 ml.) and water to give a final volume of 2·5 ml. Incubations were at 37° for 30 min. Buffers: △, potassium phosphate; ○, tris containing K_2SO_4 (40 mM).

Table 10. *Effect of potassium ions on δ-aminolaevulate dehydratase*

The incubation mixture contained: δ-aminolaevulate (5 μmoles), L-cysteine (25 μmoles), $MgCl_2$ (5 μmoles), tris buffer, pH 7·8 (160 μmoles), test compounds (final concentrations given in parentheses), enzyme and water to give a final volume of 2·5 ml. Incubation was for 30 min. at 37°. The reaction was stopped with $CuSO_4$, and porphobilinogen was determined.

Additions to standard assay mixture	Specific activity (μm-moles of porphobilinogen/ hr./mg. of protein)
None (control)	650
K_2SO_4 (1·6 mM)	1070
K_2SO_4 (4·8 mM)	2050
K_2SO_4 (16 mM)	3260
K_2SO_4 (40 mM)	4370
KCl (40 mM)	3680
KH_2PO_4–K_2HPO_4 buffer, pH 7·8 (40 mM)	4100
Na_2SO_4 (40 mM)	745

hibited by low concentrations of EDTA (Gibson et al. 1955). The enzyme isolated from *R. spheroides* was, however, not inhibited by EDTA (4 mM).

Experiments with intact cells

Effect of haemin on whole cells. The effect of haemin was examined with whole cells synthesizing either free porphyrins or bacteriochlorophyll. In these experiments iron-deficient cells were incubated in the light with glycine and α-oxoglutarate with and without iron citrate under the conditions described by Lascelles (1956). In the absence of

---

Table 11. *Effect of haemin on δ-aminolaevulate dehydratase*

The incubation mixture contained: δ-aminolaevulate (5 μmoles), potassium phosphate buffer, pH 7·8 (125 μ. moles), MgCl₂ (5 μmoles), L-cysteine (25 μmoles), haemin (final concentrations shown in parentheses), enzyme and water to give a final volume of 2·5 ml. Incubations were for 30 min. at 37°. The haemin was added with the δ-aminolaevulate after the enzyme had been preincubated for 10 min. in the reaction mixture with cysteine. The reaction was stopped with CuSO₄, and porphobilinogen was determined.

Additions to standard assay mixture	Specific activity (μm-moles of porphobilinogen/ hr./mg. of protein)
None (control)	5120
Haemin (8 μM)	4900
Haemin (20 μM)	4420
Haemin (40 μM)	2380

added iron, coproporphyrin accumulated with only slight synthesis of bacteriochlorophyll; with iron present, bacteriochlorophyll formation was considerably increased and porphyrins did not accumulate. Haemin at concentrations that inhibit δ-aminolaevulate synthetase caused a considerable decrease in porphyrin formation, but bacteriochlorophyll synthesis (measured with iron added to the incubation system) was much less affected (Table 12). Neither haematohaemin nor protoporphyrin was inhibitory, but deuterohaemin almost completely prevented the formation of both porphyrin and bacteriochlorophyll (Table 12).

Haemin did not inhibit the conversion of δ-aminolaevulate into porphyrin by cell suspensions (Table 12), providing evidence that its effect on porphyrin synthesis from glycine and α-oxoglutarate was confined to its action on δ-aminolaevulate synthetase.

DISCUSSION

R. spheroides was chosen for this work since the controlling effect of iron on porphyrin accumulation is readily demonstrable and also because it contains relatively high concentrations of δ-aminolaevulate synthetase. In micro-organisms other than Athiorhodaceae this enzyme is difficult to detect by the method described above.

Accounts of the purification of this enzyme have appeared (Kikuchi et al. 1958; Kikuchi, Kumar & Shemin, 1959), but lack details. The enzyme seems to be labile, and attempts at purification generally

---

Table 12. *Effect of haemin and other tetrapyrroles on porphyrin and bacteriochlorophyll formation by cell suspensions of* Rhodopseudomonas spheroides

Suspensions of iron-deficient cells (0·6–0·8 mg. dry wt./ml.) were incubated anaerobically in the light in 'mixture I' (containing glycine and α-oxoglutarate) or in 'mixture II' (containing δ-aminolaevulate) under the conditions described by Lascelles (1956). The final concentrations of the added tetrapyrroles are given in parentheses. Porphyrin synthesis was measured in systems containing no added iron, and bacteriochlorophyll synthesis in the presence of 10 μM-iron citrate. Incubation was for 7 hr. in Expts. 1 and 3 and for 8·5 hr. in Expt. 2. N.D., Not determined.

Expt. no.	Substrate mixture	Tetrapyrrole added	Porphyrin formed (μm-moles/ml.)	Bacteriochlorophyll formed (μm-moles/ml.)
1	I	None (control)	31	36
	I	Haemin (5 μM)	16	31
	I	Haemin (10 μM)	17	30
	I	Haemin (20 μM)	6	26
	I	Haemin (40 μM)	3	25
2	I	None (control)	34	56
	I	Haemin (20 μM)	6	47
	I	Protoporphyrin (20 μM)	33	54
	I	Haematohaemin (20 μM)	32	55
	I	Deuterohaemin (20 μM)	2	0
3	I	None	38	N.D.
	I	Haemin (20 μM)	3	N.D.
	II	None	31	N.D.
	II	Haemin (20 μM)	33	N.D.

produce low yields. Some success was attained in the present investigation, possibly as a result of the precautions taken to eliminate inhibitory materials during the fractionation. Preliminary experiments on fractionation with ammonium sulphate were generally unsatisfactory because of poor recovery. This confirmed observations made by Dr K. Gibson (personal communication). It was found, however, that the enzyme could be at least partially protected by carrying out most operations in the presence of β-mercaptoethanol. This, however, was only true if chelating agents, and particularly ones capable of binding ferrous iron, were added before the treatment with ammonium sulphate.

Apart from Cu^{2+}, Fe^{2+} was the most inhibitory metal ion of those tested. The fact that this inhibition can be prevented by using high concentrations of pyridoxal phosphate in the assay mixture suggests that the inhibition is caused by the removal of this cofactor from the system by binding to the metal.

None of the experimental findings indicate that iron is involved in the action of the enzyme, which is contrary to the situation found in avian erythrocytes (Brown, 1958a, b; Vogel et al. 1960). It would seem also that iron is not involved in the synthesis of this enzyme by R. spheroides, since it is present in similar amounts in both iron-deficient cells and those cultured with adequate iron.

The nature of the inhibition of the enzyme by haemin supports the possibility that this compound acts as a controlling factor and not simply as an enzyme inactivator. Inhibition was detectable at concentrations as low as $0.1~\mu M$. Even at the highest concentrations tested haemin did not completely inhibit the enzyme activity. This suggests that the inhibition is not the result of a simple stoicheiometric reaction between the haemin and a reactive site on the protein. It also indicates that it is not the result of an interaction with one of the substrates or cofactors. The reversibility of the inhibition caused by haemin adds additional support to the possibility that haemin acts as a controlling factor. Reversibility is a hallmark of negative-feedback systems, according to Umbarger (1961).

It is not necessary to assume that haemin exists free within the cell at any appreciable concentration for it to have a controlling effect on δ-aminolaevulate synthetase, since some haemoproteins were also inhibitory. Work by Banerjee (1962) with haemoglobin and myoglobin, and by Greengard & Feigelson (1962) with tryptophan pyrrolase, indicates that haemin is probably not as tightly bound to some haemoproteins as has been generally assumed. It seems possible, therefore, that sufficient haemin is present within the cells in equilibrium with specific haemoproteins for it to function as a controlling factor.

The experiments with whole cells support the suggestion that haemin exerts a negative-feedback control on porphyrin synthesis. In other systems where a negative-feedback control has been demonstrated, the enzymic step under control has been the first one leading to the end product, and this step is generally energy-consuming and irreversible (Umbarger, 1961). In the present case, haemin inhibits porphyrin synthesis by cell suspensions when glycine and α-oxoglutarate are the starting substrates, i.e. when δ-aminolaevulate synthetase must function. When this step is bypassed by using δ-aminolaevulate as substrate, haemin does not affect the synthesis of porphyrin. The results obtained with inorganic iron, in the present and previous investigations, are compatible with this, if it is assumed that the iron is first converted into a haem compound, which in turn exerts its controlling influence by inhibiting δ-aminolaevulate synthetase.

In whole cells, haemin inhibits porphyrin accumulation much more strongly than it does bacteriochlorophyll formation, indicating that a control exerted by haemin does not appear to interfere with the normal synthesis of bacteriochlorophyll.

It seems incongruous that, in an organism synthesizing two major tetrapyrrole derivatives, haem(in) and bacteriochlorophyll, only haem(in) inhibits the isolated δ-aminolaevulate synthetase. This may have no physiological relevance since bacteriochlorophyll is insoluble in water, and it is doubtful if it ever exists as a free molecule in the cell. The evidence indicates that the later steps in the synthesis of bacteriochlorophyll occur in the chromatophores where it functions. δ-Aminolaevulate synthetase, however, is found in the soluble fraction of the cell. Evidence was sought in extracts of R. spheroides for the occurrence of two δ-aminolaevulate synthetases, one for making haemin and the other for making bacteriochlorophyll. An analogous situation has been demonstrated in Escherichia coli: two aspartokinases have been shown, each being under the control of a different end product (Stadtman, Cohen, LeBras, De Robichon-Szulmajster, 1961). No evidence for two enzymes was found in the present instance, though it is possible that a δ-aminolaevulate synthetase inside the chromatophore might go undetected. The enzyme is not detectable in other microbial extracts, where it presumably functions since the intact cells synthesize readily detectable amounts of tetrapyrroles (B. F. Burnham & J. Lascelles, unpublished work).

The excretion of porphyrins and porphyrin precursors is sometimes observed in certain diseases of higher animals, e.g. porphyria in man. Since the excreted porphyrin represents an over-production, one of the systems controlling porphyrin biosynthesis may have broken down, allowing porphyrin and precursors to be formed continuously at the maximum rate. Gerhart & Pardee (1962) have demonstrated that it is possible to alter the active site for the inhibitor on an enzyme without altering the active site for the substrate. Such an enzyme continues to function catalytically, but it is no longer sensitive to inhibitor. It might, therefore, be useful to examine the effect of haemin on enzyme preparations from some of the diseased conditions compared with those from normal animals.

SUMMARY

1. The enzyme, δ-aminolaevulate synthetase, was purified about tenfold from extracts of *Rhodopseudomonas spheroides*.

2. Significant inhibition of δ-aminolaevulate synthetase was caused by $0.1\,\mu$M-iron protoporphyrin (haemin); the highest concentration tested (0.2 mM) inhibited the enzyme by about 87 %. Other iron porphyrins inhibited to a similar extent, whereas protoporphyrin and other metal complexes of protoporphyrin were less effective. Haemoglobin and myoglobin were also inhibitory.

3. The inhibition by haemin was not competitive with any of the substrates or cofactors, but was reversible by dilution.

4. Porphyrin formation from glycine and α-oxoglutarate by whole-cell suspensions of *R. spheroides* was inhibited by haemin, but conversion of δ-aminolaevulate into porphyrins was unaffected.

5. The characteristics of the inhibition of δ-aminolaevulate synthetase, and the results obtained with whole cells, indicate that one mechanism for control of porphyrin biosynthesis in *R. spheroides* may be through negative feedback by haemin.

6. Succinyl-coenzyme A thiokinase and δ-aminolaevulate dehydratase were purified by about 170- and 70-fold respectively from extracts of *R. spheroides*. δ-Aminolaevulate dehydratase was only slightly inhibited by haemin. It required K^+ ions for activation.

The authors thank Professor D. D. Woods, F.R.S., for his encouragement and advice. The excellent technical assistance of Miss Lynda Butler and Mrs Anne Morris is gratefully acknowledged. This work was aided by a grant from the Jane Coffin Childs Memorial Fund for Medical Research and grants to the Department from the Rockefeller Foundation and the United States Department of Health, Education and Welfare. B.F.B. was a Fellow of the Jane Coffin Childs Memorial Fund for Medical Research at the time of this work.

REFERENCES

Banerjee, R. (1962). *Biochem. biophys. Res. Commun.* **8,** 114.

Bonnichsen, R. K. (1947). *Arch. Biochem.* **12,** 83.

Brown, E. G. (1958*a*). *Nature, Lond.,* **182,** 313.

Brown, E. G. (1958*b*). *Nature, Lond.,* **182,** 1091.

Burnham, B. F. (1962*a*). *Biochem. biophys. Res. Commun.* **7,** 315.

Burnham, B. F. (1962*b*). *Biochem. J.* **84,** 15P.

Cohen-Bazire, G., Sistrom, W. R. & Stanier, R. Y. (1957). *J. cell. comp. Physiol.* **49,** 25.

Falk, J. E. (1961). *J. Chromat.* **5,** 277.

Fischer, H. & Putzer, G. (1926). *Hoppe-Seyl. Z.* **154,** 39.

Fischer, H., Treibs, A. & Zeile, K. (1931). *Hoppe-Seyl. Z.* **195,** 1.

Gerhart, J. C. & Pardee, A. B. (1962). *J. biol. Chem.* **237,** 891.

Gibson, K. D. (1958). *Biochim. biophys. Acta,* **28,** 451.

Gibson, K. D., Neuberger, A. & Scott, J. J. (1955). *Biochem. J.* **61,** 618.

Gibson, K. D., Matthew, M., Neuberger, A. & Tait, G. H. (1961). *Nature, Lond.,* **192,** 204.

Gomori, G. (1955). In *Methods in Enzymology,* vol. 1, p. 138. Ed. by Colowick, S. P. & Kaplan, N. O. New York: Academic Press Inc.

Granick, S. (1948). *J. biol. Chem.* **175,** 333.

Granick, S., Bogorad, L. & Jaffe, H. (1953). *J. biol. Chem.* **202,** 801.

Greengard, O. & Feigelson, P. (1962). *J. biol. Chem.* **237,** 1903.

Jacobs, E. E., Vatter, A. E. & Holt, S. A. (1954). *Arch. Biochem. Biophys.* **53,** 228.

Kaufman, S. & Alivisatos, S. G. A. (1955). *J. biol. Chem.* **216,** 141.

Kikuchi, G., Kumar, A. & Shemin, D. (1959). *Fed. Proc.* **18,** 259.

Kikuchi, G., Kumar, A., Talmage, P. & Shemin, D. (1958). *J. biol. Chem.* **233,** 1214.

Lascelles, J. (1956). *Biochem. J.* **62,** 78.

Lascelles, J. (1959). *Biochem. J.* **72,** 508.

Lascelles, J. (1960). *J. gen. Microbiol.* **23,** 487.

Lascelles, J. (1961). *Physiol. Rev.* **41,** 417.

Lineweaver, H. & Burk, D. (1934). *J. Amer. chem. Soc.* **56,** 658.

Lipmann, F. & Tuttle, L. C. (1945). *J. biol. Chem.* **159,** 21.

Lowry, O. H., Rosebrough, N. J., Farr, A. L. & Randall, R. J. (1951). *J. biol. Chem.* **193,** 265.

Mauzerall, D. & Granick, S. (1956). *J. biol. Chem.* **219,** 435.

Rossi-Fanelli, A., Antonini, E. & Caputo, A. (1958). *Biochim. biophys. Acta,* **30,** 608.

Schwartz, S., Berg, M. H., Bossenmaier, I. & Dinsmore, H. (1960). *Mcth. biochem. Anal.* **8,** 221.

Simon, E. J. & Shemin, D. (1953). *J. Amer. chem. Soc.* **75,** 2520.

Stadtman, E. R., Cohen, G. N., LeBras, G. & De Robichon-Szulmajster, H. (1961). *J. biol. Chem.* **236,** 2033.

Umbarger, H. E. (1961). *Cold Spring Harb. Symp. quant. Biol.* **26,** 301.

Vogel, W., Richert, D. A., Pixley, B. Q. & Schulman, M. (1960). *J. biol. Chem.* **235,** 1769.

CONTROL OF HEME SYNTHESIS BY FEEDBACK INHIBITION

Doris Karibian and Irving M. London

Department of Medicine, Albert Einstein College of Medicine
and Bronx Municipal Hospital Center, New York, New York

Received November 18, 1964

The capacity of immature erythroid cells to synthesize heme in vitro (London et al, 1950, Shemin et al, 1950, Morell et al, 1958) provides an opportunity for the study of the processes involved in the regulation of this biosynthetic mechanism in animal cells. Burnham and Lascelles (1962) have shown that preparations of deltaaminolevulinic acid (ALA) synthetase from Rhodopseudomonas spheroides are inhibited by hemin. This enzyme catalyzes the condensation of glycine and succinyl-coenzyme A to form deltaaminolevulinic acid (Shemin, 1954). The enzyme ALA dehydrase which catalyzes the condensation of ALA to form porphobilinogen (PBG) was less inhibited. With intact cells of this bacterium, however, inhibition of porphyrin synthesis by hemin was observed when glycine, but not ALA, was the precursor. These findings pointed to ALA synthetase as the site for negative feedback control of porphyrin synthesis by hemin in this bacterium.

In the studies reported here the effects of hemin on the incorporation of glycine-2-C^{14} and ALA-4-C^{14} into heme in immature rabbit erythrocytes (reticulocytes) have been examined. The results suggest that a similar control mechanism, involving feedback inhibition in the conversion of glycine to ALA, is operative in these animal cells.

Methods: Reticulocyte Preparations. New Zealand rabbits were bled repeatedly (about 30 ml daily for at least 3 days) and reticulocytes were obtained in the top 1-3 ml of packed cells following centrifugation. More prolonged series of bleeding produced reticulocytoses of 15-20%. One ml of such cell preparations plus one ml plasma were added to 8 ml of a saline solution containing the following: 0.76% NaCl, 0.039% KCl, 0.15% $MgCl_2.6H_2O$, 100 mg% glucose, 0.02 M Tris-HCl buffer, pH 7.8 or K_2HPO_4 - KH_2PO_4 buffer, pH 7.4. When a lysate was required, equal volumes of cells and cold distilled water were mixed for 1 minute, the tonicity was adjusted with 10-fold concentrated saline solution and plasma and the saline solution were added as for whole cell suspensions.

Conditions of incubation. The incubation mixture in 12 ml conical tubes included: (1) 1 ml aliquots of cell suspension or lysate; (2) 0.12 ml of hemin solution[1]; (3) penicillin and strepto-mycin 0.8 to 1.0 mg per ml; (4) glycine-2-C^{14}, 0.25 umole of 8 x 10^5 cpm/umole or ALA-4-C^{14}, 0.5 umole of 4 x 10^5 cpm/umole; (5) saline solution to give total volume of 1.2 to 1.6 ml. In control samples, 0.12 ml of the KOH-buffer-HCl solution without hemin was added. The tubes were incubated in a 37° water bath in room air or in 95% O_2-5% CO_2. At the end of incubation, they were chilled in ice,

---

[1]. Hemin solution: (a) 1.2 mg hemin was dissolved in 0.1 ml 1N KOH and diluted with 1.0 ml freshly boiled distilled H_2O and 0.1 ml 1M tris or phosphate buffer; 0.08 ml 1N HCl was added with mix-ing and the volume was made up to 2 ml with H_2O; (b) for higher concentrations, 8 mg hemin was dissolved in twice the above volumes of KOH, buffer and HCl and the volume was again made up to 2 ml with H_2O. The final concentration of hemin when 0.12 ml of solution (a) was present in an incubation mixture of 1.2 ml was 1 x 10^{-4} M.

and 10 ml of cold red cell lysate (1 vol packed cells and 1 vol
H_2O) was added to provide unlabeled heme as carrier. Hemin in
solution, equal in amount to that which had been added to the
experimental samples, was added to the control samples.

Hemin was crystallized from the hemolysate after treatment
with glacial acetic acid (Fischer, 1941). It was recrystallized
from pyridine-chloroform, and its radioactivity was measured at
infinite thickness. Nearly all experiments were carried out in
duplicate with agreement within $\pm$ 5 per cent.

Table I

Effect of Hemin on Utilization of Glycine-2-C^{14} and ALA-4-C^{14}
for Heme Synthesis in Intact and Lysed Rabbit Reticulocytes

Incorporation of Glycine-2-C^{14} into Heme	Incorporation of ALA-4-C^{14} into Heme
% Change from Control	% Change from Control
Number of experiments 42	21
Mean change -48.6	-12.2
S.E. $\pm$ 3.00	$\pm$ 4.84
$p < .001$	$.05 > p > .02$

Results: Table I presents the effects of added hemin
on the utilization of glycine-2-C^{14} and ALA-4-C^{14} for heme synthesis
by intact and lysed rabbit reticulocytes. The data are recorded as
the percentage change from the control values obtained in preparations to which no hemin was added. At this concentration ($1 \times 10^{-4}M$)

the effect of hemin on the utilization of glycine-2-C^{14} was inhibitory in all but one of the 42 experiments. The mean effect was an inhibition of nearly 50 per cent and is highly significant. The mean effect of hemin on the utilization of ALA-4-C^{14} was an inhibition of only 12 per cent and was of only marginal statistical significance. The effects of added hemin on utilization of ALA were variable and in several instances enhanced synthesis of heme was observed.

Figure 1 shows the effect of concentration of added hemin on the synthesis of heme from glycine in intact rabbit reticulocytes.

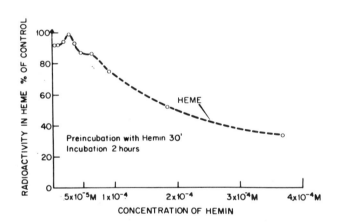

1. The effect of various concentrations of added hemin on the utilization of glycine-2-C^{14} for heme synthesis.

Inhibition is appreciable at 1 x 10^{-4} M and is progressively increased at higher concentrations.

The effects of hemin on the synthesis of heme in a long-term incubation and in a short-term incubation are presented in Figure 2. The inhibitory effect occurs rapidly and is demonstrable throughout a 24-hour period of incubation.

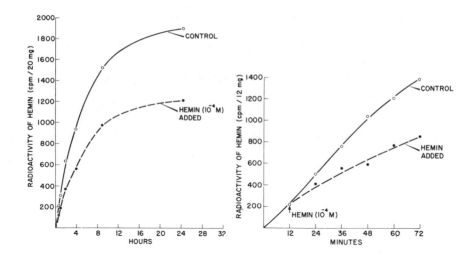

2. Inhibitory effect of hemin on utilization of glycine-2-C^{14} for heme synthesis.

The synthesis of heme with and without added hemin was studied in isotonic phosphate buffer in the range of pH 6.35 to 7.90 and in Tris-NaCl buffer, pH 7.25 to 8.70. Maximal synthesis was observed at pH 7.3-7.4 in the absence of added hemin. The inhibitory effect of hemin was observed over the full range of pH which was studied.

Discussion: The results of these studies indicate significant inhibition by hemin of the utilization of glycine for heme synthesis in rabbit reticulocytes; the effect on the utilization of ALA was variable and less significant. The principal site of inhibition by hemin appears therefore to be found among the reactions which precede the formation of ALA:

$$\text{Succinyl-CoA + Glycine} \xrightarrow[\substack{\text{Pyridoxal} \\ \text{Phosphate}}]{\substack{\text{ALA} \\ \text{Synthetase}}} \alpha\text{-amino }\beta\text{-Keto} \xrightarrow{-CO_2} \text{ALA}$$
$$\text{adipic acid}$$
$$\text{(AKA)}$$

These reactions include the activation of succinate, the activation of glycine, probably by a pyridoxal phosphate system; the condensation of activated glycine and succinate, catalyzed by ALA synthetase, to form AKA, and the decarboxylation of AKA to form ALA. It is possible that hemin may inhibit the activation of succinate or glycine, but no information is available on these possibilities at present. The decarboxylation of AKA occurs very readily; it seems unlikely, but it is possible, that hemin may influence the conversion of AKA to ALA. In the light of the studies of Burnham and Lascelles in Rhodopseudomonas spheroides, it seems most likely that a site of feedback control of heme synthesis in the rabbit reticulocyte is at the level of ALA synthetase.

The concentration of hemin within the reticulocyte at which the inhibitory effect is observed is unknown, since the extent to which the hemin can penetrate the cell and the extent of its binding within the cell are not known. It is relevant to note that free protoporphyrin, which is present in reticulocytes in a concentration of the order of 10^{-4}M, can inhibit porphyrin synthesis at this concentration in Rhodopseudomonas spheroides.

Negative feedback control of heme synthesis by heme affords a mechanism for the regulation of porphyrin synthesis. Coupled with the stimulatory effect of hemin on the synthesis of globin (Bruns and London), this control mechanism may participate in the coordination of the synthesis of heme and of globin.

This work was supported by USPHS grant HE-02803 and a grant of the Office of Naval Research Nonr 4094.

REFERENCES

Bruns, G.P. and London, I.M. (accompanying paper)

Burnham, B.F. and Lascelles, J., Biochem. J. 87, 462 (1963)

Fischer, H., Org. Syntheses 21, 53 (1941)

London, I.M., Shemin, D. and Rittenberg, D., J. Biol. Chem. 183, 749 (1950)

Morell, H., Savoie, J.C. and London, I.M., J. Biol. Chem. 233, 923 (1958)

Shemin, D., The Harvey Lectures, Series 50 (1954–1955) (Academic Press Inc., New York, 1956) p. 258

Shemin, D., London, I.M. and Rittenberg, D., J. Biol. Chem. 183, 757 (1950)

THE JOURNAL OF BIOLOGICAL CHEMISTRY
Vol. 242, No. 8, Issue of April 25, pp. 1903–1911, 1967
Printed in U.S.A.

Control of Hemoglobin Synthesis in the Cultured Chick Blastoderm*

(Received for publication, September 8, 1966)

RICHARD D. LEVERE AND S. GRANICK

From the Department of Medicine, State University of New York, Downstate Medical Center, New York, New York 11203, and The Rockefeller University, New York, New York 10021

SUMMARY

The early, de-embryonated chick blastoderm, cultured *in vitro*, closely simulates a phased culture of erythroid cells. This fact permits the study of hemoglobin synthesis from colorless erythroblast precursor cells to fully hemoglobinated erythrocytes.

When δ-aminolevulinic acid is added to colorless blastoderms, thereby by-passing δ-aminolevulinic acid synthetase, copious amounts of porphyrins, and presumably of heme, are formed. This result indicates that in the erythroid precursor cells of the early blastoderms heme synthesis is limited by the activity of δ-aminolevulinic acid synthetase.

The addition of δ-aminolevulinate also results in an increase in globin synthesis and hemoglobin formation. The enhancing effect of δ-aminolevulinic acid on hemoglobin formation is not abolished by actinomycin D but is prevented by puromycin. This result suggests that δ-aminolevulinic acid forms heme which stimulates globin synthesis at the ribosome level. It is conjectured that heme may be necessary for the appropriate folding of the globin polypeptide in the completion of its synthesis.

The hypothesis is proposed that the formation of δ-aminovulinic acid synthetase, which is under repressor control, is the limiting and controlling reaction in the formation of hemoglobin. Such a hypothesis would explain the fact that no free globin is formed and that monomeric globin and heme are formed in a 1:1 ratio.

The almost complete elucidation, over the past two decades, of the heme biosynthetic chain has provided a unique model for the study of the control mechanisms which operate to govern such a synthetic pathway. The present study was undertaken to investigate the temporal appearance of the enzymes of this biosynthetic chain in relation to progressive erythroid maturation and to study the interrelationships between heme and globin synthesis. A preliminary report has been published on some aspects of this study (1).

The first enzyme in the heme biosynthetic chain, δ-aminolevulinic acid synthetase (see Fig. 1), condenses glycine and

* This work was supported in part by United States Public Health Service Grants AM 09838 and GM 04922.

succinate to form δ-aminolevulinic acid. This enzyme has been shown by Granick (2, 3) to be rate-limiting for the entire biosynthetic chain of heme in liver cells. One of the specific questions asked in the present study was whether this enzyme also limits heme synthesis in erythroid precursor cells. The second question was, in what manner is the regulation of heme synthesis related to globin formation so that they are normally produced in a 1:1 ratio?

The chick blastoderm, cultured *in vitro*, provides an excellent system for the study of these problems. Unlike bone marrow, the blastoderm is completely devoid of myeloid and lymphoid elements. The hematopoietic tissue of the early blastoderm starts with colorless cells at a stage prior to initiation of hemoglobin synthesis and these differentiate in 24 to 48 hours into fully developed erythrocytes. Therefore, this tissue may be regarded as a phased culture of erythroid cells and its differentiation studied with respect to time.

In vivo, the blastoderm is free of hemoglobin until the embryo is at the five- to six-somite stage of development (4). At this time hemoglobin appears in the *area pellucida* and surrounding *area opaca* in a horseshoe-like pattern just lateral and posterior to the developing embryo. O'Brien (5) has shown that when young blastoderms, *i.e.* prior to the fifth to sixth somite stage, are de-embryonated and grown on a simple glucose agar medium there is inhibition of cell migration and maturation in all cells except the developing hematopoietic mesoderm. This hematopoietic mesoderm is arranged in clusters of syncytial tissue called blood islands, and is found in the horseshoe-shaped area where hemoglobin will eventually appear. The cells of the blood islands are comparable to the hemocytoblasts of mammalian bone marrow. Sabin (6) showed that these cells have the potential of developing into either the primitive line of erythrocytes or the endothelial lining cells of the extraembryonic blood vessels. When the blastoderm is cultured *in vitro*, the endothelial cells form only poorly defined tubules within which are found the nucleated erythrocytes.

Hemoglobin first appears in the cultured, de-embryonated blastoderm after 14 to 20 hours of incubation. The time of the initial appearance of hemoglobin is directly related to the age of the blastoderm at the onset of incubation. Blastoderms closer to the five-to six-somite stage develop hemoglobin earlier than blastoderms cultured at earlier stages. Maximum hemoglobin production is reached after 36 to 48 hours of incubation *in vitro*. Because the maturation from precursor cell to definitive eryth-

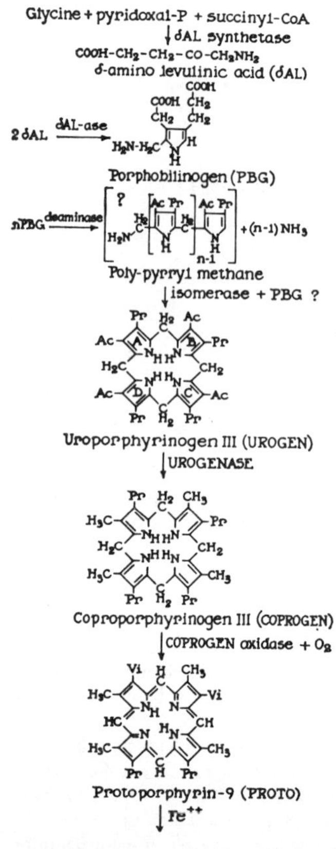

Glycine + pyridoxal-P + succinyl-CoA

$\downarrow$ δAL synthetase

COOH-CH₂-CH₂-CO-CH₂NH₂

δ-amino levulinic acid (δAL)

2 δAL $\xrightarrow{\text{δAL-ase}}$ Porphobilinogen (PBG)

nPBG $\xrightarrow{\text{deaminase}}$ Poly-pyrryl methane $+(n\text{-}1)\,NH_3$

$\downarrow$ isomerase + PBG ?

Uroporphyrinogen III (UROGEN)

$\downarrow$ UROGENASE

Coproporphyrinogen III (COPROGEN)

$\downarrow$ COPROGEN oxidase + O₂

Protoporphyrin-9 (PROTO)

$\downarrow$ Fe⁺⁺

FIG. 1. The general scheme of biosynthesis of heme. *Ac*, CH₂COOH; *Pr*, —CH₂CH₂—COOH; *Vi*, —CH—CH₂. To form porphobilinogen, 2 moles of δ-aminolevulinic acid are required.

rócyte takes less than 2 days, the cultured blastoderm simulates a phased culture of erythroid cells.

Early hematopoietic cells may also be obtained by the culture *in vitro* of cells obtained from blastoderms dissociated by trypsin. The vast majority (7) of these cultures will yield erythroid cells to the exclusion of other cell types. This system, like the culture of the whole de-embryonated blastoderms, also allows for the study of the early stages of erythroid development. However, the poor yield of mature erythrocytes and the early dedifferentiation of these cells prevents this technique from offering any advantage over the whole blastoderm system.

MATERIALS AND METHODS

All embryos used were of the White Leghorn breed, obtained from Shamrock Farms, New Jersey. Upon arrival the eggs were incubated at 37° for the desired period of time (usually 20 to 22 hours).

The yolk of each egg was placed in chick Ringer's solution (8) and the embryonic disc was removed with a circular cut through the vitelline membrane employing fine dissecting scissors. This and the succeeding steps are graphically outlined in Fig. 2. The blastoderms were dissected free of the vitelline membrane with a ball-tipped glass needle and then washed free

of any adhering yolk by gently sucking the blastoderms in and out of a wide mouthed pipette. Following this procedure, the embryos were removed from the blastoderms under a dissecting microscope, utilizing a glass needle and a fine tipped suction pipette. The de-embryonated blastoderms were then divided into symmetrical halves by an anterioposterior cut made with iridectomy scissors. One-half of each blastoderm was placed in a small Petri dish containing an agar gel medium composed of 1% agar in Earle's solution (9). Additions of various chemicals were made to the test and control media as indicated by the experiment. Prior to placing the blastoderms on the agar, the halves were washed in liquid medium of the same composition as the agar medium. The Petri dishes were then incubated at 37° in an atmosphere of 5% CO₂-95% air for the desired period of time. After incubation, the amount of porphyrins or hemoglobin in the test and control halves was determined.

Estimation of Porphyrins in Blastoderms—Porphyrins were determined qualitatively by examining the unfixed blastoderms with a Zeiss Ultraphot fluorescence microscope. The presence of orange-red fluoresence is indicative of the presence of increased amounts of uroporphyrin and coproporphyrin.

Semiquantitative Determination of Heme and Hemoglobin—Heme and hemoglobin were stained by a benzidine peroxidase stain (10) and the reaction then quantitated macroscopically and microscopically. The blastoderm halves were washed with 0.9% NaCl to free them of the agar and then were placed in the staining sloution for 3 min. The staining solution was made as follows: (*a*) 100 mg of *O*-dianisidine (3,3'-dimethoxy benzidine), (*b*) 70 ml of 95% ethanol, (*c*) 10 ml of 1.5 M acetate buffer, pH 4.7, (*d*) 18 ml of water, and (*e*) 2 ml of H₂O₂ (30%) added just before use.

Following removal from the above stain, the blastoderms were washed with distilled water. They were then dehydrated in dioxane, cleared in xylol, and finally mounted on glass slides. Each specimen was examined for the presence of brownish pink color indicative of heme or hemoglobin or both. The degree of the reaction was graded according to the following schema. Trace: stained erythrocytes visible microscopically only; 1+, positive reaction just perceptible with the naked eye; 2+, few scattered areas of faintly positive reaction; 3+, reticular pattern to positive areas, cells deeply stained; 4+, intense and extensive reaction confined to *area pellucida*; 5+, same as for 4+ with positive reaction peripherally in *area opaca*.

Quantitative Determination for Hemoglobin—The minute

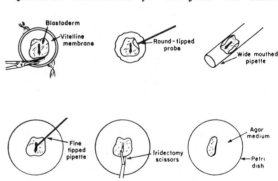

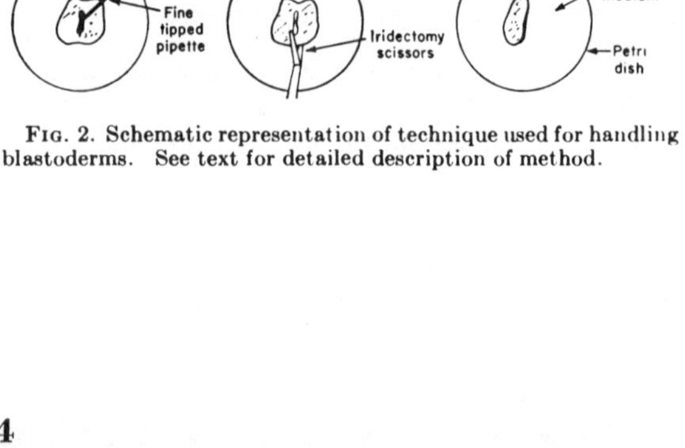

FIG. 2. Schematic representation of technique used for handling blastoderms. See text for detailed description of method.

amount of hemoglobin present in each blastoderm half was quantitated by spectrophotometry. Following incubation, the blastoderm halves were washed free of the agar with 0.9% NaCl and placed in thick walled serum hematocrit tubes (Clay-Adams) with particular attention paid to exclude excess 0.9% NaCl. At this point, if time was not available, the blastoderms were frozen at $-20°$ and kept at this temperature until used. Then, in order to hemolyze the erythrocytes, 0.2 ml of a solution of 1% digitonin in phosphate buffer, pH 7.4 (previously boiled to clear the solution), was added to each serum tube and the blastoderm ground in this solution with a nylon rod. When the blastoderm was finely suspended, 0.3 ml of phosphate buffer, pH 7.4, was added and the contents of the tube were mixed with a fine aluminium wire. The tubes were then spun for 5 min at 12,000 rpm in a Clay-Adams microhematocrit centrifuge. A thin, superficial lipid layer which appeared at this point was removed with a small piece of filter paper. Then as much as possible of the underlying clear hemolysate was removed with a 20-gauge needle and a graduated 1-ml syringe. Care was taken not to disturb the sediment. This volume of hemolysate (approximately 0.42 ml), was measured in the syringe, diluted to a constant volume with 0.05 M phosphate buffer (pH 7.4), and divided into two equal parts. Each part was placed in one of a pair of matched semimicro 4-mm wide cuvettes with a 1-cm optical path. The cuvettes were covered with Teflon caps held down by Scotch tape. Each cap had two holes, one of which was used to pass gas into the cuvette by insertion of a 23-gauge needle. Each cuvette was gassed with N_2 to remove the oxygen. Solid sodium dithionite (1 mg) was added to both cuvettes to convert the hemoglobin to ferrous hemoglobin. After obtaining a base-line difference spectrum of reduced hemoglobin

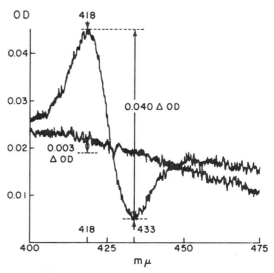

FIG. 4. Difference spectrum of ferrous hemoglobin with respect to CO-ferrous hemoglobin measured between 418 and 433 mμ. There is a net change in optical density of 0.037 corresponding to 4.20 μg of hemoglobin per ml.

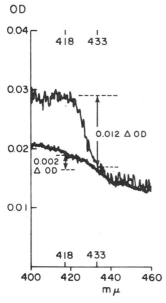

FIG. 3. Difference spectrum of ferrous hemoglobin with respect to CO-ferrous hemoglobin measured between 418 and 433 mμ. Correcting for change in optical density of 0.002 in the base-line there is a net change in optical density of 0.010 corresponding to 1.13 μg of hemoglobin per ml.

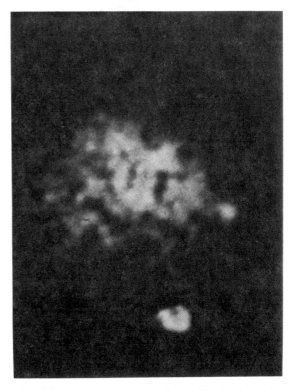

FIG. 5. Fluorescence photograph of a blood island after incubation of blastoderm with 1 mM δ-aminolevulinic acid-HCl for 2 hours. Red fluorescence is recorded as white. The intense fluorescence is indicative of copious amounts of porphyrins. × 400.

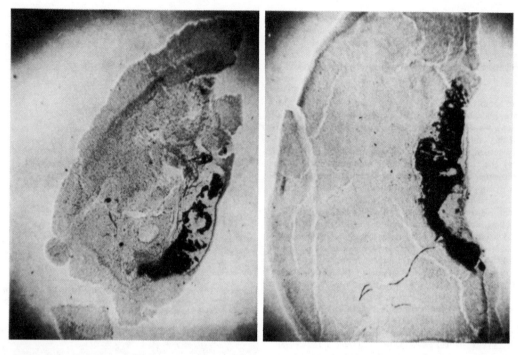

Fig. 6. Paired blastoderm halves stained with *O*-dianisidine after 14 hours of incubation *in vitro*. The half on the *right* (× 40) was incubated with 1 mM δ-aminolevulinic acid-HCl and gave a more intense reaction than did the control on the *left* (× 30).

TABLE I

Effect of δ-aminolevulinic acid on heme and hemoglobin synthesis in blastoderm halves as measured by distribution and intensity of o-dianisidine stain (after different times of incubation)[a]

Stage	14–15 hrs		16–18 hrs		18–20 hrs	
	δ-Amino-levulinic acid	Control	δ-Amino-levulinic acid	Control	δ-Amino-levulinic acid	Control
Definitive primitive streak	3+	2+	2+ 1+	Trace 0		
Head process	1+ 3+ 2+	0 Trace 0	1+ 1+ 3+ 2+ 2+	0 0 1+ 1+ Trace	2+	3+
Head fold	4+ 3+ 3+	2+ 0 1+	3+ 4+ 4+ 3+ 4+	1+ 2+ 3+ 2+ 2+	3+ 3+ 4+	2+ 3+ 2+
1–2 somites	3+	Trace	4+ 4+	1+ 4+	3+	2+
3–5 somites			3+ 4+	1+ 3+	5+	Trace

[a] See "Materials and Methods" for method of scoring.

with respect to reduced hemoglobin, one of the cuvettes was gassed with carbon monoxide. The amount of hemoglobin present was determined by measuring the difference spectrum between the ferrous hemoglobin and the carbon monoxide ferrous hemoglobin in the Soret region. The spectra were measured on a Cary model 14 recording spectrophotometer employing the 0.1 optical density full scale slide wire. The cuvette cell-holders had masks with slits (2-mm wide × 4 mm tall). The difference in absorption between 418 and 433 mµ was measured. The A_{433} (ferrous hemoglobin) to A_{418} (CO-ferrous hemoglobin) = 156,000 per hemoglobin monomer of 17,000 molecular weight.[1] Representative spectra are shown in Figs. 3 and 4. A change in optical density of 0.01 corresponds to 1.13 µg of hemoglobin per ml.

The amount of hemoglobin in the blastoderm hemolysate was then related to the nitrogen content of the hemolysate. Nitrogen was determined by a micro-Kjeldahl technique.

RESULTS

Activity of Enzymes of Heme Biosynthetic Chain

To determine the activity of the enzymes of the heme biosynthetic pathway in the chick erythroid precursor cells, blastoderm halves younger than the five somite stage were de-embryonated and incubated for 2 hours on media containing 1 mM δ-aminolevulinic acid-HCl. The corresponding control halves were incubated on regular media or on media containing 1 mM sodium succinate and 5 mM glycine.

[1] This value was derived from unpublished curves of Dr. D. L. Drabkin for which the authors are greatly indebted.

TABLE II

Effect of δ-aminolevulinic acid on hemoglobin synthesis in blastoderm halves after 24 to 26 hours incubation in vitro[a]

Stage	Amount of hemoglobin per half-blastoderm incubated with			Amount of hemoglobin incubated with			Ratio of δ-aminolevulinic acid to control (amino-acetone or no additions)[b]
	δ-Aminolevulinic acid	Aminoacetone	Nothing added to agar	δ-Aminolevulinic acid	Aminoacetone	Nothing added to agar	
	μg			*μg/mg nitrogen*			*μg hemoglobin/mg nitrogen*
Head process	0.91		0.36	9.9		3.8	2.6
	0.34		0.11	4.0		1.3	3.1
Head fold	0.45		0.39	4.5		3.8	1.2
	0.44	0.11		4.1	1.1		3.7
Head process	0.77	0.21		7.8	2.7		2.9
	0.55	0.12		5.6	1.2		4.7
	0.35	0.12		4.2	1.4		3.0
	1.00	0.74		6.8	7.5		0.9
	0.37	0.11		3.5	1.5		2.3

[a] See "Materials and Methods" for quantitative determination of hemoglobin.
[b] Average: 2.7 ± 0.8.

TABLE III

Effect of δ-aminolevulinic acid on hemoglobin synthesis in blastoderm halves after 27 to 29 hours incubation in vitro[a]

Stage	Amount of hemoglobin per half-blastoderm incubated with			Amount of hemoglobin incubated with			Ratio of δ-aminolevulinic acid to control (amino-acetone or no additions)[b]
	δ-Aminolevulinic acid	Aminoacetone	Nothing added to agar	δ-Aminolevulinic acid	Aminoacetone	Nothing added to agar	
	μg			*μg/mg nitrogen*			*μg hemoglobin/mg nitrogen*
Head fold	1.15		0.76	10.0		8.4	1.2
Head fold	0.80		0.44	8.3		4.5	1.8
3 somites	1.21		0.59	14.7		8.2	1.8
Head fold	1.32		1.26	15.0		16.1	0.9
Head process	0.80		0.42	7.5		4.0	1.9
Head fold	0.46		0.46	4.9		5.1	1.0
Definitive primitive streak	0.68		0.34	8.3		4.1	2.0
Head process	0.83		0.82	9.3		10.6	0.9
Head process	0.80	Trace		7.0	Trace		>7.0
1 somite	1.43	0.55		13.0	4.9		2.7
Head process	0.84	Trace		7.6	Trace		>7.6
1 somite	1.07	0.24		10.2	2.3		4.4

[a] See "Materials and Methods" for quantitative determination of hemoglobin.
[b] Average: 2.7 ± 1.7.

Examination with the fluorescence microscope of blastoderms incubated with δ-aminolevulinate showed an intense red fluorescence in the blood islands (Fig. 5) indicative of copious amounts of porphyrins and presumably of heme. No porphyrin fluorescence was noted in the control blastoderm halves. These results indicate that all of the enzymes of the heme biosynthetic chain exclusive of the first one, *i.e.* δ-aminolevulinic acid synthetase, are present in nonlimiting amounts in these precursor cells. As in the liver, heme synthesis is limited by the activity of δ-aminolevulinic acid synthetase.

Effect of δ-Aminolevulinic acid Synthetase Activity on Hemoglobin Formation

Knowing that heme synthesis is limited by the first enzyme of the biosynthetic chain, the next question asked was what effect does this limitation have on the production of globin? As shown by the previous experiment, δ-aminolevulinic acid can enter the blastoderm cells and cause the formation of copious amounts of porphyrins and presumably of heme. The amount of iron is not a limiting factor. When stained with α,α'-dipyyridyl the blastoderm becomes pink because of formation of the ferrous dipyridyl complex indicating a strongly positive reaction for iron. To supply heme earlier than normal, δ-aminolevulinic acid was used to by-pass δ-aminolevulinic acid synthetase. For this experiment, test blastoderm halves were grown on agar, a medium containing 1 mM δ-aminolevulinic acid-HCl. The control halves were grown either on regular medium or on agar containing 1 mM aminoacetone hydrochloride. Aminoacetone was used as a control since it is the aminoketone which, while not an intermediate in the biosynthesis of heme, most closely resembles δ-aminolevulinic acid (11).

Effect of δ-Aminolevulinic Acid as Measured by o-Dianisidine Stain—A group of 30 paired blastoderm halves were incubated for 14 to 20 hours and then stained. A representative pair is shown in Fig. 6. In 27 of the 30 experiments there was a greater

347

TABLE IV

Effect of δ-aminolevulinic acid on hemoglobin synthesis in blastoderm halves after 40 to 43 hours incubation in vitro[a]

Stage	Amount of hemoglobin per half-blastoderm incubated with			Amount of hemoglobin incubated with			Ratio of δ-aminolevulinic acid to control (aminoacetone or no additions)[b]
	δ-Aminolevulinic acid	Aminoacetone	Nothing added to agar	δ-Aminolevulinic acid	Aminoacetone	Nothing added to agar	
	μg			*μg/mg nitrogen*			*μg hemoglobin/mg nitrogen*
1 somite	4.90		1.27	44.5		5.5	8.2
Head fold	2.49		0.53	37.0		19.0	2.0
Definitive primitive streak	2.70		0.48	26.0		4.9	5.3
Head process	3.74		2.90	35.0		31.5	1.1
Definitive primitive streak	0.26		0.50	2.5		7.2	0.4
1 somite	3.75		0.80	34.0		7.5	4.5
Head process	0.49		0.50	5.5		7.2	0.8
Head process	1.59	1.24		21.0	13.0		1.6
Head fold	1.08	1.55		15.0	24.5		0.6
Head process	0.82	0.35		11.5	5.3		2.2
1 somite	0.37	1.27		5.0	16.0		0.3
Head fold	0.46	1.19		4.0	13.9		0.3

[a] See "Methods and Methods" for quantitative determination of hemoglobin.

[b] Average: 2.3 ± 1.9.

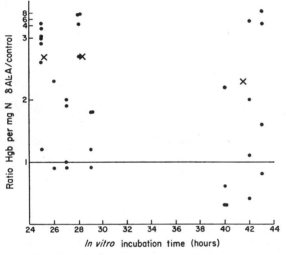

Single determination
Average value

FIG. 7. Effect of δ-aminolevulinic acid on the rate of hemoglobin formation as measured by difference spectrometry. After 24 to 30 hours of incubation, there was, on the average, 2.7 times more hemoglobin in the δ-aminolevulinic acid treated halves. With 40 to 44 hours of incubation, 2.3 times more hemoglobin was found in the test halves. ●, single determination; ×, average value.

peroxidase reaction on the halves cultured with δ-aminolevulinic acid (Table I). When the staining reaction was graded on the basis of 0.5 for trace to 5+ there was 2.1 times more heme and hemoglobin found in the test halves as compared to the controls. It should be noted that the peroxidase reaction is not specific for the heme of globin but also detects free heme and other hemoproteins. Therefore, these experiments can only suggest that

TABLE V

Effect of puromycin and δ-aminolevulinic acid on hemoglobin synthesis in blastoderm halves[a]

Puromycin	Stage	24-hr incubation		48-hr incubation	
		Puromycin + 1 mM δ-aminolevulinic acid	Nothing added to agar	Puromycin + 1 mM δ-aminolevulinic acid	Nothing added to agar
μg/ml		*μg hemoglobin/mg nitrogen*		*μg hemoglobin/mg nitrogen*	
10	Definitive primitive streak	0	1.5		
	Head process	0	9.1		
	Head process			1.8	115.0
	Definitive primitive streak			0	8.9
5	Head process	0	2.5		
	Head process	0	4.1		
	Head fold			Trace	12.2
	Head process			0	15.9
1	Head process	4.0	4.0		
	Head process	Trace	9.8		
	Head process			9.2	28.6
0.5	Head process	0	7.1		
	Head process			Trace	3.2
	Head process			5.4	73.8
0.25	Head Process	0	Trace		
	1 Somite	10.0	15.9		
	Head Process			3.9	37.4
	Definitive primitive streak			5.4	24.8

[a] See "Materials and Methods" for quantitative determination of hemoglobin.

δ-aminolevulinic acid may cause an increase in the rate of formation of hemoglobin.

δ-Aminolevulinic Acid Effect as Measured by Difference Spectrometry—In eight of nine blastoderm pairs incubated for 25 to 26 hours more hemoglobin was found in the δ-aminolevulinic acid treated halves (Table II). There was an average of 2.7 ± 0.8 times more hemoglobin in the δ-aminolevulinic acid-treated group. With 27 to 29 hours of incubation there was on the average 2.7 ± 1.7 times more hemoglobin in the δ-amino-levulinic acid-treated halves (Table III). After 40 to 43 hours of incubation (Table IV), the δ-aminolevulinic acid-treated halves had 2.3 ± 1.9 times more hemoglobin than the controls.

The ratio of hemoglobin per mg of nitrogen for the test as compared to the control blastoderm halves in the above three groups are summarized in Fig. 7.

These observations indicate that δ-aminolevulinic acid has a significant effect on the rate of hemoglobin formation in the chick blastoderm, increasing by 2 to 3 times the amount of hemoglobin formed during the first 30 hours of incubation on agar. With longer incubation the δ-aminolevulinic acid effect is less marked, because with progressive development δ-amino-levulinic acid synthetase develops spontaneously and no longer limits heme synthesis in the controls.

Effect of Puromycin and Actinomycin D on Ability of δ-Aminolevulinic Acid to Increase Rate of Hemoglobin Formation

In an attempt to define more clearly the mechanisms by which δ-aminolevulinic acid increased the rate of hemoglobin formation, either puromycin or actinomycin D was added to the agar medium alone or concurrently with δ-aminolevulinic acid.

TABLE VI

Effect of actinomycin D alone on hemoglobin synthesis in blastoderm halves incubated in vitro for 42 hours[a]

Actinomycin	Stage	Amount of hemoglobin per half blastoderm incubated with		Amount incubated with		Average ratio of actinomycin D to control
		Actinomycin D	Nothing added to agar	Actinomycin D	Nothing added to agar	
μg/ml		*μg*		*μg hemoglobin/mg nitrogen*		
0.02	Head process	0.53	0.27	11.3	5.7	
	Head process	Trace	1.27	Trace	18.5	0.2
	1 somite	0.86	6.12	11.6	74.6	
	Head process	0.13	0.72	3.1	17.1	
0.01	Head process	0.38	0.48	2.3	1.4	
	Head process	1.00	0.80	16.1	12.5	
	Head process	0.13	0.98	2.9	10.5	0.3
	Head process	Trace	1.14	Trace	26.0	
	Head process	Trace	0.92	Trace	17.0	
0.005	Head process	1.04	2.40	20.8	40.0	
	Head process	4.80	1.80	77.5	20.7	1.3
	Notochord	0.78	2.38	11.8	26.2	
	Head process	2.70	2.08	45.0	18.2	
	1 somite	6.59	2.60	89.0	33.4	
	Head fold	2.40	7.14	38.7	82.1	

[a] See "Materials and Methods" for quantitative determination of hemoglobin.

TABLE VII

Effect of actinomycin D plus δ-aminolevulinic acid on hemoglobin synthesis in blastoderm halves incubated in vitro[a]

Actinomycin	Stage	24-hr incubation		48-hr incubation	
		Actinomycin D1 + 1 mM δ-amino-levulinic acid	Nothing added to agar	Actinomycin D + 1 mM δ-amino-levulinic acid	Nothing added to agar
μg/ml		*μg hemoglobin/mg nitrogen*		*μg hemoglobin/mg nitrogen*	
0.01	1 somite	8.8	3.2		
	Head process			8.23	35.5
	Head fold			11.4	78.5
0.02	Head process	5.9	3.9		
	4 somites	8.4	14.9		
	Definitive primitive streak			8.5	31.4
	Head process	3.4	4.5		
	Head fold	2.0	2.5		
	Head fold			51.6	47.8
	1 somite			50.2	80.5

[a] See "Materials and Methods" for quantitative determination of hemoglobin.

When puromycin in concentrations from 0.5 to 10.0 μg per ml was added to the medium together with 1 mM δ-aminolevulinic acid-HCl, little or no hemoglobin was formed during 24 hours of incubation (Table V). After 48 hours, trace amounts of hemoglobin did appear in the test blastoderm halves indicating that these doses of puromycin were not lethal. In the presence of added δ-aminolevulinic acid, heme is not limiting for hemoglobin synthesis and if globin had been present hemoglobin would have been formed. In the presence of puromycin, which acts at the ribosome level to prevent protein synthesis, no globin was synthesized and no hemoglobin was formed. This experiment signifies that no free, detectable, globin is stored in precursor cells to await heme formation.

Wilt (12) treated chick blastoderms with actinomycin D and followed RNA synthesis by tracer uridine incorporation, and protein synthesis by tracer leucine incorporation. At a concentration of 2 μg per ml actinomycin D was found to inhibit RNA synthesis in 2 hours, and protein synthesis by 8 hours. It is known that high concentrations of actinomycin D not only inhibit mRNA and rRNA synthesis but also inhibit protein synthesis (13, 14). To distinguish more clearly between inhibition of RNA and protein synthesis much lower concentrations of the inhibitor were used in the present study. At concentrations of about 0.02 μg per ml, actinomycin D primarily inhibits RNA synthesis. When actinomycin D (0.02 μg per ml) was added to the agar medium supporting the blastoderm halves, the hemoglobin formed was, on the average, about one-fourth that formed in control blastoderm halves (Table VI). At 0.01 μg per ml of actinomycin D, the hemoglobin formed was one-third that of controls. At 0.005 μg per ml, no inhibition of hemoglobin formation was observed.

When 1 mM δ-aminolevulinic acid was added to the agar medium together with actinomycin D (0.01 and 0.02 μg per ml) and the blastoderm halves incubated for 24 hours, hemoglobin formation was, on the average, nearly equal to the controls

(Table VII). After incubation for 48 hours, the treated halves had, on the average, half of the hemoglobin of the untreated halves. In spite of the small number of blastoderms used in this experiment the data clearly show that the addition of δ-aminolevulinic acid to the actinomycin-treated blastoderms appreciably enhanced the formation of hemoglobin. The data also indicate that there was a decrease in hemoglobin formation in 24 hours which became more marked at 48 hours. This decrease in hemoglobin formation in the presence of 0.02 μg per ml of actinomycin and 1 mM δ-aminolevulinic acid is probably caused primarily by a relatively slow breakdown of globin messenger RNA which occurs concomitantly with an inhibition of RNA synthesis at the DNA level.

Because actinomycin D blocks messenger RNA formation presumably little messenger RNA was transcribed for globin synthesis and little messenger RNA was transcribed for the synthesis of δ-aminolevulinic acid synthetase. When δ-aminolevulinic acid was added in the presence of actinomycin, hemoglobin formation was enhanced. Since the puromycin experiment showed that no pre-formed globin was present in these cells this result suggests that globin was synthesized *de novo*. The enhanced synthesis of globin occurred presumably by the action of ribosomes and globin messenger RNA that were already present in the precursor erythroid cells. In addition, the synthesis of globin required δ-aminolevulinic acid or rather the conversion product heme.

DISCUSSION

The present studies indicate that hemoglobin synthesis in the chick blastoderm is triggered by the activation of the structural gene that forms messenger RNA for δ-aminolevulinic acid synthetase. The following observations are advanced in support of this idea.

These studies indicate that in the erythroid precursor cells of the blastoderm the rate of heme synthesis is limited by the activity of the first enzyme in the heme biosynthetic chain, δ-aminolevulinic acid synthetase. This finding is also true for heme synthesis in other cell types (1, 15). All of the other enzymes of the heme biosynthetic chain which serve to convert δ-aminolevulinic acid to heme are at nonlimiting activities in the hematopoietic mesoderm of the chick blastoderm. In the colorless erythroid precursor cells, only small amounts of heme are synthesized, sufficient for the requirements for cytochrome production. At the time of initiation of hemoglobin synthesis much larger amounts of heme are synthesized. This is associated with an increase in the levels of δ-aminolevulinic acid synthetase.

When δ-aminolevulinic acid is added to colorless erythroid precursor cells, hemoglobin synthesis occurs earlier than in controls (Tables I to IV). The greatest differences occur at earlier times of incubation, before δ-aminolevulinic acid is made at an appreciable rate by the cells themselves. As δ-aminolevulinic acid is rapidly converted to heme, it is presumed that heme is the substance which controls the rate of hemoglobin synthesis. This presumption is supported by the work of other investigators with the use of different hemoglobin-synthesizing systems. Hammel and Bessman (16) found that globin synthesis by isolated avian erythrocyte nuclei could be increased by the addition of heme. In addition, Bruns and London (17) found that hemin increased the incorporation of ^{14}C-valine into the hemoglobin of rabbit reticulocytes.

How does heme increase the rate of hemoglobin formation? Three possibilities were considered. First, heme might stimulate the synthesis, *i.e.* transcription, of messenger RNA for globin monomer formation. To test this possibility, actinomycin D was given to the cells in order to block messenger RNA formation; at the same time δ-aminolevulinic acid was given to supply heme. In spite of the presence of actinomycin D δ-aminolevulinic acid stimulated the formation of hemoglobin. From this experiment it was concluded that messenger RNA for globin and ribosomal RNA were not limiting hemoglobin synthesis and in the colorless erythroid precursor cells, messenger RNA for globin, and ribosomes must be present. This agrees with the conclusions of Wilt (12) that the time of transcription of messenger RNA for globin is at the head fold stage, several hours before active hemoglobin synthesis starts.

Another possible way to explain the fact that heme increases the rate of hemoglobin formation is to assume the presence of pre-formed globin in the colorless erythroid precursor cells. Experiments with puromycin and δ-aminolevulinic acid showed that pre-formed globin was not present in detectable amounts. Puromycin blocks protein synthesis at the ribosome level. If a pool of pre-formed globin existed the addition of δ-aminolevulinic acid leading to the formation of heme should have caused an increase in hemoglobin synthesis. In the presence of puromycin and δ-aminolevulinic acid, no hemoglobin synthesis occurred (Table V), ruling out the presence of pre-formed globin. The findings of others support this conclusion. Wilt (12) observed that puromycin prevented hemoglobin formation in the chick embryo at all developmental stages. Grayzel, Hörchner, and London (18) found that puromycin and cycloheximide blocked hemoglobin synthesis in rabbit reticulocytes in the presence or absence of added heme.

A third possibility to explain the fact that heme increases the rate of hemoglobin formation is to assume that heme is required for the appropriate three-dimensional folding of the globin polypeptide as it is synthesized on the ribosomes. Winslow and Ingram (19) have shown that the second half of the globin monomer is synthesized at a slower rate than the first half is. The iron of heme in the hemoglobin monomer is attached to a histidine in the middle of the chain (His 87 in the α chain, and His 92 in the β chain). We propose the hypothesis that globin is not released from the ribosomes unless it folds around heme to form a compact unit. This hypothesis would most simply explain the fact that no free globin is detectable in precursor erythroblasts. The fact that globin monomer is formed in a 1:1 ratio with heme would be most readily explained on the basis that heme was limiting, and heme was required for globin synthesis. Grayzel *et al.* (18) observed that 10^{-4} M heme causes the aggregation of single ribosomes to polyribosomes; this may be an additional contributory effect of heme on hemoglobin biosynthesis.

The following hypothesis summarizes what is felt to be the situation in the erythroid precursor cell. In this colorless cell are present adequate amounts of ribosomal RNA and messenger RNA for globin formation. In addition, there are present all the enzymes needed to make heme at an appreciable rate except the first enzyme δ-aminolevulinic acid synthetase which is at a limiting activity. The rate of synthesis of δ-aminolevulinic acid synthetase must be controlled by a repressor mechanism. Only when derepression occurs by the action of some unknown substance is the structural gene for δ-aminolevulinic acid synthetase stimulated to transcribe messenger RNA to form increased amounts of δ-aminolevulinic acid synthetase. The δ-aminolevulinic acid synthetase then produces δ-aminolevulinic acid which is readily converted to heme by the other nonlimiting enzymes of the heme biosynthetic chain. Heme, formed in the mitochondria, enters the cytoplasm. There it attaches to a globin monomer that is being synthesized on the polyribosomes. The monomer grows and folds into a compact unit around the heme. Then completed hemoglobin monomers detach from the ribosomes and combine to form tetrameric hemoglobin. Thus, according to this hypothesis, it is the activation of the structural gene for δ-aminolevulinic acid synthetase which is the major step that controls the differentiation of the pro-erythroblast into the mature erythrocyte.

REFERENCES

1. LEVERE, R. D., AND GRANICK S., *Proc. Nat. Acad. Sci. U. S. A.*, **54**, 134 (1965).
2. GRANICK, S., *J. Biol. Chem.*, **238**, PC2247 (1963).
3. GRANICK, S., *J. Biol. Chem.*, **241**, 1359 (1966).
4. ROMANOFF, A. L., *The avian embryo*, Macmillan, New York, 1960.
5. O'BRIEN, B. R. A., *J. Embryol. Exp. Morphol.*, **9**, 202 (1961).
6. SABIN, F. T., *Carnegie Inst. Wash. Publications*, **9**, 213 (1920).
7. ZWILLING, E., *Nat. Cancer Inst. Monogr.*, **2**, (1959).
8. RUGH, R., *Experimental embryology*, Burgess Publishing Company, Minneapolis, 1962, p. 15.
9. PARKER, R. C., *Methods of tissue culture*, Ed. 3, Harper and Row, New York, 1961, p. 57.
10. OWEN, J. A., SILBERMAN, H. J., AND GOT, C., *Nature (London)*, **182**, 1373 (1958).
11. URATA, G., AND GRANICK, S., *J. Biol. Chem.*, **238**, 811 (1963).
12. WILT, F. H., *J. Mol. Biol.*, **12**, 331 (1965).
13. REVEL, M., HIATT, H., AND REVEL, J. P., *Science (Wash.)*, **146**, 1311 (1964).
14. REICH, E., *Progr. Nucleic Acid Res.*, **8**, 184 (1964).
15. SAILLEN, R., *Helv. Med. Acta*, **30**, 208 (1963).
16. HAMMEL, C. L., AND BESSMAN, S. P., *J. Biol. Chem.*, **239**, 2228 (1964).
17. BRUNS, G. P., AND LONDON, I. M., *Biochem. Biophys. Res. Commun.*, **18**, 236 (1965).
18. GRAYZEL, A. I., HÖRCHNER, P., AND LONDON, I. M., *Proc. Nat. Acad. Sci. U. S. A.*, **55**, 650 (1966).
19. WINSLOW, R. M., AND INGRAM, V. M., *J. Biol. Chem.*, **241**, 1144 (1966).

Reprinted from the Proceedings of the National Academy of Sciences
Vol. 61, No. 2, pp. 509–513. October, 1968.

THE INDUCTION OF δ-AMINOLEVULINIC ACID SYNTHETASE IN VIVO IN CHICK EMBRYO LIVER BY NATURAL STEROIDS*

By Attallah Kappas, Chull S. Song, Richard D. Levere, Richard A. Sachson, and S. Granick

THE ROCKEFELLER UNIVERSITY, NEW YORK CITY; AND THE STATE UNIVERSITY OF NEW YORK COLLEGE OF MEDICINE, BROOKLYN

Communicated August 1, 1968

It has been shown in previous studies from our laboratories that certain natural steroids markedly enhance porphyrin synthesis, as determined by fluorescence microscopy, in chick embryo liver cells growing in primary culture.[1, 2]   In its intensity, course of development, and other characteristics, this action of steroids resembles the porphyrinogenic effect in the liver cell culture of certain drugs and foreign chemicals;[3, 4] these act *in vivo* by enhancing the *de novo* formation of δ-aminolevulinic acid (ALA)-synthetase, the rate-limiting enzyme in porphyrin biosynthesis.[5]   We inferred[6] therefore that the porphyrin-inducing action of natural steroids in tissue culture was similarly mediated through the induction of enhanced ALA-synthetase activity in the liver.   The present investigation was undertaken to test this possibility in chick embryo livers.   The results support our previous conclusion that the porphyrinogenic action which steroids manifest in tissue culture does in fact reflect a substantial increase in ALA-synthetase, which these natural compounds evoke in liver cells of the chick embryo.

Methods and Results.—Steroids were solubilized in propylene glycol containing 10 per cent N,N′-dimethylacetamide and, after sterilization by filtration through a Millipore® filter, were injected via a no. 22 needle through the air sac membrane into the yolk sacs of 16-day-old chick embryos in volumes of 0.2 ml, with appropriate solvent controls.   The potent chemical inducer of ALA-synthetase, allylisopropylacetamide, was similarly administered in various amounts to the embryo.   Eggs were then incubated at 37°C for various time periods, after which the embryos were sacrificed, and the livers were removed and homogenized in groups of two or three; ALA-synthetase was determined in duplicate by the method of Marver *et al.*[7]   The ALA produced in the reaction was estimated by the method of Mauzerall and Granick.[8]   ALA production in this assay system increased linearly between 0 and 60 minutes and was directly proportional to the amount of liver homogenate in the reaction mixtures.

A number of steroid metabolites of the 5β-H configuration known to enhance porphyrin synthesis in liver cell culture[1] greatly stimulated hepatic ALA-synthetase activity in the whole chick embryo.   Figure 1 depicts the mean levels of ALA-synthetase activity expressed in mμmoles of ALA formed/gram of liver/hour in control embryos and in a group treated eight hours earlier with 5.0 mg of the steroid metabolite 5β pregnane-3α, 17α-diol, 11,20-dione.   Control embryo livers showed detectable but low levels of ALA-synthetase activity.   This enzyme activity increased markedly after treatment with the steroid depicted in Figure 1 and reached an average level, in the experiment shown, that was approximately 20 times higher than that in controls.   The response to this steroid was variable, but only occasionally was enzyme activity less than 5–10 times the

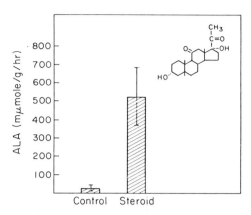

Fig. 1.—Steroid induction of ALA-synthetase in chick embryo liver. Vertical bars indicate mean enzyme activity ± 1 SD in livers of control chicks (120 embryos) and chicks (90 embryos) treated 8 hr earlier with 5.0 mg of the steroid metabolite shown in the upper right.

normal; sometimes it reached 40 or more times that of the control chicks treated with solvent alone. Similar variability in the enzyme response to allylisopropylacetamide, administered in equivalent amounts, was observed and may reflect differences of individual embryos in susceptibility to induction.

Figure 2 depicts results of an experiment showing mean levels of ALA-synthetase activity eight hours after treatment of chick embryos with several other metabolites as well as with certain precursor hormones. Optimal inducing amounts of these metabolites ranged from 2.5 to 5.0 mg/egg, though small but significant increments in enzyme activity were consistently evoked by as little as 0.1 mg/egg. Primary endocrine secretions, i.e., metabolically unaltered hormones, such as progesterone, testosterone, estradiol, and cortisol, had weak or no enzyme-stimulating activity. These relations between structure and enzyme-inducing action of steroids *in vivo* are consistent with the previously observed structural requirements for their porphyrinogenic activity in tissue culture.[1]

Incubation of liver homogenates with inducing steroids over a wide range of concentrations did not lead to an increase in ALA-synthetase activity, an indication that the steroids did not act directly by activating an inactive enzyme.

The time course of steroid stimulation of ALA-synthetase activity was studied in detail with the metabolite 5β pregnane-3α, 17α-diol,11-20-dione, whose structure is shown in Figure 1. Detectable elevations in ALA-synthetase occurred within two hours and increased sharply to reach maximum levels approximately eight hours after steroid injection into the yolk sac. After reaching maximum

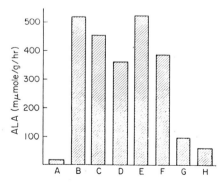

Fig. 2.—Comparative effects of various steroids on hepatic ALA-synthetase activity in chick embryos. Steroid doses were 2.5–5.0 mg/egg administered 8 hr earlier. Vertical bars indicate mean values of enzyme activity in a minimum of 24 embryos per experimental group.

Group *A*, control; group *B*, 5β pregnane-3α, 17α-diol, 11,20-dione; group *C*, etiocholanolone; group *D*, etiocholanedione; group *E*, pregnandione; group *F*, 11-ketopregnanolone; group *G*, progesterone; group *H*, testosterone.

levels, activity declined rapidly, although small elevations persisted for at least several days in chicks maintained until hatching. The reason for the rapid decline from peak enzyme activity in induced embryos is not clear; there is no evidence of formation of an inhibitor of ALA-synthetase activity in the livers of such embryos during this decline. A minimum of 85–90 per cent of the amino-ketone formed in steroid-treated embryos was determined to be ALA, rather than the related compound aminoacetone.[4] The enzyme response was proportional to the amount of steroid injected up to 5 mg; the response diminished with larger amounts of steroid. A similar effect with respect to the induction of porphyrin fluoresence has been observed in tissue culture and may be related in part to the toxic action of high doses of these steroids on hepatic cells. Certain porphyrino-genic drugs show a similar dose-response effect in the chick embryo preparation.

Substantial increases in ALA-synthetase activity were also noted in preparations of fresh mitochondria[5] isolated from the livers of chick embryos treated eight hours earlier with the steroid metabolite shown in Figure 1. The liver weights of embryos treated with steroid inducers of ALA-synthetase showed no significant differences from controls. It has been noted in mammalian liver that drugs and foreign chemicals which induce porphyria may produce substantial increases in liver weight after several days of treatment. We regard these changes as secondary ones not directly involved in the induction process.

When actinomycin D (250 µg/egg) or cycloheximide (5 µg/egg) was injected into the yolk sac together with an optimum amount of a 5β-H steroid inducer, the stimulation of ALA-synthetase in the liver was inhibited 80–96 per cent. This inhibitory effect was manifest at the earliest time period that induction generally becomes evident (2 hours); even at six to eight hours, treated embryos appeared healthy and their liver weights did not differ from those of controls. The ability of actinomycin and of cycloheximide to inhibit enzyme induction *in vivo* in the chick is consistent with their capacity to block steroid- and drug-induced porphyrin synthesis in tissue culture[2], and to block the induction of ALA-synthe-tase in rat liver[9] by the porphyria-inducing chemical allylisopropylacetamide.

Discussion.—The present study demonstrates that certain natural steroids can greatly enhance hepatic activity of the enzyme ALA-synthetase *in vivo* in the chick embryo. ALA-synthetase controls the rate-limiting step in heme formation,[5] and the steroid action described here thus confirms our earlier conclusion that the induction of ALA-synthetase by these compounds is the proximate mechanism by which they enhance porphyrin synthesis in chick embryo liver cells growing in primary culture.[1, 2] The amounts and types of steroids produced by the chick during embryogenesis are not known; however, the natural occurrence, among various species, of steroids structurally resembling those which we have shown to strongly induce ALA-synthetase leads us to suggest that certain steroids are the physiological agents which control, by induction of this enzyme, the rate of heme synthesis in the chick embryo liver. A similar conclusion, strengthened by these and previous experiments,[10] is that steroids also normally control the rate of heme and hemoglobin synthesis in the erythroid cells of chick embryo blastoderm by induction of ALA-synthetase in these cells.

The structural basis for steroid induction of hepatic ALA-synthetase has not been examined as extensively in the whole chick embryo as in the tissue-culture studies we have previously described.[1, 2]   Nevertheless, the results obtained with the compounds indicated in Figures 1 and 2, and others not reported here, confirm our earlier findings of the unique potency of 5β-H steroid hormone metabolites in inducing this enzyme.   These metabolites have generally been regarded as biologically inactive end products of hormone metabolism, but this study, as well as other observations,[11, 12] suggests that they may in fact comprise a potentially important category of active endocrine substances.

The response of the chick embryo liver to natural steroids, and to certain drugs and foreign chemicals, by enhanced production of ALA-synthetase, establishes a close analogy in the mode of action of these inducing substances in regulating heme biosynthesis in this organ.   This response may be regarded partly as a detoxification mechanism in view of the important role of heme and heme-proteins, e.g., the microsomal P-450 cytochrome system,[13] in the metabolism of drugs and other substrates.   However, the analogy in action of steroids and drugs in chick embryo liver does not necessarily extend to the effects of these agents in other species or tissues.   We have, for example, been unable as yet to enhance ALA-synthetase formation in guinea pig or rat liver by intensive administration of 5β-H steroids, although in both species this enzyme is readily induced by foreign chemicals.[5, 9]   The relative unresponsiveness of these animals to induction of ALA-synthetase by steroids probably denotes the existence of additional mechanisms for controlling heme formation that may be distinctive to the mammalian liver cell.   The rapid inactivation of certain potential inducers of ALA-synthetase, i.e., steroids, by chemical transformation or conjugation with glucuronic acid may represent such possible control mechanisms.[2]

A different type of control of heme synthesis appears to operate in erythroid cell precursors of the chick blastoderm, as we have shown in an earlier study.[10] In the latter report, 5β-H steroids significantly enhanced the rate of heme and hemoglobin formation in chick blastoderm erythroid cells grown in culture, whereas drugs and chemicals that induce hepatic porphyria were without such effect.   Regulation of the heme biosynthetic pathway in these embryonic red blood cells thus is mediated via a control mechanism responsive to certain steroids, but not to drugs or foreign chemicals.   The possibility that the repressor for the ALA-synthetase operon in avian erythroid cells may have a more structurally rigid derepressor requirement than that in avian hepatic cells has been suggested.[10]

Most recently, we have observed in preliminary experiments that the neonatal period in the rat is associated with a high degree of unresponsiveness to chemical induction of ALA-synthetase in the liver.   The response to drug induction of the enzyme gradually intensifies, reaching normal adult levels in the late postnatal period; such a response indicates that the controls on inducibility of ALA-synthetase in the neonate may be developmentally determined or adaptively related to gestational influences.

Thus the existence of differences in the types and levels of controls that are imposed on heme synthesis in various cells seems evident, and a significant influence of species and of developmental or physiological factors on these regulatory mechanisms may be anticipated.   Elucidation of the manner in which such influences are exerted would provide insight into both the pathogenesis of the heredi- tary and acquired porphyrias of man, and the normal hepatic mechanisms for the detoxification of drugs.

Summary.—This study demonstrates that certain natural steroids greatly enhance ALA-synthetase activity *in vivo* in the liver of the chick embryo. Ste- roid induction of this enzyme, which controls the rate-limiting step in heme forma- tion, confirms our previous conclusion, based on tissue culture studies, regarding the mechanism by which these compounds regulate the activity of the heme bio- synthetic pathway.

The existence of differences in the types and levels of controls imposed on heme synthesis in various cells is noted, and it is suggested that these are determined in part by specific species and tissue factors and by developmental and physiological status.

The authors are indebted to Mrs. M. Hunziker for editorial assistance and preparation of the manuscript, and to Miss Corinne Barrett for invaluable technical assistance.

* These studies were supported in part by USPHS grants AM09838 and GM04922 and N. Y. C. Health Research Council grant I-168.

[1] Granick, S., and A. Kappas, *J. Biol. Chem.*, **242**, 4587–4593 (1967).

[2] Kappas, A., and S. Granick, *J. Biol. Chem.*, **243**, 346–351 (1968).

[3] Granick, S., *J. Biol. Chem.*, **238**, PC2247–PC2248 (1963).

[4] *Ibid.*, **241**, 1359–1375 (1966).

[5] Granick, S., and G. Urata, *J. Biol. Chem.*, **238**, 821–827 (1963).

[6] Granick, S., and A. Kappas, these PROCEEDINGS, **57**, 1463–1467 (1967).

[7] Marver, H. S., D. P. Tschudy, M. G. Perlroth, and A. Collins, *J. Biol. Chem.*, **241**, 2803– 2809 (1966).

[8] Mauzerall, D., and S. Granick, *J. Biol. Chem.*, **219**, 435–446 (1956).

[9] Marver, H. S., A. Collins, D. P. Tschudy, and M. Rechcigl, Jr., *J. Biol. Chem.*, **241**, 4323– 4329 (1966).

[10] Levere, R. D., A. Kappas, and S. Granick, these PROCEEDINGS, **58**, 985–990 (1967).

[11] Kappas, A., and R. H. Palmer, *Pharmacol. Rev.*, **15**, 123–167 (1963).

[12] Kappas, A., and R. H. Palmer, *Methods Hormone Res.*, **4**, 1–19 (1965).

[13] Omura, T., and R. Sato, *J. Biol. Chem.*, **239**, 2370–2378 (1964).

Reprinted from
Biochimica et Biophysica Acta

BBA 95207

EFFECT OF PROTOPORPHYRIN ON HEMOGLOBIN SYNTHESIS

T. J. GRIBBLE AND H. C. SCHWARTZ

Department of Pediatrics, Stanford University, Palo Alto, Calif. (U.S.A.)
(Received October 26th, 1964)

SUMMARY

1. The synthesis of hemoglobin was studied in a system *in vitro* which contained ribosomes, pH-5 enzymes, and the supernatant solution prepared from rabbit reticulocytes.

2. When protoporhyrin IX was added to this "cell-free" system, the release into solution of protein labeled with [^{14}C]leucine was increased 2- to 3-fold.

3. The same effect was observed whether the protoporhyrin IX was added initially or after the reaction mixture had been incubated for 10 min.

4. The increase in the radioactivity of the soluble protein was maximal when the concentration of protoporphyrin IX was 32 μM.

5. These studies suggest that the mechanism for the release of hemoglobin from the ribosomes may be associated with the synthesis of heme from protoporphyrin IX and iron.

INTRODUCTION

In 1958, SCHWEET et al.[1] described the synthesis of hemoglobin in a ribosomal system prepared from rabbit reticulocytes. This system was unique in that a soluble product, presumably hemoglobin, was formed and released into the supernatant solution[1-3]. However, the factors which control this release mechanism are not well understood. Ionic strength, Mg^{2+}, GSH, GTP and the energy source involved in peptide-bond formation and in ribosomal stability may play a role in the release mechanism[4]. A "releasing factor" in a soluble cell fraction derived from rabbit reticulocytes has been described by LAMFROM[5]; however, no attempt to further define this factor has been reported.

PERUTZ et al.[6] have demonstrated that the heme groups lie in separate packets, which are formed by folds in the polypeptide chains. They suggested that the polypeptide chain, once it is synthesized and provided with a heme group around which it can coil, takes up its configuration spontaneously. The present studies were undertaken to determine whether the availability of heme might be a factor limiting the formation of soluble protein in a ribosomal system derived from reticulocytes. Since rabbit ribosomal systems can synthesize heme[7], protoporphyrin IX, a precursor of heme, was used in these studies. The addition of protoporphyrin IX to a ribosomal system derived from rabbit reticulocytes was found to augment the release of a soluble protein, which was probably hemoglobin.

METHODS

New Zealand, white adult male rabbits were injected daily with 1 ml of 2.5 % phenylhydrazine for 5 days and then bled by cardiac puncture on the 7th day[8]. The red cells consisted almost entirely of reticulocytes. They were washed and packed in a Krebs–Henseleit solution which contained 0.13 M NaCl, 5.2 mM KCl and 7.5 mM $MgCl_2$. The cells were lysed with four volumes of 5 mM $MgCl_2$ and gently stirred for 10 min. After the addition of 1 volume of a 1.5 M sucrose solution, containing 0.15 M KCl, the mixture was centrifuged at 12 000 $\times g$ for 10 min. The supernatant fraction was then centrifuged for 90 min at 105 000 $\times g$ in a Spinco preparative centrifuge in order to sediment the ribosomes. The supernatant solution was separated further into "pH-5 precipitate" and "pH-5 supernatant" fractions by adjusting the pH to 5.2 with 1 N acetic acid. The pH-5 precipitate was dissolved in 0.1 M Tris buffer (pH 7.5) and neutralized with 0.1 N KOH. This solution was used as the "pH-5 enzyme" fraction-. The "pH-5 supernatant" fraction was adjusted to pH 7.5 with 1 N KOH and was used as the "soluble supernatant" cell fraction[5]. The ribosomes were resuspended in Medium A which contained 0.35 M sucrose, 0.15 M KCl, 35 mM $KHCO_3$ and 4 mM $MgCl_2$, adjusted to pH 7.8 and centrifuged for 90 min at 105 000 $\times g$. These washed microsomes were resuspended in Medium A (ref. 9).

Ribosomes, pH-5 enzymes, and soluble supernatant cell fractions were freshly prepared for each experiment and added to reaction mixtures as indicated in the legends. Reaction mixtures also contained 0.25 μmoles GTP, 1 μmole ATP. 20 μmoles creatine phosphate, 200 μg creatine kinase, 1.5 μmoles reduced glutathione, 225 μmoles sucrose, 60 μmoles KCl, 25 μmoles $KHCO_3$, 2.6 μmoles Mg^{2+}, 50 μmoles Tris buffer (pH 7.5), 0.05 ml of a complete amino acid mixture[1] and 1 μC L-[*Carboxy*-14C]-leucine (New England Nuclear Corporation, specific activity 18.7 mC/mmole) in a final volume of 1.5 ml. After the reaction mixtures were incubated in a Dubnoff shaker at 37°, the soluble and ribosomal protein fractions were separated by adjusting the pH to 5.2 with 1 N acetic acid and centrifuging for 180 min at 105 000 $\times g$. The precipitate contained the ribosomal protein and the supernatant solution contained the soluble protein[5]. The radioactivity of these fractions was determined as follows. The proteins were precipitated with cold 8 % trichloroacetic acid, were washed twice with 5 % trichloroacetic acid which contained 0.05 M L-leucine. and were dissolved in 1.0 N NaOH. They were reprecipitated with 8 % trichloroacetic acid and washed a third time with hot (90°) 5 % trichloroacetic acid, which contained 0.05 M L-leucine. The precipitates were then washed twice with ethanol–ether (3 : 1, v/v), once at room temperature and once at 56°, washed twice with ether, and finally dissolved in 0.1 N NaOH. The protein concentration in an aliquot was determined by the method of LOWRY *et al.*[10] with rabbit serum as standard protein. Another aliquot was dissolved in 1 ml of hyamine and 15 ml of a liquid scintillation

Biochim. Biophys. Acta, 103 (1965) 333–338

counting solution and counted in a Tricarb liquid scintillation counter. An internal standard was added to correct quenching in each sample. The counting efficiency was 45 %. The activity was expressed as specific activity (counts/min per mg protein). Similar results were obtained when the activity was expressed as total radioactivity (total counts/min).

Protoporphyrin was prepared as the methyl ester by the method of GRINSTEIN[11]. The protoporphyrin methyl ester was hydrolyzed with 3 N HCl, dried, and stored over NaOH in a vacuum desiccator. The protoporphyrin was dissolved in 0.14 M KHCO$_3$ and pH was adjusted to 7.8 with 1.5 N HCl (ref. 12). For control flasks, 0.14 M KHCO$_3$, which had been adjusted to pH 7.8 with 1.5 N HCl, was used instead of protoporphyrin.

RESULTS

The effect of protoporphyrin on the incorporation of [^{14}C]leucine into ribosomal protein and the release of labeled protein from the ribosome was studied. Protoporphyrin was added to reaction mixtures after 10 min incubation in order to allow adequate ribosomal synthesis of protein to occur initially. At that time, protoporphyrin, dissolved in 0.14 M KHCO$_3$ (pH 7.8), was added to experimental flasks to make a final concentration of 0.12 mM and an equal volume of 0.14 M KHCO$_3$ (pH 7.8) was added to a duplicate set of control flasks. An experimental and control flask were removed after 10, 20, 30 and 60 min incubation and the radioactivity in soluble and ribosomal protein determined.

The effect of protoporphyrin on the soluble protein in a typical experiment is shown in Fig. 1. The specific activity of the soluble protein in the experimental

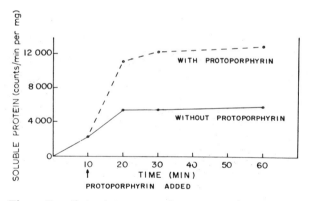

Fig. 1. Reaction mixtures contained the following cell fractions: 5.4 mg ribosomes, 7.1 mg pH-5 enzymes, and 4.1 mg soluble supernatant. Incubation conditions were as described in METHODS.

samples was twice that of the controls. The incorporation of [^{14}C]leucine into the ribosomal protein in the same experiment is shown in Fig. 2. The specific activities of the ribosomal protein in the experimental samples were slightly less than that of the controls.

This effect of protoporphyrin on the soluble and ribosomal protein was ob-

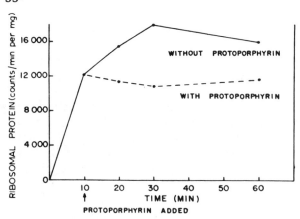

Fig. 2. Reaction mixtures contained the following cell fractions: 5.4 mg ribosomes, 7.1 mg pH-5 enzymes, and 4.1 mg soluble supernatant. Incubation conditions were as described in METHODS.

served in eight separate experiments. When protoporphyrin was added to reaction mixtures, 20–30 % of the total counts incorporated into protein were released as soluble protein. In control reaction mixtures without added protoporphyrin, 8–13 % of the total counts appeared as soluble protein. In five experiments, the activity of the ribosomal protein was slightly decreased when protoporphyrin was added; however, in three experiments no change occurred.

The effect of adding protoporphyrin at time zero was studied in five experiments. Results similar to those described above were obtained. The addition of protoporphyrin doubled the incorporation of leucine into soluble protein. There was no difference in the ribosomal protein activity between the experimental incubation mixtures containing protoporphyrin and the control incubation mixtures containing $KHCO_3$.

The effect of various protoporphyrin concentrations on the formation of soluble protein was studied. The results are shown in Fig. 3. The radioactivity of the soluble protein increased to a maximum at a protoporphyrin concentration of 32 μM. At higher protoporphyrin concentrations, the activity progressively decreased. Marked inhibition occurred at a protoporphyrin concentration of 0.64 mM.

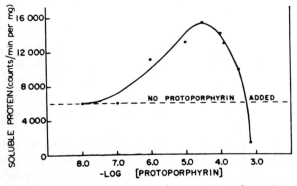

Fig. 3. Reaction mixtures contained the following cell fractions: 6.1 mg ribosomes, 6.8 mg pH-5 enzymes, and 4.5 mg soluble supernatant. Protoporphyrin was added in the concentrations indicated. Incubation conditions were as described in METHODS. Incubation time was 30 min.

Biochim. Biophys. Acta, 103 (1965) 333–338

DISCUSSION

Despite numerous investigations of hemoglobin synthesis by ribosomal systems derived from rabbit reticulocytes, the factors responsible for the release of a soluble product have not been well defined[4]. In such systems only a small per cent of the total radioactivity is found in the soluble protein. When a ribosomal system prepared from rabbit reticulocytes was studied by LAMFROM[5], 17 % of the total radioactivity incorporated into protein was released as a soluble product. She suggested that a "releasing factor" was present in the soluble cell fraction; however, no subsequent characterization of this factor has been reported.

The present studies of the release mechanism were stimulated by the description by PERUTZ et al.[6] of the intimate relationship of the heme to the tertiary structure of the globin moiety. The purpose was to determine whether protoporphyrin IX, a heme precursor, could augment the release of ribosomal protein labeled with [^{14}C]leucine. VON EHRENSTEIN AND LIPMANN[2] included hemin chloride in the ribosomal system prepared from rabbit reticulocytes which they studied, but did not investigate its particular effect on hemoglobin synthesis. In preliminary studies of ribosomal systems derived from human and avian reticulocytes, we observed that the addition of hemin chloride augmented the incorporation of [^{14}C]leucine into ribosomal protein[14] Since hemin has a low solubility at pH 7.8, protoporphyrin IX, which can be converted to heme by rabbit reticulocyte ribosomes[7], was used in the present studies.

Protoporphyrin IX, when added to a ribosomal system prepared from rabbit reticulocytes, augmented the release into solution of protein labeled with [^{14}C]-leucine by 2- to 3-fold. This increase in soluble protein occurred in the absence of marked stimulation of total protein synthesis, indicating a redistribution of radioactivity between the soluble and ribosomal protein. These observations suggest that the release of hemoglobin from the ribosomes may involve the coiling of the globin chains around the protoporphyrin and/or heme groups.

The increase in the radioactivity of the soluble protein was maximal at 32 μM protoporphyrin. It is noteworthy that this concentration is similar to the protoporphyrin concentration, 50 μM, which is optimal for the enzymic synthesis of heme *in vitro*[12].

Alternate explanations for the increase in radioactivity of the soluble protein would suggest an interference with protein synthesis by protoporphyrin. Such interference might represent a non-specific damage to the ribosomes with release of labeled fragments. The observations that protoporphyrin was usually effective when added at time zero or after 10 min of incubation, and that this effect occurred at an optimal protoporphyrin concentration make this possibility unlikely. Protoporphyrin might act like puromycin, causing the premature release of incompletely synthesized chains[13]. However, preliminary identification of the radioactive soluble product by chromatography and electrophoresis indicates that it is probably hemoglobin, and not a highly labeled intermediate or polypeptide fragment[14].

HAMEL AND BESSMAN[15,16] have recently studied the effect of hemin, deuterohemin, and hematoporphyrin on hemoglobin synthesis by nuclei from pigeon erythrocytes. They also concluded that porphyrins stimulated amino acid incorporation into globin and suggested that the prosthetic group might be linked to apoprotein synthesis in some regulatory manner. Several investigators have demonstrated that the rates of heme and globin synthesis in the rabbit are nearly equal under a variety of experimental conditions[17,18]. The present studies suggest that heme may be involved in the regulation of hemoglobin synthesis by augmenting the release of the completed molecule from the ribosomes.

ACKNOWLEDGEMENTS

    This investigation was supported in part by grants from the National Heart Institute, U.S. Public Health Service (H-7184) and the John A. Hartford Foundation. One of the authors (T.J.G.) was a predoctoral research fellow, National Institute of Arthritis and Metabolic Diseases, U.S. Public Health Service (5 Tl AM-5229) and the other (H.C.S.) is a John and Mary R. Markle Scholar in Academic Medicine.

REFERENCES

1   R. SCHWEET, H. LAMFROM AND E. ALLEN, Proc. Natl. Acad. Sci. U.S., 44 (1958) 1029.
2   G. VON EHRENSTEIN AND F. LIPMANN, Proc. Natl. Acad. Sci. U.S., 47 (1961) 941.
3   J. BISHOP, J. LEAHY AND R. SCHWEET, Proc. Natl. Acad. Sci. U.S., 46 (1960) 1030.
4   R. SCHWEET AND J. BISHOP, in J. H. TAYLOR, Molecular Genetics, Part 1, Academic Press, New York, 1963, p. 353.
5   H. LAMFROM, J. Mol. Biol., 3 (1961) 241.
6   M. F. PERUTZ, M. G. ROSSMANN, A. F. CULLIS, H. MUIRHEAD, G. WILL AND A. C. T. NORTH, Nature, 185 (1960) 416.
7   M. RABINOVITZ AND M. E. OLSON, Nature, 181 (1958) 1665.
8   H. BORSOOK, C. L. DEASY, A. J. HAAGEN-SMIT, G. KEIGHLEY AND D. H. LOWY, J. Biol. Chem., 196 (1952) 669.
9   E. B. KELLER AND P. C. ZAMECNIK, J. Biol. Chem., 221 (1956) 45.
10 O. H. LOWRY, N. J. ROSEBROUGH, A. L. FARR AND R. J. RANDALL, J. Biol. Chem., 193 (1951) 265.
11 M. GRINSTEIN, J. Biol. Chem., 167 (1947) 515.
12 H. C. SCHWARTZ, G. E. CARTWRIGHT, E. L. SMITH AND M. M. WINTROBE, Blood, 14 (1959) 486.
13 D. NATHANS, Proc. Natl. Acad. Sci. U.S., 51 (1964) 585.
14 T. J. GRIBBLE AND H. C. SCHWARTZ, in preparation.
15 C. L. HAMMEL AND S. P. BESSMAN, J. Biol. Chem., 239 (1964) 2228.
16 C. L. HAMMEL AND S. P. BESSMAN, Federation Proc., 23 (1964) 317.
17 J. KRUH AND H. BORSOOK, J. Biol. Chem., 220 (1956) 905.
18 H. MORELL, J. C. SAVOIE AND I. M. LONDON, J. Biol. Chem., 233 (1958) 923.

Biochim. Biophys. Acta, 103 (1965) 333–338

Reprinted from the Proceedings of the National Academy of Sciences
Vol. 59, No. 2, pp. 582–589. February, 1968.

STIMULATION OF GLOBIN-CHAIN INITIATION BY HEMIN IN THE RETICULOCYTE CELL-FREE SYSTEM*

By William V. Zucker and Herbert M. Schulman

DEPARTMENT OF BIOLOGY, UNIVERSITY OF CALIFORNIA, SAN DIEGO (LA JOLLA)

Communicated by Martin D. Kamen, November 16, 1967

Recent experiments have shown that hemin or heme precursors stimulate globin synthesis in reticulocytes[1,2] and in embryonic tissues,[3,4] and that hemin increases the size and amount of polysomes in reticulocytes from iron-deficient rabbits.[2] It has been proposed that heme causes the release of completed nascent globin chains from the site of their synthesis.[5,6] That this may not be the mechanism is suggested by experiments which show that the main product of a cell-free system from rabbit reticulocytes is a soluble globin dimer which can, in part, be converted to a tetramer by hemin.[7]

Since the original report by Kruh and Borsook[8] showing parallel rates of heme and globin synthesis in rabbit reticulocytes, interest has focused on the mechanism of regulation of hemoglobin synthesis. The idea has been advanced that selective release of globin chains from polysomes provides at least one point for regulating the synthesis of the globin portion of hemoglobin.[9] According to this scheme, α chains are released from polysomes only by β chains and $\alpha\beta$ dimers would constitute a first soluble intermediate, which would then be converted to hemoglobin.[10] Heme plays no role in this proposal.

We here report experimental results with an unfractionated cell-free system from rabbit reticulocytes which suggest that the function of hemin in globin synthesis is not solely in the terminal release of completed nascent chains. The results lead to the hypothesis that heme is specifically involved with an initiation process resulting in continued synthesis of new nascent chains from the amino-terminal valine, and that polysomal integrity is dependent on this function. This suggests a model for the translational control of globin synthesis by heme.

Methods.—Reticulocytes were obtained from rabbits made anemic with phenylhydrazine The cell-free system, prepared according to the proceedure of Lamfrom and Knopf,[11] has already been described.[7] Radioactivity was determined in a liquid scintillation counter with 65% efficiency for C^{14} and 21% for H^3. Total incorporation was determined with globin purified from the unfractionated system. Incorporation into nascent chains was determined with washed material which sedimented at $133,573 \times g$ for 2.5 hr. Incorporation into soluble protein was determined with the remaining supernatant. Polysome profiles were obtained by automatic monitoring of 10–25% linear sucrose gradients which had been centrifuged at $78,700 \times g$ for 3.5 hr in the Spinco SW25.3 rotor. Amino-terminal amino acid determinations were carried out using the three-cycle form of the Edman method[12] and the proceedure described by Blombäck et al.[13]

Results.— (1) *The effect of hemin on cell-free protein synthesis:* Figure 1 shows that 6.4×10^{-5} M hemin extends the period during which protein is synthesized. The effect of hemin is concentration-dependent with maximal stimulation from 3.2×10^{-5} M to 6.4×10^{-5} M. Higher concentrations were not tested. Hemin causes an initial reduction in the rate of synthesis, varying in different experiments, from 80 to 90 per cent of the rate of synthesis in the absence of hemin.

The amount of increased synthesis in the presence of hemin is variable and ranges from about 100 to 300 per cent.

It has been found that during storage at $0°C$ lysates lose their potential for stimulation by hemin much more rapidly than their protein-synthesizing ability, a fact which may account for the variability, since hemin may be interacting with a very labile component of the cell-free system.

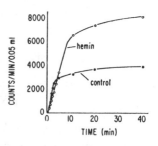

FIG. 1.—Effect of hemin on cell-free protein synthesis.

The specificity of hemin stimulation has been tested in various ways. Table 1 compares the effects of iron, protoporphyrin, and hemin in various combinations on the initial rate of amino acid incorporation and the total amount of incorporation at 20 minutes. In this experiment the initial rate lasted for three minutes in the absence of hemin and for ten minutes in its presence. Protoporphyrin ($6.4 \times 10^{-5}\ M$) had little effect with or without iron present. Iron was initially inhibitory[14] and strongly antagonized the stimulation by hemin. Hemin at various concentrations, including that used in the reticulocyte cell-free system, did not stimulate protein synthesis in cell-free systems derived from rabbit liver and regenerating rat liver. Thus it appears that hemin, and not protoporphyrin or iron, specifically stimulated protein synthesis only in a system whose major product was globin chains.

TABLE 1. *A comparison of the effects on protein synthesis of iron, protoporphyrin IX, and hemin in various combinations.*

	Per Cent Minus Hemin	
	Relative specific activity at 2 min	Relative amount protein synthesized in 20 min
− Hemin	100	100
+ Hemin	88	325
− Hemin + Fe^{++}	70	124
+ Hemin + Fe^{++}	90	142
+ Protoporphyrin IX	108	136
+ Protoporphyrin IX + Fe^{++}	80	116
+ Hemin + protoporphyrin IX	88	349

Four ml of the complete cell-free system containing 3 μc of the uniformly labeled C^{14}-amino acid mixture (sp. act. ~1 mc/mg) was incubated in the presence of the above additions for various times. Aliquots of 0.05 ml were removed and radioactivity in total protein determined as described in *Methods*. All concentrations were $6.4 \times 10^{-5}\ M$.

(2) *The effect of hemin on polysomes:* Figure 2 shows the effect of hemin in the cell-free system on the accumulation and disappearance of polysomes. It is apparent that the presence of hemin results in an increase in the proportion of polysomes to $80S$ material and stabilizes the aggregates. In the absence of hemin, complete polysome disaggregation occurs between 5 and 7 minutes, while in the presence of hemin, the polysomes are stabilized for more than 45 minutes. Hemin is not acting as a nuclease inhibitor because polysomes from a cell-free system containing hemin are as sensitive to small amounts of ribonuclease ($1\ μg/ml$) as are those from a control lysate.

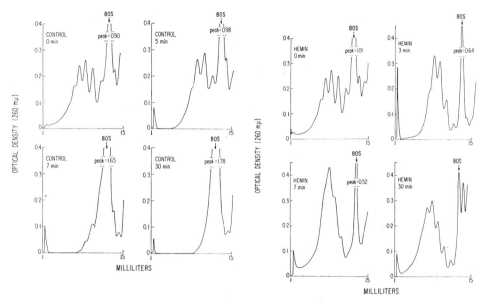

FIG. 2.—Effect of hemin on polysome distribution in the cell-free system.

(3) *The effect of hemin on the incorporation of radioactive amino acid into nascent and soluble protein:* To determine where hemin affected protein synthesis, the kinetics of incorporation of a radioactive amino acid into nascent and soluble protein was measured. A comparison of the specific activities of the nascent and soluble fractions in the presence and absence of hemin is shown in Figure 3.

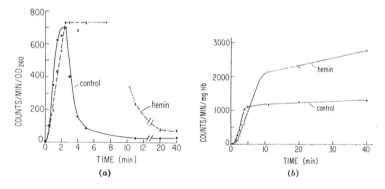

FIG. 3.—Effect of hemin on the incorporation of C[14]-amino acids into nascent chains (a) and soluble protein (b).

With or without hemin, polysomes, after a short lag, became almost equally saturated with radioactivity, but in the presence of hemin the polysomes remained saturated for a much longer time. In the absence of hemin, nascent chain release was rapid and almost complete, with 3–10 per cent of the nascent chains remaining associated with the ribosomal material (in the presence of hemin as much as 15% remained after 40 min). The remaining nascent radioactivity

TABLE 2. *The specific activities of the soluble protein and the amino-terminal valine in the presence and absence of hemin.*

| | Minus Hemin | | Plus Hemin | | | Sp. act. of amino-terminal amino acid |
	Cpm/mg hemoglobin	Cpm/μmole amino-term. amino acid	Cpm/mg hemoglobin	Cpm/μmole amino-term. amino acid	Sp. act. of protein (+ H/− H)	(+ H/− H)
Globin	26,002	8,890	76,531	25,421	2.99	2.87
α-Chains	13,725	—	34,220	—	2.49	—
β-Chains	29,076	—	65,077	—	2.24	—

One ml of the complete cell-free system was incubated for 60 min in the presence and absence of hemin with 25 μc of [C14] uniformly labeled amino acid mixture (see below). Globin was purified from each and split into α and β chains. The specific activities were determined as described in *Methods*. Protein concentration was determined by a ninhydrin assay after hydrolysis of the protein for 24 hr in 6 N HCl at 105°.

Amino acid mixture (in a total of 1000 μc): L-Ala, 80 μc; L-Arg, 70 μc; L-Asp, 80 μc; L-Glu, 125 μc; Gly, 40 μc; L-His, 15 μc; L-Ileu, 140 μc; L-lys, 60 μc; L-Phe, 80 μc; L-Pro, 50 μc; L-Ser, 40 μc; L-Thr, 50 μc; L-Tyr, 50 μc; L-Val, 80 μc.

was not bound, charged sRNA because it was not solubilized by hot trichloroacetic acid (TCA). The results show that hemin stimulated continued synthesis of nascent chains.

It appears that hemin has an effect on the incorporation of amino acids into total and soluble protein which may be attributed to a reduced rate of nascent chain release.

(4) *Evidence for increased globin-chain initiation in the presence of hemin:* De novo synthesis of α and β chains has been previously demonstrated in this cell-free system.[15] To determine whether hemin stimulates initiation of new globin chains, from the amino-terminal valine of both α and β chains as opposed to random initiation along the peptide chain, the radioactive-soluble product of the cell-free system incubated in the presence and absence of hemin was subjected to amino-terminal analysis by the Edman procedure.[12, 13] Table 2 summarizes the results from an experiment in which a mixture of C14- amino acids was used as the radioactive tracer. In the amino acid mixture, valine accounted for 8 per cent of the total radioactivity (see Table 2). In this experiment, the α and β chains were separated and their specific activities determined (Fig. 4). The effect of hemin on both the specific activities of the purified globin, α and β chains, and

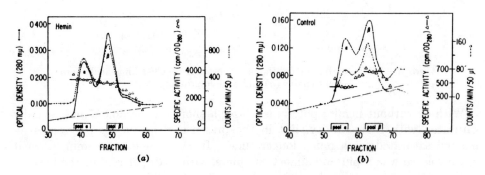

FIG. 4.—Carboxymethylcellulose chromatography[25] of globin from the cell-free system incubated in the presence (a) and absence (b) of hemin.

the amino-terminal phenyl thiohydantoin (PTH) derivative from the purified globin was determined.   It can be seen that the specific activity of the amino-terminal amino acid of the purified globin was increased in the presence of hemin and was about equal to the increased specific activity of the globin itself.   When the α and β chains were analyzed separately, it was found that hemin affected their syntheses to about the same extent, although it is apparent that approximately twice as many β chains were synthesized as were α chains, assuming no dilution of the specific activity of the latter by a free pool of α chains.[16]   There was a loss of some protein, in the step between purified globin and the purified α and β chains, since both the specific activities and the $+H/-H$ ratio decreased significantly.   Nevertheless, the radioactive protein synthesized in the presence of hemin was chromatographically identical to α and β chains.

Sufficient radioactive amino acids were added so that the amino-terminal amino acid of the purified globin could be identified by paper chromatography. The only radioactive amino-terminal amino acid detected was valine.

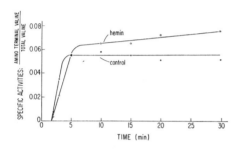

Fig. 5.—The ratio of amino-terminal C^{14}-valine to total C^{14}-valine incorporated into soluble protein in the presence and absence of hemin.

Since both the α and β chains of rabbit hemoglobin contain valine in the amino-terminal position, it is clear that hemin is not involved with random initiation of peptide chains, unless it be specifically at valine sites along the chain. Evidence that suggests this is not the case was obtained by calculating the ratios of the specific activities of amino-terminal valine to total valine incorporated in the presence and absence of hemin.   Since Figure 5 shows that this ratio does not exceed 0.083 (the value obtained from rabbit hemoglobin uniformly labeled with valine) in the presence of hemin, it seems unlikely that hemin caused chain initiation at internal valine residues of the globin chains.

(5) *Effects of puromycin and NaF on the stabilization of polysomes by hemin:* The ability of hemin to prolong cell-free protein synthesis by allowing increased chain initiation from the amino-terminal valine of both α and β chains has been shown directly and is accompanied by a pronounced stabilization of polysomes. Since initiation of α and β chains is not dependent on the existence of polysomes,[15] it seemed reasonable to determine whether hemin-mediated polysome stabilization was a result of, or a cause of, the observed increased chain initiation.   To determine this, the cell-free system was incubated in the presence of the two inhibitors of protein synthesis, puromycin and NaF.   Puromycin is known to inhibit both *in vivo*[17] and *in vitro*[18] protein synthesis by causing premature release of nascent polypeptide chains.   NaF, on the other hand, inhibits protein synthesis in the reticulocyte cell-free system by preventing chain initiation, resulting

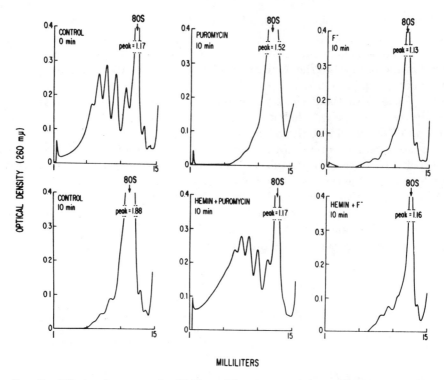

FIG. 6.—Effects of puromycin, NaF, and hemin on polysome distribution in the cell-free system.

in an inability to form the first peptide bond[19] but not the formation of internal peptide bonds.[20]   It has also been postulated that NaF inhibits the binding of mRNA to ribosomes.[21]

Table 3 shows that $1.4 \times 10^{-4}\ M$ puromycin completely inhibited protein

TABLE 3.   *Effect of puromycin and NaF on cell-free protein synthesis in the presence and absence of hemin.*

Expt.		Specific Activity (cpm/mg hemoglobin) of Soluble Protein	
		− Hemin	+ Hemin
1*	− Puromycin	1096	2493
	+ Puromycin ($1.4 \times 10^{-4}\ M$	<10	<10
2†	− NaF	2289	5030
	+ NaF ($1 \times 10^{-2}\ M$)	363	356

* A cell-free system containing 0.7 μc/ml of C^{14} uniformly labeled amino acid mix was incubated for 15 min in the presence and absence of hemin as indicated.
† A cell-free system containing 5.5 μc/ml of C^{14}-valine (sp. act. 267 mc/mmole) was incubated for 15 min in the presence and absence of hemin as indicated. The specific activity of the soluble protein was determined as described in *Methods*.

synthesis, whether or not hemin was present.   Nevertheless, as shown in Figure 6, polysomes were stabilized by hemin in the presence of puromycin.   In contrast to puromycin, NaF partially inhibited protein synthesis and hemin was without effect on this inhibition or on polysome disaggregation.

These results suggest that the hemin effect probably involves the formation of the first peptide bond. Furthermore, if the postulated mode of action of puromycin is correct, these results also demonstrate that premature release of nascent chains does not affect polysome stability, and thus the effect of hemin on polysome stability cannot depend solely on nascent chain release.

Discussion.—The reason for using an unfractionated reticulocyte cell-free system to investigate the control of hemoglobin synthesis rests on the finding that, in this system, extensive *de novo* synthesis of both α- and β-globin chains occurs. This is not the case for the totally fractionated system.[11] When hemin is added to the unfractionated system, it produces effects similar to those observed with whole reticulocytes.

It. has been demonstrated that the increased synthesis of protein in the presence of hemin is accompanied by a corresponding increase in the initiation of α- and β-globin chains from their amino-terminal valine residues, thus excluding the possibility that hemin acts nonspecifically.

In the absence of hemin, release of nascent chains is almost complete with a concomitant disaggregation of polysomes to 80S monomers. Hemin extends the period of nascent chain synthesis and polysome integrity. These two effects have been dissociated by the use of two different inhibitors of protein synthesis. When nascent chains are released prematurely from polysomes by the action of puromycin, hemin-mediated polysome stabilization is still observed. When protein synthesis is blocked with NaF, which prevents the formation of the first peptide bond, hemin is unable to stabilize the polysomes. These results are compatible with the idea that hemin is involved with a chain initiation process. In conjunction with the observed nascent chain release in the absence of added hemin, it strongly suggests that hemin does not act solely through a chain release mechanism.

Grayzel *et al.*[2] reported that hemin has no effect on the disaggregation of polysomes by puromycin in iron-deficient reticulocytes; and Williamson and Schweet[22] reported an increased rate of polysome disaggregation in the totally fractionated system in the presence of puromycin. The contrary results presented here may be unique for the unfractionated cell-free system. Nevertheless, this positive result is in accord with a function for hemin in chain initiation.

The possibility is raised that heme may play a direct role in regulating the translation of globin messenger RNA. A mechanism which would require heme for the initiation of globin messenger RNA translation would explain why heme and globin synthesis are coupled in reticulocytes, since heme biosynthesis is feedback inhibited by free heme.[23]

Although it has been demonstrated that hemin stimulates chain initiation, it is nonetheless clear that chain initiation can occur in this cell-free system in the absence of exogenous hemin. Thus, an obligatory dependence of chain initiation on hemin has not been demonstrated. It is possible that the existence of very small pools of free heme, or the availability of heme from hemoglobin[24] may suffice to explain the *de novo* synthesis observed in the absence of exogenous hemin.

It is possible that the increased chain initiation and the preservation of the polysomes caused by hemin are specifically related. Polysomes may be stabilized because increased initiation, involving heme, and ribosomal attachment to polysomes are mutually dependent.

The authors are grateful to Dr. R. F. Doolittle for his generous assistance in our amino-terminal analyses.

* This work was supported by a grant from the U.S. Public Health Service (AM 08250). William V. Zucker was supported by U.S. Public Health Service predoctoral traineeship (no. 2 TO1-GM 00702-07).

[1] Bruns, G. P., and I. M. London, *Biochem. Biophys. Res. Commun.*, 18, 236 (1965).

[2] Grayzel, A. I., P. Hörchner, and I. M. London, these PROCEEDINGS, 55, 650 (1966).

[3] Levere, R. D., and S. Granick, *J. Biol. Chem.*, 242, 1903 (1967).

[4] Wainwright, S. D., and L. K. Wainwright, *Can. J. Biochem.*, 45, 344 (1967).

[5] Cline, A. L., and R. M. Bock, in *Cold Spring Harbor Symposia on Quantitative Biology*, vol. 31 (1966), p. 321.

[6] Gribble, T. J., and H. C. Schwartz, *Biochim. Biophys. Acta*, 103, 333 (1965).

[7] Zucker, W. V., and H. M. Schulman, *Biochim. Biophys. Acta*, 138, 400 (1967).

[8] Kruh, J., and H. Borsook, *J. Biol. Chem.*, 220, 905 (1956).

[9] Baglioni, C., and B. Colombo, in *Cold Spring Harbor Symposia on Quantitative Biology*, vol. 29 (1964), p. 347.

[10] Felicetti, L., B. Colombo, and C. Baglioni, *Biochim. Biophys. Acta*, 129, 380 (1966).

[11] Lamfrom, H., and P. M. Knopf, *J. Mol. Biol.*, 9, 558 (1964).

[12] Edman, P., *Ann. N.Y. Acad. Sci.*, 88, 602 (1960).

[13] Blombäck, B., M. Blombäck, P. Edman, and B. Hessel, *Biochim. Biophys. Acta*, 115, 371 (1966).

[14] Van Stone, J., R. O. Coleman, and P. Heller, *Nature*, 210, 843 (1966).

[15] Lamfrom, H., and P. M. Knopf, *J. Mol. Biol.*, 11, 589 (1965).

[16] Shaeffer, J. R., *Biochem. Biophys. Res. Commun.*, 28, 647 (1967).

[17] Allen, D. W., and D. C. Zamecnik, *Biochim. Biophys. Acta*, 55, 865 (1962).

[18] Morris, A., R. Arlinghaus, S. Favelukes, and R. Schweet, *Biochemistry*, 2, 1084 (1963).

[19] Lin, S., R. D. Mosteller, and B. Hardesty, *J. Mol. Biol.*, 21, 51 (1966).

[20] Ravel, J. M., R. D. Mosteller, and B. Hardesty, these PROCEEDINGS, 56, 701 (1966).

[21] Dreyfus, J. C., and G. Shapira, *Biochim. Biophys. Acta*, 129, 601 (1966).

[22] Williamson, A. R., and R. Schweet, *J. Mol. Biol.*, 11, 358 (1965).

[23] Karibian, D., and I. M. London, *Biochem. Biophys. Res. Commun.*, 18, 243 (1965).

[24] Bunn, H. F., and J. H. Jandl, these PROCEEDINGS, 56, 974 (1966).

[25] Beard, N. S., and S. A. Armentrout, these PROCEEDINGS, 58, 750 (1967).

European J. Biochem. 2 (1967) 480—492

α-Chain and Globin: Intermediates in the Synthesis of Rabbit Hemoglobin

C. Baglioni and T. Campana

Laboratorio Internazionale di Genetica e Biofisica, Napoli

(Received May 20, 1967)

The synthesis of hemoglobin by rabbit reticulocytes has been studied by means of pulse-labelling and chase experiments. The reticulocyte lysate was fractionated into a top layer and a ribosomal fraction. The top layer was analysed by gel filtration on columns of Sephadex G-75. At least two intermediates which were formed after short incubations and were chased into hemoglobin were separated by gel filtration. These intermediates have been identified with α chain and globin.

α Chain and globin have also been separated by chromatography on carboxymethyl-Sephadex. This method of analysis has been used to measure the rate of appearance of these intermediates in the top layer fraction and their rate of removal in chase experiments. The presence of complete α chains on polyribosomes has been confirmed. The rate of appearance of α chains on polyribosomes and their rate of removal in chase experiments have been determined. These rates appear to be identical, suggesting that the same biosynthetic process is responsible for these rates.

The nature of the complete α chains present on polyribosomes has been investigated. These chains can be separated from peptidyl-tRNA chains by gel filtration in a sodium dodecyl sulphate-acetate buffer. This finding suggests that the complete chains are not bound to tRNA.

The experimental results support the following scheme of assembly of the hemoglobin molecule: α chains are released from polyribosomes on completion. These chains combine with β chains which are still being synthesized on polyribosomes and for this reason complete α chains are found on polyribosomes. αβ Subunits are released from polyribosomes once the synthesis of β chains is completed. The subunits then combine with heme to form hemoglobin molecules. The combination with heme may be stepwise and, in this case, intermediates containing less than one heme every peptide chain are formed. Some evidence for the existence of heme-containing intermediates has been obtained.

The significance of the combination of α chains with β chains at the polyribosome level is discussed. This phenomenon may have some regulatory function which may be of general importance in view of the similar finding that immunoglobulin light chains combine with heavy chains at the polyribosome level and that heavy chains are apparently not released independently from polyribosomes.

The assembly of a protein molecule composed of different types of peptide chains and of prosthetic groups has not so far been investigated in detail. In the present paper, the assembly of one such protein—hemoglobin—has been studied and compounds which appear to be intermediates in the assembly process have been detected.

The synthesis of hemoglobin by reticulocytes appears to be an ideal system for the study of the assembly process, since at least 95% of the protein synthesized by these cells is hemoglobin. Moreover,

the synthesis of the peptide chains of hemoglobin has been studied in detail by Dintzis [1] and other relevant information on the genetic and cytoplasmic control of hemoglobin synthesis has recently become available [2]. Completed α chains have been found to be present on polyribosomes [3,4]; this observation has led to the postulation of some regulatory mechanism at the polyribosome level [3].

Hereditary hematological diseases (α- and β-thalassemia) are known in man, in which either the β or the α peptide chain of hemoglobin respectively is not synthesized in adequate amount [5]. The finding that large amounts of an abnormal hemoglobin made up only of β chains ($β_4$) are present in patients with defective synthesis of α chains shows

---

Non-Standard Abbreviations. Trichloroacetic acid, TCA; sodium dodecyl sulphate, SDS; carboxymethylcellulose, CMC; carboxymethyl-Sephadex, CM-Sephadex.

Emzyme. Ribonuclease (EC 2.7.7.16).

that β chains can be produced and accumulated in the absence of synthesis of α chains [5]. In patients defective in the synthesis of β chains, only traces of a monomeric hemoglobin made up of a single α chain have been found [6]. This suggested that differences between the behavior of the α and the β chain existed, either in the rate of synthesis of one chain in the absence of the other, or in the stability and thus in the survival, of the isolated chains.

The synthesis of the human hemoglobin peptide chains in patients with β-thalassemia has been investigated by several authors [7—10]. They have shown that α chains are synthesized in large excess compared to β chains; however, these α chains are not found in the circulating erythrocytes of these thalassemia patients [7—10]. In some cases, complete absence of β chain synthesis has been observed in patients homozygous for thalassemia [10]. The α chains synthesized by the reticulocytes of thalassemia patients separate in starch gel electrophoresis with monomeric α hemoglobin [9]. These observations suggest that the difference in the behavior of the two peptide chains is not caused by different rates of synthesis but is most likely due to the relative stability and survival of the chains.

Once it has become clear that both hemoglobin chains can be synthesized independently of each other, the presence of completed α chains on polyribosomes cannot be explained by the regulatory mechanism previously suggested [3]. The present investigation has aimed at studying the synthesis of hemoglobin in a system in which the two chains are produced at equal rates and at discovering which compounds are intermediates in the assembly process. In a previous report, it was shown that heme does not appear to bind to the hemoglobin chains while these are being synthesised on polyribosomes and that, in the absence of heme synthesis, globin accumulates in reticulocytes [11]. These observations indicated that globin may be an intermediate in the synthesis of hemoglobin, but more direct evidence was needed to substantiate these findings. This evidence has been sought by means of pulse and of chase experiments on hemoglobin synthesis, providing a more comprehensive picture of the steps in the process of assembly of the hemoglobin molecule.

MATERIALS AND METHODS

Preparation and Incubation of Reticulocytes with ^{14}C-Labelled Amino Acids

Reticulocytes were obtained from phenylhydrazine-injected rabbits and washed with special saline as previously described [12]. The washed reticulocytes were incubated for 15 min at 37° in an equal volume of special saline containing 0.60 mg of glucose, 0.36 mg of $NaHCO_3$ and 0.24 mg of $Fe(NH_4)_2$

$(SO_4)_2$ per ml; in addition, 0.1 ml of an amino acid solution containing tryptophane, histidine and cysteine in the proportions indicated by Borsook et al. [13] was added per ml of reticulocytes. 1 μC of ^{14}C-labelled amino acids (0,666 μC/mg U.L. Mixture, New England Nuclear) were added per ml of reticulocytes and samples removed at different times. An equal volume of cold amino acid solution [13] was added in chase experiments, as indicated in the legends of the figures. Ten volumes of cold special saline were added to each sample to stop the incubation, and the reticulocytes were centrifuged at $1000 \times g$ in the cold.

Sucrose Density Gradients

Each sample was lysed by the addition of an equal volume of 0.0015 M $MgCl_2$ and diluted with three volumes of 0.01 M tris/HCl pH 7.5, 0.01 M KCl and 0.0015 M $MgCl_2$ (standard buffer). After centrifugation at $17,000 \times g$ for 15 min, the clear supernatants were layered on 15—30% sucrose density gradients prepared in standard buffer. The gradients were centrifuged at 24,000 rev./min for three hours in the SW 25 rotor of a Spinco Model L ultracentrifuge. 6 ml of the hemoglobin-containing top layer were removed from the top of the gradient and stored in the cold for further analysis. The colorless portion of the gradient (approximately 15 ml) was separated by piercing the bottom of the tube with a hypodermic needle and was collected into a flask set in ice. This last fraction was contrifuged for 15 hours at 22,000 rev./min in the Spinco 30 rotor; the pellets obtained were stored frozen for further analysis.

Analysis of the Top Layer

An aliquot of the top layer obtained from the gradient was analyzed for absorbance at 563 mμ and for counts/min incorporated into trichloroacetic acid precipitable material. Two equal portions of this top layer were analyzed on a column of Sephadex G-75 (2 cm × 100 cm) in 0.01 M phosphate, 0.001 M KCN, 0.1 M NaCl, pH 7.5. This column had been calibrated with blue dextran, rabbit hemoglobin, rabbit globin and α chain (Fig. 1). One portion of the top layer was analysed directly; hemin was added to the other portion as described previously [14]. Fractions of about 5 ml each were collected; the absorbance at 563 mμ and the amount of radioactivity present as TCA-precipitable material were determined. In some experiments, certain fractions were pooled and dialysed overnight in the cold against Dintzis starting buffer and α and β chains separated as previously described [1] after the addition of carrier globin. The fractions were analyzed for absorbance at 280 mμ and counts/min incorporated.

A third portion of the top layer was passed through small columns of CM-Sephadex C-50 in

0.01 M phosphate buffer pH 6.8 containing 100 mg of KCN per litre; the columns (4 mm × 30 mm) were kept in the cold during elution. The columns were eluted with 4 volumes of phosphate buffer pH 6.8 containing 100 mg of KCN per litre, with 5 volumes of 0.01 M phosphate buffer pH 7.9 containing 100 mg of KCN per litre and with 5 volumes of 0.05 M veronal buffer pH 8.6 containing 50 mg of hemin per litre. Each of these eluents was analysed for counts/min incorporated; absorbance at 563 mμ was determined for the 7.9 eluent. In some experiments, the

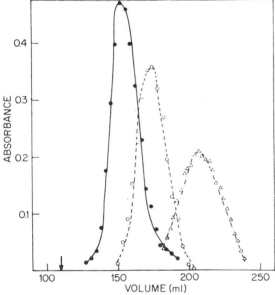

Fig. 1. *Gel filtration of hemoglobin, globin and α-hemoglobin on Sephadex G-75. α*-Hemoglobin was prepared as previously described [14]. The proteins were localised by measuring their absorbance at 563 mμ for hemoglobin (●), at 280 mμ for globin (○) and at 410 mμ for α-hemoglobin (△). The arrow indicates the point of elution of blue dextran

eluents at pH 6.8 and at pH 7.9 were also analysed by gel filtration on Sephadex G-75, as described above.

Analysis of the Polyribosome Fractions

The polyribosome pellets obtained by centrifugation of the colorless portion of the gradients were resuspended in 2 ml of standard buffer; an aliquot of 0.1 ml was removed for determination of absorbance at 260 mμ and of counts/min incorporated into TCA-precipitable material. The remainder of the fraction was digested for one hour at room temperature with 15 μg of ribonuclease; after digestion one-tenth volume of Dintzis limit buffer [1] and 40 mg of carrier globin were added to each sample. The α and β peptide chains were then separated as pre-

viously described [1]; absorbance at 280 mμ was determined for each fraction. The fractions containing each of the peptide chains were then pooled and precipitated with TCA. Each sample was washed once with 5% (w/v) TCA, with ethanol—ether (1:1, v/v) and with ether. After drying, a weighed amount of each chain was dissolved in formic acid and the counts/min incorporated were determined.

Analysis of Reticulocytes Incubated with [59]Fe

Washed reticulocytes (2.5 ml) were incubated in an equal volume of special saline containing 0.60 mg of glucose and 0.36 mg of $NaHCO_3$; one-tenth volume of an amino acid solution [13] was added. After 45 min at 37°, 10 μC of [59Fe] ferrous ascorbate (3.5 mC/mg carrier free isotope obtained from Amersham, England) in saline was added; samples were removed at various times before and after chase with $Fe(NH_4)_2(SO_4)_2$, added to a final concentration of 0.005 M. The reaction was stopped by the addition of ten volumes of cold special saline to the samples. After centrifugation of the cells at $1000 \times g$, the reticulocytes were lysed with three volumes of standard buffer and centrifuged at $17,000 \times g$ for 15 min. The clear lysate was then centrifuged for 2 hours at 39,000 rev./min in the Spinco 40.2 rotor. The supernatant was analysed on Sephadex G-75 as described above.

Analysis of Polyribosome-bound Peptide Chains

2.5 ml of washed reticulocytes were incubated for 30 min at 37° with one tenth volume of cold amino acid mixture [13] from which either arginine or valine was omitted. 5 μC of [14C]arginine or [14C]-valine were then added for three min. In some experiments, reticulocytes were incubated for 3 min with 14C-labelled amino acids as described above. Polyribosomes were then prepared by sucrose density gradient centrifugation as described previously [3]. A column (2.5 cm × 90 cm) of Sephadex G-100 in bead form was equilibrated with 0.05% (w/v) sodium dodecyl sulphate 0.1 M ammonium acetate pH 4.8 (SDS-acetate buffer) and kept at 10° [15]. The polyribosomes to be analysed were resuspended in 0.1 ml of standard buffer, and 2.4 ml of SDS-acetate buffer were added before applying to the Sephadex column. Five ml fractions were collected and analysed for absorbance at 260 mμ and counts/min. Fractions corresponding to a peak were pooled.

In experiments where reticulocytes were incubated with [14C]arginine, 20 mg of carrier rabbit globin and globin uniformly labelled with [3H]arginine [3] were added, in the proportion of approximately 20 counts/min of 3H for each counts/min of 14C. The protein was then precipitated with TCA and washed with alcohol—ether (1:1, v/v) and ether.

The dried protein was digested with trypsin and analysed by high voltage ionophoresis as previously described [3]. The spots corresponding to the arginine-containing peptides αT4, αT10 and αT14 were eluted and counted in a Packard Tri-Carb counter model 4312. Pooled fractions of [^{14}C]arginine labelled polyribosomes separated by gel filtration in SDS-acetate buffer were also analyzed by centrifugation in 5—20% (w/v) sucrose density gradients; the sucrose was prepared in SDS-acetate buffer. Gradients were centrifuged for 8 hours at 24,000 rev./min in the Spinco SW 25.2 rotor at 10°. Fractions were collected and analysed as described above.

RESULTS

Analysis of Reticulocyte Lysates by Gel-Filtration

Gel filtration on columns of Sephadex G-75 separates hemoglobin from globin and from α chain (Fig. 1). When reticulocyte lysates were prepared after a short incubation with ^{14}C-labelled amino acids (1 to 2 min at 37°) and analysed by gel filtration, the presence of at least three components of ^{14}C activity with R_F corresponding to those of hemoglobin, globin and α chain was detected. However, the peaks of ^{14}C activity were incompletely separated and were not clearly identified from the chromatographic profile (Fig. 2A).

The addition of hemin to the lysate immediately prior to the gel filtration analysis caused the disappearance of the peak with an intermediate R_F value (peak 2, Fig. 2). This seemed to support the idea that globin was present in the reticulocyte lysate and that the addition of hemin caused the conversion of globin into hemoglobin. An increase of the ^{14}C activity present in the hemoglobin peak (peak 1, Fig. 2) corresponding to the decrease of the ^{14}C activity of peak 2 was demonstrated (Fig. 2B). In addition, analysis of this peak by chromatography on carboxymethyl cellulose using the method of Dintzis [1] indicated that the ^{14}C activity was distributed between the α and β peptide chains. The peak with the lowest R_F (peak 3, Fig. 2) was identified with α chain by analysing the corresponding fractions by chromatography on CMC according to Dintzis [1]. This method of analysis separates α from β chains almost completely. The ^{14}C activity of the fractions analysed was found almost exclusively in the α chain peak (Fig. 3A).

α Globin and α hemoglobin, prepared as previously described [14] were analysed by gel filtration on Sephadex G-75; it was found that both had the same R_F value. It could not thus be established from the gel filtration analysis of the reticulocyte lysate whether heme was bound or not to the free α chains present.

Kinetic Analysis of Reticulocyte Lysates

In order to establish the sequence of events in the synthesis and assembly of the hemoglobin molecule, chase experiments were devised. After a short incubation in the presence of ^{14}C-labelled amino acids, an excess of cold amino acids was added and samples were taken at different times. The lysates obtained

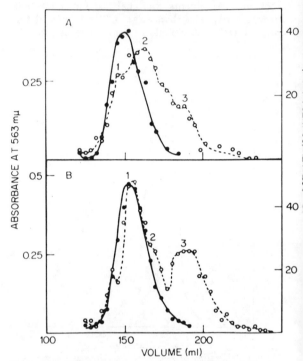

Fig. 2. Gel filtration analysis on Sephadex G-75 of the top layer fraction obtained from reticulocytes incubated for 2 min and 15 sec with ^{14}C-labelled amino acids and chased for 30 sec with cold amino acids. 1 ml of reticulocytes was incubated as described in Methods with 1 μC of ^{14}C-labelled amino acids. The cells were lysed and the lysate fractionated by sucrose density gradient centrifugation. The top layer of the gradient was divided into two 3 ml fractions: (A) analysis of the sample with no addition; (B) analysis of the sample after addition of hemin as decribed in the text. ●, Absorbance at 563 mμ; ○, radioactivity

were then fractionated into a ribosomal and a top layer fraction and the distribution of the ^{14}C activity in these two fractions was determined (Fig. 4).

As may be expected, the TCA-precipitable ^{14}C activity appeared at first in the ribosomal fraction and then in the top layer fraction. TCA-precipitable counts were chased from the ribosomal fraction by the addition of the cold amino acids and the ^{14}C activity of the top layer fraction levelled off 2 min after the chase. This showed clearly that the chase prevented further incorporation of ^{14}C-labelled

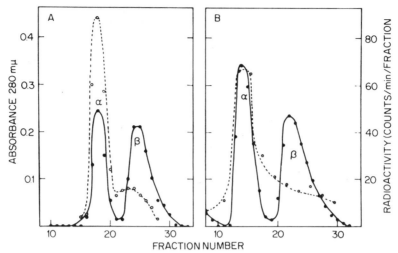

Fig. 3. *Separation of α and β chains by chromatography on carboxymethylcellulose according to Dintzis [1]. (A) Separation of the fraction eluted between 180 and 210 ml from Sephadex G-75 in the experiment shown in Fig. 2 B. (B) Separation of the fraction eluted at pH 6.8 from carboxymethyl-Sephadex as described in Methods. The top layer fraction separated on CM-Sephadex in this experiment was obtained from 0.25 ml of reticulocytes incubated for 2 min with 0.25 μC of 14C-labelled amino acids and chased for 1 min with cold amino acids as described in Methods.* ●, Absorbance at 280 mμ; ○, radioactivity

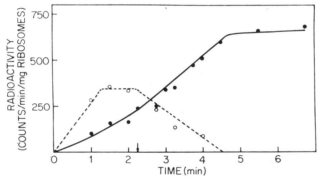

Fig. 4. *Distribution with time of specific activity in polyribosomes and top layer fraction of samples taken after different times of incubation.* 5 ml of reticulocytes were incubated with 5 μC of 14C-labelled amino acids and chased with cold amino acids as described under Methods. Aliquots corresponding to 0.5 ml of reticulocytes were taken at various times, lysed and separated by sucrose density gradient centrifugation into top layer and polyribosome fraction as described in Methods. The time of addition of cold amino acids for the chase is indicated by an arrow. Solid line, specific activity of the top layer fraction; dotted line, specific activity of the polyribosomes. To calculate the specific activity of the top layer fraction the counts/min present were divided by the mg of polyribosomes that were obtained from the corresponding lysates. The mg of polyribosomes were calculated from the absorbance at 260 mμ of an aliquot of the pellets obtained as described under Methods; the extinction coefficent of reticulocyte ribosomes has been taken from Ts'o and Vinograd [22]

amino acids. This incubation system seemed thus suitable for the study of the components intermediate in the synthesis of the hemoglobin molecule separated by Sephadex G-75 gel filtration.

Analysis of the top layer of lysates taken at different times after the chase showed a gradual decrease of the 14C activity not associated with the hemoglobin peak and a gradual increase of the 14C activity of the hemoglobin peak. After a 5 min chase, practically all the 14C activity was found in the hemoglobin peak. This shows the intermediary nature of the components which are separated from hemoglobin by gel filtration, since all the counts are chased into the final product of the assembly process.

In order to measure the intermediate components at different times before and after the chase, a quantitative method of analysis was devised. The incomplete separation of the peaks by gel filtration on Sephadex G-75 did not allow accurate measurement of different components. Carboxymethyl Sephadex (CM-Sephadex) was therefore used to separate α chain from hemoglobin and from globin. These proteins were eluted in this order when the lysate was applied to a CM-Sephadex column. α Chain was not adsorbed at pH 6.8 by the CM-Sephadex, whereas hemoglobin, which is adsorbed, was then eluted at pH 7.9. Globin was eluted at pH 8.6 by a hemin containing buffer (see Methods). It was found that the yield of globin eluted from the column was poor if the eluting buffer contained no hemin. Even when the buffer contained hemin, the yield of globin, as judged by comparison with the results of gel filtration analysis, was not as good as that of α chain and hemoglobin.

This method of analysis separated the lysates into three fractions. The first fraction was analyzed by chromatography, on CM-cellulose, which separates the α and β chain of hemoglobin. ^{14}C activity was found only in the α chain peak (Fig. 3 B). This fraction contains also some protein other than hemoglobin, since other proteins present in the reticulocyte lysate are not retained by CM-Sephadex. However, the largest fraction of the ^{14}C activity is in the α chain, since it is recovered in good yield from the chromatography on CM-cellulose. Proteins other than hemoglobin are separated from the globin chains by this chromatography.

Some fractions eluted from CM-Sephadex were also analysed by gel filtration on Sephadex G-75. The pH 6.8 fraction of samples taken immediately before and after the chase gave one peak of ^{14}C activity only, with R_F similar to that of α chain as can be seen by comparison of Fig. 5 A with Fig. 3. This confirmed that most of the ^{14}C activity of this fraction was present in α chain since ^{14}C activity in regions of the chromatogram where proteins other than hemoglobin separated was not detected. The pH 7.9 fraction and the pH 8.6 fraction gave one peak only corresponding to hemoglobin; the addition of hemine to the pH 8.6 buffer changed all the globin into hemoglobin (Fig. 5 B). This behaviour on Sephadex G-75 gel filtration of the fractions separated by chromatography on CM-Sephadex helped to establish their identity.

The lysates obtained at different times before and after the chase were analysed by chromatography on CM-Sephadex (Fig. 6). In the first few minutes of incubation, a large fraction of the ^{14}C activity incorporated is found in the α chain. After the chase, the ^{14}C activity of this fraction levels off to a small percentage of the total ^{14}C activity incorporated.

This small amount of residual ^{14}C activity of the pH 6.8 fraction may possibly be due to the presence, in this fraction, of proteins other than hemoglobin.

The specific activity of hemoglobin rises slowly at first and then more rapidly until 4 to 5 min after the chase it levels off. The ^{14}C activity found in the pH 8.6 fractions did not account for all the ^{14}C activity of the lysate not eluted with the pH 6.8 or 7.9 fractions. This was thought to be caused by a rather poor elution of globin from the CM-Sephadex. When labelled globin was prepared [14] and chroma-

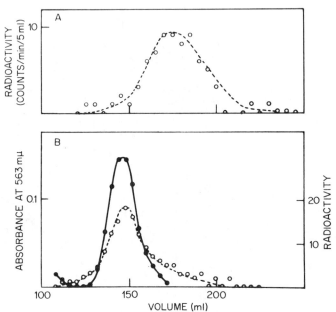

Fig. 5. *Gel filtration analysis on Sephadex G-75 of samples obtained by chromatography on carboxymethyl-Sephadex of the top layer fractions of the lysates obtained from reticulocytes incubated for 2 min with ^{14}C-labelled amino acids and chased for 30 sec with cold amino acids.* 0.25 ml of reticulocytes was incubated for 2 min with 0.25 μC of ^{14}C-labelled amino acids and chased for 30 sec with cold amino acids as described in Methods. The reticulocytes were lysed and the lysate fractionated by sucrose density gradient centrifugation and the top layer fraction chromatographed on carboxymethyl-Sephadex as described in Methods. (A) Analysis of the fraction eluted at pH 6.8; this fraction had practically no absorbance at 280 or 410 mμ and no carrier was added. (B) Analysis of the fraction eluted at pH 7.9; no carrier was added since the hemoglobin present in this fraction acted as a carrier. ●, Absorbance at 563 mμ; ○, radioactivity

tographed under the same conditions, a poor recovery was consistently observed. For this reason the difference between the counts/min of the lysate and those found in the pH 6.8 and 7.9 fraction has been plotted in Fig. 6. If these counts/min are all given by globin, the specific activity of this protein rises after that of the α chain and then levels off.

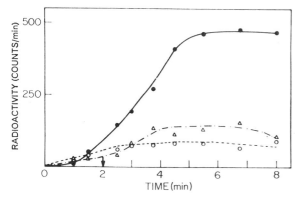

Fig. 6. *Distribution with time of ¹⁴C activity in fractions eluted from carboxymethyl-Sephadex.* 2.5 ml of reticulocytes were incubated with 2.5 μC of ¹⁴C-labelled amino acids and chased with cold amino acids as indicated in Methods. Aliquots corresponding to 0.25 ml of reticulocytes were removed at different times, lysed and fractionated by density gradient centrifugation as described in Methods. The top layer fraction was then chromatographed on small columns of carboxymethyl-Sephadex (see Methods). The arrow indicates the time of addition of cold amino acids for the chase. ●, Counts/min eluted at pH 7.9; this fraction contains the hemoglobin; ○, counts/min eluted at pH 6.8; this fraction contains the α chain; △, counts/min retained on the column; globin is present in this fraction since it is retained on columns of carboxymethyl-Sephadex at pH 7.9

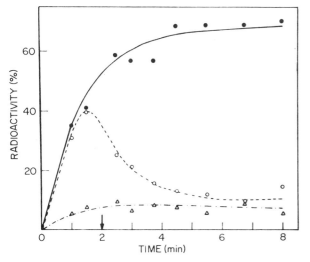

Fig. 7. *Distribution with time of per cent ¹⁴C activity of samples eluted from carboxymethyl-Sephadex.* The experiment is the same as that described in the legend to Fig. 6 (see also text for explanations). The arrow indicates the time of addition of cold amino acids for the chase. ●, Per cent of ¹⁴C activity eluted at pH 7.9; this fraction contains hemoglobin; ○, per cent of ¹⁴C activity eluted at pH 6.8; this fraction contains the α chain; △, per cent ¹⁴C activity eluted at pH 8.6; this fraction contains globin, which was not completely recovered (see text for explanations)

A different presentation of the data obtained in this experiment is shown in Fig. 7. The results are expressed as per cent of the ¹⁴C activity of the lysate present in each fraction. The ¹⁴C activity of the pH 8.6 fraction is shown in this figure. Since the recovery of this fraction is rather poor, the per cent of globin present is underestimated and the total is less than 100%. However, this figures shows even better the intermediary nature of the α chain, which contains a large amount of the counts incorporated in the first minutes and decreases after the chase.

The Search for Intermediates Labelled with ⁵⁹Fe

Having established that some intermediates in the assembly of the hemoglobin molecule do exist and that α chain and globin are presumably among

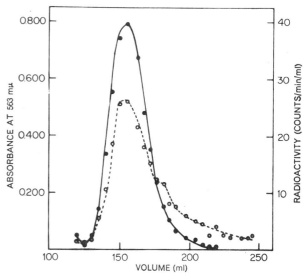

Fig. 8. *Gel filtration analysis on Sephadex G-75 of the 100,000 × g supernatant fraction obtained from reticulocytes incubated with ⁵⁹Fe.* 0.5 ml of reticulocytes were incubated with 2 μC of [⁵⁹Fe]ferrous ascorbate and chased for 30 sec with ⁵⁶Fe(NH₄)₂(SO₄)₂ as described in Methods. The cells were lysed and the lysate centrifuged at 100,000 × g for 2 hours. The supernatant was analyzed by gel filtration on Sephadex G-75 as described in Methods. ●, Absorbance at 563 mμ; ○, counts/min/ml

these, the possibility that some intermediate was formed in the assembly process which contained heme was investigated. A similar experiment (a short incubation followed by a chase) was devised using ⁵⁹Fe to label the heme groups. The lysates obtained were analysed by gel filtration on Sephadex G-75 (Fig. 8).

No indication of intermediates as clear as that obtained by experiments with ¹⁴C-labelled amino acids was obtained by incubating the reticulocytes with ^{59}Fe. The large majority of the ^{59}Fe incorporated was found in the hemoglobin peak in all the samples examined, which were taken before and after the chase with cold iron. However, a shoulder in the profile of the ^{59}Fe activity incorporated was noticed, which followed the hemoglobin peak. This shoulder was more evident in samples taken after a very short incubation. The position of this shoulder in the chromatogram corresponded to that of globin. No ^{59}Fe activity was found in the region of the chromatogram where the α chain separated. This indicated that little or no heme was found in the free α chains. Whether some other intermediate in the assembly process was formed which contained heme was not clearly shown by these experiments, although some indication of the existence of such an intermediate was obtained.

Kinetic Analysis of the Polyribosomes-bound Completed Chains

It has previously been shown that approximately 20% of the labelled protein present on polyribosomes consists of completed α chains [3]. No completed β chains were found to be present on polyribosomes [3]. To establish the function of the completed peptide chains, the polyribosomes were analysed at different times in a chase experiment. The reticulocytes were incubated with ^{14}C-labelled amino acids as in the previous experiment and cold amino acids were added after a short incubation. Samples were taken before and after the chase. The polyribosomes were prepared from each sample as described under Methods and were analysed for the presence of completed α or β chains (Fig. 9).

The method used to analyse the polyribosomes for the presence of labelled completed chains does not distinguish between chains which are completed up to the COOH-terminal amino acid and chains which are nearly completed [16]. The small amount of labelled protein which was found associated with polyribosomes was presumably not due to completed β chains, since it has been previously shown [3] that β chains are not held on polyribosomes once completed, but are immediately released. Completed α chains on the other hand were found to be present on polyribosomes already after a 1 min incubation. The amount of completed α chains on polyribosomes increased in the next minute and then seemed to level off. After the chase, the completed α chains present on polyribosomes decreased; two minutes after the chase very few completed α chains were left on polyribosomes. The rate at which α chains accumulate on polyribosomes seems to be very similar to the rate at which α chains were removed from polyribosomes after the chase. The completed α chains which are present on polyribosomes are thus not stored away but are in a dynamic equilibrium.

The Nature of the Polyribosome-bound Peptide Chains

α Chains were found in the reticulocyte lysate supernatant and on polyribosomes. The α chains found in the supernatant fraction behaved like "native" α chains prepared from rabbit globin [14]. The α chains present on polyribosomes could not be easily studied since these chains could not be removed from polyribosomes by washing. Attempts to isolate the polyribosome-bound chains in a "native" form were thus unsuccessful.

It seemed important to study the nature of the polyribosome-bound peptide chains in order to establish whether they were identical to the α chains present in the top layer fraction and could possibly

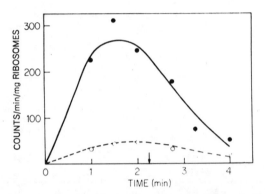

Fig. 9. *Distribution with time of specific activity in polyribosome-bound α and β chains.* 5 ml of reticulocytes were incubated with 5 μC of ^{14}C-labelled amino acids and chased with cold amino acids as described in Methods. Aliquots corresponding to 0.75 ml of reticulocytes were taken at various times, lysed and fractionated by sucrose density gradient centrifugation as described in Methods. The polyribosomes were isolated and analysed for the presence of completed chains as described in Methods. The α and β chains were separated by carboxymethylcellulose chromatography according to Dintzis [1]. The arrow indicates the time of addition of cold amino acids for the chase. ●, Counts/min/mg ribosomes of α chain; ○, counts/min/mg ribosomes of β chain

derive from these chains. To remove the peptide chains from polyribosomes, it was necessary to use an acidic buffer containing the detergent sodium dodecyl sulphate [15]. Gel filtration on Sephadex G-100 in SDS-acetate buffer was then used to separate ribosomal subunits (ribosomes were dissociated in the SDS-acetate buffer) from peptidyl-tRNA [15]. Chromatography by this method of polyribosomes labeled with ^{14}C amino acid mixture or [^{14}C]arginine resulted in the separation of two peaks of ^{14}C activity (Fig. 10). The first peak absorbed strongly at 260 mμ while the second peak had no absorbance associated with the ^{14}C activity. It has been shown that this peak contains peptidyl-tRNA [15].

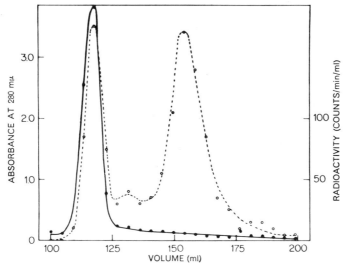

Fig. 10. *Gel filtration analysis on Sephadex G-100 of the peptide chains of polyribosomes labelled with [¹⁴C]arginine.* ●, Absorbance at 260 mμ; ○, counts/min/ml

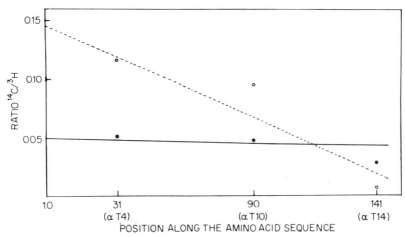

Fig. 11. *¹⁴C/³H ratio of the arginine-containing peptides isolated from the α chains present in the two peaks separated by gel filtration as shown in Fig. 10.* The position of the amino acid residues along the amino acid sequence of the α chain is indicated; in parenthesis the tryptic peptides of the α chain containing the arginines is also indicated. ●, ¹⁴C/³H Ratio of peptides obtained from the first peak; ○, ¹⁴C/³H ratio of peptides from the second peak

The ratio of the specific activity found in the two peaks when the reticulocytes were incubated with ¹⁴C-labelled amino acids or [¹⁴C]valine was found to be markedly different from that observed when the reticulocytes were incubated with [¹⁴C]arginine. The ¹⁴C activity present in the first and second peak was 23 and 77⁰/₀ respectively in experiments with [¹⁴C]-valine and 18 and 82⁰/₀ in experiments with ¹⁴C-labelled amino acids, whereas it was 35 and 65⁰/₀ in the case of reticulocytes incubated with [¹⁴C]arginine. This fact suggested that the peptide chains present in the peaks were in some way different.

The peptide chains of the second peak have been shown to be linked to tRNA molecules in double-labelling experiments in which the tRNA was labelled with ³²P [17]. It was established that peptides chains present in this peak were incomplete chains by analysing the distribution of [¹⁴C]arginine along α chain peptides, according to the method of Dintzis [1]. The peptidyl-tRNA in the second peak was digested with trypsin and the tryptic peptides separated as previously described [3]. Rabbit globin uniformly labelled with [³H]arginine was mixed with the peptidyl-tRNA prior to the tryptic digestion and the ratio $^{14}C/^3H$ evaluated for each peptide. Three arginine-containing peptides are present in the α chain of rabbit hemoglobin. One of these peptides contains the COOH-terminal arginine residue to the α chain. No [^{14}C]arginine was found in this peptide, whereas the other peptides had [^{14}C]arginine in a relative ratio close to that expected (Fig. 11).

When the peptide chains present in the first peak were analysed in the same way, it was found that the $^{14}C/^3H$ ratio in the three peptides of the α chain was relatively constant and did not show the gradient observed with the peptidyl-tRNA chains. This was a clear indication that the peptide chains of the first peak were completed chains; the fact that the COOH-terminal residue of the α-chain was labelled proved that the chains were completed to the last amino acid residue.

The fact that completed α chains separated from incomplete chains bound to tRNA could be taken as an indication that the complete chains were no longer bound to tRNA. The R_f in the gel filtration analysis of the peptidyl-tRNA is determined by the tRNA, rather than by the molecular weight of the complex [15]. However, the complete peptide chains found in the first peak separated together with ribosomal subunits, which formed when the polyribosomes were exposed to the acetate-SDS buffer. The possibility existed that the complete peptide chains were bound tightly to the ribosomal subunits and that they were separated from the peptidyl-tRNA for this reason.

To eliminate this possibility, the material present in the first and second peak was analyzed by sucrose density gradient centrifugation in SDS-acetate buffer. By this method of analysis it was shown that the ^{14}C activity present in the first peak obtained from the Sephadex G-100 column separated from the ribosomal subunits (Fig. 12). These were clearly identified on the basis of their absorption at 260 mμ and of their sedimentation coefficient. The peptidyl-tRNA gave one peak of ^{14}C activity only, with a sedimentation coefficient similar to that given by the completed peptide chains of the first peak and to that of globin which was used as a reference together with ribosomal subunits in a control gradient (Fig. 12).

The results showed that the complete peptide chains were not bound to ribosomal subunits in the SDS-acetate buffer. Attempts to remove the complete chains from intact polyribosomes by washing have so far failed, whereas removal of peptidyl-tRNA by the SDS-acetate buffer caused the release of the complete peptide chains.

DISCUSSION

The experiments described have shown that some intermediates in the synthesis of hemoglobin by rabbit reticulocytes exist. These intermediates have

33*

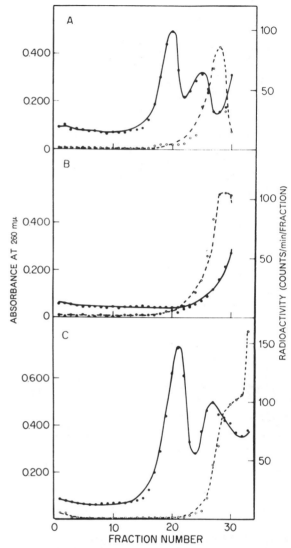

Fig. 12. *Sucrose density gradient centrifugation of the peaks separated by gel filtration on Sephadex G-100 shown in Fig 10.* (A) Peak separated between 110 and 125 ml; (B) peak separated between 145 and 175 ml; (C) control gradient mixture containing polyribosomes obtained from unincubated reticulocytes and U.L.-[^{14}C]globin. ●, Absorbance at 260 mμ; ○, counts/min/fraction

been detected by separating the post-ribosomal supernatant of rabbit reticulocytes pulse-labelled with ^{14}C-labelled amino acids on Sephadex columns. The intermediates in the synthesis of hemoglobin have a very high specific activity after a short incubation; the specific activity decreases in the intermediates after addition of cold amino acids and is chased into hemoglobin. The intermediary nature of the compounds detected has thus been clearly established.

Two of the intermediates have been identified with α globin chains and with globin. The α chains were identified by chromatography on Sephadex, CM-cellulose and CM-Sephadex. The labelled α chains found in the top layer fraction behaved like "native" α chains prepared from rabbit globin. Experiments in which reticulocytes were incubated with ^{59}Fe failed to shown any incorporation of this isotope by the α chains present in the supernatant fraction. No evidence was thus obtained to show that free α chains combine with heme. However, the sensitivity of the method of analysis is not sufficiently high to rule out that some α chains combine with heme while in the supernatant.

Another intermediate in the synthesis of hemoglobin has been identified with globin. The identification is supported by the finding that this intermediate can be changed into hemoglobin by the addition of hemine. Moreover, this intermediate behaved in chromatography on Sephadex, CM-cellulose and CM-Sephadex like rabbit globin. The fact that the combination of the peptide chains of globin with heme does not occur on polyribosomes[11] is a further argument in favour of the intermediary nature of globin in the synthesis of hemoglobin. Moreover, the previous finding that globin accumulates in reticulocytes when heme synthesis is inhibited [11] supports this hypothesis.

The experiments with ^{59}Fe have shown the possible existence of one or more heme-containing intermediates. These compounds have not been investigated in detail; since they are changed into hemoglobin by the addition of hemine, they may be intermediate compounds containing less than one heme group per peptide chain. Three classes of these compounds are to be expected, containing one, two or three heme groups every four globin chains [18]. Winterhalter [18] has shown that by gradual addition of hemine to human globin, three intermediate compounds were formed, which appeared to contain one, two and three heme groups every four globin chains. The formation of the intermediate compound containing two heme groups every four globin chains seemed to be favoured over that of the other intermediate compounds [18]. This intermediate had a molecular weight close to that of hemoglobin, but showed a tendency to dissociate into two subunits when analysed by gel filtration. Since the relative amount of this compound in the supernatant of reticulocyte lysate is extremely small, it seems likely that most of it (if it is formed in the assembly process) is in the form of an $\alpha\beta$ subunit, containing one heme every two peptide chains, and that it separates with globin in gel filtration chromatography. The experiments described have not proved conclusively, however, the existence of this or of other heme-containing intermediates.

The presence of completed α chains on polyribosomes, which has previously been described [3,16], has been confirmed. The completed α chains accumulate on polyribosomes at a characteristic rate during incubation with ^{14}C-labelled amino acids and are removed at the same rate from polyribosomes by a chase with cold amino acids. The time required to observe the maximum amount of α chains on polyribosomes is longer than the average time required to synthesise one peptide chain from the NH_2- to the COOH-terminus; this time has been estimated to be less than 30 sec [19]. This may indicate that the completed α chains present on polyribosomes are not chains which are completed during the incubation and then not released, since less time would be required to get the maximum labelling if one completed chain were retained for each terminal ribosome of polyribosomes synthesising chains. The assumption has been previously made that this mechanism is responsible for the accumulation of α chains on polyribosomes [3].

In view of the finding that free α chains are present in the top layer fraction, the hypothesis that α chains are retained on polyribosomes after they are completed is not longer tenable. Moreover, since a considerable amount of α chains are found in the top layer fraction at a time earlier than that at which the maximum level of complete α chains on polyribosomes is observed, it seems likely that α chains are first released from polyribosomes synthesising α chains and that they then become associated again with polyribosomes. According to this hypothesis, α chains become associated with polyribosomes synthesising β chains. The studies on the complete α chains present on polyribosomes have indicated that these chains are not associated with tRNA. This is compatible with the interpretation that the complete α chains come from a small pool of free α chains and become associated with polyribosomes synthesising β chains. The number of complete α chains present on polyribosomes can be estimated to be slightly less than one chain per polyribosome synthesising β chains. It may thus be thought that α chains become associated with β chains, while these are either almost completed or completed, so that no more than one β chain can interact with an α chain every polyribosome. This means that the β chain must be approximately 120 amino acids long or longer to interact with an α chain. Since a small pool of free α chains is present at all times in reticulocytes, one does not see other factors which may limit the number of complete α chains present on polyribosomes which interact with β chains, except the number of β chains available.

The idea that complete α chains are bound to incomplete β chains is supported by the observation that α chains are accumulated on and chased off the polyribosomes at about the same rate. The factor which determines these rates seems thus to be the same in both cases and it may be identified with the rate of protein synthesis.

The first step in the assembly of the hemoglobin molecule is thus presumably the combination of α chains with β chains at the polyribosome level. Once the β chains are completed they are released together with α chains as $\alpha\beta$ subunits. The failure to observe free β chains in the top layer fraction of reticulocyte lysate is in agreement with the hypothesis that in the normal assembly process of hemoglobin, β chains are only released combined with α chains. If β chains were present in the top layer fraction, these would combine with α chains because of the high affinity of these proteins [14].

The observation that β chains have a higher specific activity than α chains after short incubations [3] may be explained in the following way: the same amount of labelled amino acids is incorporated into α or β chains. The β chains, however, appear immediately in the postribosomal supernatant combined with α chains that were synthesised before the incubation started. At the same time the α chains which are synthesised combine with β chains on polyribosomes and are thus removed from the supernatant fraction. This implies that the pool of free α chains is small, since the α chains combine with β chains on polyribosomes immediately after they are synthesised. The small size of the pool is also shown by the rapid decay of the relative specific activity of α chains in the chase experiment (Fig. 7). The half life of globin seems to be longer, since in chase experiments no sharp decline in relative specific activity comparable to that of the α chain is observed. This is in agreement with the concept that heme synthesis may become a limiting step in hemoglobin synthesis and that globin may accumulate when synthesis of heme is inhibited [11]. The existence and the pool of other intermediates in the assembly of hemoglobin has not been estimated.

The observation which changed our thinking on the assembly of hemoglobin is the discovery that free α chains are short-lived intermediates in the synthesis of hemoglobin. The experiments which were devised to show that α chains are released from polyribosomes in the supernatant as intermediates have been stimulated by different observations. The recent finding that α chains are synthesised in excess by reticulocytes of individuals affected by β-thalassemia [8—10] and the older observation that a small amount of α hemoglobin is detectable in erythrocytes of patients affected by homozygous β-thalassemia [6], were important in directing our attention to the fact that α chains can be synthesised independently of the availability of β chains. The finding that light chains of immunoglobulins (presumably complete, even though this has not been shown as rigorously as for α chains of hemoglobin) are present on poly-

ribosomes synthesising heavy chains was important in providing a parallel example of an assembly process [20—21]. In cells synthesising immunoglobulins, free light chains are always found in large excess. These light chains combine with heavy chains while these are still on polyribosomes [20]. In the case of immunoglobulin chains, this can be easily shown since the polyribosomes synthesising heavy chains are heavier than polyribosomes synthesising light chains [20—21]. Thus, the two classes of polyribosomes can be separated and analysed for the presence of completed light or heavy chains separately. This has not been possible in the case of polyribosomes synthesising hemoglobin chains, since these polyribosomes have equal size. In the case of immunoglobulins, heavy chains are never found free in the supernatant fraction and are thus presumably released only when complexed with light chains. Moreover, individuals affected by myeloma synthesise either both chains of a single immunoglobulin species or one chain only, and, in this case, the chain synthesised and excreted in the urine as Bence Jones protein, is always the light chain. However, in the case of hemoglobin synthesis the β chains can presumably be released from polyribosomes independently, since patients homozygous for α-thalassemia have large amounts of a hemoglobin made up of β chains only. These β chains are apparently released in the absence of an equivalent amount of α chains.

The function of the combination, at the polyribosome level, of one type of chain with the other chains in the assembly of proteins made up of two types of chain is not yet clear. It may be supposed to be a general phenomenon, since it has been observed and clearly documented for two classes of proteins of completely different nature. It may be thought that the combination at the polyribosome level helps to assemble the protein in a correct way and that the rate of assembly may in turn control the rate of release of the protein subunits. This process seems more important in the case of the immunoglobulin chains than in the case of hemoglobin chains. There is no information available, however, on the rate of synthesis and release of β chains in the absence of α chains. The combination at the polyribosome level of the peptide chains of hemoglobin and immunoglobulin, as well as of other proteins, may thus represent a control step in the rate of synthesis of these proteins. Co-operative interactions of the types of peptide chains may be of importance for achieving the correct tridimensional structure and for speeding up in this way the rate of synthesis of one chain. Possibly the combination process may have become a built-in control step to adjust the rate of synthesis of one chain to that of the other chain.

Work carried out under the association Euratom-Consiglio Nazionale delle Ricerche — Comitato Nazionale Energia Nucleare contract No. 012-61-BIAI.

REFERENCES

1. Dintzis, H. M., *Proc. Natl. Acad. Sci. U. S.* 47 (1961) 247.
2. Baglioni, C., *XI Congress of the International Society of Haematology*, (1966) p. 413.
3. Colombo, B., and Baglioni, C., *J. Mol. Biol.* 16 (1966) 51.
4. Weatherall, D. J., Clegg, J. B., and Naughton, M. A., *Nature*, 208 (1965) 1061.
5. Motulsky, A. G., *Cold Spring Harbor Sym. Quant. Biol.* 29 (1964) 399.
6. Fessas, P., Stamatoyamnopoulos, G., and Karaklis, A., *Blood*, 19 (1962) 1.
7. Bank, A., and Marks, P. A., *Nature*, 212 (1966) 1198.
8. Marks, P. A., and Bank, A., *XI Congress of the International Society of Haematology*, (1966) p. 263.
9. Huehns, E. R., and McLoughlin, C. B., *XI Congress of the International Society of Haematology*, (1966) p. 264.
10. Bargellesi, A., Pontremoli, S., and Concini, F., *European J. Biochem.* 1 (1967) 73.
11. Felicetti, L., Colombo, B., and Baglioni, C., *Biochim. Biophys. Acta*, 129 (1966) 380.
12. Colombo, B., Felicetti, L., and Baglioni, C., *Biochem. Biophys. Res. Commun.* 18 (1965) 389.
13. Borsook, H., Deasy, C. L., Haagen-Smit, A. J., Keighley, G., and Lawy, P. H., *J. Biol. Chem.* 196 (1952) 669.
14. Baglioni, C., Campana, T., and Colombo, B., *Arch. Biochem. Biophys.* 117 (1966) 515.
15. Breler, S., Grajevskaja, R., Kirilov, S., Saminiski, E., and Shutov, F., *Biochim. Biophys. Acta*, 123 (1966) 534.
16. Baglioni, C., and Colombo, B., *Cold Spring Harbor Symp. Quant. Biol.* 29 (1964) 347.
17. Baglioni, C., and Campana, T., In preparation.
18. Winterhalter, K. H., *Nature*, 211 (1966) 932.
19. Knopf, P. M., and Lamfrom, H., *Biochim. Biophys. Acta*, 95 (1965) 398.
20. Shapiro, A. L., Scharff, M. D., Maizel, J. V., and Uhr, J. V., *Proc. Natl. Acad. Sci. U. S.* 56 (1966) 216.
21. Williamson, A. R., and Askonas, B. A., *J. Mol. Biol.* 23 (1967) 201.
22. Ts'o P. O. P., and Vinograd, J., *Biochim. Biophys. Acta*, 49 (1961) 113.

C. Baglioni and T. Campana
Laboratorio Internazionale di Genetica e Biofisica
Via Marconi 10 (Casella postale 3061)
Napoli, Italy

J. Mol. Biol. (1965) **12**, 331–341

Regulation of the Initiation of
Chick Embryo Hemoglobin Synthesis

Fred H. Wilt

Department of Zoology, University of California, Berkeley, Calif., U.S.A.

(Received 16 December 1964)

The chick embryo begins rapid synthesis of hemoglobin in the blood islands of the extraembryonic mesoderm at the seven-somite stage (34 hours incubation at 38°C). Explants of potential hemoglobin synthesizing tissues were placed in organ cultures for 2 to 72 hours. The capacity of the explants from the head-fold and later stages of the embryo to form hemoglobin was not eliminated by high concentrations of 5-bromodeoxyuridine, 5-fluorouracil or actinomycin D. However, the hemoglobin-forming system becomes somewhat resistant to 8-azaguanine after attaining the seven-somite stage. Fractionation of labeled RNA by sucrose density-gradient centrifugation showed that virtually all RNA synthesis except some turnover of 4 to 6 s RNA was eliminated within two hours after exposure to actinomycin D. This was confirmed autoradiographically. 8-Azaguanine reduced incorporation of uridine into ribosomal and messenger RNA populations by about 70%, and [8-^{14}C]azaguanine was incorporated exclusively into 4 s RNA. It is concluded that the final transcription necessary for elaboration of a complete erythrocyte containing hemoglobin may occur prior to the head-fold stage. The initiation of hemoglobin synthesis at the seven-somite stage is probably regulated at the translational level.

1. Introduction

The onset of hemoglobin synthesis in the chick embryo provides an opportunity to describe some of the factors controlling the initiation of synthesis of a specific protein during development. Experimental evidence will be presented demonstrating that the initiation of hemoglobin synthesis occurs in the absence of concomitant synthesis of high molecular weight RNA. This suggests that the final genetic transcription necessary for a complete erythrocyte containing hemoglobin occurs prior to the translation of the message into Hb polypeptides.

The developmental events leading to the onset of hemoglobin synthesis in the chick embryo are well known. On the yolk of the unincubated egg there is an inverted saucer-like sheet of about 60,000 cells. Explantation of different portions of the early blastoderm (Settle, 1954) and tracing of cell movements by carbon marking (Spratt & Haas, 1960) show that descendants of cells located near the marginal zone (a transition zone from syncytial to cellular organization located in a circular band around the blastoderm just centrad to the perimeter) are the cells which later carry out hemoglobin synthesis. For 18 to 20 hours a complex set of morphogenetic movements is carried out, which establishes a trilaminar mass of cells with the future neural axis of the embryo along its midline. Descendants of marginal zone cells now lie in the middle mesodermal layer, just lateral to what will become the posterior portion of the embryo. This mesoderm condenses at about the head-fold stage

(22 hours of incubation at 38°C) to form small compact cell aggregates, the blood islands. Some ten hours later a rapid synthesis of Hb is first detected in the blood islands. The time of onset of Hb synthesis has been determined with some precision by a number of methods: (1) the sensitive dimethylbenzidine cytochemical technique reveals Hb at the 7 to 8-somite stage (O'Brien, 1961); (2) protein-bound heme in mitochondrial-free supernatant fractions of cell extracts is first detectable by spectrophotometric methods by the 9-somite stage (Wilt, unpublished experiments); (3) an antigenic component typical of avian Hb can only be demonstrated by Ouchterlony analysis subsequent to the 8-somite stage (Wilt, 1962); (4) incorporation of $[^{59}Fe]$- and $[^{3}H]$leucine into material precipitable with anti-chicken hemoglobin antisera first occurs at the 7-somite stage (Wilt, 1962). There is some globin antigen in the blastoderm prior to seven somites, but little or no isotope is incorporated into this fraction.

It is my purpose to analyze the metabolic requirements for the initiation of Hb synthesis, with particular reference to its dependence on RNA synthesis. The experiments to be described have utilized antimetabolites and drugs to derange RNA metabolism of the blood islands, and they demonstrate that the onset of Hb synthesis does not depend on high molecular weight RNA synthesis for at least eight hours prior to synthesis of Hb.

2. Materials and Methods

(a) Culture methods

Eggs of white Leghorn chickens were used for all experiments. Blastoderms were removed from yolk and vitelline membranes by dissection in chick saline (0·7% NaCl, 0·037% KCl, 0·017% $CaCl_2$) containing 0·02 M-tris, pH 7·6 (TS). Excess tissue was trimmed to the border of the prospective sinus terminalis (the peripheral limit of blood island formation). In many experiments small pieces of area vasculosa were excised for culture, or the area pellucida was removed and only the area vasculosa was cultured. Embryos and fragments thereof were cultured on Spratt's whole egg–agar medium (Spratt & Haas, 1960) in watch glasses at 38°C. Actinomycin D, 5-fluorouracil, 5-bromodeoxyuridine, 8-azaguanine, and puromycin were incorporated into media at the levels indicated. Cultures were kept in the dark except at the actual moment of explantation of the tissue. Tissues to be exposed to inhibitors were bathed in the appropriate concentration of the inhibitor in TS at 25°C for 15 min prior to explantation. Whole egg medium was also used for determination of uptake of $[^{3}H]$uridine. Incorporation of amino acids was followed using a modified medium because of the high free amino acid content of yolk. The medium was composed of 9 parts of TS containing 0·05% glucose, $\frac{1}{2}$ part fresh egg albumin, and $\frac{1}{2}$ part of the appropriate dilution of isotope and/or inhibitor in TS.

(b) Isotope incorporation

Incorporation of isotope into acid-insoluble fractions was measured by uptake from the radioactive culture medium by pooled, trimmed embryos. Results were expressed as cts/min/embryo. The accuracy of the method depends on the ability to trim embryos to the same size. This has been checked by DNA determinations (Ogur & Rosen, 1950); variability from this source is less than 10%. Accumulation of acid-insoluble uridine was determined on groups of 2 to 3 embryos after 2 extractions with cold 5% TCA† and two extractions with cold methanol. Accumulation of acid-insoluble leucine was determined on groups of 2 to 3 embryos after 2 extractions with hot (90°C) TCA followed by two extractions with cold methanol. The residues were dissolved in 1 ml. of Hyamine (Packard Instruments) and mixed with 10 ml. of Bray's solution (Bray, 1960) prior to radioactivity determination by liquid-scintillation counting. Determinations of incorporation of radio-

† Abbreviation used: TCA, trichloroacetic acid.

activity into antibody precipitable material were carried out by the immunological procedures described previously (Wilt, 1962), followed by processing the precipitates as for leucine. The anti-Hb gamma globulin was prepared from the same antisera described previously, and showed the same apparent absolute specificity (Wilt, 1962).

(c) Sucrose density-gradients

RNA pulse-labeled with [^{3}H]uridine or [8-^{14}C]azaguanine was obtained by suspending minced fragments of embryos for 30 to 60 min at 38°C in TS containing 0·05% glucose and 10 μc/ml. of isotope. RNA was isolated by the warm phenol method (Scherrer, Latham & Darnell, 1963; Wilt, 1964), and sucrose density-gradients were run in SW39 rotors at 39,000 rev./min for 3 to 3·5 hr and processed and counted as described previously (Wilt, 1964).

(d) Histological technique

Autoradiographic determination of incorporation of [^{3}H]thymidine and [^{3}H]uridine was carried out as described by Wessells (1964a), and the appropriate controls with RNase and DNase for specificity of labeling were carried out. Histological sections (5 μ) were prepared after fixation of tissue in Bouin's solution, and stained with hematoxylin and eosin. Staining for hemoglobin was carried out by O'Brien's method (O'Brien, 1961).

(e) Materials

[^{3}H]uridine (2·2 c/m-mole), [^{3}H]thymidine (6·7 c/m-mole), and [^{3}H]leucine (5·2 c/m-mole) were obtained from the New England Nuclear Corporation. [8-^{14}C]azaguanine (2·4 mc/ m-mole) was obtained from Volk. ^{55}FeCl$_3$(7298 mc/g) was supplied by Oak Ridge National Laboratories. Actinomycin D was a gift of Merck, Sharpe & Dohme, and 5-fluorouracil was generously donated by Dr Charles Yanofsky. 5-Bromodeoxyuridine was obtained from "Calbiochem", and puromycin and 8-azaguanine were obtained from Nutritional Biochemicals.

3. Results

(a) Acquisition of insensitivity to inhibitors by blood island cells

The influence on initiation of Hb synthesis of several drugs and analogues affecting RNA metabolism was tested by culturing embryos of various stages on media containing the agents. Hemoglobin synthesis was detected both by visual inspection and staining with dimethylbenzidine. Explants were scored at 12, 24 and 36 hours after beginning the cultures, for the presence or absence of hemoglobin. Table 1 tabulates the results of this qualitative screening. Results were the same if whole embryos, de-embryonated blastoderms or fragments of area vasculosa were used. Explants were scored on a 0 to plus 3 scale for Hb. Explants on control media always gave a plus 3 response within 24 hours. As O'Brien has shown (O'Brien, 1961), 8-azaguanine effectively reduced Hb synthesis below levels detectable by these techniques (although some synthesis, about 10% of normal, can be detected by immunochemical analysis (Wilt, 1962)) if applied prior to the time of initiation of synthesis. If 8-azaguanine was not applied until after the 7-somite stage, some Hb was synthesized, but was noticeably reduced in amount. Application of 5-fluorouracil, 5-bromodeoxyuridine or actinomycin prior to the head-fold stage completely blocked subsequent hemoglobin synthesis; application of the same agents after attainment of head-fold stage allowed the occurrence of easily detectable hemoglobin synthesis (+ 2 response). Explants showed no such changing pattern of sensitivity to puromycin. It either completely blocked initiation or continuation of synthesis, or failed to do so, at all stages, depending on the concentration of puromycin used. The results suggested that derangement

TABLE 1

Inhibition of chick embryo Hb synthesis

Inhibitor	Midstreak		DPS		HF		Stage 2-S		4-S		7-S		10-S	
	+	Total	+	Total	+	Total	+	Total	+	Total	+	Total	+	Total
Actinomycin (2 μg/ml.)	0	13	0	15	9	20	12	12	13	13	5	5	3	3
5-Fluorouracil (10^{-4} M)	0	3	0	7	3	6	7	7	8	8	5	5	2	2
5-Bromodeoxy-uridine (100 μg/ml.)	0	5	0	10	15	19	7	7	6	6	5	5	2	2
8-Azaguanine (50 μg/ml.)	0	2	0	3	0	7	0	12	1	20	5	5	8	8
Puromycin (10^{-4} M)	–	–	0	4	0	7	0	4	0	3	0	4	–	–
(10^{-5} M)	–	–	8	8	8	8	5	5	5	5	9	9	2	2

Blastoderms of the ages indicated were trimmed to the limit of the sinus terminalis, de-embryonated, exposed to inhibitor dissolved in TS for 15 min, and explanted on medium containing the inhibitor at the indicated levels. The blastoderms were stained with dimethylbenzidine after 24 hr in culture. The number of blastoderms showing hemoglobin formation is designated +; the total number examined is designated "Total".

DPS, definitive primitive streak; HF, head-fold; S, somite.

of RNA metabolism up to eight to nine hours prior to initiation of Hb synthesis did not prevent the onset of this synthesis. The results of further experiments employing 8-azaguanine and actinomycin D support this hypothesis and will be analyzed further. The action of 5-bromodeoxyuridine and 5-fluorouracil also support the conclusion, and will be the subject of a subsequent communication.

(b) *Action of actinomycin*

The action of actinomycin was qualitatively similar at levels from 0·5 to 5·0 μg/ml., and the inhibition of Hb synthesis by exposure prior to the head-fold stage was irreversible after 40 minutes. Actinomycin did not completely prevent condensation of splanchnopleuric mesoderm into blood islands, although rarely did normal morphogenesis of the embryo continue for more than an hour or two. Mesodermal condensation is not necessary for some Hb synthesis, in any case (Wilt, 1965). At the usual dose level of 2 μg/ml. cell degeneration and autolysis became obvious both in whole blastoderms and histological sections after 12 hours (cf. Revel, Hiatt & Revel, 1964). The initiation of Hb synthesis takes place in treated cultures during the same time period when many cells are undergoing autolysis. Plate I(a) and (b) presents the appearance of typical explants after 24 hours in culture.

The inhibition of incorporation of [^{3}H]uridine into acid-insoluble form was rapid and profound. Within two hours after exposure to actinomycin, incorporation was reduced to 85 to 95% of control levels (five experiments), and the residual incorporation was primarily into low molecular weight RNA, as will be discussed subsequently. Figure 1 shows the nearly linear accumulation of [^{3}H]uridine on whole egg medium

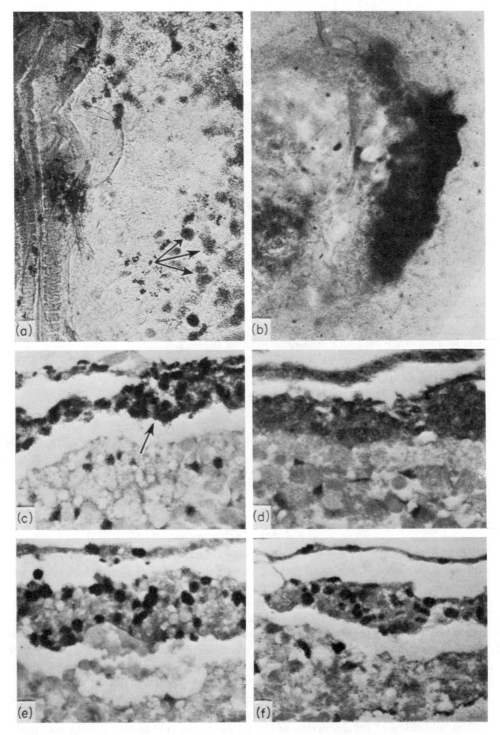

[facing p. 335

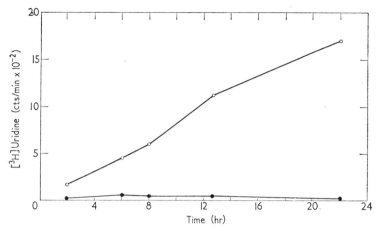

FIG. 1. De-embryonated 1-somite blastoderms were placed on whole egg–agar medium containing 1 μc/ml. of [³H]uridine. After the times indicated on the graph, 2 or 3 embryos were removed, rinsed in TS and processed for incorporation of acid-insoluble counts. Actinomycin embryos were placed on the same medium containing 2 μg/ml. of actinomycin D. Each point represents radioactive material (counts) incorporated into two de-embryonated blastoderms. —O——O—, Control; —●——●—, actinomycin treated.

in control cultures; incorporation has virtually halted within two hours after exposure to actinomycin. Variable amounts of incorporation into material sedimenting at 4 to 6 s can be detected for at least ten hours, even after cessation of net accumulation of acid-insoluble uridine. The effect of actinomycin on incorporation of leucine is shown in Fig. 2. The incorporation proceeds at near normal rates for two hours, then gradually ceases, until by eight hours there is no further net accumulation of [³H]-leucine. Subsequently, there is a reduction in amount of isotope incorporated, probably due to loss of protein into the medium by autolysis. In summary, a one-somite embryo explanted on actinomycin medium ceases synthesis of high molecular weight RNA within two hours and shows no further net accumulation of acid-insoluble leucine after eight hours. Nevertheless, substantial amounts of Hb appear under these conditions (Table 1 and Plate I(b)).

PLATE I. (a) The appearance of a whole mount of an explanted 1-somite embryo after development for 20 hr on whole-egg medium. The blastoderm was stained for hemoglobin. The dense areas surrounding the blastoderm are blood islands containing Hb. Arrows point to blood islands. Magnification ×31.

(b) The appearance of a whole mount of a 1-somite embryo after development for 20 hr on whole-egg medium containing 3·5 μg/ml. of actinomycin D. The explant was stained for Hb. Considerable accumulation of blood islands containing Hb may be observed. Magnification ×31.

(c) A fragment of the area vasculosa from a 1-somite embryo was cultured on whole-egg medium for 1·5 hr, and was then labeled with [³H]uridine for autoradiography. The arrow points to a blood island. Magnification × 288.

(d) This is the companion to the experiment of Fig. 3. In this instance the fragment was cultured on medium containing 2 μg/ml. of actinomycin before labeling and autoradiographic processing. Magnification × 288.

(e) A fragment of a 1-somite embryo area vasculosa was cultured on control whole-egg medium for 2 hr. Subsequently the tissue was labeled with [³H]thymidine and processed for autoradiography. Magnification × 288.

(f) This is the companion to the experiment shown in Fig. 5. In this case the tissue was exposed to 2 μg/ml. of actinomycin D during culture, and subsequently was labeled with thymidine and treated exactly as the tissue in Fig. 5. Magnification × 288.

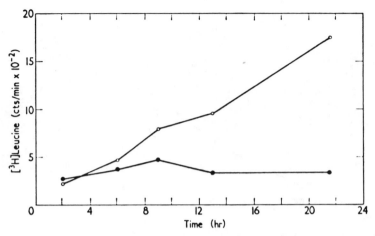

Fig. 2. De-embryonated 1-somite blastoderms were placed on albumin–agar medium containing 5 μc/ml. of [³H]leucine. At the times indicated, 2 embryos were removed, rinsed and processed for incorporation of acid-insoluble leucine. Actinomycin-treated embryos were placed on the same medium containing 2 μg/ml. of actinomycin D. Each point represents the counts incorporated into two de-embryonated blastoderms. —○——○—, Control;— ●——●—, actinomycin-treated.

Estimation of hemoglobin synthesis in inhibited cultures may be made by employing ^{55}Fe to label heme, and then determining the amount of ^{55}Fe incorporated into material precipitated by anti-Hb antibody. Results of such an experiment are shown in Table 2. There is little incorporation prior to eight hours, a time when the embryo is just forming the seventh or eighth pair of somites; subsequently incorporation is detectable, and it proceeds at about 80% of the normal rate in inhibited embryos. A similar experiment was carried out using very high levels of [³H]leucine. One-somite embryos were explanted to control and actinomycin media. Eight hours later, the controls had seven somite pairs, and both control and actinomycin embryos were transferred to media containing 20 μc/ml. of [³H]leucine. Over a four-hour period, control embryos

TABLE 2

Incorporation of ^{55}Fe into cultured blastoderms

Time in culture (hr)	Cts/min/blastoderm of antibody-precipitable material	
	Controls	Actinomycin-treated
0	30	—
4	54	33
8	56	46
12	143	109

One-somite blastoderms were trimmed to the sinus terminalis and then placed on control or actinomycin containing (2 μg/ml.) media. After the times indicated above, the blastoderms were removed, minced, and exposed to 10 μc/ml. of ^{55}FeCl$_3$ in TS containing 0·05% glucose and 0·05 M-sodium citrate for 1 hr. Tissues were then washed and frozen. Incorporation of ^{55}Fe into material precipitable by anti-Hb antibody was determined as described previously. The zero time refers to background found in 1-somite embryos heat-killed (10 min at 75°C) before exposure to isotope.

incorporated 380 cts/min/embryo of leucine into antibody-precipitable material, while 170 cts/min/embryo were detected in anti-Hb precipitates of extracts from actinomycin-treated embryos. Furthermore, microscopic observation of living and stained explants reveals an apparently normal content of hemoglobin in the erythrocytes forming in inhibited cultures. The cells of the peripheral portion of the area vasculosa, those closest the sinus terminalis, are the first to complete normal differentiation in control explants, and it is these same cells which seem to escape the actinomycin inhibition.

It might be suggested that the incorporation of acid-insoluble uridine is not sensitive enough to detect RNA synthesis by small numbers of blood island cells. This possibility was checked directly by autoradiography. Actinomycin inhibits incorporation of [³H]uridine into blood island cells within 1·5 hours after exposure to the drug, and by two hours no grains can be detected over the mesoderm. There does not seem to be an actinomycin-resistant population of cells in the blood islands (Plate I(c) and (d)). The effect of actinomycin on DNA synthesis is much less profound, as shown in Plate I (e) and (f). Incorporation of [³H]thymidine proceeds actively for at least two hours, although eventually (five to six hours) incorporation and mitosis cease.

(c) Action of 8-azaguanine

Even though derangement and inhibition of RNA synthesis by actinomycin allows some Hb synthesis to proceed, 8-azaguanine is a fairly effective inhibitor (greater than 90% inhibition if applied at the 2-somite stage) of Hb synthesis. Apparently some essential nucleic acid synthesis proceeds in the presence of actinomycin which is inhibited or deranged by 8-azaguanine. Sucrose density-gradient analysis of sedimentation of [³H]uridine-labeled RNA from cells exposed to 8-azaguanine for two hours is shown in Fig. 3. There is an inhibition of high molecular weight RNA synthesis (the level of incorporation in controls is shown in Fig. 4), just as with actinomycin, but it is less severe. Incorporation of uridine into material sedimenting at 4 to 6 s seems almost unaffected. Perhaps 8-azaguanine is incorporated into slowly sedimenting RNA in addition to producing a depression of synthesis of high molecular weight RNA. This possibility was investigated by exposing

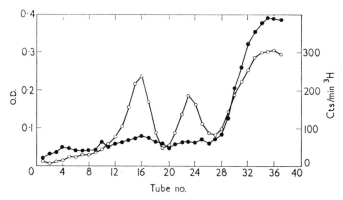

Fig. 3. 20 one-somite embryos were cultured for 2 hr in the presence of 50 μg/ml. of 8-azaguanine on whole egg medium. They were subsequently rinsed, minced and incubated with 10 μg/ml. of [³H]uridine for 45 min. The RNA was extracted by the phenol method and analyzed by sucrose density-gradient centrifugation. —●——●—, Radioactivity; —○——○—, optical density.

22

actinomycin-treated and control blastoderms to [³H]uridine and [8-¹⁴C]azaguanine. Figure 4 shows the type of pattern encountered in control cultures. The uridine labels all classes of RNA, as well as some species heavier than 28 s, as observed in other studies with chick embryo cells (Lerner, Bell & Darnell, 1963). Incorporation of 8-azaguanine is restricted to slowly sedimenting RNA. In cultures treated with actinomycin for two hours prior to labeling, uridine incorporation has been almost eliminated from all RNA types except the S-RNA region. The illustration for Fig. 5 was chosen because this is the most extensive incorporation of [³H]uridine ever encountered in

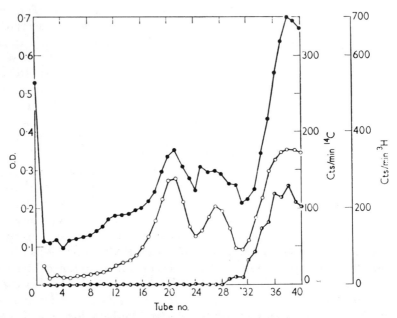

FIG. 4. 20 one-somite embryos were cultured for 2 hr on whole egg medium. They were subsequently rinsed, minced and pulse-labeled for 45 min in 10 μc/ml. of [³H]uridine and 10 μc/ml. of [8-¹⁴C]azaguanine. The RNA was extracted by the phenol method and analyzed by sucrose density-gradient centrifugation. —○——○—, Optical density; —●——●—, radioactivity ³H; —◑——◑—, ¹⁴C.

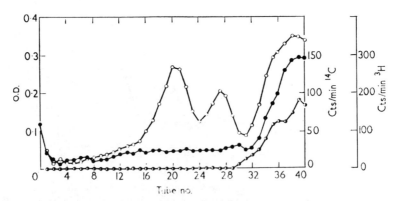

FIG. 5. The same experiment was carried out as described for Fig. 4, except that the embryos were cultured on media containing 2 μg/ml. of actinomycin D prior to labeling. —○——○—, Optical density; —●——●—, radioactivity ³H; —◑——◑—, ¹⁴C.

the presence of actinomycin, and, as such, represents the lower limit of inhibition. Again, [8-^{14}C]azaguanine incorporation occurs only in the light region of the gradient, and its incorporation in this region is only reduced by some 30 to 40% by actinomycin. 8-Azaguanine both inhibits the synthesis of high molecular weight RNA and is incorporated into material sedimenting in the region characteristic of S-RNA.

4. Discussion

The main conclusion is that some terminal limit can be set for the time of transcription of a substantial amount of messenger RNA for the terminal steps in erythrocyte differentiation; this time is about at the head-fold stage, several hours before active hemoglobin synthesis commences. Since high levels of actinomycin induce autolysis, the actual transcription time may be much earlier. For the same reason, it is not possible to assign an accurate half-life to the messengers in question, either before or after the beginning of polypeptide synthesis, except to say that it must be longer than several hours.

The assurance with which this assertion is made depends on two considerations. First, is the production of messenger RNA really eliminated in blood island cells? Both gross labeling and autoradiographic techniques indicate this is certainly so. There is no differential escape of blood island cells from actinomycin inhibition. Synthesis of high molecular weight RNA is almost completely inhibited within two hours, and profound inhibition occurs almost immediately. The conclusion is reinforced by the fact that other analogues which derange RNA metabolism display this same pattern of inhibition. The exception is 8-azaguanine, and its action is complex. It inhibits synthesis of high molecular weight RNA under the conditions used here, and 8-azaguanine is also incorporated into slowly sedimenting RNA, even in the presence of actinomycin. Levin (1963) has also found a preferential incorporation of 8-azaguanine into S-RNA of *Bacillus cereus*. Hell (1963) has reported that 8-azaguanine inhibits net synthesis of RNA and is a general inhibitor of protein synthesis in the chick embryo. The inhibition of protein synthesis may be a reflection of synthesis of counterfeit transfer RNA which does not function effectively in protein synthesis. Chantrenne & Le Clerq-Calingaert (1963) have also been led by their studies on *B. cereus* to propose that 8-azaguanine inhibits protein synthesis by acting at the level of polypeptide synthesis. Action of 8-azaguanine at the translational level would explain its inhibitory action on initiation of Hb synthesis after the 1-somite stage. Decreased sensitivity to 8-azaguanine after the 8-somite stage may be due to development of permeability barriers, and this is currently under investigation.

The second consideration affecting the conclusion is the degree of assurance that hemoglobin synthesis begins at the 7-somite stage. It is not possible, of course, to state when the first molecule of globin is made; but a variety of sensitive techniques support the conclusion that, at the least, a rapid increase in rate of Hb synthesis occurs at the 7-somite stage. The sensitivity of the system to puromycin, as well as the increase in incorporation of both ^{55}Fe and [^{3}H]leucine into antibody-precipitable material at 7-somites, indicate *de novo* Hb synthesis, rather than association of preformed heme and globin. In this connection, the observations show that actinomycin reduces the rate of Hb synthesis during the first four hours by 20 to 50%. This could either be a reduction of the number of cells making Hb, or a reduction of the rate of synthesis per cell. The histological observations favor the first alternative.

It is not uncommon to find that a differentiated system may display stability of messenger in the absence of RNA synthesis. In the reticulocyte (Marks, Burka & Schlessinger, 1962), rat liver (Revel & Hiatt, 1964), embryonic pancreas (Wessells, 1964b) and embryonic lens and skin (Scott & Bell, 1964) a high degree of messenger stability is implied. It has not been shown heretofore, however, that a message may be transcribed well in advance of its translation. Perhaps a similar situation is involved in the onset of protein synthesis following fertilization of the sea urchin egg in which RNA synthesis has been inhibited by actinomycin (Gross, 1964). Here, however, the paucity of information on the nature of the proteins being synthesized does not allow a conclusion regarding the relation of transcription time to the appearance of a *new* protein in development.

Finally, it remains to point out that a simple model may be constructed which serves as a basis for further experiments, and which explains the apparent translational regulation in this system. The lag between acquisition of actinomycin insensitivity and Hb synthesis may be due to a time-dependent delivery of essential substrate (or de-repressor) to the hemoglobin-forming machinery. Some evidence suggests that iron and ferritin levels may affect the rate of Hb synthesis (Matioli & Eylar, 1964). Perhaps the level of substrates for prosthetic group synthesis, e.g. ferritin, iron, δ-amino levulinic acid, may control the onset of rapid hemoglobin synthesis. It is suggested that there is a transfer of yolk containing ferritin (or apoferritin, iron, etc.) from endoderm to blood island cells; this can only occur after condensation of mesoderm on the endoderm at the head-fold stage. Several hours might be needed for yolk droplet breakdown and mobilization of substrate or de-repressor. Rapid Hb synthesis would await delivery of this molecule even though messenger transcription had occurred. This proposal is consistent with the observation that mesoderm cells appear yolk laden after condensation on the endoderm (Kallman & Wilt, unpublished experiments), and that removal of endoderm from mesoderm drastically reduces the level of Hb formation (Wilt, 1965).

Portions of this work were carried out while I was a Special Fellow of the U.S. Public Health Service in residence at Stanford University. I thank Drs Clifford Grobstein and Norman Wessells and their technical staffs for their help. The research was supported by grants from the National Science Foundation to me and to Dr Grobstein.

REFERENCES

Bray, G. A. (1960). *Analyt. Biochem.* 1, 279.
Chantrenne, H. & LeClerq-Calingaert, M. (1963). *Biochim. biophys. Acta*, 72, 87.
Gross, P. (1964). *J. Exp. Zool.* 157, 21.
Hell (1963). *Arch. Int. Physiol. Biochim.* 71, 817.
Lerner, A. M., Bell, E. & Darnell, J. E. (1963). *Science*, 141, 1187.
Levin, D. H. (1963). *J. Biol. Chem.* 238, 1098.
Marks, P., Burka, E. R. & Schlessinger, D. (1962). *Proc. Nat. Acad. Sci., Wash.* 48, 2163.
Matioli, G. T. & Eylar, E. H. (1964). *Proc. Nat. Acad. Sci., Wash.* 52, 508.
O'Brien, B. R. A. (1961). *J. Embryol. Exp. Morph.* 8, 202.
Ogur, M. & Rosen, G. (1950). *Arch. Biochem. Biophys.* 25, 262.
Revel, M. & Hiatt, H. (1964). *Proc. Nat. Acad. Sci., Wash.* 51, 810.
Revel, M., Hiatt, H. & Revel J.-P. (1964). *Science*, 146, 1311.
Scherrer, K., Latham, H. & Darnell, J. (1963). *Proc. Nat. Acad. Sci., Wash.* 49, 240.
Scott, R. B. & Bell, E. (1964). *Science,*, 145, 711.
Settle, G. W. (1954). Carneg. Instn. Wash. Pub. 603, Contrib. *Embryol.* 35, 221.
Spratt, N. T. & Haas, H. (1960). *J. Exp. Zool.* 144, 139.

Wessells, N. (1964a). *J. Cell Biol.* **20**, 415.
Wessells, N. (1964b). *J. Exp. Zool.* **157**, 139.
Wilt, F. H. (1962). *Proc. Nat. Acad. Sci., Wash.* **48**, 1582.
Wilt, F. H. (1964). *Develop. Biol.* **9**, 299.
Wilt, F. H. (1965). *Science,* **147**, 1588.

THE JOURNAL OF BIOLOGICAL CHEMISTRY
Vol. 244, No. 3, Issue of February 10, pp. 675–681, 1969
Printed in U.S.A.

Synthesis of Embryonic Hemoglobins during Erythroid Cell Development in Fetal Mice*

(Received for publication, September 9, 1968)

ANTONIO FANTONI,‡ ALBERT DE LA CHAPELLE,§ AND PAUL A. MARKS

From the Department of Medicine, College of Physicians and Surgeons, Columbia University, New York, New York 10032

SUMMARY

Three embryonic hemoglobins are formed in erythroid cells derived from yolk sac blood islands in fetal mice of the C57BL/6J strain. These cells provide a suitable model to study the rates of synthesis of specific proteins during the differentiation of cells. Erythroid cells differentiate initially in yolk sac blood islands from the 8th to the 10th day of gestation. (Fetal mice have a 20- to 21-day period of gestation.) These cells enter the fetal circulation and continue to develop as a relatively homogeneous population until Day 14 or 15, as indicated by a progressive decrease in the size of the nucleus, increasing pycnosis of nuclear chromatin, increasing content of hemoglobin in the cytoplasm, and decreasing content of ribosomes in the cytoplasm. The relative rates of synthesis of the three embryonic hemoglobins, Hb E_I, Hb E_{II}, and Hb E_{III}, change as these erythroid cells differentiate. The synthesis of Hb E_I, the most abundant of the hemoglobins present at Day 10, decreases markedly after Day 11, while the synthesis of Hb E_{II} proceeds at a relatively linear rate over the entire period and by Day 12 is present in the largest amount. Hb E_{III} is formed at a slower rate than Hb E_I or Hb E_{II} during the entire period from Day 10 to Day 14. Hemoglobin formation in yolk sac erythroid cells is not inhibited by actinomycin D from Day 10, while the antibiotic does inhibit RNA formation and non-heme protein synthesis in these cells. It is suggested that changes in rates of synthesis of the three embryonic hemoglobins which occur as yolk sac erythroid cells develop between Days 10 and 14 may be largely determined by factors regulating protein formation which do not require the immediate or continued synthesis of RNA.

* These studies were supported, in part, by grants from the United States Public Health Service, National Institutes of Health (GM-14552), the National Science Foundation (GB-4631), and the RGK Foundation.

‡ Supported as a Trainee in Hematology under Grant TIAM-5231 of the National Institutes of Health. Present address, Laboratorio di Biologia Animale, Comitato Nazionale Energia Nucleare, Casaccia, Rome, Italy.

§ Supported by an International Fellowship of the United States Public Health Service, National Institutes of Health. Present address, The Folkhälsan Institute for Genetics, Helsingfors, Finland.

During cell differentiation, it is characteristic that proteins are formed at different rates. The synthesis of different hemoglobins and non-heme proteins during erythroid cell development is a good example of this phenomenon. Erythroid cells derived from yolk sac blood islands in fetal mice of strain C57BL/6J form three hemoglobins (1). This erythroid cell line provides a particularly suitable system for study of relative rates of synthesis of several hemoglobins by an erythroid cell population as it differentiates.

Regulation of the types and amounts of protein synthesized can occur at the level of transcription, *i.e.* at the level of DNA and messenger RNA synthesis, and at the level of translation, *i.e.* at the level of polypeptide chain formation on polyribosomes. The latter regulation of protein synthesis is not dependent on continued RNA formation, and data have accumulated to suggest that such control mechanisms are important in determining the amounts of hemoglobin formed in erythroid cells (2–10). Thus, it has been shown that changes can be induced in the synthetic time for a globin chain in intact reticulocytes, cells which synthesize no RNA (8), and that heme and iron affect the rate of synthesis of globin (5–7, 10).

This investigation has examined the rate of synthesis of each of three embryonic hemoglobins formed in erythroid cells derived from yolk sac blood islands in fetal mice of the C57BL/6J strain. These mice have a 20- to 21-day period of gestation. Erythropoiesis occurs initially in yolk sac blood islands from the 8th to the 10th day. The erythroid cells enter the fetal peripheral blood and continue to differentiate, as a relatively homogeneous population, until Day 14 or 15. The fetal liver is a site of erythropoiesis from Day 11 to about Day 16 (11, 12). In this study, hemoglobin synthesis in yolk sac erythroid cells is shown not to be affected by actinomycin D from Day 10, although the antibiotic markedly inhibits RNA formation and non-heme protein synthesis in these cells. Between Days 10 and 14 of gestation, the relative rates of synthesis of the three embryonic hemoglobins change as yolk sac erythroid cells differentiate. The synthesis of hemoglobin E_I, the most abundant of hemoglobins present at Day 10, decreases markedly after Day 11, while the synthesis of hemoglobin E_{II} continues at a relatively linear rate over the entire period and by Day 12 it is present in the largest amount. Hemoglobin E_{III} is formed at a slower rate than hemoglobins E_I and E_{II} during the entire period from Day 10 through 14.

METHODS

Animals—Three- to four-week-old female mice of C57BL/6J inbred strain, and two- to five-month-old males of the same strain were purchased from the Jackson Laboratory, Bar Harbor, Maine. The method for obtaining dated fetal development was based on timed matings of hormonally primed immature females (13). The 1st day of gestation was counted as the morning following mating.

Preparation of Erythroid Cells—At the 10th day of gestation, erythroid cells were prepared from the peripheral blood of fetuses as follows. The pregnant uteri were removed and placed in a 1:1 mixture of Tyrode's solution and γ-globulin-free fetal calf serum (Solution A). All subsequent steps were performed at 4° with the aid of a dissecting microscope. The embryos were dissected from the uteri and washed three times with Solution A, the maternal membranes were opened by sharp dissection, and the embryo with the yolk sac attached was rapidly transferred to fresh Solution A. This procedure is associated with disruption of the umbilical cord and bleeding. Loss of embryonic blood during this procedure was kept to a minimum by rapidly transferring the embryo to fresh Solution A. Once the embryo was in fresh Solution A, the heart, neck, and dorsal aorta were incised, and blood was allowed to flow into the medium. When bleeding was completed, the embryos with the attached yolk sacs were allowed to sediment, and the supernatant solution containing blood cells was decanted. The sedimented embryos and yolk sacs were rinsed once with Solution A, and the rinse solution was combined with the decanted fluid.

At the 11th, 12th, 13th, 14th, and 15th day of gestation, erythroid cells were prepared from the peripheral blood of fetuses in a manner similar to that described above with the exception that it was not necessary to use a dissecting microscope to remove the embryos from the uterus. With these larger embryos, the yolk sac contained negligible amounts of blood relative to that present in the whole embryo. The yolk sacs were not transferred with the embryos to Solution A for bleeding.

At each day of gestation, the amount of hemoglobin remaining in the embryo and yolk sac was determined after homogenization of the embryos and yolk sacs (14). In each preparation, the amount of hemoglobin remaining in the embryos and yolk sacs was less than 5% of the total hemoglobin recovered in erythroid cells from the embryos.

In each experiment, the total number of embryos processed was recorded, and for a given experiment at least 100 embryos from 15 litters of the same day of gestation were pooled.

Cytology—Monolayer smears were prepared from each preparation of cells and stained with benzidine and with Giemsa (15). The proportion, if any, of maternal erythroid cells and of reticulocytes of fetal liver origin (both types of cells are nonnucleated and are readily distinguished from nucleated yolk sac erythroid cells) was determined by examining 500 cells on stained smears. The total number of cells was also determined. The fraction

of the total cells which were yolk sac erythroid cells multiplied by the total number of cells yielded the total number of erythroid cells in each preparation.

Incubation of Cells—Cells were washed and incubated according to the procedures previously described (16), with the following modifications. The cells were incubated in a concentration of 5 to 10×10^7 yolk sac erythroid cells per 0.3 ml, in the presence of ^{14}C-valine (1 $\mu Ci/4.8$ mμM) or ^{14}C-δ-aminolevulinic acid (0.6 $\mu Ci/40.4$ mμM). The duration of the period of incubation was 10 min at 37° unless otherwise indicated below. In preliminary studies it was shown that the rate of incorporation of ^{14}C-valine or ^{14}C-δ-aminolevulinic acid by yolk sac erythroid cells was linear for at least 15 min under these conditions of incubation. In studies designed to determine the effect of actinomycin D, the cells were incubated as previously reported (17), with the exception that in each such experiment the cells were incubated in pairs and to one of the pair ^{14}C-valine and ^{3}H-uridine were added in concentrations as previously described (17) and to the other of the pair, ^{14}C-δ-aminolevulinic acid (0.6 $\mu Ci/40.4$ mμM) was added.

Following incubation, cells were recovered and lysed by the procedures described in detail elsewhere (17).

RNA and Protein Synthesis—The rates of synthesis of RNA and of protein were determined by the procedures described by Fantoni *et al.* (17). The rates of synthesis of these macromolecules are expressed as counts per min per μg of RNA or of protein.

Electrophoresis of Embryonic Hemoglobins in Polyacrylamide Gel—Hemoglobins present in the stroma-free hemolysates were separated by electrophoresis in polyacrylamide gel (18). Hemoglobin (200 to 600 μg) in the stroma-free hemolysate was applied to the gel, and the electrophoresis was carried out in glass tubes which had an internal diameter of 8 mm. A current of 5 ma per tube was applied for 45 to 60 min, at 4°. The composition of the discontinuous polyacrylamide gel was described elsewhere (19), except that the pH of the separating gel was lowered to 7.5 (20) and the polyacrylamide concentration in the stacking gel was 2.5%.

After completion of the period of electrophoresis, the distribution of the unstained bands of hemoglobins in the gel was evaluated by determination of absorbance of the gel with a Densicord densitometer. The gel was then divided into sections by free hand with a razor blade, and each section was placed in 0.001 M phosphate buffer, pH 7.4, to elute the protein by allowing it to stand in this solution overnight at 4°. A second, and, when necessary, a third, elution was performed under the same conditions. This procedure for elution of the hemoglobin from the gel yielded recoveries of at least 75%. In initial experiments, it was shown that recovery from the gel for each embryonic hemoglobin was similar. The content of hemoglobins in the eluate, as well as the content of hemoglobin in the hemolysate applied to each gel, was determined by the method of Drabkin (14).

Characterization of Globin Chains—The globin chain composition of the hemoglobins eluted from the polyacrylamide gel was determined by chromatography on carboxymethyl cellulose in 8 M urea as described in detail elsewhere (1). In experiments designed to determine the amount of ^{14}C-valine incorporated into each of the separated hemoglobins at the different days of gestation, this previously described procedure was modified by eluting the hemoglobins from the column with the use of the same gradient of developer by mixing 50 ml of the two buffers

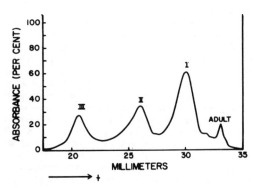

Fig. 1. Electrophoresis of hemolysate prepared from erythroid cells of 11-day fetal mouse peripheral blood. Electrophoresis was in polyacrylamide gel as described under "Methods." Four peaks correspond to hemoglobins referred to in the text as *Bands A, I, II,* and *III,* respectively. Full scale at the setting for a particular gel was taken as 100% absorbance.

(0.01 M Na₂HPO₄ and 0.02 M Na₂HPO₄, pH 6.8) with a flow rate of 2 ml per min.

Calculations of Content and Synthesis of Different Embryonic Hemoglobins—In each study the proportion of the adult type of hemoglobin present in the preparations of hemolysates of yolk sac erythroid cells was determined by measuring the amount of hemoglobin eluted following electrophoresis from the portion of the gel corresponding to *Band A* as illustrated in Fig. 1. The adult hemoglobin present in these samples was derived from maternal erythroid cells or from fetal liver erythroid cells (1, 16). In a similar manner, the proportion of the total hemoglobin represented by each of the three types of embryonic hemoglobin (*Bands I, II,* and *III,* Fig. 1) was determined. The total hemoglobin in hemolysates multiplied by the proportion of the hemoglobin recovered in each band was taken as the amount of each type of hemoglobin present and expressed as micrograms of hemoglobin per embryo or micrograms of hemoglobin per 10⁶ yolk sac erythroid cells.

Depending on the particular study, as indicated below, ¹⁴C-valine or ¹⁴C-δ-aminolevulinic acid was used as the labeled precursor of hemoglobin. The rate of synthesis of each embryonic hemoglobin was expressed as counts per min incorporated into globin eluted from carboxymethyl cellulose column when ¹⁴C-valine was used or as the counts per min incorporated into each hemoglobin separated by electrophoresis in polyacrylamide gel, when ¹⁴C-δ-aminolevulinic acid was used. The sum of the radioactivity in the three types of embryonic hemoglobins was taken as the total radioactivity incorporated into embryonic hemoglobins by the population of yolk sac erythroid cells.

RESULTS

Types of Hemoglobin in Fetal Peripheral Blood—In the present studies, the hemoglobins present in peripheral blood of fetal mice at Days 10, 11, 12, 13, and 14 of gestation were separated by electrophoresis in polyacrylamide gel. On each day, four hemoglobins were shown (Fig. 1), in agreement with previously published studies in which column chromatography was used to separate hemoglobins (1). In the earlier studies, three of the four types of hemoglobins were designated embryonic hemoglobins E_I, E_II, and E_III, and the fourth type of hemoglobin, which

was indistinguishable from the single hemoglobin present in the adult of this species, was designated adult hemoglobin. The adult hemoglobin present in these preparations before the 12th day of gestation has been shown to be derived from maternal erythroid cells (16). On Day 12 of gestation and subsequently, adult hemoglobin present in these samples is derived, in part, from liver erythroid cells which begin to enter the circulation on the 12th day of gestation (1, 16).

Since column chromatography was not suitable for analysis of multiple fetal mouse blood samples required in this study, the correspondence between the four hemoglobins separated by electrophoresis (Fig. 1) and the four hemoglobins separated by carboxymethyl cellulose column chromatography in our previous studies (1) was determined. Twelve-day fetal mouse yolk sac erythroid cells were labeled with ¹⁴C-valine, or ¹⁴C-lysine and ³H-arginine, lysates were prepared from these cells, and hemoglobins in these lysates were separated by electrophoresis in polyacrylamide gel. Globin was prepared from each of the four hemoglobins recovered from the gel following electrophoresis. The globins were chromatographed in carboxymethyl cellulose columns in 8 M urea with nonradioactive adult α- and β-globin added as carrier (1). In electrophoresis, the most rapidly migrating hemoglobin, *Band A,* contains two globin chains which correspond to α- and β-globin of adult hemoglobin (Fig. 2A). Thus, *Band A* in electrophoresis corresponds to adult hemoglobin. The second most rapidly migrating band (*Band I,* Fig. 1) appears to be composed of two globin chains, both more acidic than β-globin

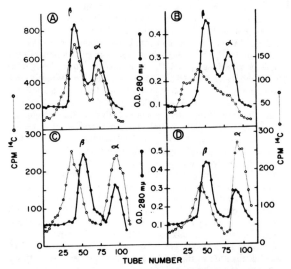

Fig. 2. Chromatography of the globins eluted from the electrophoretically separated hemoglobin bands from 12-day fetal peripheral blood. The cells from the peripheral blood of 12-day embryos were incubated in the presence of ¹⁴C-valine. Hemoglobin in the hemolysates prepared from these cells was separated by electrophoresis in polyacrylamide gel. The resulting four bands, *A, I, II,* and *III* (Fig. 1), were separately eluted. Adult mouse hemoglobin was added to each preparation as a marker. Globin was prepared from each hemoglobin and chromatographed in carboxymethyl cellulose columns as described in the text. *A* is the chromatography of globin of hemoglobin from *Band A* (Fig. 1), *B* from *Band I* (Fig. 1), *C* from *Band II* (Fig. 1), *D* from *Band III* (Fig. 1). ●——●, absorbance at 280 mμ; O– – –O, radioactivity.

(Fig. 2B). These globin chains correspond to Hb E_I. A small amount of labeled α-chain may be present in this preparation which is probably due to contamination of the gel eluate of Hb E_I with Hb E_{II} (1). The third and fourth bands (*Bands II* and *III*, Fig. 1) both contain α chains (Fig. 2, *C* and *D*) and another globin component more acidic than β chains. The β-like chains of these two hemoglobins differ from each other on the basis of the patterns of elution in parallel chromatograms. The β-like chain from *Band II* appears to be more acidic than the β-like chain from *Band III*, which would suggest that *Band II* corresponds to embryonic hemoglobin E_{II} and *Band III* to embryonic hemoglobin E_{III}. The β-like chains of hemoglobins from *Bands II* and *III* were further characterized by determining the relative amounts of ^{14}C-lysine and ^{3}H-arginine incorporated into these globin chains. The ratio of ^{14}C to ^{3}H radioactivity in the α chains prepared from hemoglobin of *Bands II* and *III* differed by 7% (Table I), but in the β-like chains of *Bands II* and *III* differed by 27%. In two other experiments, the ratio of incorporation of ^{14}C-lysine to that of ^{3}H-arginine was measured in α-globin and β-globin of adult hemoglobin and non-heme protein. In no instance did the duplicate determinations differ by more than 15%. It is likely that the β-like chain of *Band II* corresponds to *y*-globin (1). The nature of the β-like chain contained in *Band III* can be tentatively assigned as *z*-globin, although this globin chain, prepared from hemoglobin *Band III* purified by electrophoresis, has a somewhat different elution pattern than the *z*-globin, prepared from Hb E_{III} as purified by carboxymethyl cellulose chromatography. Gilman and Smithies (21) have confirmed, by means of two-dimensional starch gel electrophoresis that mouse fetal peripheral blood contains four hemoglobins and the globin composition of the four hemoglobins is, as indicated above, adult hemoglobin, composed of α and β chains; embryonic Hb E_I, *x* and *y* chains; embryonic Hb E_{II}, α and *y* chains; and embryonic Hb E_{III}, α and *z* chains.

Morphology of Erythroid Cells in Fetal Circulation—By morphological criteria, the yolk sac erythroid cells in the peripheral blood appear to differentiate as a relatively homogeneous population between Days 10 and 15 (Fig. 3). During this period, the population of yolk sac-derived erythroid cells in the fetal circulation undergoes structural changes, which include a decrease in the number of mitotic figures and condensation of nuclear chromatin; a decrease in the size of the nucleus and in the ratio of the area of nucleus to the area of the cytoplasm; and progressively less basophilic staining of the cytoplasm (presumably reflecting a decreasing content of ribosomes and RNA (17)) and an increase in the benzidine stain (stain for heme) of the cyto-

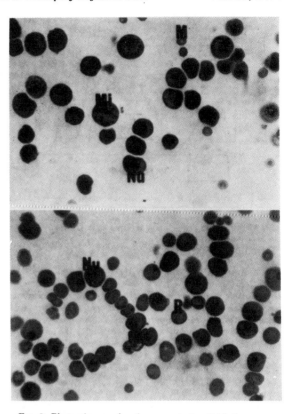

FIG. 3. Photomicrographs of representative fields from monolayer smears prepared from peripheral blood of fetal mice. *Upper*, Day 11 of gestation; yolk sac erythroid cells showing moderate condensation of chromatin (*Nu*) and frequent mitotic figures (*Mi*). A few contaminating red blood cells from the maternal circulation (*M*) are present. *Lower*, Day 14 of gestation; yolk sac erythroid cells showing advanced nuclear condensation (*Nu*). No mitotic figures are seen. Nonnucleated red blood cells of nepatic origin (*R*) are present at this stage of fetal development. × 1000.

plasm. These observations are in agreement with previous reports based on light microscopic and electron microscopic observations (11, 16, 22, 23).

Rate of Replication of Yolk Sac Erythroid Cells—The number of yolk sac erythroid cells per embryo increases each day between the 10th and 14th days of gestation. The number of yolk sac erythroid cells more than doubles between Day 10 and 11, and thereafter these cells continue to increase in number, but at a decreased rate (Table II). The yolk sac blood islands cease to be a site of active erythropoiesis by the 10th day of gestation (11, 23). The increase in the number of yolk sac erythroid cells reflects division of these cells in the circulation.[1] Data are not available as to the survival time of yolk sac erythroid cells. The increase in yolk sac erythroid cells represents a net increase.

Changes in Content of Total Embryonic Hemoglobin with Fetal Development—The content of embryonic hemoglobins, expressed

TABLE I

Incorporation of ^{14}C-lysine and of ^{3}H-arginine into globin chains prepared from electrophoretically separated hemoglobin Bands II and III

	α chain			β-like chain		
	^{14}C-Lysine	^{3}H-Arginine	^{14}C:^{3}H	^{14}C-Lysine	^{3}H-Arginine	^{14}C:^{3}H
	cpm/band			*cpm/band*		
Band II[a]	4670	615	7.6	4330	1180	3.7
Band III[a]	5620	787	7.1	2130	795	2.7

[a] *Band II* and *Band III* refer to the hemoglobin bands separated by electrophoresis in polyacrylamide gel (Fig. 1).

[1] A. de la Chapelle, A. Fantoni, and P. A. Marks, unpublished observations (manuscript in preparation, 1968).

TABLE II

Content of yolk sac-derived erythroid cells and of embryonic hemoglobins in fetal mice between the 10th and 14th days of gestation

Day of gestation	No. of experiments	Yolk sac erythroid cells × 10^6 per embryo[a]	Embryonic hemoglobins	
			μg/embryo	μg/10^6 yolk sac erythroid cells[b]
10	8	0.31 (0.25–0.40)	3.5 (3.2–4.0)	11.3
11	9	0.70 (0.48–0.85)	37.5 (24.0–67.2)	53.6
12	3	1.22 (1.05–1.45)	78.0 (52.0–104.0)	64.0
13	3	1.41 (1.07–1.81)	102.0 (83.0–121.0)	72.3
14	4	1.50 (1.47–1.53)	121.0 (60.0–178.0)	80.6

[a] Numbers represent the average of the value for all experiments, with the range of values indicated in parentheses.

[b] This value was calculated from the average values for embryonic hemoglobins per embryo and the number of yolk sac erythroid cells per embryo.

per embryo or per yolk sac erythroid cells, increases each day between the 10th and 14th days of gestation (Table II). The increment in embryonic hemoglobins is greatest between Day 10 and 11. The increase in hemoglobin content per embryo is less with each succeeding day of gestation. There is no information as to the disappearance rate of embryonic hemoglobins during this period. The changes in content of hemoglobin as determined in these studies represent net changes.

Changes in Content of Each Type of Embryonic Hemoglobin with Fetal Development—At Day 10 of gestation, Hb E_I is present in a greater amount than Hb E_{II} or E_{III} (Fig. 4). As fetal development proceeds, Hb E_{II} becomes the major embryonic hemoglobin component. On Day 10, Hb E_{II} constitutes, on the average, 35% of the total embryonic hemoglobin, and by Day 14, it accounts for, on the average, 51% of the total embryonic hemoglobin.

All three embryonic hemoglobins, expressed on a per embryo basis, increase in content at a relatively linear rate between Day 10 and 12 (Fig. 5, *left*). The content per embryo of Hb E_I and E_{II} increases at a similar rate between Day 10 and 12, while Hb E_{III} increases at a slower rate. Between Day 13 and 14, the content of Hb E_I and E_{III} remains relatively unchanged, while the rate of increase in Hb E_{II} continues at about the same rate. The amount of Hb E_I and Hb E_{III} per yolk sac erythroid cell increases between Day 10 and 11, but then tends to remain relatively unchanged between Day 11 and 14 (Fig. 5, *right*). The content of hemoglobin E_{II} per yolk sac erythroid cell rises throughout the period of study, that is, from the 10th day of gestation.

Rate of Synthesis of Embryonic Hemoglobins in Yolk Sac Erythroid Cells in Vitro—The rate of synthesis of each embryonic hemoglobin in yolk sac erythroid cells of 10-, 13- and 14-day-old fetuses was assayed by determining the incorporation of ^{14}C-

valine or ^{14}C-δ-aminolevulinic acid by these cells incubated in vitro. With the use of either ^{14}C-valine or ^{14}C-δ-aminolevulinic acid, at Day 10, Hb E_I is the most rapidly labeled of the three embryonic hemoglobins (Table III). By Day 13, Hb E_{II} is synthesized more rapidly than Hb E_I or Hb E_{III}. At each day studied, radioactivity was incorporated into Hb E_{III} at the lowest rate. These findings with respect to the alterations in relative rates of synthesis of Hb E_I, Hb E_{II}, and Hb E_{III} by yolk sac erythroid cells incubated in vitro are in agreement with the data presented above for relative changes in content of these hemoglobins in yolk sac erythroid cells as they differentiate in vivo.

Effect of Actinomycin on Hemoglobin Synthesis in Yolk Sac Erythroid Cells—It has been previously shown that hemoglobin synthesis in yolk sac erythroid cells at 11 days of gestation is not inhibited by actinomycin, although the antibiotic markedly depresses RNA and non-heme protein synthesis in these cells (17). Since the present studies are concerned with observations on cells from the 10th through the 14th days of gestation, the effect

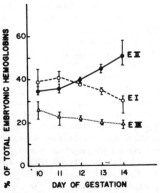

FIG. 4. Changes in the proportion of the content of the three embryonic hemoglobins in peripheral blood of fetal mice between the 10th and 14th days of gestation. O- - -O, Hb E_I; ●——●, Hb E_{II}; and △- - -△, Hb E_{III}. The *vertical bars* indicate the range of values for all studies for each day. The number of experiments performed for each day is indicated in Table I. At Day 12, the values for E_I were the same in each study; hence no range is indicated.

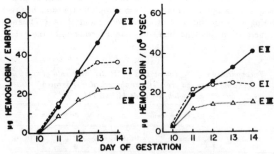

FIG. 5. Changes in the content of each of the embryonic hemoglobins in peripheral blood of fetal mice between the 10th and 14th days of gestation. *Left*, changes in content of embryonic hemoglobins expressed per embryo. *Right*, changes in content of embryonic hemoglobins expressed per 10^6 yolk sac erythroid cells. O- - -O, Hb E_I, ●——●, Hb E_{II}, △- - -△, Hb E_{III}.

TABLE III

Rates of synthesis of embryonic hemoglobins in yolk sac erythroid cells incubated in vitro

Day of gestation	^{14}C-Valine incorporation[a]			^{14}C-δ-Aminolevulinic acid incorporation[b]		
	E_I	E_{II}	E_{III}	E_I	E_{II}	E_{III}
10	42	34	24	39	37	24
13	37	51	12	28	56	18
14				24	66	10

[a] Values for incorporation of ^{14}C-valine are expressed as percentage of total radioactivity incorporated into hemoglobin which was recovered in the globin purified from each embryonic hemoglobin. The details of these procedures are described under "Methods."

[b] Values for incorporation of ^{14}C-δ-aminolevulinic acid are expressed as percentage of the total radioactivity incorporated into hemoglobin which was recovered in each embryonic hemoglobin following separation by electrophoresis as described under "Methods."

TABLE IV

Effect of actinomycin D on RNA, total protein, and hemoglobin synthesis in yolk sac erythroid cells from fetal mice at 10 days of gestation

Time[a]	RNA synthesis		Total protein synthesis		Hemoglobin synthesis	
	Control	+Actino-mycin	Control	+Actino-mycin	Control	+Actino-mycin
hrs	*cpm/0.1 mg RNA*		*cpm/0.1 mg protein*		*cpm/0.1 mg Hb*	
0	4,310		12,350		6,420	
3	5,160	282	12,590	4,460	5,340	5,820

[a] Time refers to the period of preincubation without or with actinomycin D (4 μg per ml). The cells were divided into two aliquots and one of each pair was incubated with ^{3}H-uridine and ^{14}C-valine, and the other with ^{14}C-δ-aminolevulinic acid for 10 min at 37°. The ^{14}C radioactivity incorporated into hot trichloracetic acid-insoluble material of cells incubated with ^{14}C-valine was taken as a measure of total protein synthesis; and that incorporated by the cells incubated with ^{14}C-δ-aminolevulinic acid was taken as a measure of hemoglobin synthesis.

of actinomycin on hemoglobin formation in yolk sac erythroid cells at Day 10 was determined (Table IV). Actinomycin D inhibited ^{3}H-uridine incorporation into RNA by 95% and ^{14}C-valine incorporation into total protein by 65%, but had no inhibitory effect on ^{14}C-δ-aminolevulinic acid incorporation. It was necessary to use ^{14}C-δ-aminolevulinic acid incorporation into hot trichloracetic acid-insoluble material as a measure of hemoglobin synthesis in 10-day yolk sac erythroid cells because too few cells could be harvested to permit determination of radioactivity incorporated into purified hemoglobin. To evaluate the validity of using δ-aminolevulinic acid in these experiments, the effect of actinomycin D on total protein and hemoglobin synthesis by yolk sac erythroid cells of Day 11 was determined with cells incubated with ^{3}H-valine and ^{14}C-δ-aminolevulinic acid. In these experiments, actinomycin had no effect on the incorporation of either ^{3}H-valine or ^{14}C-δ-aminolevulinic acid into hemoglobin isolated from total hemolysates by electrophoresis. ^{3}H-Valine incorporation into total protein was inhibited 44%, a figure in agreement with previously published results with 11-

day yolk sac erythroid cells (17). Actinomycin D did not inhibit ^{14}C-δ-aminolevulinic acid incorporation into total protein. Taken together, these data suggest that ^{14}C-δ-aminolevulinic acid is a valid indicator of hemoglobin synthesis in yolk sac erythroid cells under these experimental conditions and that hemoglobin synthesis is not inhibited by actinomycin D in 10-day yolk sac erythroid cells.

DISCUSSION

This paper provides evidence pertinent to the question of whether, in a single population of erythroid cells which form three distinct types of hemoglobins, the relative rates of synthesis of these proteins change as the cells differentiate. A prerequisite for this type of analysis of cell differentiation is the ability to obtain preparations of cells at different stages of differentiation. The yolk sac erythroid cells of the fetal mice provide a suitable model for this purpose because these cells appear to differentiate in a relatively homogeneous fashion in the fetal circulation as gestation proceeds between the 10th and 14th days. The present morphological evidence is in the agreement with previously published observations (16, 22) indicating that yolk sac erythroid cells differentiate as gestation proceeds. This morphological evidence includes the progressive decrease in the size of the nucleus, increasing pycnosis of the nuclear chromatin, a decrease in the size of the nucleus relative to that of the cytoplasm, increasing content of hemoglobin in the cytoplasm, and decreasing content of ribosomes in the cytoplasm. Further evidence that these cells differentiate as gestation proceeds is provided by the biochemical studies of DNA synthesis and mitotic rates[1] and of the capacity of these cells to form non-heme protein and hemoglobins (17). In the present study, there is no direct evidence that all three homoglobins are made in a single cell. This is a reasonable possibility in view of the apparent morphological homogeneity of the cell population through the various stages of differentiation between Day 10 and 14 of gestation. In addition, Matioli,[2] who used techniques for electrophoresis applied to single cells (24) has obtained direct evidence that the three types of embryonic hemoglobin are formed in a single yolk sac erythroid cell.

The present evidence indicates that as yolk sac erythroid cells differentiate, the relative rates of synthesis of the three embryonic hemoglobins change. The embryonic hemoglobin which is most abundant at Day 10, Hb E_I, is a relatively minor component by Day 14, at which time Hb E_{II} is the major embryonic hemoglobin component. These studies represent the first report of changes in the rates of synthesis of specific hemoglobins during erythroid cell differentiation in which one type of hemoglobin continues to be formed at a relatively linear rate while the rate of synthesis of the other types of embryonic hemoglobins declines.

Previous studies on the rates of synthesis of hemoglobins during erythroid cell development have been concerned primarily with the terminal phases of this process. In the later stages of erythroid cell development in chickens, Kabat and Attardi (25) found that the rate of decrease in capacity to synthesize the two types of hemoglobins present in these cells decays in a parallel fashion. In studies with cells from human subjects heterozygous for two mutations of the gene for β-globin, evidence has been obtained which was interpreted as indicating that during the end stages of erythroid cell development, *i.e.* during the maturation of reticulocytes, there is a more rapid decline in the capacity to

[2] G. T. Matioli, personal communication, 1968.

form the altered β-globin chains, β^s or β^o Arabia, relative to the decline in production of β^A (26). Similarly, in studies on the rates of synthesis of α- and β-globin chains in cells from human subjects with β-type thalassemia major, the rate of synthesis of β-globin chains declines more rapidly than that of α chains, as erythroid cells mature (27). In all of these previous studies, the experiments were performed with cells in which the capacity to synthesize all proteins was declining.

Changes in the relative rates of synthesis of hemoglobins E_I, E_{II}, and E_{III} occur during a stage of development of yolk sac erythroid cells when the formation of hemoglobin is resistant to inhibition by actinomycin D. By contrast, at the same stages of differentiation the synthesis of non-heme proteins is inhibited almost completely by the antibiotic (17).

Differential rates of degradation of the three embryonic hemoglobins could contribute to the changes in the relative amounts of these hemoglobins present in yolk sac erythroid cells at different stages of development. There have been no measurements of the survival times of the three embryonic hemoglobins. The indications of differences in relative rates of synthesis of embryonic hemoglobins in cells incubated *in vitro* (Table III) are consistent with the relative changes in content of the hemoglobins occurring *in vivo*. While different survival times for the three embryonic hemoglobins cannot be excluded, it does not appear that this is a major determinant of the changes in relative amounts of embryonic hemoglobins which occur as yolk sac erythroid cells differentiate.

Several possible alternative mechanisms can explain a relatively unchanged rate of synthesis of Hb E_{II} while that of Hb E_I and Hb E_{III} decays between Days 11 and 14. These can be considered in the context of the possibility (a) that mRNA for the embryonic globins decays at the same rate or (b) that mRNA for globin chains of Hb E_{II} (y-globin) is degraded at a slower rate than that for Hb E_I (x-globin) or Hb E_{III} (z-globin).

If mRNA for all globins decays at the same rate, the differences in relative rates of formation of the hemoglobins could result from at least one of the following mechanisms including (a) that there is continued formation of mRNA for y-globin of Hb E_{II}, but not for x- or z-globin chains of Hb E_I and Hb E_{III}, respectively. Against this possibility is the finding that all hemoglobin synthesis was resistant to actinomycin D and (b) that mRNA for α- and y-globin (Hb E_{II}), but not that for x- and z-globins, is present in excess of the number of molecules being actively translated. Under such circumstances, equal rates of decay of mRNA for different embryonic hemoglobins could occur, but mRNA is not limiting to the rate of Hb E_{II} formation. (c) Remaining templates for globins of Hb E_{II} are translated more efficiently than those for globins of Hb E_I or Hb E_{III}. This could involve a change in synthetic time for specific globin chain as the cells differentiate. It has been shown that the synthetic time for globin chain synthesis can change over at least a 2- to 3-fold range in reticulocytes, cells which form no RNA (8).

If mRNA for globins decays at different rates, then one might postulate that a selective degradation of mRNA occurs during yolk sac erythroid cell differentiation. An RNase has been described which can degrade polyribosomes in reticulocytes (28). This RNase has selectivity with respect to the structure of the RNA substrate.

Studies of several systems are providing evidence that mechanisms which do not require continued RNA synthesis are important in control of protein formation in differentiated tissues

such as lens (29, 30), sea urchin eggs (31), liver (32), and pancreas (33), as well as in erythroid cells (2–10, 34, 35). Taken together, the present evidence suggests that there are mechanisms which regulate the rates of formation of Hb E_I, Hb E_{II}, and Hb E_{III} as yolk sac erythroid cells develop which do not depend on immediate or continued RNA synthesis.

REFERENCES

1. FANTONI, A., BANK, A., AND MARKS, P. A., *Science*, **157**, 3795 (1967).
2. LONDON, I. M., TAVILL, A. S., VANDERHOFF, G. A., HUNT, T., AND GRAYZEL, A. I., *Develop. Biol.*, 1(suppl.), 227 (1967).
3. MARKS, P. A., FANTONI, A., AND DE LA CHAPELLE, A., *Vitamins Hormones*, in press.
4. MARKS, P. A., BURKA, E. R., CONCONI, F., PERL, W., AND RIFKIND, R. A., *Proc. Nat. Acad. Sci. U. S. A.*, **53**, 1437 (1965).
5. WAXMAN, H. S., AND RABINOWITZ, M., *Biochem. Biophys. Res. Commun.*, **19**, 538 (1965).
6. WAXMAN, H. S., AND RABINOWITZ, M., *Biochim. Biophys. Acta*, **129**, 369 (1966).
7. GRAYZEL, A. I., HORCHNER, P., AND LONDON, I. M., *Proc. Nat. Acad. Sci. U. S. A.*, **55**, 650 (1966).
8. CONCONI, F., BANK, A., AND MARKS, P. A., *J. Mol. Biol.*, **19**, 525 (1966).
9. KAZAZIAN, H. H., JR., AND ITANO, H. A., *Fed. Proc.*, **27**, 235 (1968).
10. GRAYZEL, A. I., FUHR, J. E., AND LONDON, I. M., *Biochem. Biophys. Res. Commun.*, **28**, 705 (1967).
11. RUSSELL, E. S., AND BERNSTEIN, S. E., in E. L. GREEN (Editor), *Biology of the laboratory mouse*, McGraw-Hill Book Company, Inc., New York, 1966, p. 351.
12. MARKS, P. A., AND KOVACH, J. S., in A. MONROY AND A. MOSCONA (Editors), *Current topics in developmental biology*, Vol. 1, Academic Press, New York, 1967, p. 213.
13. SOUTHARD, J. L., WOLFE, H. G., AND RUSSELL, E. S., *Nature*, **208**, 1126 (1965).
14. DRABKIN, D. L., *J. Biol. Chem.*, **98**, 719 (1932).
15. WINTROBE, M. M., *Clinical hematology*, Lea and Febiger, Philadelphia, 1956, p. 404.
16. KOVACH, J. S., MARKS, P. A., RUSSELL, E. S., AND EPLER, H., *J. Mol. Biol.*, **25**, 131 (1967).
17. FANTONI, A., DE LA CHAPELLE, A., RIFKIND, R. A., AND MARKS, P. A., *J. Mol. Biol.*, **33**, 79 (1968).
18. DAVIS, B. S., *Disc electrophoresis, Part II*, Bulletin of Distillation Industries, Rochester, 1963.
19. *Chemical formulation for disc electrophoresis*, Canal Industrial Corporation, Bethesda, Maryland, 1965.
20. WILLIAMS, D. E., AND REISFELD, R. A., *Ann. N. Y. Acad. Sci.*, **121**, 373 (1964).
21. GILMAN, J. G., AND SMITHIES, O., *Science*, **160**, 885 (1968).
22. CRAIG, M. L., AND RUSSELL, E. L., *Develop. Biol.*, **10**, 191 (1964).
23. CHUI, D., DJALDETTI, M., AND RIFKIND, R. A., *Proceedings of the Twelfth Congress of the International Society of Hematology, New York, 1968*, Abstract 00-5.
24. MATIOLI, G. T., AND NIEWISCH, H. B., *Science*, **150**, 1824 (1965).
25. KABAT, D., AND ATTARDI, G., *Biochim. Biophys. Acta*, **138**, 382 (1967).
26. BOYER, S. H., HATHAWAY, P., AND GARRICH, M. D., *Cold Spring Harbor Symp. Quant. Biol.*, **29**, 33 (1964).
27. BRAVERMAN, A. S., AND BANK, A., *Clin. Res.*, **15**, 462 (1967).
28. FARKAS, W., AND MARKS, P. A., *J. Biol. Chem.*, **243**, 6464 (1968).
29. PAPACONSTANTINOU, J., *Science*, **156**, 338 (1967).
30. REEDER, R., AND BELL, E., *J. Mol. Biol.*, **23**, 577 (1967).
31. HULTIN, T., *Develop. Biol.*, **10**, 305 (1964).
32. GARREN, L. D., HOWELL, R. R., TOMKINS, G. M., AND CROCCO, R. M., *Proc. Nat. Acad. Sci. U. S. A.*, **52**, 1121 (1964).
33. WESSELLS, N. K., *Develop. Biol.*, **9**, 92 (1964).
34. WILT, F. H., *J. Mol. Biol.*, **12**, 331 (1965).
35. WAINWRIGHT, S. D., AND WAINWRIGHT, L. K., *Can. J. Biochem.*, **44**, 1543 (1966).

Reprinted from *J. Mol. Biol.* (1968) **32**, 481–492

Hemoglobin Synthesis during Amphibian Metamorphosis

I. Chemical Studies on the Hemoglobins from the Larval and Adult Stages of *Rana catesbeiana*

Bernard Moss† and Vernon M. Ingram

Department of Biology
Massachusetts Institute of Technology
Cambridge, Massachusetts, U.S.A.

(*Received 4 August 1967*)

The hemoglobins of *Rana catesbeiana* tadpoles were resolved into five characteristic components by polyacrylamide gel electrophoresis. Characterization of the peptide chains of the major and of one other component showed each to have two types of chain, none of which is in common. The major tadpole hemoglobin with two valine NH_2-terminal groups has no peptide chain in common with the major frog hemoglobin. The latter has two chains beginning with glycine. No other amino acid groups appear to be available to the Edman end group reagent.

1. Introduction

Hemoglobin polypeptide chains of different amino acid sequence are synthesized during successive stages of human embryonic and fetal development (Schroeder & Matsuda, 1958; Hunt, 1959; Huehns, Dance, Beaven, Hecht & Motulsky, 1964). Analogous, although so far less well-studied changes may also occur in other vertebrates (see Solomon, 1965 for a recent review) but in no case are the significant regulatory events known. The amphibia appear to be particularly suitable experimental animals since the replacement of early hemoglobins begins in the free-living tadpole stage during metamorphosis or abruptly following administration of thyroid hormones to immature tadpoles (Herner & Frieden, 1961). Preliminary evidence indicates that thyroxine, administered to immature *Rana catesbeiana* tadpoles, induces the *de novo* synthesis of adult hemoglobin polypeptide chains and represses synthesis of tadpole hemoglobin polypeptide chains (Moss & Ingram, 1965).

Limited information is available concerning the structures of the multiple hemoglobins of *R. catesbeiana* (Baglioni & Sparks, 1963; Hamada, Sakai, Shukuya & Kaziro, 1964; Hamada & Shukuya, 1966; Riggs & Aggarwal, 1967; Stratton & Wise 1967). The present studies are concerned with the nature of the multiple hemoglobins of the tadpole stage, particularly their polypeptide chain structures, and their biochemical relationship to hemoglobins found in the adult animal. The changes in hemoglobin synthesis following the administration of L-thyroxine are reported in the accompanying paper (Moss & Ingram, 1968).

† Present address: National Institute of Allergy and Infectious Diseases, National Institutes of Health, Bethesda, Md., U.S.A.

31

2. Materials and Methods

(a) Source of animals

Larval and adult stages of *R. catesbeiana* were obtained from the Connecticut Valley Biological Supply Co., Southampton, Mass., or where specified from the Carolina Biological Supply Co., Burlington, N.C.

(b) Preparation of hemoglobin solutions

Tadpoles, anesthetized by briefly immersing in ice water or 1:3000 solution of tricaine methanesulfonate (MS222, Sandoz Pharmaceuticals, Hanover, N.J.), were decapitated at the level of the truncus arteriosus and the heart allowed to pump the blood into a small amount of heparinized Ringer's solution (6·6 g NaCl, 0·15 g KCl, 0·15 g $CaCl_2$ in 1 l. of distilled water, adjusted to pH 7·8 with $NaHCO_3$). Frogs, anesthetized with ether or by hypothermia were bled from the truncus arteriosus with a hypodermic syringe. The blood cells were washed 5 times with Ringer's solution by repeated sedimentation, resuspended in 1/2 concn Ringer's solution and lysed by freezing and thawing 3 times. The hemolysates were clarified by extraction with a 0·2 vol. of carbon tetrachloride. The aqueous layer was separated by low-speed centrifugation and additional particulate material was removed by a second centrifugation at 20,000 *g* for 15 min. All procedures were carried out at 0 to 4°C.

Heme concentration was determined as the pyridine protohemochromogen (Porra & Jones, 1963). The extinction coefficient of tadpole methemoglobin cyanide was determined from the latter value and was found to be within 1% of that obtained simultaneously for human hemoglobin. Hemoglobin concentration was then determined by diluting hemoglobin in Drabkin's solution (1·0 g $NaHCO_3$, 50 mg KCN, 200 mg $K_3Fe(CN)_6$ and water to 1 l.) and using the mM extinction coefficient of 11·5 at 540 mμ (Drabkin & Austin, 1935).

(c) Analytical polyacrylamide gel electrophoresis of hemoglobin

The disc electrophoresis method of Ornstein (1964) and Davis (1964) was used, but the reservoir buffer was modified to contain 6·32 g Tris, 3·94 g glycine and 0·10 g KCN/l. and the procedure was carried out at 2°C. Acrylamide, *N,N'*-methylene-bisacrylamide (bisacrylamide), *N,N,N',N'*-tetramethylethylene-diamine (TEMED) and glycine (ammonia-free) were obtained from Distillation Products Industries, Rochester, N.Y.

Hemoglobin samples were converted to the cyanmet form by the addition of 0·1 to 0·2 vol. of 2% $K_3Fe(CN)_6$, 0·5% KCN, 0·1% $NaHCO_3$. A solution containing 50 μg of hemoglobin in 20 μl. was layered over the concentrating gel. The current was maintained at 0·5 mA/tube until the hemoglobin entered the concentrating gel and then raised to 2 or 3 mA/tube until the hemoglobin was observed to have moved an appropriate distance, usually in about 3 hr. The gels were removed from the glass tubes, and stained overnight by immersion in 1% amido black (Hartmann–Leddon Co., Philadelphia, Pa.) in 7% acetic acid. Excess stain was removed by washing with 7% acetic acid. The gels were stained for hemoglobin by placing them in 1 M-acetic acid for 5 min and then transferring to a benzidine solution prepared by dissolving 0·2 g of benzidine dihydrochloride in 100 ml. of 0·5% acetic acid. Just before use, 0·2 ml. of 30% hydrogen peroxide was added. The gels were kept in the benzidine–hydrogen peroxide solution until the blue color developed sufficiently, usually 5 to 10 min, transferred to a solution of 0·5 M-acetic acid, 0·5 M-sodium acetate and photographed immediately.

(d) Preparative polyacrylamide gel electrophoresis of tadpole hemoglobin

A commercial apparatus (Buchler Instruments, Inc., Fort Lee, N.J.) derived from a prototype of Jovin, Chrambach & Naughton (1964) was used. The solutions described in section (c) above were used, but the elution buffer and the lower reservoir buffer contained 12·1 g Tris, 50 ml. of 1 N-HCl and 100 mg of KCN/l. (pH 8·1, 25°C). The concentrating gel was twice the volume of the sample and the resolving gel was 6 cm long. Approximately 60 mg of methemoglobin cyanide was applied in a vol. of 5 ml. The current was regulated at 20 mA until the hemoglobin entered the gel and then increased to 40 to 50 mA. The column was cooled by the circulation of water at 2°C through the jacketed glass column. The elution rate was 0·5 ml./min and 6-ml. fractions were collected.

Pooled fractions, in dialysis tubing, were concentrated by application of washed, dry Sephadex or by lyophilization.

(e) *Preparation of globin*

Hemoglobin was dialyzed against 0.001 M-Na_2HPO_4 and globin was prepared by acid–acetone precipitation according to the method of Rossi-Fanelli, Antonini & Caputo (1958) except that the precipitated globin was not dialyzed but was washed with acetone, then resuspended in water and lyophilized. Occasionally the globin was reprecipitated with acid–acetone to remove traces of heme. The concentration of globin was determined by a microbiuret procedure (Itzhaki & Gill, 1964). An $E_{1\ cm}^{1\%}$ at 310 mμ of 20.9 was obtained for tadpole globin.

(f) *Reduction and aminoethylation or alkylation of globin*

Aminoethylation of reduced globin was carried out under nitrogen in 8 M-urea as described by Raferty & Cole (1963) and modified by Jones (1964). Reagent grade urea was deionized by passage through a mixed bed ion-exchange resin (AG 501-8D, Bio-Rad Laboratories, Richmond, Calif.) and recrystallized. Ethylenimine was obtained from Matheson, Coleman & Bell, Norwood, N.J. A negative nitroprusside test in 2 to 2.5 hr indicated the reaction of all thiol groups. At this time, the pH was lowered to 2 with HCl and the globin freed of reagents by passage through a Sephadex G25 column equilibrated with 0.2 M-acetic acid. The material was lyophilized over NaOH pellets and P_2O_5 and stored at $-20°C$.

Alkylation of reduced globin was carried out in 8 M-urea with thrice recrystallized iodoacetamide according to Edelman, Benacerraf, Ovary & Poulik (1961).

(g) *Analytical polyacrylamide gel electrophoresis of globin*

All solutions were freshly prepared, 8 M in deionized urea.

(i) *8 M-Urea, pH 2.8*

The reservoir buffer contained 59.0 ml. of 90% formic acid and 6.0 ml. of 2 N-NaOH/l. The gel solutions were prepared by mixing an equal vol. of the following 3 solutions: (A) 18 g acrylamide, 0.44 g bisacrylamide in 100 ml.; (B) 17.7 ml. 90% formic acid, 1.8 ml. 2 N-NaOH, 1.7 ml. TEMED in 100 ml.; (C) 1.0 g ammonium persulfate in 100 ml. The deaerated gel solution was carefully layered with 8 M-urea containing 0.33 g of ammonium persulfate/100 ml. Excess persulfate ion was removed by a preliminary electrophoresis overnight at 2 mA/tube. In some experiments the upper reservoir buffer was made 1 mM in mercaptoethylamine (Distillation Products Industries, Rochester, N.Y.) and 0.1 M in mercaptoethanol in order to introduce thiol groups into the gel. The dry globin was dissolved in buffer containing 5% sucrose; 50 μg of protien in 10 μl. was layered over the gel and electrophoresis carried out at 1 mA/gel for 30 min and then at 4 to 5 mA for 3 to 11 hr.

(ii) *8 M-Urea, pH 9.8*

The reservoir buffers contained 43.6 g Tris, 3.2 g glycine/l. The gel solutions were prepared by mixing equal volumes of the following three solutions: (A) 21.2 g acrylamide, and 0.56 g bisacrylamide, in 100 ml.; (B) 8.72 g Tris, 0.65 g glycine, and 0.06 ml. TEMED in 100 ml.; (C) 0.28 g ammonium persulfate in 100 ml. Globin (0.1 mg) was applied in buffer containing 5% sucrose. The current was regulated at 1 mA for 20 min and then raised to 3 mA/tube for approximatley 3.5 hr.

(iii) *Discontinuous Tris–glycine, 8 M-urea*

Stock solutions were similar to those described in section (d) except that all solutions contained 8 M-deionized urea and cyanide was omitted.

(h) *Preparative polyacrylamide gel electrophoresis of tadpole globin chains in 8 M-urea*

The compositions of all buffer solutions were identical to those used for the pH 2.8 in 8 M-urea analytical gels except that the concentration of formic acid and sodium hydroxide in the reservoir buffer was doubled for use as lower reservoir and elution buffers. The gels were 3 cm high and cooled to several degrees below room temperature. A preliminary electrophoresis at 120 mA was carried out for 5 hr to remove excess persulfate. Thiol groups were introduced into the gel as described above section (g)(i) and the globin solution was made 0·1 M in mercaptoethanol. The sample was applied in 5 ml. and the current regulated at 50 mA until the protein entered the gel. The current was then increased to 120 mA. A solution, of the same composition as the gel buffer, was pumped through the elution space until the protein bands (visible as refractile zones) neared the bottom of the gel. At this time elution buffer was pumped through at a flow rate of 0·5 ml./min. The effluent was monitored at 280 mμ. The pooled fractions were dialyzed against deionized water and lyophilized.

(i) Tryptic digestion and fingerprinting

Salt-free globin was dissolved in 2% ammonium bicarbonate or dilute trimethylamine (Baglioni, 1965) and an amount of trypsin (trichloroacetic acid-precipitated, Worthington Biochemical Corp., Freehold, N.J.) equal to 1/50 of the weight of globin was added. The solution was continuously mixed for 3 hr at 38°C. The pH was then lowered to approximately 6 with acetic acid. Trypsin was denatured and the core coagulated by heating at 90°C for 5 min. Insoluble material was removed by sedimentation at 15,000 g for 30 min. Traces of ammonium bicarbonate were removed by repeated lyophilization.

The peptides were fingerprinted as described by Ingram (1958) and modified by Baglioni (1961).

(j) N-terminal analysis

N-terminal analysis was performed on 10 to 15 mg quantities of globin by the paper strip technique for the stepwise degradation of proteins, described by Fraenkel-Conrat, Harris & Levy (1955). The cyclization time was varied between 12 and 15 hr. The dried phenylthiohydantoins were dissolved in redistilled acetone and chromatographed with standard PTH† amino acids (Mann Research Laboratories, Inc., N.Y.) using the solvent systems described by Sjöquist (1959). The PTH amino acids were located on the starch impregnated paper with an iodine–azide reagent (Sjöquist, 1953).

3. Results

(a) Analytical gel electrophoresis of tadpole hemoglobins

Initial experiments confirmed the starch gel electrophoretic pattern of tadpole hemoglobins obtained by Baglioni & Sparks (1963). Greater resolution of the hemo-globins was achieved by disc electrophoresis on polyacrylamide gels (Moss & Ingram, 1965). Four or five red bands could be seen by visual inspection of unstained gels following the electrophoresis of pooled hemolysate (Plate I(a)). Only a few additional minor proteins, located nearer to the origin, could be detected by staining with amido black (Plate I(b)). The multiplicity of bands is not due to variation in the oxidation state of the heme, since prior to electrophoresis hemoglobin had been con-verted to the methemoglobin–cyanide form and additional cyanide was added to the electrophoresis buffer in order to maintain this state. The multiple bands are not artifacts produced by the discontinuous electrophoretic system, since an identical pattern was obtained with a continuous buffer. Varying the method of preparation of the hemoglobin by omission of freeze–thawing, carbon tetrachloride extraction and ferricyanide oxidation did not eliminate the minor hemoglobin bands.

Variations in the pattern of minor hemoglobin bands from individual tadpoles of identical size and appearance, obtained from the same shipment, were frequently found (Plate I(b) and (c)). Commonly an additional band (2a) just ahead of band 2 is present. Occasionally band 1 is absent. Bands 1 and 2a stain more weakly with benzidine than would be expected from the intensity of the amido black color (Plate I(c)). Sometimes band 4 (or a band of similar mobility as 4) appeared in high concentra-tion. Tadpoles with large amounts of hemoglobin 4 were only infrequently obtained

† Abbreviations used: PTH, phenylthiohydantoin; DNP, dinitrophenol.

from the Connecticut Valley Biological Supply Co., Southampton, Mass. but were regularly received in shipments from the Carolina Biological Supply Co., Burlington, N. C. The difference may reflect a subspecies variation in the tadpoles from these two sources. All structural studies were done with tadpoles from the former supplier. No systematic variations in the pattern of hemoglobin bands was found in tadpoles ranging in size from 2 to 16 g; therefore the heterogeneity and individual differences cannot be ascribed to an ontogenetic basis. Inbred stocks of *R. catesbeiana* are not available and the long developmental period makes genetic studies difficult.

(b) *Gel filtration of tadpole hemoglobins*

The minor tadpole hemoglobins were partially separated from the major hemoglobin by gel filtration on Sephadex G100. They eluted in a region suggestive of a molecular weight range between the major component and 17,000. The separation probably results from the greater dissociation of those hemoglobins present at lower concentration (Guidotti & Craig, 1963; Whitaker, 1963; Andrews, 1964). In addition, a discrete peak of non-heme protein has the elution volume expected for a 17,000 molecular weight globin polypeptide chain. However, gel electrophoresis suggested that the latter material is heterogeneous.

(c) *Preparative separation of the hemoglobin components*

Four distinct hemoglobin fractions (Plate II) were obtained by preparative poly-acrylamide gel electrophoresis. The initial two very high $A_{280m\mu}$ peaks are not proteins, as judged by their ultraviolet absorption spectra, and presumably represent gel polymerization products and excess ferricyanide (Jovin *et al.*, 1964). Proteins with low electrophoretic mobilities (e.g. peak 4) are considerably diluted because of the constant elution flow and because of the increased time in which diffusion may occur. The four hemoglobin peaks correspond to the hemoglobin bands on analytical gels (Plate II). Hemoglobin 3 contaminates peak 4 to some extent as expected from the appearance of the elution profile.

TABLE 1

Relative amounts of the four tadpole hemoglobin components

Expt no.	Hemoglobin component			
	1 (%)	2 (%)	3 (%)	4 (%)
1	4·3	27·2	64·4	4·1
2	3·7	18·0	75·3	3·0
3	10·2	18·4	67·8	3·6
4	6·0	14·8	72·2	7·0
Average	6	20	70	4

The recovery of hemoglobin following gel electrophoresis was greater than 95%. The relative percentages of hemoglobin contained in the four components appear in Table 1, obtained from the fractionation of four separate samples of pooled hemoglobin solutions.

Absorption spectra were made from the four peak fractions immediately after elution. The visible absorption maxima of all four are identical and correspond to the maxima of hemoglobin in the cyanmet form (Hamada *et al.*, 1964).

(d) *Polypeptide chain composition*

The molecular weight of tadpole hemoglobin has been determined by sedimentation to be 68,000 (Riggs, 1951). Assuming that there is one heme per subunit, as in mammalian and avian hemoglobins, the subunit molecular weight could be established by determining the percentage of iron in purified tadpole hemoglobin. The major tadpole hemoglobin (fraction 3, Plate II) was purified by preparative polyacrylamide gel electrophoresis, dialyzed against high ionic strength buffer (0.15 M-NaCl–0.005 M-Na$_2$HPO$_4$, pH 7.5), and passed through a Millipore filter. The material was dried *in vacuo* at 100°C and an iron determination was performed by Dr George Maniatis of this laboratory using 1,10-phenanthroline (Adler & George, 1965; Cameron, 1965). The subunit weights for two samples were determined to be 16,400 and 17,900. The 68,000 molecular weight molecule thus contains four atoms of iron and presumably four polypeptide chains of approximately 17,000 molecular weight.

To resolve the polypeptide chains of the four hemoglobin fractions, the heme was removed by acid–acetone precipitation, possible disulfide bonds were reduced at pH 8.6 in deionized 8 M-urea with 0.1 M-mercaptoethanol, thiol groups were blocked by alkylation with iodoacetamide or aminoethylation, and finally the dissociated chains were resolved by polyacrylamide gel electrophoresis at either acid or alkaline pH in 8 M-urea.

The electrophoresis of unfractionated tadpole globin in the Tris–glycine–8 M-urea buffers gave a multiple band pattern. The intensity of the minor bands varied somewhat with different samples of globin, possibly related to the varying amounts of the minor hemoglobins. Globin fractions, prepared from the four separated hemoglobin components, isolated by preparative polyacrylamide gel electrophoresis, were resolved into characteristic patterns (Plate III). The patterns remained the same when the globin was simply reduced, reduced and alkylated, or not reduced at all, suggesting the absence of disulfide bonds. The polypeptide chains of hemoglobin fraction 1 could not be resolved into more than a single major component. However, two prominent bands were separated for both fractions 2 and 3. Fraction 4 has been resolved into two bands that correspond to contaminating polypeptide chains of fraction 3, and a polypeptide chain separation identical to that in Plate III (b) was obtained with the alkaline continuous buffer system described in Materials and Methods section (g).

The electrophoresis of unfractionated tadpole globin in the 8 M-urea, pH 2.8 buffer gives a simple pattern that does not change with aminoethylation or alkylation. As in the alkaline 8 M-urea system, the polypeptide chains of hemoglobin 1 cannot be resolved into more than a single major band (Plate III). Globin prepared from hemoglobin fractions 2 and 3 gives rise to fast (F) and slow (S) bands. At this pH the polypeptide chains of hemoglobins 2 and 3 have similar mobilities. Slight differences in the mobilities of the F bands appeared upon prolonged electrophoresis (11 hours). One major and two minor components were resolved from fraction 4. It will be necessary to obtain the minor hemoglobin component 4 in purer form before its polypeptide chain composition can be defined.

Since proteins are separated by gel electrophoresis on the basis of size as well as charge, it was considered possible that the F bands are unaggregated chains and the S bands are aggregates of the same or different chains. This possibility was investigated by passing tadpole globin through a one-meter column of Sephadex G200 equilibrated with the same 8 M-urea, pH 2.8 buffer used for analytical electrophoresis. A single protein peak with an elution volume slightly greater than that of aminoethylated human globin was obtained, indicating the absence of aggregation.

(e) Isolation and fingerprinting of tadpole globin polypeptide chains

The polypeptide chains of the major tadpole hemoglobin were separated from each other by preparative polyacrylamide gel electrophoresis in an 8 M-urea, pH 2·8 buffer system. The proteins were recovered either by continuous elution or by slicing out the refractive bands, followed by homogenization and elution into the 8 M-urea buffer. The separated components ran as single bands upon re-electrophoresis (Plate IV). The polypeptide chains, after extensive dialysis and lyophilization, were digested with trypsin and fingerprinted. Ninhydrin staining revealed 10 to 11 spots from each chain. This number of peptides is less than that found for whole globin, and unique peptides were present in the fingerprints of each chain.

Two well-separated peaks were also obtained by chromatography of globin on IRC50 columns using non-linear urea gradients at pH 2·8; however, the recovery of S chains was poor.

(f) Differences between the hemoglobins of the tadpole and adult frog

The occurrence of certain amphibian hemoglobins in a higher molecular weight form was first described by Svedberg & Hedenius (1934) and has been further elucidated by Riggs, Sullivan & Agee (1964) and Trader & Frieden (1966). In the present studies undialyzed frog hemoglobin was stored at −20°C for four days in order to allow complete dimerization to occur. At this time approximately 70% of the hemo-

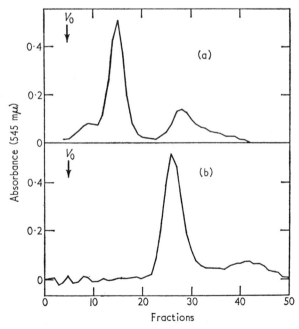

FIG. 1. Filtration of frog and tadpole hemoglobin through Sephadex G100.
Column 0·9 cm × 100 cm. Solvent: 0·1 M-NaCl, 0·1 M-Tris–HCl, 1·5 mM-KCN, pH 8·3. Hemoglobin was stored at −20°C for 4 days, diluted to approximately 3·5 mg/0·2 ml. and applied to the column. The same column was used for both hemoglobins. (a) Frog hemoglobin; (b) tadpole hemoglobin. V_0 (void volume) indicates position of nucleoprotein contained in hemolysate.

globin is in a heavy molecular weight (7 s) form. The undimerized fraction of frog hemoglobin has a molecular weight equal to that of human hemoglobin, judged by the rate of filtration on thin layers of Sephadex G100. Tadpole hemoglobin does not dimerize. The Sephadex G100 elution volume of undimerized frog hemoglobin is approximately the same as that of tadpole hemoglobin (Fig. 1). In addition to the major dimerized component, a small amount of still higher molecular weight hemoglobin is present.

Frog hemoglobin was resolved into five bands by starch gel electrophoresis at pH 9·3. Under these conditions, some of the tadpole and frog hemoglobins have similar mobilities. Better resolution has been obtained using discontinuous polyacrylamide gel electrophoresis (Plate V). The major band is the frog hemoglobin dimer.

An almost complete separation of tadpole hemoglobins from frog hemoglobins was obtained by electrophoresis on starch gel or Pevikon block at pH values near neutrality (Fig. 2). Quantitative elution from the Pevikon granules (three experiments) permitted

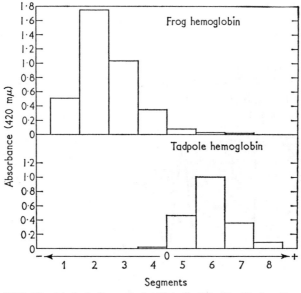

FIG. 2. Pevikon C870 (Stockholm's Superfosfet Fabrik AD, Stockholm, Sweden) block electrophoresis of tadpole and frog hemoglobins. Buffer: 0·04 M-sodium phosphate, pH 6·7. Electrophoresis was carried out at a constant voltage of 200 v for 16 hr at 2°C and then the hemoglobin was eluted from eight 1·5-cm segments.

the estimation of the maximum amounts of frog hemoglobin in tadpoles (0 to 5%) and tadpole hemoglobin in frogs (1 to 6%). The values are probably upper limits, since the small amounts of hemoglobin with overlapping mobilities may not be identical in structure.

(g) N-terminal amino acid analysis

N-terminal amino acid analysis, by a modification of the phenylthiohydantoin method of Edman, of tadpole and frog globins yielded only valine for the former and only glycine for the latter (Plate VI). In two experiments the yield of PTH amino acid was calculated as described by Fraenkel-Conrat et al. (1955) from the ultraviolet absorption. Only 1·4 to 1·6 moles of PTH amino acid per 65,000 molecular weight was

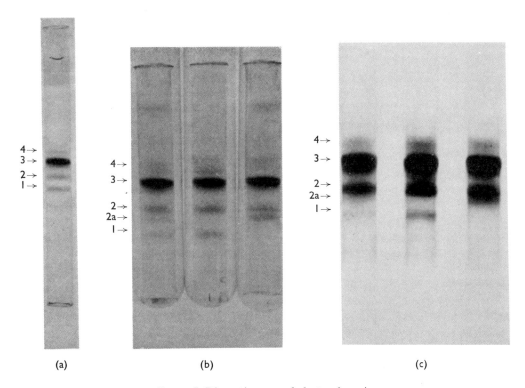

PLATE I. Discontinuous gel electrophoresis.
(a) Tadpole hemoglobin (photographed as methemoglobin cyanide). (b) and (c) Variation in the pattern of minor hemoglobins of individual tadpoles: (b) amido black stain, (c) benzidine stain. The pattern in the left gel of (b) is the most common.

[facing page 488

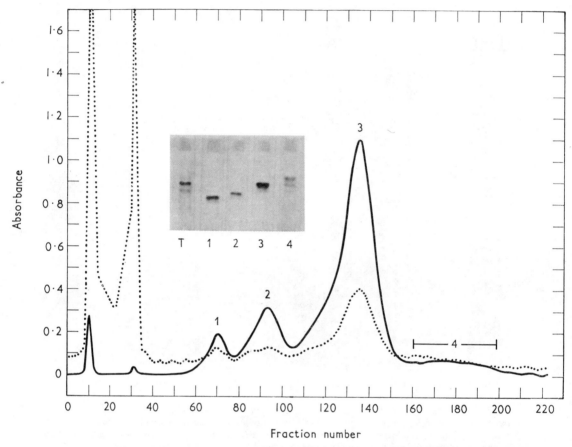

PLATE II. Preparative disc gel electrophoresis of tadpole hemoglobin.

The initial two very high $A_{280m\mu}$ peaks represent gel polymerization products and excess ferricyanide. The 4 hemoglobin peak fractions were concentrated and re-run on analytical polyacrylamide gels using the same buffer system (inset). The gels were stained with benzidine. T corresponds to the total unfractionated hemoglobin.

Acid–urea

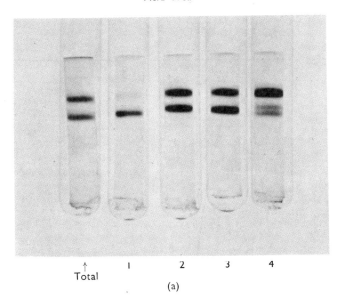

Total ↑   1   2   3   4

(a)

Alkaline–urea

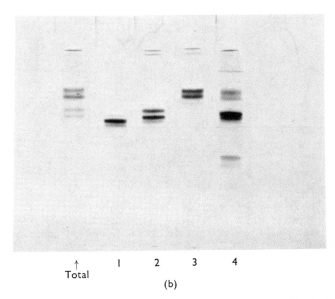

Total ↑   1   2   3   4

(b)

PLATE III. Electrophoresis of the tadpole globin polypeptide chains.
Globin was prepared from the tadpole hemoglobin components 1, 2, 3 and 4 of Plate II. Approximately 50 μg of reduced globin was submitted to electrophoresis in (a) the 8 M-urea, pH 2·8 and in (b) the discontinuous Tris–glycine, 8 M-urea, polyacrylamide gel systems. Amido black stain.

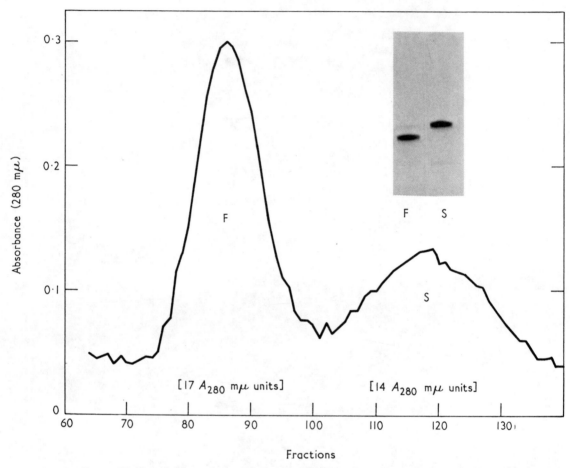

PLATE IV. Preparative polyacrylamide gel electrophoresis of tadpole globin chains.

Globin was prepared from the major tadpole hemoglobin (cyanmet form) obtained by gel filtration on Sephadex G100 in 0·1 M-NaCl, 0·1 M-Tris–HCl, 1·5 mM-KCN, pH 8·3. Electrophoresis was performed in 8 M-urea at pH 2·8. See Materials and Methods for details. The fractions indicated by the brackets were pooled, dialyzed against water, lyophilized and re-run under similar conditions on analytical gels (inset). The gels are stained with amido black.

414

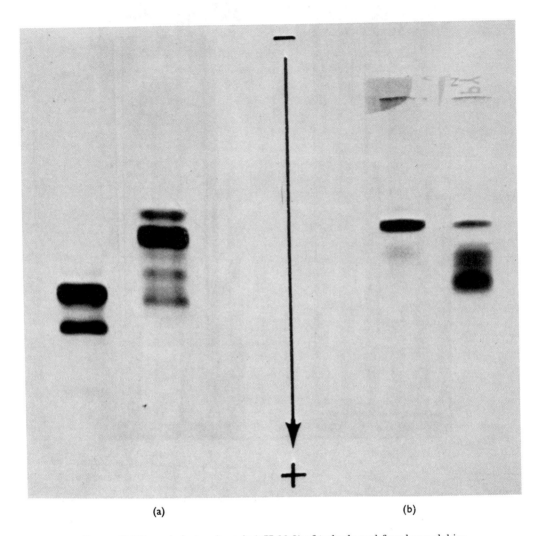

(a)   (b)

PLATE V. Disc gel electrophoresis (pH 10·3) of tadpole and frog hemoglobins.
(a) Left: whole tadpole hemoglobin. Right: whole frog hemoglobin. Amido black stain. (b) Fractions 14 to 16 (left) and 26 to 30 (right) of Plate III(a) were pooled, concentrated and dialyzed against 0·001 M-Na$_2$HPO$_4$.

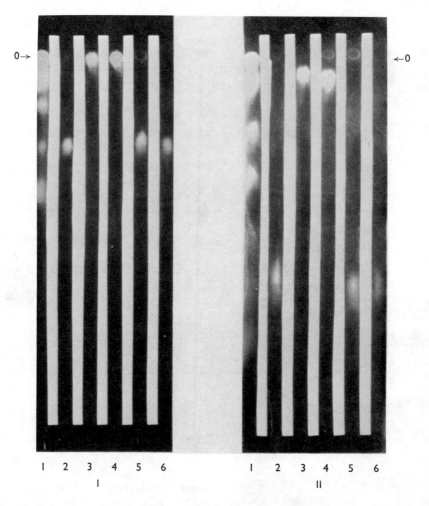

PLATE VI. Chromatographic identification of PTH amino acids. N-terminal amino acid analysis was done by the paper strip modification of the Edman technique on globin derived from human hemoglobin A and globin derived from the major tadpole and frog hemoglobins purified by filtration on Sephadex G100 columns. Descending chromatography was carried out in solvent systems I and II (Sjöquist, 1959) and the spots located by dipping the starch-impregnated papers in an iodine azide reagent (Sjöquist, 1953). O indicates the origin and, numbered from left to right, the samples contained:

(1) PTH-Leu, Val, Phe, Met, Ala, Trp, Gly, Tyr, Thr and Ser.
(2) PTH derivative of human globin.
(3) PTH-Gly.
(4) PTH derivative of frog globin.
(5) PTH derivative of tadpole globin.
(6) PTH-Val.

recovered from tadpole globin purified either by preparative gel electrophoresis or by gel filtration. Globin prepared from human hemoglobin A was analyzed simultaneously and gave an 83 to 88% recovery of PTH valine (a 100% recovery would give four moles of PTH). Correction of the values for tadpole globin by assuming the same operational losses that occurred for human globin increases the yield of PTH valine to 1·6 to 2·0 moles per 65,000 molecular weight. The results are consistent with the detection of an N-terminal amino acid on only two of the four polypeptide chains. Similarly, an uncorrected yield of 1·9 moles of PTH per 65,000 molecular weight was obtained for frog globin prepared from the major (7 s) hemoglobin isolated by Sephadex G200.

(h) *Polypeptide chains*

Evidence suggesting that there are no polypeptide chains common to the hemoglobins of the tadpole and frog has been obtained by electrophoresis of the globins on starch and polyacrylamide gels in a variety of 8 M-urea buffers (Fig. 3). Reduction, or

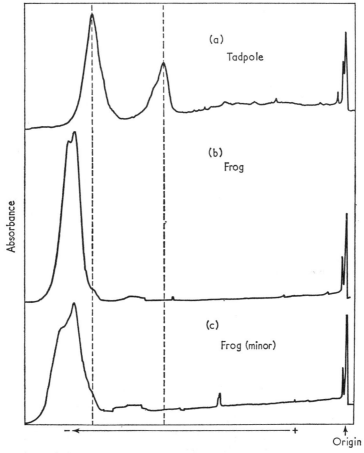

FIG. 3. Polyacrylamide gel electrophoresis of aminoethylated tadpole and frog globin in 8 M-urea, pH 2·8. (a) Tadpole globin prepared from hemoglobin purified by filtration on a 1-m Sephadex G100 column. (b) Frog globin prepared from the major hemoglobin peak obtained by gel filtration on a 1-m Sephadex G100 column. (c) Frog globin prepared from the minor hemoglobin peak obtained by gel filtration on a 1-m Sephadex G100 column. Densitometer tracings were made with a Joyce–Loebl microdensitometer. The initial deflections of the optical density tracing are due entirely to light scattering caused by the edge of the gel.

reduction and alkylation with iodoacetamide, or reduction and aminoethylation was necessary to prevent the appearance of additional frog globin bands, resulting from disulfide bond formation. Reaction with iodoacetamide, under the conditions used, did not produce additional artifactual bands, since the same pattern was obtained with simple reduction if precautions were taken to prevent the reoxidation of thiol groups. Advantage was taken of the greater cysteine content of frog globin to add extra positive charges by aminoethylation. Aminoethylated frog globin, prepared from the purified hemoglobin dimer, was resolved into two equally staining bands (Fig. 3), more clearly resolved visually. An additional faster migrating band seen only as a shoulder in the densitometer tracing, was detected in globin prepared from the minor frog hemoglobins (isolated by gel filtration on Sephadex G200). The tadpole globin polypeptide chains all have slower mobilities than the frog chains. The separation has been confirmed even when the tadpole and frog globins are mixed throughout all steps, including aminoethylation.

4. Discussion

The use of genetically undefined animals for protein structural studies presents potential problems. The tadpoles and frogs were obtained from commercial suppliers but were identified by us as *R. catesbeiana* using several criteria described by Wright (1929) and Wright & Wright (1949). Tadpoles received from commercial suppliers in different regions of the United States frequently showed differences involving the major hemoglobin components. We have therefore used only animals from a single supplier located in western Massachusetts. The only differences noted in the hemoglobin patterns from individual animals from this source involved the presence or absence of one or two minor hemoglobins (Plate I(b) and (c)). The existence of genetic differences between the larval and adult animals obtained was considered, but metamorphosing animals developed new hemoglobins electrophoretically identical to adult hemoglobins. In addition, tadpoles were induced with thyroid hormone to synthesize adult hemoglobin and the newly synthesized, radioactively labeled, hemoglobins were identical to carrier frog hemoglobins by gel electrophoresis, by electrophoresis of globin chains, by gel filtration and by fingerprinting (Moss & Ingram, 1968).

Multiple molecular species of hemoglobins are frequently found in vertebrates (Muller, 1961). In some animals, for instance in man, the hemoglobins have been shown to share a common subunit. The heterogeneity of tadpole hemoglobins results from the presence of at least four or possibly five electrophoretically distinct polypeptide chains. Two different polypeptide chains were resolved from the major (7 s) frog hemoglobin and still another chain from the minor frog hemoglobins, bringing the total number of electrophoretically distinct polypeptide chains in the hemoglobins of *R. catesbeiana* to seven or eight. Two of the polypeptide chains from the major tadpole hemoglobin have been isolated in pure form and we know from fingerprints of the tryptic digests that they have different amino acid sequences. The other electrophoretic differences are unlikely to be due to disulfide bond formation since all globins were reduced and alkylated. Deamidation would not account for the differences seen in the pH 2·8, 8 M-urea gels since the carboxyl groups are essentially uncharged at this pH. We believe, on the basis of the electrophoretic separation as well as N-terminal data, that tadpole and frog hemoglobins have no common subunits.

Although Stratton & Wise (1967) could not separate the polypeptide chains from the larval and adult hemoglobins, differences in ^{203}Hg binding suggested that the chains were not identical. Riggs & Aggarwal (1967), on the basis of amino acid analysis, have also concluded that the major hemoglobins of the tadpole and frog do not have any identical polypeptide chains.

Our Edman analysis is consistent with both tadpole and frog globins having two polypeptide chains with blocked N-terminals. This interpretation conflicts with the results reported by Hamada et al. (1964) and Hamada & Shukuya (1966) who found, for the major tadpole hemoglobin, 2·1 moles of DNP-valine and additional 2·0 moles of DNP-glycine per 68,000 molecular weight. We obtained approximately two moles of PTH-amino acid identified as PTH-valine and no PTH-glycine. Our failure to detect PTH-glycine is not due to losses, since it was recovered from the adult frog hemoglobin, analyzed simultaneously. The latter analysis indicated two moles of PTH-glycine per 65,000 molecular weight. Hamada et al. (1964) have calculated 4·1 moles of DNP-glycine for the major frog hemoglobin. It is possible that the discrepancy arises from differences in the methods of analysis, but the PTH method is preferable to the DNP method for glycine, because of the large losses by hydrolysis in the latter procedure (Hamada et al. corrected for a 70 to 73% loss). The results of Elzinga (1964) are also in conflict with those of Hamada et al. (1964), but are not entirely in accord with our own data. Elzinga found 0·93 mole of DNP-valine per 68,000 molecular weight, but no DNP-glycine, for unpurified tadpole hemoglobin and 2·1 moles of DNP-glycine for unpurified frog hemoglobin. His low yield of DNP-valine cannot be explained, except on the basis of the resistance of valine peptides to hydrolysis.

Our belief that tadpole and frog hemoglobins have blocked N-terminals has recently been strengthened by the finding of two moles of hydrolyzable acetyl groups per 65,000 molecular weight for both tadpole and frog globins (De Witt & Ingram, 1968).

It is possible that the conflicting end-group data reported by different laboratories are a result of the use of different species or subspecies of tadpoles.

We thank Dr Y. W. Kan for allowing us to see the results of his earlier experiments on the gel filtration and Edman degradation of adult R. catesbeiana hemoglobin and Miss Ann Armstrong and Mrs Roberta Berrien for technical assistance.

This work has been supported by grant number GB5181X from the National Science Foundation. One of us (B. M.) was the recipient of a Basic Science Training Fellowship, New York University School of Medicine, U.S. Public Health Service training grant 2G-466.

REFERENCES

Adler, A. D. & George, P. (1965). Analyt. Biochem. 11, 159.
Andrews, P. (1964). Biochem. J. 91, 222.
Baglioni, C. (1961). Biochim. biophys. Acta, 48, 392.
Baglioni, C. (1965). Biochim. biophys. Acta, 97, 37.
Baglioni. C. & Sparks, C. E. (1963). Developmental Biol., 8, 232.
Cameron, B. F. (1965). Analyt. Biochem. 11, 164.
Davis, B. J. (1964). Ann. N. Y. Acad. Sci. 121, 404.
De Witt, W. & Ingram, V. M. (1968). Biochem. Biophys. Res. Comm. 27, 236.
Drabkin, D. L. & Austin, J. H. (1935). J. Biol. Chem. 112, 51.
Edelman, G. M., Benacerraf, B., Ovary, Z. & Poulik, M. D. (1961). Proc. Nat. Acad. Sci., Wash. 47, 1751.
Elzinga, M. G. (1964). Ph.D. Thesis, University of Illinois, University Microfilms, Ann Arbor, Mich., no. 65–809.

Fraenkel-Conrat, H., Harris, J. I. & Levy. A. L. (1955). *Meth. Biochem. Anal.* **2**, 359.

Guidotti, G. & Craig, L. C. (1963). *Proc. Nat. Acad. Sci., Wash.* **50**, 46.

Hamada, K. Sakai, Y., Shukuya, R. & Kaziro, K. (1964). *J. Biochem., Japan*, **55**, 636.

Hamada, K. & Shukuya, R. (1966). *J. Biochem., Japan*, **59**, 397.

Herner, A. E. & Frieden, E. (1961). *Arch. Biochem. Biophys.* **95**, 25.

Huehns, E. R., Dance, N., Beaven, G. H., Hecht, F. & Motulsky, A. G. (1964). *Cold Spr. Harb. Symp. Quant. Biol.* **29**, 327.

Hunt, J. A. (1959). *Nature,* **183**, 1373.

Ingram, V. M. (1958). *Biochim. biophys. Acta,* **28**, 539.

Itzhaki, R. F. & Gill, D. M. (1964). *Analyt. Biochem.* **9**, 401.

Jones, R. T. (1964). *Cold Spr. Harb. Symp. Quant. Biol.* **29**, 297.

Jovin, T., Chrambach, A. & Naughton, M. A. (1964). *Analyt. Biochem.* **9,** 351.

Moss, B. & Ingram, V. M. (1965). *Proc. Nat. Acad. Sci., Wash.* **54**, 967.

Moss, B. & Ingram, V. M. (1968). *J. Mol. Biol.* **32**, 493.

Muller, C. J. (1961). *Molecular Evolution.* Assen, The Netherlands: Van Gorcum's Medical Library.

Ornstein, L. (1964). *Ann. N. Y. Acad. Sci.* **121**, 321.

Porra, R. J. & Jones, O. T. (1963). *Biochem. J.* **87**, 181.

Raferty, M. A. & Cole, R. D. (1963). *Biochem. Biophys. Res. Comm.* **10**, 467.

Riggs, A. (1951). *J. Gen. Physiol.* **35**, 23.

Riggs. A. & Aggarwal, S. (1967). *Int. Cong. Biochem.,* Tokyo. In the press.

Riggs, A., Sullivan, B. & Agee, J. R. (1964). *Proc. Nat. Acad. Sci., Wash.* **51**, 1127.

Rossi-Fanelli, A., Antonini, E. & Caputo, A. (1958). *Biochim. biophys. Acta,* **30**, 608.

Shroeder, W. A. & Matsuda, G. (1958). *J. Amer. Chem. Soc.* **80**, 1521.

Sjöquist, J. (1953). *Acta Chem. Scand.* **7**, 447.

Sjöquist, J. (1959). *Biochim. biophys. Acta,* **41**, 20.

Solomon, J. B. (1965). *The Biochemistry of Animal Development,* vol. 1, ed. by R. Weber. New York: Academic Press.

Stratton, L. P. & Wise, R. W. (1967). *Fed. Proc.* **26**, 808.

Svedberg, T. & Hedenius, A. (1934). *Biol. Bull.* **66**, 191.

Trader, C. D. & Frieden, E. (1966). *J. Biol. Chem.* **241**, 357.

Whitaker, J. R. (1963). *Analyt. Chem.* **35**, 1950.

Wright, A. H. (1929). *Proc. U. S. Nat. Museum,* **74**, 1.

Wright, A. H. & Wright, A. A. (1949). *Handbook of Frogs and Toads of the United States and Canada.* New York: Comstock Pub. Co.

Reprinted from *J. Mol. Biol.* (1968) **32**, 493–504

Hemoglobin Synthesis during Amphibian Metamorphosis

II. Synthesis of Adult Hemoglobin following Thyroxine Administration

Bernard Moss† and Vernon M. Ingram

Department of Biology
Massachusetts Institute of Technology
Cambridge, Massachusetts, U.S.A.

(*Received 4 August 1967*)

Hemoglobin synthesized *in vitro* by red blood cells of thyroxine-treated *Rana catesbeiana* tadpoles is shown to be identical to adult frog hemoglobin by Sephadex gel filtration, by polyacrylamide gel electrophoresis of hemoglobin and of aminoethylated globin chains, and by fingerprinting of tryptic digests. The cells responsible for the synthesis of the adult hemoglobin were identified by radioautography and could be distinguished from the red cells of non-metamorphosing tadpoles by their rounder shape, relatively larger nuclei and lower content of hemoglobin. Polyacrylamide gel electrophoresis of hemoglobin and globin polypeptide chains was also used to determine the stage at which a switch in hemoglobin synthesis occurred during natural metamorphosis.

1. Introduction

A great many biochemical changes occur during the transition of the amphibian from an aquatic larval stage to a semi-terrestrial adult form. The regulation of these events is particularly suitable for study, since amphibian metamorphosis occurs in free living organisms and can be experimentally induced by the administration of chemically defined hormones. A switch from larval to adult type hemoglobin occurs during the metamorphosis of *Rana catesbeiana* (McCutcheon, 1936; Herner & Frieden, 1961). The difference between the oxygen affinities of frog and tadpole hemoglobins (McCutcheon, 1936; Riggs, 1951) results from a change in the protein portion of the hemoglobin molecule (Herner & Frieden, 1961; Baglioni & Sparks, 1963; Hamada, Sakai, Shukuya & Kaziro, 1964). A completely different set of hemoglobin polypeptide chains is probably synthesized by the adult animal (Moss & Ingram, 1968). Preliminary experiments suggested that the repression of synthesis of tadpole hemoglobin polypeptide chains and the induction of frog hemoglobin chains occur in a sequential manner following treatment of immature tadpoles with thyroid hormone (Moss & Ingram, 1965). An early decrease in the *in vitro* amino acid incorporation by tadpole blood cells was followed by increased incorporation at 11 to 13 days following the initiation of thyroxine treatment. In the present study we show that the isotopically labeled protein synthesized at the latter time is identical to the adult frog hemoglobin by gel filtration, gel electrophoresis and fingerprinting. Combined cytological and radioautographic studies suggest that a new population of red cells is responsible for the synthesis of the adult hemoglobin.

† Present address: National Institute of Allergy and Infectious Diseases, National Institutes of Health, Bethesda, Md., U.S.A.

2. Materials and Methods

(a) In vitro *incubation of blood cells*

Washed tadpole and frog red cells were incubated at 30°C in amphibian Ringer's solution supplemented with glucose, iron and amino acids (Moss & Ingram, 1965). The corresponding [^{12}C]amino acids were omitted from the incubation mixture when isotopically labeled amino acids were used (reconstituted [^{14}C]protein hydrolysate, 1·39 mc/mg, Schwarz BioResearch, Orangeburg, N.Y.). In some experiments the iron was replaced with tracer amounts of ^{59}FeCl$_3$ (New England Nuclear Corp., Boston, Mass.). The porphyrin precursor, δ-[4-^{14}C]aminolevulinic acid (0·192 mc/mg, New England Nuclear Corp., Boston, Mass.) was also used. The reactions were stopped by chilling with cold Ringer's solution. The cells were washed, lysed, stroma removed and hemoglobin concentration determined as described in the preceding paper (Moss & Ingram, 1968).

(b) *Gel filtration, gel electrophoresis and fingerprinting*

Gel filtration and gel electrophoresis of hemoglobin, in the methemoglobin cyanide form, was carried out as previously described. The procedures for preparation and aminoethylation of globin and electrophoresis in 8-M urea, pH 2·8 buffer have also been described (Moss & Ingram, 1968). The method of Fairbanks, Levinthal & Reeder (1965) was used for radioautography of polyacrylamide gels.

(c) *Cellular radioautography*

Washed blood cells were suspended in Ringer's solution containing 1% bovine serum albumin and smears were made on gelatinized slides (Caro, 1964). The smears were air-dried and then fixed by immersion in methanol for 3 min. Unincorporated [^{14}C]amino acids were removed by successively passing the slides for 5-min periods through cold 5% trichloroacetic acid containing 1% Casamino acids (Difco Laboratories, Detroit, Mich.) and then cold 5% trichloroacetic acid. The trichloroacetic acid was removed by immersing the slides for 10 min in 3 successive baths of 70% ethanol. Cells labeled with ^{59}Fe or δ-[^{14}C] aminolevulinic acid were fixed with methanol and washed in running water for 20 min. The slides were air-dried and dipped in NTB3 nuclear emulsion (Eastman Kodak, Rochester N.Y.) and processed according to Prescott (1964). Duplicate smears following methanol fixation were stained for hemoglobin with O-dianisidine (O'Brien, 1961).

3. Results

(a) *Identification of proteins synthesized* in vitro *by blood cells of thyroxine-treated tadpoles*

(i) *Polyacrylamide gel electrophoresis*

Tadpoles were treated for 13 days by immersion with 5×10^{-8} M-L-thyroxine. Blood cells from these tadpoles usually incorporate three to four times as much [^{14}C]amino acids as red cells from untreated animals. Washed blood cells from the treated tadpoles and from an equivalent group of untreated ones were incubated for three hours in a volume of 2 ml. with 50 μc of mixed [^{14}C]amino acids. The cells were washed and a portion immediately lysed. The remaining cells were first mixed with an equal volume of chilled adult frog red blood cells, to provide fresh carrier hemoglobin, and then rapidly lysed. The lysates were stored at -20°C for four days to allow polymerization of the frog hemoglobin. Hemolysate containing 50 μg of tadpole hemoglobin or 100 μg of mixed tadpole and carrier frog hemoglobin were applied to polyacrylamide gels for electrophoresis. The gels were stained with amido black, destained, sliced longitudinally, dried and exposed to X-ray film. Densitometer tracings were obtained of both the stained gels prior to drying and the X-ray film radioautographs. There was no apparent difference in the pattern of stained proteins from control or hormone-treated tadpoles (Plate I and Fig. 1.) However, the tracings of

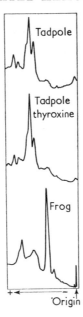

FIG. 1. Densitometer tracings of the gels shown in Plate I.

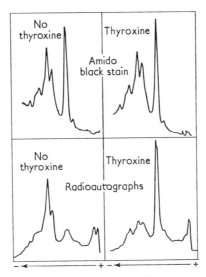

FIG. 2. Radioautography of polyacrylamide gels containing proteins synthesized by blood cells of untreated and thyroxine-treated tadpoles and added carrier frog hemoglobin.

Blood cells from untreated tadpoles and tadpoles treated with 5×10^{-8} M-L-thyroxine for 13 days were incubated in an identical manner with mixed [^{14}C]amino acids as described in the text. The cells were chilled, washed and lysed with an equal volume of unlabeled frog red cells to provide fresh frog hemoglobin carrier. Equal amounts of hemoglobin (100 μg) were applied to each gel, 963 and 3121 trichloroacetic acid-precipitable cts/min, respectively, for samples derived from untreated and thyroxine-treated tadpoles. In the upper part of the Figure are densitometer tracings made with the same density wedge, of gels stained with amido black. In the lower Figure are tracings of the radioautographs of these gels. All X-ray films were exposed for the same length of time; however, a 0 to 1/2 microdensitometer density wedge was used for the films derived from the untreated tadpoles and a 0 to 2 density wedge was used for the films derived from the thyroxine-treated tadpoles in order to magnify the former tracings 4 times.

the radioautographs are strikingly different (Fig. 2). The position of the major radioactive band in the gels containing hemolysate from thyroxine-treated tadpoles coincides precisely with the major frog hemoglobin band. The correspondence was verified by strip-scanning dried gels with a gas-flow Geiger detector and by slicing out the stained bands for scintillation counting (Moss & Ingram, 1965). It should be noted that the differences in the optical density tracings of the amido black-stained gels in Figs 1 and 2 are due to the addition of carrier frog hemoglobin to the latter. Very little radioactive material had the mobility of the major frog hemoglobin band, if fresh frog hemoglobin carrier was not used. The presence of frog hemoglobin carrier did not influence the distribution of radioactivity in gel radioautographs of hemolysates from untreated tadpoles (Fig. 2).

(ii) *Polyacrylamide gel electrophoresis of aminoethylated globin*

Aminoethylated frog globin chains can be separated from tadpole chains by polyacrylamide gel electrophoresis in a pH 2·8, 8 M-urea buffer (Moss & Ingram 1968). This technique was used to identify the polypeptide chains synthesized by blood cells

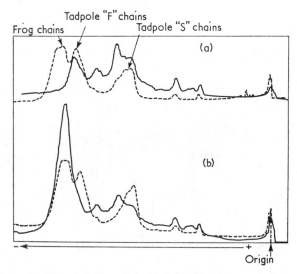

FIG. 3. Polyacrylamide gel electrophoresis of ^{14}C-labeled aminoethylated globins. Aminoethylated globin was prepared from the hemolysates described in Fig. 2 which contained carrier frog hemoglobin. Electrophoresis was carried out in 1·4 M-formate, 8 M-urea (pH 2·8) buffer. The gels were stained with amido black and radioautographs made of the sliced gels. The dashed lines represent densitometer tracings of the amido black-stained proteins; the solid lines represent the tracings of the radioautographs. (a) Globin derived from control tadpoles. (b) Globin derived from tadpoles treated with thyroxine. Densitometry of the X-ray film was done with a 0 to 3 wedge in (b) but only a 0 to 2 wedge in (a) in order to magnify the latter tracing.

of thyroxine-treated tadpoles. Unpurified ^{14}C-labeled hemoglobin was converted to globin, reduced and aminoethylated. Radioautographs of the polyacrylamide gels were made following electrophoresis (Fig. 3). The densitometer tracings indicated that the red cells of tadpoles treated for 13 days with 5×10^{-8} M-thyroxine synthesize predominantly frog globin polypeptide chains and smaller amounts of tadpole globin. Since the hemoglobin was not purified, additional radioactive peaks not corresponding to the globin chains are present. Some of this material undoubtedly represents non-globin protein but a portion may be precurser, non-acetylated globin polypeptide

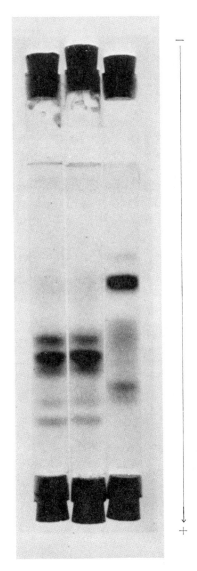

PLATE I. Polyacrylamide disc gel electrophoresis of the hemoglobin obtained from untreated tadpoles and tadpoles treated with thyroxine.

The experimental animals were treated for 13 days with 5×10^{-8} M-L-thyroxine. From left to right the hemoglobin applied to the gel came from untreated tadpoles, tadpoles treated with thyroxine for 13 days, and an adult frog.

[facing p. 496

425

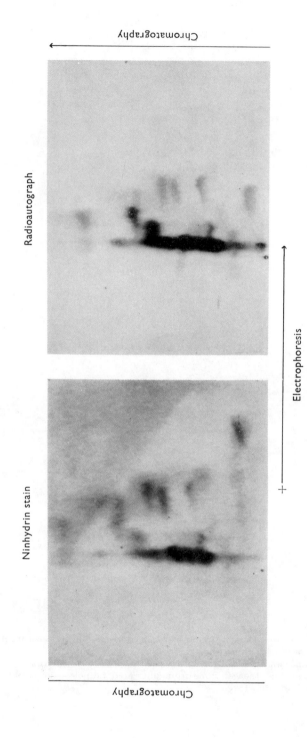

Radioautograph

Ninhydrin stain

Chromatography

Electrophoresis

+

PLATE II. Radioautography of tryptic peptides.

Aminoethylated globin was prepared from the hemoglobin dimer peak (Fig. 5(b)) and digested with trypsin. The peptides were resolved by two-dimensional electrophoresis and ascending chromatography.

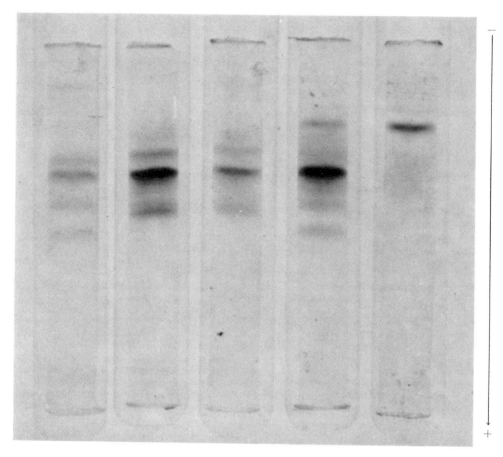

PLATE III. Polyacrylamide disc gel electrophoresis of hemoglobin from naturally metamorphosing tadpoles.

From left to right, the ratio of hindlimb to tail length is: 0·1, 0·3, 0·5, 0·7, froglet. Amido black stained.

PLATE IV. Radioautography of red blood cells from control tadpoles labeled *in vitro* with δ-[4-^{14}C]aminolevulinic acid and ^{59}Fe.

(a) A washed blood cell suspension (0·42 ml.) containing amino acids, glucose and iron was incubated for 15 min prior to the addition of 5/μc of δ-[4-^{14}C]aminolevulinic acid. After 30 min of incubation with the radioactive heme precursor, the cells were washed 3 times with cold Ringer's solution containing 0·1 mg/ml. of unlabeled δ-aminolevulinic acid. The cells were resuspended in incubation medium containing 0·1 mg/ml. of unlabeled δ-aminolevulinic acid. The cells were washed after 30 min incubation and incubated with unlabeled δ-aminolevulinic acid for a second time. After a final wash, the cells were smeared on slides, stained with *o*-dianisidine and processed for radioautography with Kodak NTB3 emulsion. The slides, coated with emulsion, were stored 5 weeks prior to developing.

(b) A blood cell suspension was incubated with ^{59}Fe and after 30 min the cells were washed and resuspended in 0·5 ml. of incubation medium containing 25 μg of FeCl$_3$ and incubated for an additional 30 min. The latter procedure was repeated again at 60 min. The cells were washed for a final time after a total of 90 min of incubation, and processed for radioautography with NTB3 emulsion. The slides were stored for 1 week prior to developing. The cells were stained for hemoglobin with *o*-dianisidine prior to radioautography, and counterstained with Wright's stain following radioautography.

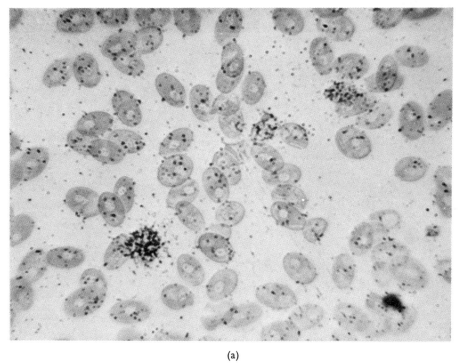

(a)

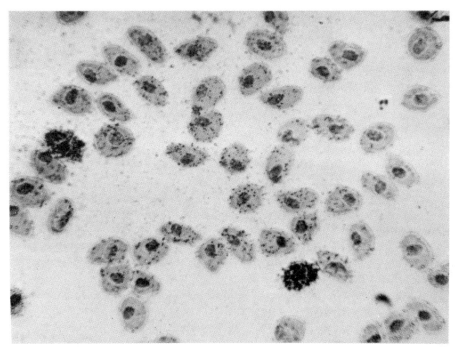

(b)

PLATE IV.

429

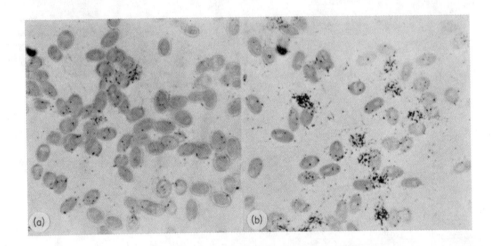

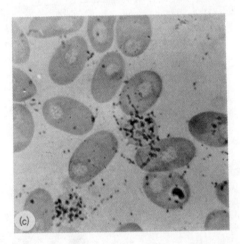

PLATE V. Radioautography of blood cells from thyroxine-treated tadpoles.

Tadpoles were treated for 12 days with 5×10^{-8} M-thyroxine. The hindleg/tail ratios were 0·6 to 0·7 for the throxine-treated tadpoles and 0·1 or less for the control animals. The tadpoles were injected intraperitoneally with 5 μc of ^{14}C-labeled amino acids and bled after 3 hr. Smears of the washed cells were stained with o-dianisidine, extracted with trichloroacetic acid and radioautographed with NTB3 nuclear emulsion. (a) 300 × magnification of cells from control (no thyroxine) tadpoles. (b) 300 × magnification of cells from thyroxine-treated tadpoles. (c) 750 × magnification of cells from thyroxine-treated tadpoles.

chains (Moss & Ingram, 1968; De Witt, Appendix to this paper). A non-acetylated chain would move slightly faster at this pH than the carrier-acetylated polypeptide. The presence of frog globin carrier does not influence the distribution of radioactivity in the radioautographs.

(iii) *Gel filtration*

The specific dimerization of the major frog hemoglobin permits its isolation from tadpole hemoglobins by gel filtration. The radioactive proteins synthesized by tadpole and frog red cells were compared by gel filtration on Sephadex G100 and G200 columns. Four major radioactive peaks were obtained from normal tadpole red cells and they corresponded in order of elution to the position of the exclusion volume, hemoglobin, 17,000 molecular weight non-heme protein (Moss & Ingram, 1968), and the total inclusion volume (Fig. 4). Radioactive material in all peaks except the last were

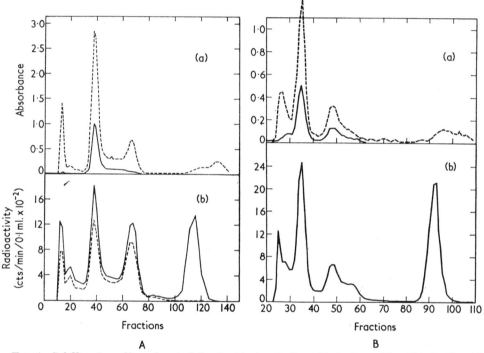

A   B

Fig. 4. Gel filtration of hemolysate following the incubation of tadpole and frog blood cells with [14C]amino acids.

Washed cells were incubated for 2 hr at 30°C with mixed [14C]amino acids. The cells were then washed, lysed and freed of stroma. Column: 2·3 cm × 100 cm G100 Sephadex. Solvent: 0·1 M-NaCl, 0·1 M-Tris–HCl, 0·0015 M-KCN, pH 8·3.

A, Tadpole blood cells. B, Frog blood cells. (a) Absorbance was measured at 545 mμ (———) and at 280 mμ (– – –). (b) Portions (0·1 ml.) were directly plated for counting (———) and precipitated by 5% trichloroacetic acid with 0·2 mg of bovine serum albumin carrier (– – –). The precipitated protein was heated at 90°C for 30 min in 5% trichloroacetic acid and collected on filters. The samples were counted with a gas-flow Geiger counter. No corrections for efficiency were made.

precipitable with hot trichloroacetic acid. The distribution of radioactive material in the three precipitable peaks, in the order of their elution, was 22·0, 38·7 and 39·3% in one experiment and 15·1, 55·7 and 29·2% in a completely separate experiment.

The elution profile of radioactive proteins synthesized by frog blood cells differed

32

in that a hemoglobin peak, corresponding to the dimerized (7 s) hemoglobin, is present and elutes early. Much less radioactive material is found in the position corresponding to the tadpole "17,000 molecular weight non-heme protein." The similarity of $A_{540 m\mu}/A_{280 m\mu}$ ratio 0·41 and 0·40, for the major hemoglobin and minor hemoglobin peaks calculated from the four most concentrated fractions, indicates that the peak tubes are of similar purity. The values for the cts/min/$A_{540 m\mu}$ are 20,200 for the major hemoglobin peak and 20,530 for the minor hemoglobin peak, suggesting that the hemoglobins which form the two peaks are synthesized at similar rates. It should be noted that different columns were used for the experiments illustrated in Figs 4(A) and 4(B). The elution volumes of tadpole and frog hemoglobins are directly compared in the preceding paper (Moss & Ingram, 1968).

Mixing experiments indicated that gel filtration could be used to separate the dimerized species of frog hemoglobin (Hb peak I) from undimerized frog hemoglobins and tadpole hemoglobins (peak II) and non-heme proteins (Fig. 5). The completeness of the separations was monitored by polyacrylamide gel electrophoresis.

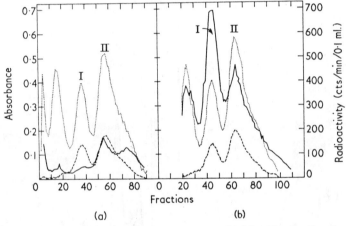

FIG. 5. G200 Sephadex gel filtration of proteins synthesized by blood cells of control (no thyroxine) and thyroxine-treated tadpoles.

The column was 2·3 cm × 100 cm equilibrated with 0·1 M-Tris–HCl, 0·1 M-NaCl, 0·0015 M-KCN, pH 8·3. Approximately 20 mg of methemoglobin cyanide was applied in 0·5 ml. of lysate. The flow rate was maintained at 0·25 ml./min. with a Mariotte flask and 10-min fractions were collected when the hemoglobin approached the bottom of the column. Radioactivity (———) was determined on 0·1-ml. portions added to 1 ml. of 1 N-NaOH containing 0·2 mg of bovine serum albumin carrier that was precipitated, after 15 min, with 1 ml. of 40% trichloroacetic acid containing 2% Casamino acids. Absorbance was measured at 540 mμ (– – –) and 280 mμ (. . . . .).

(a) Frog hemoglobin carrier and labeled hemolysate from in vitro incubation with [^{14}C]amino acids made with intact blood cells from control (no thyroxine) tadpoles. (b) Frog hemoglobin carrier and labeled hemolysate from in vitro incubation made with intact blood cells from tadpoles treated for 13 days with 5 × 10^{-8} M-L-thyroxine.

Isotopically labeled protein synthesized by blood cells both of tadpoles treated with thyroxine for 13 days and untreated tadpoles was stored with fresh frog hemoglobin carrier as previously described. Gel filtration of the frog hemoglobin carrier alone showed that 61% of the frog hemoglobin was in peak I and 39% in peak II. When labeled proteins synthesized by blood cells of tadpoles not treated with thyroxine were filtered through the same column, only 6% of the radioactive material under the two hemoglobin peaks was under peak I (Fig. 5). Significantly, 68% of the radioactively labeled hemoglobin synthesized by the thyroxine-treated tadpoles was under peak I, Fig. 5. The labeled protein under peak I was further identified as frog hemoglobin by polyacrylamide gel electrophoresis of the aminoethylated globin chains. A smaller amount of labeled tadpole globin chains was present under peak II, in addition to frog globin polypeptide chains.

(iv) *Fingerprinting of tryptic peptides*

The identity of the new protein synthesized by blood cells of thyroxine-treated tadpoles was established by comparing the radioactively labeled tryptic peptides with those of frog hemoglobin carrier. Differences between the fingerprints of tadpole and frog hemoglobins have been shown by Baglioni & Sparks (1963) and Hamada & Shukuya (1966) and confirmed in our laboratory. The protein in Hb peak I (Fig. 5) was concentrated, dialyzed, precipitated with acidified acetone, aminoethylated, digested with trypsin and fingerprinted. The radioautographs and ninhydrin-stained fingerprints showed a correspondence of all peptides (Plate II). The intensity of stain and amount of radioactivity are not related, since the former depends primarily on the number of moles of peptide and their N-terminal amino acid while the latter depends on the total number of amino acids and their specific activities. The ninhydrin-stained material that has migrated farthest is in the position of free lysine and arginine and would be expected to show up very weakly on radioautography.

(b) *The synthesis of frog hemoglobin during natural metamorphosis*

Naturally metamorphosing *R. catesbeiana* tadpoles, obtained from commercial suppliers, were bled individually and the type of hemoglobin and globin present was determined by polyacrylamide gel electrophoresis. Frog hemoglobin and globin were detected as stained bands at stages of metamorphosis corresponding to hindleg/tail ratios 0·7 to 1·0 (Plate III and Fig. 6). The transition from tadpole hemoglobin to frog hemoglobin appeared complete in froglets still bearing small tail stumps. The variation in minor hemoglobin bands, seen in Plate III, is unrelated to metamorphosis (Moss & Ingram, 1968).

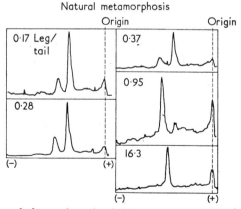

FIG. 6. Polyacrylamide gel electrophoresis of globin from naturally metamorphosing tadpoles. Discontinuous pH 2·3 buffer made 8 M in urea (Moss & Ingram, 1965). Globin has been alkylated with thrice recrystallized iodoacetamide according to Edelman *et al.* (1961). Under these conditions recovery of the fast tadpole chain appears to be incomplete; there is no separation of the major frog globin chains from each other or from the fast tadpole chain. The initial deflection of the optical density tracing is due primarily to light scattering caused by the edge of the gel.

(c) Cellular radioautography

The synthetic activities of the circulating red cells of tadpoles were measured by *in vivo* or *in vitro* incubation with [^{14}C]amino acids and the heme precursors, ^{59}FeCl$_3$ and δ-[4-^{14}C]aminolevulinic acid. Incorporation of δ-aminolevulinic acid increased linearly with time and an equal amount of labeled material was precipitated with trichloroacetic acid and extracted by acidified α-butanone (Teale, 1959). The equivalence of the two sets of values is consistent with the incorporation of this precursor into the protoporphyrin moiety of hemoglobin: however, porphyrins may bind non-specifically to proteins. Blood smears, made from cells incubated *in vitro* with δ-[4-^{14}C]aminolevulinic acid and chased with the unlabeled precursor were radioautographed with nuclear emulsion. Estimates of the number of cells with heavy grain densities were made by counting 1000 cells. Approximately 2% of the cells had heavy grain densities (Plate IV).

Tadpole red cells incorporated ^{59}Fe into butanone-extractable material for several hours at a linear rate; however, most of the counts were stromal. Approximately 5% of the red cells had heavy grain densities following pulse–chase type experiments (Plate IV). Similarly, less than 5% of the red cells were heavily labeled with [^{14}C]-amino acids following either a three-hour *in vivo* labeling period or a 30-minute *in vitro* incubation. The red cells were identified by o-dianisidine staining for hemoglobin.

More than 10% of the circulating red cells from tadpoles treated for 12 days with 5×10^{-8} M-L-thyroxine had heavy grain densities following either *in vivo* or *in vitro* incubation with [^{14}C]amino acids. The protein synthesizing cells were distinguished from inactive cells and from the majority of labeled cells of untreated tadpoles by their appearance (Plate V). Typically they are rounder, stain more lightly with o-dianisidine and have relatively larger nuclei than the red cells of untreated tadpoles (see also the Appendix to this paper).

4. Discussion

We have demonstrated that hemoglobin synthesized *in vitro* by red blood cells of thyroxine-treated *R. catesbeiana* tadpoles is identical to adult hemoglobin by four criteria: (1) Sephadex gel filtration; (2) polyacrylamide gel electrophoresis of hemoglobin; (3) polyacrylamide gel electrophoresis of aminoethylated globin polypeptide chains; (4) fingerprinting of tryptic digests. The results were obtained using ^{14}C-labeled hemoglobin at a time before sufficient adult hemoglobin accumulated in the total red blood cell population to permit detection as stained bands. At this time relatively little tadpole hemoglobin was still synthesized.

The anomalous electrophoretic mobility of the newly synthesized adult hemoglobin in the absence of frog hemoglobin carrier deserves comment. Following lysis of frog red cells, dimerization of the major frog hemoglobin occurs possibly by specific disulfide bond formation (Riggs, Sullivan & Agee, 1964; Trader & Frieden, 1966). The major frog hemoglobin band on polyacrylamide gel is this dimer (Moss & Ingram, 1968). Dimerization of adult hemoglobin synthesized by red cells of thyroxine-treated tadpoles did not occur in the absence of carrier because of the low concentration of adult hemoglobin or possibly because of the absence of factors catalyzing the specific disulfide bond formation. The inability of stored frog hemoglobin to act as carrier suggests that dimerization is irreversible. Problems arising from incomplete dimerization were avoided in our experiments by the addition of a constant amount of fresh frog hemoglobin carrier. Herner & Frieden (1961) reported that during natural or induced metamorphosis of *R. grylio* tadpoles a gradual change in the paper electrophoretic mobility of the hemoglobin occurred until at last the mobility of the adult hemoglobin was attained. The latter experiments suggest the possibility that novel hemoglobins with intermediate mobilities may be synthesized during metamorphosis. Under our experimental conditions, the major hemoglobin made following repression of tadpole hemoglobin synthesis was the definitive adult hemoglobin. The hemoglobin with intermediate mobility found by Herner & Frieden (1961) may be und'merized adult hemoglobin, since the 7 s dimer was not detected (Trader & Frieden, 1966). The latter experiments were not done with isotopically labeled protein, and carrier frog hemoglobin was not added.

Cellular radioautography indicated that only a small proportion of the circulating red cells of normal tadpoles have substantial hemoglobin synthetic activity. It is likely, by analogy with erythropoiesis in mammals, that the active cells are young and have recently arrived in the circulation. The cells responsible for the synthesis of the adult hemoglobin, following thyroxine treatment, could be identified by radioautography since primarily frog hemoglobin is synthesized at this time. The latter cells had morphological characteristics associated with immaturity such as round shape, relatively large nuclei and in addition had a lower content of hemoglobin in the cytoplasm, as demonstrated by lighter staining with o-dianisidine. Only rarely did a red cell of untreated tadpoles have the very immature appearance found in approximately 10% of the red cells of thyroxine-treated tadpoles. We do not know whether the cells that synthesize adult hemoglobin are derived from stem cells that are clonally distinct from tadpole erythropoietic cells. The shift in erythropoietic locus during metamorphosis, described by Jordon & Speidel (1923) and the sequence of amino acid incorporation suggesting the repression of tadpole hemoglobin synthesis followed by induction of adult hemoglobin synthesis (Moss & Ingram, 1965) are consistent with a clonal selection theory. Thyroxine may have no direct action on the hemoglobin structural genes, but may cause directly or indirectly the inhibition of proliferation or maturation of the larval cell line. This would lead to a decline in tadpole hemoglobin synthesis. Simultaneously or subsequently, thyroxine may stimulate the proliferation of a new cell line which synthesizes adult frog hemoglobins.

After submission of this manuscript we became aware that Hollyfield (1966) detected the appearance of small erythrocytes with light cytoplasm and prominent nuclei in metamorphosing *R. pipiens* tadpoles.

We thank Miss Ann Armstrong for her excellent technical assistance and Mrs Roberta Berrien for assistance with one experiment. We are grateful to Professor Alexander Rich for permission to use his Joyce–Loebl microdensitometer.

This work has been supported by grant no. GB5181X from the National Science Foundation. One of us (B.M.) was the recipient of a Basic Science Training Fellowship, New York University School of Medicine, U.S. Public Health Service training grant 2G466.

REFERENCES

Baglioni, C. & Sparks, C. F. (1963). *Developmental Biol.* 8, 232.

Caro, L. G. (1964). In *Methods in Cell Physiology,* ed. by D. M. Prescott, p. 327. New York: Academic Press.

Edelman, G. M., Benacerraf, B., Ovary, Z. & Poulik, M. D. (1961). *Proc. Nat. Acad. Sci., Wash.* 47, 1751.

Fairbanks, G., Jr., Levinthal, C. & Reeder, R. H. (1965). *Biochem. Biophys. Res. Comm.* 20, 393.

Hamada, K., Sakai, Y., Shukuya, R. & Kaziro, K. (1964). *J. Biochem., Japan,* **55**, 636.
Hamada, K. & Shukuya, R. (1966). *J. Biochem., Japan,* **59**, 397.
Herner, A. E. & Frieden, E. (1961). *Arch. Biochem. Biophys.* **95**, 25.
Hollyfield, J. G. (1966). *J. Morphol.* **119**, 1.
Jordan, H. E. & Speidel, C. C. *J. Exp. Med.* (1923). **38**, 529.
McCutcheon, F. H. (1936). *J. Cell. Comp. Physiol.* **8**, 63.
Moss, B. & Ingram, V. M. (1965). *Proc. Nat. Acad. Sci., Wash.* **55**, 1616.
Moss, B. & Ingram, V. M. (1968). *J. Mol. Biol.* **32**, 48.
O'Brien, R. A. (1961). *Stain Tech.* **36**, 57.
Prescott, D. M. (1964). In *Methods in Cell Physiology,* ed. by D. M. Prescott, p. 365. New York: Academic Press.
Riggs, A. (1951). *J. Gen. Physiol.* **35**, 23.
Riggs, A., Sullivan, B. & Agee, J. R. (1964). *Proc. Nat. Acad. Sci., Wash.* **51**, 1127.
Teale, F. W. J. (1959). *Biochim. biophys. Acta,* **35**, 543.
Trader, C. D. & Frieden, E. (1966). *J. Biol. Chem.* **241**, 357.

APPENDIX

Microcytic Response to Thyroxine Administration

WILLIAM DE WITT†

Department of Biology,
Massachusetts Institute of Technology,
Cambridge, Massachusetts, U.S.A.

It has been shown in the preceding paper that the increased rate of protein synthesis was associated with a cell type which differed from the mature red blood cells in size and shape. Since these morphologically distinct cells were induced by thyroid hormone, it was of interest to examine the kinetics of their appearance. In addition, an enriched preparation of the new cell type has been obtained, and it is concluded that these cells are indeed synthesizing frog hemoglobin.

Rana catesbeiana tadpoles (see Paper I in this series) were maintained in water to which thyroxine had been added at a concentration of either $2 \cdot 5$ or $5 \cdot 0 \times 10^{-8}$ M. At various times three to five tadpoles were injected intraperitoneally with 5 µc of algal [^{14}C]protein hydrolysate (New England Nuclear). After 24 hours the red cells were harvested and lysed and their hemoglobin extracted as described by Moss & Ingram (1965). The hemoglobin concentration was determined spectrophotometrically, and incorporation of radioactivity was measured as described in the main paper.

Cellular radioautography

Groups of three to five tadpoles were injected intraperitoneally with $12 \cdot 5$ µc [*methyl*-^{3}H]thymidine. The animals were killed 24 hours later, and the blood cells were collected, pooled and washed in cold heparinized Ringer's solution. Blood smears were stained with o-dianisidine, washed and radioautography performed as described. The slides were exposed for two weeks.

Separation of red blood cells

Partial separation of the newly synthesized red cell population from mature red blood cells was obtained using silicone fluids according to a procedure developed by Kovach, Marks, Russell & Epler (1967). A silicone mixture containing five parts of Dow Corning 550 fluid and one part of Dow Corning 710 fluid (v/v) was used. Packed

† Present address: Department of Biology, Williams College, Williamstown, Mass., U.S.A.

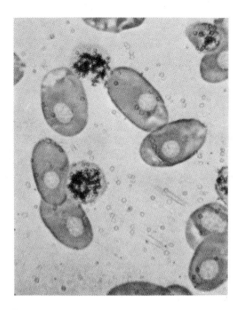

PLATE I. Radioautographs of circulating blood from tadpoles treated with $2 \cdot 5 \times 10^{-8}$ M-thyroxine for 23 days.

Tadpoles were injected intraperitoneally with $12 \cdot 5$ μc of [³H]thymidine 24 hr prior to bleeding. Washed cells were smeared, stained with o–dianisidine and radioautographed. (Focused on cells.)

[facing p. 502

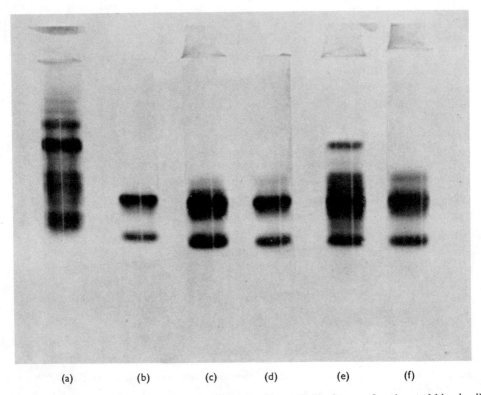

PLATE II. Benzidine-stained polyacrylamide gels of hemoglobin from unfractionated blood cells and from the enriched preparation of new cells. Red cells were washed, fractionated on silicone fluids and hemoglobin was extracted as described in the text.

Hemoglobin (a) from adult frog; (b) from normal tadpoles; (c) from enriched preparation of new cells obtained from tadpoles treated for 16 days with $2 \cdot 5 \times 10^{-8}$ M-thyroxine; (d) from unfractionated blood of the same tadpoles; (e) from enriched preparation of new cells obtained from tadpoles treated with $2 \cdot 5 \times 10^{-8}$ M-thyroxine for 23 days, showing the slow, dimerized frog hemoglobin band; (f) from unfractionated blood of the same tadpoles.

blood cells were diluted tenfold with cold, amphibian Ringer's solution, and then carefully added to a 5 mm × 50 mm siliconized glass test tube containing 0·2 ml. of the silicone mixture. The tube was centrifuged in the cold at 3000 g in a clinical centrifuge for ten minutes. The less dense, immature red cells banded above the silicone mixture, while the mature red cells pelleted beneath the silicone. Separated cell preparations were examined by cellular radioautography, and hemoglobin was also extracted and examined on polyacrylamide gels (Moss & Ingram, 1968). Attempts to refractionate the enriched cell samples on 550 fluid led to considerable cell damage.

Data on the *in vivo* incorporation of [^{14}C]amino acids and [^{3}H]thymidine by circulating blood cells are summarized in Table 1. Tadpoles were treated with 5×10^{-8} M-thyroxine in the first experiment and $2·5 \times 10^{-8}$ M-thyroxine in the second. The latter concentration, although reducing the rate of metamorphosis, allowed the tadpoles to survive to a more advanced stage as judged by the hindleg/tail ratio. In both experiments, cellular radioautographs of circulating blood cells show that the percentage of red blood cells actively incorporating [^{3}H]thymidine decreased to very low levels after a number of days of thyroxine treatment, and then increases greatly. The first experiment also demonstrates, as expected (Moss & Ingram, 1965), a correlation between the decrease in the number of cells actively incorporating [^{3}H]thymidine and the reduced ability of the peripheral blood to incorporate [^{14}C]amino acids *in vivo*. The general morphology of the new cells is shown in Plate I (see also Moss & Ingram, 1968, Plate V(c)). The immature red blood cells from normal tadpoles tend to be oval in shape and larger than the thyroxine-induced cells.

A three- to tenfold enrichment of the newly induced cell type, as determined by counting the percentage of red cells labeled with [^{3}H]thymidine in radioautographs, was obtained by the use of silicone fluids (Table 1).

Hemoglobin, extracted from unfractionated blood cells and from preparations of enriched new cells obtained after tadpoles had been given $2·5 \times 10^{-8}$ M-thyroxine for

TABLE 1

Distribution and synthetic activities of the immature red cells

	Average hindleg/tail ratio	[^{14}C]Amino acids/mg Hb (cts/min)	Red blood cells† labeled with [^{3}H]thymidine (%)	^{3}H-labeled red cells†/total red cells after enrichment (%)
Days on 5×10^{-8} M-thyroxine				
0	0·06	716	2·2	
8	0·12	147	0·6	
13	0·21	185	0	
16	0·49	407	1·1	
Days on $2·5 \times 10^{-8}$ M-thyroxine				
0	0·06	—	1·0	2·6
10	0·20	—	2·0	3·7
16	0·34	—	0·1	1·0
23	0·63	—	3·6	8·4

The blood from 4 tadpoles was pooled for each time point; only 3 tadpoles were used for the 23-day experiment.

† In each case a total of 1000 to 2000 red blood cells was counted.

16 and 23 days, was examined by electrophoresis on polyacrylamide gels (Plate II).
A hemoglobin band, corresponding to that of the major frog hemoglobin, is visible in
the enriched preparation of blood cells from tadpoles treated with thyroxine for 23
days. It represents 5·3% of the total hemoglobin, as calculated from microdensitometer tracings of the benzidine-stained polyacrylamide gels. This percentage is in
reasonably good agreement with the figure (8·4%) of tritiated red blood cells counted
in radioautographs of the enriched preparation, although this calculation may be
somewhat distorted by the apparent difference in size of the two cell types. The slow
major frog hemoglobin band appears in its characteristic position because this particular hemoglobin dimerizes in solution to form an eight-chain molecule. If the
concentration is too low, however, this dimerization cannot occur and the hemoglobin
occupies a different, faster position (as in Plate II(f)). The dimerized frog hemoglobin
band is not visible in the hemoglobin preparations on the sixteenth day in either
whole blood or in the enriched sample, because at this lower thyroxine concentration
frog hemoglobin synthesis in the circulating blood is delayed.

The morphology of the microcytic cells found in the present experiments suggests
that they are not normal members of the erythrocytic series or that they are not
normally released into the circulation in such numbers. Perhaps the release of these
cells is caused by the extreme metabolic stress of accelerated metamorphosis.

We are indebted to Miss Ann Armstrong for valuable technical assistance. This research
was supported by a grant no. GB5181X from the National Science Foundation.

REFERENCES

Kovach, J. S., Marks, P. A., Russell, E. S. & Epler, H. (1967). *J. Mol. Biol.* **25**, 131.
Moss, B. & Ingram, V. M. (1965). *Proc. Nat. Acad. Sci., Wash.* **55**, 1616.
Moss, B. & Ingram, V. M. (1968). *J. Mol. Biol.* **32**, 481.

Reprinted from Science, December 8, 1967, Vol. 158, No. 3806, pages 1330-1332
Copyright © 1967 by the American Association for the Advancement of Science

Erythrocyte Transfer RNA: Change during Chick Development

*Abstract. Radioactive aminoacyl transfer RNA's isolated from erythrocytes
in the blood of 4-day-old chick embryos and from reticulocytes of adult chickens
were analyzed by chromatography on methylated albumin kieselguhr and freon
columns. Embryonic and adult methionyl transfer RNA's showed qualitative and
quantitative differences in both chromatographic systems. The patterns for arginyl,
seryl, and tyrosyl transfer RNA's in the two cell types were similar, while the
leucyl transfer RNA patterns suggested a difference.*

Structural modification of transfer RNA (tRNA) may play a regulatory function in cell differentiation and metabolism (*1*). With methylated albumin kieselguhr (MAK) chromatography, Kano-Sueoka and Sueoka (*2*) demonstrated an alteration in leucyl-tRNA after bacteriophage T2 infection of *Escherichia coli*; this finding was confirmed by Waters and Novelli (*3*), using the reversed-phase chromatography developed by Kelmers et al. (*4*). Kaneko and Doi (*5*) found a change during sporulation of *Bacillus subtilis* in the elution pattern of valyl-tRNA from MAK columns.

To look for changes in specific tRNA's during development, we used avian immature red cells as a test system and compared the chromatographic profiles of aminoacyl-tRNA's from red cells present in the blood of 4-day-old chick embryos and of reticulocytes of adult chickens. The techniques in this study were MAK (*2*) and freon columns (*6*). Of the five aminoacyl-tRNA's examined, only the methionyl-tRNA gave a strikingly different elution pattern.

Adult chickens (White Leghorn) were made anemic by daily injection (for 5 days) of 15 mg of phenylhydrazine [in 0.1M tris(hydroxymethyl)amino-methane (tris) buffer, pH 7.2] and were bled on the 6th day. Eggs from the same strain were incubated at 37°C for 4 days, and blood cells were collected by bleeding the embryos. Blood cells from either source were washed twice with 0.145M NaCl, 5 × 10^{-4}M KCl, and 0.0015M MgCl$_2$, and once with 0.145M NaCl, 5 × 10^{-4}M FeCl$_2$, and 0.01M phosphate buffer (pH 7.4); 0.12 ml of packed embryonic cells was suspended in the latter medium supplemented with glucose (200 mg/ml) with a total volume of 0.5 ml. For adult cells, 0.5 ml of packed cells was similarly incubated in a total volume of 2.0 ml. To cells previously incubated at 38°C for 10 minutes, [14]C- or ^{3}H-labeled amino acid (5 to 10 μc) and the 19 remaining nonradioactive amino acids (1 μmole of each)

were added. After incubation for an additional 12 minutes, cycloheximide (10^{-4}M) was added to inhibit protein synthesis (*7*) and thus prevent the transfer of amino acids from aminoacyl-tRNA's. After 10 minutes more, the cells were lysed by suspension in 5 volumes of 0.01M tris, 0.01M KCl, and 0.0015M MgCl$_2$ containing 15 mg of purified bentonite per milliliter (*8*) and by repeated freezing (in a mixture of dry ice and acetone) and thawing. The lysate was extracted with half volume of carbon tetrachloride, and the upper phase was shaken for 15 minutes with an equal volume of twice-distilled, buffer-saturated phenol. The aqueous phase was extracted again with phenol, and traces of phenol were removed with cold, peroxide-free ether. The solution was then adjusted to 0.1M with sodium acetate buffer (4M, pH 6), and then 2 volumes of cold ethanol were added. After several hours at −20°C, the precipitated RNA was collected by centrifugation, washed with cold ethanol, and dried. The yields of tRNA from the above-mentioned volumes of packed cells were 1.3 optical density (O.D.) units (260 mμ) and 0.85 O.D. units for embryonic and adult cells, respectively.

The MAK column (1 by 3 cm) was similar to that of Kano-Sueoka et al. (*2*); it contained 1 g of kieselguhr and 0.25 ml of 1-percent methylated albumin, because only small quantities of material were available for analysis. The second change was the use of a shallower gradient of 0.20 to 0.65M NaCl (250 ml in total volume).

The freon column used was a modification of the method of Weiss et al. (*6*). Radioactive aminoacyl-tRNA's, together with 5 mg of carrier unlabeled tRNA's (*9*), were applied to a column (0.5 by 250 cm). Elution was effected with a concave NaCl gradient containing 0.01M sodium acetate and 0.01M MgCl$_2$ (pH 4.5) at room temperature. Fractions (2 ml) were collected at 12-minute intervals.

Optical density was measured at 260 mμ on alternate fractions. A sample (1 ml) of each fraction was then mixed with 10 ml of Bray's solution (*10*), and the radioactivity was measured in an Ansitron liquid-scintillation counter.

Aminoacyl-tRNA's isolated from erythrocytes of 4-day-old chick embryos and from reticulocytes of adult chickens were compared first by chromatography on the MAK column and then on the freon column. The specific tRNA's examined were: arginine, leucine, methionine, serine, and tyrosine. Typical results of the MAK chromatographs are shown in Fig. 1. With the exception of the methionyl-tRNA, which gave a clear alteration in the elution profiles, there were no significant differences in the profiles between the aminoacyl-tRNA's from the two

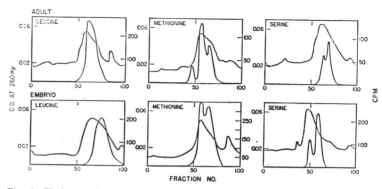

Fig. 1. Elution profiles of aminoacyl-tRNA's of blood cells from embryonic and adult chickens on MAK columns. Dotted lines, optical density at 260 mμ; solid lines, radioactivity. Amino acids labeled with ^{14}C were used in the preparation of all aminoacyl-tRNA's.

sources. Under the present chromatographic conditions, both the adult- and the embryonic-cell methionyl-tRNA showed two major peaks in MAK chromatography. However, a dramatic change during development in the proportion of methionyl-tRNA in the two major peaks was observed. The ratio of the areas under the peaks which was 1.1 in the embryonic cells shifted to 3.8 in the adult cells.

Figure 2 shows the elution patterns of the aminoacyl-tRNA's on the freon column. The better resolution of this chromatographic system revealed the presence of multiple peaks for several of the amino acids tested (arginine, leucine, and methionine). No significant difference was observed between the elution patterns of the embryonic and adult cells of the amino acids arginine, leucine, serine, and tyrosine. However, the elution profiles of the methionyl-tRNA's from cells of the two different developmental stages showed a striking alteration. Although both the adult and the embryonic methionyl-tRNA's gave two resolvable peaks, the proportions of the two peaks differed. The ratio of the peaks was 1.3 for the embryonic cells and 2.7 for the adult cells. These results were similar to those found with the MAK column. In addition, the two peaks for the embryonic cells were further apart; a small third peak was observed, but its significance is doubtful.

The chromatograph of leucyl-tRNA from avian reticulocytes differed strikingly from that from *E. coli* B on both the MAK and the freon columns. A typical elution profile of the bacterial leucyl-tRNA on the latter column is shown in Fig. 3. There were at least four major peaks in the bacterial system, but only two were detected in the avian system. Moreover, the elution profiles of adult and embryonic

leucyl-tRNA's appeared to differ slightly. The two embryonic peaks were further apart. However, the significance of this difference is not clear at the moment.

Thus, the analysis of aminoacyl-tRNA's from immature erythrocytes of chick embryos and from reticulocytes of adult chickens by chromatography on the MAK and freon columns has revealed that the elution pattern for methionyl-tRNA changes during development, whereas the patterns for the four other amino acids studied remain essentially unaltered with a possible difference for leucyl-tRNA. However, it is possible that changes in other untested tRNA's may exist. The fact that remarkably similar elution patterns of the other aminoacyl-tRNA's were observed apparently eliminates the possibility of ribonuclease activity as a major factor in the observed change in methionyl-tRNA. In a later experiment, we examined the embryonic methionyl-tRNA with the use of the same ^{14}C-methionine sample as we had used for the adult tRNA in Fig. 2. Because the expected embryonic pattern was observed, it seemed unlikely that the difference illustrated

in Fig. 2 is due to contamination in the ^{3}H-methionine. The identical elution profiles obtained either by ^{14}C-, ^{3}H-, double-, or single-labeling techniques (as in the case of tyrosyl-tRNA) demonstrated that these profiles are reproducible and reliable.

The actual mechanism and biological significance of this change are not clear at the moment. The observed modification in methionyl-tRNA during development may be a change of either the tRNA molecules or of the specificities of the aminoacyl-tRNA synthetases involved. The tRNA may also be involved in the regulation of protein synthesis at the translational level (*1*). Moreover, our finding is of particular interest because N-formyl-methionyl-tRNA from *E. coli* plays a crucial role in the initiation of protein synthesis in bacteria (*11*). Two methionyl-tRNA's of *E. coli* have been reported (*12*); one of these can be converted to N-formyl-methionyl-tRNA, and the other does not accept formyl groups. Our finding that methionyl-tRNA's are modified during development agrees with the expectation based on the model of regulation that a change in tRNA molecules may lead to an alteration in their functional capacity and thus may affect translation.

JOHN C. LEE
VERNON M. INGRAM
Department of Biology,
Massachusetts Institute of Technology,
Cambridge 02139

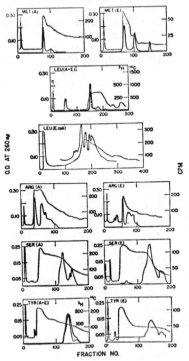

Fig. 2 (right). Elution profiles of aminoacyl-tRNA's on freon columns. Avian aminoacyl-tRNA's were prepared as described. The following samples were prepared with ^{14}C-labeled amino acids: arg (A), arg (E), leu (E), met (A), ser (E), and tyr (A), whereas leu (A), met (E), ser (A), and tyr (E) were acylated with ^{3}H-labeled amino acids. *Escherichia coli* leucyl-tRNA was prepared as described by Kano-Sueoka and Sueoka (*2*). Dotted lines, optical density at 260 mμ; solid lines, radioactivity. (In the double-labeling experiments, ^{14}C is shown by a solid line, and ^{3}H is shown by a dashed line.)

References and Notes

1. N. Sueoka and T. Kano-Sueoka, *Proc. Nat. Acad. Sci. U.S.* **52**, 1535 (1964); B. N. Ames and P. Hartman, *Cold Spring Harbor Symp. Quant. Biol.* **28**, 569 (1963); G. S. Stent, *Science* **144**, 816 (1964).
2. T. Kano-Sueoka and N. Sueoka, *J. Mol. Biol.* **20**, 183 (1966).
3. L. C. Waters and G. D. Novelli, *Proc. Nat. Acad. Sci. U.S.* **57**, 979 (1967).
4. A. D. Kelmers, G. D. Novelli, M. P. Stulberg, *J. Biol. Chem.* **240**, 3979 (1965).
5. I. Kaneko and R. H. Doi, *Proc. Nat. Acad. Sci. U.S.* **55**, 564 (1966).
6. J. F. Weiss, A. D. Kelmers, M. P. Stulberg, *Fed. Proc.* **26**, 2667 (1967).
7. L. Felicetti, B. Colombo, C. Baglioni, *Biochim. Biophys. Acta* **119**, 120 (1966).
8. H. Fraenkel-Conrat, B. Singer, A. Tsugita, *Virology* **14**, 541 (1961).
9. *Escherichia coli* B was obtained from Calbiochem, Los Angeles, California.
10. G. A. Bray, *Anal. Biochem.* **1**, 279 (1960).
11. K. A. Marcker and F. Sanger, *J. Mol. Biol.* **8**, 835 (1964).
12. B. F. C. Clark and K. A. Marcker, *ibid.* **17**, 394 (1966); D. A. Kellogg, B. Doctor, J. Loebel, M. W. Nirenberg, *Proc. Nat. Acad. Sci. U.S.* **55**, 912 (1966).
13. We thank Miss Joanne Wirsig and Mrs. Leslie D. Schroeder for technical assistance. Supported by grant AM 08390 from NIH.

25 October 1967